The Rules of the Game

The Rules of the Game: International Money and Exchange Rates

Ronald I. McKinnon

The MIT Press
Cambridge, Massachusetts
London, England

This book was set in Palatino by Compset Inc. and was printed and bound in the United States of America.

Library of Congress Cataloging-in-Publication Data

McKinnon, Ronald I.
  The rules of the game : international money and exchange rates / Ronald I. McKinnon.
    p.   cm.
  Selected journal articles and essays from books published from the 1960's to the present.
  Includes index.
  ISBN 0-262-13318-0 (hc : alk. paper)
  1. International finance—History—19th century. 2. International finance—History—20th century. 3. Foreign exchange rates—History. I. Title.
HG3881.M396   1996
332.4'5—dc20   95-36690
                                                              CIP

In Loving Memory of Lois and Ian McKinnon

Contents

III International Monetary Reform

Preface

The initial concept of this book was simply to assemble my published work in international finance. These selected essays, from the 1960s to the present, were to show how at least one economist had thought over time on such great issues as optimal currency areas, the operation of the postwar world dollar standard compared to the pre-1914 gold standard, and the breakdown in 1971–73 of the par-value system into floating exchange rates with which we are now so familiar.

However, the process of pruning old essays prompted a much sharper focus and led to the writing of new material. Indeed, I have convinced myself—and, I hope, the reader—that the essays have become a coherent book. The theme is financial volatility—in exchange rates, interest rates, and price levels—as related to the nature of international monetary arrangements. How international monetary systems have worked in the past, from gold to the dollar to the European Monetary System, suggests what "rules of the game" could be feasible and desirable in the future. The last chapters offer an up-to-date statement of my views on international monetary reform.

But dating remains important, particularly for the older essays. Although slightly updated for stylistic consistency, they are a record of what at least some people thought before the days of time inconsistency, "rational" expectations, forward-looking asset prices, and so forth. However, I have not included old essays that are not fully consistent with my recent writings—or that seem to have been superseded by events. In particular, I have not reproduced several articles dating back to the early 1970s containing my proposals for international monetary reform. But their spirit remains very much alive in this book.

The last chapter offers a synthesis of those proposals, combined with theory and data from the modern era, to spell out new rules of the game for a more tranquil—and more efficient—international financial system in the future.

I would like to thank the persistent but forbearing editors of the MIT Press, Terry Vaughn, Ann Sochi, and Kathleen Caruso; my wife, Margaret, who helped with many of the chapters going back into the 1960s; and generations of Stanford students who were subject to many of the essays through my lectures in international finance.

In particular, Kenichi Ohno, now a professor of economics at Tsukuba University in Japan, not only helped with this book's essential empirical work on the nature of business cycles under the floating-rate dollar standard, but is also my coauthor on the companion work, *Dollar and Yen: A Macroeconomic Approach to Resolving Conflict between the United States and Japan,* to follow also from the MIT Press. This detailed case study of the sometimes volatile economic interaction between Japan and the United States from the early 1950s to the 1990s lends additional empirical and conceptual support for the ideas advanced here on reforming the world's money machine.

1 Introduction

Generalized financial volatility is capitalism's Achilles' heel. And nowhere is the problem of controlling such volatility more acute than in monetary and exchange relationships across countries: the central theme of this book. Among the principal players, this international volatility is more or less restrained by rules and understandings—not all of which are written down or unambiguous. Beginning with the gold standard in the late nineteenth century, these conventions are analyzed in historical perspective to the present in chapters 2 through 9. Then, presuming that the industrial economies will remain highly open in trade and finance, subsequent chapters investigate how to better avoid financial disorder into the twenty-first century.

At Bretton Woods in 1944, the authors of the Articles of the International Monetary Fund sought to prevent a recurrence of the disastrous monetary, exchange-rate, and price-level fluctuations of the 1920s and 1930s, which eventually transmitted the Great Depression around the world. With the associated outbreak of protectionism in the foreign trade of every important country, international commerce imploded: by 1933 world trade had fallen to one-third of what it had been in 1929.

Since World War II, the rules governing monetary relationships among industrial countries succeeded in preventing another Great Depression. But, as I shall show, these rules differ(ed) in many essentials from those negotiated at Bretton Woods, and they have gone through three major transformations since then. Nevertheless, these changing international monetary arrangements underlay successive negotiating rounds under the General Agreement on Tariffs and Trade for reducing trade barriers on a worldwide basis—culminating in the founding of the World

Trade Organization in late 1994. Today, international trade has recovered to (relative) levels not seen since the heyday of the international gold standard before 1914, and gross (though not net) international capital flows are much greater now than then. Countries newly opened to the market system with modest wages but high absorptive capacity for new technologies—such as Asia's famous newly industrializing countries, whether Taiwan and Korea three decades ago, or China and Indonesia now—can still use the existing trading mechanism as a springboard to rapid economic growth. In this sense, the postwar monetary regimes have been successful.

However, among the older industrial countries, this trade-led economic expansion has been uneven. By common consensus, the period from 1950 to 1973 was Western capitalism's most successful age.[1] Trade expansion was the engine of remarkable economic growth and, at least until the late 1960s, domestic price levels were anchored by the exchange-rate regime. Stable prices and exchange rates were associated with more rapid growth in foreign trade (albeit from repressed levels) and in output per capita in North America, Europe, and Japan than they had been in any period before or since (Maddison 1989). Why this period should have been so successful is still the subject of unresolved debate (Abramovitz 1986), which explains the considerable effort in this book to pin down what the actual rules of the game were under this fixed-rate dollar standard, and precisely how they came into existence in ways that differed substantially from what the Bretton Woods treaty had envisioned.

Subsequently, the international monetary system has been plagued with excess volatility in various forms—even as it has become more open. After the collapse of the dollar-based system of fixed exchange rates in 1971–73, the sharp upsurge in exchange rate volatility—whether measured day to day, month to month, or year to year—continues to the present day—as shown rather dramatically in figure 1.1 for monthly changes in the yen/dollar, mark/dollar, and mark/yen exchange rates. The rules of the monetary game among the mature industrial countries have also been less effective in promoting domestic price-level stability coupled with sustained growth. From the early 1970s into the mid-1980s, a synchronized international business cycle saw two major worldwide inflations leading to two painful disinflations. Since then, with a change in the rules of the game (as shown

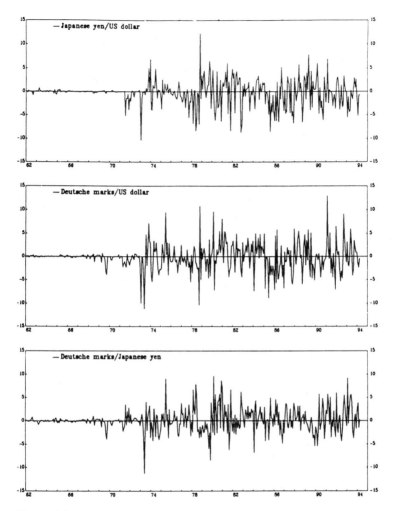

Figure 1.1
Volatility of nominal exchange rates, 1962–94 (percentage changes from previous month).

in chapters 2 and 22), the world business cycle has been less pronounced. However, periods of overvalued exchange rates lasting months or years have contributed to major economic downturns in Britain, Canada, in continental Europe, and Japan—as exemplified by Japan's sharp industrial slump in 1993–95.

Apart from the inflationary 1970s, a startling upsurge in volatility of long-term interest rates in the industrial countries in the

1980s and 1990s—even in periods of relative price-level tranquil-lity—puzzles central bankers everywhere. True, the dismantling of exchange controls on capital account permits freer portfolio diversification among the industrial countries than in the 1950s and 1960s. But today's volatility in long-term interest rates is inordinately high by the standards of previous eras, such as the pre-1914 gold standard, where capital could flow freely across national boundaries. Summarizing and slightly updating to 1994 the more extensive data in chapter 3, table 1.1 compares interest volatility for both short and long rates under the gold standard (1879–1913), the dollar standard (1950–70) and floating exchange rates (1973–94). In both Britain and the United States, volatility in long-term interest rates since 1973 has been eight to ten times as high as it was under the classical gold standard before 1914, and two to four times as high as during the fixed-rate dollar standard of the 1950s and 1960s.

This interest-rate volatility continues unabated. After a sharp fall in long rates in 1993, their sudden rise in 1994 prompted cen-tral bankers in Britain, Canada, the United States, and some Euro-pean countries to tighten their domestic monetary policies by

Table 1.1
Interest Rate Volatility[a] in Historical Perspective: Britain and the United States

		Britain	United States
Mean Annual Interest Changes			
Long-term Bonds	Gold standard	0.07	0.14
	Dollar standard	0.45	0.29
	Floating	0.99	1.05
Short-term Bills	Gold standard	0.98	1.01
	Dollar standard	0.77	0.69
	Floating	2.05	1.57
Mean Monthly Interest Changes			
Long-term Bonds	Gold standard	0.03	0.03
	Dollar standard	0.09	0.08
	Floating	0.34	0.26
Short-term Bills	Gold standard	0.50	0.40
	Dollar standard	0.16	0.14
	Floating	0.53	0.39

[a]Mean absolute change in end-of-period interest rates (in percentage points). Periods: International gold standard, 1879–1913; dollar standard, 1950–70; float-ing exchange rates, 1973–94.

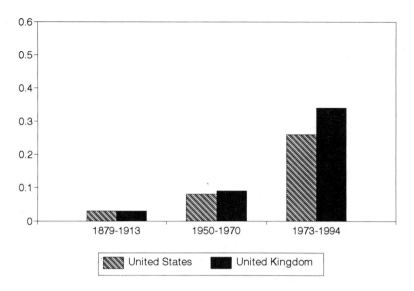

Figure 1.2
Volatility in long-term interest rates (mean absolute monthly charges).

raising short rates to calm the apparent inflationary fears of investors holding assets at the long end of the maturity spectrum. The resulting crash in the capital values of bonds in 1994 exceeded in value the collapse of the stock market in October 1987. For dramatic effect, this heightened monthly volatility in long-term interest rates under floating—in comparison to the gold and dollar standard when exchange rates were fixed—is shown in figure 1.2.

Apparently, investors in long-dated bonds are responding to this volatility by demanding a higher risk premium for holding them. Thus, while 1990s price levels are quite stable, average real long rates of interest seem high by historical standards. A century ago, the real yield on British consols stayed close to 3 percent (see chapter 3).

1.1 Financial Volatility Versus Comparative Advantage

If severe enough, exposure to financial volatility from the international economy undermines the analytical and political cases for individual nations to maintain free trade in goods and services as well as in financial assets. Both the Ricardian principle of comparative advantage in the exchange of goods and the Smith-ian principle of the gains from specialization in production being limited by the size of the market presume that international trade per se does not aggravate domestic financial uncertainty—in price levels or interest rates—beyond ordinary commercial risk associated with new or more varied products. Ricardo and Smith—as well as modern writers on gains from trade—presume(d) that international trade was just an extension of domestic trade within the domain of a single currency and without exchange risk.

Thus it is not surprising that exchange-rate risk between countries on different monetary standards is a prime cause of the rise of modern protectionism. Rather than old-fashioned statutory tariffs, the new protectionism takes the form of quantitative restrictions (quotas or market-sharing agreements), undue regulatory restraints, and privately tailored "antidumping" suits as well as the formation of regional trading blocs. Much of the rationale for this new protectionism can be linked to the desire to insulate particular product markets from the effects of exchange-rate fluctuations (see chapter 18).

Of course, more extreme volatility in the international monetary system could drive countries to insulate themselves even more. In the 1930s, direct controls over international trade and capital flows became commonplace. For example, by becoming protectionist and insular at the outset of the Great Depression, Argentina avoided the severe downturn felt by other economies selling primary products on world markets.

But concern with international monetary stability has a positive side. Suppose a stable international monetary standard is somehow established, with low financial volatility in the countries adhering to it. By remaining open to international trade and capital flows, each member country can then better anchor its own monetary policy. Under both the pre-1914 gold and post-1949 fixed-rate dollar standards, most countries succeeded in reducing domestic financial volatility and stabilizing their macroeconomies—as shown in chapter 6 for the dollar standard.

In these serendipitous circumstances, a policy of free trade is twice blessed. By maintaining a fixed exchange rate, each national economy gains from more efficient specialization in international goods markets à la Ricardo and Smith *and* also gains from better monetary stability than it could manage on its own. The political economy for sustaining the international standard then falls into place. In each country, politicians will see it in their interest to adhere to the more stable external monetary standard. And, as more countries fix themselves to it, the international standard's collective appeal is enhanced.

How to achieve this state of financial bliss is not simple. Nor is it primarily a question of writing down a set of equations, or a tightly specified how-to-do-it manual. Instead, the political economy of international monetary systems, good and bad, can only be understood in historical perspective.

1.2 Organization

The twenty-one essays in the body of the book are divided into three parts.

Part I provides an analytical history of international monetary standards from gold to the dollar in chapters 2 through 9. Its first essay, "The Rules of the Game: International Money in Historical Perspective," establishes the organizing principle for comparing monetary regimes past and present, and ultimately for part III on international monetary reform.

The technique developed in chapter 2 for analyzing and comparing different international monetary regimes is unusual. I wanted to avoid a purely historical narrative with little structure other than being chronological. But I could not devise a general algebraic model with different sets of parameters to distinguish one regime from another without suppressing many of their essential economic characteristics. Instead, for each "coherent" international monetary regime (including treaties themselves) since the late nineteenth century, I list in a separate box its important rules of the game as understood by the principal players. The supporting text is used to justify why these particular rules accurately reflect the monetary order in question, and to draw contrasts and similarities across regimes. Chapter 2's seven rule boxes cover

1. The International Gold Standard, 1879–1913

2. The Bretton Woods Agreement in 1945: The Spirit of the Treaty

3. The Fixed-Rate Dollar Standard, 1950–70

4. The Floating-Rate Dollar Standard, 1973–84

5. The Plaza-Louvre Intervention Accords for the Dollar Exchange Rate, 1985–95

6. The European Monetary System in 1979: The Spirit of the Treaty

7. The European Monetary System as a Greater Deutsche Mark Area, 1979–92

These rules, sometimes called monetary orders, have governed relationships among the industrial countries at the center of the world economy; they were often adopted by less developed economies on the periphery. After these rules are laid out, subsequent chapters in part I analyze how the resulting monetary systems actually worked in practice. How successful was each international regime in stabilizing national price levels and exchange rates, while curbing business cycles, so that economic integration in goods and factor markets could proceed unimpeded?

Part II, "Optimum Currency Areas and Exchange-Rate Flexibility," addresses a central analytical question facing each country. What are the net benefits of giving up exchange-rate flexibility in order to join a common monetary standard with fixed exchange rates? Is a flexible exchange rate a useful shock absorber for adjusting net trade balances to capital flows? These questions define the central theme in chapters 10 through 18.

The analytical framework established by the essays in parts I and II sets the stage for part III, "International Monetary Reform." These more prescriptive essays—chapters 19 through 22—encompass both the European Monetary System and, more generally, the reconstruction of monetary arrangements among the major industrial countries including Japan and the United States. The last chapter, "From Plaza-Louvre to a Common Monetary Standard for the Twenty-First Century," was expressly written to be this book's capstone—synthesizing much of the earlier material I had written on international monetary reform with lessons learned from recent experience. After first updating rule box 5 to give a snapshot of what the rules governing monetary relationships among the industrial countries were as of 1995, chapter 22 offers rule box 8:

8. A Common Monetary Standard for the Twenty-First Century (CMS21)

Rule box 8 encapsulates my proposal for reforming the monetary relationships among the industrial countries in the late 1990s to eventually establish (restore) a par-value system for exchange rates. Because CMS21 builds on today's monetary understandings—or norms—that govern monetary interactions among the industrial countries, it is evolutionary rather than revolutionary. No comprehensive international conference or treaty—like that signed in Bretton Woods, New Hampshire, in 1944—is needed or recommended in order to reduce volatility in exchange rates, price levels, and interest rates. But the new rules in CMS21 draw heavily on lessons from the past—particularly the pre-1914 gold standard and the post-1949 dollar standard—as well as from the more recent travails of the European Monetary System.

1.3 A Reader's Guide

The book's organization allows readers two complementary lines of attack. Those wanting a compact discussion of the rules of the game past, present, and future can simply read chapters 2 and 22: there, the main theme on the organization of the world's monetary system is contained in the eight rule boxes analyzed in the texts of these two chapters. For easy reference, all eight rule boxes are also appended at the end of the book (p. 527).

Those with more time may also wish to start with chapter 2 but then dip into historical issues on how each system worked (part I), and corresponding theoretical debates on exchange-rate flexibility (part II), before finishing with issues of international monetary reform in part III. To help readers taking this longer route, a brief overview of the remaining chapters is provided below.

Chapter 3 compares interest-rate and price-level volatility under different exchange-rate regimes. In particular, the very high volatility in long-term interest rates under floating is compared to the virtual absence of such fluctuations under the international gold standard. Chapter 4 explains why balance-of-payments adjustment under the international gold standard worked so smoothly, even though the common price level was not all that stable.

My early writing on the postwar dollar standard (chapter 5, "Private and Official International Money: The Case for the Dollar," 1969) shows how at least one economist actually thought about the fixed-rate dollar standard then prevailing. Contrary to the trend of the 1960s, when both monetarists and Keynesians increasingly favored more flexible exchange rates, this essay defends the logic of credible par values based on the dollar—the world's dominant vehicle and invoice currency. The important caveat, however, was that the United States correctly play its asymmetrical role as the key currency country, that is, understand the appropriate rules of the game for differentiating its behavior from that of the other industrial countries.

Despite my best efforts, the dollar-based par-value system broke down anyway in 1971–73! Chapters 6 through 9 demonstrate the inherent instability of the floating-rate dollar standard when this monetary asymmetry persists: the U.S Federal Reserve more or less ignores the strength or weakness of the dollar in the foreign exchanges, but other countries try to smooth—albeit not very successfully—fluctuations in their dollar exchange rates. Because countries in the rest of the world collectively increased their money supplies when the dollar was weak and contracted when it was strong, business cycles were more synchronized on a worldwide basis from 1971 through the mid-1980s. These worldwide business cycles were generally more virulent than those experienced in the two decades before or the decade since.

After 1985–87 under the Plaza-Louvre Accords (discussed in chapter 2), the United States played a major role, in concert with other countries, in helping iron out major swings in the dollar exchange rate. Because this greater symmetry allowed the industrial countries to avoid expanding or contracting their monetary policies together, worldwide business cycles became less pronounced (chapter 22). This is not to deny that exchange-rate and interest-rate volatility remain extremely high, or to deny that individual countries subsequently suffered economic downturns from severe exchange overvaluations—as in Japan in 1986–87 and again in 1993–95. But worldwide stability improved.

Part II starts off by developing the theory of optimum currency areas—now enjoying revived popularity—in chapters 10 and 11. They reflect my perceptions in the early 1960s, *before* we had had the experience with worldwide floating, of how the world should be divided into currency blocs. Chapter 11 suggested that Western Europe was definitely an optimum currency area as of 1963, but that a floating exchange rate between a European bloc and, say, a North American bloc might be desirable. However, the world has changed since then. The upsurge in international financial flows suggests that the optimum currency area, in the sense of the domain over which fixed exchange rates and a common monetary policy are desirable, is now much wider. (Indeed, the analysis in chapter 22 would link all the industrial countries, which don't depend on inflationary monetary policies for revenue, under a common monetary standard.)

In chapter 12, "Floating Foreign Exchange Rates, 1973–74: The Emperor's New Clothes," written in 1975, and also in chapters 13 through 17, written later, I try to explain why exchange volatility in practice was so unexpectedly high once the par-value system broke down—much higher than I and others had previously believed to be likely, as exemplified by my own analysis in chapter 11 of the desirability of a floating exchange rate between Europe and the United States.

Chapters 13 and 14, written in the early 1980s, deal with the vexing question of the exchange rate and the trade balance—and why economists are wrong to treat the exchange rate among financially open economies as an instrumental variable for adjusting the trade balance. (This controversial issue will be dealt with in more analytical and empirical depth in McKinnon and Ohno [forthcoming].) This doctrinal dispute arises from the failure to distinguish between "insular" and "open" economies in historical perspective, and in cross section. In effect, those economists (still most of the profession) who treat the exchange rate as an instrumental variable for controlling trade deficits are using theoretical models that apply only to insular economies, that is, those not naturally well integrated with their principal trading partners.

The last essay in this second section, chapter 18 on the new interbloc protectionism, then makes the key argument that fluctuating currency values have encouraged the rise of modern protectionism—more in the form of quantitative restrictions and market-sharing agreements than of statutory tariffs. After 1971, floating rates encouraged the devolution of the multilateral trading mechanism into regional trading blocs within which partner countries try, without always succeeding, to maintain exchange stability.

In part III, chapter 19 on the problem of European monetary integration fills a serious gap in the current theory of optimum currency areas. Exchange-rate stability within a natural currency area is greatly to be wished. But can this best be secured by going all the way to a common currency? Or should nations simply agree to fix exchange rates within narrow bands under a common monetary standard, where national monies continue to circulate independently?

In either case, transition problems can be acute. But the state of the public finances in general, and the size of the overhangs of national debts in particular, poses a more fundamental constraint. Whether or not the Western European Union should adopt a common currency is a case in point. In chapter 19, I argue that the outstanding huge national debts in Western Europe cannot feasibly be managed at the national level *unless* the governments in question retain the right to issue their own national currencies. Hence, the Europeans are better off to leave national monies in circulation and aim for a well-articulated common monetary standard.

Chapters 20 through 22 sketch what the "rules of the game" should be to sustain a common monetary standard *symmetrically*. First, participating governments should agree on a nominal anchor for their monetary policies in terms of a common price level defined in terms of tradable goods. Then, in the steady state, relatively modest variations in relative short-term interest rates can confine exchange rates indefinitely within narrow bands. The asymmetry that plagued the old dollar standard and still plagues the European Monetary System—of having the nominal anchor depend on the monetary policy of just one country—can then be avoided.

These last chapters are written with the broader objective of tethering the relative values of the U.S. dollar, Japanese yen, and the German mark—while securing their common purchasing power in terms of a broad producer price index—in such away as to create a new monetary standard that other countries large and small would find attractive. The same principles would apply for containing intra-European exchange-rate fluctuations within even narrower target zones. In chapter 22, the pros and cons of alternative parity arrangements—such as the (unsatisfactory) EMS bilateral parity grid—are explored in pursuit of this broader objective.

1.4 Philosophical Disclaimer

Most readers will quickly realize that these ideas on international monetary reform are not in the generally accepted mainstream. Most economists still reject the idea of reestablishing par values for exchange rates across the world's important trading countries. But the advocacy of unrestricted floating, so common in the 1950s and 1960s (Friedman 1953; Meade 1955; Johnson 1972), is more in abeyance in the 1990s. Chastened by the unexpectedly extreme exchange fluctuations since 1971–73, most economists now support a middle position: they advocate "managed" no-par floating for most countries. Although agreeing that governments should iron out major exchange-rate misalignments, most writers don't want governments to commit themselves to some new regime of fixed exchange rates.

The philosophy behind this now dominant middle way is worth spelling out; see Corden (1994, chap. 16). It rests on two related assumptions about the fundamentals governing exchange rates among sovereign countries. First, with the possible exception of tight regional groupings such as the core countries within the European Monetary System, important nominal variables—including monetary policy and price-wage inflation—inevitably evolve independently within each nation state. Insofar as national price levels diverge in the long run, offsetting adjustments in nominal exchange rates will be needed. Second, real shocks—terms of trade changes, shifts in net international capital flows, political instability, and so on—hit individual economies differently. In order to maintain full employment and "balanced" international trade, national governments should be free to offset these short-run shocks by discretionary monetary and fiscal policies supported by adjustments in exchange rates if need be.

In summary, today's prevailing view is for national governments not to commit themselves to fixed nominal exchange rates within narrow (hard) bands because this ties their hands in ways that prevent necessary and desirable adjustments in the balance of payments or aggregate demand in the future. And if governments fail to understand this, the wide-open international capital market will prevent such fixed exchange-rate commitments from being effective. Speculators will anticipate (perhaps incorrectly) those exchange-rate adjustments governments might want to make, and massive speculative capital flows will undermine any putative par values that the government announced.

A few economists would take managed floating one step further by confining "real" exchange-rate movements within soft target zones. Not only would these soft zones be very wide, but their desired central rates would have to be continually recalculated according to changing circumstances. John Williamson is the leading proponent of soft target zones for limiting extreme exchange-rate misalignments (Williamson 1985; Williamson and Miller 1987; Williamson and Henning 1994). Essential to this scheme is that the nominal exchange rate be continually nudged toward the equilibrium real exchange rate as the fundamentals change—whether they be differential inflation, or trade imbalances beyond those that could be financed by sustainable net capital flows (which Williamson offers to calculate). Indeed, he has spawned a cottage industry where numerous authors estimate equilibrium real exchange rates for various developed and developing economies (Williamson 1994). To hit these moving targets for the real exchange rate, however, a country needs to retain flexibility in its nominal exchange rate into the more distant future—which Williamson's soft target zone would not constrain.

Nested within this prevailing wisdom favoring exchange flexibility, authors who advocate fixed nominal exchange rates carefully limit themselves to special cases of full-scale monetary unification—such as the adoption of a common currency in Europe (chapter 19), or a currency board with complete dependence on some foreign money (chapter 16). W. M. Corden (1994, 305) summarizes the prevailing ethos as follows: "The choice is between the regime that now prevails for almost all the developed and many developing countries, namely managed floating, and a solid regime in the form of a monetary union or currency board."

After making the same distinction, that the only feasible options are no-par floating or complete monetary union, Barry Eichengreen (1993, 1354) asserts that "the one alternative that is not viable is fixed exchange rates between distinct national currencies." In his recent comprehensive survey of the literature on exchange rates, Obstfeld (1995) comes to more or less the same conclusion.

This book's philosophy differs from that undergirding the case for managed floating. Indeed, part III makes the case for reestablishing a common monetary standard—where national currencies remain in circulation under the control of national governments but nominal exchange rates remain indefinitely fixed within narrow bands. And the last chapter provides specific details on how a worldwide par-value system could be established in a consistent fashion.

What assumptions underlie this disparity between my perspective and that of economists favoring managed floating? (The reader will only get a complete idea by reading this book from beginning to end!) The differences are more empirical than theoretical, and they depend on how one compares past and present monetary standards.

First, I explain the unusually high degree of volatility in today's financial markets by the fact that major trading countries are on separate national monetary standards, while the now massive flows of financial capital have an unrestricted international range. Because international investors, perhaps acting purely defensively, must guess how governments will separately manage their national monetary policies, a casino effect is created (chapter 3). Ordinary considerations of commercial profitability and risk, which financial systems can accommodate efficiently within a single currency domain, are swamped by concern with how exchange rates and interest rates in neighboring countries are going to evolve vis-à-vis those at home. The failure of industrial countries to precommit to a common monetary standard, where nominal exchange rates in the (distant) future are likely to be close to what they are today, leads to excessive volatility in exchange rates and long-term interest rates in every national capital market. The adverse consequences for long-run productivity growth and price-level stability outweigh the advantages of having more exchange-rate flexibility in the short run.

Second, the historical record suggests that it is not that difficult technically for countries to harmonize their national monetary policies if the rules of the game are consistent with price-level stability and are well understood. Through the discipline of a common monetary standard, equilibrium real exchange rates stabilize and national price levels align themselves so as to make flexibility in nominal exchange rates unnecessary and national macroeconomic autonomy less expedient. Rather than a disruptive force, unrestricted—and possibly speculative—international flows of short-term capital then become the balance wheel of international payments adjustment once exchange-rate par values become credible.

Third, although political opposition to international monetary harmonization is substantial, national interests properly understood are not in conflict. Rather this political barrier results from the doctrines of economists, who influence politicians and officials, being either wrong or misapplied (chapter 20).

From the 1960s well into the 1970s, the principal argument favoring floating exchange rates was to secure national macroeconomic autonomy in order that each country could achieve its preferred trade-off between inflation and unemployment—see Johnson (1972), as quoted in chapter 13. If country A had a taste for high inflation and low unemployment, why should it be locked into the same monetary standard as country B, which feared inflation and would tolerate unemployment more easily? Fortunately, the economics profession subsequently rejected the existence of any sustained trade-off between inflation and unemployment: the (in)famous Phillips Curve. Because it is now widely agreed that efficiency is better served by opting for zero or low inflation, the idea of binding nations together under a common monetary standard—provided that it is well anchored—is more acceptable than it was a generation ago.

But an important doctrinal hang-up remains: whether or not the exchange rate should respond to real shocks hitting the economy in the short run. The complex issues are discussed in more detail in chapter 20. But the leading edge of philosophical dispute on the subject revolves around the old transfer problem—which was debated by J. M. Keynes and Bertil Ohlin in the 1920s. Suppose exchange rates in a no-par system could be counted on to adjust the "right" way—a big presumption in itself. If there is a new net capital flow from country X to country Y—warranting a consequential current account surplus in X and deficit in Y—are major changes in relative prices necessary to effect the transfer, and would these be facilitated by a discrete change in the nominal exchange rate between the two countries? My distinguished colleague Paul Krugman would answer strongly in the affirmative (1991, 46):

During the 1980s a number of economists, most prominently Robert Mundell and Ronald McKinnon, questioned the need for real exchange rate changes as part of the adjustment process. It took a while before it was clear that the two RMs differed from the standard view, but eventually it emerged that their position was essentially a replay of Bertil Ohlin's side of the classic debate over the transfer problem— which has nothing to do with monetary issues and the integration of capital markets. And the question they raise is an empirical one: are world markets for goods and services sufficiently well integrated, or with sufficient substitution in demand and supply, so as to allow transfers to be effected with minor changes in relative prices?

As I read the evidence, the answer is a clear no for trade among the United States, Japan, and Europe. Within Europe a better case can be made for immaculate transfers that do not require real exchange rate changes, but even here the problems caused by German unification show that the inability to adjust exchange rates imposes some real costs.

Generally, I don't dispute the sense of this quotation except for the phrase that "the classic debate over the transfer problem . . . has nothing to do with monetary issues and the integration of capital markets." Krugman fails to recognize that only countries on a common monetary standard and fixed exchange rates can sustain capital-market integration sufficient to more or less equalize real interest rates. And, in turn, a fully integrated capital market smooths and limits the modest relative price changes arising out of some new capital flow from X to Y. In chapter 4, this point is made by looking at how successful the pre-1914 gold standard was in facilitating enormous capital transfers from Britain to the rest of the world with no change in nominal exchange rates and little change in real rates. In the 1980s and 1990s, with Japan the great creditor country and the United States the great debtor, more or less random fluctuations in the yen/dollar exchange rate have been highly disruptive to each country's macrostability in general, and to the smooth transfer of capital between them in particular; this point will be elaborated in McKinnon and Ohno (forthcoming).

How might we bridge this philosophical gap between Krugman-Williamson et al. and McKinnon-Ohno? The efficient integration of both commodity and factor markets across countries depends heavily on the nature of international monetary arrangements in place. Under no-par floating with continual fluctuations in relative currency values since 1971, integration is bound to be imperfect—in which case any new capital transfer from X to Y may be facilitated by some (additional) exchange-rate change. But this only indicates that the money machine itself is out of order and integration is incomplete. Chapter 2 begins the study of what rules governing international money have worked well in the past and could foster international economic integration in the future.

Note

1. For obvious reasons, I hesitate to say "golden age."

References

Abramovitz, Moses. 1986. "Catching Up, Forging Ahead, and Falling Behind." *Journal of Economic History* 46: 385–406.

Corden, W. M. 1994. *Economic Policy, Exchange Rates, and the International System.* Chicago: University of Chicago Press.

Eichengreen, Barry. 1993. "European Monetary Integration." *Journal of Economic Literature* 31(3) (September): 1321–57.

Friedman, Milton. 1953. "The Case for Flexible Exchange Rates." In *Essays in Positive Economics,* 157–203. Chicago: University of Chicago Press.

Johnson, Harry. 1972. "The Case for Flexible Exchange Rates, 1969." In *Further Essays in Monetary Economics,* 198–228. Cambridge: Harvard University Press.

Krugman, Paul. 1991 "Has the Adjustment Process Worked?" *Policy Analysis in International Economics 34* (October). Washington, DC: Institute for International Economics.

Maddison, Angus. 1989. *The World Economy in the 20th Century,* Paris: OECD.

McKinnon, Ronald I., and Kenichi Ohno. Forthcoming. *Dollar and Yen: A Macroeconomic Approach to Resolving Conflict between the United States and Japan.* Cambridge: MIT Press.

Meade, James E. 1955. "The Case for Variable Exchange Rates." *Three Banks Review,* 27(3) (September): 3–27.

Obstfeld, Maurice. 1995. "International Currency Experience: New Lessons and Lessons Relearned." *Brookings Papers on Economic Activity* 2: 119–208.

Williamson, John. 1985. "The Exchange Rate System." *Policy Analyses in International Economics* 5. Rev. ed. Washington, DC: Institute for International Economics.

————, ed. 1994. *Estimating Equilibrium Exchange Rates.* Washington, DC: Institute for International Economics.

Williamson, John, and C. R. Henning. 1994. "Managing the Monetary System." In *Managing the World Economy: Fifty Years after Bretton Woods,* ed. P. Kenen. Washington: Institute for International Economics.

Williamson, John, and Marcus Miller. 1987. "Targets and Indicators: A Blueprint for the International Coordination of Economic Policy." *Policy Analysis in International Economics* 22. Washington, DC: Institute for International Economics.

I

International Monetary Standards: From Gold to the Dollar

2

The Rules of the Game: International Money in Historical Perspective

No world central bank issues a separate currency for commerce across national boundaries. Instead, a "system" of national monies works more or less well in providing a medium of exchange and unit of account for current international transactions, as well as a store of value and standard of deferred payment for longer-term borrowing and lending.

How do national governments and banking institutions interact to provide international money for merchants and investors? By necessity, this monetary interaction changes with time, place, political cirumstances, and financial technology. To better understand its historical evolution, let us follow Robert Mundell and distinguish between a monetary "system" and a monetary "order":

A *system* is an aggregation of diverse entities united by regular interaction according to some form of control. When we speak of the international monetary system we are concerned with the mechanisms governing the interactions between trading nations, and in particular the money and credit instruments of national communities in foreign exchange, capital, and commodity markets. The control is exerted through policies at the national level interacting with one another in that loose form of supervision that we call co-operation.

An *order*, as distinct from a system, represents the framework and setting in which the system operates. It is a framework of laws, conventions, regulations, and mores that establish the setting of the system and the understanding of the environment by the participants in it. A monetary order is to a monetary system somewhat like a constitution is to a political or electoral system. We can think of the monetary system as the *modus operandi* of the monetary order. (Robert Mundell 1972, p. 92)

Originally published in *Journal of Economic Literature* 31, 1 (March 1993): 1–44. Reprinted with permission.

More informally, an international monetary order is often called "the rules of the game"—terminology initially used in the 1920s to describe accepted rules governing the pre-1914 international gold standard.[1] In contrast, periods of great international turmoil and change—say from 1914 to 1945—defy any such consistent characterization (Barry J. Eichengreen 1985a). Otherwise, the rules of the game were (are) generally discernable—even when not written down or formally codified.

Mundell's distinction between a monetary system and a monetary order suggests a useful way to focus the scope of this review. Instead of covering the workings of international monetary systems—their success in promoting trade and the efficient allocation of capital, limiting the world business cycle, aligning national price levels, avoiding inflation or deflation, and so on—I shall confine my main line of analysis to comparing monetary *orders*. In chronological succession, the main rules of the game for member governments under each monetary order are separated from the ongoing text by a series of seven rule boxes:

1. The International Gold Standard, 1879–1913

2. The Bretton Woods Agreement in 1945: The Spirit of the Treaty

3. The Fixed-Rate Dollar Standard, 1950–70

4. The Floating-Rate Dollar Standard, 1973–84

5. The Plaza-Louvre Intervention Accords for the Dollar Exchange Rate, 1985–95

6. The European Monetary System in 1979: The Spirit of the Treaty

7. The European Monetary System as a Greater Deutsche Mark Area, 1979–92

Building on the ideas of authors writing at the time and subsequently, each box sets out my best assessment of the rules governing exchange-rate objectives, official reserve holdings, convertibility commitments, adjustments in domestic monetary policies, the choice of a "nominal anchor" for the price level, and so on, for its historical period. The boxes are comparably arranged more or less in parallel. For example, in each box the first rule(s) defines exchange-rate objectives while the last (or next to last) defines the anchor rule. The reader in a hurry, or one wanting an initial overview of what the paper contains, can simply compare rule boxes, listed together in the appendix.

But the selection of rules to go into each box is by no means uncontroversial. The accompanying text evaluates the practical robustness of each set of rules within its historical era, and then compares their essential features across regimes down to the present day. From historical contrasts and parallels, the rationale for the international monetary rules prevailing in any one era is more readily understood. Sometimes the rules change as a reaction to how events in an earlier period are interpreted. The Bretton Woods Agreement of 1945 sought to change the basic operating principles of the international gold standard (John Williamson 1983).

Less obviously, the way in which an international monetary system actually works may differ enormously from the written or intended rules in the treaty on which it is apparently based. The intention to treat all nations symmetrically in the written articles of the Bretton Woods Agreement of 1945 (The "Spirit of the Treaty" in box 2) was followed by the asymmetrical Fixed-Rate Dollar Standard (Ronald McKinnon 1969; C. Fred Bergsten 1975; and Peter Kenen 1983) whose rules are encapsulated in box 3. The formal symmetry of the EMS treaty of 1979 (the "Spirit of the Treaty" in box 6) was followed by a regime more akin to a Greater Deutsche Mark Area (Massimo Russo and Giuseppe Tullio 1988; Francesco Giavazzi and Alberto Giovannini 1989) as summarized in rule box 7. Drawing a distinction between the intended rules incorporated into a founding treaty and the actual rules of the game as it was subsequently played under the cover of that treaty turns out to be of central analytical importance.

Since 1973, the major blocs—Europe, the United States, and Japan—have ostensibly been on a regime of "floating" exchange rates. Yet, in rule boxes 4 and 5, we see two distinct sets of governing rules. Early in 1985, there was a major regime change separating the floating-rate dollar standard from the more recent Plaza-Louvre Accords.

First, however, let us look at the pre-1914 gold standard for which there was no collective "founding treaty" nor major regime changes. Countries opted unilaterally to follow similar rules of the game that proved remarkably robust.

2.1 The International Gold Standard, 1879–1913

Why limit our study of the gold standard to the years 1879–1913? Britain, with a few interruptions, had already been on gold for

Rule Box 1
The International Gold Standard, 1879–1913

All Countries

    I. Fix an official gold price or "mint parity," and convert freely between domestic money and gold at that price.

   II. Do not restrict the export of gold by private citizens, nor impose any other exchange restrictions on current or capital account transacting.

  III. Back national banknotes and coinage with earmarked gold reserves, and condition long-run growth in deposit money on availability of general gold reserves.

  IV. In short-run liquidity crises from an international gold drain, have the central bank lend freely to domestic banks at higher interest rates (Bagehot's Rule).

   V. If Rule I is temporarily suspended, restore convertibility at traditional mint parity as soon as practicable—if necessary by deflating the domestic economy.

  VI. Allow the common price level (nominal anchor) to be endogenously determined by the worldwide demand for, and supply of, gold.

---

more than a century. By 1879, however, the gold standard had become *inclusively international*—covering all the major industrial economies, and most smaller agrarian ones. By the mid 1870s, France had abandoned bimetallism in favor of gold; the German Empire discarded a silver-based currency and, by using its indemnity from the Franco-Prussian war of 1871, also adopted gold. In 1879, the U.S. returned to gold after the suspension of gold convertibility in the Civil War. Although threats of inconvertibility recurred from 1879 onward, Western European countries and the United States maintained their official gold parities without significant interruption for 35 years. But in August 1914, the international gold standard ended abruptly—almost overnight (Gustav Cassel 1936) as the warring European countries declared their currencies inconvertible into gold and into each other.[2]

Box 1 provides a highly simplified view of the rules of the game for the prewar gold standard. Rules I, II, and III assure the convertibility of domestic currency into gold at a fixed price on the one hand, and, by allowing free international arbitrage, into foreign exchange within a very narrow band—known as the "gold points"—on the other. In the late 19th century, these three rules were generally well understood (Barry J. Eichengreen 1985b, pp. 3–4), usually had the force of written law in all the participating countries, and were virtually automatic in their day-to-day implementation.

In addition, important *implicit* rules—active and passive—also governed the behavior of central banks and treasuries under the international gold standard.

On the active side, rules IV and V summarize the most empirically important: the national central bank's role as a lender of last resort (Walter Bagehot 1873) and the obligation to restore the traditional mint parity "in the long run" should an unforeseen crisis force a (temporary) suspension of gold convertibility. At the national level at least, the gold standard was more of a managed system than is commonly believed.

On the passive side, rule VI precluded each government from exercising any enduring influence over its own national price level. Notwithstanding the important role of Britain, to be discussed below, this passive reliance on the world market for gold to determine the common price level (the nominal anchor) reflects the essential symmetry of the international gold standard. In contrast to the asymmetrical way the game was (is) played in more recent times (rule boxes 3, 4, and 7 below), the six rules in box 1 applied *symmetrically* to all participating countries.

But how the gold standard game was actually played is not uncontroversial. Hence, it is worthwhile reviewing how well the six rules, hypothesized in box 1, held in practice.

Gold Points and Gold "Devices"

From the way exchange rates behaved, one can infer whether traditional mint parities were effectively violated, or if governments impeded international gold flows. If rules I and II hold continuously, triangular arbitage keeps the exchange rate between any pair of national currencies within a very narrow band, the "gold points." Consider the algebraic model used by Pablo Spiller and Robert Wood (1988):

X is the uniform dollar price (mint parity) of one ounce of "fine" gold as paid or charged by the U.S. Treasury (20.646 dollars).

Y is the uniform official pound sterling price (mint parity) of one ounce of fine gold as paid by or charged by the Bank of England (4.252 pounds).

S_t is the cable spot exchange rate in dollars per pound at time t.[3]

T_{ub} is the total transactions cost per ounce of gold shipped from the United States to Britain.

T_{bu} is the total transactions cost per ounce of gold shipped from Britain to the United Sates.

It is then profitable to import gold into Great Britain if and only if

$$S_t > \frac{X}{Y - T_{ub}} \tag{1}$$

and to import gold into the United States if and only if

$$S_t < \frac{X - T_{bu}}{Y}. \tag{2}$$

Suppose sterling is strong in the foreign exchanges. Then (1) shows that the larger the transactions costs of importing gold into Britain, the further sterling's dollar value can increase above the ratio of mint parities, i.e., above $X/Y = 4.856$ dollars/pound. Similarly, when sterling is weak, (2) shows it can fall below this ratio according to the transactions costs of importing gold into the United States.

But how big was this band of variation between the gold points defined by (1) and (2)? The upper panel of Table 2.1 shows the implications for exchange rates between pairs of national monies. Because of the higher transport cost for gold, Oskar Morgenstern (1959) estimated that the band was "normally" a little over one percent for the U.S. dollar against any European currency while only 0.5 to one percent within Europe. Although comparable, these bands were smaller than those established in the 1950s and 1960s under Bretton Woods or in the 1980s within the EMS—see Table 2.1 for a comparison.

But were the gold points defined by (1) and (2) well maintained in practice? For the period 1899–1908, Truman Clark (1984) claimed that inequalities (1) and (2) were violated quite often—with gold sometimes moving in the "wrong" direction. In contrast, Lawrence Officer (1986) reexamined Clark's data and found

Table 2.1
Bilateral Fluctuation Bands for Exchange Rates

	Parity	Lower Limit	Upper Limit
Gold Standard (1879–1913)			
Sterling ($/£)	4.856	4.827	4.890
Franc (FF/$)	5.183	5.148	5.215
Mark (DM/$)	4.198	4.168	4.218
Fixed-Rate Dollar Standard (1950–70)			
Sterling ($/£)	2.800	2.772	2.828
Franc (FF/$)	4.937	4.887	4.986
Mark (DM/$)	4.200	4.158	4.242
Yen (Yen/$)	360.0	356.4	363.6
European Monetary System (1979–92)			
Franc (FF/DM)	2.310	2.258	2.362

Source: Alberto Giovannini (1989).

that violations were infrequent because the gold points themselves were highly variable. The transactions costs T_{ub} and T_{bu} change through time and differ from each other—depending on varying transport fees for shipping and insurance, the length of a gold voyage (the time a merchant's capital was tied up), and the varying interest rates prevailing in each financial center. Moreover, in order to detect a violation, these stochastic gold points have to be matched exactly in time with the corresponding quotation for S_t.

Just looking at the time-series properties of S_t itself, Pablo Spiller and Robert Wood (1988) estimate that gold arbitrage costs were highly variable, as Officer had suggested. More importantly, for the period 1899 to 1908 on which they had detailed data, Spiller and Wood find that S_t was kept within the narrow range of $4.83750 to $4.90125 per pound, which was remarkably close to Morgenstern's range of 4.827 to 4.890 for just 1879 (table 2.1). Because the gold-based system itself succeeded in keeping the exchange rate within such a narrow band, the argument over whether or not the gold points were "violated" seems moot.

Nevertheless, "gold devices" were used. To cushion gold losses, governments might temporarily raise their effective buying price for gold—thus violating rule I. For example,

Throughout 1891, a year in which the Bank [of England] had considerable difficulty in controlling the discount market, the Bank manipulated its prices, both for gold bars and gold coin, to supplement its Bank Rate policy. (W. M. Scammell 1965, p. 112)

Later from 1896 to 1910, Scammell notes that the Bank of England again used such gold devices quite extensively. Even so, the dollar/sterling exchange rate remained within the narrow margins calculated by Spiller and Wood.

The Bank of England manipulated the gold points considerably less than its counterparts on the continent (Arthur Bloomfield 1959). Indeed, a few governments were not legally bound to convert at any price: in France, Belgium, and Switzerland, convertibility was at the authorities' option. And Alberto Giovannini (1986) notes that the Reichsbank often dissuaded German commercial banks from exporting gold for profit—a violation of rule II. Compared to other European central banks, the Bank of England relied more on frequent changes in its official discount rate to protect its gold reserves. Many countries and firms held sterling deposits in London, reflecting Britain's central role in the world capital market. Thus the Bank of England was more anxious to keep its notes close to their official mint parity.

One could argue that the gold devices actually improved the acceptability of the gold standard by keeping the domains of national monetary circulation somewhat segregated—thus giving national authorities greater flexibility in dealing with short-run banking crises. Otherwise falling transport costs—and more rapid transit—for gold would have narrowed the range of variation for S_t far below the one percent that Morgenstern observed for 1879—and of course further below what Spiller and Wood actually found for the period 1899–1908. If the gold devices had not already existed, they likely would have had to be invented.

I suggest that the difference between a central bank's buying and selling prices for gold be made somewhat greater than hitherto, say 2 percent, so there would be this difference between the gold points irrespective of the actual costs of transporting gold. (John Maynard Keynes 1930, p. 291)

Keynes's two percent band was indeed adopted in Bretton Woods Articles in 1945—albeit in a slightly different format as we shall see.

In conclusion, government gold devices did not significantly undermine rules I and II—contrary to what was sometimes alleged. True, gold devices slightly widened the band of experienced exchange-rate variation. This permitted greater—although still modest—short-term interest-rate differentials across countries. Provided that nations adhered to rule V, however, the (minor) use of gold devices made it easier for governments to defend their gold stocks, stay "close to" their traditional mint parities, and maintain virtually fixed exchange rates from 1879 to 1914.

Credibility in the Short Run and in the Long Run: The Restoration Rule

In contrast to the rules governing the Bretton Woods Agreement after World War II, the outstanding characteristic of the pre-1914 gold standard was the commitment to exchange stability in the long run. This is incorporated in rule V in box 1, what I shall call the *restoration rule*. When any country's mint parity had to be suspended—either in a minor way through the use of gold devices or through periods of outright inconvertibility when the government withdrew from the gold market altogether—the presumption was that full gold convertibility would eventually be restored at the traditional (pre-trouble) parity.

Following each of the British suspensions of convertibility in 1847, 1857, and 1866, the traditional mint parity was restored shortly thereafter (Michael Bordo 1984a, 1984b). Even with interruptions from major wars, this ethic usually prevailed. After the Napoleonic wars, the British government finally restored its traditional mint parity in 1821. Following a 17-year suspension during the American Civil War and its aftermath, the U.S. went back to gold in 1879 at its traditional mint parity.

Because of rule V, a government could more easily maintain the gold cover for its currency—i.e., implement rule III—without having to contract the domestic money supply. If a government increased its buying price for gold, international investors anticipated that this increase would be temporary—and that gold's future price would be lower and closer to the traditional mint parity. Short of a major crisis such as a full-scale war, they did not extrapolate further increases in the price of gold. Thus the government could easily attract gold bullion from domestic or foreign residents with modest manipulations of the gold points.

Similarly, if domestic interest rates increased because of gold losses, international investors would see little exchange risk in increasing their holdings of marketable securities denominated in that currency—at least for the industrialized countries at the center of the system. For given foreign interest rates, small increases in short-term domestic interest rates could easily attract financial inflows to cover an incipient payments deficit because of the high degree of credibility of the gold points.

Although exchange rates stayed within a remarkably narrow band from 1879 to 1913, precisely how credible were these gold points in the minds of international investors? Alberto Giovannini (1993) provides an ingenious test by looking at the boundedness of short-term interest rates that is implied by the gold points. Suppose the spot exchange rate S_t (dollars/pounds sterling) was credibly confined within the bounds defined by inequalities (1) and (2)—based on Lawrence Officer's (1986) data on the transactions costs of shipping gold between the United States and Britain. If the observed gold export point from the United States, $\overline{S}$, is widely held to be the maximum value that the exchange rate can take over the maturity of a short-term financial instrument—say a 90-day prime commercial bill denominated in dollars—and if other sources of risk are small, then the American interest rate can never exceed:

$$\overline{R}_t = (1 + R_t^*)(\overline{S}/S_t) - 1 \tag{3}$$

where R_t^* is the interest rate on an equivalent 90-day sterling bill. Similarly, the American interest rate could not fall below

$$\underline{R}_t = (1 + R_t^*)(\underline{S}/St) - 1 \tag{4}$$

where $\underline{S}$ is the gold important point for the United States. Using (3) and (4), Giovannini calculated continuous interest-rate bounds $\overline{R}_t$ and $\underline{R}_t$ from 1889 to 1899, and then checked whether or not the U.S. short-term interest rate fell within these bounds, i.e., whether or not $\underline{R}_t < R_t < \overline{R}_t$. He found that the dollar rate of interest almost always stayed within its credibility bounds. Equally interesting, if the calculation is repeated comparing French or German commercial bills against sterling, the franc and Reichsmark interest rates almost always stayed within their credibility bounds—even in periods when short-term interest rates were quite volatile. (In addition, Giovannini found substantial positive co-movement in short-term interest rates internationally.)

Because of this high degree of credibility under the pre-1914 gold standard, short-term capital flows, more than gold flows themselves, became the key swing variable for balancing international payments while keeping exchange rates stable. For example, if any one country developed a substantial trade deficit that was not matched by a sufficient inflow of long-term capital, a modest increase in its short-term interest rate vis-à-vis sterling would generate a balancing inflow of short-term capital. In contrast, the relatively modest gold flows that did occur responded to shifts in the demand for money relative to the availability of new gold supplies in different parts of the financially integrated world economy (Donald McCloskey and J. Richard Zecher 1976). [Au. note: See chapter 4 below.]

Rule V of the classical gold standard was essential for the regressive exchange-rate expectations that generated stabilizing short-term capital flows. When future exchange rates became less certain in the interwar period, and in the 1970s and 1980s under floating exchange rates, short-term capital flows became destabilizing "hot" money. But the literature does not always recognize the importance of the long-term commitment embodied in rule V. In his scathing criticism of Winston Churchill for returning Britain to gold in 1925 at her traditional mint parity, John Maynard Keynes (1925) did not concede that Churchill was following a well-defined tradition.[4]

Bagehot on Central Banks

In *Lombard Street* (1873), Walter Bagehot persuasively described how central banks should act as lender of last resort under an international gold standard—a principle that subsequently became generally accepted.[5] Bagehot's dictum is summarized as rule IV in box 1. In pursuing this role as the lender of last resort, the central bank could either maintain an excess gold reserve above that legally necessary to back its current note issue (practiced more by continential European countries) or resort more quickly to changing the official discount rate (practiced more by Britain) without violating the rules (Richard Sayers 1957). Indeed, central banks felt no compunction about sterilizing gold inflows in order to build up "excess" reserves.

Continuing increases in their reserve ratios were . . . usually followed by reductions in discount rates, but such reductions appear to have reflected, not the awareness by central banks that such action might help other countries, and thus indirectly their own, to maintain stable exchange rates, but rather such considerations as to minimize holdings of a nonincome-earning asset like gold or to maintain contact with the money market for technical reasons. Indeed, I can find no clear-cut evidence that any central bank ever lowered its discount rate following gold inflows from abroad because of an explicit desire to play, or even because of an awareness of, the "rules of the game." (Arthur Bloomfield 1959, pp. 23–24)

Asymmetrically, interest rates were increased quickly in response to a sharp gold outflow. But in the case of *both* an external and an internal drain,

We must look first to the foreign drain, and raise the rate of interest as high as may be necessary. Unless you stop the foreign export, you cannot allay the domestic alarm. The Bank will get poorer and poorer, and its poverty will protect or renew the apprehension. And at the rate of interest so raised, the holder . . . of the final bank reserve must lend freely. Very large loans at very high interest rates are the best remedy for the worst malady of the money market when a foreign drain is added to a domestic drain. (Walter Bagehot 1873, pp. 27–28)

In such a crisis, this extension of large loans to British commercial banks meant that the domestic assets of the Bank of England were actually increasing as its gold reserve declined: the impact of the gold loss on domestic stocks of circulating bank notes or deposits was (partially) offset or sterilized—as per rule IV. Fluctuations in the national money supply were thereby smoothed. More generally during 1880 to 1914, Arthur Bloomfield (1959) provides striking evidence that European central banks' foreign assets (gold, foreign exchange, and silver) and domestic assets (discounts, advances, and securities) usually moved in opposite directions—as Bagehot's rule would suggest.

In the case of *every* central bank the year-to-year changes in international and domestic assets were more often in the *opposite* direction (34 percent of the time). (Arthur Bloomfield 1959, pp. 48–50)

In interpreting the breakdown of the short-lived gold standard in the interwar period, an influential study by the League of

Nations (Ragnar Nurske 1944) claimed that the principal countries broke the rules of the game by at least partially sterilizing
gold flows. To support this contention, Nurske showed that
domestic and foreign assets moved in opposite directions during
the brief return to the gold standard in the interwar period.
Whereas he claimed that the understood rule during the pre-
1914 classical period was that central banks *reinforce* the effects
of international gold flows on the domestic money stock: changes
in their domestic assets were positively correlated with changes
in official gold stocks. And some authors (Alberto Giovannini
1986) have continued to analyze whether Nurske's nonsterilization rule—or its stronger version inclusive of a reinforcement
effect—was followed during the classical period.

But Nurske's supposed "rule" conflicts directly with Bagehot's
well-established operating principle, and conflicts with Bloomfield's data on how central banks actually behaved in the late
19th century. Thus *no implicit or explicit rule against sterilizing gold
inflows existed under the classical gold standard*—as long as the
traditional mint parity itself was not undermined. In fact, central
banks operated in the international and domestic capital markets, sometimes borrowing or lending directly from each other
(Arthur Bloomfield 1959), to *mitigate* or smooth the effects of
gold flows on domestic money stocks.

To be sure, in noncrisis times, one would not expect sterilization to take place. In the financially integrated world economy
of the late 19th century, suppose an (ongoing) increase in the
demand for the domestic money—distributed between notes and
deposits—in any one country. Then under rule III, the increase
in note issue would be met by a corresponding increase in the
central bank's gold reserves from inflows through the balance
of payments; whereas the increase in deposit money would, at
least in part, be met by an expansion of the central bank's domestic assets. Nurske's positive association between the domestic
and foreign assets of the central bank would hold. But this positive association is not itself a "rule" reflecting conscious policy
by the central bank to reinforce the effect of international gold
flows on the domestic money supply. Rather, it is an endogenous
response to an increase in the domestic demand for money.[6]

In summary, the popular textbook view of the classical gold
standard as an automatic, self-equilibrating balance-of-payments

adjustment mechanism is correct only if one narrowly interprets rules I, II, and III. But from rules IV and V, we understand
that the classical system was *managed*. Diverse countries, which
were not always on good terms politically, adhered to the rules
remarkably well—but from the rather limited perspective of national monetary management linked to a common external standard. National central bank and Treasury authorities continually
undertook discretionary action—subject to the overriding consideration that gold convertibility be maintained in the long term.

> Discretionary judgment and action were an integral part of central
> banking policy before 1914, even if monetary management was not
> oriented toward stabilization of economic activity and prices in the
> broader modern sense. (Arthur Bloomfield 1959, p. 26)

The Endogenous Nominal Anchor

I have drawn up the six rules in box 1 as if they applied *symmetrically* to all countries on the classical gold standard. True, the
British capital market, "managed" by the Bank of England, was of
great value in providing essential finance that helped individual
countries better maintain their gold parities. From rule VI, however, the common price level was still autonomously or automatically determined by the worldwide supply of and demand for
gold.

Apart from the essential randomness of major new gold discoveries, on the supply side there was a systematic tendency for
the common price level—what gold would buy in terms of a
broad basket of other goods and services—to be equilibrated in
the long run. During times of general deflation in the world
economy, new (marginal) gold mines would find it profitable
to increase production, and gold would be attracted away from
nonmonetary uses—such as jewelry. Similarly, as long as countries maintained their official gold parities, there was a natural
brake on worldwide inflation as marginal gold mines were
driven out of production and nonmonetary uses became more
attractive. This supply-side tendency toward equilibration of the
common price level was well known to classical authors such
as John Stuart Mill (1848), and has been more fully articulated
by Robert Barro (1979). Barro showed formally that the common

price level would tend toward complete stability in the long run only if the price of gold relative to a basket of all other commodities was constant.

On the demand side, major shocks occurred continually. In the 1870s and 1880s when countries rushed to (re)join the gold standard, the increased demand for monetary gold caused deflationary pressure in the world economy (Robert Barskey and J. Bradford De Long 1991). Against this, throughout the 19th century up to 1914, the demand for monetary gold was continually reduced by the rapid growth of deposit money on top of an ever-narrowing gold base (Robert Triffin 1964).

But no national monetary authority, not even Britain's, took responsibility for monitoring worldwide growth of this deposit money in order to stabilize the common price level. British monetary policy did not determine the nominal anchor for the system as a whole. Indeed, the common price level was surprisingly variable in the short and intermediate runs (Richard Cooper 1982)—although without any discernable trend in the long run (Roy W. Jastram 1977). Thus, Keynes's vivid metaphor,

> During the latter half of the 19th century the influence of London on credit conditions throughout the world was so predominant that the Bank of England could almost have claimed to be the conductor of the international orchestra (John Maynard Keynes 1930, p. 274),

seems overdrawn (Barry J. Eichengreen 1987). Without demoting the Bank of England to the role of a triangle player in the international orchestra, as Donald N. McCloskey and J. Richard Zecher (1976) playfully did, in the main the British abided by the same monetary rules—including rule VI—as did other industrial countries.

Compared to the marked asymmetry of the rules governing the postwar dollar standard, the symmetry of the pre-1914 gold standard's monetary order increased its political appeal as an exchange mechanism at the micro level. Insofar as all countries remained symmetrically tied to gold, with the common price level determined endogenously, no one country had to be the nominal anchor. (In effect, relying on gold resolved the "Nth country" or "redundancy problem" to be analyzed in our discussion of the fixed-rate dollar standard below.) Whence the great macroeconomic advantage of the international gold standard. By limiting the discretionary power of each national monetary authority to inflate its own or the common price level, or to accommodate external inflationary shocks, the problem of time inconsistency in macroeconomic policies was neatly resolved (Michael Bordo and Finn Kydland 1990; George Alogoskoufis and Ron Smith 1991; George Alogoskoufis 1992).

But this great advantage of the gold standard was also its weakness. Because no government took discretionary action to offset random changes in the demand for, or supply of, monetary gold, the system was prone to sharp (worldwide) liquidity squeezes; and the common price level was much more volatile in the short and intermediate runs than, say, under the fixed-rate dollar standard discussed below (Richard N. Cooper 1982).

Even so, the depth of the London capital market, and the unilateral British commitment to free trade in the late 19th century, were essential to the overall success of the classical gold standard in integrating the world economy. Under "permanently" fixed exchange rates and a virtually common monetary policy, the prices of tradable commodities were about as well aligned internationally as they were within any one country (Donald N. McCloskey and J. Richard Zecher 1976; Charles Calomiris and Robert Hubbard 1987). When measured by wholesale price indices, purchasing power parity across national currencies generally prevailed (Ronald McKinnon 1988b). Except for very small but increasing risk premia as one moved further outward from the center of the world capital market in London, nominal interest rates tended toward equality on a worldwide basis. Thus, from 1879 to 1914, "real" rates of interest across highly diverse industrial and raw materials producing countries were effectively equalized (Lance Davis and Robert Huttenbach 1986) to a degree not seen before or since.[7]

2.2 Bretton Woods in 1945: The Quest for National Macroeconomic Autonomy

From 1943 to 1945, American and British negotiators, among whom J. M. Keynes was the dominant intellectual influence, worked continuously to draw up a new postwar monetary order. Not only did they all seek to escape from the tyranny of gold per se, but Keynes also wanted to prevent the reestablishment of *any* common international monetary standard that would again limit the autonomy of national governments to determine their own monetary policies.

There should be the least possible interference with internal national policies, and the plan should not wander from the international "terrain." (John Maynard Keynes 1943, p. 19)

What caused this major philosophical change? The abortive British attempt to reestablish an international gold standard from 1925 to 1931 was widely seen as having aggravated the Great Depression. Anticipating Britain's return to her prewar parity, the pound appreciated about 10 percent real (15 percent nominal) vis-à-vis the dollar from 1924 to 1925. Keynes guessed that this left sterling 10 percent overvalued, and that the British policy of tight money necessary to maintain this external parity was responsible for the industrial depression which Britain suffered in the remainder of the 1920s.

Unwilling to deflate further to maintain high interest rates in the face of heavy unemployment, Britain devalued sharply in September 1931 after a run on her slender gold stock—and discontinued any official gold parity. Undervaluing the pound then put greater pressure on those countries still on gold to deflate in order to keep their legally required gold covers for domestic note issue. The U.S. finally devalued in 1933, France three years later. In each case, delay in trying to defend official gold parities *before* devaluing greatly aggravated the mounting deflationary and protectionist pressure in the world economy.

The external constraint was binding in significantly more instances than the standard accounts of the period allow. . . . Stemming a run on banks would have required intervention by the lender of last resort. Only by affirming its willingness to provide emergency liquidity to the banking system, and backing words with deeds, could central banks have contained bank runs. But a rapid increase in domestic credit threatened to produce a loss of international reserves. For central banks whose reserves were at the statutory minimum, this would have represented a breach of the gold standard statutes and a fatal blow to confidence in the exchange rate [gold parity]. (Barry J. Eichengreen 1990, pp. 106 and 108)

As is well known, through deflation and protectionism the international economy collapsed. By 1933 foreign trade had fallen to one-third its 1929 level, and controls on international capital flows had proliferated. Runs on banks were transmitted around the world—with the most severe banking crises first in Germany and then in the United States. The world capitalist system could not mount a sustained peacetime economic recovery for the remainder of the 1930s.

The economic debacle of the 1930s gave birth to the doctrine (John Maynard Keynes 1936) that each country should have free rein to manage its own macroeconomy. Rather than submitting to some international standard, exchange rates were to be sufficiently flexible to support nationally selected inflation and employment objectives (James Meade 1951). But to prevent a recurrence of the beggar-thy-neighbor policies of the 1930s, exchange rates were to be sufficiently stable to permit the resumption of normal world trade. Thus did the need for some form of controlled flexibility in exchange rates dominate the Bretton Woods negotiations.

The Bretton Woods system of fixed but adjustable par values was intended to provide exchange stability without the rigidity of the gold standard. (Edward Bernstein 1989, p. 29)

I have endeavored to encapsulate the 20-odd articles of Bretton Woods in 1945, and "the spirit of the treaty," into the six rules contained in box 2.

Unlike the other five rules in box 2, rule VI promising national macroeconomic autonomy has no precise counterpart in the written Bretton Woods articles. Yet, national macroeconomic autonomy is central to what the negotiators wanted (John Williamson 1983). Indeed, rule II supports this autonomy by binding a country to maintain its par value only in the short run, leaving open the possibility that exchange rates could change substantially in the long run. In effect, the "restoration" rule of the classical gold standard (rule V in box 1), with its strong(er) commitment to long-term exchange stability, was reversed. But this reversal is logically consistent with retaining exchange controls on capital account—as per rule III in box 2—to isolate national financial markets. Indeed, Keynes intended to extend the British wartime system of exchange controls to other countries after the war.

There is no country which can, in future, safely allow the flight of funds for political reasons or to evade domestic taxation or in anticipation of the owner turning refugee. Equally, there is no country that can safely receive fugitive funds, which constitute an unwarranted

Rule Box 2
The Bretton Woods Agreement in 1945: The Spirit of the Treaty

---

All Countries

I. Fix a foreign par value for the domestic currency by using gold, or a currency tied to gold, as the numéraire; otherwise demonetize gold in all private transacting.

II. In the short run, keep exchange rate within one percent of its par value; but leave its long-run par value unilaterally adjustable if the International Monetary Fund (IMF) concurs.

III. Free currency convertibility for current-account payments; use capital controls to dampen currency speculation.

IV. Use national monies symmetrically in foreign transacting, including dealings with the IMF.

V. Buffer short-run payments imbalances by drawing on official exchange reserves and IMF credits; sterilize the domestic monetary impact of exchange-market interventions.

VI. National macroeconomic autonomy: each member government to pursue its own price level and employment objectives unconstrained by a common nominal anchor or price rule.

---

import of capital, yet cannot safely be used for fixed investment. For these reasons it is widely held that control of capital movements, both inward and outward, should be a permanent feature of the postwar system. (John Maynard Keynes 1943, p. 31)

Against this, the United States wanted to keep its capital market open to foreigners—with private banks taking the major role in clearing international payments. Thus Keynes had to back down from the idea of maintaining generalized exchange controls. Nevertheless, under the IMF's Article VIII as finally negotiated (incorporated as part of rule III in box 2), he did persuade the Americans to limit each member's official obligation to maintain a convertible currency to *current* transactions—understood to include normal trade credit:

No member shall, without the approval of the Fund, impose restrictions on the making of payments and transfer for current international transactions. (IMF, Article VIII, July 22, 1944)

For a given distribution of the world's capital stock, the international monetary order was intended to sustain allocative efficiency in (multilateral) trade in goods (John Williamson 1983). However, the negotiators did not support microeconomic liberalism to the extent of envisaging a reintegration of the world's capital markets as they had been in the late 19th century. Keeping national capital markets segmented was seen as necessary for pursuing the overriding principle of national macroeconomic autonomy.

The Buffer Stock Approach to Exchange Reserves

Counterfactually, suppose that tight restrictions over international capital movements had been retained in the postwar, and nations had pursued autonomous macroeconomic policies where the domestic monetary consequences of international payments imbalances were sterilized (rule V in box 2). How did the Bretton Woods negotiators in 1945 imagine international payments would get balanced in the short run when exchange rates remained fixed?

Seasonal, cyclical, or any unusual shortfall in a country's net export earnings would be covered out of its official exchange reserves supplemented by that country's access to short- and intermediate-term official credits from the International Monetary Fund. Thus evolved the buffer stock rationale—rule V in box 2—for the management of official exchange reserves.

> The use of liquid reserves as a buffer for temporary discrepancies in the balance of payments should be the normal operation of the international monetary system from day to day, or rather from year to year, exchange rates being thus held stable in the short run. That is the general function of what we may call "international liquidity," including in this term not only gold and exchange reserves but also the drawing facilities (quotas) provided by the Fund. . . . When the liquid reserves of some particular country or countries are depleted, then—and only then—is the time to take measures to correct the balance of payments. Measures of (internal) inflation or deflation are excluded for this purpose, unless they happened to be required for domestic stability. We are then left with . . . commercial policy in the wide sense on the one hand, and exchange rate adjustments on the other. (Ragnar Nurske 1947, pp. 80 and 81)

This remarkable shift from the 19th-century "monetary backing" view of exchange reserves (rule III of the international gold standard) to the modern "buffer stock" approach (rule V of

Bretton Woods) had, by 1945, become accepted by virtually all writers on the subject.[8] It paralleled the shift away from accepting a common external monetary standard, where the national money supply was endogenous and the national price level was determined in common with that of other countries. It also presupposed that short-term private capital flows would no longer be the stabilizing swing variable in international payments.

Symmetry in the Choice of Par Values

Note that our six rules in box 2, like the written articles themselves, are intended to apply symmetrically to all nations signing the Bretton Woods treaty—including the determination of exchange-rate par values as summarized by rule I.

According to Article IV of the Bretton Woods Agreement, exchange rates were to be maintained within one percent of their par values. However, a member country with a payments imbalance could change its official parity to correct a "fundamental disequilibrium" in its balance of payments. Unlike the European Monetary System after 1979, the country in question could *unilaterally* apply to the IMF to change its par value (rule II in box 2) without having to negotiate directly with other member countries. And it was imagined that the IMF, representing the collective interest of all other countries, would readily acquiesce if some disequilibrium existed and the country in question was not trying to gain an unfair competitive advantage over its neighbors.

But what was to be the numéraire against which such controlled exchange rate changes were to be measured? Although gold was no longer the fundamental asset behind the issue of national monies, it—rather than the U.S. dollar—was intended to be the official numéraire in which par values were defined in the 1945 agreement. Article IV, Section I(a) reads:

Expression of par values. The par value of the currency of each member country shall be expressed in terms of gold as a common denominator or in terms of the United States dollar of the weight and fineness in effect on July 1, 1944.

The importance of gold as the numéraire was later obscured when virtually all countries except the United States chose to define their par values in terms of U.S. dollars. However, John

Williamson interprets Article IV to mean that a dollar devaluation or appreciation

(a) was legally possible; (b) did *not* automatically change the par value of any other currency in terms of gold; and (c) did change the parities of other currencies in terms of the dollar. (John Williamson 1977, p. 4)

Williamson suggests that the neutral gold numéraire was chosen to give the United States the symmetrical option to change its exchange rate along with other countries. This symmetry is also captured in box 2's rule IV by which all national currencies were, pro forma, treated more or less equally in defining contributions to, or drawing resources from, the newly created International Monetary Fund. Although gold was chosen as a conveniently neutral numéraire for defining par values for exchange rates, because these rates themselves were to be adjustable, gold was not seen as the fundamental asset restraining national money issue and determining the common price level in the late-19th-century sense. Nor, in 1945, was any one national money supposed to become a dominant "key" currency in the system as a whole.

2.3   The "Fixed-Rate" Dollar Standard, 1950–70

Despite the fact that the articles of the 1945 Bretton Woods Agreement were not significantly amended until the mid 1970s, the world monetary system had, by 1950, evolved into a fixed-rate dollar standard. For 20 years after 1949, very few adjustments in exchange par values occurred: France twice in 1957–58, Germany in 1961, Britain in 1967, Germany and France in 1969—all very modest changes by modern standards. For Japan, its par value remained unchanged at 360 yen/dollar from 1949 to 1971! In effect, virtually fixed exchange rates and a common price level for tradable goods were reimposed, and the macroeconomic autonomy of each participating country was again constrained by an international monetary standard. Thus, the spirit of the largely unwritten rules on how the game was actually played from 1950 to 1970 differed enormously from what the negotiators had intended in 1945.

Instead of treating all nations symmetrically—as embodied in the rules for the pre-1914 gold standard (box 1) and envisaged

Rule Box 3
The Fixed-Rate Dollar Standard, 1950–70

Industrial Countries Other than the United States

I. Fix a par value for the national currency with the U.S. dollar as the numeraire, and keep exchange rate within 1 percent of this par value indefinitely.

II. Free currency convertibility for current-account payments; use capital controls to insulate domestic financial markets, but begin liberalization.

III. Use the dollar as the intervention currency, and keep active official exchange reserves in the U.S. Treasury Bonds.

IV. Subordinate long-run growth in the domestic money supply to the fixed exchange rate and to the prevailing rate of price inflation (in tradable goods) in the United States.

V. Offset substantial short-run losses in exchange reserves by having the central bank purchase domestic assets to partially restore the liquidity of domestic banks and the money supply (Bagehot's Rule).

VI. Limit current account imbalances by adjusting national fiscal policy (government net saving) to offset imbalances between private saving and investment.

The United States

VII. Remain passive in the foreign exchanges: practice free trade with neither a balance-of-payments nor an exchange-rate target. Do not hold significant official reserves of foreign exchange, and (passively) sterilize the domestic monetary consequences of other countries' foreign exchange interventions.

VIII. Keep U.S. capital markets open to foreign governments and private residents as borrowers or depositors.

IX. Maintain position as a net international creditor (in dollar denominated assets) and limit fiscal deficits.

X. Anchor the dollar (world) price level for tradable goods by an independently chosen American monetary policy based on domestic credit expansion.

in the 1945 Bretton Woods treaty (box 2)—the inherent asymmetry of the fixed-rate dollar standard requires writing down one set of rules for countries other than the United States, and a different set for the United States itself. Recognizing this inherent asymmetry, box 3 summarizes the essential rules of the fixed-rate dollar standard according to two criteria. First, it portrays how, in the main, the game was actually played from 1950 to 1970 before the commitment to fixed exchange rates broke down. Second, box 3 also reflects those rules that would have been necessary and sufficient for the fixed-rate dollar standard to have continued indefinitely after 1970. (Thus box 3 omits any rule requiring the dollar to be convertible into gold—a necessary omission for the dollar standard to continue indefinitely; Robert Triffin 1960; Ronald McKinnon 1969.) Each of the 10 rules in box 3 endeavors to satisfy both criteria.

Let us first develop a conceptual rationale for the asymmetrical role of the United States. In the lower panel of box 3, rules VII through X resolved what Mundell called the "redundancy" problem:

Only $N-1$ independent balance of payments instruments are needed in an N-country world because equilibrium in the balances of $N-1$ countries implies equilibrium in the balance of the Nth country. The *redundancy problem* is the problem of deciding how to utilize the extra degree of freedom. (Robert A. Mundell 1968, p. 195)

Because of the demonetization of gold in all private transacting, and its virtual demonetization in official transacting, the redundancy problem arose in a strong form after World War II. All N currencies in the system were *potentially* independent national fiat monies. The amount of each fiat money in circulation was no longer automatically determined by its base of monetary gold, nor were exchange rates tied down by traditional gold parities. Thus gold was no longer the "Nth" currency whose purchasing power—based on the endogenous supply of, and demand for, gold—determined the common price level: the nominal anchor as per rule VI in box 1.

In the absence of a purely international money like gold, the redundancy problem could be resolved neatly by designating one country's money to be the Nth currency. The Nth country would then eschew exchange-rate and other balance-of-payments objectives, but it alone could exercise monetary independence in order to provide a nominal anchor for the system as a whole—i.e., as per American adherence to rule X in box 3.

For the fixed-rate dollar standard to be compatible with the incentives of the other $N-1$ countries, however, the United States had to behave correctly as the Nth country—not only in providing a stable nominal anchor (to be discussed more fully later on), but also by being suitably passive in other dimensions.

Rules VII and VIII in box 3 reflect the passive side: as the Nth country, the United States had to allow the other $N-1$ countries freedom of action to determine various facets of their balance of payments—exchange rates, official holdings of (dollar) reserves, net current-account surpluses, and so on.

In setting par values for exchange rates, all other countries chose the dollar as numeraire—as per rule I in box 3. Insofar as each country intervened to preserve its one percent exchange margins (two percent band), only the dollar was used as the intervention currency (rule III). Thus, in order to prevent conflict in the selection of exchange-rate targets, the United States remained passive in the foreign-exchange markets—as per rules VII and VIII. Once $N-1$ independent exchange rates were chosen against the Nth currency, triangular arbitrage in open exchange markets would determine the complete constellation of $N(N-1)/2$ cross rates—including the effective exchange rate of the Nth country (Ronald McKinnon 1979, ch. 2). This principle that the U.S. not have an independent exchange-rate policy was respected until, in 1971, President Nixon insisted that the dollar be devalued. Although Nixon acted according to the spirit of Bretton Woods Articles that permitted exchange-rate flexibility (John Williamson 1977), dollar devaluation violated the unwritten rules of the game of the fixed-rate dollar standard.

Dollar Exchange Reserves: A Soft Buffer

Beyond the setting of exchange rates, which remained largely fixed anyway, American passivity also extended to the balance of payments. Other countries controlled their individual balances of payments—and consequential buildup of dollar reserves—by the ease or tightness of their domestic monetary policies. Although constrained by the fixed exchange-rate obligation under rule I, rule V still permitted plenty of latitude for each country to adjust its foreign reserve position by altering its domestic monetary policy.

For example, from 1950 to 1967, Japan kept its exchange reserves at modest levels—less than $2 billion with a negligible gold component—by allowing domestic credit expansion by the central bank to satisfy virtually all the growing demand for money in Japan's extremely high-growth economy (Ronald McKinnon 1974). In contrast, the Bundesbank maintained a much tighter rein on domestic central bank credit in Germany—thus inducing a more rapid buildup of foreign exchange reserves to over $8 billion by 1967—with a significant gold component. Indeed, Donald Mathieson (1971) calculated that virtually the whole of the secular increase in the German monetary base in the 1950s and 1960s can be accounted for by German official purchases of U.S. dollars, which were then either held as reserves or paid out as official German capital transfers abroad.

Thus, under rule VII in box 3, the center country was to remain passive no matter what the foreign "demand" for dollar exchange reserves might be—whether modest as in the Japanese case or high as in the German. Under the classical gold standard, the supply of international reserves in the form of gold or its close substitutes determined the world price level because such reserves were backing for the issue of domestic money. In contrast, in a pure key-currency regime,[9] the center country could and should allow other countries' official claims in that currency to be demand-determined to *any* level. Because such reserves were no longer closely related to domestic money issue in the center country or the periphery, they did not determine the rate of inflation or deflation for the system as a whole. Instead, official dollar reserves were better viewed as a soft buffer—or simply as a residual.

In a widely discussed article, "The Dollar and World Liquidity: A Minority View," published in *The Economist* in 1966, Emile Despres, Charles Kindleberger, and Walter Salant argued more generally that the open American capital market (as per rule VIII) was a giant financial intermediary providing liquidity services *both* to foreign governments—mainly through their "voluntary" holdings of U.S. Treasury bonds and bills—and to individuals and firms through their buildup of dollar bank deposits. Despres, Kindleberger, and Salant criticized the U.S. Department of Commerce (worried about potential American gold losses) for treating this buildup of liquid dollar claims owned by foreigners as an American balance-of-payments "deficit"—thus incorrectly connoting a disequilibrium in need of correction.

That the supply of dollar reserve assets is *demand* determined was implicit within the Despres, Kindleberger, and Salant view of the U.S.A.'s role as an international financial intermediary. This is a major claim in favour of the dollar standard, provided that the U.S. pursues a policy of monetary stability—an argument first put forward by McKinnon (1969) . . . [Au. note: See chapter 5 below.]

It should be clear that the stability of the world price level, under the pegged rate dollar standard extant until Spring 1973, required stability of the internal value of the dollar. A stable U.S. price level would provide the link between the monetary and real spheres, much as gold was supposed to have done so under the gold standard. But with the dollar standard, and given a stable U.S. price level, it was the stable prices of *all* U.S. traded goods and services which governed the world price level. (Paul Hallwood and Ronald MacDonald 1986, pp. 165–66)

Indeterminateness in the postwar buildup of dollar exchange reserves would be benign—i.e., would minimize financial stress in the system as a whole—as long as the world price level was pinned down by rule X in box 3. The United States *actively* exercised "the extra degree of freedom" associated with Mundell's redundancy problem to stabilize the purchasing power of the dollar in terms of a broad basket of tradable goods and services.

American Monetary Independence

Unlike the Bank of England, which could not control the common price level under the pre-1914 gold standard, the U.S. Federal Reserve System had sufficient freedom of action to anchor the common price level under the postwar dollar standard. It could follow rule X in box 3 if it so chose. First, unlike all other countries, the U.S. government was not obligated to intervene directly in the foreign-exchange markets; thus it did not need continually to adjust its domestic monetary base to support such interventions. Second, other industrial countries held their official reserves mainly in U.S. Treasury bonds—thus satisfying rule

III—which, in practice, was a fairly well-established convention. These demand-determined reserves could then grow to any level without threatening a run on the U.S. gold stock, whose official price was fixed at $35 per ounce—a (nominal) obligation under the Bretton Woods Agreement but *not* one of the 10 rules for a successful fixed-rate dollar standard outlined in box 3.

(In the 1960s, intense schizophrenia afflicted the managers of the system. They were uncertain whether to follow rule box 2 or rule box 3, or to respect the residual dollar-gold convertibility constraint that fitted neither set of rules. The historical origins of this schizophrenia and the associated "Triffin Dilemma" are analyzed below.)

But rule III has a further important aspect. The accumulation or decumulation of dollar exchange reserves by foreign central banks would not affect the American monetary base. Only foreign holdings of "nonmonetary" U.S. Treasury bonds would change. Therefore, exchange interventions by foreign central banks were "passively" or automatically sterilized from changing the American money supply (Alexander Swoboda 1978; Ronald McKinnon 1982). Foreign money supplies definitely were affected by exchange intervention by foreign governments, but the American money supply was not—as reflected by rule VII.

Even if the Fed had unhindered control over the U.S. money supply, was the demand for it fairly predictable? As long as exchange rates were not expected to change collectively against the dollar (rule I), international currency substitution for or against the dollar would not be a problem—and was not in the 1950s and 1960s (Ronald McKinnon 1984 and 1988a). In the absence of institutional changes within the United States itself, i.e., "financial innovations," the effective demand for narrow money in the form of U.S. $M1$ was fairly stable.

In summary, by controlling the supply of base money in dollars and by being able to estimate the demand for it without reference to what was going on in the foreign exchanges or in other countries, the U.S. Federal Reserve was unique among central banks in being able to stabilize its own price level *unilaterally*—inclusive of tradable goods as approximated by the American producer price index. In the other industrial countries, by contrast, trends in money growth were endogenously determined according to rule IV.

The schematic diagram in figure 2.1 summarizes how the fixed-rate dollar standard fitted together to determine trends in aggregate money growth and inflation in the world economy. For the U.S. on the one hand and the rest of the industrial world (*ROW*) on the other, the arrows show the direction of causation as established in a series of Granger statistical tests performed by Kong-Yam Tan (1984).

In the system portrayed in figure 2.1, the American money supply, M^{us}, is the dominant control variable. The joint interaction with Y^{us} (American real output) and M^{us} determines the American price level for tradable goods—as denoted by P^{us}. Through the fixed exchange rate, the price level for tradables in the rest of the world, P^{row} is determined at a common level with the United States. Much weaker is the direct link from Y^{us} to Y^{row}. Instead, foreign real output is dominated by domestic supply-side determinants of growth in postwar Europe and Japan (Kenichi Ohno 1987). As *ROW*'s output increases at the common price level anchored by the United States, the demand for *ROW* money also increases causing (incipient) balance-of-payments surpluses abroad. Finally, in this chain of causation, M^{row} increases endogenously to accommodate the increased demand for it.

Official Schizophrenia: Exchange-Rate Rigidity and the Dollar Price of Gold

In order to preserve national macroeconomic autonomy, the designers of the Bretton Woods Agreement intended, in 1945, to retain exchange-rate flexibility in the long run—as per rule II in box 2. If so, why did exchange rates among the principal industrial countries remain so rigid in practice from 1950 to 1970—as per rule I in box 3?

First, after a one-time round of European devaluations in 1949 to offset greater wartime and postwar inflation vis-à-vis the

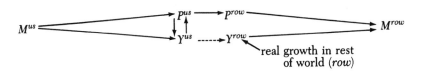

Figure 2.1
The fixed-rate dollar standard.

United States, there was more or less successful macroeconomic stabilization in Europe under the Marshall Plan. By September 1950, the Marshall Plan's most important progeny—the European Payments Union (EPU)—was established for clearing payments multilaterally within Europe by using the U.S. dollar both as the unit of account and the means of settlement. Thus, each European central bank found it convenient to maintain an exactly fixed dollar exchange parity—without even a narrow band[10]—in setting its net EPU payments imbalances every month (Jacob Kaplan and Günther Schleiminger 1989). More importantly, the greater financial stability and openness of the United States compared favorably to the relative lack of confidence in the finances of the other industrial economies.

In Japan in 1949–50, there was a similar dollar-based price-level stabilization under the Dodge Plan. Thus, the European countries and Japan wanted fixed dollar exchange rates to help anchor their national monetary policies and price levels. To secure more efficient disinflation with less unemployment, they found it convenient to lean on the superior financial reputation of the United States throughout the 1950s.

(Much later, after the fixed-rate dollar standard had collapsed into the high inflation of the 1970s, this process was again replicated within Europe. After the formation of the European Monetary System (EMS) in 1979, those European countries with higher inflation leaned on Germany—and by the by-then-superior reputation of the Bundesbank—to provide a nominal anchor for their price levels, as shown in rule box 7 below.)

Second, in the 1960s, after the EPU was terminated and after financial recovery in Europe and Japan, capital-account transactions were progressively liberalized—as per rule II in box 3. This openness inhibited governments from even considering any change in their (dollar) par values for fear of provoking large anticipatory capital flows. Similarly, governments other than the American could not conduct independent monetary policies without provoking large offsetting capital movements (Pentti Kouri and Michael Porter 1973). In effect, foreign central banks had to adjust growth in their national money supplies to support exchange intervention—i.e., in the long run, intervention had to be nonsterilized to be effective (*Jurgensen Report* 1983). Thus, willy-nilly, governments continued to follow rule IV in box 3 in the 1960s—even after doubts arose about the efficacy of relying on American monetary policy as the nominal anchor for the system as a whole.

Official schizophrenia over exchange-rate flexibility carried over to America's residual but still vexing link to gold: the commitment to convert dollar balances held by foreign central banks and treasuriers at $35 per ounce. This "rule" fitted into neither box 2 nor box 3. Instead it was an unanticipated outcome of using gold as a passive numéraire in setting exchange par values under Article IV of the 1945 Bretton Woods Agreement (rule I, box 2). Once all other countries had formally specified their par values in terms of dollars, the United States accidentally found itself as the only major country with a pro forma commitment to convert its currency into gold.

Residual or not, was this gold link a constraint on American monetary independence? In the 1950s by and large, the answer was no. U.S. gold stocks were large relative to outstanding official dollar claims. Because of the strong financial reputation of the United States and the dollar's special role in the EPU, foreign central banks preferred, on average, to build up interest-bearing dollar claims rather than converting them into (sterile) gold.

By the early 1960s, however, we have the emergence of the famous "Triffin Dilemma" (Robert Triffin 1960). Even when American monetary policy remained perfectly satisfactory in anchoring the common price level of tradable goods through the mid 1960s, the rapid voluntary build up of foreign dollar claims relative to the limited American gold stock gave speculators a one-way bet: the U.S. would always put a dollar floor under the price of gold but could not prevent a collective run on the dollar from forcing a price increase. No problem existed as long as there was no run on the dollar, but the threat of a run artificially increased the demand for gold vis-à-vis dollars in such a way that a run could be precipitated. Indeed, some Europeans like Charles de Gaulle actively used official gold conversions to try to drive the world off the de facto dollar standard. Whence the Triffin Dilemma, and why this dollar-gold link does not fit into a consistent set of rules (box 3) for the fixed-rate dollar standard.[11]

In the 1960s, this ambiguity in the rules of the game kept American politicians like Presidents Kennedy and Johnson awake at night worrying about American gold losses (Robert Solomon 1977). For a brief window of time in the early 1960s, it had the perhaps salutary effect of making American monetary policy more conservative, i.e., less inflationary, than many academic economists wanted. By 1968, however, the U.S. had made it progressively more awkward for foreign central banks to convert their dollar assets into gold. More negatively, concern for continued gold losses induced the United States to impose mild restrictions on capital outflows—such as the interest rate equalization tax—contrary to rule VIII in box 3. Although these capital-account restrictions were sufficiently porous so as not to undermine the overall integrity of the dollar standard, clearly the managers of the system had become very schizophrenic.

Adjusting to Cyclical Fluctuations in International Payments

Although foreign money growth was largely endogenous in the longer run (figure 2.1), how did governments in Europe and Japan adjust to cyclical imbalances in international payments given the "unexpected" rigidity in exchange rates? For the years 1950 to 1967, Michael Michaely (1971) studied the reaction of eight industrial countries[12] to cyclical changes in their gross official reserve positions—i.e., dollar holdings, gold, and net positions with the International Monetary Fund. Outside of the United States, he found overall compliance of domestic monetary policy to the exchange rate—as per rule IV in box 3. The domestic money supply moved in the same direction—or the discount rate moved in the opposite direction—as the change in official exchange reserves.

In a further remarkable parallel with Bloomfield's 1959 analysis of the classical gold standard, Michaely also found for the dollar standard that

> Countries tend to regard as their external target not so much the attainment of balance-of-payments equilibrium as the avoidance of deficits. . . . The loss of reserves is viewed with concern, but their accumulation . . . is viewed with satisfaction or indifference. (Michael Michaely 1971, pp. 63–64)

Fortunately, the accumulation of "excess" exchange reserves by countries with balance-of-payments surpluses could be easily accommodated under a pure dollar standard if they held non-monetary U.S. Treasury Bonds (rule III), which was largely true in practice. In contrast, the excessive accumulation of gold reserves by one or more countries under an international gold standard could lead to worldwide deflation that was particularly noticeable in the 1880s and early 1890s—not to mention the deflationary debacle that occurred from 1929 to 1933, as discussed above. Thus, the fixed-rate dollar standard was inherently less subject to liquidity crises than the classical gold standard—and thus was much less prone to cyclical variations in the common price level (Richard N. Cooper 1982). As long as the United States prevented the common price level from falling irrespective of the buildup of dollar reserves by foreign governments, deflation was not a problem.

Bagehot's rule, i.e., rule V in box 3, was also followed by Europe and Japan in the 1950s and 1960s.

The central bank's domestic assets do show, in most countries, a clear tendency to rise with a fall in the country's external reserves, and vice versa. (Michael Michaely 1971, p. 40)

When the European and Japanese governments intervened to buy and sell dollars to maintain their dollar exchange rates, in the short run national central banks partially sterilized the domestic monetary consequences of these (cyclical) imbalances in international payments. Michaely found that, rather than letting the domestic money supply contract fully by the amount of some "external drain" (in Bagehot's terminology), the central bank would lend to commercial banks to partially offset the effect of a balance-of-payments deficit on the domestic money supply. By keeping the central bank's discount window open, albeit for lending at a penalty rate, this procedure was virtually automatic (Ronald McKinnon 1979, ch. 10). If the commercial banks lost reserves in the foreign exchanges, they automatically appeared at the window for (partial) replenishment.

Internal versus External Balance

What about the potential conflicts between "internal" balance—the level of employment, output, and so on—and "external" balance in international payments? Following James Meade's seminal extension of Keynesian macroeconomics to open economies in 1951, textbooks down to the present day emphasize the importance of exchange-rate flexibility as a separate policy instrument for controlling international payments—thus freeing demand management to take care of domestic output and employment—presumably at a stable price level.[13] If the government was handicapped by a fixed exchange rate, Robert A. Mundell (1962) analyzed the further need to assign monetary policy to external balance while fiscal policy was assigned to balance aggregate demand in the domestic macroeconomy.

In his detailed empirical study of the 1950s and 1960s, however, Michaely found that such textbook conflicts seldom occurred.

> The requirements of external and internal balance tended much more often to provide policy indications in the same direction, or at least not to contradict each other, rather than to point in opposite directions. As a result of this, and the general lack of enthusiasm to employ budgetary policy, the use of the much discussed "policy mix," which would assign monetary policy to balance-of-payments adjustment and fiscal policy to achieve high employment (where the two targets call for policies in opposite directions), is a rarity rather than a common phenomenon. (Michael Michaely 1971, p. 63)

During the 1950s and 1960s when the theory behind the standard textbook dilemma of how best to maintain internal and external balance simultaneously was developed (Harry Johnson 1958; W. E. G. Salter 1959), the empirical issue was largely moot. This theorizing on the need for more exchange-rate flexibility was prompted by numerous sterling crises in the 1950s and 1960s—which reflected attempts by the British government, under the strong influence of British Keynesians, to be more inflationary than the confines of the dollar standard allowed. But Britain was not typical. Most countries, such as Japan, willingly accepted the subordination of national monetary policy to an international standard because of the absence of any conflict between external and internal balance.

> Until 1967–68, Japan's postwar monetary policy was able to pursue simultaneously three policy goals—stable prices, full employment, and balance of payments equilibrium—because there were no trade offs among these goals. It may be that, of the three, balance of payments equilibrium was given the highest priority (but) . . . there was no contradiction between this and the other two goals. (Yoshio Suzuki 1986, p. 119)

This lack of conflict between domestic and foreign balance under the fixed-rate dollar standard is superficially puzzling. True, monetary policies in countries other than the United States were subordinated to maintaining the exchange rate—as per rule IV. Unlike the classical gold standard, however, exchange controls on capital flows were still quite restrictive in Japan and in many European countries in the 1950s and 1960s—as permitted under rule II. Thus, unlike the gold standard, there was no "automatic" private finance for persistent current account deficits or surpluses. If investment tended to be greater than saving in country A, this would eventually result in an uncovered current-account deficit which, under the fixed-rate dollar standard, could not be eliminated by exchange depreciation. (Under the pre-1914 gold standard, countries could cover large trade surpluses or deficits by offsetting flows of private capital.)

In the 1950s and 1960s, the matter was essentially resolved by each country's maintaining a rough balance between aggregate national saving and investment. After the end of the Marshall Plan in 1952, persistent net capital transfers—and thus trade imbalances—among the industrial economies remained very small well into the 1970s. Fluctuations in investment and saving were highly positively correlated *within* countries (Martin Feldstein and Charles Horioka 1980; Jeffrey A. Frankel 1986)—unlike the late 19th century and unlike the 1980s to follow.

But what was the mechanism by which intracountry savings and investment remained roughly balanced? In a major empirical study, Tamin Bayoumi (1990) shows that *private* saving and investment within each country were not well correlated in the 1960s into the early 1970s. (When net international capital transfers were very large under the pre-1914 gold standard, private saving and investment were similarly uncorrelated.) However, Bayoumi also showed that government fiscal surpluses, i.e., net government saving, were inversely related to the private saving-investment gap in each country. Therefore, to complete the rules of the game for the fixed-rate dollar standard, box 3 incorporates this fiscal offset into rule VI for countries other than the United States, and into rule IX for the United States itself. In the 1950s and 1960s, fiscal policy was actively adjusted to keep each country's current account surplus (deficit) small—which obviated the need for large capital transfers from one country to another. This, in turn, made the system consistent with the retention of (modest) capital controls (rule II) by countries other than the United States.

After the Fall: The Failure to Agree on New Rules for Setting Par Values, 1971–74

The calamitous events ending the worldwide commitment to maintain par values in exchange rates have been well chronicled by the Federal Reserve's Robert Solomon (1977). Following the advice of economists throughout the United States who were worried about America's loss of international competitiveness, President Nixon insisted in August 1971 that the dollar be devalued—and imposed a temporary import surcharge of 10 percent until, at the Smithsonian Institution in December 1971, new exchange parities were declared to value the dollar some 10 to 20 percent less against other important currencies.[14] But the always tenuous Smithsonian par values broke down completely in early 1973, and the currencies of the major industrial blocs of North America, Europe, and Japan have been floating against each other ever since.

In 1973 and 1974, finance ministries and central banks—convened under the auspices of the so-called Committee of Twenty (C-20)—entered into strenuous negotiations to consider monetary reforms leading to a new set of par values. Under its terms of reference, the C-20 was to propose a new world monetary order that was more symmetrical (not dollar based) and which permitted more exchange-rate "flexibility" for individual countries including the United States than the apparent rigidity of the old fixed-rate dollar standard. But these terms of reference proved impossible to negotiate—as John Williamson (1977) analyzed comprehensively in *The Failure of World Monetary Reform, 1971–74*. In effect, in reasserting the principles of international symmetry and greater national macroeconomic autonomy while still trying to establish par values for exchange rates, the C-20 was renegotiating in the original spirit of the Bretton Woods articles—as summarized by our six rules in box 2. Still under the sway of Keynes's views as of 1943–44, officials and academic economists in 1973–74 had not really changed their mind-set for 30 years.

But the same problems that prevented the flexible and symmetrical monetary order contained in box 2 from being effective after 1945, to be replaced by the rigid and asymmetrical fixed-rate dollar standard contained in box 3, were even more apparent by the early 1970s.

First, there was the "hot" money problem. Having exchange rates stable in the short run at some given par value could not be reconciled with having them adjustable in the long run in order to allow national macroeconomic autonomy. As long as world financial markets remained (modestly) open, speculative hot money flows would tend to anticipate any discrete change in official par values.[15] And, certainly by 1973–74, the negotiators did not want a return to the draconian exchange controls that Keynes had in mind in 1943.

Second, the negotiators refused to recognize the nature of Mundell's redundancy problem. In an N-country world without any generally accepted purely international money such as gold, there can only be $N-1$ independent official targets for the exchange rate, balance of trade, balance of payments, and so on. Symmetry, in the sense of each of the N countries choosing its targets independently, is simply impossible.

Roughly speaking, two approaches can resolve this redundancy problem. One is to require detailed negotiations among all N countries for each of the $N-1$ targets in each category—something that only a close-knit group like the European Monetary System temporarily achieved in the limited sphere of setting par values for exchange rates before September 1992 (see boxes 6 and 7 below). But even the EMS does not negotiate over other balance-of-payments targets. Among countries that were more loosely related politically, a monetary order requiring continual mutual negotiations on a worldwide basis is neither possible nor desirable.

The alternative solution to the redundancy problem is both simple and elegant. If a natural candidate exists, assign one of the N countries to be the passive Nth country, and leave the other $N-1$ countries responsible for setting their par values and balance-of-payments targets independently. That corresponds precisely to the 10 rules for the fixed-rate dollar standard from 1950 to 1970 (box 3). But this was the monetary order from which the United States was trying to escape! Thus, the C-20 negotiations collapsed in 1974 for essentially the same reason that prompted President Nixon to devalue the dollar in 1971.

Concern for the "overvalued" American exchange rate from about 1968 onward reflected the slipping American resolve to continue anchoring the common price level (rule X, box 3). By caving in to domestic political pressure to be more "expansionary," the U.S. Federal Reserve allowed the American producer index to begin increasing at about 3.5 percent per year from 1968 to 1972, whereas from 1951 to 1967 inflation had averaged closer to only 1 percent per year. Other countries, notably Germany, were thereby induced to violate rule IV by attempting a sufficiently tight money policy to reduce their inflation rates below that prevailing in the United States—whence the cumulative "overvaluation" of the dollar that so concerned President Nixon and his advisors. Anticipating dollar devaluation, "hot" money flowed out of the United States in 1970–71. The result was an excessive buildup of dollar exchange reserves and money growth abroad that further hastened the collapse of the fixed exchange-rate regime. [Au. note: See chapter 7.]

But this collapse of dollar-based par values was hardly inevitable. If the U.S. Federal Reserve System had continued to anchor the common price level, and if the Americans had not asserted their legal right to adjust the dollar exchange rate as promised by the Bretton Woods Articles, the fixed dollar exchange parities could have continued indefinitely once the residual commitment to gold convertibility was terminated. Clearly, the discrepancy between the unwritten rules in box 3 and the legal obligations in box 2 eventually proved lethal for the par value system.

2.4   The Floating-Rate Dollar Standard, 1973–84

But not lethal for the dollar standard itself! Even the traumatic breakdown of fixed exchange rates in 1971–73 did surprisingly little subsequently to disturb the conventions for using the dollar as international money for official and private purposes (Ronald McKinnon 1979). Under floating (as well as fixed) exchange rates, economies of scale are such that "the use of a currency as (international) money itself reinforces that currency's usefulness" (Paul Krugman 1984). This reinforcing circularity makes displacement unlikely short of war, exchange controls, or massive inflation, in the center country.[16]

Table 2.2, adapted from Peter Kenen (1983) and Paul Krugman (1984), conveniently identifies six international monetary roles for the dollar—depending on whether it is used for private or official purposes. For compactness of discussion, the dollar's usefulness as "a standard of deferred payment"—so important for the operation of long-term capital markets (Charles P. Kindleberger 1972)—is combined with the discussions of its unit-of-account and store-of-value roles.

As an international *medium of exchange,* the dollar has remained the dominant vehicle currency for interbank clearing for more than 90 percent of spot and forward transactions in the private foreign exchange markets (Peter Kenen 1983). Today, if a Swedish bank wants to buy sterling with marks, it must first buy dollars with marks, and then sterling with dollars.

Such indirect exchange arises because of the great economies of scale (Alexander Swoboda 1968; K. Alec Chrystal 1977) involved in interbank trading. Parallel to our earlier analysis of official interventions in terms of Mundell's redundancy problem, suppose there are N national currencies to be traded in purely private foreign-exchange markets. Then symmetrical trading in any pair of them would involve organizing and maintaining $N(N-1)/2$ foreign exchange markets at every term to maturity. However, if all trading takes place against a single reference or Nth currency, the number of such markets can be reduced to $N-1$. This economy of scale is particularly pronounced in using the dollar as the vehicle for organizing *forward* exchange (and option) markets where trading naturally thins out quickly for more distant maturities.

Forward markets, in particular, are universally structured with the dollar as the settlement medium. The vast bulk of trade in spot markets is also done through the dollar, although here a number of cross markets

Table 2.2
Roles of an International Currency

	Private	Official
Medium of exchange	Vehicle	Intervention
Unit of account	Invoice	Peg
Store of value	Banking	Reserve

do exist between major currencies, notably within Europe (including Japan). (K. Alec Chrystal 1987, p. 131)

Because of the dollar's dominance as a private vehicle currency, it is still commonly used for official *intervention.* Central banks, other than the U.S. Federal Reserve System, often act to smooth or otherwise directly influence the foreign-exchange value of their own monies in terms of dollars. Even without any officially announced dollar peg, direct official intervention in the foreign exchanges has been about as extensive since 1973 as it was under the old system of fixed parities (John Williamson 1976; Esther Suss 1976). But the United States typically remained relatively passive—although after February 1985, the U.S. Federal Reserve System did occasionally intervene in concert with other central banks under the Plaza-Louvre Accords (rule box 5 below).

In the various attempts to smooth exchange fluctuations within Europe—the "snake-in-the-tunnel" of the 1970s and within the European Monetary System after 1979, the U.S. dollar was often the intervention currency. Although the dollar had been supplanted largely by the deutsche mark as the principal intervention currency within Europe in the 1990s (rule box 7), it still remains the dominant currency for official transactions elsewhere.

Aside from this interbank transacting, however, how prevalent is the dollar as an international *unit of account* for invoicing commodity trade among the industrial countries? The prices of homogeneous commodities can be quickly arbitraged across international boundaries and are immediately flexible on an hour-to-hour basis. Thus their worldwide (dollar) price is registered at a centralized basing point or commodity exchange—such as the spot market for oil in Rotterdam, or the futures markets in metals and basic foodstuffs in Chicago or New York. Because of this natural centralization of the trading mechanism for auction-market goods, much like the centralization of the foreign-exchange interbank market itself, the U.S. dollar is the invoice currency of choice.[17]

Finally, the dollar's role as an international *store of value* arises naturally out of its convenience for official intervention, as a private vehicle currency generally accepted in interbank transacting as the prevailing currency of denomination for primary commodities, and from its generalized use as a standard of deferred payment in international debt transactions.[18] Table 2.3 shows that the bulk of the world's "active" exchange reserves are still U.S. dollar claims held by foreign central banks or treasuries. Similarly, private gross claims in the Eurocurrency markets by banks in Europe are still largely in dollars—although table 2.3 also shows that the dollar's share in the late 1980s is somewhat less than during the "high" dollar standard before 1971. Despite Japan's rise to prominence as the world's dominant net creditor with large current-account surpluses after 1980, and also as an international financial intermediary borrowing short in order to further increase its long-term lending in the late 1980s, George Tavlas and Yuzuru Ozeki (1992) show that the yen remained surprisingly little used in these transactions. For example, they show that Japanese short-term liquid liabilities to the rest of the world remain largely dollar denominated.

What then was the upshot of this entrenched role of the dollar in private markets for the behavior of national governments once the commitment to the par-value system broke down? Although after March 1973 is commonly referred to as the period of "floating" exchange rates, this terminology is deceptive. Not only did official interventions continue, but they exhibited systematic rules or patterns. These are set out in rule box 4—The Floating-

Table 2.3
The Dollar as an International Store of Value (dollar percentage shares)

	1965	1970	1975	1980	1985	1990
Private interbank money: Cross-border claims in the Eurocurrency market[a]	83.5	77.1	73.7	67.9	69.4	60.1[c]
Official reserves of foreign exchange[b]	66.4	77.2	79.5	68.6	65.0	56.4[d]

[a]Bank for International Settlements (BIS), *Annual Report(s)*.
[b]IMF *International Financial Statistics* (1983 supplement on reserves) and *Annual Report(s)*.
[c]For 1988 only, which was the last year the BIS provided currency of denomination for claims in the Eurocurrency market.
[d]For 1990, the dollar share of foreign-exchange reserves would fall to 49.6% if official holdings of European Currency Units (ECUs) are treated as a separate reserve asset.

Rate Dollar Standard, 1973–1984—and, after a significant regime change, in The Plaza-Louvre Intervention Accords for the Dollar Exchange Rate, 1985–1992 in rule box 5 below.

From March 1973 to February 1985, governments followed rules of the game surprisingly similar to what they had been before—as one can readily see by comparing box 3 for the fixed-rate dollar standard to box 4 for the floating-rate dollar standard. The United States continued as the relatively passive center country, while the other (industrial) countries remained actively interventionist in the foreign exchanges. In effect, the continued importance of the dollar as international money induced foreign governments to "have a view" of what an appropriate dollar exchange rate should be in terms of their own currencies while, for the most part, the United States conducted its monetary policies independently of what was going on in the foreign exchanges.

The upper panel of box 4 gives the rules governing countries other than the United States after 1973. In contrast to box 3, however, rule I in box 4 only commits the foreign government to smoothing short-run fluctuations in its dollar exchange rate—with no well-defined commitment to some longer-term par value. As per rule V, the "target" for the dollar exchange rate can drift indefinitely such that the long-run path of other countries' domestic price levels now diverges from that of the United States. But without any credible commitment to a par value, immediate pressure on the domestic currency to move sharply against the dollar in the foreign exchanges can be enormous, whence rule IV. If its national currency weakens sharply against the dollar, the foreign government responds by temporarily contracting its domestic money supply—and vice versa.

What were the macroeconomic consequences of this nonsterilization policy? After 1970 the dollar tended to be simultaneously either weak or strong against the currencies of most other industrial countries. Because of the attempt to smooth these fluctuations by foreign central banks, the collective "world" money supply became highly variable. From 1971 through early 1985, world money tended to increase when the dollar was weak, and then fall below its trend when the dollar was strong (Ronald McKinnon 1982, 1984, 1988a; Paul de Grauwe 1989). This collective monetary response to fluctuations in the dollar exchange

Rule Box 4
The Floating-Rate Dollar Standard, 1973–84

Industrial Countries Other than the United States

I. Smooth near-term fluctuations in dollar exchange rate without committing to a par value or to long-term exchange stability.

II. Free currency convertibility for current payments, while eventually eliminating remaining restrictions on capital account.

III. Use the dollar as the intervention currency (except for some transactions to stabilize intra-European exchange rates), and keep official exchange reserves mainly in U.S. Treasury bonds.

IV. Adjust short-run growth in the national money supply to support major exchange interventions: reduce when the national currency is weak against the dollar and expand when it is strong.

V. Set long-run growth in the national price level and money supply independently of the United States, and allow corresponding secular adjustments in dollar exchange rate.

The United States

VI. Remain passive in the foreign exchanges: free trade with neither a balance of payments nor exchange-rate target. Do not hold significant official reserves of foreign exchange, and (passively) sterilize the domestic monetary consequences of other countries' foreign-exchange interventions.

VII. Keep U.S. capital markets open to foreign governments and private residents as borrowers or depositors.

VIII. Pursue monetary policies independent of the foreign-exchange value of the dollar and of the rate of money growth in other industrial countries—without trying to anchor any common price level.

---

rate explains why the world business cycle was more synchronized and so pronounced from 1971 to the mid 1980s (Kenichi Ohno 1987; Matti Viren 1992). Apart from the effects of oil shocks, the two worldwide inflations of the 1970s were caused by prior expansions in "world" money associated with dollar weakness, and worldwide output contracted sharply in 1981–82 because of the sudden fall in foreign money growth associated with the dollar's surprising strength. [Au. note: See chapters 7 and 9.]

How could this unfortunate cyclical behavior in "world" money from (incipient) fluctuations in the dollar exchange rate have been dampened? Suppose, contrary to rule VI, box 4, after 1971 the United States behaved more symmetrically with respect to other countries in stabilizing the dollar exchange rate—as advocated by Ronald McKinnon (1974 and chapter 8). Then, the American money supply would have contracted when the dollar was weak to offset the expansion in foreign money supplies—and vice versa. Fluctuations in the aggregate money supply, in world prices and output, and in the dollar exchange rate, would thereby have been dampened. In the event, the regime change that occurred differed from this guideline in important respects—although American behavior did indeed become more "symmetrical" after 1984.

2.5 The Plaza-Louvre Intervention Accords for the Dollar Exchange Rate, 1985–95

The rapid appreciation of the dollar in 1981–84, particularly against the mark (figure 2.2a) and the EMS bloc, was widely characterized as a "bubble" (Paul Krugman 1985; Jeffrey A. Frankel 1985)—but was no less disruptive to American foreign trade for all that. By February 1985, the dollar's last upward fling of about 20 percent from June 1984 finally provoked the U.S. government to cast aside its previous hands-off foreign exchange policy. The other industrial countries, particularly the Europeans, were distressed by again being forced separately into an unduly tight monetary policy in order to dampen upward pressure on the dollar (rule IV, box 4). This depressing influence on their economies contributed to what was then called "euro-sclerosis." Hence, the stage was set for the "Plaza Sea-Change of 1985" (Kathryn Dominguez and Jeffrey A. Frankel 1993a).

The Switch to Concerted, Discrete Interventions

The dominant characteristics of the new regime, which I have dubbed The Plaza-Louvre Intervention Accords for the Dollar Exchange Rate, 1985–1992 in rule box 5 (revised slightly and updated to 1995 in this book), did not emerge all at once. Still, even as early as February 1985, there were abrupt breaks from the

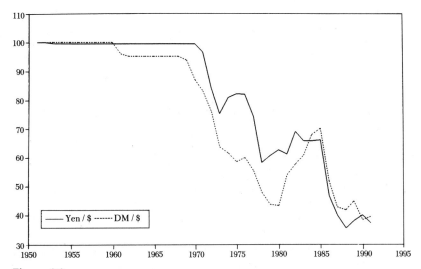

Figure 2.2a
Nominal exchange rate, 1951 = 100 (annual data).

old regime. First, the American government ended its passivity in the foreign exchanges and actively intervened not only to stop the dollar's sharp rise, but to engineer a major devaluation. Second, foreign governments, instead of intervening singly or piecemeal to sell dollars according to conditions in their own foreign-exchange markets, now coordinated their interventions with the U.S. Federal Reserve System in a way that was obvious to all market participants. The common direction and intent of this official intervention *in dollars,* with the dollar's exchange rates against yen and marks being the benchmarks, was clearly signaled. The principle of concerted, open intervention as per rule III in box 5 was established at the outset.

Using hitherto confidential and extraordinarily detailed daily data from the central banks themselves, Piero Catte, Giampaolo Galli, and Salvatore Rebecchini (1992, 1994) studied the magnitude and timing of official interventions by 16 governments from February 1985 through the end of 1991. They found that:

1. "Interventions by the G-3 were rare and concentrated in time."

2. "The three countries never pursued conflicting intervention policies vis-à-vis the dollar. Whenever one of the three was in the market to, say, support the dollar, the other two were either doing the same thing or nothing."

Rule Box 5
The Plaza-Louvre Intervention Accords for the Dollar Exchange Rate, 1985–95

Germany, Japan, and the United States (G-3)

  I. Set broad target zones for the mark/dollar and yen/dollar exchange rates of ± 12 percent. Do not announce the agreed-on central rates, and leave zonal boundaries flexible.

 II. If disparities in economic "fundamentals" among the G-3 change substantially, adjust the (implicit) central rates.

III. Intervene in concert, but infrequently, to reverse short-run trends in the dollar exchange rate that threaten to pierce zonal boundaries. Signal the collective intent by not disguising these concerted interventions.

 IV. Practice free currency convertibility on current and capital account, and hold official exchange reserves symmetrically in each other's currencies. U.S. government to begin building up its reserves in marks, yen, and possibly other convertible currencies.

  V. Sterilize the immediate domestic monetary impact of foreign-exchange interventions by leaving short-term interest rates unchanged.

 VI. Assign domestic monetary policy to achieve a zero or low rate of price inflation—as measured variously by the domestic CPI, or WPI, or GNP deflator. Do not commit to any one national price index, or attempt to coordinate inflation targets internationally.

VIa. If national inflation rates undershoot or overshoot their targets, rebase the price level for targeting next period's inflation. Allow cumulative drift in the national price level from past errors in forecasting inflation rates.

Other Industrial Countries

VII. Support, or not oppose, interventions by G-3 to keep the dollar within designated mark and yen zones. Buy dollars with the national curency, or with yen and marks, when the dollar is weak—and vice versa.

3. "The timing of the (intervention) clusters were almost always coincident for two of the three countries (in the G-3)."

From this general pattern, they then define a discrete episode of concerted intervention to be when (i) at least two of the G-3 central banks start to intervene together, and (ii) at least one of these two central banks continues to intervene with interruptions lasting no more than five working days. Of the 17 concerted interventions from 1985 to 1991, 16 were "leaning against the wind" in the sense of trying to reverse sharp trends in the dollar exchange rate. Nevertheless, these episodes were infrequent: a whole year could be missed, e.g., 1986; and, outside the authors' sample, only one occurred in 1992—from July 20 to August 11 when 13 central banks intervened massively to support the dollar (*New York Times*, 21 July and 12 Aug. 1992).

How successful were these concerted interventions? For their 17 episodes from 1985 to 1991, Pietro Catte, Giampaola Galli, and Salvatore Rebecchini conclude:

Interventions were successful in the sense that they always reversed the trend of the dollar relative to the yen and the DM, although in four cases, for only a few weeks. Eight of the nine major turning points of the dollar in the period coincided exactly with periods of concerted intervention. (1994, p. 217)

The last recorded episode when this chapter was first written in late 1992, in the summer of 1992, seems to have been moderately successful. By November, the mark, at 1.58 to the dollar, was trading well above its late-summer (and all-time) high of 1.40; and the yen, at 123 to the dollar, was trading modestly above its late-summer high of 119—which had also been briefly touched in late 1988.

Thus the evidence showing the existence of open, concerted intervention—as encapsulated in rules III and VII in box 5— seems persuasive for 1985–92—and continued into 1995 as analyzed in chapter 22. The changed behavior of the United States is further substantiated by the American buildup of foreign exchange reserves—as per rule IV. From 1978 through 1984, U.S. reserves ranged between $6 billion and $10 billion, but by 1989–92 they had been built up to betweeen $45 billion and $50 billion (IMF 1992). Perhaps because the Plaza-Louvre regime of foreign-exchange intervention was more symmetrical than the floating-rate dollar standard that preceded it, business cycles were less highly synchronized across countries after 1984 (Kenichi Ohno 1992) as discussed in chapter 22.

Do Target Zones Exist?

In box 5, however, the evidence supporting the existence of rules I, II, and V is more problematic. Whether unannounced target zones are operative (rules I and II), and whether exchange interventions are effectively sterilized (rule V), is less clear. Informed insiders may disagree over the robustness of these three rules and whether or not they are a good representation of official behavior over the 1985–92 period.

Certainly, in February 1985, the main concern was to get the overvalued dollar down—rather than coming to any understanding to maintain informal target zones in the future (I. Mac Destler and C. Randall Henning 1989). Moreover, with the dollar so far out of alignment in February 1985, participating governments subsequently adjusted their monetary policies to help engineer dollar devaluation. Throughout 1985, U.S. money growth was high compared to that in Germany and Japan. Thus, in 1985 and perhaps 1986, rule V of box 5 was not followed: the concerted interventions to sell dollars for yen and marks were not effectively sterilized. At the Plaza Hotel meeting on September 22, 1985, in New York, finance ministers simply ratified what had already happened the previous February. The U.S. government would continue to intervene in concert with the European and Japanese governments to drive the dollar down further—which they did again in October. U.S. monetary policy remained easier, and the dollar continued to drift down through 1986.

In February 1987, the meeting of the G-7 finance ministers in the Louvre in Paris provided the first substantial indications of an official attempt to establish target zones. Because of growing concern with a possible run on the dollar, the official communique agreed that the dollar should be stabilized around "current levels" (Kathryn Dominguez and Jeffrey A. Frankel 1993a). Only much later was it revealed (Yoichi Funabashi 1988, pp. 183–87) that the Louvre participants had after all set a "reference range" of five percent around then current levels of 1.825 marks/dollar and 153.5 yen/dollar. But then, over the next five years, continual "rebasing" of even these targets seems to have occurred. Almost immediately, in April 1987, the yen fell below its Louvre range and was rebased at 146 yen/dollar (Kathryn Dominguez and Jeffrey A. Frankel 1993a); these authors nicely summarize the ebb and flow of the dollar exchange rate and official interactions from 1985 to 1991. In 1992, Germany's extraordinarily tight monetary policy, and the high interest rates associated with the fiscal problems of unification, marked a change in a "fundamental" (in the sense of rule II, box V) that apparently induced the G-3 to accept a stronger mark. The mark rose to 147 to the dollar before provoking the concerted defense of the dollar in the summer of 1992.

In summary, for rule I in box 5, I have simply adopted the suggestion of C. Fred Bergsten (1993) that the G-3 are behaving as if they had a target of ±12 percent for the mark/dollar and yen/dollar exchange rates. And rule II, box 5, suggests that even this relatively modest objective is subject to "rebasing" should there be a change in macroeconomic "fundamentals." Modest and flimsy though they may be, these target zones seem to have kept the dollar's exchange rates within narrower ranges from 1987 through 1992 (and 1995)—compared to the more volatile experience of the 14 years after 1973. Dare one hope that this Plaza-Louvre regime has also suppressed the dollar's long-run tendency to depreciate? (Between 1971 and 1992, the dollar fell from 4 to about 1.58 marks, and from 360 to about 123 yen.) If so, stabilizing the world price level—in the sense of rule VI, box 5—may now be feasible. [Au. note: Obviously, this statement, written in 1992, was premature.]

The Sterilization Issue

Of great analytical interest is the remaining loose end in box 5: How robust empirically is rule V—the sterilization rule? In the absence of explicit international coordination of the G-3's domestic monetary policies, sterilization of exchange interventions is a necessary condition for being able to implement rule VI (the anchor rule): the ability of each of the G-3 countries *individually* to orient each domestic monetary policy toward long-run price stability while keeping exchange rates within a narrow range.

During concerted interventions Pietro Catte, Giampaola Galli, and Salvatore Rebecchini (1994) could find no systematic evidence of supporting changes in interest rates: "... in several cases, interest rate differential did not change or changed in the wrong direction" (p. 206). Similarly, in the last massive concerted intervention in July–August 1992 to support the dollar, the Bundesbank if anything seemed to behave perversely by tightening further while the Federal Reserve System retained its easy money stance.

Yet, this effectiveness of sterilized interventions seems quite contrary to what economists (including this writer) had previously believed. Before 1985, it was thought that effective intervention in the foreign exchanges had to be conducted in concert with monetary policy with supporting interest rate adjustments. As long as international capital flows were unrestricted, the exchange rate was not itself seen as an independent policy instrument. And this theoretical consensus was officially recognized in an empirical study commissioned by the G-7 at the Versailles economic summit in 1982. The resulting *Jurgensen Report* (Mar. 1983) found that the effect of sterilized intervention was at most small and transitory—a result also found by Kenneth Rogoff (1984), Dale Henderson and Stephanie Samson (1983), and other authors using pre-1985 data.

In an econometric study of sterilized intervention with two structural equations, Kathryn Dominguez and Jeffrey A. Frankel (1993a, 1993b) distinguish between portfolio and expectations effects. If domestic money supplies do not change, net purchases of dollars in a concerted intervention will tend to withdraw U.S. government bonds from private circulation and increase foreign bonds: the portfolio effect. But then the very announcement of a concerted intervention might well induce people to believe that the (monetary) fundamentals will be different in the future: the expectations effect. While both effects are positive, the authors find the expectations effect to be much more important than the portfolio effect. And they found that the impact of "news" regarding official intentions became much more pronounced in influencing exchange rates after 1984.

In conclusion, the switch to concerted, open intervention— which is well telegraphed to the exchange markets—seems to be the key to the modest "success" of the Plaza-Louvre regime from 1985 through 1992 (and 1995). In a world of great exchange-rate uncertainty, where traders' knowledge of future fundamentals of the economic policies of each participating country is incomplete and perhaps ill-formed, infrequent but concerted interventions can play a useful signaling role—even when sterilized. But without more direct coordination of national monetary policies, the range of exchange-rate fluctuations is likely to remain uncomfortably large.

2.6 The EMS, the Marshall Plan, and the Postwar Dollar Standard: Resolving a Historical Puzzle

This chapter has focused on *worldwide* international monetary orders: "frameworks of laws, conventions, and regulations" (Robert A. Mundell 1972) that establish alternative settings in which international monetary systems worked themselves out from the late 19th century to the present day. However, a complete evaluation of the strengths and weaknesses of the corresponding international monetary systems for promoting trade, integrating world capital markets, containing business cycles, securing price stability, and so on, requires a book-length manuscript. Going beyond the rules of the game per se is beyond the scope of this chapter, but is picked up in succeeding ones.[19]

To secure exchange stability and freer trade on a more limited basis, monetary orders can also be established for purely *regional* country groupings. Without explanatory text, boxes 6 and 7 outline the rules of the game for the European Monetary System.[20] The symmetry of the treaty setting up the EMS in 1979 (box 6), which evolved into a greater Deutsche Mark area (box 7), so closely parallels the symmetry of the 1945 Bretton Woods Agreement (box 2), which evolved into the fixed-rate dollar standard (box 3), that interested readers can provide their own textual explanation! Even so, the operating rules of the EMS remain closer in spirit to the 1979 treaty (at least up to September 1992) than did the operating rules of the dollar standard in the 1950s and 1960s adhere to the spirit of Bretton Woods in 1945. Indeed, for the EMS, the first five rules in each of boxes 6 and 7 are the same—although the continuing German predominance in providing the nominal anchor may not have been intended by the EMS negotiators in 1979.[21]

This parallel highlights what, for the author, was a major historical puzzle. Between 1945 and 1950, what caused such a

Rule Box 6
The European Monetary System (EMS) in 1979: The Spirit of the Treaty

---

All Member Countries

    I. Fix a par value for the exchange rate in terms of the European Currency Unit, a basket of EMS currencies weighted according to country size.

   II. Keep par value stable in the short run by symmetrically limiting range of variation in each bilateral exchange rate to 2.25 percent on either side of its central rate.

  III. When an exchange rate threatens to breech its bilateral limit, the strong-currency central bank must lend freely to the weak-currency central bank to support the rate.

  IV. Adjust par values in the intermediate term if necessary to realign national price levels—but only by collective agreement within the EMS.

   V. Work symmetrically toward convergence of national macroeconomic policies and unchanging long-run par values for exchange rates.

  VI. Keep free convertibility for current-account payments.

 VII. Hold reserves mainly as European Currency Units with the European Fund for Monetary Cooperation, and reduce dollar reserves. Avoid holding substantial reserves in other EMS currencies.

VIII. Repay central bank debts quickly from exchange reserves, or by borrowing from the European Fund for Monetary Cooperation within strict longer-term credit limits.

  IX. No member country's money is to be a reserve currency, nor is its national monetary policy to be (asymmetrically) the nominal anchor for the group.

---

dramatic shift away from the spirit of the original Bretton Woods Agreement? How did the influential politicians and economists, who in 1945 fully intended to maintain long-term exchange flexibility and national macroeconomic autonomy, manage to put the world on to a fixed-rate dollar standard by 1950—and one that successfully anchored the common world price level for almost 20 years? Figure 2.2b shows that inflation rates in the WPIs (our best measure of tradable goods prices) of the United States, Germany, and Japan, were very low and virtually the same until 1971.

Rule Box 7
The European Monetary System as a Greater Deutsche Mark
Area: 1979–92

All Member Countries

    I. through V. Same as in EMS "Spirit of the Treaty" (Box 6).
    VI. Avoid using the credit facilities of the European Fund for Monetary Cooperation.

Member Countries Except Germany

    VII. Intervene intramarginally, within formal bilateral parity limits, to stabilize the national exchange rate vis-à-vis the DM. Increasingly intervene in DM rather than dollars.
    VIII. Keep active exchange reserves in interest-bearing DM open-market instruments such as Euromark deposits, as well as in dollar Treasury bonds.
    IX. Adjust short-term national money growth and/or short-term interest rates to support exchange market interventions—whether intramarginal or at the bilateral parity limits.
    X. Keep adjusting long-term money growth so that domestic price inflation (in tradable goods) converges to, or remains the same as, price inflation in Germany.
    XI. Progressively liberalize capital controls.

Germany

    XII. Remain passive in the foreign-exchange markets with other European (EMS) countries: free trade with neither a balance-of-payments nor an intramarginal exchange-rate target.
    XIII. Keep German capital markets open to foreign governments or private residents as borrowers or depositors.
    XIV. Sterilize (perhaps passively) the effects of German or other EMS countries' official interventions in the European foreign-exchange markets on the German monetary base.
    XV. Anchor the DM (EMS) price level for tradable goods by an independently chosen German monetary policy.

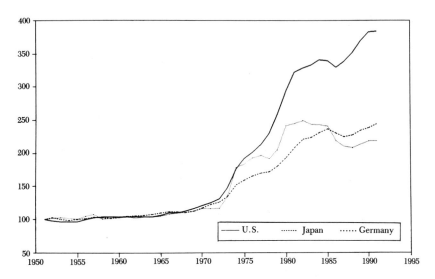

Figure 2.2b
Wholesale price indices, 1951 = 100 (annual data).
Source: IMF International Financial Statistics.

True, a key-currency system based on the most economically important country—if that country maintains an open capital market and a fully convertible currency—is a convenient way of solving the redundancy problem and providing a medium of exchange, unit of account, and store of value for international transacting (table 2.2). But at least the first two of these monetary functions could have been satisfied if the system had evolved directly to some form of a "flexible-rate" dollar standard as approximated by box 4.

Something more was required: a major historical-institutional event—one that the Bretton Woods negotiators did not anticipate in 1945—to give the industrial economies a tremendous if unintended push toward the fixed-rate dollar standard. The Marshall Plan was formally begun in April 1948 with the express purpose of using American financial assistance to restore intra-European trade and financial stability—both of which were in great disarray (Herbert Mayer 1969; Alan Milward 1984). But not until September 1950 was the monetary centerpiece of this great effort, The European Payments Union (EPU), finally completed (Jacob J. Kaplan and Günther Schleiminger 1989) for 16 European countries.

As described above in the text on the fixed-rate dollar standard, the EPU restored multilateral current-account convertibility among Western European currencies by enthroning the dollar as a unit of account for calculating debit and credit balances for each member, and as the fundamental means of settlement. Thus, after 1949, European countries (and Japan) preferred to keep their dollar exchange parities fixed in order to (1) simplify book-keeping in actually clearing international payments; and (2) improve the credibility of their still-fragile domestic anti-inflation policies by relying on an external nominal anchor.

To maintain these dollar parities indefinitely, each European country had to subordinate its domestic monetary policy to the fixed exchange rate. More by accident than design, therefore, in 1950 the United States suddenly found itself to be the only major country with an independent monetary policy. As the more financially stable "outsider," the U.S. alone had the monetary independence to provide a nominal anchor for the group—which it managed to do successfully for almost 20 years (figure 2.2b).

In the extreme, one could argue (Ronald McKinnon 1993) that the original Bretton Woods Articles of 1945 never came into effect! In 1946–48, the International Monetary Fund did virtually nothing to alleviate the great postwar financial crises in Europe or Japan (Charles P. Kindleberger 1987, p. 57). Unbridled inflation and severe currency inconvertibility led to bilateralism and disruption in trade within Western Europe, and by late 1947 many felt that the postwar recovery might prove abortive (Peter Coffey and John Presley 1971). Superseding anything the IMF was doing, the Marshall Plan began in April 1948 with the definite objective (conditionality) of restoring macroeconomic stability and multilateral payments convertibility—more or less in that order—in Europe. Thus it was the Marshall Plan, particularly the monetary institutions of the EPU, that cast the die for the rules of the game for the fixed-rate dollar standard outlined in box 3.

But this historical accident, which provided the monetary underpinning for the unprecedented trade-led growth in world GNP in the 1950s and 1960s (Angus Maddison 1989), eventually proved insufficient. Although enormously successful in practice, the unwritten rules of the game necessary to keep the fixed-rate dollar standard going differed too much in spirit from its legal cover, i.e., the 1945 Bretton Woods Articles. In 1970–71, facing the clamor for dollar devaluation and greater exchange flexibility, the schizophrenic American government would not disinflate the American economy in order to defend the most successful international monetary regime the world has ever known.

Suppose some latter-day Walter Bagehot had fully articulated the rules for the fixed-rate dollar standard, much as Bagehot himself articulated coherent rules for the Bank of England to follow in maintaining the 19th-century gold standard. Further suppose that our modern Bagehot convinced the American government it was in its own best interest to maintain price-level stability—as per the anchor rule (rule X, box 3)—while demonetizing gold. Conceivably, the remarkable monetary and exchange stability of the 1950s and 1960s could have continued indefinitely. Understanding what the rules actually are, and the obligations of the various players, can be extremely important.

Although not suffering nearly the same degree of schizophrenia as the fixed-rate dollar standard, the European Monetary System has a similar potential weakness: dependence on the monetary policy of just one country to provide the nominal anchor for the system as a whole. This flaw seemed to be particularly noticeable in the summer and fall of 1992 when excessively tight German monetary policy not only forced Britain and Italy to suspend par values for their exchange rates, but also unduly depressed the whole European economy including Germany's. Absent any agreement on a common currency, making the EMS more symmetrical with a common price rule, while keeping nominal exchange rates within narrow bands, might well be preferred (Ronald McKinnon 1992).

Similarly, to rescue multilateralism in the GATT and prevent the world from devolving into regional trading blocs, restoring global exchange stability among the major industrial countries is imperative. The still fragile Plaza-Louvre Accords could be a good beginning—provided that the rules, as provisionally laid out in box 5, are well understood.

2.7   Symmetry and the Anchor Rule: A Concluding Note

Assigning the anchoring job to just one national monetary authority—as with the successful EMS of the 1980s, or the highly successful postwar fixed-rate dollar standard of the 1950s and

1960s—can be remarkably effective in particular historical circumstances. If the anchor country's economic predominance is combined with greater financial stability, other countries will then voluntarily stabilize their exchange rates against the anchor currency. But such "natural" asymmetry need not persist indefinitely. Besides future financial upheavals beyond the control of the central bank in the anchor country, it may fail to play by the (appropriate) rules—and, to the great detriment of the other members, abuse its extra degree of freedom.

However, more symmetrical rules of the game for coordinating national monetary policies still require a stable nominal anchor. Agreements that narrow the range of exchange-rate variation without, at the same time, pinning down the common price level are unsatisfactory. Vaguely specified international monetary obligations could undermine the ability of national monetary authorities to stabilize their own price levels individually. Worse, informally targeting exchange rates asymmetrically could, inadvertently, generate business cycles that are synchronized across countries—as per the analysis of the floating-rate dollar standard, 1973–1984.

By taking the anchoring mechanism out of the hands of any one country or national central bank, the international gold standard before 1914 was more symmetrical. The common price level was determined by the relative price of gold vis-à-vis a broad price index of all other goods and services—which proved (accidentally?) to have remarkably stable value in the very long run. In the short and intermediate runs, however, sharp worldwide liquidity squeezes made the common price level uncomfortably variable cyclically. Lacking discretionary control over the monetary base for the gold standard as a whole, national monetary authorities were virtually helpless in avoiding sharp cyclical fluctuations in worldwide economic activity.

Without making the nominal anchor the responsibility of either one country or nobody, can we do better in some new, and more symmetrical, international monetary order? Participating countries could define a common price index whose stabilization is the domestic objective of each national central bank; and if that objective was roughly achieved, the central banks could also maintain fixed par values for their exchange rates. Among industrial countries, empirical evidence (Ronald McKinnon and

Kenichi Ohno 1989) suggests that producer price indices tend
to satisfy these dual criteria—but consumer price indices or GNP
deflators need not. That is, when nominal exchange rates remain
fixed (within narrow bands) for long periods of time—as under
the international gold and fixed-rate dollar standards—producer
(or wholesale) price indices align themselves across countries
remarkably well. But new rules of the game, based on a common
producer price index as the nominal anchor, are a story for
chapter 22 below.[22]

Notes

I would like to thank Barry Eichengreen, Jeffrey Frankel, Christina Gerberding,
Randall Henning, John Hussman, Bernhard Herz, Kenichi Ohno, David Robinson, Jürgen Schröder, John Williamson, and an anonymous referee for insightful comments. This work was supported by the Center for Economic
Policy Research at Stanford.

1. The expression "Rules of the Game" is often attributed to J. M. Keynes
(Arthur Bloomfield 1959, p. 47; Barry J. Eichengreen 1985b, p. 14). In his "Economic Consequences of Mr. Churchill" (1925, p. 220), Keynes once referred to
the "rules of the gold standard game" that were then forcing the Bank of
England to curtail credit. Nevertheless, Keynes did not literally list systematically what he thought the important rules were—nor have subsequent authors
using this popular expression.

2. The United States itself remained formally on gold until 1933.

3. From the development of cable communications in the 1870s, exchange rates
in both foreign centers were the same—at least by the late 1890s. In the earlier
history of the gold standard, however, the assumption of a unified foreign
exchange market need not be appropriate (Maria Cristina Marcuzzo and Annalisa Rosselli 1987, 1991).

4. Keynes's criticism, that the traditional British mint parity overvalued sterling
relative to the dollar, was enormously influential—probably inducing the interwar gold standard to abort somewhat sooner than it would have otherwise.
More importantly, the ethic contained in rule V was abandoned in the Bretton
Woods Articles drafted in 1943–45—and in most subsequent proposals for
reducing variance in exchange rates. Although the articles aimed to rein in
short-run exchange volatility, countries remained free to adjust their exchange
parities in the longer run.

5. See Bordo (1984b) for a nice discussion of Bagehot's ideas. Unlike the major
European countries, which had established central banks before 1879, the
United States had no central bank until 1913. But the United States also suffered
more financial stress—bank panics and more volatile short-term interest
rates—from 1879 to 1913.

6. The fact that Bloomfield's data are annual, spanning several crisis periods,
may well account for the negative correlation between domestic and foreign

assets that he observed, whereas, within shorter time periods during which there was no crisis, one would expect a positive association. I am indebted to an anonymous outside referee for this important distinction.

7. Purchasing power parity, and thus the equalization of "real" interest rates, held only when measured in terms of wholesale (tradable) price indices. Otherwise different rates of productivity growth could lead to international differences in price movements when measured in terms of consumer or other price indices with nontradable components.

8. Between the wars, this buffer stock view of international reserves had already become widely accepted by Keynes and others. See Barry J. Eichengreen (1990a and 1990b, ch. 10) for references.

9. The (limited) American commitment to convert officially held dollar balances into gold meant that the postwar monetary regime was more complicated, and more fragile, than the pure fixed-rate dollar standard portrayed in box 3. Indeed, the authorities worried about the unrestricted buildup of official dollar reserves, and various substitute arrangements for creating reserve assets were tried or proposed—but generally proved unsuccessful in displacing the dollar (Hans Genberg and Alexander Swoboda 1993).

10. As long as central banks clear international payments directly, exact dollar parities are both feasible and convenient. Only when exchange markets become more open is a narrow band necessary to devolve the business of clearing international payments to commercial banks (Ronald McKinnon 1979). Within Europe, this devolution was not fully completed until December 1958, when the EPU was finally abolished; only then did European countries adopt the two-percent bands around their dollar parities associated with the Bretton Woods Agreement.

11. In the early 1960s, at least one prescient commentator argued strongly for demonetizing gold so as to open up the possibility that its market price could fall as well as increase. See *Collected Papers of Emile Despres*, edited by Gerald Meier (1973). That of course would have resolved the Triffin Dilemma and eliminated this particular ambiguity in the fixed-rate dollar standard—although the problem of unintended rigidity in exchange rates would have remained.

12. Belgium, France, Germany, Japan, Netherlands, Sweden, the U.K., and the U.S. Michaely analyzes the United States and finds that the Fed did not systematically react to America's balance-of-payments position—unlike the other seven countries, which did react to their balance of payments.

13. This extensive literature was previously reviewed for the *Journal of Economic Literature* (Ronald McKinnon 1981a).

14. In that fateful August, President Nixon also ended the commitment of the U.S. Treasury to redeem dollar assets owned by foreign governments in terms of gold. Since 1968, however, foreign pressure to request conversion had been diminished by the development of a two-tier market in gold that insulated official transactions at $35 per ounce from the private market, where higher prices had begun to prevail (Kenneth Dam 1982).

15. Even if par values adjust smoothly according to some version of the crawling peg (John Williamson 1965), an open economy without capital controls

could well suffer from greater dynamic instability if it allowed its exchange parity to crawl according to commonly accepted indicator rules (Ronald McKinnon 1981b).

16. Because of disruptions from World Wars I and II, the dollar eventually displaced sterling's similarly entrenched international role (Benjamin Cohen 1971)—but not without fomenting disorganization in the international economy (Charles P. Kindleberger 1973). Now, however, no natural "successor" to the dollar is in the offing.

17. However, "brand-name" manufactures from industrial countries are typically invoiced in the currency of the exporter (Sven Grassman 1973, 1976; Ronald McKinnon 1979).

18. The buildup of less-developed countries debt in the 1970s was largely in the form of dollar-denominated syndicated loans from the Eurocurrency market. In the 1980s and 1990s, the spectacular buildup of American net debt to the rest of the world is denominated in dollars. The "privilege" of going into international debt so heavily in your own currency is one that is open only to the center, or Nth currency, country.

19. There is an interesting alternative to the purely historical approach of analyzing how international monetary systems work. For alternative sets of monetary rules of the game, how the corresponding international monetary system would respond to realistically formulated economic shocks can be simulated on a computer—see Warwick McKibbin and Jeffrey Sachs (1991).

20. In setting up the rules of the game for the EMS, I have been greatly helped by the advice of Bernhard Herz of the University of Tübingen and his paper (coauthored with Werner Roger) "The EMS Is a Greater Deutschemark Area" (1992).

21. Although the predominance of Germany as the anchor country is accepted by almost all commentators on the subject, a few question the strength of this asymmetry (Paul de Grauwe 1991; Michele Fratianni and Jürgen von Hagen 1990). Any doubts on this score, however, must have been dispelled by the events of September 1992 when the Bundesbank refused to acquiesce to partner requests to ease what in retrospect looks like excessively tight German monetary policy. This forced Britain and Italy to devalue and float their currencies, thus violating rules I and II of box 7.

22. The case for a common price rule and more symmetry in fixing nominal exchange rates is contained in Ronald McKinnon (1984, 1988c, and 1990). In such a multiple-currency regime, an ingenious way of not having to rely on a single anchor country is suggested by Peter Bofinger and Christina Gerberding (1988).

References

Acheson, A. L. K., Chant, J. F., and Prachowny, M. F. J. *Bretton Woods revisited.* Toronto: U. of Toronto Press, 1972.

Alogoskoufis, George S. "Monetary Accommodation, Exchange Rate Regimes and Inflation Persistence," *Econ. J.,* May 1992, pp. 1–20.

Alogoskoufis, George, and Smith, Ron. "The Phillips Curve, The Persistence of Inflation, and the Lucas Critique: Evidence from Exchange-Rate Regimes," *Amer. Econ. Rev.*, Dec. 1991, *81*(5), pp. 1254–75.

Bagehot, Walter. *Lombard street.* 1873; reprinted by the Hyperion Press Inc., Westport, CT, 1979.

Bank for International Settlements. *Annual report(s).*

Barro, Robert J. "Money and the Price Level Under the Gold Standard," *Econ. J.*, Mar. 1979, *89*(353), pp. 13–33; reprinted in Eichengreen 1985b.

Barsky, Robert B., and De Long, J. Bradford. "Forecasting Pre-World War I Inflation: The Fisher Effect and the Gold Standard," *Quart. J. Econ.*, Aug. 1991, *106*(3), pp. 815–36.

Bayoumi, Tamin. "Saving-Investment Correlations," *IMF Staff Papers*, June 1990, pp. 360–88.

Bergsten, C. Fred. *The dilemmas of the dollar: The economics and politics of United States international monetary policy.* NY: NYU Press, 1975.

———. "The Collapse of Bretton Woods: Implications for International Monetary Reform," in Bordo and Eichengreen, 1993.

Bergsten, C. Fred, Halm, George, Marchup, Fritz, and Roosa, Robert. *Approaches to greater flexibility of exchange rates: The Burgenstock papers.* Princeton: Princeton U. Press, 1970.

Bernstein, Edward. "The Search for Exchange Stability Before and After Bretton Woods," in *The future of the international monetary system: Change, coordination or instability?* Eds.: Omar F. Hamouda, Robin Rowley, and Bernard M. Wolf. Aldershot, Eng.: Edward Elgar, 1989, pp. 27–34.

Bloomfield, Arthur. *Monetary policy under the international gold standard, 1880–1914.* NY: Federal Reserve Bank of New York, 1959.

Bofinger, Peter, and Gerberding, Christina. "EMS: A Model for World Monetary Order?" *Intereconomics*, Sept./Oct. 1988, pp. 212–19.

Bordo, Michael D. "The Classical Gold Standard: Some Lessons for Today," *Federal Reserve Bank of St. Louis Review*, May 1984a.

———. "The Gold Standard: The Traditional Approach," in *A retrospective on the classical gold standard, 1821–1931.* Eds.: Michael D. Bordo and Anna J. Schwartz. Chicago: U. of Chicago Press, 1984b, pp. 23–113.

Bordo, Michael, and Eichengreen, Barry, eds. *Retrospective on the Bretton Woods system.* Chicago: U. of Chicago Press for the NBER, 1993.

Bordo, Michael, and Kydland, Finn E. "The Gold Standard as 'Rule'." NBER Working Paper, May 1990.

Calomiris, Charles, and Hubbard, Robert Glenn. "International Adjustment Under the Classical Gold Standard." Unpub. ms. Northwestern U., May 1987.

Cassel, Gustav. *The downfall of the gold standard.* London: Frank Cass and Co. 1936; 2nd impression 1966.

Catte, Pietro, Galli, Giampaola, and Rebecchini, Salvatore. "Exchange Rates Can Be Managed!" *International Economic Insights,* Sept./Oct. 1992, pp. 17–21.

———. "Concerted Interventions and the Dollar: An Analysis of Daily Data." Rinaldo Ossola Memorial Conference, in *The International Monetary System.* Eds. P. Kenen, F. Papadia, and F. Saccomonni. Cambridge: Cambridge U. Press, 1994, pp. 201–40.

Chrystal, K. Alec. "Demand for International Media of Exchange," *Amer. Econ. Rev.,* Dec. 1977, *67*(5), pp. 840–50.

———. "Changing Perceptions of International Money and International Reserves in the World Economy," in *The reconstruction of international monetary arrangements.* Ed.: Robert Z. Aliber. NY: St. Martin's Press, 1987, pp. 127–50.

Clark, Truman A. "Violations of the Gold Points, 1890 to 1908," *J. Polit. Econ.,* Oct. 1984, *92*(5), pp. 791–823.

Coffey, Peter, and Presley, John R. *European monetary integration.* London: Macmillan, 1971.

Cohen, Benjamin J. *The future of sterling as an international currency.* London: Macmillan, 1971.

Cooper, Richard N. "The Gold Standard: Historical Facts and Future Prospects," *Brookings Pap. Econ. Act.,* 1982, (1), pp. 1–45; reprinted in Richard N. Cooper, *The international monetary system.* Cambridge, MA: MIT Press, 1987.

Dam, Kenneth W. *The rules of the game: Reform and evolution in the international monetary system.* Chicago: U. of Chicago Press, 1982.

Davis, Lance E., and Huttenbach, Robert A. *Mammon and the pursuit of empire: The political economy of British imperialism, 1860–1912.* Cambridge: Cambridge U. Press, 1986.

de Grauwe, Paul. *International money: Post-war trends and theories.* Oxford: Oxford U. Press, 1989.

———. "Is The European Monetary System a DM-Zone?" in *Evolution of the international and regional monetary systems.* Eds.: Alfred Steinherr and Daniel Weiserbs. London: Macmillan, 1991, pp. 207–27.

Despres, Emile, Kindleberger, Charles, and Salant, Walter. "The Dollar and World Liquidity: A Minority View," *The Economist,* Feb. 5, 1966, pp. 526–29.

Destler, I. Mac, and Henning, C. Randall. *Dollar politics: Exchange rate policy making in the United States.* Washington, DC: Institute for International Economics, 1989.

Dominguez, Kathryn, and Frankel, Jeffrey A. *Intervention policy reconsidered.* Washington, DC: Institute for International Economics, 1993a.

———. "Does Foreign Exchange Intervention Matter? Disentangling the Portfolio and Expectations Effects," *Amer. Econ. Rev.,* Dec. 1993b, *83*(5), pp. 1356–69.

Eichengreen, Barry J. "International Economic Cooperation in Historical Perspective: A View from the Interwar Years," in *International economic policy coordination.* Eds.: Willem H. Buiter and Richard C. Marston. London: Cambridge U. Press, 1985a, pp. 139–77.

————. "Editor's Introduction," in *The gold standard in theory and history*. Ed.: Barry J. Eichengreen. NY: Methuen Press, 1985b, pp. 1–36.

————. "Conducting the International Orchestra: Bank of England Leadership Under the Classical Gold Standard," *J. Int. Money Finance*, Mar. 1987, *6*(1), pp. 5–29.

————. "International Monetary Instability Between the Wars: Structural Flaws or Misguided Policies?" in *The evolution of the international monetary system*. Eds.: Yoshio Suzuki, Junichi Miyake, and Mitsuaki Okabe. Tokyo: U. of Tokyo Press, 1990a, pp. 71–116.

————. *Elusive stability*. Cambridge: Cambridge U. Press, 1990b.

Feldstein, Martin, and Horioka, Charles. "Domestic Saving and International Capital Flows," *Econ. J.*, June 1980, *90*(358), pp. 314–29.

Frankel, Jeffrey A. "International Capital Mobility and Crowding-out in the U.S. Economy," in *The increasing openness of the U.S. economy*. Ed.: R. W. Hafer. Federal Reserve Bank of St. Louis, 1986, ch. 2, pp. 33–67.

————. "The Dazzling Dollar," *Brookings Pap. Econ. Act.*, 1985 (1), pp. 199–217.

Funabashi, Yoichi. *Managing the dollar: From Plaza to the Louvre*. Washington, DC: Institute for International Economics, 1988.

Fratianni, Michele, and von Hagen, Jürgen. "German Dominance in the EMS: The Empirical Evidence," *Open Economies Review*, 1990, *1*, pp. 67–87.

Frenkel, Jacob A., and Mussa, Michael L. "The Efficiency of Foreign Exchange Markets and Measures of Turbulence," *Amer. Econ. Rev.*, May 1980, *70*(2), pp. 374–81.

Genberg, Hans, and Swoboda, Alexander. "The Provision of Liquidity in the Bretton Woods System," in Bordo and Eichengreen, eds., 1993, pp. 269–306.

Giavazzi, Francesco, and Giovannini, Alberto. *Limiting exchange rate flexibility: The European monetary system*. Cambridge, MA, and London: MIT Press, 1989.

Giovannini, Alberto. "'Rules of the Game' During the International Gold Standard: England and Germany," *J. Int. Money Finance*, Dec. 1986, *5*(4), pp. 467–83.

————. "How Do Fixed Exchange Rate Systems Work: Evidence from the Gold Standard, Bretton Woods, and the EMS," in *Blueprints for exchange role management*. Eds.: Marcus Miller, Barry J. Eichengreen, and Richard Portes. Centre for Economic Policy Research. London: Academic Press, 1989, pp. 13–46.

————. "Bretton Woods and Its Precursors: Rules Versus Discretion in the History of International Monetary Regimes," in Bordo and Eichengreen, 1993, pp. 109–47.

Grassman, Sven. "A Fundamental Symmetry in International Payments Patterns," *J. Int. Econ.*, May 1973, *3*(2), pp. 105–06.

————. "Currency Distribution and Forward Cover in Foreign Trade: Sweden Revisited," *J. Int. Econ.*, May 1976, *6*(2), pp. 215–21.

Hallwood, Paul, and MacDonald, Ronald. *International money, theory, evidence, and institutions*. Oxford: Basil Blackwell, 1986.

Henderson, Dale, and Samson, Stephanie. "Intervention in Foreign Exchange Markets: A Summary of Ten Staff Studies," *Fed. Res. Bull.*, Nov. 1983, *69*, pp. 830–36.

Herz, Bernhard, and Werner, Roger. "The EMS Is a Greater Deutschemark Area," *Europ. Econ. Rev.*, Oct. 1992, *36*(7), pp. 1413–25.

International Monetary Fund. *The International Monetary Fund 1945–1965*, Vol. 3: "Documents." Washington, DC, 1969.

———. *Annual report 1990.* Washington, DC.

———. *International financial statistics*, Washington, DC. 1992.

Jastram, Roy W. *The golden constant: The English and American experience, 1560– 1976.* NY: John Wiley, 1977.

Johnson, Harry G. "Toward a General Theory of the Balance of Payments," in *International trade and economic growth.* By Harry G. Johnson. London: George Allen & Unwin, 1958, pp. 153–68.

Jurgensen report. Working Group on Exchange Market Intervention, Mar. 1983.

Kaplan, Jacob J., and Schleiminger, Günther. *The European payments union: Financial diplomacy in the 1950s.* Oxford: Clarendon Press, 1989.

Kenen, Peter. "The Role of the Dollar as International Currency." *Occasional Paper.* No. 13, Group of Thirty. New York, 1983.

Keynes, John Maynard. *The collected writings of John Maynard Keynes.* Vol. 4. *A tract on monetary reform.* London: Macmillan, [1923] 1971.

———. "The Economic Consequences of Mr. Churchill," in *The collected writings.* Vol. 9. *Essays in persuasion.* London: Macmillan, [1925] 1972, pp. 207–30.

———. *The collected writings.* Vol. 6. *A treatise on money: The applied theory of money.* London: Macmillan, [1930] 1971.

———. *The collected writings.* Vol. 7. *The general theory of employment, interest, and money.* London: Macmillan, [1936] 1973.

———. "Proposals for an International Clearing Union," in *The international monetary fund, 1945–65.* Vol. III: "Documents," Washington, DC, [Apr. 1943] 1969.

Kindleberger, Charles P. "The Benefits of International Money," *J. Int. Econ.*, Sept. 1972, *2*(4), pp. 425–42.

———. *The world economy in depression: 1929–39.* Berkeley: U. of California Press, 1973.

———. *Marshall Plan days.* Boston: Allen & Unwin, 1987.

Kouri, Pentti, and Porter, Michael. "International Capital Flows and Portfolio Equilibrium," *J. Polit. Econ.*, May–June 1974, *82*(3), pp. 443–67.

Krugman, Paul. "The International Role of the Dollar: Theory and Prospect," in *Exchange rate theory and practice.* Eds.: John F. O. Bilson and Richard C. Marston. Chicago: U. of Chicago Press, 1984, pp. 261–78.

————. "Is the Strong Dollar Sustainable?" in *The U.S. dollar: Recent developments*. Federal Reserve Bank of Kansas City, 1985, pp. 103–32.

Maddison, Angus. *The world economy in the 20th century*. Paris: OECD, 1989.

Marcuzzo, Maria Christina, and Rosselli, Annalisa. "Profitability in the International Gold Market in the Early History of the Gold Standard," *Economica*, Aug. 1987, *54*(215), pp. 367–80.

————. *Ricardo and the gold standard: The foundations of the international monetary order*. Translated by Joan Hall. NY: St. Martin's Press, 1991.

Mathieson, Donald J. "Portfolio Balance and International Finance." Ph.D. Dissertation, Stanford U., 1971.

Mayer, Herbert C. *German recovery and the Marshall Plan 1948–1952*. NY: Edition Atlantic Forum, 1969.

McCloskey, Donald N., and Zecher, J. Richard. "How the Gold Standard Worked, 1880–1913," in *The monetary approach to the balance of payments*. Eds.: Jacob A. Frenkel and Harry G. Johnson. London: Allen & Unwin, 1976, pp. 357–85.

McKibbin, Warwick J., and Sachs, Jeffrey D. *Global linkages: Macroeconomic interdependence, and cooperation in the world economy*. Washington, DC: Brookings Institution, 1991.

McKinnon, Ronald I. "Private and Official International Money: The Case for the Dollar," *Essays in international finance*, no. 74. International Finance Section, Princeton U., Apr. 1969.

————. "A New Tripartite Monetary Agreement or a Limping Dollar Standard?" *Essays in international finance*, no. 106. International Finance Section, Princeton U., Oct. 1974.

————. *Money in international exchange: The convertible currency system*. NY: Oxford U. Press, 1979.

————. "The Exchange Rate and Macroeconomic Policy: Changing Postwar Perceptions," *J. Econ. Lit.*, June 1981a, *19*(2), pp. 531–57.

————. "Monetary Control and the Crawling Peg," in *Exchange rate rules*. Ed.: John Williamson. Macmillan, 1981b, pp. 38–49.

————. "Currency Substitution and Instability in the World Dollar Standard," *Amer. Econ. Rev.*, June 1982, *72*(3), pp. 320–33.

————. *An international standard for monetary stabilization*. PA 8, Institute for International Economics, Washington, DC, 1984.

————. "Money Supply versus Exchange-Rate Targeting: An Asymmetry between the United States and Other Industrial Economies," in *Macro and micro policies for more growth and employment*. Ed.: Herbert Giersch. Tübingen: J.C.B. Mohr, 1988a, pp. 245–64.

————. "An International Gold Standard Without Gold," *The Cato Institute*, Fall 1988b, *8*(2), pp. 351–73.

————. "Monetary and Exchange Rate Policies for International Financial Stability: A Proposal," *J. Econ. Perspectives*, Winter 1988c, *2*(1), pp. 83–103.

―――. "Interest Rate Volatility and Exchange Risk: New Rules for a Common Monetary Standard," *Contemp. Policy Issues*, Apr. 1990, *8*(2), pp. 1–17.

―――. "A Common Monetary Standard or a Common Currency?" Presented to American Economic Association, Jan. 1992.

―――. "Bretton Woods, The Marshall Plan, and the Postwar Dollar Standard," in Bordo and Eichengreen, 1993, pp. 593–604.

McKinnon, Ronald I., and Ohno, Kenichi. "Purchasing Power Parity as a Monetary Standard," in *The future of the international monetary system: Change, coordination or instability?* Eds.: Omar F. Hamouda, Robin Rowley, and Bernard M. Wolf. Aldershot, Eng.: Edward Elgar, 1989, pp. 42–67.

Meade, James E. *The balance of payments.* London: Oxford U. Press, 1951.

―――. "The Case for Variable Exchange Rates," *Three Banks Review*, Sept. 1955, *27*(3), pp. 3–27.

Meier, Gerald M. *International monetary reform: Collected papers of Emile Despres.* NY: Oxford U. Press, 1973.

Michaely, Michael. *The responsiveness of demand policies to balance of payments.* NY: Columbia U. Press, 1971.

Mill, John Stuart. *Principles of political economy.* Boston: Little Brown, 1848.

Milward, Alan S. *The reconstruction of Western Europe 1945–51.* London: Methuen, 1984.

Morgenstern, Oskar. *International financial transactions and business cycles.* Princeton: Princeton U. Press, 1959.

Mundell, Robert A. "The Appropriate Use of Monetary and Fiscal Policy for Internal and External Stability," *IMF Staff Papers*, Mar. 1962, *9*(1), pp. 70–77.

―――. "The Redundancy Problem and the World Price Level," in *International economics.* Ed.: Robert A. Mundell. NY: Macmillan, 1968, pp. 195–200.

―――. "The Future of the International Financial System," in Acheson, Chant, and Prachowny, 1972, pp. 91–103.

Nurske, Ragnar. *International currency experience.* Geneva: League of Nations, 1944.

―――. "Conditions of International Monetary Equilibrium," in *Essays in international finance*, no. 4. Princeton U., Spring 1945; reprinted in *Readings in the theory of international trade.* Eds.: Howard S. Ellis and Lloyd A. Metzler. Blakiston, 1949, pp. 3–34.

―――. "International Monetary Policy and the Search for Economic Stability," *Amer. Econ. Rev.*, May 1947, *37*, pp. 569–80; reprinted in *Equilibrium and growth in the world economy: Economic essays by Ragnar Nurske.* Eds.: Gottfried Haberler and Robert M. Stern. Cambridge: Harvard U. Press, 1961, pp 72–86.

Officer, Lawrence H. "The Efficiency of the Dollar-Sterling Gold Standard, 1890–1908," *J. Polit. Econ.*, Oct. 1986, *94*(5), pp. 103–73.

Ohno, Kenichi. "The Exchange Rate and Prices in Financially Open Economies." Ph.D. Dissertation, Stanford U., 1987.

———. "Estimating Yen/Dollar and Mark/Dollar Purchasing Power Parities," *IMF Staff Papers*, Sept. 1990, pp. 700–25.

———. "Exchange Rate Regimes and Economic Structure." Center for Research in Economic Growth, Memo. 304, Stanford U., May 1992.

Rogoff, Kenneth. "On the Effects of Sterilized Intervention: An Analysis of Weekly Data," *J. Monet. Econ.*, Sept. 1984, *14*(2), pp. 133–50.

Russo, Massimo, and Tullio, Giuseppe. "Monetary Policy Coordination within the European Monetary System: Is There a Rule?" in *Policy coordination in the European monetary system*. Occasional Paper 61, International Monetary Fund, Washington, DC, Sept. 1988.

Sachs, Jeffrey D. "Is There a Case for More Managed Exchange Rates?" in *The U.S. dollar: Recent developments*. Federal Reserve Bank of Kansas City, 1985, pp. 185–212.

Salter, W. E. G. "Internal and External Balance: The Role of Price and Expenditure Effects," *Econ. Record*, Aug. 1959, *35*, pp. 226–38.

Sayers, Richard S. *Central banking after Bagehot*. London, Oxford U. Press, 1957.

Scammell, W. M. "The Working of the Gold Standard," *Yorkshire Bull. Econ. Soc. Res.*, May 1965, pp. 32–45; reprinted in Eichengreen 1985b, pp. 103–19.

Solomon, Robert. *The international monetary system, 1945–76*. NY: Harper & Row, 1977.

Spiller, Pablo T., and Wood, Robert O. "Arbitrage During the Dollar-Sterling Gold Standard, 1899–1908: An Economic Approach," *J. Polit. Econ.*, Aug. 1988, *96*(4), pp. 882–92.

Suss, Esther C. "A Note on Reserve Use under Alternative Exchange Rate Regimes," *IMF Staff Papers*, July 1976, *23*(2), pp. 387–94.

Suzuki, Yoshio. *Money, finance, and macroeconomic performance in Japan*. New Haven: Yale U. Press, 1986.

Swoboda, Alexander. "The Eurodollar Market: An Interpretation," *Essays in international finance*, no. 64. Princeton U., 1968.

———. "Gold, Dollars, Euro-dollars, and the World Monetary Stock Under Fixed Exchange Rates," *Amer. Econ. Rev.*, Sept. 1978, *68*(4), pp. 625–42.

Tan, Kong-Yam. "Flexible Exchange Rates and Interdependence: Empirical Implications for U.S. Monetary Policy." Ph.D. Dissertation, Stanford U., 1984.

Tavlas, George, and Ozeki, Yuzuru. *The internationalization of currencies: An appraisal of the Japanese yen*. Occasional Paper 90, International Monetary Fund, Washington, DC, Jan. 1992.

Triffin, Robert. *Gold and the dollar crisis*. New Haven: Yale U. Press, 1960.

———. "The Evolution of the International Monetary System: Historical Reappraisal and Future Perspectives," *Studies in international finance*, no. 18. Princeton U., June 1964.

Viren, Matti. "McKinnon's Currency Substitution Hypothesis: Some New Evidence," *Economica Internazionale*, 1992.

Williamson, John. "The Crawling Peg," *Essays in international finance*, no. 50, Princeton U., 1965.

———. "Exchange-Rate Flexibility and Reserve Use," *The Scand. J. Econ.*, 1976, *78*(2), pp. 327–39.

———. *The failure of world monetary reform, 1971–74*. Great Britain: Thomas Nelson and Sons, 1977.

———. "Keynes and the International Economic Order," (1983) in *Political economy and international money: Selected essays of John Williamson*. NY: NYU Press, 1987, pp. 37–59.

3

Exchange Risk and Interest-Rate Volatility in Historical Perspective

3.1 Introduction

Under flexible exchange rates, governments do not commit themselves to maintain par values with other national monies into the distant future. Under fixed exchange rates, governments strive (not always successfully) to preserve historic par values of their national monies in terms of foreign exchange or some common international monetary standard. What are the implications for the behavior of interest rates? The key difference between these two general classes of exchange-rate regimes is the commitment, under fixed rates, to subordinate domestic monetary policy to long-term exchange stability.

This short paper focuses on the remarkable increase in the volatility of *long-term* interest rates in the world's major industrial economies since 1973, when the postwar commitment to maintain dollar exchange parities finally collapsed. First, the evidence on interest-rate volatility under floating exchange rates (1973 to 1990) is compared to the more stable behavior of interest rates during the earlier fixed-rate regimes—the classical gold standard (1879 to 1913) and the Bretton Woods dollar standard (1950 to 1970). Then, I examine whether or not the differing behavior of long-term interest rates across these different historical epochs

Originally published, in slightly longer form, in *Greek Economic Review* 15, 2 (December 1993): 29–44. Part of this chapter also appeared in "Dollar Devaluation, Interest Rate Volatility, and the Duration of Investment in the United States" in *Technology and the Wealth of Nations*, ed. N. Rosenberg, R. Landau, and D. Mowery (Stanford University Press, 1992), 281–326, with David Robinson. Reprinted with permission.

can reasonably be attributed to the exchange-rate regimes themselves. Apart from the increased exchange risk under floating, did the rules of the classical gold standard differ significantly from those of Bretton Woods?

3.2 The Evidence

Under the classical gold standard, nominal exchange rates were confined within their gold points—a band width of less than 1 percent (see table 2.1), which was expected to last into the distant future. Without exchange controls and with the completion of the transoceanic cable telegraph in the 1870s, financial capital was both free to move and highly mobile internationally in the late 19th century—more so than for some decades after World War II. For the period 1879 to 1913, figure 3.1 shows that long-term interest rates remained low, close together, and little changed through time. Yields on prime grade U.S. railway bonds remained near 4 percent, those on British consols near 3 percent or slightly less; yields on French rentes and on other European long-term bonds (not shown in figure 3.1) were in between.

In sharp visual contrast to figure 3.1 on the classical gold standard, figure 3.2 portrays the modern experience with long-term interest rates on the government bonds of Japan, the United States, Germany, and the United Kingdom. From 1973 to 1990, interest rates were much higher, often over 12 percent, volatility was much greater, and dispersion of interest rates across countries was high: a differential of 5 to 6 percentage points between the United States and Britain on the one hand, and Germany and Japan on the other, was not unusual. Figure 3.2 also shows that, during the dollar standard of the 1950s and 1960s, long-term interest rates[1] were closer together and less volatile—at least until 1969–71, when the fixed rate system came under pressure.

Suppose we define interest-rate volatility more precisely as the mean absolute change, monthly or annual, in percentage points of bond yields over the period in question. This will be the primary meaning of the word "volatility." Alternatively, we also measure volatility as the standard deviation of monthly or annual changes in interest rates from their mean change in the period in question.[2] For the United States and Britain, respec-

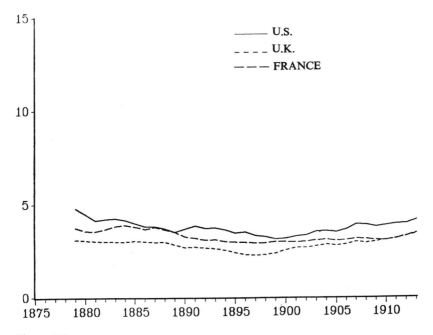

Figure 3.1
Long-term interest rates: Gold standard, 1879–1913.
Source: See data appendix.

tively, tables 3.1 and 3.2 compare interest-rate volatility under the classical gold standard to the Bretton Woods dollar standard, and no-par floating since 1973.

From either monthly or annual data, table 3.1 shows that interest-rate volatility on American long-term bonds of the highest quality was 8 to 9 times higher under floating as under the classical gold standard, and 3 to 4 times higher under floating as under Bretton Woods. The British data in table 3.2 are strikingly similar. Long-term interest rates varied hardly at all under the classical gold standard and varied significantly more under the Bretton Woods dollar standard. However, when measured on a monthly basis, volatility in British long-term gilt-edged bonds since 1973 has been about four times higher than it was in the 1950s and 1960s, and more than twice as high as when measured by year-to-year changes. (If interest-rate volatility is measured by standard deviations, tables 3.1 and 3.2 show that these remarkable differences in exchange-rate regimes are still evident.)

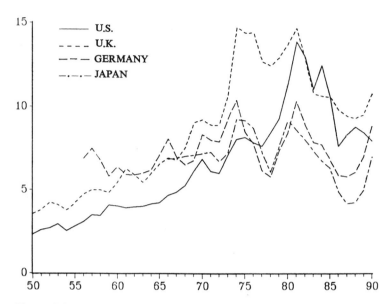

Figure 3.2
Long-term government bond yields, 1950–90.
Source: See data appendix.

The unusually high variance in exchange rates since 1973 is now well recognized, but the extraordinary volatility in long-term interest rates is sometimes forgotten.

Short-term interest rates were also shown as more volatile under floating compared to the earlier fixed-rate standards—although the differences are not as systematically large as in the case of long rates. For annual data on the United States and Britain, tables 3.1 and 3.2 show that volatility in short rates under floating was about twice as large as under the earlier fixed-rate standards. Measured by monthly changes in short-term interest rates, however, the Bretton Woods dollar standard was the least volatile compared to either floating or the classical gold standard. Although long rates remained remarkably stable, the classical gold standard exhibited month-to-month volatility in short-term interest rates which was high by the standards of Bretton Woods—but was not so high by modern standards.

We don't have such similarly comparable data over the three historical epochs for Germany and Japan. Indeed, their internal bond markets were not really free of government control until

Table 3.1
U.S. Interest-Rate Volatility (summary statistics of historical comparisons)

		Mean Absolute Change[a]	Standard Deviation[b]
Annual data			
Short-term	Gold standard	1.01	1.35
	Bretton Woods	0.69	0.77
	Floating	1.65	1.93
Long-term	Gold standard	0.14	0.20
	Bretton Woods	0.29	0.30
	Floating	1.11	1.41
Monthly data			
Short-term	Gold standard	0.40	0.58
	Bretton Woods	0.14	0.21
	Floating	0.44	0.74
Long-term	Gold standard	0.03	0.04
	Bretton Woods	0.08	0.12
	Floating	0.28	0.40

Source: See data appendix.
[a]Annual measures are based on end-of-year interest changes in percentage points. Monthly measures are based on end-of-month changes in percentage points. Periods: Gold standard 1879–1913; Bretton Woods 1950–1970; floating 1973–1990.
[b]Standard deviations are calculated from the period's mean interest rate.

about 1960 in Germany, and somewhere in the 1970s in Japan. Nevertheless, table 3.3 shows that month-to-month volatility in German long-term bonds more than doubled from the 1960s to floating after 1973. Table 3.3 also shows that month-to-month volatility in long-term interest rates in Japan after 1973 was as high as that in the United States and Germany.

Is there a tendency for volatility in long-term interest rates to diminish as experience with floating exchange rates accumulates? With the possible exception of Britain, table 3.3 also shows that long-rate volatility in the industrial countries was about as high from the late 1980s into the early 1990s as it was from the mid 1970s into the early 1980s. The "completion" of the European Monetary System (EMS) by the late 1980s succeeded in creating a zone of exchange-rate stability around Germany. But German capital markets were not effectively insulated from extra-European financial flows. Table 3.3 shows that volatility in German long-term interest rates from 1985 to 1990 was as high as it was from 1973 to 1984.

Table 3.2
British Interest-Rate Volatility (summary statistics of historical comparisons)

		Mean Absolute Change[a]	Standard Deviation[b]
Annual data			
Short-term	Gold standard	0.98	1.29
	Bretton Woods	0.77	0.92
	Floating	1.89	2.24
Long-term	Gold standard	0.07	0.09
	Bretton Woods	0.45	0.48
	Floating	0.97	1.43
Monthly data			
Short-term	Gold standard	0.50	0.72
	Bretton Woods	0.16	0.31
	Floating	0.51	0.76
Long-term	Gold standard	0.03	0.04
	Bretton Woods	0.09	0.12
	Floating	0.36	0.47

Source: See data appendix.
[a]Annual measures are based on end-of-year interest changes in percentage points. Monthly measures are based on end-of-month changes in percentage points. Periods: Gold standard 1879–1913; Bretton Woods 1950–1970; floating 1973–1990.
[b]Standard deviations are calculated from the period's mean interest rate.

3.3   Coincidence or Cause and Effect?

How can we best explain this upsurge in long-term interest-rate volatility after 1973 as compared to the earlier periods when a worldwide monetary standard prevailed?

One hypothesis, difficult to refute, is to argue that the exchange-rate regime itself is not a causal factor determining volatility in long-term interest rates. We simply live in riskier times than those of the Bretton Woods dollar standard after 1950, or those of the international gold standard before World War I. And this increased risk shows up *coincidentally* in the higher level of interest rates, and in their greater volatility at the longer end of the maturity spectrum. Putting this coincidence hypothesis a bit more subtly to make it even more difficult to refute, one could say that those risk factors, perhaps in the form of diverging national macroeconomic policies that caused the Bret-

Table 3.3
Volatility in Long-Term Interest Rates: Cross-Country Comparisons from 1950 to 1990 (mean absolute monthly changes in percentage points)

Period	U.S.	Britain	Germany	Japan
Bretton Woods				
50.02–69.12	0.085	0.091	—	—
60.02–69.12	0.092	0.112	0.087	—
No-Par Floating				
73.01–90.12	0.282	0.355	0.198	0.227
73.01–84.12	0.293	0.408	0.202	0.202
85.01–90.12	0.258	0.251	0.192	0.279

Source: IFS Statistics of the International Monetary Fund.
Note: Unfilled entries indicate that the country in question did not have an open long-term bond market in that period.

ton Woods par-value system to break down, are also responsible for the increased volatility of interest rates.

I take a different tack. Let us allow for the possibility that the ways in which exchange-rate regimes themselves are organized strongly affect interest rates. What then are the relevant features of international exchange-rate agreements, or the lack thereof, that could most plausibly influence the volatility of interest rates in national capital markets?

Suppose that the countries in question are sovereign over their own national monetary policies. National central banks or treasuries remain responsible for domestic note issues and for regulating and controlling the reserve positions of domestic commercial banks. Then, the nature of the exchange-rate regime will strongly influence the strength or weakness of any country's willingness to adhere to the same monetary policies, with a common rate of price inflation, as its neighbors.

If this commitment to a common monetary standard is weak, managers of international bond portfolios will continually switch among securities denominated in differing national currencies in response to new information on how the longer-run evolution of national price levels might diverge—thus anticipating corresponding adjustments in future exchange rates. This continual portfolio switching among dollar, sterling, mark, and yen assets would then strongly affect spot exchange rates if they were free to float (Frenkel and Mussa 1980). And I claim it will also strongly increase the volatility of long-term interest rates—although not necessarily of short rates.

Before analyzing the "rules of the game" of the classical gold standard and of the Bretton Woods dollar standard for containing this risk from diverging national monetary policies, consider exchange risk under no-par floating where pressure to coordinate national monetary policies is minimal.

3.4 Real Exchange Rate and Relative Price-Level Risk

Let us break the risk characteristics of no-par floating into two components. The first component is *real exchange-rate risk:* the extent to which the nominal exchange rate differs from purchasing power parity. PPP is defined as the exchange rate that would align national price levels of a very broad basket of internationally tradable goods. During past periods with a common monetary standard and fixed exchange rates, broad wholesale (producer) price indices remained closely aligned internationally. In the 1950s and 1960s when their exchange rates were virtually unchanged, price levels in Germany, Japan, and the United States remained very close; see figure 2.2 in chapter 2 above. One can show a similar commonality in national price-level movements under the classical gold standard (McKinnon 1988b and chapter 4 below).

Under no-par floating, in contrast, short-term volatility in real exchange rates is high on a month-to-month or quarter-to-quarter basis: nominal exchange rates fluctuate while national price levels change relatively little. But the more striking characteristic of the modern experience is the extent to which national price levels have been misaligned for prolonged periods. For 1975 to 1989, figures 3.3 and 3.4 (taken from Ohno 1990) compare movements in the actual yen/dollar and mark/dollar exchange rates to the path(s) of their estimated purchasing power parities (PPPs)—those rates which would have aligned either producer price indices or unit labor costs between the United States and Japan or Germany.[3]

Deviations from PPP of 20 percent in either direction have been sustained, sometimes for years, with individual spikes ranging up to 40 percent. In the now worldwide markets for goods and many services, these are tremendous swings in the international competitiveness of any country's merchants and manu-

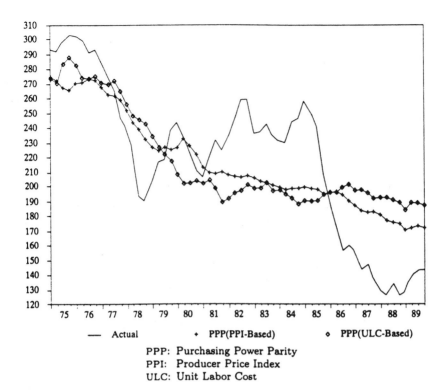

Figure 3.3
Actual and PPP yen/dollar rates, 1975–89.
Source: Kenichi Ohno, "Estimating Yen/Dollar and Mark/Dollar Purchasing Power Parities," *IMF Staff Papers,* 1990.

facturers. Manufacturers whose country's real exchange rate suddenly appreciates can experience a sudden decline in profitability, as did those in Japan from the sudden appreciation of the yen in 1986–87, and did those in the United States in 1981–85 with the appreciation of the dollar.

But can't such real exchange rate risk be effectively hedged if forward markets for foreign exchange are fairly complete? Unfortunately, no. Even if international financial markets permit industrialists to freely adjust their net foreign exchange positions to virtually any term to maturity, forward commodity markets for brand-name manufactured goods remain seriously incomplete. Thus, industrialists planning long-term investments in plant and equipment in various parts of the world cannot fully

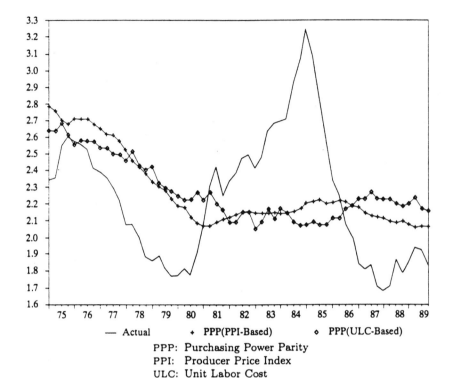

— Actual   ◆ PPP(PPI-Based)   ◇ PPP(ULC-Based)

PPP: Purchasing Power Parity
PPI: Producer Price Index
ULC: Unit Labor Cost
SOURCE: Kinichi Ohno, "Estimating Yen/Dollar and Mark/Dollar
Purchasing Power Parities," *IMF Staff Papers* (forthcoming), 1990.

FIGURE 11.2 Actual and PPP Yen/Dollar Rates

hedge real exchange-rate risk (McKinnon 1979, 1988a). Without
forward commodity contracts in hand, industrialists find they
must live with substantial residual exchange risk even when
their forward positions in foreign exchange are optimized ex
ante.

What are the implications for the behavior of interest rates of
this largely unhedgeable[4] real exchange rate risk? If farmers or
industrialists issuing securities to finance new physical investments are subject to a higher probability of default, the risk
premia demanded by the holders of these securities will increase.
Thus, real exchange-rate risk contributes to the higher *level* of
"real" interest rates in the 1980s into the 1990s compared to the
late 19th century or the 1950s and 1960s. But real exchange-rate

risk, i.e., unexpected deviations from PPP, does not itself directly explain why long-term interest rates should be so much more *volatile* under floating. To better explain this increased volatility, another component of exchange risk becomes important.

The second, and less well recognized, component is what I shall call *relative price-level risk*. Even if we suppose that exchange rates always equaled their PPP values so that real exchange-rate risk was absent, the choice of a currency with which to finance a long-term investment is still nontrivial if there is no common international monetary standard. The price level of country *A* could still evolve quite differently, and unpredictably, from that in country *B*. From 1973 to 1990, figure 2.2 in chapter 2 shows that price inflation in the United States was more than 50 percent higher than that in Germany and Japan, while the dollar was depreciating—albeit erratically—by a similar order of magnitude. (In the 1950–69 period of fixed exchange rates, inflation in all three countries' wholesale price indices was virtually the same—less than 1 percent per year.)

Relative price-level risk hampers business firms trying to decide whether to issue long-term bonds denominated in dollars, marks, yen, or in some other currency. A company that issues dollar bonds, bearing a substantially higher interest rate than yen bonds, could be saddled with a higher real debt burden if American price inflation relative to that in Japan turns out to be substantially lower than that forecast by the current long-term interest differential. Conversely, a company fortunate enough to issue yen bonds would find itself with a substantially lower real debt burden. This enhanced possibility of corporate bankruptcy also serves to raise risk premia and the general level of interest rates.

3.5 The Casino Effect in Portfolio Choice

But what about volatility per se? By destabilizing the portfolio preferences of international investors—trust funds, insurance companies, wealthy individuals, and so on—relative price-level risk also directly increases the variability of long-term interest rates.

Under flexible exchange rates, international investors must continually guess the course of, say, the yen/dollar or mark/

dollar exchange rates into the indefinite future. Even if PPP held day-to-day, investors in long-term dollar, yen, or mark bonds are still required to estimate future exchange rates among dollars, yen, or marks, i.e., how the three national price levels will evolve relative to each other in the long run. But the three fiat monies have no intrinsic purchasing powers other than what their respective central banks manage to establish. In this guessing game, portfolio managers must continually project forward the relative ease or tightness of monetary policies in Germany, Japan, and the United States over 10 to 20 years—the terms to maturity of the bonds that they hold.

Absent exchange controls, financial assets denominated in yen, marks, dollars, sterling, and so on are also close substitutes as international stores of value at any term to maturity. They are easily bought and sold in national capital markets, with the proceeds easily reconverted into any designated national currency. Thus, relatively small changes in expected relative yields—the rate of interest on country A's bonds less the expected depreciation of A's currency against those of B, C, D, and so on, can cause a substantial shift in portfolio preferences across bonds denominated in different currencies: what I shall call the "casino effect." This explains the high variability in spot exchange rates on the one hand *and* in long-term interest rates on the other. This casino effect is an easily recognized extension of the asset approach to exchange-rate determination (Frenkel and Mussa 1980) to encompass the determination of longer-term interest rates in the bond market. Both exchange rates and long-term interest rates then exhibit "virtual" random walks in the short and intermediate runs.[5]

Why omit short-term interest rates from the casino effect? In a regime of floating exchange rates, each country follows an independent monetary policy—at least in principle. As a short-run operating guideline, most central banks target some short-term interest rate, on treasury bills, federal funds, or something similar. This tends to smooth out fluctuations in short-term interest rates in response to shifts in international portfolio preferences. Alternatively, one can consider short-term interest rates to be caught in national liquidity traps in the face of shifting international risk assessments (McKinnon 1990 and chapter 17). Either way, the volatility of short-term interest rates should increase rather less than the volatility of long rates increases in moving from a par-value system to greater exchange-rate flexibility.

3.6 The Dollar Standard versus the Gold Standard

In comparison to the more recent experience with no-par floating, both the Bretton Woods dollar standard (1950–70) and the gold standard (1879 to 1913) succeeded in containing volatility in long-term interest rates. Although these two international monetary standards operated differently in some important respects, what were their common elements that successfully anchored the long-term capital markets?

First, both successfully reduced relative price-level risk in the long run. Countries were bound to a common monetary standard so that their price levels evolved similarly through time. Thus the probability was considered small that, 10 to 20 years hence, the exchange rate of country *A* with country *B* would differ greatly from the then current exchange rate.

Second, the classical gold and postwar dollar standards were fully international, encompassing *all* the financially important countries. Unlike the regional character of today's European monetary system, no alternative liquid financial asset—with significantly different monetary characteristics—existed into which international investors could conveniently and continually shift. Bonds denominated in sterling, dollars, marks, and so on, bore the same risk of general price-level inflation or deflation.

What is the principal lesson from these historical experiences with fixed rates in comparison to no-par floating? As long as all important countries with freely convertible currencies are credibly committed to the same worldwide monetary standard, holders of long-term bonds need not be so nervous. They need not continually reassess country *A*'s monetary policy in terms of *B*'s in order to adjust their portfolios of liquid financial assets in keeping with changing perceptions of the evolution of the exchange rate. True, the common rate of commodity price inflation might still remain uncertain. However, unless some obviously persistent worldwide price inflation seemed in the offing, arbitrage between bonds (with worldwide markets) and relatively illiquid nonmonetary assets—such as real estate or inventories of commodities—was too inconvenient to appeal to

Table 3.4
Price Level Volatility: United States, West Germany, and Japan

Period		Annual Change	Standard Deviation
United States			
Bretton Woods	1951–69	0.9	1.7
Floating	1973–88	5.6	3.8
West Germany			
Bretton Woods	1951–69	0.7	1.5
Floating	1973–88	3.6	3.0
Japan			
Bretton Woods	1951–69	0.5	2.4
Floating	1973–88	2.3	6.2

Source: IMF, *International Financial Statistics.*
Note: Annual change is calculated as the time coefficient of the log of the variable on a time trend. Standard deviation is the standard error of the estimate of the fitted equation $lnP_t = a + blnP_{t-1}$ where P_t is the Wholesale Price Index in year t.
  Cooper (1982) performs similar calculations for the United States during the gold standard period of 1879–1913. He derives an annual average change of 0.1 and a standard deviation of 5.4.

international portfolio managers. Thus their portfolio preferences were more stable, the volatility of long-term interest rates was much less, and risk premia in the level of each country's interest rates were lower.

However, the two standards were not identical. Tables 3.1 and 3.2 show that volatility in long-term bond rates was substantially lower under the classical gold standard than under Bretton Woods.

Could the success of the late 19th-century system in keeping long-term interest rates lower and more stable be because the common price level was better anchored? Although the common price level exhibited virtually no trend over the whole period from 1879 to 1913, cyclical fluctuations—as measured by national wholesale price indices (WPIs)—were severe and sometimes prolonged (figure 3.5). Richard Cooper (1982) calculated that the standard deviation of annual changes in the American WPI from 1879 to 1913 was 5.4, which is high in comparison to a standard deviation of just 1.7 from 1950 to 1969. Indeed, a glance at figure 2.2 in chapter 2 indicates that the common price level under the postwar dollar standard from 1950 to 1970 was remarkably

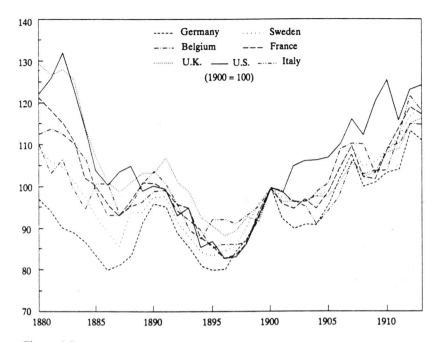

Figure 3.5
Wholesale prices, 1879–1913 (1900 = 100).
Source: See data appendix.

stable. But price-level volatility again became high under the floating-rate dollar standard—as shown in table 3.4.

Instead, a more promising explanation is that the commitment to *long-term* exchange stability was stronger under the classical gold standard than under the dollar standard. Nations made firm long-term commitments to return to their traditional gold parities even if gold convertibility had to be temporarily suspended because of some panic or run. Thus investors had *long-term confidence* in, say, what the dollar/sterling exchange rate was expected to be 20 years hence—although occasionally they might face some *near-term uncertainty* as to whether or not the exchange rate would be contained within the gold points next week or next month.

However, figure 3.5 also shows that U.S. price level exhibited virtually no trend over the whole 1879–1913 period: increasing at 0.1 percent per year, which is indistinguishable from measurement error. Superimposed on the classical gold standard's sharp

cyclical fluctuations, however, wholesale prices drifted down
from the 1870s to 1896 by about two percent a year; and upward
thereafter to 1913 by about the same amount, as shown in figure
3.5. Whether or not any of these price-level movements should
have been expected and thus registered in interest rates has been
a matter of long-standing curiosity: the so-called Gibson paradox
(Fisher 1930; Barsky 1987). But they were not so registered, as
figure 3.1 suggests. Instead, the nature of the exchange-rate regime, rather than the classical gold standard's success in anchoring the price level(s), could be more important in minimizing
volatility in long-term interest rates. First, the classical gold standard was fully international, encompassing all the financially
important countries. No alternative liquid financial asset—with
significantly different monetary characteristics—existed into
which international investors could conveniently and continually
shift. Bonds denominated in sterling, dollars, francs, and so on,
bore the same risk of general price-level inflation or deflation.
Unless some obviously persistent general price inflation seemed
in the offing, arbitrage between bonds (with worldwide markets)
and relatively illiquid nonmonetary assets, such as real estate or
inventories of commodities, was too inconvenient to appeal to
international portfolio managers.

Second, nations made firm long-term commitments to return
to their traditional gold parities even if gold convertibility had
to be temporarily suspended because of some panic or run. Thus
investors had long-term confidence in, say, what the dollar/
sterling exchange rate was expected to be twenty years hence,
although occasionally they might face some near-term uncertainty as to whether or not the exchange rate would be contained
within the gold points next week or next month. Thus did the
classical gold standard avoid the continual churning of asset
portfolios that we now associate with free international capital
mobility. Because of the absence of long-term exchange risk
across otherwise economically and politically diverse countries,
long-term interest rates remained low and uniform.

In contrast, the Bretton Woods Articles of 1945 required that
nations adhere to par values for their currencies in the short run,
but explicitly left open the possibility that those par values could
be adjusted in the future if a "fundamental disequilibrium"

should develop in a country's international payments. Fortunately, this provision's potentially adverse expectations effect, towards increasing the volatility of the long-term capital markets, was muted by the way the system worked in practice. Because of the greater monetary stability of the American economy and the operations of the Marshall Plan in 1949–51, most industrial countries opted simply to simply peg their currencies to the dollar "indefinitely" after 1950. After exchange controls were loosened and international financial arbitrage revived in the 1950s, it became progressively more awkward to change those dollar pegs without provoking an anticipatory speculative run on the currency whose devaluation was contemplated. Thus, most governments tried to avoid changing their par values, and surprisingly few changes occurred in practice.[6] Nevertheless, some residual uncertainty remained because of the "promise" of long-term exchange-rate flexibility and national monetary autonomy in the 1945 agreement.

Thus the rules of the classical gold standard anchored exchange rates in the long run more securely than did the dollar standard. Correspondingly, long-term interest rates were less volatile under the gold standard than under the dollar standard (tables 3.1 and 3.2). But both fixed exchange-rate standards avoided the continual churning of asset portfolios and the very high volatility in, and levels of, long-term interest rates that we now associate with no-par floating.

Data Appendix

Gold Standard

Long-Term Interest Rates.
United States: Unadjusted index number of yields on U.S. Railroad Bonds from Macaulay, *The Movements of Interest Rates, Bond Yields, and Stock Prices in the United States Since 1856*, 1938.

United Kingdom: Yield on consols from F. Capie and A. Weber, *A Monetary History of the United Kingdom 1870–1982*, vol. 1, 1985.

France: Annual average yield on 3 percent Rentes from S. Homer, *A History of Interest Rates*, 1977.

Post War

i. Long-Term Government Bond Yields.
United States: 10-year government bonds, Citibase series
FYGT10.
Japan: Long-term government bonds (seven years and over)
from IMF, *IFS* line 61.
Germany: Public authority bond yields (at least three years
to maturity) from IMF, *IFS* line 61.
United Kingdom: 20-year government bonds from IMF, *IFS*
line 61.
ii. Wholesale Prices and Exchange Rates: *International Financial
Statistics*, International Monetary Fund (various issues).

Notes

John Hussman, Kenichi Ohno, and David Robinson all contributed to the ideas
and contents of this chapter.

1. Because the domestic long-term bond markets in Germany and Japan were
not yet decontrolled to permit open-market trading throughout much of the
1950s and 1960s, their interest-rate plots in figure 3.2 are incomplete.

2. This standard-deviation measure of volatility is less sensitive to overall
trends in the level of interest rates.

3. How best to estimate (absolute) PPP exchange rates remains contentious,
but alternative statistical techniques lead to estimates similar to those appearing
in figures 3.3 and 3.4 (McKinnon and Ohno 1989; Ohno 1990). More basically,
substituting long-term moving averages of the yen/dollar and mark/dollar
rates for the PPP rates in figures 3.3 and 3.4 would show similarly large
deviations of current exchange rates from these long-term trends.

4. That real exchange-rate risk can be only partially hedged, even when forward
markets in foreign exchange are highly developed, is discussed in McKinnon
(1979) and in chapters 4 and 18.

5. Insofar as both exchange rates and long-term interest rates are (weakly)
bounded in the long run, they are not pure random walks (Robinson 1990).

6. From 1950 to 1969, France devalued three times, Britain once by 15 percent,
and Germany appreciated by 5 percent (figure 2.2 in chapter 2). But even these
discrete changes are small relative to commonly observed annual exchange-
rate movements under no-par floating.

References

Barsky, Robert B. (1987). "The Fisher Hypotheses and the Forecastability and
Persistence of Inflation," *Journal of Monetary Economics*, (January) 19 (1), 3–34.

Cooper, Richard (1982). "The Gold Standard: Historical Facts and Future Prospects," in *Brookings Papers on Economic Activity*, I, 1–45; and reprinted in R. N. Cooper, *The International Monetary System* (Cambridge, Mass.: The MIT Press).

Fisher, Irving (1930). *The Theory of Interest* (New York: Macmillan).

Frenkel, Jacob, and Mussa, Michael (1980). "The Efficiency of Foreign Exchange Markets and Measures of Turbulence," *American Economic Review*, (May) 70, 374–381.

McKinnon, Ronald I. (1979). *Money In International Exchange: The Convertible Currency System* (Oxford: Oxford University Press).

——— (1988a). "Monetary and Exchange Rate Policies for International Financial Stability: A Proposal." *Journal of Economic Perspectives*, (Winter), 83–103.

——— (1988b). "An International Gold Standard Without Gold," *Cato Journal*, (Fall), 8 (2), 351–373.

——— (1990). "Why Floating Exchange Rates Fail: A Reconsideration of the Liquidity Trap," *Open Economies Review*, (Fall), 1, 229–250.

McKinnon, R., and Ohno, K. (1989). "Purchasing Power Parity as a Monetary Standard," Ch. 7 in Hamouda, Rowley, and Wolf (eds.), *The Future of the International Monetary System* (Edward Elgar).

Ohno, Kenichi (1990). "Estimating Yen/Dollar and Mark/Dollar Purchasing Power Parities," International Monetary Fund *Staff Papers* (September).

Robinson, David (1990). "Is the Exchange Rate a Random Walk?," Economics Dept., Stanford University, unpublished, (November).

4   An International Gold Standard without Gold

What can history tell us about the desirability, and feasibility, of maintaining fixed exchange rates between national currencies when capital is highly mobile? The workings of the international gold standard from the late 1870s to August 1914 provide the best example we have. Unlike the Bretton Woods system of pegged exchange rates in the 1950s and 1960s, or the residual controls of today's European Monetary System, no exchange controls impeded gross flows of financial capital. Moreover, net transfers of capital between countries were huge: Large net trade surpluses (deficits) opened and closed continually with no adjustments in nominal exchange rates and, by modern standards, with little change in real exchange rates. World trade grew rapidly.

Nevertheless, fixed exchange rates in general, and the gold standard in particular, remain as unpopular among American economists today as they were with the Populists who almost succeeded in electing William Jennings Bryan president in 1896. From 1873 onward America's acquiescence to the discipline of the gold standard and to British dominance of the international capital market was always somewhat grudging (Hale 1988). Even the formation of the Federal Reserve System in 1913 was an attempt to make American control over domestic money and credit somewhat more independent of international influences.

But this discrediting of fixed exchange rates, and subsequent refusal to bend American monetary policy toward maintaining a common international monetary standard, reflects, in part, a

Originally published in *Cato Journal* 8, 2 (Fall 1988): 351–373. Reprinted with permission.

misassessment of the late 19th-century experience. How well the process of balancing payments between countries actually worked when exchange rates were fixed and capital markets were integrated has not been sufficiently distinguished from systemwide instability associated with gold itself.

In this chapter I will contrast the classical Hume-Ricardo-Mill model of international payments adjustment under the gold standard—still the dominant textbook approach—with the modern (revisionist) view based on more integrated goods and financial markets. The case for or against flexible exchange rates largely depends on which of these perspectives one accepts.

First, however, I want to assess how well the 19th-century gold standard anchored the world price level. The problem of worldwide inflation and deflation is somewhat distinct from whether fixed exchange rates, based on mutual monetary adjustment, are desirable.

4.1 The World Price Level

For the period before 1914, data on wholesale prices are much easier to obtain than is direct information on output and employment. Roy Jastram (1977) pieced together a long time series, based on both British and American price data, to show that the real purchasing power of gold over a general basket of primary commodities and simple manufactures was virtually the same at the beginning of World War I as it had been at the end of the Napoleonic wars a century earlier. Indeed, British data going back to the 18th century show a remarkable absence of any trend in gold's purchasing power.

A second characteristic of the gold standard—at least from the late 1870s to 1913 when exchange rates were securely fixed—was the strength of international arbitrage in markets for tradable goods other than precious metals. Table 4.1 shows that the wholesale price levels of the United States, Great Britain, Germany, and France fell *in parallel* by the order of 40 to 50 percent from 1873 to 1896, and then rose by a similar amount from 1896 to 1913. At a more microeconomic level, McCloskey and Zecher (1976) provide additional evidence that the absolute prices of individual commodities were generally aligned internationally about as well as they were among different regions within the same country.

Table 4.1
Wholesale Price Indexes for the United States, United Kingdom, Germany, and France. Selected Years, 1816–1913

Year and Period	United States	United Kingdom	Germany	France
Indexes (1913 = 100)				
1816	150	147	94	143
1849	82	86	67	94
1873	137	130	114	112
1896	64	72	69	69
1913	100	100	100	100
Changes (%)				
1816–1849	−45	−41	−29	−33
1849–1873	67	51	70	30
1873–1896	−53	−45	−40	−45
1896–1913	56	39	45	45

Source: Cooper (1982, p. 8).

Thus, in the late 19th century, the world economy was successfully unified to the extent that prices of a broad basket of tradable goods were aligned across countries. When nominal exchange rates were securely fixed by mutual monetary adjustment, international commodity arbitrage was sufficiently robust to create purchasing power parity (PPP): Any one national currency had about the same real purchasing power in domestic markets for tradable commodities as it did abroad. (This was most unlike our recent experience with floating exchange rates.) Since one may then talk sensibly about a common world price level, can the mechanisms of the gold standard per se be credited with systematically stabilizing it over the long run—as Jastram's statistics might suggest?

Barry Eichengreen (1985, p. 7) clearly summarizes the classical view of how the common price level was anchored:

[Mill's] assumption was that the flow supply of newly mined gold would be responsive to relative prices. As the world economy expanded and the demand for money grew, downward pressure would be placed on the world price level. As the prices of other commodities fell in terms of the numeraire commodity gold, new supplies would be elicited by its rising value. . . . Similarly, to the extent that deflation causes the price of jewelry to fall in terms of gold coin, jewelry will be presented at the Mint for conversion into coin, increasing the quantity of coin in circulation and moderating the downward pressure on prices.

Robert Barro (1979) provides an algebraic exposition of these two forces and notes that "the determination of the absolute price level amounts to the determination of the relative price of the reserve commodity." Was then the price of gold relative to other commodities naturally constant so as to prevent secular change in the common price level?

From table 4.2, Robert Triffin's (1964) analysis suggests the contrary. In the 19th century, only massive increases in the circulation of credit money (notes and deposits) prevented unending price-level deflation. Triffin shows that by 1885 token currency and demand deposits already constituted about 65 percent of the money supplies of Britain, France, and the United States, and that this proportion increased to 87 percent by 1913. Thus during this period, the mixed system had become largely a gold bullion standard with relatively slender reserves for meeting international payments concentrated in national treasuries and central banks.

These financial innovations were only loosely regulated at the national level. No authority with a worldwide view—not even the Bank of England—was monitoring or controlling the aggregate stock of credit money with an eye to stabilizing the world's price level. The fact that the world's price level was approximately the same in early 1914 as it was before the Napoleonic Wars, therefore, seems to be largely accidental.

This absence of a dependable gold anchor for the common price level becomes evident once one looks at price movements over shorter time periods. In his thorough study of economic fluctuations under the pre-1914 gold standard, Richard Cooper (1982, p. 6) notes that

Price stability was not attained, either in the short run or in the long run, either during the gold standard proper or over a longer period during which gold held dominant influence. In fact, in the United States short-run variations in wholesale prices were higher during the prewar gold standard than from 1949 to 1979. The standard deviation of annual movements in (wholesale) prices was 5.4 percent in the earlier period and only 4.8 percent in the latter period.

For longer-term cyclical fluctuations of a decade or two, Cooper offers the wholesale price index data in table 4.1 for the United States, Great Britain, Germany, and France. The great deflations of the early 19th century were relieved only by the

Table 4.2
Comparative Evolution of Money and Reserve Structure, 1885 and 1913

	Three Countries[a]		Eleven Countries[b]		World	
Money and Reserves	1885	1913	1885	1913	1885	1913
In Billions of U.S. Dollars						
1. Money supply	**6.3**	**19.8**	**8.4**	**26.3**	**14.2**	**33.1**
a. Gold	1.4	2.0	1.8	2.7	2.4	3.2
b. Silver	0.7	0.6	1.0	1.2	3.0	2.3
c. Credit money	4.1	17.2	5.6	22.4	8.8	27.6
i. Currency[c]	*1.6*	*3.8*	*2.3*	*5.9*	*3.8*	*8.1*
ii. Demand deposits	*2.6*	*13.3*	*3.3*	*16.5*	*5.0*	*19.6*
2. Monetary reserves	**1.0**	**2.7**	**1.5**	**4.0**	**2.0**	**5.3**
a. Gold	0.6	2.1	0.9	3.2	1.3	4.1
b. Silver	0.4	0.6	0.6	0.8	0.7	1.2
3. Total gold and silver	**3.1**	**5.4**	**4.3**	**7.9**	**7.4**	**10.8**
a. Gold	2.0	4.1	2.7	5.9	3.7	7.3
b. Silver	1.1	1.2	1.6	2.0	3.7	3.5
In % of Money Supply						
1. Money supply	**100**	**100**	**100**	**100**	**100**	**100**
a. Gold	23	10	21	10	17	10
b. Silver	11	3	12	5	21	7
c. Credit money	66	87	67	85	62	83
i. Currency[c]	*25*	*19*	*27*	*22*	*27*	*25*
ii. Demand deposits	*41*	*67*	*39*	*63*	*35*	*59*
2. Monetary reserves	**16**	**14**	**18**	**15**	**14**	**16**
a. Gold	9	11	11	12	9	12
b. Silver	7	3	7	3	5	4
3. Total gold and silver	**49**	**27**	**51**	**30**	**52**	**33**
a. Gold	32	21	32	22	26	22
b. Silver	17	6	19	8	26	11

Source: Triffin (1964, p. 56).
[a]United States, United Kingdom, and France.
[b]United States, United Kingdom, France, Germany, Italy, Netherlands, Belgium, Sweden, Switzerland, Canada, and Japan.
[c]Including subsidiary (nonsilver) coinage, except in the last column.

discovery of gold in California in 1849 and in Australia in 1851, and deflation was interspersed with depressions from 1873 to 1896 as more nations joined the gold standard, thereby causing a general shortage of gold reserves, which was not relieved until the South African and Yukon discoveries of the late 1890s. The inflations from 1849 to 1873 and from 1896 to 1913 were substantial, although not high by modern standards.

Periodic convertibility crises were a natural consequence of the buildup of credit money relative to the narrowing gold base. An "internal drain" within a country—not infrequently within some regions of the United States—could be triggered by a bank panic in which people rushed to cash in bank notes or deposits for gold. An "external drain" could arise out of (incipient) gold losses to foreigners through the balance of payments. Indeed, the development of central banking was largely a response to numerous convertibility crises. Whence Walter Bagehot's famous dictum of 1873 that when a gold run developed, the national central bank should raise its discount rate to attract foreign funds, but then lend freely to domestic financial institutions to mitigate their reserve losses.

In summary, convertibility crises did not arise mainly because the gold standard was "international"—that is, because nations maintained fixed nominal exchange rates with each other and had to subordinate domestic money growth to the balance of payments. Individual countries could even, on occasion, meet an internal drain somewhat better if they could borrow in the London capital market. In the 19th century the world gold standard was less than fully stable because of the uneasy coexistence of gold and credit money. Moreover, the collective supply of the latter was not under the control of any supernational monetary authority that assumed responsibility for stabilizing the common price level.

4.2 Two Views of International Adjustment

In the integrated world economy with fixed exchange rates of the late 19th century, the world price level and economic conditions were determined by cyclical fluctuations in the overall supply of and demand for gold and by uneven secular growth in gold-based credit monies. But how did payments between individual countries remain in balance?

The classical theory comes down from the full-bodied gold standard and price-specie flow mechanism of David Hume (1752). Sometimes called the Ricardo-Mill adjustment mechanism, it remains the standard textbook approach to interpreting how the gold standard worked. This theory presumes that gold movements themselves were instrumental in balancing international payments through their effects on net trade flows. If a country developed a payments deficit, a loss of gold to the outside world would force an internal deflation that induced a rise in exports and fall in imports, and vice versa for surplus countries.

The classical approach was extended to include the mixed system of the later 19th century, characterized by a narrow gold base and a larger superstructure of credit money. Under the "classical" rules of the game, central banks or treasuries were not to sterilize: A gold inflow would be allowed to expand the domestic money supply by some multiple of the inflow itself, and vice versa. (But see chapter 2 for showing how the actual rules of the game permitted partial sterilization in practice.) In Great Britain these rules were formalized under the Bank Act of 1844 where note issue by the Bank of England was restricted one-for-one to any marginal changes in its gold reserves. Thus, internal inflation or deflation was ensured so as to maintain external equilibrium through changes in the net trade balance.

Consider a more precise example of a disturbance in the flow of international payments, say, a new ongoing transfer of long-term capital from country A to country B. According to classical theory, adjustment would occur because gold flows in the same direction as the capital transfer and the resulting fall in A's money supply would induce general price-level deflation—across both tradable goods and nontradable services—in country A and correspondingly general inflation in country B.

From the mid-18th century into the early 19th century, transport costs were perhaps such that only gold could be easily arbitraged to have a common price in both foreign and domestic markets (Marcuzzo and Rosselli 1987). Following gold movements, the prices of commodities other than precious metals could then fall in country A as they rose in country B, as might be predicted by the quantity theory of money applied on a purely national basis. (By the late 19th century, however, international markets in potentially tradable commodities were too unified for such divergent price movements to occur.)

In particular, the price of tradable goods produced in country A, measured at the prevailing fixed exchange rate, would decline relative to those produced in country B. This decline in A's terms of trade—the cheapening of A's export products relative to B's—is then seen (in the classical perspective) to be a principal mechanism by which A's exports increase and imports decrease so as to create a trade surplus. This surplus is the "real" counterpart of the capital transfer. Later authors in the classical tradition—from Viner (1937), Taussig (1927), and Keynes (1923, 1930) down to Friedman and Schwartz (1963)—place additional emphasis on absorption (and possibly income) decreases in country A and increases in country B. But induced changes in the relative prices of A's tradables vis-à-vis B's remained important for balancing international payments.

From this classical description of the adjustment mechanism, therefore, comes the popular image of the gold standard: In different countries domestic inflation rates continually moved in *opposite* directions. The stability of national price levels (and possibly employment and output) was hostage to (arbitrary) shifts in the international distribution of gold reserves arising out of disturbances in foreign trade or in capital flows. More generally, the classical view suggests that fixed exchange rates sacrifice domestic macroeconomic stability to the need for balancing international payments.

The revisionist view of how international payments remained balanced begins with the observation that the classical adjustment mechanism is inconsistent with price-level data of the sort displayed in table 4.1. Instead of moving in opposite directions, national price levels moved up and down together over periods of several years (Triffin 1964; Cooper 1982), as did prices of individual tradable commodities (McCloskey and Zecher 1976; Dick and Floyd 1987). Indeed, therein lay the attractiveness of the fixed-rate 19th-century system: It provided a common international standard of value.

When exchange rates were fixed for a long period, generalized commodity arbitrage became sufficiently strong to prevent the prices (exclusive of tariffs) of any particular tradable good (for example, cotton shirts) from differing significantly more across countries than they did interregionally within a country.[1] Similarly, overall price levels of tradable goods, as measured by national wholesale price indices, remained aligned and did not change in a Humean fashion in response to gold flows.

With changes in relative national price levels thus restricted, what was the adjustment mechanism for the large net transfers of real capital from one country to another from 1870 to 1913? How did capital-receiving countries, such as those of North and

South America, develop trade deficits while the capital-donating countries, largely in Western Europe, generated corresponding trade surpluses?

By the late 19th century, a large and sophisticated international capital market centered in London had developed by both short-term trade bills of exchange and longer-term bond and equity issues that could be, and were, purchased by foreigners as well as Britons (Arndt and Drake 1985). Through modest adjustments in relative interest rates, expenditure patterns across countries were coordinated so as to match trade surpluses and deficits with net capital flows (Whale 1937; Williamson 1964). In effect, the international integration of capital markets complemented the integration of markets in tradable goods so that little or no net gold flows—let alone changes in exchange rates—were necessary to effect these capital transfers. Adjustments in international payments were similar to adjustments within a country or a single currency area.

Consider the flotation of a large new issue of American railway bonds in the 19th-century London capital market. Under the classical adjustment mechanism, this transfer would be treated as an exogenous force inducing gold to flow into the United States, causing inflation, and out of Great Britain, causing deflation. From the revisionist perspective of integrated financial and goods markets, however, the capital transfer would naturally reflect an upward propensity to spend for goods and services in the United States coupled with a similar reduction in Great Britain. That is, British financial saving, which would otherwise be transmuted to domestic investment, would simultaneously be diverted to support an increase in spending in the United States. So the changes in national levels of absorption (aggregate spending) would naturally create a British trade surplus with the United States that was a counterpart of the net capital transfer.

To the extent the British trade surplus fell short of (or exceeded) the total proceeds from the issue of railway bonds, an offsetting inflow (or outflow) of short-term capital to London would be the residual balancing item. Indeed, short-run interest rates could well adjust so that the funds were kept on deposit in London until disbursed "smoothly" through time to finance the American trade deficit. Only very small changes in international interest differentials would be necessary to maintain this payments balance as long as exchange rates remained credibly fixed.

In contrast to the classical view, gold flows would not be an instrumental or "forcing" variable in this adjustment process. Indeed, the initial flotation of railway bonds need not have any predictable impact on net gold flows, although they might respond ex post to differing rates of national income growth and increases in money demand (Abramovitz 1973; McCloskey and Zecher 1976).

What happens to relative prices in the revisionist adjustment process? Here it is important to distinguish between (1) the terms of trade: the relative price of a broad basket of British exports (largely manufactures) and American exports (largely primary products in the 19th century); and (2) the prices of tradable goods relative to nontradables within Great Britain and within the United States.

The classical adjustment mechanism does not distinguish between (1) and (2). That is, forced gold flow, causing general price deflation in Great Britain and general price inflation in the United States, tends to lower British prices across the board relative to their American counterparts, with the possible exception of precious metals that can be easily arbitraged. Thus, the classical theory presumes that Great Britain's terms of trade would deteriorate, which imposes a secondary burden on the capital-donating country. Also, because some British goods have higher transport costs and are less tradable than other goods, their relative prices would fall further. The reverse pattern would hold in the United States.

In the revisionist view based on a more integrated world economy, however, there is no presumption that the terms of trade need change as a result of a capital transfer as long as exchange rates are fixed so that the law of one price holds for each tradable good. Although the relative prices of nontradables might be bid up in the United States and down in Great Britain, there is a presumption that all such changes would be moderate and possibly only temporary. To effect even large net transfers of capital, the "need" for broad changes in relative commodity prices would seem quite modest in final equilibrium when trade and capital movements are balanced.[2]

4.3   The Law of One Price under Fixed and Floating Exchange Rates

One common justification for allowing exchange rates to float (Frenkel 1987) is to provide greater flexibility in allowing the prices of goods and services of country A to vary collectively vis-à-vis those in country B. In modern industrial economies, the invoice prices of manufactures, which are largely brand-specific, are quite rigid or "sticky" in the currency of the country where they originate (Grassman 1973; McKinnon 1979) and, temporarily, in the destination country. Thus a sudden (unexpected) depreciation of A's currency will (i) violate the law of one price in a narrow sense: The same brand-name good will sell for days or weeks at a lower price in country A than the price in country B evaluated at the current exchange rate; (ii) violate the law of one price in a broad sense: the prices of A's products similar (in the sense of models of monopolistic competition) to those in B will be sold at lower prices, possibly for many months or quarters; and (iii) products unique to A will sell at lower prices compared with those unique to B, perhaps for several years if the depreciation were to persist.

In all three senses, the sudden depreciation of A's currency turns the terms of trade against country A. Moreover, under floating exchange rates with given national money supplies (present and future), the "normal" effect of an ex ante transfer of financial capital from A to B is to depreciate A's currency against B's (Johnson 1956). Thus, under floating, one expects a "forced" deterioration in A's terms of trade in response to a capital outflow—a deterioration similar to that posited by the classical theory of adjustment to a capital outflow under the gold standard. A modern example was the large 1980–84 depreciation of European currencies against the dollar in response to a flow of private capital into the United States. Thus, in a regime of floating exchange rates, there is a strong presumption that the terms of trade will turn against the transferor and in favor of the transferee.

But is such an abrupt change in relative prices, particularly in the terms of trade, warranted if economies could potentially be integrated under fixed exchange rates? Is the acute sensitivity of a floating exchange rate to shifts in international portfolio preferences a "correct" response for facilitating a trade surplus for A and a deficit for B? The late 19th-century experience with fixed exchange rates suggests otherwise: Capital flowed from Europe to Canada and the United States without inducing or requiring substantial increases in the North American terms of trade—certainly nothing like the U.S. dollar's 40 to 50 percent appreciation in the early 1980s.[3]

4.4   Alternative Pure Trade Models of the Transfer Problem

For a moneyless world, pure trade theory offers several formal models based on barter and continuous full employment. To supplement historical experience, these models can throw additional light on how relative prices, including the terms of trade, should change in response to a capital transfer.

However, the implicit monetary mechanism that underlies, or is at least consistent with, the pure trade model must be made explicit.[4] All of the pure trade models reviewed below assume that the law of one price for tradable goods always holds in both the narrow and broad senses discussed above. To this extent, therefore, these models implicitly assume a regime of fixed exchange rates (or a single currency area) linking foreign and domestic economies. This assumption, nevertheless, leaves open the possibility that terms of trade between dissimilar goods may vary. Although exchange rates are (implicitly) fixed, the prices of nontradable services, the provision of which requires close geographic proximity, may still vary.

In his article "Presumption and the Transfer Problem," Ronald Jones (1975) built a model with two trading economies. Each produced and consumed a nontradable commodity with prohibitively high international transport costs, an exportable (the other's importable), and an importable (the other's exportable) whose relative prices were free to vary. Because each produced nontradables as well as close substitutes for the other's exportables, Jones's model effectively assumed that the two were industrially diversified (as opposed to monoproduct) economies.

While fully mobile within each country, neither labor nor capital were internationally mobile in two important respects. First, there was no direct ongoing factor movement across national boundaries. To encapsulate the transfer problem, Jones did consider a one-time increase in the flow of capital out of the home country that was experiencing reduced domestic expenditures and corresponding increases abroad. But he assumed no ongoing financial linkage that would equalize interest rates between the two countries. Second, Jones did not assume that the two countries needed to be in the factor price equalization region: Trade alone does not equalize factor prices.

Instead, Jones simply posited that all three goods were gross substitutes in production and consumption within each country—with given, possibly heterogeneous, factor supplies. The two economies were integrated in trade flows but not in factor markets, thus leaving relative commodity prices free to vary.

Jones then demonstrated (1975, p. 265) that the transferor's or home country's terms of trade deteriorate if and only if

$$m_2^* + \theta^* m_3^* > m_2 + \theta m_3. \tag{1}$$

The m parameters are expenditure propensities (arising out of the capital transfer), asterisks represent the foreign country, commodity 2 is the home importable (foreign exportable), and commodity 3 is the nontraded good in each country. An alternative inequality condition could be restated in terms of commodities 1 (the home country's exportable) and 3. If (1) holds, the home country's terms of trade P_1/P_2 fall during the transfer—the orthodox presumption.

The parameters θ and θ^* are complex and reflect price substitution effects across the three commodities within each country. They would be identical if the two countries were symmetrically diversified in their production and consumption characteristics. Suppose they were so diversified.

Whether inequality (1) is satisfied, therefore, largely depends on whether each country's marginal propensity to spend on its own exportable exceeds the trading partner's propensity to spend on the same good (the partner's importable), that is, whether $m_2^* > m_2$. The fall in home country expenditures tends to reduce the relative price of the foreign exportable (P_2 tends to fall relative to P_1), but the rise in expenditures abroad tends to raise its relative price. And which effect is stronger remains an open empirical question for industrially diversified economies. There is no theoretical presumption that the terms of trade of the transferor need deteriorate, that is, for (1) to hold, unless one makes more specialized assumptions about patterns of production and consumption.

Paul Krugman (1987a, 1987b), for example, makes such specialized assumptions in order to support the orthodox (classical)
presumption that the terms of trade of the transferor will deteriorate. In the modern context, he asks: "Suppose the United States
were to increase tax revenues (reduce the fiscal deficit) by 100
billion dollars and stop borrowing that much in the international
capital market. For the U.S. trade balance to improve by a similar
amount, would the terms of trade have to turn against the
United States?"

Krugman then assumes that the United States produces only
one good, some of which it exports and most of which it consumes at home. The United States does not produce import
substitutes while it consumes imports nor is there a distinct
category of nontradables. In contrast to the Jones model, the
industrial structure in Krugman's model is not diversified. The
rest of the world (ROW) is similarly a monoproduct economy.
ROW consumes most of the single good it produces, while exporting the rest, and consumes some of the American good. (In
common with the Jones model, however, Krugman's does not
assume that factor markets are integrated with a tendency toward
factor price equalization.)

With this analytical machinery based on nondiversified (monoproduct) economies in place, the orthodox presumption seems
very strong: As the American trade balance adjusts to the reduced
capital inflow, the terms of trade are likely to turn against the
United States. Specifically, Krugman shows that the orthodox
presumption will hold if and only if

$$m + m^* < 1 \tag{2}$$

where the m parameters are now distinguished from inequality
(1) above. Here, m is the more narrowly defined marginal propensity to import of the United States. (The m parameter is identical
to the marginal propensity to spend on importables, $m2$ above,
only in monoproduct economies.) Parameter m^* is ROW's similarly defined marginal propensity to import. Krugman provides
empirical evidence to suggest that m and m^* are each much less
than 0.5. Indeed, if one looks only at the share of imports in
either American or ROW GNP, they are 0.2 or less, although
Krugman recognizes that marginal propensities are likely to be
a bit higher.

So (2) appears to be satisfied in practice, leading Krugman to take the orthodox view that the American terms of trade must deteriorate if the trade deficit is to be reduced by the full hypothetical increase in tax revenues. Further, because domestic prices of manufactured tradables are "sticky" in the United States and in ROW, he suggests some large nominal devaluation of the dollar would be justified to bring about the needed reduction in the American terms of trade. (This leaves open the important question of whether the requisite American fiscal adjustment is imminent, and whether dollar devaluation should precede, coincide with, or follow the $100 billion tax increase.)

But remember that inequality (2) is a sufficient condition for the orthodox presumption only if one accepts Krugman's simplifying assumption that both the United States and ROW are mono-product economies. If, instead, both economies are diversified in the sense of Jones (1975) or Dornbusch (1975), then (2) may hold even if the orthodox presumption is invalid. Even though observed import shares in GNP are quite small, the transfer can be effected without having the terms of trade turn against the United States. Jones's model, based as it is on diversified free-trade economies, better represents the industrial world today as well as that of the late 19th century, although not necessarily in the intervening decades.

Left unanalyzed is the more naive, but commonly held, view that dollar devaluation alone—without a complementary change in the fiscal deficit—will reduce the dollar value of the American trade deficit. More generally, the old elasticities approach (Bickerdike 1920; Robinson 1939; Metzler 1949) suggested that exchange rate changes themselves have a systematic effect on net trade balances. That this latter presumption is false for open, diversified economies is demonstrated analytically in Dornbusch (1975) and McKinnon and Ohno (1986) and is borne out by the failure of the American trade deficit to respond to dollar devaluation from 1984 to 1988.

4.5 An Exchange-Rate Dilemma When Factor Markets Are Not Integrated

Barter models of exchange suggest that the terms of trade need not move substantially to bring about a capital transfer between economies with diversified foreign trade in goods and services.

Whether the change in the terms of trade is negative or positive, the point at which final equilibrium is achieved remains unknown a priori. Unlike what Krugman's model suggests, using the nominal exchange rate as an instrument to influence the terms of trade during the transfer process seems neither necessary nor desirable.

When foreign and domestic factor markets are not integrated, however, the price of the domestic nontradable must still decrease (relative to tradables) in the transferor's economy and increase within the transferee's. In his pure trade model, Jones (1975) derives this unambiguous result algebraically, but it is clear intuitively under a fixed exchange-rate regime. The capital transfer is associated with reduced spending in the home country, pressure from which then reduces the prices (using foreign exchange as the numeraire) of those goods and services not arbitraged in international markets. The home trade balance then improves as resources are released from the nontradables sector to produce more exportables and importables—with the reverse adjustment occurring abroad.

Now return to monetary economies where nominal prices may be quoted in different currencies. In addition, suppose that the domestic currency prices of both nontradables and domestically produced tradables are "sticky" at home and abroad. When the capital transfer occurs, would movement in the nominal exchange rate help speed the necessary adjustments in equilibrium relative prices by overcoming this price stickiness? Specifically, would the orthodox policy of having the home country devalue its currency reduce the relative prices of nontradables without causing "false" changes in other relative prices, and without impeding the process by which expenditures are naturally reduced at home and increased abroad? The short answer is "no." If substantial devaluation occurs, incidental price and absorption effects both go in wrong directions.

First, *the primary effect of devaluation is to reduce the transferor's terms of trade with the transferee—and not raise the relative price of tradables to nontradables within the home country while reducing it abroad.* The domestic currency prices of direct imports are typically sensitive to the exchange rate, even though prices of the great mass of domestically produced exportables and import substitutes are not. With full pass-through, a devaluation may quickly raise import prices vis-à-vis those of domestically produced tradables.[5] The law of one price is violated and the terms of trade turn against the transferor in the three senses discussed above. But there is no presumption that the terms of trade should or need to change in final equilibrium; thus, these price "misalignments" likely will need to be corrected at a later stage in the transfer process. In the short run, the devaluation introduces confusing noise into the price system.

At the same time, the devaluation succeeds in raising the prices of tradables relative to nontradables only in a limited, fragmented way. The prices of direct imports increase, but not the overall prices of domestically produced tradables. More important, the extreme changes observed in the mark/dollar and yen/dollar exchange rates in recent years—sometimes nearly 40 or 50 percent—seem to be much too high (see below) for any conceivable warranted adjustments in the average price of tradables relative to nontradables.

Second, *a devaluation may induce absorption to adjust the wrong way in both the transferor's and transferee's economies, and thus impede the capital transfer.* Because domestic invoice prices are sticky, they do not jump with the exchange rate. But they do adjust with a lag, albeit quite long. After devaluation by the transferor, expectations of ongoing domestic inflation will increase, raising the private propensity to spend for goods and services in that country. Similarly, expectations of deflation in the transferee will reduce people's propensity to spend there (McKinnon and Ohno 1986; Kim 1987). These perverse absorption effects then delay the emergence of the transferor's trade surplus, which is the real counterpart of the transfer of financial capital. (See chapter 14 for a more precise treatment of perverse absorption effects.)

4.6 Alternative Exchange-Rate Systems and the International Integration of Factor Markets

However, if factor markets between economies with similar levels of technical proficiency are effectively integrated, even the relative prices of tradables and nontradables need not adjust significantly when a transfer occurs. The ongoing international arbitrage in markets for tradable goods and in financial capital keeps both economies in the "factor-price equalization region." Because the nontradable goods industry in each country is then a price taker in factor markets facing the same real wage and real rental rate on capital, the relative price of nontradables need not change as their output varies during the transfer process (Samuelson 1971).

Whether international monetary arrangements support the ongoing arbitrage in goods and financial markets necessary to keep economies in, or close to, the equalization region is an open question. One condition is that the law of one price holds in international markets for tradable goods. A second is that financial arbitrage must be effective in equalizing *real* interest rates—nominal rates minus anticipated price inflation—across countries.

Unfortunately, both conditions have been continually violated under the system of fluctuating exchange rates we have observed over the past 15 years. Internal price and wage stickiness in the major industrial economies implies that unexpected changes in exchange rates continually disrupt commodity market arbitrage: The law of one price is violated in both the narrow and broad senses. This failure of tradable goods markets to remain integrated, that is, the failure of purchasing power parity between national monies, reduces indirect pressure to equalize factor prices across countries.

More subtly, *direct financial arbitrage—even today's massive (gross) capital flows among Europe, Japan, and the United States—fails to equate real interest rates across countries as long as exchange rates float and (relative) purchasing power parity is violated.* Because goods markets are imperfectly integrated, national rates of price inflation can differ from expected changes in exchange rates, which may dominate differences in nominal interest rates (Frankel 1986). For example, from 1981 to mid-1985, the dollar was obviously overvalued against the yen and mark by the PPP criterion, and survey data showed that financiers expected the dollar to depreciate (Frankel and Froot 1987). Thus, U.S. nominal interest rates remained much higher than in Japan or Germany, even though national rates of price inflation were not much different. Real interest rates were not equalized—at least not ex post facto.

As a result, the modern system of fluctuating relative currency values severely impairs the allocative efficiency of the international capital market. Countries go through alternating cycles of underinvestment or overinvestment in tradable goods industries, depending on whether their currencies are overvalued or under-

Table 4.3
Proportions of Merchandise Trade to National Product for Major
Developed Economies

Ranked by Economic Size in 1984	Pre–World War I	1950s	1984
United States	11.0	7.9	15.2
Japan	29.5	18.8	24.2
Germany	38.3	35.1	52.8
France	35.2	n/a	40.2
United Kingdom	43.5	30.4	47.0
Italy	28.1	25.0	44.6
Canada	32.2	31.2	47.3

Source: Wolf (1987).

valued by the PPP criterion. The increased exchange risk inhibits industrial investment everywhere.

Here, the 19th-century system, based on fixed exchange rates and mutual monetary adjustment to provide a common standard of value, seems much preferred. Arbitrage in internationally tradable goods then became sufficient to approximate the law of one price. In financial markets the commitment to fixed nominal exchange rates had two related effects. First, nominal interest rates were closer together and, on average, lower. Second, price inflation was more uniform across countries. International financial arbitrage could succeed in keeping real interest rates closer together.

But is the present degree of economic integration among the principal industrial economies sufficient to warrant establishing a common monetary standard with fixed exchange rates? Table 4.3 indicates that the intensity of merchandise trade in the 1980s is again comparable to what had been achieved by 1913. With the elimination of exchange controls in Europe and Japan, arbitrage pressures in international financial markets seem at least as great as they were before World War I. If exchange rates were to become credibly fixed once more, commodity and financial arbitrage should again serve to keep industrial nations within, or close to, the region of factor price equalization.

Moreover, table 4.4 indicates that the average net transfer of capital out of the U.K. between 1905 and 1914 was more than half of net national saving—proportionately much higher than

Table 4.4
Net Capital Outflows

	Gross National Savings	Gross Domestic Fixed Investment	Current Account
United States 1985	16.5	18.6	−2.9
Japan 1985	31.4	27.5	3.7
West Germany 1985	22.2	19.5	2.2
United Kingdom 1905–14	16.0	7.0	8.0

Source: Wolf (1987).

the large trade surpluses generated by Japan and Germany (or trade deficit of the United States) in the mid-1980s. In this sense, the "need" for broad changes in relative prices to help effect capital transfers would seem to be less now than in the earlier era. And, among modern industrial economies, this paper suggests that exchange rate changes can be ambiguous, even perverse, in bringing about whatever adjustments in relative prices that might be needed to keep net trade balances in line with warranted net capital flows.

4.7 Lessons from the 19th Century

The strengths and weaknesses of the 19th-century gold standard must be carefully assessed to draw any useful lessons for present-day monetary arrangements.

Consider the positive side first. By binding nations together—albeit sometimes grudgingly—with what was a common price level, the system completely avoided the sudden and dramatic changes in relative international competitiveness characteristic of floating rates in the 1970s and 1980s. This common monetary standard permitted a much more efficient international allocation of capital: Financial arbitrage could better succeed in equalizing real interest rates while keeping European and North American economies within (or close to) the region of factor price equalization.

Moreover, the reality of international adjustment was quite different from its usual treatment in modern textbooks. Large net transfers of capital from country A to country B did not require a major deflation for A to run a trade surplus, nor a major inflation for B to run a trade deficit. At unchanged nominal exchange rates, capital transfers took place quite smoothly with apparently little need for one country's price level to change in any substantial way vis-à-vis another's. In short, that the gold standard was truly international was its greatest virtue.

But worldwide deflation or inflation was a problem for the 19th-century system because the underlying base of gold and credit monies was not properly anchored. Much American Populist hostility at the time—with present-day echoes—was concerned with strong deflationary pressure and recurrent depressions from the 1870s to the mid-1890s. Because these pressures were not peculiar to the United States, fixed exchange rates per se, requiring American monetary policy to adjust to an international standard, have been "unfairly" identified as creating excessive domestic cycles of inflation or deflation. Rather, the problem lay with basing the international standard on gold.

Now North America, Western Europe, and Japan are as mutually dependent on trade and finance as were the former two a century ago. If exchange rates were again credibly fixed through mutual monetary adjustment, the "natural" nominal anchor for the system as a whole would be the common price level over internationally tradable goods, which can be approximated by wholesale or producer price indices. And, through joint management of the underlying base of national credit monies, the triumvirate could keep the new international monetary standard more stable than its 19th-century counterpart (see chapters 20 and 22).[6]

Notes

1. Only when exchange rates float freely and, thus, unpredictably is the law of one price systematically violated, as it has been in recent years (Isard 1977; Levich 1986).

2. This difference between the classical and the revisionist perspective parallels the famous 1929 debate between J. M. Keynes and Bertil Ohlin on whether the war reparations owed by Germany to the rest of Europe would necessarily turn the terms of trade against Germany and thus impose a secondary burden on the German economy beyond the transfer itself. By emphasizing the need for Germany's terms of trade to decline in order for a German trade surplus to develop, Keynes took the classical position on how the capital transfer would be effected.

Ohlin was the "revisionist." He argued as if the German economy was more fully integrated into the rest of Europe. The fall in absorption in Germany, coupled with a rise in the capital-receiving countries, would effect the transfer without substantially turning the terms of trade against Germany.

In retrospect, who was right seems to be more of an empirical question—how open was the postwar Germany economy—than a theoretical one. For the principal articles and rejoinders of Keynes and Ohlin, see *Economic Journal* 39 (1929): pp. 1–7, 172–82, and 400–408.

3. For evidence on the Canadian experience, see Dick and Floyd (1987).

4. As Samuelson (1971, pp. 327–28) noted, "Analytically, the discussion [of the transfer problem] remained confused, because models involving effective demand and financial considerations were rarely carefully separated from those involving pure barter." And in a series of articles beginning in the early 1950s, Samuelson himself could not make up his mind whether the orthodox presumption was correct: that a financial transfer would turn the terms of trade significantly against the transferor. To this day, a satisfactory general equilibrium model, incorporating real and financial considerations, remains to be constructed.

5. Unlike other industrial economies such as Germany, immediate pass-through into the domestic prices of direct imports is not typical of the United States (Knetter 1988). Despite changes in the dollar exchange rate, exporters to the United States prefer to keep their dollar price quotes to American customers rather more rigid—perhaps because of the American economy's large size, and the dollar's central position in the world monetary system.

6. See McKinnon (1984, 1988) for an overall description of how mutual monetary adjustment could be organized; and McKinnon and Ohno (1986) on the specific question of how "starting" exchange rates could be set so as to bring national price and wage levels into approximate alignment.

References

Abramovitz, Moses. "The Monetary Side of Long Swings in U.S. Economic Growth." Memorandum 146. Center for Research on Economic Growth, Stanford University, 1973.

Arndt, Helmut, and Drake, Peter. "Bank Loans or Bonds: Some Lessons of Historical Experience." Banca Nazionale del Lavoro *Quarterly Review* (December 1985): 373–92.

Bagehot, Walter. *Lombard Street*. Reprint of 1915 edition. New York: Arno Press, 1969.

Barro, Robert. "Money and Price Level under the Gold Standard." *Economic Journal* 89 (March 1979): 13–27.

Bickerdike, C. F. "The Instability of Foreign Exchange." *Economic Journal* 30 (March 1920): 118–22.

Cooper, Richard N. "The Gold Standard: Historical Facts and Future Prospects." *Brookings Papers on Economic Activity* (1982): 1–45. Reprinted in

Richard N. Cooper, *The International Monetary System*. Cambridge: MIT Press, 1987.

Dick, Trevor, and Floyd, John. "Canada and the Gold Standard: 1871–1913." Manuscript. July 1987.

Dornbusch, Rudiger. "Exchange Rates and Fiscal Policy in a Popular Model of International Trade." *American Economic Review* 65 (December 1975): 859–71.

Eichengreen, Barry. "Editor's Introduction." In *The Gold Standard in Theory and History*, pp. 1–36. Edited by B. Eichengreen. New York: Methuen Press, 1987.

Frankel, Jeffrey, and Froot, Kenneth. "Using Survey Data to Test Standard Propositions Regarding Exchange Rate Expectations." *American Economic Review* 77 (March 1987): 93–106.

Frenkel, Jacob A. "International Capital Mobility and Crowding Out in the U.S. Economy." In *The Increasing Openness of the U.S. Economy*, pp. 33–69. Edited by R. Hafer. Federal Reserve Bank of St. Louis, 1986.

———. "The International Monetary System: Should It Be Reformed?" *American Economic Review* 77 (May 1987): 205–10.

Friedman, Milton, and Schwartz, Anna. *A Monetary History of the United States, 1867–1960*. Princeton: Princeton University Press, 1963.

Grassman, Sven. "A Fundamental Symmetry in International Payments Patterns." *Journal of International Economics* (May 1973): 105–6.

Hale, David. "Will We Hate Japan as We Hated Britain?" *The International Economy* 2 (January/February 1988): 84–91.

Hume, David. *Of the Balance of Trade*. 1752. Reprinted in *Writings on Economics*. Edited by E. Rotwein. Madison: Wisconsin University Press, 1955.

Isard, Peter. "How Far Can We Push the Law of One Price?" *American Economic Review* 67 (1977): 942–48.

Jastram, Roy. *The Golden Constant: The English and American Experience, 1560–1976*. New York: John Wiley and Sons, 1977.

Johnson, Harry. "The Transfer Problem and Exchange Stability." *Journal of Political Economy* 64 (June 1956): 212–25.

Jones, Ronald. "Presumption and the Transfer Problem." *Journal of International Economics* 5 (1975): 263–74.

Keynes, John M. *A Tract on Monetary Reform*. London: Macmillan, 1923.

———. "The German Transfer Problem." *Economic Journal* 39 (March 1929): 1–7.

———. *A Treatise on Money*. London: Macmillan, 1930.

Kim, Yoonbai. "International Transfers of Capital and the Role of the Terms of Trade." Economics Department, Stanford University, February 1987.

Knetter, Michael. *Export Price Dynamics: Theory and Evidence*. Ph.D. dissertation, Stanford University, 1988.

Krugman, Paul. "Adjustment in the World Economy." *Occasional Paper 24*, Group of 30, 1987a.

————. "Exchange Rates and International Adjustment." Manuscript. September 1987b.

Levich, Richard. "Gauging the Evidence on Recent Movements in the Value of the Dollar." In *The U.S. Dollar: Recent Developments, Outlook, and Policy Options*, pp. 1–28. Federal Reserve Bank of Kansas City, 1986.

Marcuzzo, Maria, and Rosselli, Annalisa. "Profitability in the Early History of the International Gold Standard." *Economica* 54 (August 1987): 367–80.

McCloskey, Donald, and Zecher, Richard. "How the Gold Standard Worked: 1880–1913." In *The Monetary Approach to the Balance of Payment*. Edited by Jacob A. Frenkel and Harry G. Johnson. London: Allen and Unwin, 1976.

McKinnon, Ronald I. *Money in International Exchange: The Convertible Currency System*. New York: Oxford University Press, 1979.

————. *An International Standard for Monetary Stabilization*. Washington, D.C.: Institute for International Economics, 1984.

————. "Monetary and Exchange Rate Policies for International Financial Stability: A Proposal." *Journal of Economic Perspectives* 2 (Winter 1988): 83–103.

————. "Purchasing Power Parity as a Monetary Standard." Economics Department, Stanford University, October 1988.

McKinnon, Ronald I., and Ohno, Kenichi. "Getting the Exchange Rate Right: Insular Versus Open Economies." Economics Department, Stanford University, December 1986.

Metzler, Lloyd A. "The Theory of International Trade." In *A Survey of Contemporary Economics*, pp. 210–14. Edited by H. Ellis. Philadephia: Richard Irwin for the American Economic Association, 1949.

Ohlin, Bertil. "The Reparation Problem: A Discussion." *Economic Journal* 39 (June 1929): 170–78.

Robinson, Joan. "The Foreign Exchanges," in *Essays on the Theory of Unemployment* (1937). Reprinted in *Readings in the Theory of International Trade*, pp. 83–103. Edited by H. Ellis and L. A. Metzler. Homewood, Ill.: Blakiston, 1950.

Samuelson, Paul. "On the Trail of Conventional Beliefs about the Transfer Problem." In *Trade, Balance of Payments, and Growth*. Edited by Jagdish Bhagwati, et al. Amsterdam: North-Holland, 1971.

Taussig, Frank W. *International Trade*. New York: Macmillan, 1927.

Triffin, Robert. "The Evolution of the International Monetary System: Historical Reappraisal and Future Perspectives." *Princton Studies in International Finance*, no. 18, June 1964.

Viner, Jacob. *Studies in the Theory of International Trade*. New York: Harper and Brothers, 1937.

Whale, Philip B. "The Working of the Prewar Gold Standard." *Economica* 6 (February 1937): 18–32.

Williamson, Jeffrey G. *American Growth and the Balance of Payments, 1820–1913.* Chapel Hill: University of North Carolina Press, 1964.

Wolf, Martin. "The Need to Look to the Long Term." *Financial Times,* 16 November 1987.

5   Private and Official International Money: The Case for the Dollar, 1969*

It is worth much to the world to have an established and fully coherent monetary mechanism that is both understood and adhered to by national authorities because they believe it to be mutually beneficial. This essay favorably interprets the American dollar as international money, based on what have become virtual conventions of international exchange, requiring very little alteration in our existing political and economic institutions. The implications of an international dollar standard for economic policy and welfare are then drawn.

5.1 Introduction

The demand for international money has two important components: (1) reserve assets held by official institutions such as central banks and treasuries, and (2) private holdings of internationally liquid assets by individuals and by financial and nonfinancial corporations. Official reserves have dominated academic and governmental thinking on international "liquidity," as evidenced by the prolonged negotiations within the Group of Ten resulting in the Special Drawing Rights (SDRs) facility of the International Monetary Fund. SDRs would be used exclusively by governmental institutions.

In his most recent book, *Our International Monetary System: Yesterday, Today, and Tomorrow*, Robert Triffin reiterates the need

*Date added to the original title for the benefit of modern readers.
Originally published, in slightly longer form, in *Essays of International Finance*, no. 74 (International Finance Section, Department of Economics, Princeton University, 1969), 3–34.

for deliberate expansions in world liquidity, but confines his attention to official institutions (Yale University Press, Random House, 1968, pp. 88–102) and does not discuss the problem of private international money. He envisages that SDRs, or a somewhat broader facility, will eventually replace gold and national currencies in official reserves. Indeed, one of the points of unanimous agreement among the confreres in the Group of Ten deliberations was that the use of the dollar—and the concomitant deficits in the balance of payments of the United States—should cease or greatly diminish once the new international facility is ratified.

However, the dollar is, internationally, much more than an official reserve asset. Besides being the vehicle currency, which governments use to enter the foreign-exchange market to peg their own exchange rates, there are enormous private holdings by foreigners of short-term dollar claims on American banks and additional pyramided claims on Euro-dollar banks. Indeed, the spectacular growth of the Euro-dollar market—and more recently of dollar-denominated Euro-bonds—has consolidated the dollar's role as *the* dominant international money. It is used as a numeraire and as a means of finance for both trade in goods and trade in securities. It is the center of the world's international capital market where both official and private institutions borrow and lend.

Given this second "nonofficial" role of the dollar, this essay analyzes a number of issues related to the dichotomization of our thinking on official and private international liquidity. We shall investigate the determinants of private and official demand for international money in section 5.2. There it is demonstrated, among other things, that floating exchange rates are not a solution to the general liquidity problem, as is commonly thought. The demand for international money would continue to exist and possibly be augmented under floating rates. Moreover, there is a need to establish a single financial instrument, most conveniently dollars, as international money.

Having established the international demand for money, the mechanism for supplying dollars to the rest of the world is developed in section 5.3. What ensures that the foreign demand for international money in real terms—after price-level deflation—can be satisfied by the apparently "random" balance-of-payments deficits of the United States? It is demonstrated that a systematic and probably adequate mechanism for supplying international money does in fact exist. However, the workings of this mechanism are not recognized by American authorities in their policies for international payments, particularly in their restrictions on outflows of capital.

Finally, after establishing that a dollar standard can be nonexploitive and a most efficient practical instrument for providing badly needed international money, we shall investigate the implications for American monetary, fiscal, and exchange-rate policy in section 5.4. Peripherally, economic policy in other countries, particularly regarding exchange rates, will also be examined. It seems at first glance that many complications would arise in domestic monetary and fiscal policy if American authorities finally recognized that they are responsible for the health of the international monetary mechanism. This chapter contends that such is not the case. Full recognition of international obligations would, on net balance, simplify American economic policy. In the recent past, foreign-exchange and internal-policy mistakes have been compounded by continual failure to recognize the true strength and international status of the dollar, to the detriment of all concerned.

5.2 The Demand for International Money

The demand for official reserves is usually associated with the pegging of exchange rates at preassigned levels and the free convertibility of external transactions. With these commitments, a national authority must buy back its own currency by selling foreign exchange if the price of foreign exchange rises; and it must buy foreign exchange with its own currency if the price of foreign exchange falls. Exchange rates can then be kept within the narrow range prescribed by the International Monetary Fund without resorting to controls in imports or other direct interventions. To be able to buy and sell freely, national authorities hold reserves of convertible foreign exchange.

Dollar Reserves and Exchange Stabilization

In the postwar period, outside of the sterling area, the vehicle currency commonly used as foreign exchange has been the

American dollar. There is a legal reason for this which in turn reflects underlying economic forces. Legally, under the Articles of Agreement of the International Monetary Fund, member countries are obligated to peg their currencies either to gold or to the currency of a country that is pegged to gold. Among major countries, only the United States has opted to peg its currency directly to gold. Other noncommunist industrial countries have pegged their currencies to the American dollar within a margin of 1 per cent on either side of parity. Thus, all countries—other than the United States—are obligated to buy and sell dollars in the foreign-exchange market to maintain the international value of their currency. The United States retains the residual obligation to buy and sell gold within 1/4 of 1 percent of $35 per ounce. Since the gold crisis of March 1968, the Government of the United States has restricted its buying and selling of gold to foreign central banks.

This asymmetrical relationship of the United States to the rest of the world has distinct administrative advantages. The Fund's mandate to maintain stable exchange margins is made easier by having one anchor or reference currency to which all the others are pegged. Each government directly maintains the range of 2 percent (1 percent on either side of parity) for the rate of exchange between its currency and dollars; and the resulting private arbitrage maintains a range of 4 percent for the exchange rate between any pair of nondollar currencies (2 percent on either side of parity). The obligations of national authorities in the foreign-exchange market are, therefore, simply and unambiguously defined. For example, no decisions have to be made as to whether France or Germany is responsible for the rate of exchange between francs and marks, as long as both maintain their official parity with the dollar.

Under the current system of pegging within 1 percent of dollar parities, it is perhaps instructive to illustrate with a numerical example the maximum variation of 4 percent possible between nondollar currencies. Suppose the parity dollar-price of pounds is $2.40 and the parity dollar-price of francs is $.20. Therefore, at parity, 12 francs exchange for 1 pound. Suppose now that pounds move to their minimum dollar price of $2.376 and francs to their maximum dollar price of $.202. Triangular arbitrage by private speculators in pounds, dollars, and francs will then drive the franc-pound rate to 11.76, which is just 2 percent *below* the parity rate of 12.

In contrast, if pounds move to their maximum dollar price of $2.424 and francs to their minimum dollar price of $.198, then private arbitrage will drive the franc-pound rate to 12.24, which is just 2 percent *above* parity. Thus, a complete range of variation of 4 percent of parity is possible between francs and pounds. Of course, only a maximum 2-percent variation is possible between pounds and dollars or between francs and dollars.

However, with more than one reference currency, the 4-percent variation would *not* be automatically maintained if the reference currencies varied with respect to each other. Indeed, increased but not complete exchange flexibility—as advocated by many economists—would still require the use of a single reference currency for maintaining unambiguous, if increased, exchange margins. In the pre-1914 gold standard, gold provided this point of reference. However, in the absence of any desire to perpetuate the gold standard, it is convenient to settle on one major national currency as the reference point. Thus, the United States is left without an exchange-rate policy of its own with respect to other national currencies, since they are all responsible for maintaining parity with the dollar.

This singular position of the United States is of great convenience to all concerned and is the proximate cause for other countries holding "working" dollar balances for intervening in the market for foreign exchange. Nevertheless, the legal mechanism should not obscure the underlying real strength of the dollar. After World War II, the dollar was the only major currency that was freely convertible and had the best reputation for maintaining its value in terms of a representative bundle of internationally traded goods. It became the most convenient numeraire for official settlements among currencies of limited convertibility. Since major European currencies returned to a higher degree of convertibility in 1958, foreign private corporations and individuals have exercised this increased leeway to acquire and hold dollar balances. The dollar is used increasingly to denominate international economic transactions, even those not directly associated with the United States. Thus, the international use of the dollar is not dependent on the rules of the International Monetary Fund, which themselves represent underlying economic forces. Nevertheless, these rules do conveniently formalize the central role of the dollar in exchange stabilization.

Flexible Exchange Rates

Pegged exchange rates and the desire to maintain external convertibility contribute to the demand for official reserves. Nevertheless, it would be naive to suppose that freely flexible or floating exchange rates would eliminate this demand. Nations would still find it desirable to maintain contingency reserves even with no official parity in their exchange rates.

Authorities in Korea find it convenient to hold foreign exchange against the possibility of failure of the national rice crop. The French government finds it convenient to hold gold and foreign exchange, which is usable to support the flow of domestic expenditures (absorption) in case of events like those of May 1968. Both countries have a positive demand for liquid reserves for contingencies seen in a broader sense than that of simply maintaining parity in the rate of exchange. Thus, increased exchange-rate flexibility, going so far as to eliminate formal parities altogether, would reduce but not eliminate official demands for international liquidity.

Although floating exchange rates might ease official demands for international money, they would *increase* private demand. This is an important point to establish. The usual debate on the merits or demerits of floating exchange rates omits consideration of private demands for international money and focuses on the reduction of official demand—the latter being indeed likely to occur. A most interesting exception is the discussion by Fritz Machlup in *International Payments, Debts and Gold*. In "The Mysterious Numbers Game," he develops several arguments, based on optimal-inventory considerations (Charles Scribner's Sons, 1964, pp. 267–76), for increased private holding of foreign exchange to substitute for official holdings if floating exchange rates were introduced. These arguments can be extended in a multi-country world to show how private traders would concentrate their transactions in the most suitable major currency in order to economize on inventory-carrying costs and to minimize the informational uncertainty arising from floating rates.

Even in a world where exchange rates change infrequently, the development of the Euro-dollar and Euro-bond markets and the international use of the New York money market are evidence of the convenience of having a single numéraire, store of value, and medium of exchange for international transactions. As long as confidence is maintained in the dollar value of other national currencies, they remain good but not perfect substitutes for international money (dollars). That is, mark, sterling, or franc balances—whether held by domestic nationals or foreigners—are near-money as far as international transactions are concerned. However, floating exchange rates, leading to wider short-term variations in dollar values, would make other national currencies less good substitutes for holding dollars to finance the international flow of commerce. Correspondingly, the foreign private demand for holding dollars would increase under floating exchange rates.

These are not arguments against flexible exchange rates. Once one carefully defines the optimal size of a currency area, then an exchange rate with no fixed parity may be the preferred method of solving the adjustment problem in external payments. Then, too, in the case of domestic monetary instability associated with chronic inflation, it is folly for even small nations to maintain an official parity. What is suggested is that floating exchange rates will not eliminate the foreign demand for American dollars. Consequently, floating rates will not eliminate "deficits" in the international payments of the United States as currently measured.

The "liquidity" definition of the American deficit roughly measures the annual increase in short-term dollar claims held by both private and official foreigners, plus losses of monetary gold. If the world moved toward a regime of floating exchange rates, increases in the demand for privately held dollars may offset decreases in the demand for officially held dollars or gold. Thus, the net impact on the liquidity measure of the deficit could go in either direction. If there were significant economies of scale in national holdings of exchange stabilization funds as compared to individual private holdings, one could conceive of the "deficit" under the liquidity definition actually increasing. That is, additions to private holdings of dollars as the world economy grows would be greater than reductions in official holdings under a system of flexible exchange rates.

The "official-settlements" definition of the deficit is confined to measuring annual increases in dollar holdings of official foreigners plus annual gold losses. Under this definition, the introduction of a regime of floating exchange rates would, in the long run, reduce the American deficit without eliminating it. In the short run, the elimination of official intervention to maintain parities may lead some foreign authorities to liquidate "excessive" existing dollar holdings, thereby leading to a temporary surplus in American payments under the official-settlements definition. This short-run effect is a matter of conjecture, given the apparent instability of official portfolio preferences. Nevertheless, in the absence of official parities, official institutions would have some demand for dollar holdings which would eventually grow with world income and lead to deficits in American payments under the official-settlements definition. Indeed, for certain classes of foreign banking institutions, it might be difficult to distinguish official from private holdings.

The important point is that floating exchange rates are not a solution to the international liquidity problem in the sense of eliminating or even reducing the demand for international money. That is, there still would be the "problem" of providing international money even if it is largely privately held. Academic debate on flexible exchange rates has generally not distinguished the "adjustment" problem from the "liquidity" problem. The debate is relevant for the former but only peripherally so for the latter. Flexible exchange rates, then, are not an alternative to the development of institutions that provide international money. Since the American "deficit" is the vehicle by which international money is created, it would not, in the long run, be ended by generally floating exchange rates.

Gold and the Confidence Problem

Although dollars are widely held officially and privately as working balances, some governments and a few individuals have elected to hold their longer-term "precautionary" balances in the form of gold. If in fact the dollar is basically a superior monetary asset, as is claimed here, why is there any significant demand for gold by both governments and individuals? (One must remember that, unlike national monetary systems where coins and hand-to-hand currency are a significant proportion of outstanding money, foreign holdings of dollars are generally held in large quantities in interest-bearing form—as facilitated by the presence of the Euro-dollar market.)

There is, of course, the long history of gold's serving both a national and international monetary function. Internationally, the use of money is still a matter of convention, so history remains psychologically important. But international monetary history of the last century and a half is one of shifting from the direct use of gold—sometimes supplemented by silver—to the use of fiat money, first with gold backing and then without. Robert Triffin (see table 4.2 in chapter 4 above) provides interesting statistics on the extent to which this substitution has taken place. In the great era of the gold standard, 1815–1913, commodity money—gold or silver—was 67 percent of total national money outstanding in 1815 but had been reduced to 13 percent of the total by 1913. It was replaced by fiat paper money and deposits. In the international sphere, holdings of fiat money relative to gold have varied more sporadically, with international holdings of sterling being important prior to 1931 and dollars beginning in 1945.

Because of the formal American commitment to buy and sell gold at a fixed price, and the long international history of gold, one naturally thinks of gold as the "ultimate" monetary asset. It is easy to concede that the dollar has superior short-run liquidity properties as a vehicle currency both privately and publicly, and also to concede that it pays an attractive rate of interest, which gold does not. Even with such concessions, most bankers and civil servants, and some eminent and influential academicians like Robert Roosa and Arthur Burns, hold to the thesis that the demand for dollars as international money requires the tie to gold. But is this really so, and what are the implications of the gold tie?

In congressional testimony in 1959, Triffin pointed out the consequences. If international supplies of gold are fixed and increments to international liquidity are largely satisfied by a buildup in foreign holdings of dollars, the underlying system is unstable. As foreign holdings of dollars increase with a monetary gold supply which is relatively stationary, doubts arise about the American ability to convert gold into dollars at the fixed price. Speculative attempts to convert dollars into gold, in anticipation of a sharp rise in the price of gold, multiply. The overall convertibility of the dollar-based system becomes threatened, as it was by the gold rush of March 1968. From Triffin's now very familiar argument, American policymakers face an impossible dilemma. If they try to reduce the deficit as defined by the Department of Commerce, the growth of international liquidity would be halted and convertibility threatened. If they let the deficit run, the system becomes increasingly unstable and convertibility is threatened anyway.

There are two nonexclusive schools of thought for solving the dilemma. One is to replace the dollar/gold-exchange standard with an international money whose issue is controlled by an international institution. The prolonged negotiations over the development of Special Drawing Rights are the result of this influential view. However, as mentioned in the introduction, SDRs are envisaged (even under their widest conception) to be official instruments only. The rapidly growing demand for private international liquidity and an official vehicle currency has been completely outside of the negotiations. Here, it suffices to note that SDRs are not sufficient to replace dollars as international money.

The other school of thought suggests that the demand for international liquidity in the form of dollars can be satisfied and stabilized by demonetizing gold in the sense that central banks will no longer enter the private gold market as either buyers or sellers. This view is subscribed to in this essay and rests on two premises: (1) the provision of international money is a "natural" monopoly associated with one independent financial instrument, and (2) the dollar is preferred to gold as an international monetary asset. The first premise rests on Gresham's Law. Any system with more than one money linked together by a nominally fixed price is unstable, as exemplified by the dollar-gold standard. This line of thought, again mainly in terms of official reserve preferences, is more fully developed by Robert A. Aliber in "Gresham's Law, Asset Preferences, and the Demand for International Reserves" (*Quarterly Journal of Economics*, November 1967). Incidentally, the fact that a single national currency is used as a natural monopoly does not mean the banks of that country are given monopolistic advantages.

The second premise of the superiority of the dollar bears some examination. International transactions in commodities and securities are largely denominated in dollars, without effective gold clauses. The dollar has superior liquidity value in its use as a vehicle currency on both private and official account, whereas gold is not used at all. It is a superior store of value in the sense that dollar holdings bear a substantial rate of interest even for sight obligations in the Euro-dollar market. Longer-term obligations bear higher rates. So for all the textbook properties of money—as a numeraire, as medium of exchange, and as a store of value—the dollar dominates gold. It is now incorrect to think in historical terms of gold being the ultimate asset.

As pointed out by many writers, the speculative demand for gold now is similar to the demand for any easily storable metal whose floor price is fixed but whose ceiling price is not. By assessing the limited size of the American gold stock, speculators believe there is some significant probability that the official price of gold can be forced upward by buying pressure. One cannot lose by taking a long position in gold with these ground rules. One can lose, however, if the ground rules are changed so that the price of gold can dip below $35 per ounce as well as rise above it. This change in the rules would greatly reduce the monetary attractiveness of gold and would cause some substantial private dishoarding and probably a significant fall in its free-market price. More importantly, this demonetization of gold would stabilize the demand for international money in the form of dollars.

The current two-price system for gold is a partial but not complete movement toward demonetization. It is partial because the official communiqué (March 17, 1968) is ambiguous as to whether a floor price for gold of $35 per ounce in the free market will be supported. It is too early to tell what the ultimate effect will be. Nevertheless, even this limited step has the effect of establishing the dollar as the unit of account in official reserve holdings, which are not effectively denominated in dollars irrespective of what happens to the price of gold on the free market. (SDRs would also be effectively denominated in dollars if they are ever issued.)

The fact that the Union of South Africa and major European holders of gold have recently put pressure on banking authorities to guarantee the floor price is an indication of the dependent status of gold. The apparent willingness of European central banks to give such a guarantee to put a $35-per-ounce floor price under South African gold sales does not augur well for the demonetization process. In part, it nullifies the action taken the previous March, and private traders can now speculate with more impunity by holding gold. Whether or not the essential strength of the dollar is recognized by American authorities and full demonetization is carried out remains to be seen. The international demand for dollars can, and does, exist in the face of uncertainty in gold policy. However, greatly increased stability in official and private portfolio preferences for dollars would be introduced if the gold link were completely broken.

5.3   The Supply of Dollars

With heavy official and private international demand for dollars, what governs the supply response? Common to all monetary mechanisms, there remains the control problem of satisfying the "real" (price-deflated) demand for money while maintaining a stable price level and steady growth in world commerce. Would not the world's money supply become subject to the vicissitudes of American payments deficits under a dollar standard? What ensures that the supply of international money expands pari passu with the size of the world economy, but that there is no flood of unwanted holdings of dollars? In order to establish the properties of a pure dollar standard, let us assume gold is fully demonetized.

There is potentially much more order in the process of supplying dollars than initially meets the eye. One wants the "Euro-dollar/New York banking system" to be highly elastic or responsive to the needs of countries that get into temporary difficulties—such as Canada in 1962, Italy in 1963–64, or France in 1968. Thus, large short-term lending potential would be desirable. At the same time, the long-run trend in foreign holdings of dollars should match the potential growth of world real income. This trend could be adjusted upward if the income elasticity of the world demand for international money were greater than unity. Even though the money supply is capable of elastic short-term expansion to meet liquidity crises in particular countries, the aggregate holdings of international money should not depart far from this long-term trend in *either* direction. A completely passive supply mechanism that expands or contracts with the state of demand for nominal money is not a sufficiently stabilizing influence on international prices or real income flows.

Asset Preferences and Money Creation

The "liquidity" definition of the deficit in American external payments includes both capital and current account and approximately measures the change in private and official holdings of short-term dollar assets by foreigners if gold is demonetized. However, holdings of international money (these short-term dollar assets) can change with or without a change in the *net* position of foreigners. Changes in their net asset position depend on the size of a properly defined deficit or surplus on *current* account of the United States. From a purely bookkeeping point of view, there is always an offset on capital account to any entry on current account. That is, a surplus on current account by the United States means that Americans are acquiring claims on foreigners, once long- and short-term capital movements are netted out.

In the absence of long-term capital inflows into the United States, an American deficit on current account increases the supply of international money by increasing short-term dollar assets in the hands of foreigners. In doing so, the current deficit also increases the net asset position of foreigners. In contrast, pure financial intermediation, where foreigners sell long-term bonds in New York but maintain short-term American bank balances with the proceeds, leads to the creation of international money without any change in the *net* asset position of foreigners.

In the whole postwar period, the United States has run surpluses on current account rather than deficits. In the absence of covering long-term outflows of capital, these surpluses would have diminished the liquid asset holdings of foreigners. The fact that outflows of long-term capital have generally exceeded the American surplus on current account is not merely a fortuitous circumstance but directly reflects the asset-preference functions of official and private foreigners. In order to build up their liquid-asset positions, foreigners borrow long in New York. This process of financial intermediation more than offsets the current surplus to permit the international money supply to grow at or close to the desired rate. A more complete account of this intermediation process is given by E. Despres, C. Kindleberger, and W. Salant in "The Dollar and World Liquidity—A Minority View" (*The Economist*, February 5, 1966, pp. 526–29). However, the net total of liquid and illiquid claims on the United States held by foreigners is steadily becoming more negative as the American surplus on current account continues—which can be perfectly consistent with portfolio equilibrium in a growing world economy.

Financial intermediation is not the only way in which the rest of the world adjusts to the American surplus on current account. The size of the current surplus is not autonomously given but depends in significant measure on the elasticity of the financial mechanism. For many countries, the availability of American long- and short-term lending determines their demand for imports, and hence the size of the current surplus itself, since the United States is an important world exporter. This demand for imports financed by American lending can operate directly on American exports, or indirectly through increasing exports of third countries, which in turn increase their imports from the United States. In summary, the surplus on current account of the United States, the desired holdings of liquid assets by foreigners, and the net asset position of foreigners, vis-à-vis Americans, are all jointly determined.

The Supply Elasticity and Liquidity Needs

This complicated exercise in portfolio choice requires more detailed investigation—empirical and theoretical—than can be carried out within the confines of this essay. Nevertheless, the underlying elasticity of the supply mechanism is very great. The development of borrowing facilities in the Euro-dollar market seems to have offset the more negative effects of direct controls or taxes on American lending abroad. Otherwise, such controls would have seriously disrupted the supply mechanism. The controls themselves are a measure of the misunderstanding by American officials of the international role of the dollar.

On private account, if foreigners have an immediate need to hold international money, they can borrow at long term either directly from New York banks or, if turned away there, from

Euro-dollar banks. If they have an excess of short-term international liquidity, they can restrict their "normal" longer-term borrowing so as to permit their holdings of liquid balances to decline. The short-term elasticity of the mechanism depends on having large stocks of outstanding loans and securities through which changes in short-term preferences for liquidity can be easily handled. The large and growing real size of the market for short- and long-term dollar securities seems to be increasingly able to accommodate these demands.

What controls desired *official* balances of international money? Is the elasticity of the supply mechanism sufficiently responsive? With fixed-exchange-rate obligations, official holdings of dollars can only be controlled indirectly through domestic monetary and fiscal policy. For example, if excess liquidity in dollars takes the form of excess demand for francs by private individuals, then the French authorities must step into the market and acquire dollars. The obligations to maintain fixed exchange rates and free convertibility give the French government no other immediate choice.

National authorities can react to the acquisition of short-term dollar claims by direct reinvestment in longer-term dollar securities or they can leave them in liquid form. The existence of a well-developed international market gives them wide portfolio choice. If the authorities do not care to acquire dollar assets on a net basis, they can encourage internal monetary expansion. Indeed, the process of creating francs in order to buy dollars would naturally augment the domestic money supply if the authorities followed a passive monetary policy. This internal monetary expansion works on both capital and current account to reduce excess dollar accumulation. Fortunately, in a highly developed international capital market, much of the adjustment could be confined to changes in the flow of securities without sharp repercussions on the commodity market.

As long as national authorities have scope for considerable changes in the size and composition of their dollar holdings—which a highly developed international capital market would give them—they have some independent, though limited, scope for internal monetary policy under a system of both fixed exchange rates and free convertibility. Any country that deems it inadvisable to accept any restraint arising from external considerations is probably outside the "optimal currency area" defined

by exchange rates fixed in dollar terms. In this case, a floating
exchange rate would be the correct policy to restore sovereignty
over internal monetary policy and, externally, over holdings of
exchange reserves. However, as discussed above, even without
a fixed external parity, a country would aim to hold some contingency reserves of dollars, which it could "buy" in the free foreign-
exchange market with its own currency.

Long-Run Stability

The elasticity of the mechanism for supplying dollars seems
potentially adequate to service the needs of both private and
official foreigners so as to maintain free and convenient convertibility in international transactions. However, there remains the
important longer-run issue of keeping the world price level of
tradable goods determinant and stable while avoiding cycles in
income and employment. Fortunately, the preeminence of the
United States in the world economy and the highly diversified
nature of its exports permits it to influence broadly world prices
of tradable goods. Correspondingly, the trade balance is not tied
to the ebb and flow of a small number of commodities. Indeed,
maintaining a stable real value for the American dollar in terms
of American tradable goods is sufficient to maintain the liquidity
value of the dollar for the rest of the world. The prices of foreign
tradable goods cannot rise much above or fall below their American equivalents without inducing longer-run expansions or contractions in the balance of trade of the United States. These
movements in the American balance of trade in turn induce international monetary contractions or expansions through American
surpluses or deficits, respectively, of the "outside" variety, which
in the long run maintain the prices of foreign tradable goods
close to American levels.

This process of long-run equilibration working through the
American trade balance is analogous to one once hypothesized
for the 19th-century gold standard. Deflation would be halted
because gold production would be stimulated as factor prices fell.
Similarly, gold mining would be halted in periods of inflation,
forcing a monetary contraction. Of course, this equilibrating
mechanism did not work at all in the textbook fashion because
of the vagaries of the mining industry and the fact that new gold

discoveries might bear little or no relationship to the state of inflation or deflation in the world. Indeed, as Robert Triffin points out, variations in the rate of money creation were necessary to compensate for the variations in gold output! So the gold mechanism itself was hardly a long-run stabilizing influence.

Fortunately, the mechanism for creating internationally held dollars is based broadly on the production of thousands of goods and does not depend on the vicissitudes of production in any one industry. Therefore, it is potentially a much more stable and sensitive mechanism than the old gold standard. Much, of course, depends on the nature of internal American monetary and fiscal policy, which we treat in detail in section 5.4. It is conjectured there that the maintenance of internal-price-level stability with full employment in the United States makes it possible for the rest of the world to enjoy also such stability if it cares to avail itself of the opportunity.

5.4 Towards Abolition of American Balance-of-Payments Policy

There is another role in the United States can usefully play that is complementary to the provision of international money. In a world of N countries, if $N-1$ have targets for their balances of payments which they successfully achieve, this automatically determines the payments position of the Nth. (In a two-county world, if country A fixes the size of its payments surplus or deficit, this determines the international-payments position of country B. By similar reasoning, one can generalize to N countries.) Unless at least one of the N countries reacts passively or sponge-like to the policies of the others, a high probability of conflict arises. The absence of a degree of freedom is targeting balances in international payments has been christened the "redundancy problem" by Robert Mundell.

The Redundancy Problem

Conflict can arise out of inconsistent accounting definitions of surplus and deficit. Indeed, under current accounting practices, the sum of the world's deficits can exceed substantially the sum of the world's surpluses in the presence of short-term capital movements. Countries receiving inflows of short-term capital often do not register them as such, whereas short-term outflows of capital are duly registered. Therefore, even if all N countries were aiming for a state of balance in the accounting of their international payments, they could not achieve it.

More important, the problem is aggravated because nations typically wish to build up private and public reserve holdings as their economies grow, and to do so they must aim for surpluses—even when defined under a consistent set of accounting definitions. Even with adequate reserves, nations in surplus are frequently unwilling to alter their policies for political or psychological reasons. At least one *major* country must be willing to run deficits so as to provide an offset. The logical choice of country is, of course, the one country whose currency is used to supply international liquidity. The liquidity and redundancy problems can then be handled simultaneously.

An important part of the American position in this respect is its favorable balance sheet regarding other countries. American claims on foreigners amount to about $120 billion, whereas foreign claims on the United States amount to approximately $60 billion, albeit in more liquid forms. This uniquely large stock of both net and gross assets permits great flexibility in changing external-payments flows of the United States in any one year. Thus, the United States is ideally suited for playing the role of both banker and sponge.

The abolition of any conscious target in international payments is consistent with the lack of an exchange-rate policy available to the United States. As pointed out in section 5.1, redundancy exists in exchange rates as well. It proved very convenient in the postwar period to let $N-1$ countries in the world fix their exchange rates vis-à-vis a single anchor currency—the American dollar. The dollar was then used as a stabilization vehicle for these $N-1$ rates, and each country had a well-defined commitment in the foreign-exchange market. To maintain consistency, the United States became the Nth country without an exchange-rate policy of its own.

If, in spite of its inability to alter the relative value of its currency, the United States adopts targets in international payments, policymakers will be induced to try either (1) direct intervention in international trade in goods and securities, or (2) the bending of internal monetary and fiscal policy to alter the flow of international payments. Neither technique is acceptable. The first endangers free convertibility, as is well illustrated by the web of controls on capital outflows. The second is inappropriate in a country where only 5 percent of its total output is exported. Monetary and fiscal policy are far too important instruments to be geared to events in the small foreign-trade sector.

More fundamentally, we have argued that the state of American external payments is largely a function of the portfolio preferences of foreigners. Therefore, only the most detailed controls—completely inconsistent with worldwide convertibility—will stop foreigners from exercising these preferences. Exchange-rate changes are preferable to direct controls, but it is vital for the United States to play its Nth-country role with neither a payments target nor an exchange-rate policy. Additionally, because of foreign demand to increase dollar holdings, it is very doubtful whether the United States dollar is overvalued in terms of foreign currencies from what it should be under floating exchange rates.

How real is this redundancy problem, or is it merely a figment of academic imagination? Reading the *New York Times* in the month of June 1968, we note that most of the world's principal trading countries (Britain, Canada, France, Japan, and the United States) imagined themselves simultaneously to be going through external-payments crises, some mild and some severe. This leaves Germany and Italy to be on the other side of the fence, but there are no counterbalancing signs of joy from them on the financial pages. They remain watchful and wary. The *Wall Street Journal* publishes articles on the loss of American competitiveness in world markets; at the same time, Europeans read and are deeply affected by J. J. Servan-Schreiber's *Le Défi Américain* (*The American Challenge*), which tells of the growing technological superiority of the United States over Europe.

It is clear that we should extricate ourselves from the almost comic situation of major world traders setting mutually inconsistent goals in international payments. If some countries wish, unrelentingly, to build up excess liquidity through balance-of-payments surpluses year after year, an elastic financial system should be able to accommodate them without having this accumulation upset everybody else. (Even as late as January 1968, in the face of enormous surpluses, the Germans went ahead and substantially raised border taxes on imports. They were reduced only with great reluctance in December 1968, in the face of a substantial crisis.) The simple way out is for the United States to abandon completely any payments targets of its own and to permit the other $N-1$ countries in the world to set their own payments targets unhindered.

This abandonment should take the form of removing all American restrictions or taxes on portfolio purchases, direct investments, or bank lending abroad, as well as avoiding the tying of foreign aid and the hindering of imports of goods and services. It would also imply that the Department of Commerce should publish international-payments statistics much as it now does but *without* adding up any subset of accounts as a measure of the "deficit." This last entry should be omitted as a casualty to a changing technology.[1] There is no plausible definition of a deficit in the balance of payments of the Nth country which is also a reserve center. Fritz Machlup, in "The Mysterious Numbers Game," gives an account of the impossibility of suitably defining the deficit of the United States and of the changing views of those who tried it.

American Internal Policy

The proposal for abandoning policies of the United States regarding exchange rates and the balance of payments should in no sense be interpreted as abandoning international obligations in terms of foreign aid or other economic assistance. Indeed, it is out of respect for the valuable international role that the United States is uniquely suited to play, that it should maintain a passive policy with respect to its balance of payments. However, the United States would have an increased obligation to maintain stable internal policies. It would be the balance wheel of the world economy. As such, maintenance of stability in the prices of tradable goods is highly important, as is the avoidance of cyclical fluctuations in income and employment.

Monetary policy should be more stable than in the past, with the Federal Reserve System enjoined to create money—broadly defined—at a constant predictable rate associated with the growth of American output in real terms. Foreigners as well as domestic participants in the capital market could then better accommodate themselves to what was a known and established policy. Such episodes as great monetary liberality in 1965, followed by a "crunch" in the summer of 1966, followed by periods of excessive expansion in 1967 and 1968, should be avoided. The important point is that there need be no conflict between internal- and external-policy goals, of the kind commonly outlined in textbooks on foreign-trade theory, as far as the United States is concerned.

Notice that the policy advocated here is, in some respects, the opposite of that advocated by Richard Cooper (*The Economics of Interdependence: Economic Policy in the Atlantic Community,* McGraw-Hill, 1968). He suggests that in a world of growing interdependence, policies of the United States and other countries should increasingly be consciously geared to the outside world. For example, unemployment in France should enter American decision-making. The opinions of European bankers should be heeded. In practical terms, one implication might be that, in the frequent meetings of the Board of Governors of the Federal Reserve System, general economic conditions throughout the world would be weighed in detail in setting the immediate course of American monetary policy.

In contrast, it is suggested here that the United States abandon policy consciously directed at the outside world and concentrate on maintaining a stable internal economy toward which the rest of the world can accommodate itself. A multiplicity of policy goals leading to numerous short-run shifts in policy, whose full consequences are uncertain, can easily lead to destabilizing behavior. Steady and predictable monetary expansion by the Federal Reserve is one way of dealing with this uncertainty domestically and of also providing an independent point of reference for the rest of the world. The United States is in an enormously powerful position, which its own balance-of-payments accounting fails to recognize. The conscious use of this enormous power for maintaining internal stability would make the United States and the rest of the world better off.

Exchange-Rate Policy in the Rest of the World

It was mentioned in section 5.2 that policy regarding exchange rates was *not* the dominant determinant of the demand for international liquidity in a world where private holdings of international money are important. However, flexible exchange rates can be a convenient device for adjusting the balance of payments of certain classes of countries and may also prove convenient for permitting independent domestic monetary policies. Some countries may wish completely floating exchange rates; others might optimally increase the band limits (defined in terms of dollars) within which their rates fluctuate without official intervention. Rigid rates within a few blocs of countries may well be desirable as a basis for building a unified currency system. Again, the United States can remain passive in all of this.

Passivity in American policy regarding its balance of payments can preserve worldwide convertibility in the face of a wide variety of exchange-rate policies on the part of other nations. For example, if any country wishes to build up substantially its exchange reserves by maintaining an undervalued exchange rate or an equivalent complex of "border" taxes and subsidies on imports and exports, this can normally be handled by accommodating American deficits. The willingness of the United States to do this relieves much of the pressure on those neighboring countries which cannot themselves create international reserves. The experience with Germany and France in the late 1950s and early 1960s is a case in point. Large reserves were built up by these two countries with free convertibility fairly easily maintained—even enhanced—as the United States ran more or less equivalent "deficits" as the Nth country.

However, flexible as the dollar standard is when the United States plays its passive role correctly, there are some exchange-rate policies on the part of other countries that are inimical to worldwide convertibility. If, for example, one major trading country not only maintains a set of policies that lead to continuous reserve acquisition over a long period (which can be handled by the dollar system if gold is demonetized), but also takes measures in banking and tax policy that have the effect of strongly accelerating this reserve acquisition, then the pressure on neighboring countries can become intolerably great. (This pressure is made even greater, of course, if American authorities lose their "cool" and try to strengthen controls on outflows of capital.) The neighboring countries lose their dollar reserves and can then be forced into imposing trade restrictions or devaluing. In fact, one can imagine one sufficiently strong surplus country forcing a whole chain of devaluations for all major trading countries other than the United States, the last not having an exchange rate to change. Nth-country passivity is not sufficient in the presence of strong "neighborhood" effects.

In this kind of situation, there is substantial likelihood of a breakdown in international agreements prohibiting trade restrictions and tariff increases. The neighboring countries are likely to lose control of their internal economic policies. Furthermore, substantial devaluations vis-à-vis the dollar may throw the international use of the dollar into question—although, again, it may not if the United States is not frightened further into abandoning a passive policy in the face of increases in its imports and decreases in its exports.

The moral of this fable is easy to see. Some collective pressure on the one country whose currency is badly undervalued is necessary to avoid an upheaval. If a formal large appreciation cannot be negotiated, then a general move toward flexible exchange rates—the abandonment of fixed parities—is desirable. Under the last policy, international holdings of dollars on private account would be of enhanced importance.

In a world of recurrent crises in the gold market and the foreign-exchange markets, it is all too easy to forget the great progress that has been made under the dollar system. Rapid growth of world trade in goods and securities has been enormous by any historical standard. These crises should not obscure the fact that a little adroit tinkering with the system can permit growth to continue even faster without the crises. Completing the demonetization of gold, correcting one or two exchange rates which are badly out of line, and removing American restrictions on outflows of capital while keeping stable domestic prices would be sufficient. It would be tragic if recurrent crises were to inculcate the psychology of an inevitable collapse in the dollar standard. There are no handy alternatives.

Note

1. In 1976, the U.S. Department of Commerce did indeed stop publishing any official measure of the U.S. balance-of-payments "deficit."

6

Sterilization in Three Dimensions: Major Trading Countries, Eurocurrencies, and the United States

While monetarists and Keynesians disagree over the relative strengths of monetary and fiscal policies in influencing aggregate demand, neither school disputes the desirability of national control over each country's supply of money. Both Keynesians such as James Meade and monetarists such as Milton Friedman have long advocated freely floating exchange rates, in part to secure greater national monetary autonomy. Insofar as parity commitments may force governments to buy or sell domestic currency for foreign exchange, sterilization of any impact on the domestic monetary base has been accepted intellectually in the postwar period, and has also been the avowed goal of monetary authorities. The Bretton Woods system explicitly permitted national intervention to block or slow international capital movements (as long as convertibility on current account was not directly affected) in order to facilitate domestic sterilization operations.

This paper reexamines the basis for venerating national autonomy in monetary matters, and then suggests how governments might go beyond the Smithsonian or subsequent agreements on exchange-rate parities to delimit sterilization activities in a systematic way. The objective is to promote more symmetrical mutual adjustment in international payments, even as monetary stability in individual countries is enhanced rather than sacrificed.

The sterilization of deficits or surpluses in international payments can be conveniently considered on three levels. First, there

Originally published, in slightly longer form, in *National Monetary Policies and the International Financial System*, ed. Robert Z. Aliber (University of Chicago Press, 1974), 231–249. Reprinted with permission.

is the direct impact on the domestic money supply, other than that of the reserve center, of countries whose governments enter the market for foreign exchange by buying or selling domestic currency. What is the proper scope of offsetting domestic open-market operations, rediscounting, or other individual actions by these national central banks?

At the second level, the form(s) in which European countries and Canada and Japan hold their dollar reserves has important monetary implications. The acquisition by foreign governments of U.S. Treasury bills can influence the U.S. money market. Re-depositing official reserves in the Euro-dollar market can have a sharp "multiplier" effect on the growth of Euro-dollar deposit liabilities. This rather neglected aspect of international steriliza-tion also warrants systematic investigation.

On yet a third level, the autonomy of the reserve currency center, the United States, is brought into the open. Without at-tracting any attention from academic economists, the Federal Reserve System has, almost subconsciously, sterilized the impact of "official settlements" deficits on the U.S. monetary base through-out the postwar period. That the center country should exercise considerable autonomy is hardly surprising. However, I shall try to show that neither international adjustment nor U.S. monetary stability need be well served by full sterilization of month-to-month imbalances in U.S. international payments.

For convenience, sterilization problems are discussed on each of these three levels, although the three are not fully independent.

6.1   The Stabilizing Influence of the International Economy: 1950 to the Mid 1960s

Arguments for a high degree of exchange-rate flexibility, or for sterilization of the impact of government foreign-exchange oper-ations on the domestic monetary base, assume that national mon-etary autonomy leads to greater stability and higher growth than would a more dependent monetary policy. It is believed that shocks or business cycles are transmitted internationally in a destabilizing fashion and are in some sense "large" relative to purely national disturbances in income and employment. The breakdown and extraordinary fluctuations in international eco-nomic relations in the interwar period have been projected to carry over, albeit in lesser degree, to the post–World War II period.[1] A dependent economy, the reasoning goes, is more likely to be destabilized than smoothed by international flows of goods and capital over which it has little direct control—flows that may hinder policies to handle economic crises of purely domestic origin.

It is difficult to design a direct and comprehensive empirical test of the "international transmission hypothesis," and it is impossible to specify statistically the quantitative influence of alternative exchange rate mechanisms on the transmission process. There is, however, indirect empirical evidence for the period 1950–68, which casts considerable doubt on the traditional view of the destabilizing influence of the international economy on developed and less developed countries.

Other things being equal, the transmission hypothesis implies that economies more open to foreign trade should be *less* stable than those that are relatively closed. In the analysis to follow, "instability" is measured by the variance of "real" components of Gross Domestic Product across a variety of countries for which the OECD has tabulated annual statistics comparably deflated for price changes. The statistical sample includes 13 developed and 15 less-developed countries.[2] The variance of these components of GDP about their *logarithmic* trends measures national instability for each country. That is, define Y_i to the ith component of GDP—say real gross investment—for a given country and then fit:

$$\log Y_{ti} = a_{oj} + a_1 t + e_{ti} \qquad i = 1, 2, \ldots 5$$

$$t \text{ is an index of time over} \qquad (1)$$
$$\text{annual observations.}$$

Our measure of instability through time is simply the estimated standard error of (1), as denoted by S_i, where:

$$S_i = \frac{\sum e_{ti}^2}{n - 2}$$

The S_{ij} were calculated for each country j in each of five categories: gross investment (GI), machinery and equipment expenditures (ME), exports (E), imports (M), and aggregate gross domestic product.[3] Within any one of these five categories, the S_{ij}

have the advantage of being directly comparable across countries because they are ratios measuring percentage variation around a logarithmic trend. And countries do indeed differ by this measure: the less developed countries exhibit approximately twice as much instability as do the wealthy ones. Moreover, there are significant variations within each group.

Why bother with four different measures of instability in addition to Gross Domestic Product, when GDP itself seems a more comprehensive measure that includes investment and trade flows? For many countries—particularly the poorer ones—all of GDP is not reestimated directly every year, and coverage of private consumption is quite poor. Indeed, GDP may simply be extrapolated from five-year benchmarks and so smooth the annual fluctuations that we are trying to measure![4] In contrast, exports, imports, gross investment, and machinery-equipment expenditures are usually measured directly annually, and do show much more volatility in rich as well as in poor countries.

The measure of instability S_i can be related to the "openness" of each economy to foreign trade. Ignoring capital flows, simply the ratio of exports to GDP, E/Y, is used to measure openness. For any given country this ratio is calculated at the midpoint of the interval within the 1950–68 period over which annual observations on S_i were available. Then S_{ij} was regressed on E/Y across countries to obtain the results in table 6.1 below.

Somewhat surprisingly, table 6.1 indicates that openness to foreign trade may well *reduce* economic instability experienced in individual countries! The coefficient of E/Y in the first four equations—on major components of GDP—is significantly negative. The coefficient of E/Y is still negative although not significantly so in the GDP equation, but available statistics on aggregate Gross Domestic Product are inadequate for measuring annual fluctuations for reasons discussed above.

The mere absence of correlation between openness and instability should be sufficient to cast doubt on the old transmission hypothesis. Hence a negative association between openness and instability is more than sufficient.

This negative association may be explainable by some other unspecified "third" factor related to both the dependent and the independent variables used in the statistical regressions reported in table 6.1. However, adding additional explanatory variables

Table 6.1
Instability Indices for Both Developed and Developing Countries (figures in parentheses are t ratios)

Gross investment	S_{GI}	$= .121 - .148\dfrac{E}{Y}$	$R^2 = .1438$	$n = 26$
		(7.51) (2.01)		
Machinery-equipment expenditures	S_{ME}	$= .199 - .321\dfrac{E}{Y}$	$R^2 = .1559$	$n = 23$
		(5.4) (1.97)		
Imports	S_{M}	$= .133 - .221\dfrac{E}{Y}$	$R^2 = .245$	$n = 25$
		(7.48) (2.73)		
Exports	S_{E}	$= .103 - .175\dfrac{E}{Y}$	$R^2 = .3056$	$n = 25$
		(8.48) (3.18)		
Gross Domestic Product	S_{GDP}	$= .0282 - .00789\dfrac{E}{Y}$	$R^2 = .0064$	$n = 27$
		(6.67) (.402)		

Source: OECD data described in text.
Notes: S_i is an index of instability; E/Y is the ratio of exports to Gross Domestic Product; n is the number of countries in the sample.

such as wealth per capita or country size does not change the results qualitatively, although the explanatory power attributed to E/Y is usually reduced as the list of other closely related "independent" variables grows. Similarly, disaggregation into rich and poor countries reduces the variance in the S_i to be explained and the statistical degrees of freedom, but the coefficients of E/Y generally retain their negative signs.[5] Of course, causality can go in either direction—openness can lead to stability, and stability can lead to openness. They were not, however, antithetical in the period 1950–68.

Merely relating openness to stability in investment and trade flows does not establish anything directly about exchange-rate systems or monetary policy. Michael Michaely has recently done a painstaking empirical analysis of the monetary and fiscal policies followed by nine industrial economies[6] from 1950 to 1966. All had similarly pegged exchange rates under the Bretton Woods system, so that all generated measurable payments deficits or surpluses from time to time. To what extent did their need to maintain external balance conflict with the need to secure full employment or combat domestic inflation within each country? Since countries in deficit were often those facing inflationary pressure at home, and vice versa, there was no policy dilemma. When not pointing in the same direction, Michaely found the state of the balance of payments to be rather neutral with respect to domestic needs. "Conflict" cases were rare.

> It should be noted . . . that the frequency of conflicts between the requirements of domestic targets—mainly the target of high employment—and the requirements of balance-of-payments equilibrium is not as high as the attention paid to these clashes in recent discussions would suggest. The impression that such a contradiction is of an overriding concern is probably due in large part to the recent experience of the United States, where from the late 1950s to the mid-1960s a high rate of unemployment accompanied a persistent balance-of-payment deficit. But this experience is by no means commonly shared: in most other major countries, the requirements of external and internal balance tended more often to provide policy indications in the same direction, or at least not to contradict each other, rather than to point in opposite directions.[7]

Even the United States in the late 1950s and early 1960s may not be an exception to Michaely's rule. With the benefit of hindsight, we know that both the "liquidity" and "official settlements" definitions of a deficit may be inappropriate for a reserve-center country, where foreign demand to hold claims in its currency is high and rising. It is doubtful that an excess supply of dollars did flow to the rest of the world in the later 1950s and early 1960s—although the belief of its existence probably made U.S. policymakers too reluctant to deal with domestic unemployment.

In summary, the international economy seems to have helped rather than hindered national economic stability from 1950 to the mid-1960s. Countries connected by stable trading relationships, and which do not experience business cycles or national upheavals in unison, can be expected to exercise a smoothing effect on each other through the statistical law of large numbers. International monetary chaos in the 1970s may, of course, reverse this effect, as it did in the interwar period. Indeed, the evident maladjustment in exchange rates in the late 1960s and early 1970s, due to inflationary pressure emanating from the United

States, has caused the international economy to become less stable. Nevertheless, mutual monetary adjustment is potentially consistent with the maintenance of economic stability within each country, if the "rules of the game" can be sufficiently well defined for the United States as well as for other industrial countries. Unfettered national autonomy may be both unnecessary and unwise.

6.2 The Composition of Reserves and Neighborhood Effects

But is it enough to set sustainable exchange rates and to agree to let short-run disequilibria in international payments influence significantly the stock of money within each major trading country? Under a pure gold standard, where no asset other than gold is used internationally, no further constraints on national policy would seem necessary. Central banks would hold only gold, and one country's losses would be another's gain—aside from new gold production. The outstanding deposit liabilities of the commercial banks would be closely tied to national gold reserves. Exchange controls would be absent, and capital could move more freely from one country to another, or from bank deposits in one national currency to deposits denominated in any other national currency, with a concomitant change in the gold position of the countries involved in either case.

This rather disarming simplicity has been absent from the international gold-dollar exchange standard that lasted until 1968, and from the pure dollar standard that now concerns us. National central banks no longer are confined to a single reserve asset in the form of economically inert yellow metal; rather, they can choose from a plethora of dollar assets with varying degrees of liquidity, exchange guarantees, and the like. By convention, most of the huge dollar reserves now extant are held in the form of U.S. Treasury bills, which were purchased for the accounts of foreign central banks in the open New York bill market by the Federal Reserve. But foreign central banks can and do hold demand and time deposits in New York, as well as Euro-dollar deposits in London. What are the monetary implications of these various possibilities for holding reserves, when disequilibria in the balance of international payments occur?

First, if a surplus in an industrial European country were merely the counterpart of an "official-settlements" deficit in the United States, there would be a marked asymmetry in the adjustment process. The purchase of dollars by the European central bank with domestic high-powered money would cause the monetary base of the European country to expand, but would normally result in a reduction only in the stock of U.S. Treasury bills held by Americans. The U.S. monetary base would not contract. Therefore, the full burden of short-run adjustment would fall on the European country, and the world's money supply would increase because of this "accident" in international payments.

Let us, however, defer consideration of the asymmetrical position of the United States, and consider balance-of-payments relationships among other major trading countries. For example, what are the monetary implications of a balance-of-payments deficit in France, which corresponds to a surplus in Germany? Clearly, all European countries are closely connected in foreign trade so that such neighborhood effects are important.

If both the French and the German central banks operate instantaneously to convert reserve losses and gains into changes in their holding of U.S. Treasury bills, and if both allow their domestic monetary bases to reflect these reserve changes as described above, then mutual adjustment would occur as if a pure gold standard were operating. German monetary policy would become easier as French policy became tighter. In this circumstance, the German surplus would *not* lead to any net increase in international reserves or in the world's money supply, as measured by the sum of national money supplies.[8] The use of the dollar as an intervention currency to maintain exchange-rate parities, where both central banks quickly convert dollar bank deposits into U.S. Treasury bills, would leave the U.S. Treasury bill market unaffected. Mutual adjustment would be appropriately balanced between, and focused on, the two European countries in which the disturbance occurred.

But this happy consistency can easily be upset by the selection of dollar-reserve assets that differ as between France and Germany. Suppose that the Bank of France were in the habit of holding U.S. Treasury bills, while the German Bundesbank decided to invest gains in its reserves in higher-yield Euro-dollars on deposit in London. In order to finance the French payments deficit, the Bank of France sells U.S. Treasury bills in the New York capital market, and pays the Bundesbank by a check drawn on the resulting demand deposit in the Federal Reserve Bank of New York. Then the Bundesbank deposits the dollars with Barclays in London.

Many avenues for further flows of funds are now open. Perhaps the simplest is for Barclays to purchase U.S. Treasury bills, in which case we get harmonious results derived earlier when both central banks bought and sold U.S. Treasury bills directly. Barclays would be only a neutral intermediary for the Bundesbank in the purchase of U.S. Treasury bills sold by the Bank of France, and there would be no net monetary expansion resulting from the German-French payments imbalance.

However, the Bundesbank's deposit with Barclays was made in the expectation of a higher rate of return than that on U.S. Treasury bills. Hence, the circuit is more likely to be completed by Barclays' lending to some borrower who will pay a higher rate of return—which could be anywhere in the Euro-dollar market. Suppose that the German surplus were caused by a relatively high interest-rate policy in Germany, a policy that induces Barclays to lend the newly deposited dollars to German commercial banks. Dollars are still in excess supply vis-à-vis marks; and the German commercial banks sell these dollars to the Bundesbank, which is still obliged to defend its foreign-exchange parity by selling high-powered marks in return. This currency pyramiding then leads to a secondary expansion in the German monetary base, with further expansionary rounds being quite possible. Pyramiding stops only when the Euro-dollars leak out into the official reserves of countries willing to hold U.S. Treasury bills, or come into the hands of private individuals in Europe who are willing to acquire direct financial claims on the United States inclusive of U.S. Treasury bills. Clearly, it is the willingness of Europeans to hold direct dollar claims on the United States that eventually sterilizes the currency pyramiding in Europe.

In order to sharpen the point at issue, let us temporarily assume that France and Germany are the only two countries in the world outside of the United States. London is not a country—merely

a financial intermediary. Moreover, only the Bank of France—
and not private Europeans—holds U.S. Treasury bills or other
direct short-term dollar claims on the United States. Assume that
France develops a deficit and Germany develops a corresponding
surplus. There is an incipient tendency for the French monetary
authorities to sell their U.S. Treasury bills and take the proceeds
to supply dollars to the Bundesbank, which in turn redeposits
with Barclays in London. Barclays reinvests in Europe. What
will the final equilibrium look like? Currency pyramiding will
stop only when (1) the German monetary base has fully expanded
so as to eliminate the payments imbalance between France and
Germany; and (2) the French reserves of U.S. Treasury bills, as
well as the French domestic monetary base, are restored to their
initial levels. Germany has borne the full burden of monetary
adjustment, and the sum of the nation's money supplies has
risen. This result violates the symmetry property of the pure
gold standard described earlier, and the world's aggregate
money stock is much less stable.

   Is there any evidence that this "European" pyramiding is important empirically in the more complicated world of many countries, each of which uses differentiated rules of thumb for reserve
assets? The International Monetary Fund publishes a statistical
series that compares the direct short-term dollar liabilities of the
United States (to foreign governments) with the dollar holdings
that foreign governments count as part of their exchange reserves.[9] The difference is due to pyramiding and has been growing steadily. Official dollar reserves held outside of the United
States exceed direct U.S. dollar liabilities to foreign governments
by approximately $2,586 million in 1967, $7,517 million in 1969,
$19,590 million in 1971, and $33,417 million at the end of 1972.
This phenomenon became widely noted when, in a scandal of
sorts, it was pointed out that the Bank for International Settlements (BIS) had been active in accepting dollar deposits from
European governments, and then relending in the Euro-dollar
market at a time when the BIS's official clients were being flooded
with dollars.[10] Since then understandings have been reached to
curb the BIS's (unwitting) role in the pyramiding process. Nevertheless, the IMF's statistics indicate that the pyramiding of official
reserves continues at a rather astonishing rate.

What then can we conclude about neighborhood effects? Central banks of major trading countries might well agree to deal in a common dollar-denominated reserve asset which is also a direct—as opposed to an intermediate—claim on the United States. U.S. Treasury bills seem to meet this need reasonably well, but they are by no means perfect for this role, as is shown below. (Unfortunately, Regulation Q makes U.S. bank deposits less attractive than they should be.) The common use of U.S. Treasury bills allows mutual adjustment to be confined to the countries experiencing payments imbalances, if neither of these countries is the United States. In addition, the pyramiding of official reserves that can result from intra-European payments imbalances would be effectively sterilized if foreign central banks hold only direct dollar claims on the United States. Uncontrolled fluctuations in the monetary base are thereby dampened.

6.3   On Sterilizing the Federal Reserve

Is it realistic to suppose that foreign central banks would agree to deal in a single "direct" dollar asset on the one hand, and also allow international deficits or surpluses to influence their domestic money supplies on the other? Until 1966, important elements of such a system did exist, as noted above. The main source of instability in the earlier period arose from the confidence problem associated with holding two reserve assets—gold and dollars. Fortunately, gold is no longer actively traded among central banks, and that particular problem is no longer with us. But confidence in U.S. monetary policy has been badly shaken and must be restored if a purely dollar-based system is to work in a consistent and stable fashion.

Two aspects of the current situation pose problems for the United States that did not exist in the earlier halcyon days. First, it is no longer accepted by Americans themselves—let alone by foreigners—that the Federal Reserve knows how to run a stable monetary policy. Second, the international economy is now "larger," as measured by either trade or financial flows, relative to the economy of the United States. Both problems suggest that the United States might do better to pursue a less autonomous monetary policy in the future.

Consider first the knowledge gap in monetary management. The public's expectations regarding future price inflation are now much less stable than they have been throughout most of the postwar period. Hence, the traditional "Keynesian" precepts of monetary management, where "the" absolute level of nominal rates of interest (on short- or long-term securities) is accepted as a measure of ease or tightness, are highly suspect. Indeed, the attempt to use an expansionary monetary policy to reduce high nominal rates of interest, initially arising from a failure to provide tax finance for the Vietnam war in 1965, led to the loss of monetary control in the United States in the late 1960s. Inflationary expectations were kindled, and nominal rates of interest rose higher still. Fortunately, in 1969–70, the Federal Reserve decided against indefinite monetary expansion to reduce rates of interest. The authorities are now somewhat sadder, and only slightly wiser, about the reliability of interest rates as monetary indicators.

The alternative "monetarist" approach focuses on steady expansion, say 6 percent a year, in some well-defined monetary aggregate as a means of assuring monetary stability. Whether the aggregate chosen is M_1, M_2, or the monetary base—defined as commercial bank reserves plus outstanding currency—is not supposed to matter much as long as smooth growth is maintained over fairly long periods of time. The social value of such a firm commitment by the Federal Reserve may be very high indeed because of its dampening influence on the inflationary expectations of both Americans and foreigners for the indefinite future.

But the monetarist model still leaves an uncomfortable hiatus in guidelines for monetary policy in the short run. In the United States, at least, the exercise of month-to-month control over monetary aggregates has proved very difficult technically for three related sets of reasons:

1. Each of the three aggregates can move quite differently for several months at a time. M_1 can be rising 2 percent a year, while M_2 rises at 8 percent. These divergent movements are particularly noticeable during cycles of bank disintermediation and reintermediation due to interest-rate restrictions such as Regulation Q.

2. Statistical estimates of the monetary aggregates come out with surprisingly long lags and large "revisions." These adjustments to the data, perhaps several months after the fact, are

often of the same order of magnitude as the incremental changes that monetary authority wants to know initially.[11] Deseasonalization procedures are particularly suspect.

3. Finally, deficits and surpluses in U.S. international payments have recently been great enough to obscure even further the "correct" definition of the monetary aggregates. Foreigners are now significant holders of bank deposits in the United States; and only recently has there been a systematic attempt to separate these foreign holdings from those of U.S. nationals.[12] The impact of Euro-currency transactions on the American monetary aggregates has also been ambiguous and subject to sizable retrospective revisions.

Undeniably, these "technical" difficulties make the monetarist model difficult to use for purposes of the short-run monetary management. But then the use of nominal rates of interest as policy targets seems even more treacherous. Indeed, the fragmentation in the structure of interest rates observed in early 1972, where U.S. Treasury bills yielded 3 1/2 percent while high quality long-term corporate bonds yielded 7 1/2 percent, weakens the interest-rate model even further.

If the Federal Reserve does not have purely domestic guidelines for short-run management of the money supply that are commonly acceptable, perhaps a more conscious effort to adjust to short-run changes in the balance of international payments would have a more stabilizing influence in the United States than is commonly supposed. Such a conclusion would hardly be surprising if applied to any European country. But American academic economists and central bankers have, in the postwar period, become accustomed to virtually complete autonomy in monetary matters. The large size of the U.S. economy, the relatively small foreign-trade component, and the unique position of being the Nth country whose central bank is not directly obligated to buy and sell foreign exchange, have all been important in allowing the United States to exercise monetary independence. Full sterilization of balance-of-payments deficits and surpluses has been practiced almost subliminally.

The institutions of the international dollar standard have made automatic sterilization particularly easy as a technical matter. Consider the case of an official-settlements deficit by the United States where the surplus country—say France—elects to increase its holdings of U.S. Treasury bills. The Bank of France initially acquires dollar deposits with Chase Manhattan in New York that are then used to purchase U.S. Treasury bills in the open market for the French government. More commonly, the Bank of France is likely to transfer its dollar deposits to the Federal Reserve Bank of New York, which in turn acts as an agent of the French government in purchasing the Treasury bills on the open market. Let us call this last procedure "policy Alpha." In neither case is there any net diminution of the U.S. monetary base. Only the stock of U.S. Treasury bills held by Americans declines. In effect, there has been full sterilization of the U.S. international deficit.[13]

How could those procedures be changed so that full sterilization of the U.S. balance-of-payments deficit is no longer automatic? Suppose the Bank of France agreed to transfer all its newly acquired claims on U.S. commercial banks to the Federal Reserve Bank of New York. If nothing else is done, the reserves of American commercial banks decline: that is, the American monetary base contracts. But the French government still wants interest-bearing assets. If the U.S. government—Federal Reserve—issues bills new to the market from its own portfolio to the Bank of France, instead of purchasing existing Treasury bills on the open market, there is no offsetting expansion in the U.S. monetary base. The stock of outstanding U.S. Treasury bills held by Americans on private account would remain unchanged. Let us call this policy of no sterilization "policy Beta."

There are various combinations of policies Alpha and Beta that the Federal Reserve can follow when a deficit in the balance of payments occurs. A case can be made, however, for giving Beta something more than a zero weight in the formulation of short-term monetary policy. A presumptive operating rule could easily be designed to allow an unusually large deficit to reduce the U.S. monetary base to some degree—not necessarily on a dollar-for-dollar basis, but significantly. Short-term rates of interest would then be pushed up slightly, and capital would be attracted to the United States. In short, U.S. monetary policy would consciously facilitate mutual adjustment in international payments among the major trading countries.

What is being suggested is that the Federal Reserve give some credence to what might be called "a monetary interpretation of balance-of-payments disequilibria." That is, deficits and surpluses in international payments are often themselves indicative of an excess supply of or demand for money domestically—unless exchange-rate parities are seriously misaligned. Given the absence of other guidelines for short-run policy, the balance of payments could well contain valuable information that even the center country should not ignore continuously.

Let us take an example. At the beginning of 1971, accelerated monetary expansion in the United States triggered incredibly large official-settlements deficits that were fully sterilized, that is, not allowed to interfere with the monetary expansion. There was a resurgence of inflationary expectations in the United States, a rise in long-term bond rates, and finally wage and price controls were instituted on 15 August 1971. At the beginning of 1971, exchange-rate parities were hardly at "equilibrium" levels. Nevertheless, it seems that the Fed erred in totally sterilizing the large balance-of-payments deficits, even if it had only been concerned with monetary stability within the United States.

Thus far we have been discussing the knowledge gap in the formulating of short-run American monetary policy. Does the greatly increased size of the international economy also make a difference to the degree of autonomy that the United States can now wisely exercise?

Consider the market for U.S. Treasury bills, which, as we have seen, have been a useful and relatively efficient vehicle for the holding of dollar reserves by foreign central banks. As of 30 April 1972, there were approximately $68 billion worth of Treasury bills held outside the Federal Reserve System by commercial banks, private financial or nonfinancial corporations, and so on. Foreign central banks and other official institutions held close to $30 billion or almost 44 percent of these outstanding Treasury bills.[14] Purchases and sales of U.S. Treasury bills by foreign central banks could well dominate the bill market. Indeed, their acquisition of $10 billion or so worth of Treasury bills in the year prior to 30 April 1972 was probably a major factor in driving the yield on Treasury bills down below 4 percent in early 1972—in contrast to long-term corporate bonds that returned 7 1/2 percent. Unlike most of the postwar period, foreign official purchases of some classes of dollar securities are now large enough to affect yields in U.S. financial markets quite significantly.

Well, what difference does it make, anyway? Unfortunately, foreign official purchases of dollar securities can now aggravate balance-of-payments disequilibria in a way that would not have happened in the early postwar period. Suppose that the United States has a deficit that is completely sterilized, and foreign central banks buy U.S. Treasury bills in the open market. These purchases drive down short-term interest rates in the United States so that private capital is then induced to flow abroad. The U.S. balance-of-payments deficit is aggravated—at least in the short run—and foreign central banks must acquire more dollar assets and interest rates go down further. The system has become unstable—at least for some short periods.[15]

Hence, the very size of current foreign holdings of dollars, and capital flows in the international economy, provide reason for giving more weight to a Beta policy. An unusual balance-of-payments deficit would then lead to some contraction in the U.S. monetary base that has, as its counterpart, some *new* net issue (sale) of Treasury bills by the Federal Reserve. Short-term rates of interest are maintained or even increased in the United States. Private capital then flows so as to equilibrate rather than to destabilize the international balance of payments. Asymmetrical adjustment, in the sense that foreign money supplies expand while the U.S. does not contract, is avoided.

Of course, to say that the balance of payments should be given some weight in the short run is not to advocate exclusive reliance on it. Nor should the U.S. authorities stop trying to get the appropriate smooth expansion in monetary aggregates over longer periods. However, adherence to full and automatic sterilization of short-run imbalances in international payments could well be reconsidered by the United States.

6.4 Monetary Reform: A Concluding Note

My analysis of the sterilization problem—for dependent economies, Euro-currencies, and the United States—has focused on the need for mutual adjustment of money supplies at each of these three levels. It has stressed the need for consistent "rules of the game" to guide monetary management in individual countries—including the reserve center—assuming that the degree of flexibility in exchange rates was subject to international control. The overall objective was, simply, to stabilize the international supply of money.

Unfortunately, most of the issues explored above—presumptive rules against fully sterilizing payments imbalances, restraints on the composition of dollar assets, and so on—have been outside the purview of international monetary agreements actually concluded, such as those at Bretton Woods or the Smithsonian Institution. They have been outside the scope of entirely new proposals such as the one presented by the U.S. Secretary of the Treasury in the fall of 1972. Instead, official efforts have focused more narrowly on the important problem of designing a consistent set of foreign-exchange parities (as well as on the creation of official reserve assets).

Even with the successful negotiation of a parity system, however, there remains a pressing residual need to have mutual adjustments in national money supplies, as long as central banks continue to buy and sell foreign exchange. Stabilizing operating rules may develop without formal agreement, as for example, the tendency from 1950 to 1966 toward partial sterilization of payments imbalances by countries other than the United States. However, there are so many reciprocal costs and benefits, and so many quid pro quos—particularly as they involve constraints on American monetary policy—that more formally negotiated agreements could be of great social benefit.

Notes

The author is indebted to Donald Mathieson, Edward Shaw, and John Scadding for their valuable comments.

1. For a fairly recent example of this kind of projection, see Rudolph Rhomberg, "Transmission of Business Fluctuations from Developed to Developing Countries," *IMF Staff Papers*, March 1968.

2. The developed countries considered are the United States, Canada, the United Kingdom, Sweden, Denmark, Norway, France, West Germany, Belgium, Netherlands, Italy, Austria, and Japan. The developing countries include Chile, Brazil, Argentina, Bolivia, Mexico, Uruguay, Colombia, Peru, Pakistan, the Philippines, South Korea, China (Taiwan), Israel, Greece, and Thailand.

Ideally, quarterly data compiled in a similar manner for all countries are desirable. Unfortunately, developing countries seldom publish quarterly data, and often the accounts of one country are compiled in a different manner from those of another country. While little has been done about the lack of quarterly data, the OECD has recently attempted to standardize annual national accounts across countries. The data for the developing countries are found in the OECD, *National Accounts of Less Developed Countries, 1950–66* (published July 1968); and OECD, *Latest Information on National Accounts of Less Developed Countries* (published 1971). The data for the developed countries are taken from the OECD, *National Accounts Statistics, 1950–68*.

3. These results were part of a larger project done by Donald Mathieson of Columbia University and myself, the details of which are reported more comprehensively in "Instability in Underdeveloped Countries: The Impact of the International Economy," in *Nations and Households in Economic Growth: Essays in Honor of Moses Abramovitz*, ed. Paul A. David and Melvin W. Reder (New York: Academic Press, 1974).

4. Again, for a more detailed discussion of this rather unexpected statistical problem, see Mathieson and McKinnon (note 3 above).

5. The reader is referred to Mathieson and McKinnon for disaggregation and further analysis of the regression equations used in table 6.1.

6. Belgium, France, Germany, Italy, Japan, Netherlands, Sweden, United Kingdom, and the United States.

7. Michael Michaely, *The Responsiveness of Demand Policies to Balance of Payments: Postwar Patterns* (National Bureau of Economic Research, Columbia University Press, 1971), p. 63.

8. Presuming that the ratio of reserves to outstanding deposits held by private nonbank public is approximately the same for the commercial banks in either country.

9. *International Financial Statistics*, International Monetary Fund, December 1973, p. 23. I have ignored the much smaller holdings of sterling that are also included in this series.

10. See, for example, Fritz Machlup, "The Magicians and Their Rabbits," *Morgan Guaranty Survey*, Morgan Guaranty Trust Company, May 1971, pp. 3–13.

11. For a description of this problem and the one preceding, see Milton Friedman, "Monetary Aggregates and Monetary Policy" (mimeographed), University of Chicago, June 1971.

12. A. E. Berger and Anatol Balbach, "Measurement of the Domestic Money Stock," *Federal Reserve Bank of St. Louis Review*, May 1972, pp. 10–23.

13. Even in the less common case where the Bank of France continued to hold demand or time deposits with Chase Manhattan, there would be no shrinkage in the American monetary base. Foreigners would simply own more of M_1 or M_2.

14. All data taken from the *Federal Reserve Bulletin*, June 1972. A problem exists in ascertaining the exact official holding of Treasury bills by foreigners because there are other "certificates of indebtedness" that are not broken out separately.

15. The same argument has been elaborated in greater detail by Donald Mathieson in "Dollars, Deficits, and Foreign Central Bank Portfolio Decisions" (mimeographed), March 1972, and to whom I am obviously deeply indebted.

7   Currency Substitution and Instability in the World Dollar Standard

Should foreign-exchange considerations or observed growth in the money supplies of other industrial countries significantly influence the domestic monetary policy of the United States? The received wisdom of both monetarist and Keynesian economists and the revealed preferences of U.S. policymakers has been to try—often unsuccessfully—either to suppress international influences or to ignore them. Both groups define policy targets in terms of growth rates in purely *domestic* monetary aggregates, or in terms of domestic (dollar) rates of interest.

Indeed one of the main objectives of Milton Friedman's persuasive advocacy (1953) of floating exchange rates was to secure, without the use of exchange controls or other trade distortions, national monetary autonomy for all countries—whether they be the United States, Germany, Canada, or Brazil. This point of view has been vigorously espoused by both Keynesians such as James Meade (1955) and monetarists such as Harry Johnson (1972); it was influential in persuading policymakers to accept (albeit under pressure) the advent of floating exchange rates among industrial countries in 1973—followed by formal legal ratification through amendment of the IMF's Articles of Agreement in 1976. And monetarists have a strategy for exercising this autonomy: each country pursues its own fixed monetary growth rule as if the demands for national monies were stable and independent of one another.

In contrast, the admittedly casual empirical evidence presented below suggest a radically different view: the national (convertible) monies of an inner group of industrial countries are highly

Originally published in *The American Economic Review* 72, 3 (June 1982): 320–333. Reprinted with permission.

substitutable in demand according to anticipated exchange-rate movements. This international currency substitution destabilizes the demand for individual national monies so that one can't make much sense out of year-to-year changes in purely national monetary aggregates in explaining cycles in purely national rates of price inflation.

However, all is not necessarily lost for the monetarist view. The world demand for money seems relatively stable. By considering a crude index of a "world" money supply (confined to the convertible currencies of industrial countries), the two great outbreaks of international price inflation in the 1970s become explicable. The world money supply exploded in 1971–72 and again in 1977–78 (well before the two oil crises of 1973 and 1979). Speculation against the U.S. dollar was combined with exchange interventions by foreign central banks (to prevent the dollar from falling) that directly expanded money supplies in Europe and Japan. How this inflationary pressure was divided among countries depended on relative exchange-rate movements in each case, but the impact on the world price level was unambiguous. Even for the United States itself, this tentative measure of changes in the world money supply explains the great (dollar) price inflations of 1973–74 and 1979–80 much better than does any domestic American monetary aggregate.

But why didn't the American money supply decrease as people shifted out of dollars into foreign monies? First, the American monetary authorities were operating myopically under a fixed domestic money growth rule over a monthly or quarterly time horizon. Secondly, in the very short run, the U.S. money stock did not contract automatically in response to official exchange intervention. Because the United States is the reserve-center country under the world dollar standard, even massive dollar interventions by foreign central banks are usually sterilized of any impact on the American monetary base—as described in the theoretical model given below.

But the sterilization appropriate for the strong dollar standard under the fixed exchange rates of the 1950s and 1960s (chapter 5 above) is less benign under today's managed floating and volatile exchange-rate expectations. I conclude by briefly discussing how American monetary policy should be suitably "internationalized" in order to better stabilize both the international and American price levels.

7.1 The Evidence

The usual procedure would be to present an ostensibly complete structural model of the international macroeconomy, and then estimate the individual parameters by using elaborate econometric techniques only loosely related to the theoretical model. The nature and quality of the data would not be discussed, but the unprocessed statistical series might be available from the author upon special request.

Here, I follow a different strategy. First unprocessed but standardized data on the industrial countries' national money supplies, price levels, and foreign exchange reserves are compiled from the *International Financial Statistics* of the International Monetary Fund (IMF). Without trying to build a comprehensive model of income, employment, or price levels in the world economy, two extreme cases where international currency substitution seemed to lead to a loss of monetary control are identified. Then a very short-run and highly simplified analytical model is developed to explain what happened in those two episodes and, possibly, in other less easily identified cases.

The money supplies, whose rates of change appear in table 7.1, are defined narrowly to include currency and mainly non-interest-bearing checking accounts—although some countries do include deposits bearing fixed rates of interest in this M1 category. Precisely which of these convertible currencies are the strongest substitutes for one another, and which should enter with the heaviest weights in any index of world money, is not addressed. Nevertheless, table 7.1 includes the principal monies that are used for invoicing world trade and for denominating internationally liquid wealth in the Euromarkets. But Eurocurrency deposits per se are omitted because they are more like bonds in bearing an equilibrium market rate of interest and in not being usable by nonbanks for making payments to third parties (Helmut Mayer 1979). In short, I am interested in a narrow definition of money in the spectrum of financial assets, but one which has effective potential as an international medium of exchange and standard of value.

Table 7.1
World Money Supply Increases: Ten Industrial Countries (percentage changes between year-end stocks)

	U.S.	Canada	Japan	U.K.	Germany	France	Italy	Netherlands	Belgium	Switzerland	Weighted World Average
(GNP weights 1970)	(.5174)	(.0432)	(.1042)	(.0648)	(.0989)	(.0804)	(.0491)	(.0167)	(.0137)	(.0115)	
1960	0.6	4.0	36.6	0.4	7.2	14.1	13.6	6.7	1.9	5.0[a]	7.03
1961	3.3	12.7	18.4	2.0	14.5	15.5	16.0	7.7	7.7	15.3	8.18
1962	2.5	4.3	16.6	-5.0	6.8	18.1	17.6	7.5	7.2	11.3	6.23
1963	3.2	7.3	34.6	14.5	7.2	14.5	13.6	9.3	9.6	7.3	9.43
1964	4.7	9.4	13.0	3.2	8.5	8.3	7.5	8.0	6.6	6.5	6.57
1965	4.8	14.3	18.2	3.9	7.7	9.4	16.4	10.0	7.1	3.8	7.88
1966	2.4	7.3	13.9	0.0	1.9	7.8	13.3	6.8	6.6	3.8	4.72
1967	7.5	4.0[a]	14.1	7.6	10.0	4.8	15.7	6.2	3.2	6.7	8.38
1968	8.1	0.6	13.3	3.9	7.6[a]	8.0	11.9	11.4	7.2	11.9	8.26
1969	3.3	-4.2	20.6	0.0	5.3	-2.5	15.9	8.1	-6.0	11.0	4.96
1970	4.3	1.8	16.8	9.3	8.6	11.4	27.4	11.8	7.0	11.0	8.19
1971	6.5	13.1	29.7	15.2	12.8	11.8	19.0	15.0	11.1	18.4	11.77
1972	9.1	12.2	24.7	14.0	14.1	14.9	17.3	17.6	15.2	5.7	12.73
1973	5.7	8.8	16.8	5.1	1.7	9.8	24.3	0.0	7.5	0.0	7.65

1974	3.0	1.5	11.5	10.8	10.7	15.2	9.4	12.2	6.2	-3.3	6.51
1975	5.5	19.0	11.1	11.0[a]	14.3	12.6	13.4	19.7	15.7	4.4	9.22
1976	5.9	1.5	12.5	11.3	3.3	7.5	18.8	8.2	7.0	10.5	7.36
1977	8.2	10.4	8.2	21.5	12.0	9.3[a]	21.4	13.2	8.3	0.6	10.27
1978	8.2	7.0	13.4	16.4	14.2	11.1	26.6	4.1	5.9	19.7	10.98
1979	8.0	1.4	3.0	9.1	3.2	11.9	23.7	2.8	2.5	-1.3	7.60
1980	5.3	10.7	-2.1	3.9	4.0	6.4	12.9	6.0	0.3	-0.5	4.88

Source: All data are non-interest-bearing M_1 and are taken from line 34 of the *International Financial Statistics*: 1975–80 data from the February 1982 issue, and 1960–74 data from the 1981 yearbook.
[a]Implies a discontinuous series where arbitrary averaging was used.

Annual percentage growth rates in the nominal money supplies of the ten industrial countries in table 7.1 are then averaged using weights corresponding to their nominal GNP in 1970—the last year of more or less fixed exchange rates and the midpoint of my 20-year data series. This aggregation procedure for measuring the growth in world money neatly avoids incorporating continual exchange rate fluctuations (Harold Van Cleveland and Bruce Brittain 1976), and ignores national differences in GNP growth and in growth in real money stocks. The United States enters with a heavy unchanging weight of .5174. More importantly, no econometric attempt is made to distinguish the international moneyness of, say, the Italian lire from that of the German mark.

Nevertheless, the weighted average of world money growth appearing in the right-hand column of table 7.1—with a trend rate of about 8 percent per year—clearly reveals the monetary consequences of the two major episodes of "bear" speculation against the dollar: (1) 1971–72: the anticipated collapse of official dollar parities under the Bretton Woods and then the Smithsonian agreements; and (2) 1977–78: the attempt by officials in the Carter Administration to talk the dollar down, culminating in the massive stabilization program of November 1, 1978.[1]

During both these major episodes (and in a host of minor ones), foreign central banks were heavily intervening—but to varying degrees—to prevent their currencies from appreciating against the dollar. Because of passive sterilization by the Federal Reserve (as explained below), the American money supply was undiminished even as foreign money supplies rose substantially above their trends. Thus, the world money supply rose unusually rapidly to between 10 and 13 percent per year in 1971–72 and again in 1977–78: the far right column in table 7.1.

These international losses of monetary control were followed—with lags of uncertain duration—by inflationary explosions in 1973–74 and 1979–80, as one can see from the price-level data in table 7.2. Using the same 1970 GNP weights, one can aggregate wholesale price levels internationally to get a weighted world average price index in the right-hand column of table 7.2. In measuring international inflationary pressure, wholesale indices come closer than consumer price indices do to providing a common denominator of tradable goods.

Table 7.2
World Price Inflation: Ten Industrial Countries (percentage changes from past year's period average)

	U.S.	Canada	Japan	U.K.	Germany	France	Italy	Nether-lands	Belgium	Switzer-land	Weighted World Average
(GNP weights 1970)	(.5174)	(.0432)	(.1042)	(.0648)	(.0980)	(.0804)	(.0491)	(.0167)	(.0137)	(.0115)	
1960	0.1	0.1	0.1	1.3[a]	1.1	3.6[c]	0.9	−2.5[d]	1.1	0.6[d]	0.6
1961	−0.4	1.1	0.1	3.8	1.5	3.0	0.1	−1.2	−0.1	0.2	.5
1962	0.2	2.8	−1.6	2.1	3.5	0.5	3.1	1.2	0.7	3.5	.7
1963	−0.4	1.9	1.7	1.2	0.4	2.8	5.3	2.5	2.5	3.8	.8
1964	0.2	0.4	0.2	2.9	1.1	3.6	3.2	6.2	4.7	1.3	1.1
1965	1.3	2.1	0.7	3.7	2.4	0.7	1.6	3.5	1.0	0.5	1.5
1966	3.3	3.5	2.4	2.8	1.8	2.7	1.6	4.5	0.6	1.9	2.9
1967	.2	1.8	1.8	1.2	−1.0	−0.9	−0.1	0.0	0.0	0.3	.3
1968	2.4	2.2	0.9	3.9	−0.7	1.7	0.3	1.1	1.2	0.1	1.5
1969	4.0	4.7	2.1	3.4	1.8	10.7	3.9	0.0	3.4	2.9	4.0
1970	3.6	1.4	3.6	7.1	4.9	7.5	7.3	6.4	6.0	4.1	4.4
1971	3.3	1.2	−0.8	9.0	4.3	2.1	3.4	1.0	1.9	2.2	3.1
1972	4.5	7.0	0.8	5.3	2.6	4.6	4.1	4.0	4.1	3.6	4.1
1973	13.1	21.5	15.9	7.3	6.6	14.7	17.0	12.4	7.4	10.7	12.9

Table 7.2
(continued)

	U.S.	Canada	Japan	U.K.	Germany	France	Italy	Netherlands	Belgium	Switzerland	Weighted World Average
1974	18.9	22.1	31.3	23.4	13.4	29.2	40.7	13.6	20.1	16.2	21.9
1975	9.2	6.7	3.0	24.1	4.7	-6.1	8.5	7.5e	4.5	-2.3	7.5
1976	4.6	5.1a	5.0	17.3	3.7b	7.4	23.8	7.8	7.1	-0.7	6.6
1977	6.1	7.9	1.9	19.8	2.7	5.6	16.6	5.8	2.4	0.3	6.6
1978	7.8	9.3	-2.5	9.1	1.2	4.3	8.4	1.3	-2.0	-3.4	5.6
1979	12.5	14.4	7.3	12.2	4.8	13.3	15.5	2.7	6.3	3.8	11.1
1980	14.0	13.4	17.9	16.3	7.5	8.8	20.1	8.2	5.8	5.2	13.5

Source: All data are wholesale price indices from *International Financial Statistics* (various issues), line 63.
aSeries based on industrial output prices.
bNew series based on industrial product prices.
cSeries based on industrial goods prices (tax included).
dSeries based on home and import goods prices.
eNew series based on final product prices.

Were foreign exchange interventions responsible for this loss of monetary control? Those increases in the (gross) foreign-exchange reserves of different countries that are associated with increases in their domestic monetary bases are hard to identify. Table 7.3 presents data on the direct dollar liabilities of the U.S. government—almost all in the form of U.S. Treasury bonds and bills—to the governments of Canada, Japan, and Western Europe. (Rather arbitrary valuation changes in monetary gold stocks have nothing to do with foreign-exchange intervention, and the physical quantities of gold held by industrial countries have been relatively stationary. Hence gold positions as well as

Table 7.3
Dollar Liabilities of the United States Government to Foreign Central Banks and Official Agencies (in billions of U.S. dollars; year-end stocks)

	Canada[a] (1)	Japan[b] (2)	Western[c] Europe (3)	Total (1) to (3)	Annual Percentage Change (5)
1963	1.79	1.59	8.51	11.89	
1964	1.81	1.50	9.32	12.63	+6.2
1965	1.70	1.57	8.83	12.10	−4.4
1966	1.33	1.47	7.77	10.57	−14.5
1967	1.31	1.45	10.32	13.08	+23.7
1968	1.87	2.26	8.06	12.19	−7.3
1969	1.62	2.61	7.07	11.30	−7.9
1970	2.95	3.19	13.61	19.75	+74.8
1971	3.98	13.78	30.13	47.89	+142.0
1972	4.25	16.48	34.20	54.93	+14.7
1973	3.85	10.20	45.76	59.81	+8.9
1974	3.66	11.35	44.33	59.34	−0.8
1975	3.13	10.63	45.70	59.46	+0.2
1976	3.41	13.88	45.88	63.17	+6.2
1977	2.33	20.13	70.75	93.21	+47.6
1978	2.49	28.90	93.09	124.48	+33.5
1979	1.90	16.36	85.60	103.86	−19.9
1980	1.56	21.56	81.59	104.71	+0.8

Source: All data from *International Financial Statistics*.
[a]Line 4aad, *IFS* (United States).
[b]Because direct U.S. liabilities to the Japanese government were not available, the virtually identical series on total Japanese reserves in foreign currency was used—line 1d.d, *IFS* (Japan).
[c]Line 4abd, *IFS* (United States).

Special Drawing Rights are ignored in table 7.3.) Because the industrial countries (unlike LDCs) tend *not* to diversify their offical reserves into Eurodollar deposits or foreign exchange assets other than dollars, the buildup of direct dollar claims on the U.S. government is a good approximation of their cumulative intervention in the foreign exchanges. Of course, under the asymmetrical world dollar standard, the U.S. government itself has negligible net accumulations of foreign-exchange reserves.

Fortunately, in interpreting the crude data in table 7.3, the very sharp run-ups of foreign-exchange reserves by Western Europe and Japan in 1970–72 and 1977–78 are so striking that one need not quibble about whether or not direct dollar claims on the United States are an inclusive measure of foreign-exchange intervention. From virtually zero growth in the 1960s, the rate of foreign-exchange accumulation rose to about 70 percent per year in 1970–72. After another quiescent period of zero growth, foreign-exchange accumulation again rose to about 40 percent per year in 1977–78—before falling back to zero net growth. These marked increases in foreign reserves are sufficient to explain the sharp increases in money supplies in Europe and Japan that dominated world money growth in 1971–72 and 1977–78, as portrayed in table 7.1.

To be consistent with the idea of a stable aggregate demand for "world money," the resulting world price inflation—after a one- or two-year lag—should be quite general in 1973–74 and again in 1979–80 as seems to be true in table 7.2. By comparison, individual rates of growth in national money supplies are—by themselves—quite puzzling as explanations of national inflation rates. For example, in 1978 Switzerland's money growth was 19.7 percent and the American money growth was "only" 8.2 percent; yet the United States experienced price inflation at about 13 percent in 1979–80, whereas Switzerland's rate was only about 4.5 percent. *In general, growth in the world money supply is a better predictor of American price inflation than is U.S. money growth.* Switzerland avoided the same inflationary pressure by letting its currency appreciate.

While not conclusive, the data are at least consistent with the idea that national monies are substitutable to the extent of making national money demand functions appear quite unstable if foreign exchange considerations are ignored. In the 1980s, it seems highly questionable for even the center country, the United

States, to pursue a purely nationalistic monetary rule irrespective of whether money supplies of other convertible currency countries were sharply expanding or contracting—or irrespective of whether the dollar was falling or rising in the foreign-exchange market.

7.2 A Model of the World Demand for Money

Following Alexander Swoboda (1978), consider only two countries: the United States issues dollars and the rest of the world (ROW) issues a single convertible currency called *rowa*. The ROW is an analytical abstraction only for industrial countries other than the United States. However, demand for either of these two non-interest-bearing monies could well originate, in part, with third countries whose own currencies are inconvertible and which are not formally part of the analysis. Nevertheless, dollars are mainly demanded for monetary circulation in the United States, and *rowa* for monetary circulation in ROW. The margin of substitutability between the two remains to be described.

A complete picture of international inflation would link money creation to realized price and possibly output increases—with differing variable lags. Such a complex process cannot be captured within a simple analytical framework. Focus instead on the much narrower problem of how changing exchange-rate expectations immediately influence the demand for *rowa* relative to dollars and the total supply of world money. In analyzing these monetary disturbances in the very short run, assume that national price levels, real incomes, and the spot exchange rate are all given. Fixing the spot exchange rate between dollars and *rowa* roughly reflects the current propensity of ROW government to intervene by "leaning against the wind" to prevent any immediate sharp changes. (Prior to 1973, it would have represented an attempt to maintain an official parity.) This presumed short-run stability in the spot exchange rate under managed floating allows us to aggregate the two national money stocks, and define the world's nominal money stock, M^w, to be

$$M^w = M + SM^*, \tag{1}$$

where M is U.S. money stock (dollars), M^* is ROW money stock (*rowa*), and S is dollars/*rowa*.

Although the spot exchange rate is stable within a very short time horizon of a few days, private expectations of future exchange-rate movements may be quite volatile from time to time. Let s represent the expected change in S, averaged into the near future of "several weeks." The parameter s is equal to the discount on the dollar in the forward exchange market, which reflects anticipated dollar depreciation,

$$s = E\{dS/dt\} = (F - S)/S, \tag{2}$$

where F is the forward exchange rate.

Fluctuations in s are given *exogenously* to the model. They may reflect pure foreign-exchange disturbances as when the American Treasury Secretary suggested early in 1977 that the dollar was overvalued; or they may vary simultaneously with changing assessments of future American monetary policy vis-à-vis ROW monetary policy. Indeed, historical evidence suggests that exchange-rate movements (beyond the very short-run official commitment to managed floating) are highly sensitive to perceived or actual changes in monetary policy (Peter Bernholz 1981). Without spelling out all the mechanisms by which s could change, the analysis begins rather arbitrarily with an expectations shock in the form of a discrete change in s.

Perfect Capital Mobility

With free Euromarkets and the absence of sustained exchange controls that separate national markets in interest-bearing securities, for analytical purposes suppose the international bond market is "perfect." After taking expected exchange-rate changes, s, into account, investors are indifferent between investing in short-term dollar or *rowa* bonds. Define this common nominal world yield on bonds to be i^w: the opportunity cost of holding money in the demand function for world money.[2]

$$M_d^w/P = L(i^w, Y^w), \tag{3}$$

where $Y^w = Y + Y^*$ is given world income, and P is the given world price level.

With P and Y^w given in the very short run, the demand function describes how i^w must vary to accommodate any changes in the world's money supply. The function L describes Keynesian liquidity preference on a global scale.

As a first approximation, we shall ignore any direct effect that changes in s might have on i^w or on the *world* demand for money. This would require a more complete macro-model specifying how s influences expected world price inflation. Hence s does not appear in world money demand—equation (3). But s directly affects individual money demands and the rates of interest on dollar bonds and on *rowa* bonds. Assume that

$$i = i^w + (1 - \alpha)s \qquad (4)$$

$$i^* = i^w - \alpha s \qquad (5)$$

where (4) is interest rate on dollar bonds and (5) is interest rate on *rowa* bonds.

Suppose $\alpha = B/B^w$ is the financial weight of the United States in the world capital markets as measured by the (given) ratio of dollars to total bonds outstanding. For the single term to maturity in equation (4), a rise in s (the expected dollar depreciation) will force up the dollar rate of interest by $(1 - \alpha)s$. In the 1950s and early 1960s, during the "strong" dollar standard and American financial predominance, α was likely close to unity: as $\alpha \to 1$, $i \to i^w$ for any given s. The interest rate on dollar bonds dominates our hypothetical world rate of interest, and changes in s have a negligible impact on interest rates in the American money market.

In the 1980s, on the other hand, the financial importance of the United States in the world's bond market has been reduced so that α may be closer to, say, one-half. In this latter case, an increase in s leads to a more symmetrical adjustment: the (short-term) rate of interest on dollar bonds is forced up by $s/2$ and that on *rowa* bonds is forced down by $s/2$. In this more symmetrical situation, nominal rates of interest in U.S. money markets are no longer determined solely by domestic influences. The dollar rates of interest on federal funds or U.S. Treasury bills become even more treacherous as short-run indicators of monetary ease or tightness.

Finally, consider two strong implications of the perfect capital mobility assumption embedded in equations (4) and (5):

$i - i^* = s$ (Fisher Open Condition)   (6)

$i^w = \alpha i + (1 - \alpha)i^*$ (Integrated Capital Market)   (7)

The short-term interest differential accurately reflects expected exchange-rate movements, and the world interest rate is simply a weighted average of the two national interest rates. Clearly, these are very strong implications of the perfect capital markets assumption, and this dominance of the foreign exchanges in domestic interest-rate determination may not be valid during much of the 1960–80 period. Nevertheless, in the two extreme episodes of 1971–72 and 1977–78 when expectations of dollar depreciation were highly developed, this simplifying assumption gives insight into how currency substitution actually occurred and is consistent with interest-rate movements actually observed (see chapter 13 below).

A Two-Stage Money Demand Function

This consistent weighting of the United States and ROW in the international bond market makes the world demand for money independent of *s*. However, the *distribution* of demand between dollars and *rowa*, for any given M_d^w, will be highly sensitive to expected changes in the exchange rate. Let β be the dollar share of world money such that

$$M_d = \beta(s; Y/Y^w)M_d^w,$$ (8)

$$SM_d^* = (1 - \beta)M_d^w,$$ (9)

where (8) is demand for dollars and (9) is demand for *rowa*.

In effect we have a two-stage money demand function. The first stage—equation (3)—describes the world demand for money, and the second stage—equations (8) and (9)—divides that demand between the two currencies. In the short run, the share of dollars in M_d^w declines with *s*, and the share of *rowa* increases commensurately so as to keep the total demand for world money constant for any given world interest rate. Hence $\partial\beta/\partial s < 0$ is a convenient measure of pure *currency substitution* between dollars and *rowa*. On the other hand, in the short run, α is insensitive to *s* because interest rates on bonds adjust to compensate their owners.

The first channel through which an increase in s raises M_d^* and reduces M_d is when large commercial banks, and possibly some nonfinancial multinationals, shift their non-interest-bearing working balances from dollars into *rowa* to reduce direct losses from anticipated dollar devaluation. Ordinarily, a rather small proportion of each country's non-interest-bearing money stock would be owned by such trade-oriented institutions. Hence this direct form of currency substitution, Channel One, may well be significant without being dominant.[3]

Instead, the indirect route, Channel Two, which utilizes our strong assumption of perfect mobility in the international bond market, is likely to lead to greater substitution between the two monies and to create a larger capital outflow from the United States. Let us take a simple example. In a situation where $\alpha = 1/2$, suppose s increases from 0 to 6 percent because the American Secretary of the Treasury decides that the dollar is overvalued. The "perfect" international bond market quickly adjusts to these new exchange-rate expectations: the incipient arbitrage pressure to move out of dollar bonds into *rowa* bonds causes interest rates to adjust immediately: i rises by three percentage points, and i^* falls by three percentage points. At this stage, significant capital outflows need not occur if expectations are commonly held, and interest rates adjust immediately so as to eliminate the incentives for profiting from international arbitrage in interest-bearing securities.[4]

Currency substitution induced by these interest-rate changes occurs indirectly. American transactors naturally try to sell non-interest-bearing dollar cash balances and buy dollar bonds when i jumps upward by three percentage points—and foreign transactors sell *rowa* bonds and buy *rowa* cash balances. But this arbitrage from money to bonds tends to decrease i and increase i^* so as to reduce $i - i^*$ below s, thus creating temporary pressure in the international bond market. In our example, the interest differential falls incipiently below six percentage points. Then international bond arbitragers do the rest: they sell dollar bonds and buy *rowa* bonds to preserve $i - i^* = s$. This additional capital outflow from the United States is exactly equal to the reduced demand for dollar cash balances and to the augmented demand for *rowa* cash balances. Because most domestic transactors (money owners) in the United States and in ROW are influenced by these interest-rate changes, this indirect form of currency substitution may well be the most important quantitatively. *Massive capital flows can easily be induced even when the interest differential remains "correctly" aligned to reflect accurately the change in expected exchange depreciation.*

Throughout the above analysis of money demands, I have assumed that the authorities maintain the spot exchange rate at S. Indeed, this provided part of the analytical basis for our world money demand function—equation (3). The next step is to look more explicitly at the short-run supply mechanism arising out of this foreign-exchange intervention.

7.3 The Supply of International Money

The supply of world money is under the joint control of the U.S. Federal Reserve System and ROW bank, which is the single hypothetical central bank representing the other convertible currencies. Because the United States is the reserve center, only the ROW bank directly enters the foreign exchange market to smooth the spot exchange rate, S. How such intervention may, in turn, influence the money supply (monetary base) of either country is important to spell out—as has been done by Lance Girton and Dale Henderson (1976), Robert Heller (1976), Alexander Swoboda (1978), and Richard Marston (1980). However, none of these authors has focused on my main theme: how currency substitution potentially destabilizes the world's money supply even when the world's aggregate demand for money is stable.

For simplicity, I ignore fractional reserve banking and the separate existence of commercial banks: at this level of abstraction no significant conclusions would change from building them into the model. Hence, the *rowa* component, M^*, of the world's money supply held by nonbanks is simply direct claims on ROW bank; and M is dollar claims of nonbanks on the Federal Reserve. The sum of these central bank liabilities is world money as defined by equation (1).

Reflecting the workings of the international dollar standard, (10) is a simple balance sheet equation showing both the domestic and foreign assets upon which *ROW* bank expands the *rowa* money supply:

$$M^* \equiv A^* + M_r/S + B_r/S, \tag{10}$$

where A^* is domestic (*rowa*) assets, M_r is dollar deposits with the Fed, and B_r is U.S. Treasury bonds owned by ROW bank.

Equation (11) is the balance sheet identity showing the assets and liabilities of the Federal Reserve System:

$$M + M_r \equiv A, \tag{11}$$

where A is domestic (dollar) assets.

From (10) and (11), the world's monetary base is simply the sum of domestic assets held by each central bank plus nonmonetary U.S. Treasury bonds held by ROW bank.

$$M + SM^* = M^w = A + SA^* + B_r. \tag{12}$$

The important asymmetry in the world system hinges on how ROW bank (with the concurrence of the Fed) chooses to hold its dollar reserves. If as a result of foreign-exchange intervention, ROW bank purchases U.S. Treasury bonds B_r in the open market, then the world money supply increases—according to equation (12)—as long as the domestic asset positions of each central bank are fixed. This closely corresponds to actual practice as shown by foreign holdings of U.S. treasury bonds in table 7.3. However, if ROW bank chooses to build up and hold direct depository claims on the Fed, M_r, the world's money supply would remain unchanged because the reduction in dollar holdings by nonbanks (the dollar money supply) is offset by a rise in the *rowa* money supply. How ROW bank holds its dollar reserves is important, and the consequences of each alternative are explored below.

The Nonsterilization of Exchange Interventions

If a central bank purchases foreign exchange, the domestic monetary base initially expands and the foreign monetary base potentially contracts. Under the present system of managed floating, should governments remain free to influence their exchange rates directly without accepting these immediate monetary consequences? Central banks often take offsetting actions—through open-market operations, changed reserve requirements, or rediscounting—to sterilize the domestic monetary impact of these official interventions.

Within our simple model of the world dollar standard, ROW bank would have to consciously contract its domestic assets in order to sterilize the influence of a buildup in its foreign assets. Clearly, sterilization would make it much more difficult for ROW bank to meet its exchange-rate target. Moreover, Hans Genberg and Swoboda (1981) provide evidence that when sterilization occurs in Europe and elsewhere, it is only partial. Hence, let us assume for analytical purposes that ROW bank does not sterilize: A^* is constant as foreign-exchange intervention takes place.

To impose a nonsterilization rule on the Federal Reserve System (in response to ROW bank's interventions) requires more than keeping domestic assets A constant—or on a predetermined Friedman growth path. Dollar claims accumulated by ROW bank should be allowed to contract the American money supply in the hands of the nonbank public. And having ROW bank build up dollar claims M_r—perhaps interest bearing—on the Federal Reserve System would be the simplest technique. Although in practice, the direct deposits of foreign central banks with the Fed are only transitory, let us provisionally assume that ROW bank holds all its exchange reserves in this form, that is, assume that $B_r = 0$ and $M_r > 0$.

What then are the monetary consequences of discretionary shifts in either central bank's domestic asset position (A or A^*) or in exogenous changes in the relative attractiveness of dollars versus *rowa* as denoted by the parameter s? From equation (12) and the assumption that $B_r = 0$, the relevant money multipliers are

$$dM^w/dA = dM^w/d(SA^*) = 1, \text{ and}$$
$$dM^w/ds = 0. \tag{13}$$

By varying its domestic assets by one dollar, each central bank has exactly the same impact on the world's money supply: one dollar. From our world money demand function, equation (3), each has an equal impact on the world rate of interest, i^w. In addition, the world's money supply is independent of s—any changes in the expected rate of dollar devaluation. The nonsterilization procedure prevents flights from one currency to another from upsetting the world's stock of money—while allowing the authorities to automatically track this changing demand for each national money. This last result can easily be seen by computing the multiplier effect of a change in s for each national currency:

$$dM/ds = (d\beta/ds)M^w = -\Delta M_r < 0. \tag{14}$$

The stock of dollars changes according to our currency substitution parameter $d\beta/ds$ weighted by the world's money stock: a change that in turn is equal to the international flow of capital, ΔM_r. The American money stock changes dollar for dollar according to the reduced demand for it—neither more nor less. Similarly, the stock of *rowa* increases symmetrically by as much as the stock of dollars decreases.

$$dM^*/ds = (d\beta/ds)M^w/S = \Delta M_r/S > 0. \tag{15}$$

In response to open-market operations in domestic assets by either central bank, the individual money multipliers are:

$$dM/dA = dM/d(SA^*) = \beta(s); \tag{16}$$

$$dM^*/d(A/S) = dM^*/dA^* = 1 - \beta(s). \tag{17}$$

Domestic credit expansion by either central bank has exactly the same effect on national money supplies, as well as on the world money supply. However, when A increases, capital flows out of the United States by $(1 - \beta)\Delta A$, and when A^* increases, capital flows into the United States by βA^*. The M_r adjusts by the amount of each capital flow.

What room then does our stabilizing rule of no sterilization leave for discretionary monetary policy on the part of our two countries? Although each national money supply changes endogenously with official foreign-exchange intervention, the monetary base for the world as a whole still depends on the domestic components of each country's monetary base, A and A^*. Without generating net international capital flows, secular rates of growth in A and SA^* could be designed roughly to equal the increase in demand for world money at a constant price level (see my 1974 article and chapter 22), whereas random short-run shifts in demand between national monies by private speculators would be fully accommodated by official intervention in the foreign exchanges *without* losing control over the world's money supply.

Passive Sterilization and Increasing Currency Instability

Our short-run analysis simply assumed that ROW bank intervenes to maintain S, the spot exchange rate. I am not necessarily advocating such intervention, although a carefully delimited case can be made for it (chapters 20 and 22). More important is to ensure that intensive official intervention of the kind that occurred in the 1970s does not result in further inadvertent losses of international monetary control in the 1980s. Under the workings of the dollar standard, however, foreign official interventions have been conducted so as to leave the supply of dollars relatively unchanged while foreign money supplies—and the weighted world average money supply—have fluctuated erratically (see table 7.1).

To demonstrate what happens when sterilization occurs, suppose foreign-exchange interventions result in only transitory and negligible changes in M_r—deposits of ROW bank with the Federal Reserve—such that $M_r \simeq 0$. Instead such deposits are used immediately to buy U.S. Treasury bonds, B_r. In practice, foreign central banks from industrial countries hold almost all their foreign-exchange reserves in nonmonetary U.S. government bonds or bills as indicated in table 7.3. These may be purchased directly with dollar demand deposits in U.S. commercial banks (which are not represented in the model) or the Federal Reserve itself simply acts as a broker by immediately buying U.S. Treasury bonds on account for ROW bank in response to incipient increases in M_r. Either method results in *sterilization* because the dollar money supply in the hands of the nonbank private sector is insulated from foreign official transactions.[5] It is *passive* because the Federal Reserve is not consciously sterilizing with offsetting changes its own domestic asset position. Rather, the American money supply is insulated from changes in official reserves by the willingness of foreign central banks to hold nonmonetary U.S. government debt.

In contrast, the supply of *rowa* outstanding responds fully to foreign exchange interventions by ROW bank. Our assumption of perfect capital mobility ensures that ROW bank cannot successfully manipulate A^* to offset these changes.

The equilibrium world money supply arising out of this asymmetrical sterilization procedure can then be calculated by substituting equations (9) and (10) into equation (12) to eliminate B_r in order to get

$$M^w = A/\beta(s). \tag{18}$$

The world money supply now is solely a function of the *domestic* asset position of the Federal Reserve Bank[6] and of the share of dollars in M^w; it does not depend at all on the domestic asset position of ROW bank.[7] (In contrast, A^* had an equivalent impact on M^w in the nonsterilization case.) Furthermore, the impact of A on world money increases according to the multiplier $1/\beta$. Suppose the U.S. share in world money β is decreasing perhaps because the other convertible currencies are becoming more important with fewer exchange controls. Then actions by the Federal Reserve to change A are increasingly magnified in their international impact.

This magnified Federal Reserve multiplier by itself need not lead to a loss of international monetary control. If, in the long run, the Federal Reserve calculates the growth in demand for dollars correctly, that is, $\Delta M = \beta \Delta M\,{}^w_d$, and then increases A commensurately, the world's money growth remains determinate and potentially noninflationary. But the system is hardly fail-safe if the Federal Reserve makes even minor miscalculations regarding the growth in demand for dollars.

In the 1950s and early 1960s under the fixed exchange rates of Bretton Woods, a Federal Reserve policy of passive sterilization of foreign official interventions—coupled with monetary policy based purely on domestic indicators—could justifiably be called "benign neglect" of the rest of the world (see chapter 5). First β was probably close to unity because only a limited number of foreign currencies were convertible on capital account so that the dollar dominated the supply of "international money"; and secondly, exchange rates were—by and large—convincingly fixed so that expected fluctuations leading to international currency substitution were minimal.

However, with managed floating, more volatile exchange-rate expectations, and a secular decline of the share of dollars in world money in the 1970s and 1980s, the old strategy of benign neglect is more questionable. Indeed, differentiating equation (18) with respect to the expected exchange-rate change, we have

$$dM^w/ds = (-A/\beta^2)(d\beta/ds) > 0. \tag{19}$$

The supply of world money is now more sensitive to expected changes in exchange rates because β has declined, and because the degree of currency substitution $d\beta/ds$ has likely increased.

An increase in expected dollar depreciation causes a multiple capital outflow from the United States, a multiple expansion in the *rowa* money supply—but no offsetting contraction in the supply of dollars because of passive sterilization. This is the simple analytics underlying the two explosions in the world money supply in 1971–72 and again in 1977–78 shown in table 7.1.

7.4 Policy Implications

Within the context of my simple two-country model of managed floating and perfect capital mobility, the solution to international currency instability is straightforward: the Federal Reserve System should discontinue its policy of passively sterilizing the domestic monetary impact of foreign official interventions. Instead, a symmetrical nonsterilization rule would ensure that each country's money supply mutually adjusts to international currency substitution in the short run, without having official exchange interventions destabilize the world's money supply. Then, long-run monetary control could be secured by coordinated domestic asset expansion by each central bank: increases in A and A^* that match each country's share of world money, and which, together, just satisfy the demand for M^w at an approximately stable international price level.

However, we do not live in a simple two-country world. In reality, ROW is a hodgepodge of countries whose governments intervene continually, and most hold at least some reserves in U.S. Treasury securities. Only a modest number of the 140 countries in the world have currencies that are convertible on current account, and even fewer extend convertibility to capital-account transactions. At most, systematic monetary cooperation with the United States can only extend to a very small inner group: those countries that are sufficiently large and stable to offer monies that significantly compete with dollar cash balances internationally. Elsewhere I have suggested (1974 and 1980 as synthesized in chapter 22) that Germany, Japan, and the United States are capable of jointly bringing the world's supply of convertible money under control through a mutual nonsterilization pact *and* agreed-on rates of domestic credit expansion by each of the three central banks. In acting optimally under a continuing world dollar standard, this triumvirate would still follow a monetary policy of benign neglect (passive sterilization) with respect to dollar interventions by other countries.[8]

A critic might well argue that a more basic problem is "dirty" floating: the continued propensity of central banks to intervene directly despite the absence of official par-value obligations. If the governments of industrial countries agreed not to intervene at all in the foreign exchanges, and if each followed fixed domestic monetary growth rules, control over the world's money supply would be secured automatically. Such a nonintervention agreement would seem easier to negotiate than a nonsterilization pact.

Unfortunately, the noninterventionalist solution implicitly presumes that the demand for each national money is stable. But governments in increasingly open economies are unable to risk prolonged upward or downward movements in their currencies (particularly against the dollar) because of the possibility of cumulative currency substitution in favor or against the national currency (table 7.1), and also the unsettling direct effects that major exchange-rate movements have on the domestic economy. For a fiat money without intrinsic value, the direct stabilization of its international purchasing power in the short run may be viewed (possibly correctly) as an important first line of defense in stabilizing its domestic purchasing power in the longer run.

Even in the United States itself, which is a huge relatively closed economy, expected dollar depreciation and international currency substitution in 1971–72 and again in 1977–78 substantially reduced the demand for dollars. Measured growth in American $M1$ thus seriously understated the degree of inflationary pressure in the system—pressure that was more accurately reflected in the "world" money supply series appearing in table 7.1. The doctrine of "domestic monetarism," where the Federal Reserve System keys on some purely American monetary aggregate such as $M1$ or $M2$ and ignores the foreign exchanges, is increasingly inefficient for preventing global inflation or deflation—and for stabilizing American income and prices.[9]

7.5 Addendum: The Great Deflation of 1981–82

Over 1979–81, money growth ($M1$) slowed down more drastically in Germany, Japan and Switzerland—countries providing substitute international reserve currencies to the dollar—than did growth in American $M1B$. True to its doctrine of domestic monetarism, the Federal Reserve System chose to ignore this monetary contraction occurring abroad.

What forced the Swiss, German, and Japanese central banks to let their monetary growth rates fall so sharply? World monetary demand shifted sharply away from their monies (and that of several other smaller countries) toward dollars. On the positive side, it became likely in 1980 that a new "free-market" government would be elected in the United States which would have much lower inflation targets. And there was political turmoil in Europe: the threat in Poland of a Russian invasion and the election in France of a socialist government predisposed to expropriate private wealth. The dollar—previously battered in 1977–78—surged upward on the world's foreign exchange markets in 1980–81 and on into 1982. After watching their currencies depreciate quite sharply, these three central banks entered to prevent further price-level disalignment by selling dollars and repurchasing their own currencies thus contracting that part of world money ($M1$) denominated in Swiss francs, marks, and yen. There was no automatic offsetting expansion in the American monetary base to accommodate the increased demand for dollars because of the passive sterilization associated with the normal operations of the world dollar standard.

Thus has speculation in favor of the dollar in 1980–81 imposed unduly sharp deflation on the world economy, just as speculation against the dollar in 1971–72 and again in 1977–78 fueled the two great inflations of the 1970s.

Notes

I would like to thank John Cuddington and James Powell for helpful comments.

1. This unfortunate official perception that the dollar was overvalued was based on an emerging U.S. trade deficit in 1977. However, one can explain (see chapter 13) the deficit on fiscal grounds rather than on exchange-rate or price-level disalignment. The initial tendency for the dollar to fall led to a loss of monetary control in the United States, and a much bigger dollar devaluation than the authorities wanted.

2. Throughout the analysis, the subscript d represents demand. Thus M_d^w is the ex ante world money demanded at the going interest rate, where M^w is the actual stock of world money in existence.

3. Bruce Brittain (1981) provides some independent evidence that the velocities of money in Germany and the United States are inversely related according

to the interest differential between dollar and DM bonds. Marc Miles (1978) concludes that currency substitution exists between Canada and the United States also based on the interest differential that incorporates expected changes in exchange rates, whereas Arturo Brillembourg and Susan Schadler (1979) compute semielasticities of substitution between the dollar and a number of other currencies.

4. Notice that the forward discount on the dollar would instantaneously go to 6 percent to match the interest differential. Our assumption of perfect capital mobility eliminates the need to consider the forward market separately.

5. Anatol Balbach (1978) describes comprehensively how official reserve transactions impinge—or fail to impinge—on the American monetary base.

6. This result is similar to that of Swoboda (1978), who, however, did not make β an endogenous variable that might fluctuate with s.

7. Increases in A^* will result in offsetting decreases in B_r so as to leave the *rowa* money supply unchanged. With A^* fixed, capital flows depend directly on A and β according to $dB_r/dA = (1 - \beta)/\beta$.

8. Consider one further caveat to even this partial solution for stabilizing the world's supply of money. Our two-country theoretical model assumed perfect capital mobility. Yet we know that both the German and Japanese authorities have imposed controls on capital movements from time to time. In the presence of current-account surpluses or deficits (which were not present in the analytical model presented above), sterilization by the Bundesbank or Bank of Japan may be justified insofar as either is simply acting as an international financial intermediary because normal flows of private capital have been disrupted. Rescinding the assumption of "perfect" capital mobility, however, requires a more elaborate analytical model yet to be developed.

9. The doctrine of "domestic Keynesianism," where the government keys on some domestic nominal rate of interest (possibly insulated from the international economy by exchange controls), is likely to be even more inadequate (see my 1979 book and my 1980 article). However, a full treatment of the Keynesian approach requires an analysis of open-economy fiscal policy under the world dollar standard. That is a story for another time.

References

Balbach, Anatol, "The Mechanics of Intervention in Exchange Markets," *Federal Reserve Bank of St. Louis Review*, February 1978, *60*, 2–7.

Bernholz, Peter, "Flexible Exchange Rates and Exchange Rate Theory in Historical Perspective," unpublished, March 1981.

Brillembourg, Arturo T., and Schadler, Susan, "A Model of Currency Substitution in Exchange-Rate Determination, 1973–78," *IMF Staff Papers*, September 1979, *26*, 513–42.

Brittain, Bruce, "International Currency Substitution and the Apparent Instability of Velocity in Some Western European Economies and in the United States," *Journal of Money, Credit and Banking*, May 1981, *13*, 135–55.

Friedman, Milton, "The Case for Flexible Exchange Rates," in *Essays in Positive Economics*, Chicago: University of Chicago Press, 1953, 157–203.

Genberg, Hans, and Swoboda, Alexander K., "Gold and the Dollar: Asymmetries in World Money Stock Determination, 1959–1971," unpublished, April 1981.

Girton, Lance, and Henderson, Dale W., "Financial Capital Movements, and Central Bank Behavior in a Two-Country, Short-Run Portfolio Balance Model," *Journal of Monetary Economics*, January 1976, 2, 33–62.

Heller, Robert, "International Reserves and World-Wide Inflation," *IMF Staff Papers*, March 1976, 23, 61–87.

International Monetary Fund, *International Financial Statistics*, Washington, various years.

Johnson, Harry, "The Case for Flexible Exchange Rates," in *Further Essays in Monetary Economics*, Winchester: Allen and Unwin, 1972, 198–222.

McKinnon, Ronald, "Private and Official International Money: The Case for the Dollar," *Princeton Essays in International Finance*, No. 74, Princeton University, 1969.

———, "A New Tripartite Monetary Agreement or a Limping Dollar Standard?," *Princeton Essays in International Finance*, No. 106, Princeton University, 1974.

———, *Money in International Exchange: The Convertible Currency System*, New York: Oxford University Press, 1979.

———, "Dollar Stabilization and American Monetary Policy," *American Economic Review Proceedings*, May 1980, 70, 382–87.

———, "The Exchange Rate and Macroeconomic Policy: Changing Postwar Perceptions," *Journal of Economic Literature*, June 1981, 19, 531–57.

Marston, Richard, "Cross Country Effects of Sterilization, Reserve Currencies and Foreign Exchange Intervention," *Journal of International Economics*, February 1980, 10, 63–78.

Mayer, Helmut W., "Credit and Liquidity Creation in the International Banking Sector," *Economic Papers #1*, Bank for International Settlements, November 1979.

Meade, James E., "The Case for Variable Exchange Rates," *Three Banks Review*, September 1955, 27, 3–27.

Miles, Marc, "Currency Substitution, Flexible Exchange Rates, and Monetary Independence," *American Economic Review*, June 1978, 68, 428–36.

Swoboda, Alexander, "Gold, Dollars, Euro-Dollars, and the World Money Stock under Fixed Exchange Rates," *American Economic Review*, September 1978, 68, 625–42.

Van Cleveland, Harold, and Brittain, Bruce, *The Great Inflation: A Monetarist View*, Washington: National Planning Association, 1976.

8   Why U.S. Monetary Policy Should Be Internationalized

No one doubts that the world economy is in serious trouble, but the monetary origins of the disorder are not well understood. Mainline Keynesian and monetarist theories suggest that by floating its exchange rate, each nation can—and should—freely exercise national monetary autonomy. These theories induce policymakers to ignore valuable information provided by the foreign-exchange markets and by monetary events in other countries.

Fortunately, practical central bankers in today's increasingly open economies do not always stick with these insular doctrines. For example, in the 1970s both the Bank of England and the U.S. Federal Reserve System (the Fed) abandoned their (Keynesian) targets for domestic interest rates because of unexpected domestic inflationary pressure and because of even more pronounced depreciation of their national moneys on the foreign exchanges.

In 1979, both central banks realized that disinflation was imperative, and each then adopted the monetarist principle of prespecified (and declining) rates of *domestic* money growth as their new operating target. Subsequently both countries were hit with unexpectedly sharp exchange appreciations—sterling in 1979–1980 and the dollar in 1980–1982—that converted disinflation into depression. Again chastened, each central bank wisely abandoned rigid adherence to domestic monetarism—the Federal Reserve being somewhat more explicit in suspending its M1 (currency in circulation plus checking account deposits) target

Originally published in *To Promote Peace: U.S. Foreign Policy in the Mid-1980s*, ed. Dennis Bark (Hoover Institution, Stanford University, 1984), 57–68.

in October 1982. But the result is an apparent analytical vacuum regarding the future conduct of monetary policy.

There is a way out. By shifting the focus of monetary policy from a national to a carefully specified international level, each central bank can avoid severe and disruptive exchange-rate disalignments. But more is required of the Fed because it is at the center of the world dollar standard. To stabilize world prices successfully and avoid the boom-and-bust cycles characteristic of the recent past, the Fed must act as the balance wheel of the international system—explicitly compensating for shortfalls or excesses of monetary growth in other hard-currency countries such as Germany and Japan.

8.1 Dollar Appreciation and the Slump of 1981–82

Before examining the reconstruction of the international system, let us try to understand why the slump of 1981–82 was worldwide. Embracing accepted monetarist doctrine in October 1979, the Fed slowed money growth in the United States without reference to the foreign exchanges or monetary conditions in other industrial countries. Annual growth in M1 fell moderately from about 8 percent in 1977–79 to about 5 to 6 percent from 1980 to October 1982. But such a moderate decline in U.S. money growth does not explain the severe slump in the industrial economies, accompanied by a global banking crisis arising from economic deterioration in less developed debtor nations. What went wrong?

In late summer 1980, the dollar unexpectedly began to rise against other hard currencies (see figure 8.1). The origins of this sharp appreciation now seem partly political and partly economic. The anticipated election of a conservative U.S. president strengthened political support for Fed Chairman Paul Volcker's policy of disinflation. Dollar assets suddenly looked more attractive to multinational firms, Arab sheikhs, foreign central banks, and others—particularly those that had reduced their dollar holdings (in favor of European currencies or yen) during the great dollar depreciation of 1977–78.

In Europe, the Polish crisis threatened German banks and European military security. In early 1981, France elected a social-

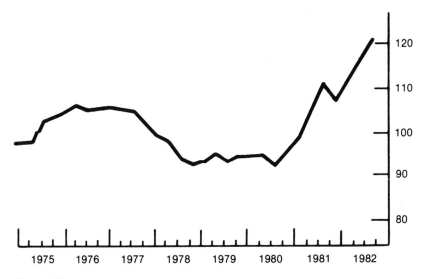

Figure 8.1
The power of the dollar (average trade-weighted value of the dollar measured against seventeen currencies of major industrial trading partners; 100 equals the average in 1975).
Source: International Monetary Fund, *International Financial Statistics,* 1983.

ist government—with an inflationist bent—that promised to tax and expropriate private wealth. In several smaller European economies, unsustainable welfare burdens precipitated political and financial crises. Thus over 1980–82, political and economic accidents prompted investors to move from European currencies into dollars.

With U.S. encouragement, the Tokyo capital market was first opened to foreign borrowers in 1980. Because interest rates abroad seemed excessively high to the Japanese government, however, it prevented yields on yen loans and deposits from rising to international levels. The resulting capital outflow exceeded the Japanese trade surplus, causing the yen to depreciate against the dollar. Despite the competitiveness of Japanese exports in U.S. markets, this unfortunate financial imbalance caused the yen to stay weak until November 1982, when dollar interest rates finally decreased and the Japanese political crisis was resolved with the selection of Yasuhiro Nakasone as prime minister.

8.2   The Fed's Blind Spot

These seemingly nonmonetary and largely unforeseeable events aggravated the great dollar appreciation of 1980–82; they also had grave monetary consequences. The upsurge in foreign demand for U.S. Treasury securities, industrial bonds, equities, bank deposits, real estate, and so on, indirectly increased the demand for money in the United States. But the Federal Reserve had committed itself to a fixed rate of domestic monetary growth. With increased demand and unchanging supply, the result was unexpectedly tight money.

In the United States, the resulting deflationary pressure worked, in part, through the overvalued dollar. Between 1980 and the fall of 1982, the dollar rose about 20 percent against the yen and 25 percent against the mark. But Germany and Japan had much lower rates of domestic price inflation over the same period. The result was a loss of international competitiveness by those U.S. industries most exposed to foreign trade—manufacturing, mining, farming. They became severely depressed, leading to an unfortunate outbreak of protectionist sentiment.

Because the dollar had far overshot its norm in the foreign-exchange market, people began to anticipate—incorrectly, for all of 1981 and most of 1982—that the dollar would depreciate to its purchasing power parity. But this expectation contributed to keeping short-term interest rates on dollar assets much higher than on yen or mark assets, a further source of deflationary pressure in interest-sensitive industries in the United States. Instead of falling in response to the upsurge in foreign demand for U.S. financial assets, U.S. interest rates initially moved in the wrong direction because the dollar had been allowed to appreciate too much.[1]

If the Fed followed an internationalist monetary policy, a stable exchange rate would be an important monetary target. Then upward pressure on the dollar in the foreign exchanges (against other hard currencies) would clearly signal that U.S. monetary policy was too tight. In the United States, money supply would automatically expand, allowing interest rates to fall and rebalance the international bond market without having the dollar overshoot its appropriate value in the foreign exchanges.

8.3 The Impotence of Foreign Central Banks

But why should foreign economies become depressed just because the U.S. Fed fails to respond correctly? At first glance, one might expect offsetting inflationary pressure in those industrial economies whose currencies had become undervalued. Unfortunately, the overvalued dollar triggered two sources of deflationary pressure abroad in addition to the depression emanating from the United States.

First, after watching their monies depreciate, some foreign governments worried about a possible run on their currency and about provoking increased U.S. protectionism. Many resisted depreciation by intervening in foreign-exchange markets to repurchase their own currency (with dollar reserves), thus contracting their domestic money growth. In Germany and Japan during 1980–81, growth in M1 fell sharply and magnified the worldwide deflationary effect of the Fed's more modest slowdown (see figure 8.2).

Second, the *private* sectors in foreign countries usually have dollar debts exceeding dollar assets, reflecting the facts that the United States is an international creditor and that the dollar is the dominant international reserve currency. An unexpected appreciation of the dollar tends to increase foreigners' debt burdens measured in their own currency and so curtails private

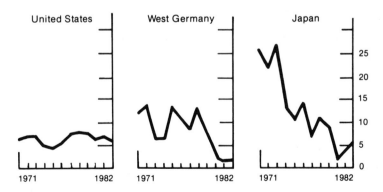

Figure 8.2
Swings in money supply (annual percentages in M1).
Source: Federal Reserve Bank of St. Louis.

spending. Indeed, massive private bankruptcies could result from a depreciation of the domestic currency. For heavily indebted less developed countries, this reduction in net wealth is further aggravated when world depression reduces the dollar prices of their primary products.

In summary, with heavy speculative pressure in favor of the dollar and no compensating action by the Federal Reserve System, foreign monetary authorities are hard-pressed to avoid an ensuing depression. If a central bank intervenes successfully to prevent exchange depreciation, its domestic money supply contracts. Simply letting its domestic currency depreciate may provoke harmful protectionism in the United States and make the financial position of its dollar-indebted private sector precarious.

Obversely, foreign central banks are no better able to avoid worldwide inflation on their own. The two great inflationary explosions of the 1970s can be traced to speculation *against* the dollar, leading to dollar devaluation and uncontrolled monetary growth in other industrial countries (see chapter 7). The open U.S. economy felt the full impact of each inflationary episode.[2]

8.4   The Need to Coordinate Central Bank Policies

Sustained recovery—where future cycles of inflation and deflation are avoided—is only possible if the principal central banks jointly agree:

1. to avoid major misalignments in exchange rates and sudden changes in the international competitiveness of different countries; and

2. to adopt a new international standard for controlling world money growth in order to stabilize the prices of internationally traded goods and thus allay inflationary (or deflationary) expectations for the future.

Fortunately, among the world's 150-plus countries, only a small group (from Western Europe, Japan, and North America) provides effectively convertible (hard) monies usable for international trade and capital flows. And only among these countries is agreement necessary or indeed even possible. Because the deutsche mark is the central hard currency of the European

Monetary System (EMS), "Germany" will be a shorthand designation for "Europe" in the following discussion. Countries such as the United Kingdom and Switzerland, currently not members of the EMS, would be welcome members of a broader agreement.

To simplify discussion, however, let us concentrate on how monetary relationships among the larger economies of the United States, Germany, and Japan should be harmonized.

8.5   A New Operating Principle for the Fed

Because Germany and Japan intervene continually to mitigate misalignments in their dollar exchange rates, their monetary policies are already significantly internationalized. Still, since 1970 Germany and Japan have suffered unduly large fluctuations in their currency's exchange rate and in their national money supply that magnified world business cycles. The crux of the problem is the failure of the Federal Reserve System to support these well-intentioned foreign interventions.

If the Fed contracted the U.S. money supply when foreign central banks were induced to buy dollars because their own currencies had appreciated unduly or if it expanded U.S. money when foreign central banks had to sell dollars, the system would be more stable. Exchange rates would move within a much narrower range. Most important, growth in the *sum* of the money supplies of hard-currency countries would be smoother: the Fed would naturally increase U.S. money when foreign money growth decreased, and vice versa. The international cycle of boom and bust, which we have experienced since 1970, would be greatly dampened.

In general and nontechnical terms, how could the Fed best announce its new operating principle—without panicking the always panicky gnomes of the financial community? British journalist Samuel Brittan has kindly volunteered what the Fed's spokesman should say:

In fixing its short-term monetary growth objectives, the Fed now intends to take into account the overseas as well as the domestic demand for dollars ... When the dollar was particularly strong against other currencies, the money supply target would be increased; when it was weak the target would be reduced. (*Financial Times*, 12 July 1982)

This much the Federal Reserve System could do without any formal pact with foreign central banks and without any new legislation from the U.S. Congress.

8.6   A Tripartite Monetary Agreement?

A formal agreement for harmonizing monetary policies among the three countries might make this new procedure securer. The Bundesbank, Bank of Japan, and U.S. Federal Reserve could jointly agree to fix a trend rate of growth in the monetary base for the system as a whole, while encouraging (offsetting) variances in national money growth rates according to the international ebb and flow of demand for each of their currencies as indicated by pressure on their exchange rate. Targeting base money growth would be designed to stabilize a broad price index of internationally traded commodities, an index that could be common to all three countries once exchange-rate fluctuations diminished.

Although not to be underestimated, the technical difficulties of implementing such a pact are no greater than trying to run each national monetary policy separately without the cooperation of foreign central banks. Changing international asset preferences has made the demand for each national money too unstable for independent national monetary policies to be successful. And a formal tripartite agreement, signed with due pomp and circumstance, would dramatically signal international investors that their future would be secure whether they be in yen, deutsche marks, or dollars.

Milton Friedman objects that the political difficulties of securing such agreement are overwhelming:

The economic objections to the proposal are dwarfed by the political objections. A verbal agreement is possible, but a credible and enforceable one, next to impossible. But even if it were, the proposal involves giving great and essentially discretionary powers to an international body independent of any political control by citizens of each member-country short of withdrawal from the agreement.[3]

Yet to successfully circumscribe the autonomy of central banks as Friedman wants requires that the monetary authorities be given the correct guidelines: rules that, if followed systematically, would indeed succeed in stabilizing the domestic economy. To this end, stabilizing the exchange rate against other hard currencies is a necessary condition (even for the U.S. economy of the 1980s). Moreover, it is relatively easy to monitor whether central bankers do stabilize exchange rates.

Somewhat more difficult to agree on, and to monitor, is the appropriate rate of growth in "world" money: the weighted sum of monetary aggregates. But this problem is very similar to that already faced by each national authority operating independently. Should one target M1 or M2 or M3? How can the short-run rate of growth of any broad monetary aggregate be stabilized when money multipliers vary unpredictably? For international coordination, I have shown that emphasizing control over the joint monetary base is a way of potentially finessing these ambiguities.[4] (See also chapter 22.)

Apart from these rather arcane technical questions of monetary control, however, the U.S. government would be more politic with its allies if ongoing monetary cooperation succeeded in preventing sharp fluctuations of the dollar against other hard currencies and prevented the accompanying cycles of worldwide inflation and deflation of the past dozen years with which we are all too familiar.

8.7   Recovery in 1983

Unduly sharp deflation and dollar overvaluation precipitated the worldwide slump of 1982. Starting from this disequilibrium, how should the monetary policies of Germany, Japan, and the United States be ideally coordinated to overcome depression on the one hand and correct the overvalued dollar on the other? (Readers may judge for themselves how much the policies actually followed differed from this ideal.)

Getting out requires some carefully formulated, once-and-for-all monetary expansion (in 1983) above the normal trend of monetary growth in this triumvirate. Because near-term inflationary expectations were sharply reduced in the United States, one expects an upward shift in the demand for base money in dollars that the Fed should accommodate.

To allay legitimate fears of future inflation, however, any monetary expansion in 1983 is best coupled with the Fed's adopting a more internationalist operating procedure: one that convincingly limits future monetary growth in the world system in general and in the United States in particular. Subsequent monetary growth in the three countries (the Fed could hypothetically explain) would slow to a normal rate designed to secure zero price inflation in a broad basket of internationally traded manufactured goods and primary commodities. Moreover, the Fed would make clear that extraordinary monetary expansion in the United States would only continue as long as the dollar remained overvalued against the yen and the mark and the threat of dollar price inflation was minimal. This strategy is fully credible only if the Bundesbank and the Bank of Japan agree *not* to expand until the dollar is properly aligned.

In summary, monetary expansion for the system as a whole should always be concentrated in that country whose currency is unusually strong in the foreign exchanges.

What if international investors become disturbed, dump dollars in favor of yen and marks, and thus precipitate a further sharp devaluation of the dollar? When the dollar exchange rate becomes approximately correct in terms of marks and yen, the three central banks would simply switch roles: monetary growth would be curtailed in the United States and be increased in Germany or Japan, depending on whose currency was the strongest.

This plan requires that the three central banks agree on an "equilibrium" set of dollar/yen and dollar/mark exchange rates for approximately aligning national price levels, as they have evolved into early 1983. It does *not* involve any mercantilist juggling of exchange rates for the purpose of fully eliminating bilateral trade surpluses or deficits between any pair of countries. To a considerable extent, surpluses and deficits in current balance-of-payments accounts are a natural and desirable consequence of allowing capital to flow freely from one country to another. They are heavily influenced by fiscal deficits or surpluses in each trading partner.

For all the ills of the international economy in 1983, the unexpectedly sharp deflation in the United States has brought its basic inflation rate much closer to those prevailing in Germany and Japan. Consequently, once dollar/yen and dollar/mark exchange rates are appropriately realigned in the course of our once-

and-for-all monetary expansion, future significant exchange adjustments would likely be unnecessary and unwise.

8.8   Fiscal Deficits and International Competitiveness

But monetary policy, however well managed among the three countries, cannot do the whole job. The sorry state of the public finances in the United States will continue to disrupt the international economy. By appropriating almost all personal savings, the federal budget deficit of over $200 billion severely damages domestic industry through high U.S. interest rates that crowd out productive investment. And the Japanese government is inhibited from relaxing interest-rate ceilings in Tokyo, with the unfortunate consequences discussed above.

Massive dissaving by the federal government literally forces the U.S. economy to rely on the savings of other nations. High rates of interest attract financial capital from Japan, Europe, and the Third World, thus forcing greater real appreciation of the dollar in foreign exchanges. The resulting decline in U.S. net exports merely reflects the trade deficit necessary to absorb capital from abroad. The trade deficit is thus caused and dominated by the much larger U.S. fiscal deficit.

Without the benefit of a Japanese trade surplus and savings transfer to the United States, real rates of interest in the United States would be even higher—making economic recovery more difficult. But the burden of absorbing this foreign capital falls disproportionately on U.S. tradable goods industries, which are understandably upset.

In short, correcting the trade deficit and preventing a severe outbreak of protectionism require that the United States put its fiscal house in order. This would free surplus Japanese saving to provide yen-dominated finance for the Third World—a more appropriate role for Japan as a natural international creditor.

8.9   Conclusion

Among financially open economies, the exchange rate indicates when national monetary policies are relatively too tight or too easy. Since 1980, the overvalued dollar has been sending a clear signal to U.S. monetary authorities that they should ease up

relative to their German and Japanese counterparts. Criticism of
the Fed for unduly rapid monetary expansion in 1982 and in 1983
was unwarranted. There is scope for harmonizing the monetary
policies of Germany, Japan, and the United States with great
mutual benefit—even if the United States' fiscal problem is not
satisfactorily resolved.

Notes

1. For readers interested in a more technical description of the failure of interest
rates to adjust correctly, leading to an overshooting of the exchange rate, see
chapter 17.

2. For a fuller examination of foreign-exchange-based inflation in the 1970s
under the world dollar standard, when there is speculation against the dollar,
see Ronald McKinnon, "Currency Substitution and Instability in the World
Dollar Standard," *American Economic Review*, June 1982, pp. 320–33.

3. Milton Friedman, "Monetary Policy for the 1980s," in John H. Moore, ed.,
To Promote Prosperity: U.S. Domestic Policy in the Mid-1980s (Stanford: Hoover
Institution Press, 1984), chap. 2.

4. For the specific technical procedures by which monetary coordination
among the U.S. Federal Reserve, the Bank of Japan, and the Bundesbank could
be carried out in practice, see chapters 20 and 22.

9 Money Supply versus Exchange-Rate Targeting: An Asymmetry between the United States and Other Industrial Economies

9.1 Introduction

For floating exchange rates from the early 1970s to 1985, this paper identifies a fundamental asymmetry in the conduct of monetary policy by the United States on the one hand, and the principal European economies as well as Japan on the other.

Following a changing mix of purely domestic American monetary indicators, the Federal Reserve System, typically, did not adjust U.S. money growth to stabilize the dollar exchange rate before 1985. Indeed, more often than not, American monetary expansion was negatively correlated with the strength of the dollar in the foreign-exchange markets: easing when the dollar was weak and tightening when it was strong so as to exaggerate exchange-rate fluctuations.

In contrast, from 1971 to 1985 West Germany (representing the continental European bloc) and Japan, on average, adjusted their domestic money growth to be correlated positively with the strength of their currencies against the dollar in the foreign exchanges. In effect, the Bundesbank, other European central banks, and the Bank of Japan opted, although with but limited success, to stabilize their dollar exchange rates: on average, they increased domestic money growth when their currencies were appreciating and contracted with exchange depreciation.

Originally published in *Macro and Micro Policies for More Growth and Employment*, ed. H. Giersch (J. C. B. Mohr, 1988), 245–264. Part of this chapter also appeared in "The U.S. Price Level and the Dollar Exchange Rate," *Macroeconomics, Agriculture, and Exchange Rates*, ed. P. Paarlberg and R. Chambers (Westview Press, 1988), 81–120. Reprinted with permission.

This asymmetry has important implications for monetary control within the United States and for the nature of the international business cycle. I shall argue that, by being excessively "nationalistic" in ignoring information contained in the foreign exchanges in the 1970s and early 1980s, the Federal Reserve System did a rather poorer job of stabilizing the domestic American price level, while needlessly aggravating exchange-rate fluctuations and business cycles in the world economy.

Subsequently, a regime change might have occurred. Starting in 1985 with the Plaza Hotel accord, European central banks and the Bank of Japan kept their money growth rates quite low through 1987 despite the dollar's fall in the foreign exchange. The Federal Reserve System shifted from high money growth in 1985–86 to very low growth in 1987—apparently because of the run on the dollar in that year. Although this 1985–87 monetary response pattern to floating exchange rates differs substantially from the earlier experience, it is too recent to be analyzed in the body of this paper. (But it is analyzed in chapters 2 and 22: the Plaza-Louvre Accords of rule box 5.)

Nevertheless, the earlier experience, where the Fed virtually ignored the strength or weakness of the dollar in the foreign exchanges from 1971 to early 1985 while other central banks did systematically respond, is of great interest in its own right—and could happen again. So let us analyze this asymmetrical floating-rate dollar standard (rule box 4, chapter 2).

9.2 The International Dollar Standard

As is well known, the Bretton Woods system of fixed exchange rates lasting from 1945 to 1971 was, in reality, a dollar standard. In order to peg their currencies to the dollar within a narrow band, industrial countries other than the United States intervened continually in the foreign exchanges and adjusted their domestic money growth to support their dollar parities. In contrast, the United States (as the Nth country) was uniquely free to pursue purely domestic monetary objectives without having to react so directly to pressures in the foreign exchanges—although the gold convertibility constraint occasionally put weak indirect pressure on the American monetary authorities.

With the advent of floating exchange rates in the early 1970s, it is rather surprising that asymmetric elements of the old fixed-rate dollar standard persisted. The dollar remained the invoice currency for a high proportion of international trade (particularly in primary commodities) and the important currency of denomination for cross-country capital flows (McKinnon 1979). Hence, monetary authorities in other industrial countries, more open than the United States, found that preserving either internal price level stability or international competitiveness required that they try to smooth their dollar exchange rates.

When portfolio disturbances emanated from the United States, other industrial countries behaved as if they were acting collectively: they expanded when the dollar was weak and contracted when it was strong (chapter 7). Each was also anxious to offset any domestic portfolio disturbance that would move its dollar exchange rate out of line with those of other industrial competitors.

9.3   Some Evidence of Monetary Asymmetry

These effects are not easy to measure unambiguously. The more successful central banks are in stabilizing their dollar exchange rates, the less correlation between exchange rates and domestic money growth can one observe. The covariance that remains may be quite sensitive to the choice of time period—weeks, months, or quarters—within which the correlation is measured. There are many definitions of exchange rates, money supplies, and so forth. Hence, the statistical procedures used here are only indicative, and must be interpreted with caution.

Figure 9.1 shows the International Monetary Fund's index of the nominal or "effective" dollar exchange rate, "merm," weighted against 17 other industrial countries. Fluctuations in such a broad measure of the dollar exchange rate are likely dominated by portfolio disturbances in the American financial markets, rather than those in specific foreign countries. What then were (are) the reaction functions of central banks?

Let quarterly percentage rates of change in M1 measure the monetary response of each central bank, and then correlate these with quarterly percentage changes in the IMF's effective dollar exchange rate. It turns out that within-quarter correlations are not high, and become progressively lower as one disaggregates to (noisier) monthly and weekly data. However, using five-quarter moving averages of both changes in the effective dollar exchange

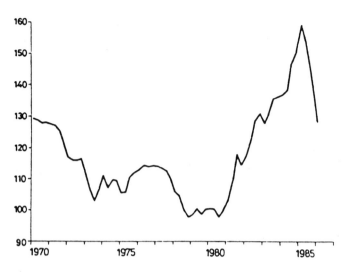

Figure 9.1
U.S. nominal effective exchange rate (1980 = 100).
Source: IMF (various issues).

and national money-growth rates yields the strikingly negative correlations shown in figure 9.2 and tables 9.1 or 9.2.

Figure 9.2 shows the collective monetary response of the seven principal industrial countries other than the United States: the U.K., Canada, France, Germany, Italy, Japan, and the Netherlands. Among convertible-currency countries providing portfolio alternatives to holding dollar assets, these seven dominate the stock of transactions balances in the form of M1—and thus are simply called the "rest of the world" or ROW.

Without taking relative exchange-rate movements[1] into account, how can one unambiguously aggregate over the seven countries to calculate *percentage growth* in ROW money? For the 1970–85 period from which the data are taken, define money growth in the rest of the world to be

$M^{ROW} = \Sigma(w^i M^i) \ i = 1, 2, \ldots, 7$
where M^i = growth in M1, and   (1)
$\qquad w^i$ = relative weight (GNP for 1977) of ith country
$\qquad$ such that $\Sigma w^i = 1$

And this measure of growth in ROW money is that which is plotted in figure 9.2.

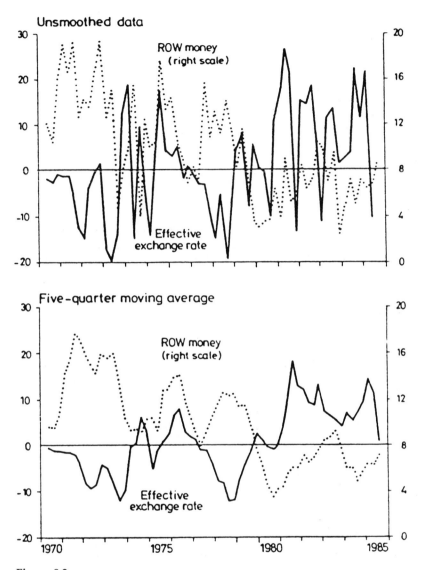

Figure 9.2
Rate of change for U.S. effective exchange rate and the rest of the world money (percentage per year).
Source: IMF (various issues); Federal Reserve Bank of St. Louis (various issues).

Table 9.1
The Dollar Exchange Rate and Money Growth in the United States, Japan, and Germany: Correlation Matrix for the 1970.IV–1986.II Period

	Not detrended				Detrended			
	E^{US}	M^{US}	M^{JA}	M^{GE}	E^{US}	M^{US}	M^{JA}	M^{GE}
E^{US}	1				1			
M^{US}	−0.417*	1			−0.690*	1		
M^{JA}	−0.405*	−0.245	1		−0.388*	0.486*	1	
M^{GE}	−0.499*	0.112	0.452*	1	−0.455*	0.514*	0.156	1

Source: As for figure 9.2.
*Significant at the 5 percent level or better.
Notes: Data contain 63 observations on quarterly percentage changes smoothed by a five-quarter moving average. The E^{US} is the "merm" weighted IMF definition of changes in the dollar exchange rate against 17 other industrial countries: foreign currency/dollars. The Ms are changes in narrow money supplies taken from the Federal Reserve Bank of St. Louis.

Table 9.2
The Dollar Exchange Rate and Money Growth in the United States, Japan, and Germany: Correlation Matrix for the 1970.IV–1984.IV Period

	Not detrended				Detrended			
	E^{US}	M^{US}	M^{JA}	M^{GE}	E^{US}	M^{US}	M^{JA}	M^{GE}
E^{US}	1				1			
M^{US}	−0.008	1			−0.519*	1		
M^{JA}	−0.620*	−0.195	1		−0.168	0.338*	1	
M^{GE}	−0.562*	0.102	0.457*	1	−0.341*	0.423*	0.026	1

Source: As for table 9.1.
Note: See table 9.1. This time there are only 57 observations.

The IMF uses a slightly more complicated aggregation procedure to construct its merm-weighted 17-country index of the foreign currency value of the dollar—call it E^{US}. "Merm" reflects an econometric procedure that leads to something very close to a trade weighted exchange-rate index. But virtually any other broad index of the dollar's foreign-exchange value yields roughly the same results.

Figure 9.2 shows this correlation between changes in ROW money and changes in the dollar exchange rate broadly defined. In the upper panel, the simple correlation in unsmoothed quarterly data is −0.280. However, if one smooths the percentage changes in ROW money and the dollar exchanage rate over five quarters, this negative correlation increases sharply to −0.599 and is highly visible in the lower panel of figure 9.2. When the dollar is strong (rising), ROW central banks cut their collective money growth to resist further increases, and vice versa.

The fundamental asymmetry of the "dollar standard" can be seen in tables 9.1 and 9.2, where Japan and Germany are now separated out—but still representative—of the "rest of the world." The monetary correlations of the United States, Japan, and Germany to fluctuations in the IMF's broad index of the dollar exchange rate are displayed.

Depending on whether the smoothed data are detrended or not, tables 9.1 and 9.2 show that U.S. money growth either responds perversely to the dollar exchange rate or not at all. That is, M^{US} is either uncorrelated or negatively correlated with E^{US}—as is visually (barely) evident in figure 9.3. Money growth in the United States could well be increasing above normal when the dollar is weak: indeed excessive monetary expansion by the U.S. Federal Reserve System could sometimes be what drives the dollar down, and vice versa.

In contrast, the Bundesbank and the Bank of Japan exhibit a stabilizing response to fluctuations in the dollar exchange rate: M^{GE} or M^{JA} are each also negatively correlated with E^{US}, as one would expect from the analysis of ROW money contained in figure 9.2. So they tend to contract when the dollar is strong and expand when it is weak.[2]

Because growth in American M1 was unusually high during the great "engineered" fall of the dollar over 1985–1986, I did this same correlation analysis in table 9.2 (as in table 9.1) but excluded these "extreme" 1985–86 observations which are so visible in figure 9.3. (Au. note: 1985–86 should be excluded because of the change to the Plaza-Louvre regime.) One still gets negative, albeit weaker, correlation between M^{US} and E^{US} in table 9.2. It seems fair to conclude that the American monetary authorities were not oriented toward stabilizing the dollar in the foreign exchanges from 1971 through early 1985—unlike the Bundesbank and the Bank of Japan.

This asymmetry implies that money-market disturbances in the United States tended to be amplified in the world economy by the reactions of foreign central banks (Swoboda 1978; and

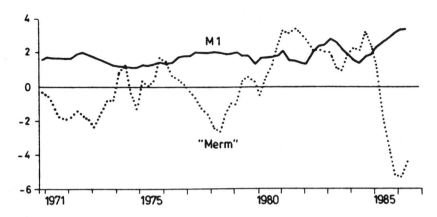

Figure 9.3
Rate of change for the U.S. money supply (M1) and the "merm" exchange rate (percent per year for smoothed data).
Source: IMF (various issues); Federal Reserve Bank of St. Louis (various issues).

chap. 7). If unusually strong American monetary expansion incidentally caused the dollar to depreciate, foreign central banks also expanded their money supplies, thus causing inflationary pressure in the world system as a whole. Tables 9.1 and 9.2 also indicate some positive correlation between American and foreign money growth—more so for Europe (represented by Germany) than for Japan.

9.4 Monetary Rules for the United States: Money Supply versus the Exchange Rate

Because the Fed (unlike other central banks) has not keyed on stabilizing the dollar exchange rate in any sustained way in the postwar period, domestic American money growth has been independently or "exogenously" determined in this important respect. Did this unique degree of freedom enable the Fed to do a better job of stabilizing the American economy from 1971 to 1985?

For the period of floating exchange rates that began in the early 1970s (and called the floating-rate dollar standard in chapter 2), I shall argue the converse. Pressure on the dollar exchange rate informed the Fed about unexpected shifts in demand for dollar assets in general, and about effective future changes in the demand for U.S. money in particular. By ignoring this information, the American central bank did a rather worse job of stabilizing the internal American price level[3] than if the Fed had followed a monetary rule requiring it to help other countries stabilize the dollar exchange rate.

To illustrate this hypothesis, let us first test how well purely domestic U.S. money growth predicted future changes in the American price level (P)—measured by changes in either the American WPI (producer price index) or the American GNP deflator. Consider the following equation regressing current quarterly changes in U.S. prices on quarterly changes in American M1 over the preceding three years, i.e., lagged 12 quarters.

$$P = C + \Sigma(a_{-t}M_{-t}) \qquad t = 1, 2, \ldots, 12 \qquad (2)$$

Equation (2) tests the principle of *domestic monetarism:* whether the domestic money supply by itself controls variations in the domestic price level within a three-year time frame.

For the period of fixed exchange rates of the 1960s ending in the first quarter of 1973, table 9.3 shows that domestic monetarism worked rather well for the United States. In the regressions on either the American GNP deflator or on the WPI, the sums of the coefficients on the money supply variable were 0.98 and 1.62 respectively, with highly significant t-statistics. Serial correlation in the residuals was absent. No wonder American monetarists became convinced that, because the domestic demand for money was sufficiently stable, imposing a constant growth rule for the supply of money would itself smooth major cyclical variations in domestic prices!

However, with the advent of floating exchange rates, the principle of domestic monetarism collapsed. Running exactly the same regression contained in (2) from the second quarter of 1973 to the last quarter of 1984, the first two equations in the middle panel of table 9.3 indicate that the coefficients on the U.S. money supply became insignificant—as does the R^2 for the equation as a whole. Furthermore, the residuals now show serial correlation, as if some major explanatory variable had been omitted.

Could the "missing" variable be the dollar exchange rate? Knowing that the exchange rate is a forward-looking asset price (Frenkel and Mussa 1980), let us include it as a second explanatory variable in our single equation regression:

Table 9.3
The United States: Regressions of Price Levels on Domestic Money and the Dollar Exchange Rate

Dependent Variable	M^{US}	E^{US}	$\bar{R}^2$	S.E.R (Percentage points)	D.W.	Period
DEF^{US}	0.98 (8.24)		0.61	0.26	2.03	1962.II–1973.I
WPI^{US}	1.62 (5.58)		0.47	0.64	2.07	1962.II–1973.I
DEF^{US}	0.44 (1.12)		0.11	0.58	0.78	1973.II–1984.IV
WPI^{US}	0.81 (0.70)		−0.04	1.73	0.98	1973.II–1984.IV
DEF^{US}	0.57 (1.91)	−0.34 (−4.87)	0.55	0.41	1.33	1973.II–1984.IV
WPI^{US}	1.20 (1.35)	−1.07 (−5.17)	0.49	1.12	2.21	1973.II–1984.IV
DEF^{US}	−0.52 (−1.37)		0.09	0.73	1.32	1973.II–1986.IV
WPI^{US}	−1.13 (−1.24)		0.03	1.77	0.87	1973.II–1986.IV
DEF^{US}	0.20 (0.52)	−0.35 (−4.90)	0.41	0.59	1.96	1973.II–1986.IV
WPI^{US}	0.43 (0.50)	−0.93 (−5.99)	0.48	1.30	1.79	1973.II–1986.IV

Source: As for figure 9.2.
Notes: Data are quarterly rates of change. OLS regressions run as a 3rd order polynomial distributed lag on right-hand side variables: 12 lagged observations over three years. Regression coefficients are the sum of the 12 estimated coefficients for each lag with t-statistics in parentheses. DEF^{US} is the U.S. GNP deflator and M^{US} is the American M1 both taken from the Federal Reserve Bank of St. Louis. WPI^{US} is the U.S. producer price index and E^{US} is "merm" weighted dollar exchange rate against 17 industrial countries (foreign currency/dollars) both taken from IMF. The "correct" sign for E^{US} is negative.

$$P = C + \Sigma(a_{-t}M_{-t}) + \Sigma(b_{-t}E_{-t}) + v \qquad t = 1, 2, \ldots, 12 \qquad (3)$$

Because E is defined as foreign currency/dollar, the expected sign for the b-coefficients is negative: a fall in the dollar exchange rate indicates price inflation to come in the American economy. And the middle panel of equations in table 9.3 show the sum of the b-coefficients to be significantly negative: -0.34 for the GNP deflator and -1.07 for the WPI. That is, a one percent appreciation in the dollar exchange rate would eventually reduce P^{DEF} by 0.34 percent. Because the WPI consists more of internationally tradable goods, it is even more sensitive eventually increasing virtually one-for-one with the dollar exchange rate.

After any change in E^{US}, the peak impact on the American WPI occurs after about 8 quarters have elapsed (9 or 10 quarters for the GNP deflator). Using smoothed data, figure 9.4 shows the strong negative correspondence between movements in the WPI, GNP deflator, and the dollar exchange rate 8 quarters earlier.

Even the a-coefficients for the money supply look more sensible (although still not quite significant statistically) once the dollar exchange rate is included as an explanatory variable in table 9.3 for the period from 1973.II to 1984.IV.

However, this effect is much less marked once the more "extreme" 1985–1986 observations on U.S. money supply and exchange-rate movements are included in the regressions displayed in table 9.3's bottom panel.[4] (And we now know—chapter 2—that there was a regime change after 1984: from the floating-rate dollar standard to the Plaza-Louvre Accords.)

Changes in the American money supply are just not very good in predicting (cyclical) changes in the American price level over a three-year period. This is not to deny, of course, that money-supply variables dominate the American price level (and exchange rate) over much longer periods.

9.5 An International Model of American Price Inflation

The effect of the exchange rate on the American price level in (3), and displayed in figure 9.4 and table 9.3, seems much greater than what can be explained by direct arbitrage in international commodity markets. American exports and imports together still amount to less than 20 percent of GNP. Just looking at the "pass

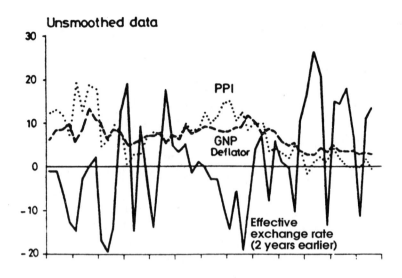

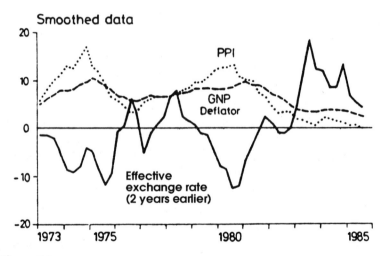

Figure 9.4
U.S. effective exchange rate, PPI and GNP deflator (percent per year).
Source: IMF (various issues); Federal Reserve Bank of St. Louis (various issues).

through" effects of exchange-rate changes on the dollar prices of goods entering American foreign trade—assuming international inflation to be given exogenously—greatly understates the ultimate inflationary impact of, say, a dollar devaluation. There are two additional money-market considerations associated with changes in E^{US} (McKinnon 1984) that impinge on the American price level.

First, in the financially more open American economy of the 1970s and 1980s, foreign-exchange assets are the most important portfolio alternative to holding money or bonds denominated in dollars. Because the advent of floating made future exchange rates more uncertain, the demand for dollar assets generally became much more volatile. In moving from the 1950s and 1960s to the 1970s and 1980s, the demand for narrow U.S. money could well have been destabilized—as evidenced by the collapse of the domestic monetarist model of the American economy.

However, the dollar exchange rate in terms of a collection of foreign "hard" monies is a convenient index of when the demand for U.S. M1 is shifting (McKinnon 1984): the dollar exchange rate shifts down when the direct and indirect demand for U.S. money falls, and vice versa. Hence, by measuring shifts in money demand, the dollar exchange rate acts as good indicator of inflationary or deflationary pressure to come *within* the American economy, as per equation (3).

Second, we know that dollar depreciation generally induces monetary expansion abroad[5] (and vice versa) as shown in figure 9.2. In the world economy, this inflationary impact from an increase in ROW money then reinforces the initiating inflationary impulse in the United States. And the inflationary pressure is distributed across countries depending inversely on whose currencies are appreciated relative to the others.

For the period of floating exchange rates from 1971 to 1985, we have established (table 9.3) that the dollar exchange rate is a very good indicator of future inflation or deflation in the United States. Can this proposition then be generalized for other industrial countries? In particular, would the dollar/mark or dollar/ yen exchange rates have given good predictions of future price inflation in Germany and Japan?

No, because of the fundamental asymmetry of the world system. Monetary disturbances in either the supply of or demand for dollars originate in American financial markets and then spread out to other industrial countries associated with changes in dollar exchange rates. Hence, the mark or yen tends to be strong against the dollar coinciding with periods of inflationary pressure in the world economy as in the 1970s, and tends to be weak in times of deflationary pressure, as in the early 1980s.

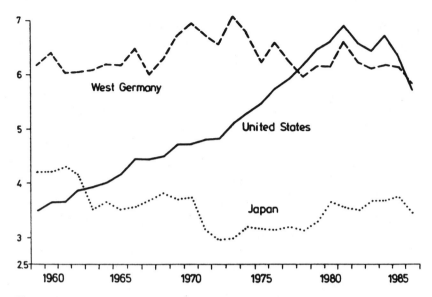

Figure 9.5
M1 velocity for the U.S., Japan, and Germany, 1959–86.
Source: Federal Reserve Bank of St. Louis (various issues).

Thus a depreciation of the mark or yen generally has not been followed by inflation in the German or Japanese economies. Rerunning regressions in the form of (3) using either German or Japanese data yields inconclusive results for the sign of the dollar/mark exchange rate on the German price level, and for the dollar/yen exchange rate on the Japanese price level.

In summary, any effects of changes in the dollar/mark or dollar/yen on future changes in the German and Japanese price levels tend to be offset by inflationary or deflationary pressure from the opposite direction in the world economy.[6]

9.6   A Concluding Note on Optimal Monetary Policy

From 1971 into 1985, the problem with international monetary instability clearly lay with the failure of the Federal Reserve System to adjust U.S. money growth toward maintaining a more stable dollar exchange rate. With monetary disturbances emanating from the United States, foreign central banks faced a dilemma. Either they allowed their dollar exchange rates to float "cleanly" and thus more violently than even those changes we have observed, or they tried to smooth such exchange-rate fluctuations by expanding their domestic money supplies when the dollar was weak (and vice versa) thus aggravating the international cycle of inflation and deflation.

Even from the narrow point of view of an American monetary nationalist, the domestic U.S. price level would have been better stabilized if the Fed had consciously keyed on stabilizing the dollar exchange rate in formulating its domestic monetary strategy. Greater symmetry would then be introduced into the international system: when the dollar tended to be weak, U.S. money growth would contract as foreign money growth expanded. Not only would this more symmetrical response by the Fed smooth fluctuations in the dollar exchange rate and the American price level, but the international cycle of inflation and deflation would also be ameliorated.

Fortunately, the Fed has recently taken some significant steps in this direction. In 1987, U.S. money growth slowed dramatically in response to the run on the dollar—unlike the earlier episodes of a weak dollar in the 1970s. Moreover, The Fed's Vice Chairman Manuel Johnson (1988) recently articulated a new monetary strategy where rates of growth in domestic monetary aggregates were to be deemphasized as monetary indicators. Instead, more weight was to be given to prices determined in forward-looking auction markets—including the dollar exchange rate and the dollar prices of primary commodities, which are also determined in world markets. As of early 1988, the signs are promising that U.S. monetary policy is becoming more internationally oriented. (Au. note: I was unduly optimistic!)

Appendix on World Monetary Variables and U.S. Price Inflation under Floating Rates

Because of the inverse correlation between the strength of the U.S. dollar and money growth in the rest of the world under "dirty" floating, the explanatory variable E in equation (3) already captures much of the impact of worldwide inflationary or deflationary pressure. But can the Fed obtain yet more useful information about the future American price level by looking directly at money growth in other industrial countries?

I have argued that changes in the demand for dollar assets in general, and for U.S. money in particular, are manifested in the foreign-exchange market in two ways: (1) under predominantly "clean" floating, by fluctuations in the average dollar exchange rate against other major currencies; and (2) when other countries' central banks act to smooth their dollar exchange rates, by fluctuations in foreign money growth.

In the latter case, changes in growth of foreign "hard" moneys—which are to some extent substitutible for dollars in international asset portfolios (chapter 7)—may itself have an additional inflationary impact on internationally tradable goods in the world at large. The remarkable positive correlation in cycles of price inflation across the industrial countries then feeds back on the U.S. price level.

So foreign money growth, under the world dollar standard, both reflects changing money demand in the United States and has its own supply-side effect on the world price level. And the simple regression models presented below cannot pretend to disentangle these two effects.

Tables 9A.1 and 9A.2 present the results of running regression equations of the form:

$$\dot{P}^{US} = C + \sum_{i=0}^{n} \dot{M}^{W}_{-1} + u, \text{ or}$$

$$\dot{P}^{US} = C + \sum_{i=0}^{n} \dot{M}^{ROW}_{-1} + v$$

(A1)

$\dot{M}^{W}$ is percentage growth in the "world" money, including U.S. M1 with a heavy weight, for annual data; and $\dot{M}^{ROW}$ is money growth in the 10 industrial countries other than the United States.

In the 1970s through 1984, world money does much better than U.S. money in predicting either the U.S. WPI or the GNP deflator: the regression coefficients for $\dot{M}^{W}$ are highly significant. The effect of world money on American tradable goods prices (table 9A.1) is greater than its effect on the American GNP deflator (table 9A.2) as one would expect.

Even ROW money by itself does considerably better than U.S. money by itself in predicting U.S. prices as—tables 9A.1 and 9A.2 based on quarterly data make clear. Moreover, the explanatory power of U.S. money improves substantially when ROW money

Table 9A.1
World Money and U.S. Tradable Goods Prices (WPI) under Floating Exchange
Rates: 1973.II to 1984.IV (quarterly data, t-statistics are in parentheses)

$\dot{M}^W$	$\dot{M}^{ROW}$	$\dot{M}^{US}$	$\dot{E}^{US}$	$\bar{R}^2$	SER (Percentage points)	D.W.
3.11 (5.49)				0.45	1.12	1.80
	1.49 (4.73)			0.39	1.32	1.69
		0.81 (0.70)		−.04	1.73	0.98
			−0.84 (−6.02)	0.50	1.21	1.95
1.06 (0.77)			−0.62 (−1.86)	0.46	1.25	2.05
	0.03 (0.05)		−0.80 (−2.60)	0.46	1.25	2.05
		1.20 (1.35)	−1.07 (−5.17)	0.49	1.12	2.21
	1.83 (5.38)	2.38 (2.39)		0.42	1.29	2.01

Notes: $W\dot{P}I$ is dependent variable: growth in the U.S. wholesale price index as defined by line 63 of IFS. $\dot{M}^W$ is percentage growth in world (narrow) money: 11 industrial countries. $\dot{M}^{ROW}$ is percentage money growth in 10 countries other than U.S. $\dot{M}^{US}$ is U.S. narrow money: M1. E is the IMF's in index of the dollar exchange rate: foreign currency/dollars "merm" weighted against 17 other industrial countries. Data are log differences of quarterly averages. OLS regressions are run as an unconstrained third-order polynomial distributed lag on the right-hand-side variables: lagged 12 quarters excluding concurrent one. The regression coefficients above are the sum of the 12 estimated coefficients for each lag.

is included as an additional explanatory variable (tables 9A.1 and 9A.2)—as if it were indeed proxying for shifts in the domestic demand for American M1.

In summary, money growth in the rest of the world does seem to be important, and there is a prima facie case for the Fed to take other countries monetary policies into account when formulating its own.

Under present world monetary arrangements, however, the dollar exchange rate seems to dominate these world and ROW

Table 9A.2
World Money Variables and U.S. GNP Price Deflator under Floating Exchange
Rates: 1973.II to 1984.IV (quarterly data, t-statistics are in parentheses)

$\dot{M}^W$	$\dot{M}^{ROW}$	$\dot{M}^{US}$	$\dot{E}^{US}$	$\bar{R}^2$	SER (Percentage points)	D.W.
0.76 (3.87)				0.50	0.43	1.22
	0.36 (3.40)			0.48	0.45	1.20
		0.44 (1.12)				
			−0.30 (−6.15)	0.53	0.43	1.23
−0.32 (−0.79)			−0.24 (−2.47)	0.66	0.36	1.70
	−0.19 (−1.06)		−0.30 (−3.27)	0.64	0.37	1.67
		0.57 (1.91)	−0.34 (−4.87)	0.55	0.41	1.33
	0.44 (3.92)	0.62 (1.87)		0.52	0.43	1.39

Notes: $\dot{DEF}^{US}$ is dependent variable: growth in U.S. GNP deflator $\dot{M}^W$ is percentage growth in world narrow money: 11 industrial countries. $\dot{M}^{ROW}$ is percentage
money growth in 10 countries other than U.S. $\dot{M}^{US}$ is U.S. narrow money: M1.
$\dot{E}^{US}$ is the IMF's index of the dollar exchange rate: foreign currency/dollars
"merm" weighted against 17 other industrial countries. Data are log differences
of quarterly averages. OLS regressions are run as an unconstrained third-order
polynomal distributed lag on the right-hand-side variables: lagged 12 quarters
excluding concurrent one. The regression coefficient above are the sum of the
12 coefficients for each lag.

money supply variables. Suppose E is added as an additional
explanatory variable, and regressions are run in the format:

$$\dot{P}^{US} = C + \sum_{i=0}^{n} \dot{M}^W_{-1} + \sum_{i=0}^{n} \dot{E}^{US}_{-i} + u, \text{ or}$$

$$\dot{P}^{US} = C + \sum_{i=0}^{n} \dot{M}^{ROW} + \sum_{i=0}^{n} \dot{E}^{US}_{-i} + v$$

(A2)

Then, tables 9A.1 and 9A.2 show that the E variables remain
significant with (correct) negative signs, but M^W and M^{ROW} become insignificant with sometimes the wrong signs. This domi-

nance of the dollar exchange rate is undoubtedly related to its inverse correlation with the world money variables. Therefore, the Fed could treat the dollar exchange rate as its primary signal of when American monetary policy was too tight or too easy *provided that* the reactions of foreign central banks remain similar to what they have been in the past. [Au. caution: The regime change to Plaza-Louvre (rule box 5) in 1985 only became evident after this was written.]

Notes

I would like to thank Kenichi Ohno for his great help in completing this paper.

1. However, the absolute level of ROW money—as distinct from its percentage rate of change—cannot be unambiguously aggregated without specifying exchange rates at every data point. See McKinnon (1984) for a discussion of this aggregation problem.

2. In the German and Japanese cases, I have also done these correlations substituting the mark/dollar or yen/dollar exchange rates respectively for E^{US}—and by substituting the German "merm" or the Japanese "merm." The resulting statistical correlations with national money growth using these "own" exchange rates are weaker—although generally of the same sign as in tables 9.1 and 9.2. Because their individual (dollar) exchange rates may be somewhat more influenced by money-market disturbances in Germany and Japan than is E^{US}, they are a less pure reflection of money-market disturbances emanating from the United States which foreign monetary authorities try to smooth.

3. What the central bank's ultimate goals should be are, of course, not fully resolved. However, monetary economists generally agree (see, for example, Friedman 1968) that the most that can be feasibly accomplished is to ask the central bank to stabilize the purchasing power of the money it issues. In this paper, I interpret this dictum narrowly to mean targeting some broad index of the domestic price level in domestic-currency prices—such as the WPI or GNP deflator. However, because the exchange rate itself defines the purchasing power of domestic money over a broad range of foreign goods whose invoice prices in foreign currencies might be sticky, exchange-rate stabilization *per se* could also be given a heavy weight in the central bank's objective function.

4. Some readers may be justifiably concerned that the whole analysis so far has relied on M1 to measure "the" money supply. Because of the erratic behavior of the velocity of American M1 in the 1980s in comparison to the 1970s (figure 9.5), many American monetarists have switched over to M2 as their preferred aggregate, and, in February 1987, the Fed itself dropped any official target for M1. However, if the regressions in table 9.3 are rerun substituting U.S. M2 for U.S. M1, the results (not reported in this paper) are even worse for the domestic monetarist model for the period of floating exchange rates. The regression coefficients on the money supply even have the wrong signs.

5. The dollar depreciation beginning in March 1985 could be a partial exception. Because of the unusual "engineered" nature of the dollar's fall, foreign central

banks retained tight monetary stances throughout 1985 into early 1986. Rather than resisting the fall by expanding their money supplies as they did in the past, foreign central banks tried to accommodate the wishes of the American government by staying fairly tight so that their own currencies would appreciate. The result was significant internal deflation in Japan and Germany (McKinnon 1988), which mitigated the "normal" inflationary pressure in the U.S. one would expect from such a large devaluation of the dollar.

6. The one significant exception to this offsetting process seems to be the extreme appreciation of the yen and mark since February 1985. Because this was engineered by maintaining relatively tight money in Europe generally and in Japan, ROW money growth and inflationary pressure in the world economy has been less than in previous dollar depreciations. Hence, the internal fall in the Japanese and German price levels (WPIs) has been remarkably greater (McKinnon 1988) than in their previous experience with appreciating currencies.

References

Federal Reserve Bank of St. Louis, *International Economic Conditions*. St. Louis, Missouri, various issues.

Friedman, Milton, "The Role of Monetary Policy." *The American Economic Review*, Vol. 58, 1968, pp. 1–17.

Frenkel, Jacob, and Michael L. Mussa, "The Efficiency of the Foreign Exchange Market and Measures of Turbulence." *The American Economic Review*, Vol. 70, 1980, pp. 374–381.

International Monetary Fund (IMF), *International Financial Statistics*. Washington, various issues.

Johnson, Manuel H., "Current Perspectives on Monetary Policy." Paper presented at the Conference on Dollars, Deficits and Trade at the CATO Institute, Washington 25th February 1988.

McKinnon, Ronald I., *Money in International Exchange: The Convertible Currency System*. New York 1979.

———, "Currency Substitution and Instability in the World Dollar Standard." *The American Economic Review*, Vol. 72, 1982, pp. 320–333.

———, *An International Standard for Monetary Stabilization*. Institute for International Economics, Washington 1984.

———, "Monetary and Exchange Rate Policies for International Financial Stability: A Proposal." *Journal of Economic Perspectives*, Vol. 2, Winter 1988, pp. 83–104.

Swoboda, Alexander K., "Gold, Dollars, Euro-Dollars, and the World Money Stock under Fixed Exchange Rates." *The American Economic Review*, Vol. 68, 1978, pp. 625–642.

II

Optimum Currency Areas and Exchange-Rate Flexibility

10   Optimum Currency Areas

In a recent note, Robert A. Mundell (1961) has suggested that little in the way of a systematic attempt has been made to define the characteristics of an area over which it is optimal to have a single currency regime, or—what is almost the same thing—a fixed exchange-rate system with guaranteed convertibility of currencies. The extensive literature on the relative merits of fixed versus flexible exchange rates has been rendered somewhat sterile by this omission. Existing national boundaries have been implicitly used to define the single currency area to which flexible external exchange rates would or would not be applied. However, when different possibilities for the grouping of nations in single currency areas exist, as in the EEC, or when resource mobility is low within individual countries, Mundell demonstrates that it is necessary to ask what economic characteristics determine the optimum size of the domain of a single currency. I shall develop the idea of optimality further by discussing the influence of the openness of the economy, i.e., the ratio of tradable to nontradable goods, on the problem of reconciling external and internal balance, emphasizing the need for internal price-level stability.

"Optimum" is used here to describe a single currency area within which monetary-fiscal policy and flexible external exchange rates can be used to give the best resolution of three (sometimes conflicting) objectives: (1) the maintenance of full employment; (2) the maintenance of balanced international payments; (3) the maintenance of a stable internal average price

Originally published in *The American Economic Review* (September 1963): 717–725. Reprinted with permission.

level. Objective (3) assumes that any capitalist economy requires a stable-valued liquid currency to ensure efficient resource allocation. Possible conflicts between (1) and (2) have been well discussed in the literature, especially by J. E. Meade (1951), but joint consideration of all three is not usually done. For example, J. L. Stein (1963) explicitly assumes internal price-level stability in his discussion of optimal flexibility in the foreign exchange rate. The inclusion of objective (3) makes the problem as much a part of monetary theory as of international trade theory. The idea of optimality, then, is complex and difficult to quantify precisely, so what follows does not presume to be a logically complete model.

"The ratio of tradable to nontradable goods" is a simplifying concept that assumes all goods can be classified into those that could enter into foreign trade and those that do not because transportation is not feasible for them. A physical description of both tradable and nontradable goods would correspond to that given by R. F. Harrod (1957, pp. 53–56). This overly sharp distinction between classes of tradable and nontradable goods is an analytically simple way of taking transportation costs into account. By tradable goods we mean: (1) exportables, which are those goods produced domestically and, in part, exported; (2) importables, which are both produced domestically and imported. The excess of exportables produced over exports will depend directly on the amount of domestic consumption, which is likely to be small when exportable production is heavily specialized in few goods. Similarly, the excess of importables consumed over imports will depend on the specialized nature of imports. Therefore, the value of exportables produced need not be the same as the value of importables consumed, even in the case of balanced trade where the values of imports and exports are equal. However, the total value of tradable goods produced will equal the value of tradable goods consumed under balanced trade. Thus, the expression "the ratio of tradable to nontradable goods" can apply unambiguously to production or consumption.

10.1 A Simple Model

Ideally, one would like to consider a large group of countries jointly and then decide how they should be divided up into optimum currency regions. The analytical framework for such a task does not exist, so it is necessary to consider a much narrower problem and hope it throws light on the general one—besides being of interest in itself. Consider a well-defined single currency area in which we wish to determine whether or not there should be flexible exchange rates with the outside world. The outside world is itself assumed to be a single currency area, which is very large.

If the area under consideration is sufficiently small, we may assume that the money prices of the tradable goods in terms of the outside currency are not influenced by domestic exchange rates or domestic currency prices.[1] In actual practice, the domestic money prices of tradable goods will be more closely tied to foreign prices through existing exchange rates than will the domestic money prices of the nontradable goods. Under this invariance assumption, i.e., fixed foreign-currency prices, the terms of trade will necessarily be immune to domestic economic policy. Some justification is given for this in R. Hinshaw (1951), even for fairly large countries. We now inquire into whether external exchange-rate flexibility or internal fiscal-monetary expansion or contraction is more suitable to maintaining external balance, i.e., shifting production and expenditures between the tradable and nontradable goods.

Case 1

Suppose exportables X_1 and importables X_2 together make up a large percentage of the goods consumed domestically. Suppose further a flexible exchange-rate system is used to maintain external balance. The price of the nontradable good, X_3, is kept constant in terms of the domestic currency. Exchange-rate changes will vary the domestic prices of X_1 and X_2 directly by the amount of the change. Thus, if the domestic currency is devalued 10 percent, the domestic money prices of X_1 and X_2 will rise by 10 percent and thus rise 10 per cent relative to X_3. The rationale of such a policy is that the production of X_1 and X_2 should increase, and the consumption of X_1 and X_2 should decline, improving the balance of payments. Direct absorption reduction from the price rise in tradable goods may have to be supplemented by deliberate contractionary monetary-fiscal policy, if unemployment is small. Substantial theoretical justification for considering relative price changes between tradable and nontradable goods to be more important than changes in the terms of trade for external balance is given by I. F. Pearce (1961).

From case 1, it is clear that external exchange-rate fluctuations, responding to shifts in the demand for imports or exports, are not compatible with internal price-level stability for a highly open economy, objective (3). In addition, such a policy by itself may not succeed in changing relative prices or affecting the trade balance. In a highly open economy operating close to full employment, significant improvement in the trade balance will have to be accomplished by the reduction of domestic absorption, i.e., real expenditures, which is the only possible way of keeping the price of X_3 constant in terms of the domestic currency. Thus, a substantial rise in domestic taxes may be necessary whether or not there is any exchange-rate change. In the extreme case where the economy is completely open, i.e., all goods produced and consumed are tradable with prices determined in the outside world, the only way the trade balance can be improved is by lowering domestic expenditures while maintaining output levels. Changes in the exchange rate will necessarily be completely offset by internal price-level repercussions with no improvement in the trade balance.

To restate the core of the argument: if we move across the spectrum from closed to open economies, flexible exchange rates become both less effective as a control device for external balance and more damaging to internal price-level stability. In fact, if one were worried about unwanted speculative movements in a floating exchange rate in case 1 of an open economy, a policy of completely fixed exchange rates (or common currency ties with the outside world) would be optimal. Blunt monetary and fiscal weapons that evenly reduced expenditures in all sectors could be counted on to improve immediately the trade balance by releasing goods from domestic consumption in the large tradable goods sector. Exportables previously consumed domestically would be released for export; imports would be directly curtailed, and domestically produced importables made available for substitution with imports. The reduction of expenditures in the relatively small nontradable goods sector would initially only cause unemployment which, depending on the degree of interindustry resource mobility and price flexibility, might eventually be translated into more production in the tradable goods sectors, and possibly improve the trade balance in the longer run. The smaller this nontradable goods sector, the smaller will be the immediate impact of reducing expenditures on employment and total production, and thus the more efficient this policy of expenditure reduction will be as a device for improving external balance (the surplus of production over expenditures).

Any region within a common currency area faced with a loss of demand for its products will be forced to cut its expenditures through a loss of bank reserves and regional income, thus eventually correcting the trade balance. A separate currency region with fixed exchange rates may have to carry out the cutback of expenditures more through deliberate policy if bank reserve losses are effectively sterilized. In either case, the immediate reduction in real income cannot be avoided if the trade balance is to be improved.

Case 2

Suppose the production of nontradable goods is very large compared to importables and exportables in the given area. Here the optimal currency arrangements may be to peg the domestic currency to the body of nontradable goods, i.e., to fix the domestic currency price of X_3 and change the domestic price of the tradable goods by altering the exchange rate to improve the trade balance. A currency devaluation of 10 percent would cause the domestic prices of X_1 and X_2 to rise by 10 percent, but the effect on the general domestic price index is much less than in case 1.

The desired effect of the relative price increase in the tradable goods is to stimulate the production of tradable compared to nontradable goods and thus improve the trade balance. On the other hand, if monetary-fiscal policy is primarily relied on to reduce domestic demand to maintain external balance, unemployment will be much higher. Much of the immediate impact of the reduction of expenditures will be in the extensive nontradable goods industries. If there are any rigidities in resource mobility, the trade balance will not improve much in the first instance. Through this policy, it may be actually necessary to achieve a fall in the domestic money prices of X_3, the numerous nontradable goods, before sufficient expansion in the production of X_1 and X_2 can be obtained. Since a major component of X_3 will be labor services, it may be necessary to lower wage costs vis-à-vis the domestic money prices of X_1 and X_2, which are fixed by the inflexible external exchange-rate system. Such a policy would contain all the well-known Keynesian difficulties of getting labor to accept a cut in money wages. In addition, a successful policy of lowering prices of the numerous X_3 goods would have a large impact on the average domestic price level. Effectively, we would have permitted the tail (tradable goods) to wag the dog (nontradable goods) in pursuing restrictive monetary and fiscal policies, with fixed exchange rates to improve the trade balance, for a small proportion of tradable goods.

Our open economy of case 1 somewhat resembles what Stein (1963) has called a "conflict" economy. In a conflict economy, export production is sufficiently large to dominate the generation of domestic income, and thus fluctuations in both are positively correlated. Therefore, with a fixed exchange rate, periods having low income will also have unfavorable trade balances, and vice versa. For income stabilization, objective (1), Stein concludes that a floating exchange rate will be optimal for a conflict economy in a Keynesian environment. The foreign-exchange rate would then rise at the top of the cycle and fall at the bottom. These exchange-rate changes will stimulate domestic production and income at the bottom of the cycle and damp them at the top. But it is precisely in this case of a highly open economy that exchange-rate changes will mean great fluctuations in internal price levels—sufficiently great, that any effects of exchange-rate changes on domestic production may be small. However, there may still remain a direct policy conflict between objectives (1) and (3) in the use of a floating exchange rate. Certainly, the liquidity value of the domestic currency will depend directly on the short-run fortunes of the export commodity(ies) for a floating exchange rate.

Qualifications

The sharp distinction between tradable and nontradable goods makes the above model analytically much easier to work with; but in practice there is a continuum of goods between the tradable and nontradable extremes. The relaxation of this sharp distinction does not invalidate the basic idea of the openness of the economy affecting optimum economic policies, but the empirical measurement of the ratio of tradable to nontradable goods becomes more difficult. Some kind of weighting system for determining the total production in each category might be possible. Certainly, knowledge of total imports and exports would give one a good lead in determining total production of exportables and importables. In addition, the idea of openness would have to be modified when the area was large enough to affect external prices.

10.2 Monetary Implications of the Model

The above discussion has been concerned with the way by which relative price changes in tradable and nontradable goods can be brought about, and the conditions under which monetary and fiscal policy can be used efficiently to maintain external balance. Minimizing the real cost of adjustments needed to preserve external balance hinged to a large extent on minimizing necessary fluctuations in the overall domestic price level. Thus the argument is very much concerned with the liquidity properties of money, and it is worthwhile to look at some of the more general monetary implications of the model. Suppose X_1, X_2, and X_3 are classes of goods rather than single goods as in the Pearce model. One of the aims of monetary policy is to set up a stable kind of money whose value in terms of a representative bundle of economic goods remains more stable than any single physical good. Indeed, it is the maintenance of this stable value that gives money its liquidity properties. The process of saving and capital accumulation in a capitalist system is greatly hampered unless a suitable numéraire and store of value exists. It may be still more difficult if a more desirable money is available from another source, e.g., from a larger currency area. This latter possibility is discussed below.

If the area under consideration is sufficiently large so that the body of nontradable goods is large, then pegging the value of the domestic currency to this body of nontradable goods is sufficient to give money liquidity value in the eyes of the inhabitants of the area in question. It may not be sufficient from the viewpoint of potential investors in the outside world. However, if the area is large, what outside investors think need not be an overriding consideration. Efficient internal capital accumulation and full employment are more important than external capital movements. If, under these circumstances, trade patterns are so unstable that substantial relative price changes in tradable and nontradable goods are required to maintain external balance and full employment, then flexible external exchange rates may well be optimal. Resulting internal price changes will not destroy the value of the domestic currency as money.

If the area under consideration is small so that the ratio of tradable to nontradable goods is large and the prices of the former are fairly well fixed in the outside currency, then the monetary implications of pegging the domestic currency to the nontradable goods are less satisfactory. Such a class of nontradable goods may not constitute a typical bundle of economic goods. The class of importables may be more representative, and a currency pegged to maintain its value in terms of importables into a small area may have a higher liquidity value than one pegged to the domestically produced nontradable goods. However, pegging a currency of a small area to maintain its value in terms of a representative bundle of imports from a large outside area is virtually the same thing as pegging it to the outside currency. Alternatively, if we have a number of small areas that trade extensively with each other, and each pegs its currency to a representative bundle of imports, then each currency will be pegged to the others. To maintain the liquidity value of individual currencies for small areas, a fixed exchange-rate system is necessary. In addition, capital movements among small areas are more needed to promote efficient economic specialization and growth than free capital movements among large, economically developed areas. Contractual arrangements for such movements are greatly facilitated by a common currency. These arguments give us some insight into why each of the fifty states in the United States could not efficiently issue its own currency, aside from the inconvenience of money changing.

If we have a small area whose currency is not convincingly pegged in terms of the currency of a larger area, and so on this account its liquidity value is less, then domestic nationals will attempt to accumulate foreign bank balances. This will occur even though the marginal efficiency of investment in the small area is greater than that outside. As long as the functions of savings and investment are specialized, savers will attempt to accumulate cash balances in the more liquid currency. The illiquidity of domestic currency may also reflect monetary mismanagement as well as small size. In either case, we would expect small countries with weak currencies to have a tendency to finance the balance-of-payments deficits of larger countries with more desirable currencies. Thus, we have capital outflows from countries where the need for capital may be rather high and which arise from "monetary" rather than "real" considerations. Authorities in such countries are generally forced to maintain rather strict exchange controls unless the currency can be pegged in a convincing fashion to that of the larger area.

The above argument is relevant to the use of uncontrolled floating exchange rates. This device of maintaining external balance will only work well when the currency in question has liquidity value of the same order as that of the outside world—or the world's major currencies. This condition was approximately satisfied in the case of the Canadian dollar up to 1961. However, a floating exchange rate for the Korean won may lead to less satisfactory results. If the official rate were made equal to the black-market rate and there were no further exchange restrictions, there would still be a capital flight out of Korea into currencies with superior liquidity value, aside from problems of political stability. A floating exchange rate in itself is not a sufficient control device and does not necessarily eliminate the need for exchange controls.

By contrast, short-term capital flows among currencies of approximately equal liquidity value are less likely with a floating exchange rate because of the exchange risk and the liquidity equivalence. The possibility of carrying out different degrees of easy or tight monetary policy in different countries is greater as capital flows would not be so responsive to interest-rate differentials. Once the world is divided into a number of optimal-sized currency areas permitting efficient internal capital accumulation, the desirability of short-term capital flows among areas well developed economically becomes less great, and it becomes desirable to insulate the monetary policies of the areas from each other in order that monetary policy may be used more freely to support full employment. However, it does not make any sense to advocate a floating exchange-rate system without first defining the optimal domains of individual currencies.

Suppose we look at the problem of a depressed subregion of a common currency area. Consider the case of West Virginia where nontradable goods are largely labor services. We have an illustration of an excess supply of nontradable goods and an excess demand for the tradable goods because of internal price rigidities. Thus, in this sense West Virginia has an ex ante balance-of-payments deficit even though in an ex post accounting sense there is a balance-of-cash flow in and out of the state. Would the adjustment of external balance and internal full employment be facilitated if West Virginia were incorporated as a country with its own currency? To the extent that the ratio of tradable to nontradable goods was high, such a monetary system would have little chance of success. A devaluation would be associated with a large domestic price-level increase and hence money illusion would not be much help in getting labor to accept a cut in real wages (Mundell 1961, p. 663). Labor unions would still continue to bargain in terms of U.S. dollars. In addition, a West Virginian currency tied to a representative bundle of nontradable goods would not be an entirely acceptable store of value. There undoubtedly would be attempts by West Virginians to accumulate U.S. bank balances. However, if the depressed area were substantially larger, with a small proportion of production in tradable goods, a separate monetary system might be preferable as a device for maintaining full employment and external balance in the absence of factor mobility.

10.3   A Concluding Note on Factor Mobility

The idea of factor mobility has two distinct senses: (1) geographic factor mobility among regions; (2) factor mobility among industries. I think it is fair to say that Mundell (1961) had interpretation (1) primarily in mind. His discussion of optimum currency areas in large measure is aimed toward having high geographic factor mobility within each single currency area and using flexible external exchange rates to make up for the lack of factor mobility among areas. Thus, for a given amount of geographic factor mobility in the world, this method of division into currency areas would maximize the possibility of world income and employment, subject to the constraint of maintaining external balance. Of course, the currency arrangements themselves would affect factor mobility, so the extent of factor mobility has to be considered ex post. Once we consider problems of factor immobility among industries, it may not be feasible to consider slicing the world into currency areas along industrial groupings rather than geographical groupings. However, from our above discussion, an optimal geographic size still exists even when we are only concerned with interindustry factor immobility.

Consider the special but perhaps common case of factor immobility between regions, each with its own specialized industries, the case where it is difficult to distinguish geographical and interindustrial immobility. Suppose there is a rise in the demand for the products of region A and a decline in the demand for goods of region B. The value of the marginal products of the potentially mobile factors of production in region B in B-type industries will fall, and rise in region A in A-type industries. Now if the possibility of developing or extending A-type industries in B is feasible, then need for factor movement between A and B is not great. The existing immobility between regions can be accepted through monetary arrangements giving both regions their own currencies, thus permitting more flexibility in enabling each area to pursue monetary and fiscal policies geared to internal stability. But if B cannot easily develop A-type industries, then factor movements to A may be the only thing that will prevent a large fall in the unit incomes of potentially mobile factors of production in B. So a policy aimed directly at overcoming the immobility of factor movements between A and B may be optimal, and perhaps the two should be joined in a common currency area. This argument becomes stronger when one considers small areas trying to develop industries in which economies of scale or indivisibilities are very great instead of efficiently moving factors elsewhere.

In a world where trade patterns are not perfectly stable, there will always be the problem of changing the world pattern of resource use among various industries to preserve external balance, full employment, and efficient resource use. In the simple model given in section 10.1 above, we considered the optimum extent of a currency area in terms of its size and structure, i.e., the ratio of tradable to nontradable goods, in promoting shifts in resources among various industries. The model accepted the degree of internal resource immobility among industries as an obstacle to be overcome as smoothly as possible. The arguments given there for applying flexible exchange rates to optimal-sized currency areas to efficiently overcome factor immobility hold in the main, whether the degree of internal mobility among industries is large or small. Such factor immobility among industries is a painful fact of economic life that has to be overcome as efficiently as possible. However, this criterion of size and openness of a single-currency economy in facilitating interindustry production shifts certainly has to be balanced with purely geographic factor-mobility considerations in determining the optimum extent of a currency area.

Notes

1. If we apply this assumption to the standard elasticities model, then both the elasticity of foreign demand for home exports η_f and the elasticity of foreign supply of home imports ϵ_f are assumed infinite. Thus a devaluation, i.e., a rise in the foreign exchange rate k, would always improve the trade balance, B, by an amount proportional to the sum of the home elasticity of demand for imports and the home elasticity of supply of exports, η_h and ϵ_h respectively, i.e.,

$$\frac{dB}{dk} = Z(\epsilon_h + \eta_h)$$

where Z is the value of exports in the case of balanced trade. The trouble with this standard model is that η_h and ϵ_h depend on the amount of domestic absorption permitted in the course of devaluation as well as on the openness of the economy, and it is difficult to make explicit what internal price repercussions may occur since the body of nontradable goods does not enter explicitly in the model. Assuming both η_f and ϵ_f to be infinite is different from the usual simplification that both supply elasticities, ϵ_f and ϵ_h, are infinite, and in my opinion is more appropriate to the consideration of most small areas.

References

R. F. Harrod, *International Economics*, 5th edition. Cambridge 1957.

Randall Hinshaw, "Currency Appreciation as an Anti-Inflationary Device," *Quart. Jour. Econ.*, Nov. 1951, 65, 447–62.

J. E. Meade, *The Theory of International Economic Policy*. Vol. I, *The Balance of Payments*. London 1951.

Robert A. Mundell, "A Theory of Optimum Currency Areas," *Am. Econ. Rev.*, Sept. 1961, *51*, 657–64.

Ivor F. Pearce, "The Problem of the Balance of Payments," *Internat. Econ. Rev.*, Jan. 1961.

Jerome L. Stein, "The Optimum Foreign Exchange Market," *Am. Econ. Rev.*, June 1963, *53*, 384–402.

11

Optimum World Monetary Arrangements and the Dual-Currency System

The economic dependence of any given geographical area on the outside world is of great importance in determining the optimal nature of its currency system. For economically developed areas, size is roughly inversely related to economic dependence on the rest of the world through foreign trade. Compare the economy of the United States to the combined economies of Belgium and Luxembourg. In 1962, American exports amounted to 4.67 percent of national income; exports from Belgium-Luxembourg amounted to 44.01 percent of their combined incomes. Most goods produced in a large economic area will be consumed in that same area. The domestic price structure of these goods that do not enter foreign trade will be mainly determined by economic forces within the area in question. A domestic currency will be liquid (i.e., will have the traditionally desirable properties of money: medium of exchange, numéraire, etc.) if it maintains a stable value in terms of some price index of these purely "domestic" goods, since these domestic goods account for the great bulk of economic consumption and production. Fluctuations in the prices of internationally traded goods will not affect the value of the domestic currency to domestic nationals for a "large" currency area with a relatively closed economy.[1]

At the other extreme, consider a "small" and very open economy like that of Peoria, Illinois. The fraction of domestically produced goods in domestic consumption is small, and the majority of prices of economic goods traded in Peoria are determined in the United States. If there were a separate domestic

Originally published, in slightly longer form, in Banco Nazionale del Lavoro *Quarterly Review* 67 (December 1963): 3–33. Reprinted with permission.

currency, say the Peorian dollar, the liquidity value of this currency would not be very high if its value were maintained in terms of purely Peorian goods. In order to induce Peorian citizens to take the Peorian dollar seriously as money (i.e., as a unit of account, store of value, etc.), the Peorian authorities would have to convincingly peg it to the U.S. dollar since most goods traded in Peoria will have their prices fixed in terms of U.S. dollars. However, if the Peorian authorities do convincingly peg the Peorian dollar to the U.S. dollar, they will have lost essential control of their own money supply. In other words, to take full advantage of economic integration with the U.S., there will also have to be a common integrated securities market, and thus the structure of interest rates in Peoria cannot be significantly different from the given interest rate structure in the U.S. If there were any differences, these would induce large capital movements, which could easily break the fixed exchange rate and thus seriously disturb the stability of trade in real goods and services between Peoria and the U.S. It is absolutely essential for Peoria to maintain full integration with the U.S. to preserve its standard of living. Thus, the Peorian authorities find they must keep the supply of the Peorian dollar just at the level where the interest-rate structure inside Peoria is the same as outside, which is a product of years of accumulated wisdom by the U.S. Federal Reserve System. They find they cannot make independent decisions regarding the creation of Peorian dollars. The continued existence of the Peorian dollar may be a useful sop to civic-minded politicians in the city, but it could easily be dispensed with once Peorian citizens became psychologically able to stand the loss.

11.1 The Position of the EEC and Western Europe

As some of the smaller economies of Western Europe, e.g., Benelux and Denmark, become more fully integrated through lowering of barriers to commodity trade, an optimal long-run monetary policy may run along the lines of the Peorian experience. On the other hand, some writers such as James Meade[2] have suggested that the progressive removal of direct restrictions on commodity trade will "disarm" devices that have been hitherto used (among other purposes) to control international payments within the EEC. Thus he argues that the need for floating exchange rates is even more pressing in order that external balance can be maintained without hampering domestic monetary and fiscal policies to attain full employment objectives in each country, or without forcing a reversion to trade restrictions in crisis times. Without trying to minimize the difficulties of achieving full economic integration, one can say that his proposal does not face squarely what economic integration implies, viz.: (a) if the increase in trade within the EEC continues at its current rapid rate, economic interdependence will soon be very large indeed (see table 11.1) and member countries will find the scope for independent monetary or fiscal policy to be increasingly limited whether or not there exists a floating exchange rate; and (b) a continuously changing exchange rate is essentially a device for forcing changes in current account commodity trade. For example, a devaluation will increase exports and diminish imports in order to balance the whole of international payments including capital flows. However, as each country becomes more dependent on the other for its most vital economic needs, the sacrificial adjustment of trade in goods and services to capital flows becomes increasingly objectionable and more perverse in its welfare effects. There is an increasing need for capital flows to be the adjusting variable; and a floating exchange rate makes the integration of securities markets across countries very difficult. Integrated securities markets are necessary to permit capital movements to adjust smoothly. This point is discussed in more detail below. (c) Exchange-rate adjustments themselves come to have less proportional effect on commodity trade as integration continues, since an increasing proportion of the economic goods traded within each country will have their price determined in the community at large and will be relatively immune to domestic economic influences.

This loss of effectiveness in exchange-rate changes, (c) above, is a direct result of the process of integration. Increasing attention is paid to prices in community-wide terms rather than those denominated in a single national currency. Money illusion, which had operated so as to get people to accept relative price changes via domestic currency price changes, becomes increasingly small. Any exchange-rate change will have an immediate significant impact on the price level of domestically traded goods denominated in the domestic currency since such a high proportion of goods have their prices determined outside the country in

question. Money illusion is destroyed as domestic nationals realize this and begin to make their economic production and buying
decisions in terms of a European-wide monetary standard. In the
absence of fixed rates, it is likely that a single national currency of
a large country with "sound" monetary management, e.g., the
German mark, would become the dominant commonly accepted
monetary standard by which individuals make their economic
decisions. Good money would drive out bad. However, with
convincingly fixed exchanges the dominance of any one currency
is unnecessary and the introduction of a common "European"
currency can be easily facilitated. This European (non-Gaullist)
outlook in economic affairs is of course inextricably part of the
political aims of the community. It has the complementary economic effect of improving efficient resource allocation since there
will be a common monetary standard by which profit and loss
calculations can be made for private investment decisions on a
European basis. This is one benefit of the process of economic
integration, providing the EEC Development Fund insures that
no major region remains chronically depressed or undeveloped
because of lack of social overhead investments.

   As integration proceeds in the trading of goods, I have tried
to show that the need for a common monetary standard becomes
more pressing and changes in exchange rates become both less
desirable and less effective. How then are external payments to be
kept in balance? In (b) above, it was noted that capital movements
have to begin to play the role of the adjusting variable since it
becomes increasingly undesirable to force changes in commodity trade patterns. Since the need for a system of convincingly
pegged exchange rates becomes more pressing, both to insure
stabilized commodity trade and integrated capital markets, its
accomplishment will mean that national monetary authorities
will lose effective control of their money supplies for the same
reasons that the Peorian central bank lost its control. The interest-
rate structure across countries in the EEC will become necessarily
determined by the need for balancing international payments
among members.

   Is this concomitant of integration the potential complete loss
of independent national control of monetary policy, and to a
lesser extent, fiscal policy, an intolerable opportunity cost for

the EEC countries? Unfortunately, the answer may be *yes* unless a great improvement is made in the current status of financial integration in the community. The reasons for this bear some detailed examination. We have seen that national monetary policies as manifested in national interest-rate structures will be virtually completely subordinated to maintaining intracommunity payments. Given the present primitive state of financial integration within the EEC, the interest differentials required to get balancing capital movements from time to time may have to be very large. They could easily move perversely with domestic economic requirements regarding full employment and inflation. For example, a country with a balance-of-payments deficit may find itself forced to contract the domestic money supply to maintain a high interest-rate structure in the face of unemployment—which may even be community-wide. The difficulty is much like that found in the working of the gold standard unassisted by international securities markets. As integration of trade in commodities proceeds and additional successes are achieved in encouraging labor mobility, the likelihood of different conditions of inflation and recession existing across member countries should become less (although not be eliminated altogether), and, as we have seen, the possibilities for differently tailored national monetary and fiscal policies to fit purely national needs also become less. Thus, the former effect should ameliorate the latter. Common monetary and fiscal policies will eventually be sufficient. However, the lack of financial integration may prevent these common policies from being executed if significant interest-rate differentials are required for balancing international payments.

Once financial integration becomes highly developed, as was finally accomplished within the United States in this century, the problem disappears. Banks throughout the United States hold wide portfolios of nationally marketable assets. Any regional shortage of cash that might arise can easily be financed by selling securities without significantly increasing the interest rate offered to do so. The essentially common interest-rate structure means that profitability considerations governing investment decisions will not be distorted by different regional interest rates, i.e., borrowing costs. Presumably, an upgrading of the social profitability of investment decisions is one of the main benefits of economic integration. The smooth functioning of these securities markets requires that many financial institutions—insurance companies, banks, etc.—develop rules of portfolio selection that are nonregional in character. For the EEC a convincingly pegged set of exchange rates is one prerequisite but the growth of "European," essentially non-national, corporations is another. Securities issued by these companies should be among the first to have equal liquidity value anywhere in the EEC. In this sense, a vertically integrated trade structure is complementary to the production of "European" securities. But it is very doubtful that such a natural evolution in the existence of European securities will be sufficient by itself to smooth the possibilities for intercountry money transfers and common monetary and fiscal policies. This is particularly true as long as national monetary authorities hold tight control over important financial institutions such as banks and deliberately limit capital transfers.

Professor James Ingram has a very penetrating discussion of the success of American financial integration among the various states and, recently, with Puerto Rico.[3] Nobody in Puerto Rico knows what the domestic money supply is or worries about inconvertibility or consciously holds exchange reserves. In the middle nineteenth century, financial integration in the U.S. was a less conspicuous success as frontier banks continuously found themselves short of cash and with portfolios of assets they could not market in the east. From time to time, there were waves of regional bank failures. James Ingram considers that the Federal Reserve System came into existence about the time integrated financial markets became completely effective. They suggest that the Fed does not have to make any significant balancing payments among areas because of the marketability of financial assets the banks now have. Undoubtedly the issue of federal government securities also created a very useful interest-bearing liquid asset with which the banking system can be stocked. Given the greater barriers to comprehensive financial integration that now exist in Europe, more deliberate policies in addition to simply removing direct controls on capital movements and creating a common European currency may be necessary. A useful step may be for a central monetary authority within the EEC to issue EEC bonds in return for a fraction of the national debt of each member country. Thus an international security market in "governments" would be created. These "governments" would be a useful quid pro quo in the shifting of cash balances. This additional flexibility would make it much easier for the national governments to turn over their money-issuing power to an EEC authority. This transfer of power is discussed more fully in the last section on transitional problems.

The process of integration in commodity trade has progressed rapidly within the EEC—see table 11.1 below.[4]

Commodity exports (without services) relative to national (international?) income have been taken as a crude measure of interdependence. The year 1952 was chosen as a base point by which to measure the current position (1962) on the premise that most of the distortions in world trade due to World War II had been removed by 1952. The remaining trends should give a rough picture of normal (Cold War) evolution of trade patterns, given the political transformation taking place in Europe. Intra-EEC trade has risen by over 50 percent measured as a fraction of the rapidly growing EEC income. The community as a whole has become slightly more self-sufficient regarding countries outside Western Europe, to which exports dropped about 10 percent measured as a fraction of EEC income. EEC exports to the U.S. and Canada grew but remained quite small in these terms. Intra-EEC exports as a fraction of national income (8.06 percent) would rise if certain periphery countries now part of EFTA (European Free Trade Association) were added. Table 11.2 (page 260) gives the combined position of the EEC and EFTA.

We can see that both groups taken together are surprisingly highly integrated (more so than either the EEC or the EFTA by

Table 11.1
EEC Trade as a Percentage of EEC National Income

	1952	1962
Total EEC National Income (unadjusted billions American dollars)	79.83	168.34
Intra-EEC Exports/EEC National Income	5.37%	8.06%
EEC Exports to Outside World/EEC National Income	12.64%	12.26%
EEC Exports Outside Western Europe/EEC National Income	7.48%	6.72%
EEC Exports to U.S. and Canada/EEC National Income	1.20%	1.65%

Note: See note 4.

Table 11.2
Combined Position of EEC and EFTA

	1952	1962
Combined EEC-EFTA National Income (unadjusted billions American dollars)	135.72	269.96
Intra-EEC–EFTA Exports/National Income	8.77%	11.27%
EEC–EFTA Exports to Outside World/National Income	10.67%	8.81%
EEC–EFTA Exports to U.S./National Income	.87%	1.51%
Intra-EFTA Exports/EFTA National Income	3.93%	3.96%

Note: See note 4.

itself) and there is a strong trend toward further integration. Also, there is a strong trend for the group as a whole toward *less* integration with the outside world. If Britain is excluded from the EFTA for purposes of this calculation, then the figure of 11.27 percent for 1962 for intracommunity trade *rises* to 13.10 percent; external dependence drops to 7.96 percent from 8.81 percent. This significant change reflects the fact that other EFTA countries are much more closely integrated to the EEC than is Britain. The case of Britain will be examined in some detail later on. It should be remembered that currency arrangements themselves will affect the degree of integration.

Combining this empirical analysis with the previous conceptual discussion, it appears that both the level of integration now achieved in Western Europe and the strong trend toward further integration would mean a single currency system encompassing most of Western Europe (with the possible exception of Britain) is rapidly becoming necessary. However, the political possibilities for accomplishing this are greater within the EEC, and it must be the leader. One may have once viewed the two opposing schools of thought, floating exchange rates and fixed rates with financial integration, as alternative means of balance-of-payments control within the Common Market. However, I have tried to show that floating exchange rates become a weaker and less desirable control device as integration increases. Further, to be fully efficient, economic integration requires a concomitant financial integration with a single monetary standard and interest-rate structure. The idea that this financial integration can be avoided through floating exchange rates, while complete economic integration on the American model is achieved, is illusory. The main reason that the intra-European payments system has not yet run into difficulty, given the present system of rigid exchange rates without financial integration, is the soothing balm of the large American balance-of-payments deficits. All European governments have been running overall balance-of-payments surpluses of *varying* degrees which they have used to build up dollar balances. However, these unintended overdoses of American medicine can only be considered a temporary fortunate coincidence for the intra-European payments system. A start must be made on workable European financial integration to provide a payments system for less fortunate but normal circumstances. Without this financial integration, it will be difficult to preserve even the present state of liberalized commodity trade within the EEC, let alone make the future advances so necessary for both political and economic welfare.

11.2   The EEC and the United States: A Dual-Currency World?

The optimum single-currency system for the EEC and most surrounding EFTA countries which are highly integrated with it does not extend to North America. See table 11.3 below.

Either the U.S. alone or Canada and the U.S. combined would form a highly self-contained economy showing a trend toward *increasing* autarky. From 1952 to 1962, there has been about a 10 percent reduction in the fraction of national income earned by exports to the outside world. Direct exports to Western Europe are very small, using the national income measuring rod, only 1.37 percent for the U.S. and 1.58 percent for the combined economies in 1962. Again, if Britain is excluded from Western Europe, these direct export figures drop to 1.13 percent and 1.19 percent, respectively. Conversely, we have similar percentages using Western European income as the yardstick—see tables 11.1 and 11.2. Since the U.S. is not highly integrated with Western Europe, and vice versa, most of the arguments and suggestions for a common currency system in Western Europe can be reversed when applied to relations between the two large areas. In fact, a floating exchange rate between the U.S. dollar and an EEC currency would work well, ignoring for the moment the purely transitional problems. These transitional problems are (1) the adjustment in the exchange rate for any possible overvaluation of the dollar before floating could work smoothly; (2) the position of the large dollar balances currently held by Western Europeans, and other contractual arrangements of various kinds that are denominated in terms of American dollars; and (3) the financial dependence of Europe on the New York securities markets.

Measurement of economic integration by the export/national income ratios should be tempered by a concern for intercountry capital flows. Such flows may be very important for countries without well-organized securities markets of their own. Access to these markets may be valuable even if there is no net capital flow in or out of the country in question. For example, Europeans enter New York securities markets both as buyers and sellers. Of course, large net capital flows reflecting genuine differences in the social profitability of investment will increase the importance of having access to such a market. Thus if one were to weight the importance of financial integration in the above exports/national income ratios these ratios would be shown to understate the interdependence of Western Europe and the United States, and probably to overstate the interdependence among Western European countries.

Although this "perverseness" of financial integration compared to commodity trade is very real at present, it is basically artificial and unnecessary. It simply reflects (a) the absence of a single large currency area in Europe; (b) the restrictions still maintained by European national governments on capital movements; and (c) the development of financial institutions in New York which has not been interrupted by wars and political upheavals of the kind experienced in Europe. The prior existence of specialized financial institutions in New York where economies of large size are important probably greatly hinders the development of equivalent embryonic European institutions. European reliance on the Euro-dollar market is testimony to the absence of a single European currency of sufficiently high liquidity value. The development of a financially integrated single-currency system in Europe, which we have already seen is necessary for balancing intra-European payments, would remove much of the artificial financial dependence on New York. A floating exchange rate would give further impetus toward reducing this dependence. However, there still remain difficult transitional problems which will be considered later in the chapter.

Recently (July 28, 1963), a report to the American government by the Brookings Institution very briefly introduced the notion of a dual-currency system connected by a floating exchange rate as a "second-best" solution if efforts to increase world liquidity are unavailing. This evoked an anguished, but probably prepared, disclaimer from the Under Secretary of the Treasury, Robert Roosa. However, Mr. Roosa's concern was with what I have called the transitional problems—principally the large overseas holdings of American dollars. From a long-run point of view, this floating exchange rate would indeed be the *optimal* solution, provided Europe evolves a single-currency system of liquidity value comparable to that of the American dollar. Since these two large currency areas are not at all closely integrated in commodity trade, a floating exchange rate that continuously changed the prices of goods that entered foreign trade vis-à-vis domestically traded goods, would make virtually no significant impact on average domestic price levels within either area. The profitability of exporting will rise and importing will fall in the areas whose currency was devalued, and vice versa for the other area. This high elasticity of response of the small foreign-trade sector connecting each large area makes the changing exchange rate a fairly efficient control device. Relatively small exchange-rate changes would be required to induce a given proportionate change in the trade balance.

Precisely because the foreign-trade sector is small, continuous alteration of the prices of commodities that enter foreign trade by a floating exchange rate need not have a significant disruptive effect in either large currency area. Short-term capital flows and portfolio investment, which can only be imperfectly hedged, may be reduced, but between large economically developed areas this should be an insignificant economic loss. Very often these portfolio flows are *not* the result of a different social profitability of investment in one large region as compared to another. Rather, they may be the result of different monetary authorities attempting to follow different interest-rate policies at the same time; or they may be speculative movements anticipating exchange rate changes. Thus, these investment flows between large areas with separate currency systems do not necessarily improve the allocation of investment resources between these areas. However, direct investment should not be hampered significantly by a floating exchange rate, and this is the vehicle by which technical information and production know-how are transmitted. For direct investment, actual cash outlays are very small relative to the average rates of return that can be earned on such investment. This increased exchange risk would be a relatively minor consideration for direct investment even though it may be considerable for portfolio investment. As long as both the EEC and the U.S. have virtually equally desirable currencies, there is no reason to fear a chronic flow of portfolio investment in one direction—as one would expect to find from an underdeveloped country to the United States.

Because portfolio investment flows would be less sensitive to interest-rate differentials, and because a changing exchange rate itself would have only a minor disturbing effect on economic activity, different monetary policies tailored to meet domestic needs could be easily carried out with a floating exchange rate. A low-interest-rate policy in one area could be used against unemployment and a high-interest-rate policy in the other against inflation, if need be. The resulting small capital flows cause the low interest rate area's currency to depreciate but this is quite bearable as the resulting disruption in foreign commodity trade would be small in its economy-wide impact. It is anomalous, even pathetic, that the small American foreign-trade sector—see table 11.3—with the much smaller direct trade connection with Western Europe, should be allowed to greatly influence American monetary and fiscal policy. The gains in the value of output to be had from restoring full employment and full capacity are far greater than the dollar value of the whole foreign sector—and this foreign sector need only suffer some inconvenience from the floating exchange rate. This would not be the case if both areas were highly integrated in their commodity trade. Also, since the U.S. and the EEC are not highly integrated, the probability is much greater that there will exist different conditions of inflation or depression in each area compared to the probability of such differing conditions existing among the highly integrated countries of the EEC. Thus it is more important for the U.S. and EEC to be able to use independent monetary and fiscal policies freely, and a floating exchange rate permits them to do so with very low opportunity costs.

Paradoxical as it may seem, it is clear that a high degree of integration between the financial markets of the EEC and U.S.

Table 11.3
Position of the United States and Canada

	1952	1962
U.S. National Income (unadjusted billions American dollars)	292.0	457.5
Total U.S. Exports/National Income	5.15%	4.67%
U.S. Exports to EEC/National Income	0.65%	0.78%
U.S. Exports to Western Europe/National Income	1.13%	1.37%
U.S. Exports to Western Europe excluding U.K./National Income	.87%	1.13%
Canadian National Income (unadjusted billions American dollars)	19.15	28.39
Total Canadian Exports/National Income	23.15%	20.89%
Canadian Exports to U.S./National Income	12.58%	12.36%
Other Canadian Exports/National Income	10.55%	8.52%
Combined Canadian–U.S. National Income	311.5	486.0
Total Net Exports/Combined National Income	4.62%	4.12%
Total Exports to Western Europe/Combined National Income	1.47%	1.58%
Total Exports to Western Europe excluding U.K./Combined National Income	1.01%	1.19%

Note: See note 4.

may *not* be optimal with a floating exchange rate. We would not want capital flows to be sensitive to interest-rate differentials in order that independent monetary policies be feasible. The maintenance of exchange controls on European capital movements and the recent (July 1963) forced imposition of taxes on foreign security purchases by President Kennedy should serve to reduce interest rate sensitivity in the future. An all-or-nothing situation may be desirable. That is, we should either have (1) total financial and economic integration with fixed exchange rates—the optimal internal EEC solution; or (2) a floating exchange rate with limited financial integration—the EEC-U.S. optimal solution. For many countries, the adjustable peg system without financial integration (which they have backed into) gets the disadvantages of both (1) and (2). Countries are inhibited from using monetary policy, or even fiscal policy, vigorously to satisfy domestic needs, and they shrink from using the exchange-rate adjustment until their difficulties become very great. They do not get the full advantage of the division of labor associated with economic integration or complete control of internal full employment. This unsatisfactory middle ground of the adjustable peg may be the concomitant of a country not having (1) or (2) as clear alternatives—a problem which fortunately neither the EEC nor U.S. face.

Appendix

Other Major Trading Nations

The above discussion on optimizing world currency arrangements has dealt with what might be considered the two extreme cases: the relationship among the increasingly integrated Western European countries on the one hand and the relationship between the U.S. and the EEC-EFTA on the other. Again, ignoring transitional problems, the optimal solutions for both these extreme cases are easy to see. The positions of most other countries in the Western world are somewhere in between and less straightforward to diagnose. It seems likely that many small countries will find it optimal to peg their currency to either the EEC currency or the American dollar because of their economic dependence on one bloc or the other and their desire to maintain the liquidity values of their own currencies. The problem of choosing is only really relevant for the advanced countries, which permit free foreign-exchange transactions by all private citizens and have fairly stable domestic price levels so that prices are used as a means of controlling resource allocation. Those countries with extensive exchange controls and continuous internal inflation tend to have their foreign trade more or less directly administered by their governments. Thus, the choice of a particular price system in the form of a peg to a major bloc is not pressing and not sustainable. Presumably, internal inflation will continue to be the dominant factor forcing continuous changes in the prices of their currencies compared to either of the large blocs. The cases of three advanced countries where prices and monetary systems are important are discussed below.

Canada

The Canadian case is interesting because Canada tried a floating exchange rate prior to 1962, and it appeared to work rather well in balancing international payments. Canada is a highly open economy, as table 11.3 shows. We note that Canadian economic dependence on the U.S. has remained very high while its interdependence with the outside world has declined significantly in the ten-year period 1952–62. In 1962, the average integration level with the U.S.—12.37 percent of its production going to the U.S.—was similar to integration so far achieved in Western Europe; see table 11.2. However, Western Europe has a strong trend toward further integration while there is no such trend between Canada and the U.S. Whether there would have been such a trend if Canada had a common currency system with the U.S. is impossible to divine. This is not the place to give a detailed analysis of Canada's position, but some casual empiricism would suggest that the Canadian experience gives some support for a single North American currency system. Certainly, the range of fluctuation in the exchange rate for the Canadian dollar was small after 1952—about 8 percent. This exchange-rate stability existed while there was a large fairly smooth capital flow from the U.S. into Canada, although the Canadian dollar had to appreciate significantly in the period 1950–52 to accommodate this inflow. The machinations of Canadian politicians in 1961 aimed at disrupting the capital flow into Canada were largely motivated by the belief that the Canadian dollar was overvalued, and they tried to "talk it down." Further ham-fisted tactics involving attempts to tax American investors early in 1963 have greatly weakened the smooth workings of capital flows between the two countries. However, they do highlight certain difficulties in Canada's carrying out a separate monetary policy even with a floating exchange rate.

Generally, the conditions of inflation and recession in the postwar United States were reflected in Canada, and there was no need for significantly different monetary and fiscal policies in Canada as compared to the U.S. In fact, the Canadian authorities used their scope for independent monetary and fiscal policies (given to them by the floating exchange rate) rather badly after 1956. Interest rates on Canadian government bonds were kept about a point and a half above the American equivalent from 1957 to the beginning of 1962. This attracted a capital inflow from the U.S., which largely replaced Canadian financing but had the additional effect of keeping the value of the Canadian dollar high, which hampered export expansion and encouraged imports. Economic stagnation which existed in the U.S. in this period was much greater in Canada, where per capital real incomes did not rise and unemployment was much higher.

Great Britain

One unique aspect of the Brookings report was the idea of a pound-dollar peg, with both floating in terms of the EEC currency as an alternative to improving world liquidity arrangements. From a short-term point of view this seems reasonable, since both currencies are probably slightly overvalued and need the opportunity to embark on expansionary monetary and fiscal policy without being hampered by foreign balance constraints. However, from a longer-run point of view, what the monetary position of Britain should be is not so clear, as table 11A.1 shows.

Although the fastest-growing part of an otherwise declining foreign-trade sector is direct exports to the EEC, total exports to both the EEC and the EFTA countries are not high by other standards, i.e., the

integration achieved among EEC and other EFTA countries—see table
11.2. British exports to the U.S. and Canada, using the national income
yardstick, have grown a little but still remain moderately small. Exports
to the sterling area show a drastically declining trend but still remain
a large component of total trade.

There seem to be at least three alternatives, assuming the sterling
area remains tied to Britain: (1) the pound-dollar peg; (2) a pound-
EEC-EFTA currency peg; (3) a separately floating British pound. One
great difficulty in making a choice is that the choice itself will likely
have some effect on the future development of trade patterns. The
short-run solution of a floating pound-dollar may inhibit the potential
future British integration with Western Europe, contrary to Britain's
long-run economic and political interests. Alternative (3) has the same
difficulty as (1) but brings up the question of whether the pound sterling
area is sufficiently "large" in the sense that I have used the term. Is
the foreign-trade sector sufficiently small that continuous balance can
be achieved through relatively small fluctuations in the exchange rate?
The Canadian experience indicates that Britain is sufficiently "large"
and, with more prudent monetary policy than Canada used, could
probably successfully float the pound without any immediate difficulties, although the rest of the sterling area, with their heavy capital
needs, might not go along with a floating pound.

The real dilemma for Britain is whether or not to aim for the possibility of unhampered use of monetary and fiscal policy for short-run
objectives, i.e., the floating exchange rate, or try for the longer-run
objective of integration with one of the larger blocs. Modern technological developments seem to make economies of scale increasingly important so that truly *competitive* capitalism can only function efficiently
within a large market area. However, the transition period would be
difficult because of the short-run need to maintain the free use of
monetary and fiscal policy.

Table 11A.1
Position of Great Britain

	1952	1962
British National Income (unadjusted billions American dollars)	35.69	63.0
Total Exports/National Income	20.15%	16.86%
Exports to EEC/National Income	2.27%	3.21%
Exports to EFTA/National Income	2.06%	2.05%
Exports to U.S. & Canada/National Income	2.17%	2.30%
Exports to Sterling Area/National Income	9.65%	5.97%

Note: See note 4.

Japan

The position of Japan is similar to that of Britain as it has a moderately large and fairly open economy, but it could potentially gain a good deal with more complete integration with an outside bloc. Japanese exports to the U.S. have been growing relatively fast even in terms of its rapidly growing national income. Exports to Western Europe have been growing much less quickly. As yet, Japan is not heavily integrated through trade into either large bloc although the statistics given in table 11A.2 probably understate Japanese dependence on international trade. The ability of the Japanese to get critical raw materials and advanced capital goods—largely from North America—has been crucial for its rapid economic growth. Only recently has the Japanese government taken some modest steps to liberalize the importation of manufactured consumer goods. Thus, export earnings have been largely used to buy only the most necessary "hardcore" imports. Further reciprocal trade agreement between Japan and the North Atlantic countries could mean a continued relative expansion in Japanese foreign trade relative to Japanese national income. Such an evolution implies that the extensive direct controls Japanese authorities now exercise over commodity trade would have to be liberalized to the point where Japan could become a full-fledged member of GATT (the General Agreement on Tariffs and Trade).

However, given the present highly managed nature of the Japanese currency (including controls of capital movements), a free foreign-exchange market with a floating exchange rate would not work too well. The foreign-trade sector would not be responsive to continuous price changes in the yen, both internally and externally where Japanese exports still face administrative restrictions on the part of many countries. The optimal interim solution would seem to be to maintain the yen-dollar peg with continued management of the yen as the main control device. In the future, as liberalization of direct controls proceeds, a decision to try for complete economic integration with North America might be made if the political conditions were right. This integration could be viable if it took place both in the capital markets

Table 11A.2
The Position of Japan

	1952	1962
Japanese National Income (unadjusted billions American dollars)	13.73	43.66
Total Exports/National Income	9.25%	11.27%
Exports to U.S./National Income	1.71%	3.23%
Exports to Western Europe/National Income	1.31%	1.58%

Note: See note 4.

and in commodity trade, as is necessary in the case of Western Europe. Indeed, access to American capital markets is probably quite important for Japanese economic development. Thus, even in the absence of complete economic integration with the U.S., the Japanese government should try, as best it can, to maintain the yen-dollar peg in a dual-currency system.

Notes

The author is deeply indebted to Professor Emile Despres for providing ideas and advice that appear throughout the chapter. However, Despres should not be implicated in all the policy conclusions.

1. For a more precise and detailed discussion of this idea, see my "Optimum Currency Areas," in *American Economic Review*, September 1963: 717–25 (chapter 10 above).

2. James E. Meade, "The Case for Variable Exchange Rates," *Three Banks Review*, No. 27 (Sept. 1955), and "The Future of International Trade and Payments," *Three Banks Review*, No. 50 (June 1961).

3. James Ingram, *Regional Payments Mechanisms: The Case of Puerto Rico*, University of North Carolina Press, 1962.

4. This and subsequent tables were constructed from information provided in the *Monthly Bulletin of Statistics* of the United Nations, and *International Financial Statistics* of the International Monetary Fund. The Export/National Income ratio has ambiguities as a measure of "integration," particularly when more than two countries are involved. Nevertheless, it has some intuitively satisfying meaning, particularly when trends are important. Note that national income is used in the denominator and not gross national product and that some of the national income statistics for 1962 are preliminary.

12　Floating Foreign-Exchange Rates 1973–74: The Emperor's New Clothes

The relative merits of fixed versus floating exchange rates can be seriously debated only if both are feasible as alternative economic policies. During most of the postwar period, for example, both options have been open bilaterally to Canada and the United States. However, major industrial countries are now experiencing markedly differential rates of price inflation that generate expectations of incipient price and cost misalignments in the future. Hence, the clearing of foreign-exchange transactions apparently requires continuous changes in relative currency values to avoid exorbitant losses in currency convertibility and in the freedom of international trade in goods and services. Return to a parity system óf fixed rates is out of the question, unless it were to be preceded by domestic monetary reforms and international monetary cooperation of a far-reaching kind beyond the purview of this chapter[1]—and probably beyond that of most monetary authorities as well.

Though economists recognize the imperial necessity of floating rates at the present time, our experiences in 1973–74 have been surprising. The models of international trade and monetary adjustment developed in the 1950s and 1960s to portray continuous flexibility on the one hand, and the impact of major appreciations and depreciations on the balance of trade on the other, seem seriously deficient. In discharging my obligation to do "an assessment of recent experience concerning floating exchange rates," I shall concentrate on the unexpectedly

Originally published, in slightly longer form, in *Carnegie Rochester Conference Series on Public Policy*, ed. K. Brunner and A. Meltzer (North-Holland, 1976), 79–114. Reprinted with permission.

large daily, monthly, and quarterly fluctuations in exchange rates among major currencies that continue to the present writing. Their consequences for the "misalignment" of international price levels, in the sense of purchasing power parity, and for the allocative efficiency of commodity trade are then explored.

However, the macroeconomic repercussions of exchange-rate fluctuations on domestic price inflation, on real output and employment, or on each country's trade balance are omitted. Hence no attempt is made to review the efficacy of the elasticities approach versus the absorption approach versus the monetary (asset-adjustment) approach to the balance of payments. Instead, I concentrate more on the direct microeconomic causes and consequences of instability in the foreign exchanges. Foreign-exchange transactions are analyzed in section 12.2 from the point of view of the direct participants: banks, multinational corporations, and individuals, whether they be hedgers, commercial traders, or speculators.

Writers in the 1950s and 1960s who espoused freely floating exchange rates—Friedman (1953), Sohmen (1961), Johnson (1972), and Machlup (1972) are taken to be representative authors for this purpose—did not foresee certain peculiar characteristics of the present (1974) system of floating rates:

1. Current movements in spot exchange rates of 20 percent quarter-to-quarter, 5 percent week-to-week, or even 1 percent on a day-to-day basis are now not unusual, although they are very large by historical standards.[2]

2. Concomitantly, bid-ask spreads in the spot market have widened significantly from the 1960s.

3. Bid-ask spreads in forward markets have risen relatively more sharply—particularly in longer-term contracts, where trade has tended to diminish. Interbank forward trading—although not necessarily bank-customer forward trading—may have declined. Floating rates have not induced any noticeable expansion in the facilities for forward trading across pairs of currencies, or in longer-term contracts.

4. Forward rates have been poor predictors of future spot rates.[3]

5. Some commercial banks have suffered severe foreign-exchange losses, and a few have gone bankrupt.

6. Official intervention has continued at a level as high as or higher than under the old fixed-rate system.[4]

These points more or less describe the state of the foreign exchanges during 1973 and 1974, after the breakdown of the Smithsonian Agreements. While volatile hourly and daily changes in exchange rates are difficult to portray graphically, weekly quotations from February 1973 for the German mark in U.S. dollars are provided by Chicago's International Monetary Market (figure 12.1). Not only are the weekly and quarterly movements large for this particular exchange rate, but they seem cyclical without a pronounced trend.

One might contrast this volatility and the high cost of foreign-exchange transactions in 1973–74 with a statement made by Machlup (1972, p. 70) that is indicative of his feeling about the smoothness of adjustment in a flexible-rate system:

Under a system of greater flexibility such serious misalignments of exchange rates would never, or hardly ever, arise, and expectations of change would be confined to minuscule adjustments. Profits from small changes can be only small, inviting only moderate speculation, which can be easily discouraged, if this is wanted, by relatively minor differentials in interest rates.

Machlup was not alone. Other notable writers such as Friedman, Johnson, and Sohmen have maintained similar views on the gradualness of adjustment under floating rates, which they contrasted favorably with the sharp discrete changes and one-way speculative frenzies of the old pegged-rate system. Under floating rates, it was imagined that forward markets and hedging facilities would expand to offset future uncertainty; private speculation would stabilize the spot and forward markets. In contrast, the fragmentary evidence from the 1973–74 period points in the opposite direction.

Though floating exchange rates are recognized as a necessity at the present time, why has past theorizing failed to comprehend the present "disordered" and high-cost state of the markets for foreign exchange as described by points (1) through (6) above? The easiest explanation is that the world has been subject to a

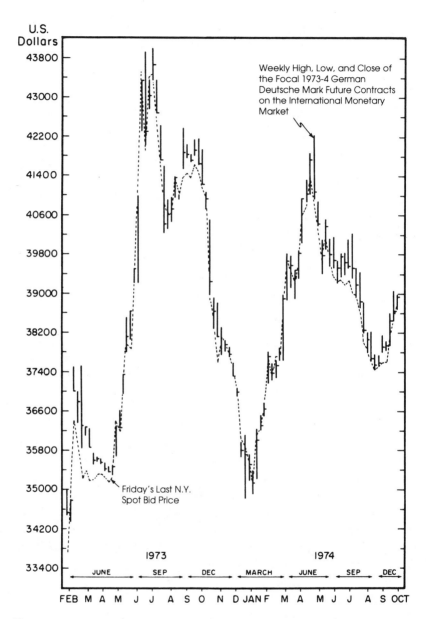

Figure 12.1
Weekly high, low, and close of the focal 1973–74 German deutsche mark future
contracts on the International Monetary Market.

number of unpredictable shocks—general inflation emanating from the United States, delayed dollar devaluation, a grain crisis, an oil crisis, and so on. Such successive shocks, and the consequent difficulty in making a full evaluation of their economic consequences, have made smoother, lower-cost operation of the foreign exchanges impossible.

Alternatively, if a purist takes official reserve turnover as a significant indicator of intervention (Williamson 1974), it might suggest that the no-par system has not settled down because governments continue to intervene. The coalescence of private expectations regarding correctly aligned exchange rates is interrupted because official intervention is so unpredictable. Thus the current system of dirty floating hardly constitutes a pure test of how freely flexible exchange rates might behave.

Both the "exogenous-shock" and the "purist" explanations are consistent with the a priori reasoning that Machlup, Friedman, and others have used to justify a system of uninhibited floating. Indeed, both explanations likely have some validity. I would submit, however, that an important institutional element was lacking from the earlier defenses of floating rates, the importance of which has only now become apparent. The questions of *who* was to be a stabilizing speculator, and *what* would be the source of private capital for such speculations, were never directly addressed. Rather, this particular issue was superseded by a rough-and-tumble debate over whether private speculation would be stabilizing or destabilizing. An implicit consensus had been reached that there would be no restraints on the availability of private speculative capital on the huge scale needed.

The contrary hypothesis, advanced here, is that the supply of private capital for taking net positions in either the forward or spot markets is currently inadequate. Exchange rates then move sharply in response to random variations in the day-to-day excess demand by merchants for foreign exchange. Once a rate starts to move because of some temporary perturbation, no prospective speculator is willing to hold an open position for a significant time interval in order to bet on a reversal—whence the large daily and monthly movements in the foreign exchanges and high bid-ask spreads. Bandwagon psychologies result from the general unwillingness of participants to take net positions against near-term market movements.

Thus, the problem seems not to be one of excessive destabilizing speculation, but rather one of the absence of speculation over time horizons longer than a day or two.

12.1 Banking Risk versus Currency Risk

Perhaps implicit in the traditional theory of flexible rates, the commercial banks were the natural candidates for the role of stabilizing speculators. After all, the principal spot and forward markets for foreign exchange are interbank markets. Expertise in the foreign exchanges is largely confined to employees of the large banks and, to a lesser extent, multinational corporations.[5] Whatever tentative speculative efforts were made, however, seem to have been cut short by a rash of bank failures for those on the losing end. Governments and central banks have now pressed commercial banks to balance more strictly their net position in foreign exchange. Hence, commercial banks are restricted—and perhaps correctly so—from taking speculative positions.

Official restraints on net foreign-exchange positions of commercial banks parallel similar restraints on their domestic loan portfolios and liquidity reserves that have long been regulated. Most banking textbooks emphasize the uneasy trade-off between the unique role of the commercial banks to provide a secure *means of payment* against their more general role as financial intermediaries between savers and investors—a role that ordinarily demands aggressive investment and money-market behavior. The commercial banks can attract capital easily by issuing money—legal tender often guaranteed by the state. In return, the government sees fit to limit their aggressiveness in the capital market—possibly reducing immediate real yields in the economy—by safety-first regulations designed to secure money as a means of payment. In addition, reserve requirements permit control over the nominal money base and, ultimately, official control over the nominal price level.

In the international sphere, excessive speculative risk in the foreign exchanges might also impair the security of deposits in purely domestic currency. Hence central banks may well limit the net foreign-exchange exposure of their commercial banks to, say, 20 percent of their owners' equity. This and similar constraining regulations are designed to reduce "banking risk"—the possibility of insolvency on the part of the custodians of the domestic money supply.

However, banking risk pervades international as well as domestic trade. Central banks have largely withdrawn from trading one currency for another at a known parity. But responsibility to clear foreign currencies remains with the commercial banks—who provide currencies on demand to depositors or honor forward commitments requiring the trade of domestic for foreign money. Large shifts in relative currency values, or the imposition of unexpected foreign-exchange controls, militate toward a risk-avoidance view of securing interbank payments in international monies against default. It is one thing for a nonbank individual or firm to risk holding a foreign currency unhedged against exchange-rate changes: this "currency risk" was indeed envisaged by proponents of flexible exchange rates as a real social cost of doing international business. It is quite another matter, however, for the nonbank firm to be continually worried about the insolvency of the bank on which it has a foreign-currency claim. The currency risk was foreseen by the old literature but the banking risk was not. Hence a fairly strong case can be made for banks that specialize in foreign-currency transactions to maintain balanced positions that limit their speculative activities and so reduce the banking risk to other firms and individuals.

This point has been recognized by the managements of major commercial banks, and, with a slightly longer lag, by central banks. Large American banks rather quickly responded to the currency fluctuations beginning in 1973 by requiring that their foreign-exchange dealers more strictly limit their net open position in any one foreign currency at the end of each trading day. In addition to this general stricture, balance requirements have been imposed at every maturity in spot and forward trading; a short forward position can no longer be balanced by a long spot position in the same currency. However, the Federal Reserve Bank has not yet tried to formally regulate the foreign-exchange positions of American commercial banks.

On the other hand, European commercial banks have, traditionally, been more willing to take net positions in foreign exchange if only to serve their relatively greater volume of foreign-exchange transactions. Foreign-exchange dealings have been thought by some to be an "art" in which European financial institutions have particularly great expertise. However, in response to a few commercial-bank failures and other large foreign-exchange losses, European central banks have now promulgated a series of directives that formally limit the net foreign-exchange positions of their commercial banks. Instead of learning how to speculate successfully in a floating-rate system as time passes, commercial banks are becoming more conservative nonspeculators: negative learning by doing. Thus it is not surprising that central banks have been partially drawn back into the market to take balancing positions in foreign exchange although they no longer have parity obligations.

From this angle, one sees a bit better the social advantages of a central bank's "speculating" to maintain an official parity, as was done under the Bretton Woods system. Even when a central bank was eventually forced to adjust discretely its pegged rate, and so take large bookkeeping losses, commercial banks could bail themselves out and get what foreign exchange they needed to cover their commitments at a known price. Similarly, multinational corporations could also easily take defensive positions against discrete appreciations or depreciations. Thus private positions in foreign exchange had not to be balanced so closely on a continuous basis. The willingness of governments to take large losses under Bretton Woods did secure the safety of the payments mechanism to a degree greater than was recognized by academic economists. In effect, some of the losses that used to be borne by central banks have now been shifted to commercial banks and firms. The resulting fear of bankruptcy has impaired confidence in interbank clearing domestically and internationally.

In summary, the withdrawal of central banks from their parity commitments has shifted the currency risk of exchange-rate changes to private speculators as expected, but brought also an increase in banking risk (insolvency) that was not anticipated. This increase in banking risk has reduced the supply of capital available for currency speculation.

12.2   Forward Trading and the Capital Constraint

Banking risk is related to another common theme in the literature on floating exchange rates: private trading in the forward markets for foreign exchange would expand once central banks withdrew from their parity commitments. However, a good part of the increase in demand for forward cover that floating rates might have portended seems to have been shifted to the spot market. Firms wishing to hedge simply buy (or sell) foreign currencies ahead of their needs and hold them spot in the form of interest-bearing assets in the Eurocurrency market (Krul 1974). Facilities for forward trading per se do not seem to have expanded as predicted.[6]

Many academic treatises have stressed the irrelevance of forward markets for hedging commodity trade because a trader could always purchase foreign currency spot and hold it until needed. However, in times of payments uncertainty and fear of default by firms or banks with forward contracts, a substantial asymmetry arises. The implicit or explicit margin required by banks of their customers in order to make a forward commitment would normally rise with the fear of unexpected oscillations in exchange rates—currency risk. Since the cost of the margin requirement is likely to be substantial (unless covered by implicit seigniorage from non-interest-bearing demand deposits), the firm wishing to hedge may find it more advantageous to hold foreign currency spot where, implicitly, the margin requirement is 100 percent but full interest compensation is paid. While the standard textbook analysis gives no reason to believe that holding spot is preferable to buying forward, currency risk raises the margin costs of forward contracting and shifts nonbank firms to holding spot. In addition, the desire of each commercial bank to maintain balance in foreign currency at every forward maturity makes organization of forward trading more awkward.

On the other side of the coin, firms may doubt the ability of banks to meet forward payments; hence banking risk leads them to *prefer* to hold foreign currencies spot—aside from the higher costs of forward contracting. There is always a good chance that current deposits in foreign currency can be quickly withdrawn if the solvency of the bank providing the deposits comes into question; whereas a company holding forward contracts, which mature in several months, is helpless if the delivering bank appears on the brink of insolvency.

In summary, the threat of default from either currency risk or banking risk effectively shortens the term structure of forward financing in the foreign exchanges. This shortening manifests itself in higher bid-ask spreads in forward quotations, but perhaps more importantly in a shift by firms to hedging by holding spot foreign exchange—largely in Eurocurrency markets.

Well, what difference does it all make? The standard textbook analysis would suggest none: forward contracting and holding foreign exchange spot were thought to be exactly equivalent. However, there is a *capital constraint* that has been made rather more acute by the current turn of events. Companies who want foreign currency in the future must find 100 percent of the capital in the present and convert spot. Forward contracting might in the old days have required only a 5 percent to 10 percent margin. Either more of a company's equity or more of its borrowing capacity now has to be utilized in hedging spot. A company's ability to be venturesome and exploit other profitable investment opportunities is thereby reduced.

How does this shortening of term influence the capital constraint facing commercial banks overall? Instead of a series of relatively longer-term forward commitments, the meeting of which can be planned with due deliberation, the banking system now finds itself extending very short-term credit and issuing current deposits (withdrawable virtually on demand) in foreign currencies to those customers who otherwise might have taken less liquid forward positions. Thus pressure on the "owned" capital of the banks magnifies their liquidity problems; the volume of business that they are able to conduct on attractive terms declines. In short, the heightened uncertainty has increased the capital requirements of both banks and their customers and restricted the scope of their operations. The social costs of shifting from forward to spot are of some consequence, contrary to what past literature on forward markets in foreign exchange might have suggested.

This capital constraint on the ability of banks to meet demands on them has, of course, been further exacerbated by the need to recycle "hot" oil money in huge quantities with an unduly short term structure. Hence the oil crisis further reduces the capability of the commercial banks to act as stabilizing speculators. This unfortunate complication, which greatly increases the uncertainty already plaguing financial markets and threatens the structure of international commodity trade, could hardly have been foreseen in the past literature on flexible exchange rates and forward trading. Thus the oil problem is exogenous to my main theme and will not be analyzed further.

12.3 Multinational Corporations and Other Nonspeculators

What ever happened to the multinational corporations, those ogres of speculative runs under the old fixed-rate regime? Surely these giants of unlimited international wealth and power need not hesitate to take a net position in this or that currency if it appears to be seriously "misaligned" (Machlup's terminology). However, the division of labor seems important to them: they prefer to be merchants and manufacturers rather than foreign-exchange speculators. Many companies have clearly defined policies against speculation in the foreign exchanges.

More strongly perhaps, evidence exists of excessive hedging of items on the multinationals' balance sheets. The current profusion of literature on the translation problem across a firm's balance sheets denominated in several currencies seems aimed at complete risk avoidance. Yet rigid adherence to either of the two main accounting rules for translation—the monetary-nonmonetary method or the current-noncurrent method—coupled with a desire to hedge against foreign-exchange losses in a formal accounting sense, can inadvertently aggravate foreign-exchange risk in the true economic sense and reduce profits.

Insofar as multinationals are now reluctant to take net positions in foreign exchange for reasons adumbrated above, hedging future imports or exports of goods and services requires that they hold spot positions in foreign exchange that must be fully financed—and so impinge seriously on the multinationals' capital constraint. Given the current state of the stock market and the financing needs of ordinary business, the freeing of capital for speculative purposes in the foreign exchanges can hardly be given a high priority by big companies whose existence in the long run depends on their expertise in manufacturing or commerce.

With both commercial banks and multinationals minimizing their net foreign-exchange exposure, it is not evident that private individuals have sufficient capital, knowledge, or ease of access to the market to take up the slack. Commercial banks have never made it easy for individuals who were not major depositors to take speculative positions. The International Monetary Market of the Chicago Mercantile Exchange does cater to individuals, but it is not booming. The contractual obligations for actual delivery of foreign exchange are complex, and trading in foreign currencies is not a game that nonspecialists can easily play.

12.4 Speculating without International Money

Beyond these institutional restraints on banks, multinational corporations, and individuals, there may be a somewhat deeper explanation of the inadequate availability of private speculative capital in the current environment. I refer to the problem of the "riskless asset" alias the "home currency" alias "international money."

Let us first distinguish arbitrage from speculation since the former seems not to present difficulties under floating rates. Define arbitrage to take place at a single point in time, where traders (mainly banks) simply buy and sell foreign exchange to make cross rates among $n-1$ currencies consistent with the $n-1$ bilateral exchange rates of each with an nth currency. The nth can be chosen arbitrarily without having the properties of international money. As is well known, the total number of exchange rates to be arbitraged in an n-country world is $n(n-1)1/2$. Accurate multilateral arbitrage across currencies is, of course, a *necessary condition* for efficient multilateral trade in goods and services. However, it is not sufficient once intertemporal international resource allocation is considered.

Arbitrageurs seem to operate reasonably efficiently under the present system of symmetrically floating exchange rates. An increase in the bid-ask spread in foreign currencies from 1972 to 1974 suggests slightly greater costs—salaries of foreign-exchange traders, bank capital, and so forth—from floating in comparison to the old pegged-rate system. However, serious multilateral inconsistencies in spot exchange rates are not evident. Continued intervention by various governments in the foreign exchanges has not seemingly provoked any obvious conflict in international economic policies.[7] Of course massive failures by commercial banks in any one country, or official restraints on free convertibility in making payments, could hinder arbitrage—but this has yet to happen.

Let us define "speculation" to be the purchase of one currency for another (forward or spot) in order to hold an open position *through time* in anticipation of a favorable change in relative currency prices. In arbitrage, the emphasis is on multilateral currency trading at one point in time,[8] whereas the risk and gain in speculating comes primarily from the way exchange rates move through time—perhaps over extended periods. A peculiar combination of expertise in the foreign exchanges, knowledge of economic policies in particular countries, and access to finance is required for speculation to be privately profitable and socially stabilizing.

The recent sharp but largely reversed movements in exchange rates seem to be prima facie evidence of the absence of stabilizing speculation.[9] If so, what in the current system of generally floating rates and differing national price inflation militates against successful speculation, although not against successful arbitrage? Official restraint on the net foreign-exchange positions of commercial banks is one obvious candidate; private uncertainty about the future of national monetary policies is another. In the latter category, private speculation is rendered more difficult in the absence of any recognized international money that could otherwise act as a stable and liquid international store of value. *Speculators need a haven, a relatively riskless asset, from which they can operate.*

To tackle this last point analytically, the concept of international money is divided into an unrestricted and into a somewhat more limited meaning. The free international circulation of gold coins, whose value in exchange depends simply on their weight and fineness, is an example of unrestricted international money. If, in addition, one places strict limits on fiduciary national monies issued at par with international money, the exchange-rate problem simply disappears. Relative national monetary values become unalterably fixed. Hence, the concept of unrestricted international money is *not* analytically useful for analyzing the present system of floating exchange rates. One can imagine (with some difficulty) the European Monetary Union recalling all national currencies of member countries, and issuing its own notes and deposits that were recognized as the sole legal tender in

Europe: international money in an unrestricted form over a limited number of countries.

The existence of international money since World War II, however, has taken a more limited form. The United States dollar was not legal tender or a medium of exchange for purely domestic transactions in most important countries. Indeed, in countries with freely convertible currencies, the *domestic currency* itself serves as international money in the sense that nonbank firms and individuals can write checks on demand deposits in domestic currency in order to meet international payments. By and large, individuals and firms that are domestic residents need not hold checking accounts abroad in foreign currencies, and generally find such overseas accounts to be inconvenient as long as the domestic currency remains freely convertible into foreign exchange. Exporters typically invoice their overseas sales in terms of the domestic currency as long as it is convertible.[10]

However, the position of banks is quite different. They are responsible for converting domestic into various possible foreign currencies as intermediaries for their nonbank customers. To facilitate currency conversions, a typical commercial bank will hold a fairly wide portfolio of checking accounts abroad in foreign currencies with correspondent banks. In order to limit the number of separate accounts and the diversity of foreign-exchange commitments that can be easily "covered," the commercial banks in, say, Sweden may well concentrate their overseas checking accounts in recognized international currencies—such as the U.S. dollar—in which a high proportion of interbank trading is organized. Thus, instead of holding checking accounts in Australian dollars to service customers dealing with Australia, a Swedish commercial bank may use U.S. dollar deposits as an intermediary claim on Australian dollars. In this sense, U.S. dollars (as well as British sterling balances) have served as "bank money" in the postwar period even though they may not be held by nonbank firms and individuals.

In forward trading, the use of an intermediary currency such as U.S. dollars is even more pronounced. Indeed a forward market between Swedish kronor and Australian dollars is unlikely to exist—even at short maturities—because of an insufficient volume of transactions. Hence, if a Swedish importer wants to buy Australian dollars forward with kronor, he first sells forward the kronor for U.S. dollars, and then sells U.S. dollars forward for Australian dollars through contracts that mature at the same point in time. Quite possibly, the Swedish importer will not undertake this dual transaction directly: his agent—a Swedish commercial bank—purchases forward Australian dollars against U.S. dollars while selling kronor against U.S. dollars. Thus the commercial bank may be left with the dual commitment in the interbank market in forward foreign exchange, whereas the Swedish importer simply has the forward obligation to sell Swedish kronor for Australian dollars to his banking agent.

We see, therefore, the importance of having a relatively riskless asset like U.S. dollars that can be used as "bank" money or more generally. Indeed, with $n(n-1)\ 1/2$ exchange rates in a system of n convertible currencies, it is unlikely that well-developed spot markets will exist for each cross rate—let alone that there will be forward trading between each pair of currencies at several different maturities. How well has the U.S. dollar served in this intermediary role as a relatively riskless bank asset? From 1950 to 1966 its real value, measured in terms of internationally tradable goods and services, was well maintained (McKinnon 1971); the dollar was an attractive store of value and numeraire for longer-term international transactions. Moreover, the dollar was virtually fully liquid in facilitating private international transactions on current or capital account, and dollar assets bore an attractive interest yield. For official interventions to peg exchange rates and to acquire reserves, the U.S. dollar was the most convenient vehicle currency because official par values were established in U.S. dollars. Since the late 1960s, however, high and variable American price inflation has made the U.S. dollar less useful as a "riskless" interbank foreign-exchange asset, but not so much as to supplant its intermediary role in the interbank market with some other currency.

Temporarily putting aside the important empirical question of the stability of the U.S. dollar, consider how private speculation would be conducted if a stable international money—defined in our limited sense—existed. Although one might still live in a world of n fluctuating currencies, speculators—whether banks or nonbanks—are now free to specialize in particular bilateral relationships between each of the other currencies and the international money in question. The breadth of market information required of any one trader is thereby reduced; the international money serves as a convenient repository (riskless asset) for defining the speculator's equity and his profits.

Let us illustrate with two commonly cited historical examples of smoothly floating exchange rates: the Austro-Hungarian gulden from 1879 to 1892, and the Canadian dollar from 1950 to 1962. In the first case,[11] British sterling served as international money, allowing free access to the London capital markets; in the latter case, the U.S. dollar served as the home currency, and the New York capital market was a source of finance to the Canadian economy.

If an individual speculator wanted to be short in gulden, he could do so conveniently by going long in sterling with funds raised or normally held in London. Of course, the speculator would have to follow weather reports on Austrian crops, chart the Austrian money supply, understand Austrian tariff policy, and follow Austria's numerous military imbroglios with diplomatic and strategic insight. Having mastered that, he could safely take his profits in sterling and not worry about being long in sterling half the time. He did not need to be directly concerned with the $n-2$ exchange rates between gulden and currencies other than sterling. The presence of secure international money, therefore, allowed the speculator to specialize in knowing Austria—a reasonably big job in itself. The consequent reduction in informational uncertainty increased the availability of capital for taking open positions in 1879–92 gulden. Similarly, in 1950–62, speculators could conveniently use the U.S. dollar to take open positions against the Canadian dollar.

Hence, the correct analytical interpretation of the satisfactory Austrian and Canadian experiences with speculation is not quite the obvious one that they were alone in floating while the rest of the world was mainly on fixed rates. Even if most countries had been floating their exchange rates in the 1879–92 or 1950–62 periods, the presence of secure international money—sterling or U.S. dollars—would economize on information (provide a riskless asset) and allow speculators to specialize in one currency by always taking their positions in that currency against international money.

Put differently, in a regime of several floating currencies—say, lire, marks, and dollars—would a speculator always go short in that currency that was judged to be the "weakest" while simultaneously going long in that judged to be "strongest"? No, because of the fundamental problem of *timing* based on rapidly changing market information. Having studied the Italian situation with decentralized care, he may find a particular point in time opportune to take a short forward position in lire against U.S. dollars—which is the one currency in which complete forward markets exist against all others. A while later (perhaps never), the German situation may develop favorably enough (according to our speculator's research) to warrant taking a long forward position in marks against U.S. dollars. His net dollar position is now zero. However, he did hold an open long position in dollars for a significant time period whose exact duration was uncertain after his lire transaction. Put more extremely, in the day-to-day or even the hour-to-hour smoothing of random exchange fluctuations, a speculator with highly specialized information on particular countries would prefer to deal only with the intermediary currency if he knew it to be safe.

From the above reasoning, the potential supply of speculative capital for the smoothing of foreign-exchange markets in 1973–74 is much reduced by the decline in the United States dollar as stable international money. For example, to go short in French francs for a year hence, in which currency should one be long at the end of that period? American monetary policy could go awry in the interim and greatly depreciate the U.S. dollar vis-à-vis some average basket of currencies or some representative bundle of tradable goods. Our potential foreign-currency speculator now needs expertise in several currencies in order to find a proper offset for his potential short position in francs. The increased uncertainty reduces his willingness to commit his own equity, and limits his capacity to borrow for speculative purposes.

In short, the markets for foreign exchange can tolerate diversity in $n-1$ national monetary policies without drying up the supply of speculative capital if and only if the nth currency is known to be stable. (Of course, the more erratic and uncertain the monetary policy in any of the $n-1$ countries, the more binding becomes the capital constraint on speculators in that particular currency.) On the other hand, if no consensus is reached on what is stable international money, there may be endless surges from one currency to another to find a home. Hot money flows—whether by multinationals or Arabs—are essentially defensive rather than speculative; they serve to widen rather than dampen fluctuations in relative currency values.

12.5 The Role of Central Banks in a No-Parity System

In summary, we have a dual explanation of why "stabilizing" private speculation has not developed in the way the old literature on flexible foreign-exchange rates seemed to portend—even on an hour-to-hour basis, let alone quarter-to-quarter. In the very short run, commercial banks are the only private institutions with convenient access to the foreign-exchange markets for taking transitory open positions as dealers. However, they are now unwilling to incur banking risk that jeopardizes their positions as custodians of the payments mechanism—and are increasingly inhibited by central banks from taking such risks. This basic monetary function of the banks prevents high potential profits, from short-run smoothing of foreign exchange transactions, to attract them into making a stable market as dealers on a daily or hourly basis. However, do we want anything other than fairly conservative financial institutions to be responsible for clearing international payments—or domestic payments for all that?

But nonbanks would have access to the spot and forward exchange market (using the banks as intermediaries) to hold open positions for longer-run speculations—say weekly, monthly, or yearly. Aside from the capital constraint on all risky enterprise, these longer-run speculations are inhibited by uncertainty (as distinct from actuarial risk) on how individual national central banks might conduct their monetary policies. In particular, the absence of a generally accepted riskless asset (international money in a limited form) makes decentralized speculation in any particular currency very difficult, and greatly increases the implicit price demanded for such risk-taking.

Hence central banks have been attracted back into the foreign-exchange markets in a big way because (1) they have a potential comparative advantage in long-run speculations through their control of national monetary policy; (2) they can enter the interbank market for foreign exchange in the short run without being hampered by capital constraints and default risk.

Notes

I would like to thank Sven Grassman and Allan Meltzer for helpful comments.

1. The monetary conditions for reestablishment of a successful parity system have been explored by the present author (1974, 1977).

2. For a more detailed statistical analysis of short-term movements in spot exchange rates, see Hirsch and Higham (June 1974).

3. For example, none of the principal turning points in the wide movements in the dollar-mark exchange rate in February 1973, in July 1973, in January 1974, or in May 1974 could be predicted from looking at forward rates.

4. See John Williamson (1974) for statistics on the turnover of official reserve holdings.

5. The relative wages of experienced foreign-exchange traders have been bid up sharply under the floating-rate regime.

6. Since the above was written, an important caveat should be added. Sven Grassman has direct information that forward contracting by Swedish banks with their nonbank retail customers approximately doubled (measured as a proportion of spot trade) from 1972 to 1974. This is not inconsistent, however, with a drying up of interbank forward trading as per Krul's analysis.

7. Somewhat to my surprise, as in an earlier paper (McKinnon 1969 and chap. 5) I had suggested that official interventions at cross-purposes would be likely in the absence of a parity system.

8. However, a finite time interval is required to conduct any arbitrage transaction.

9. A "perfect markets" theorist might object on the ground that the exchange markets were efficiently absorbing significant but contradictory bits of relevant information.

10. See Sven Grassman (1973, ch. 2) for empirical verification that exporters from convertible-currency countries typically invoice in their own currencies.

11. Described in interesting detail by Leland Yeager (1969).

References

Friedman, Milton. "The Case for Flexible Exchange Rates," pp. 157–203, in M. Friedman, *Essays in Positive Economics*. Chicago: University of Chicago Press, 1953.

Grassman, Sven. *Exchange Reserves and The Financial Structure of Foreign Trade.* Stockholm: Saxon House, 1973.

Hirsch, Fred, and David Higham. "Floating Rates—Expectations and Experience," *Three Banks Review,* June 1974.

International Monetary Fund. *International Financial Statistics* (various issues).

———. *Annual Report,* 1974.

Johnson, Harry. "The Case for Flexible Exchange, 1969," pp. 198–228, in H. Johnson, *Further Essays in Monetary Economics*. Allan and Unwin, 1972.

Kasper, Wolfgang. "The Effects of Exchange-Rate Changes: Recent International Currency Experience," Canberra. August, 1974 (processed).

Kouri, Pentti, and Michael Porter. "International Capital Flows and Portfolio Equilibrium," *Journal of Political Economy*, May/June, 1974.

Krul, Nicholas. "Floating Exchange Rates and Euromarkets," prepared for a conference, What Have We Learned From a Year of Greater Flexibility of Exchange Rates? Williamsburg, Virginia, May 1974.

Machlup, Fritz. *The Alignment of Foreign Exchange Rates*. New York: Praeger, 1972.

McKinnon, Ronald I. "Private and Official International Money," *Essays in International Finance*, No. 74, Princeton University, April 1969.

———. "Monetary Theory and Controlled Flexibility in the Foreign Exchanges," *Essays in International Finance*, No. 84, Princeton University, April 1971.

———. "A New Tripartite Agreement or a Limping Dollar Standard?" *Essays in International Finance*, No. 106, Princeton University, October 1974.

———. "Beyond Fixed Parities: The Analytics of International Monetary Agreements," pp. 42–53, in Robert Z. Aliber (ed.), *The Political Economy of International Economic Reform*. London: Macmillan, 1977.

Sohmen, Egon. *Flexible Exchange Rates*. Chicago: University of Chicago Press, 1961.

Williamson, John. "Exchange-Rate Flexibility and Reserve Use," Departmental Memorandum, IMF (Processed), August 29, 1974.

Yeager, Leland. "Fluctuating Exchange Rates in the Nineteenth Century: The Experiences of Austria and Russia," pp. 61–90, in R. Mundell and A. Swoboda, *Monetary Problems of the International Economy*. Chicago: University of Chicago Press, 1969.

13   The Exchange Rate and Macroeconomic Policy: Changing Postwar Perceptions

13.1   Introduction

Everybody understands that Western industrial economies have become more open to foreign trade in the last 30 years. International competition is increasingly pervasive—indeed overwhelming—in national markets for manufactured goods. Financial decisions by governments, whether by the central banks or by fiscal authorities, are now made with a heightened concern for the reactions of gimlet-eyed international bankers. However, the theoretical training of policymakers in how the exchange rate is determined, and its role in domestic macroeconomic policy, has lagged behind this internationalization process. The consequences have been ill-chosen monetary and exchange-rate policies in the United States, Britain, and elsewhere during the 1970s.

In organizing an explanation for this lag, in section 13.2, below, I develop the concept of an *insular economy:* one with limited financial and commodity arbitrage with the outside world but one not closed to foreign trade. This concept formed the implicit basis for the macroeconomic models, developed in the 1940s through the 1960s—whether they be Keynesian or monetarist—and for the old elasticities approach to official manipulation of a pegged exchange rate to preserve balanced trade. It underlay the arguments used in favor of floating exchange rates. But these older insular models break down when the economy becomes more open.

Originally published in *Journal of Economic Literature* 19, (June 1981): 531–557. Reprinted with permission.

The second half of the chapter reviews modern theories applicable to more open economies, with particular emphasis on the monetary approach to exchange-rate determination. Although an important step forward in our understanding of turbulent foreign-exchange markets of the 1970s, this newly received wisdom implicitly retains an important degree of insularity: separable demand functions for each national money are assumed to be "stable." And, this presumed stability underlies the case for freely floating exchange rates.

However, as international switching among convertible currencies increases, central banks find it more difficult to avoid stabilizing the exchange rate and adjusting the domestic money supply to support official interventions. Otherwise, changes in international portfolios may undermine insular national monetary policies based on either the stabilization of domestic interest rates or fixed targets for national monetary growth. In section 13.2 below, this point is illustrated with two recent unfortunate episodes in macroeconomic policymaking:

1. the 1977–78 fall of the dollar against the yen and most European currencies, with a consequential loss of monetary control in the United States and the world at large, resulting in price inflation on an international scale; and

2. the sharp 1979–80 real appreciation of sterling, with a liquidity squeeze in the London financial markets, leading to a collapse in British manufacturing output.

First, however, let us contrast how open the industrial economies have become with the situation prevailing when the older models of exchange-rate adjustment were developed.

The Increasing Openness of Industrial Economies

Not only had world imports and exports been severely truncated between 1930 and 1945, but tariffs, quotas, and exchange controls on current account transactions still proliferated in the late 1940s and 1950s. Also, as a legacy of the 1930s, policymakers expected flows of imports and exports to be quite unstable. Thus it seemed reasonable, in theory and in practice, to continue insulating the domestic economy from expected "shocks" originating in international trade. However, under fixed exchange rates and the strong dollar standard, the collective international economy of the 1950s and 1960s turned out to be more stable, on average, than were individual national economies (Mathieson and McKinnon 1974). Internal fluctuations in investment and government spending were smoothed by access to relatively stable world markets for imports and exports.

The General Agreement on Tariffs and Trade (GATT) and the commitment to currency convertibility under the International Monetary Fund (IMF) ultimately succeeded in sweeping away most trade restrictions among Western industrial economies—although less developed countries became more protectionist. Table 13.1 shows that if one uses the ratio of exports to GNP as a measure of openness, the process of becoming more open accelerated between 1965 and 1979 compared to the period 1951 to 1965. Germany's and Italy's ratios increased the most whereas, alone among the large trading countries, Japan's ratio was stationary—although it did move from detailed import controls to almost complete trade liberalization. Because the government (nontradable) sector's share in GNP grew rapidly in all countries, table 13.1 tends to understate substantially the extent to which domestic markets in manufactured goods have become interdependent. Moreover, except for agriculture where amounts traded are still often negotiated by governments, *potential* cross-country arbitrage in commodities is now much higher due to trade liberalization—and this increasing potential of uninhibited trade cannot be captured by data on actual trade flows.

Because of its huge internal market, the United States was once the archetypal "insular" economy, and much of modern macro theory was fashioned for it. Reliance on imported manufactured goods was minimal: from the 1950s through 1965, exports were only 5 percent of American GNP. However, by mid 1980 this ratio had doubled and—except for government and the provision of localized services—all American industries feel competitive pressure from abroad.

American holdings of financial assets no longer completely dominate the international capital market. For example, foreigners held 2 percent of outstanding U.S. government debt in 1951, 6 percent in 1965, and 19 percent at the end of 1979. Indeed, in several years during the 1970s, foreign monetary authorities

Table 13.1
Exports as a Proportion of GNP: Ten Industrial Countries

	1951	1965	1979
Canada	.23	.19	.29
France	.17	.14	.21
Germany	.16	.20	.27
Italy	.12	.17	.25
Japan	.13	.11	.13
Netherlands	.47	.45	.52
Sweden	.31	.23	.31
Switzerland	.27	.30	.34
United Kingdom	.25	.18	.29
United States	.05	.05	.09

Source: International Monetary Fund, *International Financial Statistics,* 1980 Yearbook and later monthly issues, Country Tables, line 90c ÷ line 99a.

absorbed *most* new net debt issued by the U.S. Treasury. Rates of interest in the United States are now strongly influenced by such foreign purchases, and by expected exchange rate changes of the dollar vis-à-vis other convertible currencies.

But the U.S. is not alone in becoming financially more open. The development of the Eurocurrency market now enables both firms and governments to borrow (or lend) internationally, on a large scale, for long periods in a variety of convertible currencies. Clearly, the international integration of capital markets in the 1980s parallels that prevailing in world trade in goods and services, whereas in the late 1940s national capital markets were segmented by exchange controls, and Eurocurrency transacting did not yet exist.

13.2 The Insular Economy

The Keynesian revolution began in *The General Theory* (1936) with no references to the foreign exchanges or to the international economy.[1] "Keynesian macro theory focused on the national economy, and the national government was, explicitly or implicitly, asserted to be the natural form of organization for achieving macroeconomic stability" (Lindbeck 1979, p. 1).

In the course of the breakdown of the international economy in the 1920s and 1930s, great shocks were transmitted from one market economy to another. Yet Keynes probably made the correct tactical simplification to focus his new macroeconomic schema for recovery on the single nation state and to leave to his students the details of preserving such autonomy from international influences. *The General Theory* analyzed the monetary or fiscal means for stimulating or otherwise manipulating aggregate demand nationally without simultaneously trying to handle awkward questions of currency convertibility, exchange reserves, tariff protection, and the macro policies of other countries. To the present day, this closed-economy approach dominates basic textbooks in macroeconomics, although writers often tack on a last chapter about the balance of payments.

However, balance-of-payments crises continued to demand attention. Under the strong influence of Fritz Machlup (1943) and James Meade (1951), a distinctly subsidiary branch of macroeconomics developed in the field of international finance—but, again, the prototype was an autonomous nation state, which happened to engage in foreign trade. How could potentially disruptive shocks coming through the balance of payments be insulated from the domestic economy—by capital controls, exchange-rate changes, or even tariffs and import quotas—so as to leave the decks clear for domestic demand management? If foreign shocks did filter through, how could national monetary and fiscal policies best offset them while maintaining a balance in foreign payments? In short, the international economy was treated as a potential source of instability, much like variations in the private propensity to invest were treated. This Keynesian version of the "international disequilibrium system" (Mundell 1961) focused on both kinds of disturbances. It had no self-equilibrating mechanisms in the form of asset or price adjustments to maintain a balance in foreign payments or in domestic output and employment. In this context, official manipulation of the exchange rate was seen to be the principal instrument for controlling the balance of payments which, in practice, meant controlling the trade balance.

The Keynesian Disequilibrium System

The prevailing theoretical consensus of the 1950s is succinctly summarized in the famous 1955 Trevor Swan diagram, which is reproduced in figure 13.1. Define the nominal exchange rate

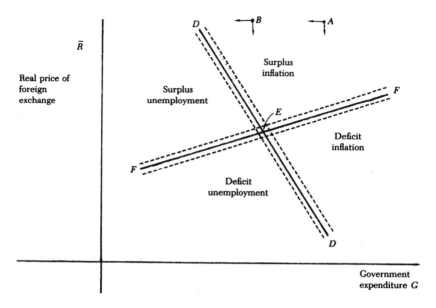

Figure 13.1
Policies for internal and external balance: The Keynesian disequilibrium system.

R to be the domestic currency cost of one unit of foreign currency. The authorities control R directly by posting an (adjustable) official parity, and then buying or selling foreign exchange for domestic currency at the official rate. Because price levels in each country remain stable in the Keynesian framework, any change in R is roughly equivalent to a change in $\bar{R}$: the "real" exchange rate appearing on the vertical axis of figure 13.1.

$$\bar{R} = \frac{\text{Domestic currency}}{\text{Foreign currency}} \times$$

$$\frac{\text{Foreign price or cost index}}{\text{Domestic price or cost index}}. \tag{1}$$

The horizontal axis represents instruments such as monetary or fiscal policy that operate directly on domestic aggregate demand. Let us refer to these collectively as "government expenditure" as denoted by G. Again, because of the assumption of domestic price stability, anticipated or unanticipated increases in government expenditure increase domestic real output and employment.

In figure 13.1 the *FF* line represents the locus of *G* and $\bar{R}$ associated with external balance, and the *DD* line the locus of $\bar{R}$ and *G* associated with domestic balance—some prespecified level of "full" employment below which price inflation is not a problem. The authority can now fine-tune $\bar{R}$ and *G* to achieve both foreign and domestic equilibrium at point *E*—the intersection of the two curves. The prevalence of "shocks" in the private domestic economy and foreign sector continually shifts both the *DD* and *FF* curves as shown by the dashed lines in figure 13.1; hence, omniscient authorities in the national government must continually vary *G* and $\bar{R}$ to preserve foreign and domestic balance. This approach remains the centerpiece of the macroeconomic analysis of open economies taught in the main elementary textbooks (Kindleberger and Lindert 1978; Caves and Jones 1977; Sodersten 1981).

An interesting refinement is called the "assignment problem" or, in Robert A. Mundell's terminology, "the principle of effective market classification" (1960, p. 250). Suppose instead of jointly moving both policy instruments toward *E* in figure 13.1 each is targeted according to its greater relative strength: the exchange rate is assigned to external balance by having $\bar{R}$ decrease if a trade surplus is perceived, and *G* is reduced if, say, labor shortages appear along with incipient price inflation. Almost all authors have assumed that the exchange rate has the greater comparative advantage in influencing external balance through the current account, and this is reflected in figure 13.1 by having *DD* drawn more steeply than *FF*.

Starting from a trade surplus and inflation at point *A* in figure 13.1, under this principle both $\bar{R}$ and *G* would be reduced until these imbalances are eliminated at point *E*. But beginning from disequilibrium at *B*, government expenditures would initially be reduced before eventually increasing when final equilibrium is achieved. Although not assured when adjustment lags are present, such decentralized policymaking should otherwise converge to *E* if the beginning policy assignment is made "correctly."

Why bother with this indirect decentralized route to full policy equilibrium, and thus accept some chance it will not converge properly? The authorities may not be so omniscient after all. In particular, they may know neither the exact slopes nor the positions of the internal and external balance schedules in figure 13.1. But authorities can recognize an external deficit or incipient internal imbalance. And these qualitative indicators are sufficient to set individual policy instruments in motion according to the prearranged assignment.

But the Keynes-Meade model depicted in the Swan diagram of figure 1 requires something more than a depression-based hangover of stable price expectations. In effect, the economy in question must be relatively *insulated* from international influences in three important respects:

(1) The share in GNP of foreign trade in goods and services is not high, or substantial trade barriers—high tariffs and quota restrictions—limit the importance of international commodity arbitrage. Hence (planned) exchange-rate changes can occur without immediate offsetting repercussions on the domestic price level.

(2) The international capital market is not functioning freely, or exchange controls limit private capital movements, so that private portfolio adjustments are insufficient to finance automatically current-account deficits or surpluses. Conversely, with current-account deficits or surpluses kept close to zero, net domestic wealth holdings of financial or real assets are not much influenced by the foreign sector.

(3) The national monetary system is insulated from the foreign exchanges. On the supply side, official purchases and sales of foreign money to maintain the exchange rate are sterilized so as to offset their impact on the domestic monetary base. On the demand side, short-term money-market rates of interest are not influenced by expected exchange-rate movements, nor are domestic currency holdings subject to other international disturbances.

These three assumptions define what I call the insular economy: where commodity and financial arbitrage with the outside world is limited as it was in the late 1940s and early 1950s. Nevertheless, the insular economy still engages in (possibly restricted) foreign trade, and even if its share in GNP is not high, that trade can still be very important. Foreign payments crises can easily arise, but they are dealt with by trying to keep the *current account* of the balance of payments close to zero. The exchange rate is assigned to control foreign payments, and it is viewed as an instrument essentially separate from domestic monetary policy.

The Advocacy of Floating Exchange Rates and the Insular Economy

Economists are accustomed to monetarists and Keynesians exchanging thunderbolts over whether monetary or fiscal policy is the stronger in influencing aggregate demand, whether the Phillips Curve exists, whether price inflation incurs high social costs, whether the demand for money is "stable," and so on. Surprisingly, however, neither school disputes the desirability of national autonomy in the field of macroeconomic policy; by implication, I shall argue that both tacitly accept the insular economy as a building block for their macroeconomic schema.

To be sure the concept of an optimum currency area (Mundell 1961; McKinnon 1963, and chapter 10) was generally recognized to apply to (very) small and highly open countries: Panama is better off to maintain a fixed exchange rate with the U.S. dollar and to give up the idea of national monetary autonomy; in the context of free trade within the European Economic Community, few would dispute the efficacy of Belgium's fixed exchange rate with the deutsche mark and the subordination of Belgian macroeconomic policy to maintaining it. But for "major" industrial economies, Keynesians such as James Meade (1955) and monetarists such as Milton Friedman (1953) and Harry Johnson (1972) have argued for floating exchange rates as if the economy under consideration were insular, as defined above. Indeed, in terms of Mundell's old principle of effective market classification (but not necessarily his present views), floating is a natural way of automatically assigning the exchange rate to take care of external balance so that national authorities suffer minimal inconvenience in getting on with domestic macroeconomic stabilization— whether or not they approach it from a Keynesian or monetarist point of view.

I quote from "The Case for Flexible Exchange Rates, 1969" by Harry Johnson, because it is usually pungent and more contemporary than the earlier articles of Friedman or Meade, while being in broad agreement with both. First comes the primacy of national macroeconomic autonomy.

The fundamental argument for flexible exchange rates is that they would allow countries autonomy with respect to their use of monetary, fiscal and other policy instruments, consistent with the maintenance of whatever degree of freedom in international transactions they chose to allow their citizens, by automatically ensuring the preservation of external equilibrium. (Johnson 1972, p. 199)

Next comes his presumption that nations remain insulated from each other by standards of domestic trade and commerce. This economic insularity is the basis for his argument against fixed exchange rates.

The argument for fixed exchange rates is that they will similarly encourage the integration of the national markets that compose the world economy into an international network of connected markets with similarly beneficial effects on economic efficiency and growth ... In the international economy the movement of labour is certainly subject to serious barriers created by national immigration policies (and in some cases restraints on emigration as well), and the freedom of movement of capital is also restricted by barriers created by national laws. The freedom of movement of goods is also restricted by tariffs and other barriers to trade ... The existence of these barriers means that the system of fixed exchange rates does not really establish the equivalent of a single international money, in the sense of a currency whose purchasing power and usefulness tends to equality throughout the market area. (Johnson 1972, p. 202)

All three authors envisaged that the international adjustment mechanism set in motion by flexible exchange rates is toward balanced trade. With the imperfect integration of international factor markets and the consequent absence of sustained private international borrowing and lending, the exchange rate adjusts to balance the flow of imports and exports:

A rise in the exchange rate produced by a tendency toward a surplus makes foreign goods cheaper in terms of domestic currency, even though their prices are unchanged in terms of their own currency, and domestic goods more expensive in terms of foreign currency, even though their prices are unchanged in terms of domestic currency. This tends to increase imports, reduce exports, and so offset the incipient surplus. (Friedman 1953, p. 162).

Balanced trade, rather than internationally aligned price levels or interest rates, has the center stage in defining the "equilibrium" exchange rate. And, I believe, this approach is logically consistent for economies that are somewhat insulated from each other with respect to commodity and financial arbitrage. To be sure, the advocates of floating recognize that general inflation will eventually make devaluation inevitable but this merely highlights another potential argument for flexible exchange rates. Johnson emphasizes the advantages for macroeconomic autonomy of differing rates of price inflation that allow countries to select different trade-offs on their (national) Phillips curves:

On the one hand, a great rift exists between nations like the United Kingdom and the United States, which are anxious to maintain high levels of employment and are prepared to pay a price for it in terms of domestic inflation, and other nations, notably the West German Federal Republic, which are strongly averse to inflation. Under the present fixed exchange-rate system, these nations are pitched against each other in a battle over the rate of inflation that is to prevail in the world economy, since the fixed rate system diffuses that rate of inflation to all the countries involved in it. Flexible rates would allow each country to pursue the mixture of unemployment and price trend objectives it prefers, consistent with international equilibrium, equilibrium being secured by appreciation of the currencies of "price-stability" countries relative to currencies of "full-employment" countries. (Johnson 1972, p. 210)

How innocent we were! However, by 1968 this view was no longer espoused by Milton Friedman. He had already given his well-known presidential address suggesting that the not-so-long-run Phillips Curve was vertical (Friedman 1968), or positively sloped, and additional price inflation would not buy reduced unemployment. But the Johnson view was more typical in ascribing to the different national inflation rates permitted by flexible exchange rates (in the presence of currency convertibility) a significant "advantage" for differing national employment goals.

How was private speculation treated in this early and persuasive advocacy of floating? These authors did not have the hindsight of experiencing floating in the postwar period, except for the atypical experience of Canada between 1952 and 1962. Friedman and Johnson, as well as Fritz Machlup (1972) and J. E. Meade (1955), believed that private speculative capital and private hedging facilities would be ample to smooth week-to-week exchange fluctuations to a level comparable to, say, that experienced under the 2-percentage-point band of the old Bretton Woods Agreement. Moreover, all were elasticity optimists: once private stabilizing speculation moved the exchange rate to this "correct" position, a balance between commodity imports and exports would quickly reassert itself as merchants and manufacturers responded. Insofar as speculators understand that commodity merchants do respond elastically, there should be no shortage of stabilizing private capital to smooth unwarranted shortrun fluctuations. The job of the speculator was to study the underlying "real" supply and demand considerations prevailing in the major markets for imports and exports—such as strikes, crop failures, or technological changes. Then the exchange rate that balanced the flow of commodity trade would be quickly established.

There are logical difficulties with this "nonmonetary" view of exchange stability but, unfortunately, none were identified in the ensuing heated debate. Friedman's critics implicitly accepted the premise of the insular economy and the "elasticities approach" (see below) to adjusting the net trade balance. But they attacked the idea that private speculation—whether in foreign exchange, copper, or soybeans—was naturally stabilizing. Conjuring up visions of Swiss gnomes and "hot money" flows, several theoretical examples of destabilizing speculation—conveniently reviewed by Robert M. Stern (1973, chap. 2)—were designed to show that such antisocial speculators could still make profits. However, Friedman's original contention held sway:

People who argue that speculation is generally destabilizing seldom realize that this is largely equivalent to saying that speculators lose money, since speculation can be destabilizing in general only if speculators on the average sell when the currency is low in price and buy when it is high. (Friedman 1953, p. 175)

On such basic (nonmonetary) principles as this did the advocates of floating win the great debate of the 1960s.

The Elasticities Approach to the Exchange Rate and the Balance of Trade

For an insular economy, what is the particular association between the controlled exchange rate R and external balance that is consistent with the Keynes-Meade model of figure 13.1? What determines the "equilibrium" exchange rate under the free floating envisaged by Friedman and Johnson? Not surprisingly, the answer is the familiar elasticities approach to the balance of trade that was developed in parallel by several authors (Robinson 1937; Machlup 1939, 1940; Haberler 1949). Rather than deriving the elasticity conditions necessary for a devaluation to improve the trade balance, I simply list the basic equations underlying the traditional elasticities model in its simplest form.

First, one specifies the foreign payments objective of the national authorities purely in terms of the net trade balance:

$$B = X \cdot P_x/R - Z \cdot P_z \tag{2}$$

where B is an ongoing flow of private payments on commodity account measured, for convenience, in units of foreign exchange; X is the physical volume of domestic exports and P_x is their price in domestic currency; Z is the physical volume of domestic imports and P_z is their price in units of foreign currency; R is the nominal (and real) exchange rate as defined above.

Second, the insular domestic economy is assumed to have a stable internal price level. Foreign trade is a sufficiently small activity, or quotas and exchange controls sufficiently restrict international commodity arbitrage, so that the general purchasing power of money is invariant to exchange-rate changes. But the specific prices of those few goods that are traded, X and Z, are uniform on foreign and domestic markets at the prevailing exchange rate. Therefore, both the domestic supply of exports and the demand for imports are simple functions of their domestic *money* prices:

$$X = S(P_x) \quad \text{Domestic supply}$$
of exports with   (3)
elasticity $\epsilon > 0$.

$$Z = D(R \cdot P_z) \quad \text{Domestic demand}$$
for imports with   (4)
elasticity $\eta < 0$.

Because foreign trade is a fringe activity, cross-price elasticities are not incorporated in (3) and (4): the domestic price of importables is not an important argument in the export function, and vice versa. Hence, the effect of a devaluation on the trade balance is calculated only in terms of "own" price elasticities.

How do foreign trading partners respond to a discretionary change in R? First, note that it is domestic authorities who are implicitly presumed to manage R. More generally, in a two-economy model, only one country can independently establish the common exchange rate—and the nationalistic approach embedded in figure 13.1 tends to treat the rest of the world as being passive.

Second, to be consistent with the possibility of "Keynesian" unemployment due to deficiencies in aggregate demand, one cannot suppose that international prices are parametrically given as if our insular economy was a trivially small factor in world markets. Otherwise, aggregate demand for domestic output would not be effectively limited. Hence, the common way of closing the model is to specify (limited) net export and import functions for the rest of the world as if it too were an insular economy with a stable domestic price level:

$$Z = S^*(P_z) \qquad \text{Foreign supply of} \qquad \qquad (5)$$
exports with elasticity $\epsilon^* > 0$.

and

$$X = D^* (P_x/R) \qquad \text{Foreign demand for} \qquad \qquad (6)$$
imports with elasticity $\eta^* < 0$.

Foreign demand and supply responses depend on foreign currency prices, as if the purchasing power of foreign money was also determined independently of the exchange rate.

Equations (3) through (6) are written without directly specifying levels of real income, or real expenditures in each country. How can such an omission be justified? Suppose each national government prespecifies the output level (through its control over aggregate demand) in each country. Then, any income generated by, say, a depreciation and expansion of domestic exports would be offset in its effect on domestic output and employment by a cutback in government expenditures or a rise in taxes. This highly specialized assumption allows us to omit income repercusions from equations (3) through (6). In effect, this procedure presupposes that the economy is kept close to the internal balance line, DD, in figure 13.1.

For algebraic simplicity, let us calculate dB/dR near the point where the trade is exactly balanced, i.e., where

$$X \cdot P_x/R = Z \cdot P_z. \tag{7}$$

Imposing (7) is also consistent with the notion that final "equilibrium" in foreign payments is at a point where $B = 0$. The impact of a small devaluation on the trade balance can then be obtained by differentiating (2) with respect to R, and then substituting for the resulting dX/dR, dP_x/dR, dZ/dR, and dP_z/dR from equations (3) through (6) to get[2]

$$\frac{dB}{dR} = Z \cdot P_z \left[-1 - \frac{\eta^*(\epsilon + 1)}{(\epsilon - \eta^*)} - \frac{\eta(\epsilon^* + 1)}{(\epsilon^* - \eta)} \right], \tag{8}$$

where η and η^* are the domestic and foreign demand elasticities (defined to be negative) from equations (4) and (5), whereas ϵ and ϵ^* are the domestic and foreign supply elasticities (defined to be positive) from equations (3) and (6). Loosely speaking, the greater the absolute numerical values of these four elasticities, the more likely it becomes that a devaluation will improve the trade balance. More precisely, a well-known *sufficient condition* for $dB/dR > 0$ may be stated in terms of demand elasticities alone:

$$|\eta| + |\eta^*| > 1.$$

Whatever the supply elasticities may be, if the response of domestic users of imports to an increase in domestic money prices—and that of foreign importers to a fall in foreign money prices—were even modestly elastic, a devaluation will improve the trade balance.

This presumption that $dB/dR > 0$ underlies the Swan diagram portrayed in figure 13.1. The fact that the external balance line FF slopes upward and to the right reflects the positive influence of R on the trade balance, along with the negative influence of G. Without support of demand management, however, the pure price effects of exchange-rate changes must be much stronger for the trade balance to respond favorably to devaluation.

To summarize, the elasticities approach relates the exchange rate to the trade balance in a way that is quite plausible in an insular economy where the purchasing power of domestic money is independently established. The absence of any sustained capital flows to accommodate trade surpluses or deficits makes the state of the current account (mainly the trade balance) a legitimate direct concern of public policy. The exchange rate is essentially an instrument to induce "expenditure switching" (Johnson 1961), away from imports and exports toward home goods with an elasticity of response described in equation (8). But what is special about the standard model embedded in equations (3) through (6) are the necessary supporting changes in total managed expenditure. Devaluation is (implicitly) accompanied by controls over aggregate demand that reduce domestic absorption and release goods for export once expenditure switching occurs. To push the argument to an extreme, the government controls its own budget as well as private investment expenditures so the trade balance responds favorably to devaluation. Such detailed fiscal and financial interventions (not always successful) were not uncommon in the late 1940s in Western Europe and Japan.

13.3 The Open Economy

Today the international capital market is more integrated—particularly for short-term transacting—and the typical industrial country is much more open to commodity trade than is the prototype insular economy on which the elasticities approach is based. And governments no longer presume or desire to control the level of aggregate investment in the Keynesian mode. Indeed, in many industrial economies, the authorities are unable to determine the fiscal deficit precisely, and the perceived desirability of discretionary fiscal policy is lessened. Exchange rates are now market-determined to a greater degree, but fairly heavy official intervention is the rule. How should these changed conditions modify how national governments view "external balance" and the exchange rate?

To reflect the greater integration of international capital markets analytically, assume that the international bond market—inclusive of interest-bearing bank deposits—is "perfect": individual firms and governments can borrow on the same terms internationally and domestically. To be sure, nominal rates of interest differ across currencies but, by assumption, these only reflect different expected rates of price inflation or exchange-rate movements. The "real" cost of capital internationally and domestically is the same. Consequently the state of the current account is no measure of external balance or imbalance and provides no signal either that the exchange rate should be changed or that the government should provide accommodating finance to maintain the current one. Rather, any deficit or surplus on current account merely measures the gap between national saving and investment, rather like the gap that may exist within any single American state.

Secondly, with the new neoclassical macroeconomics, assume that the level of domestic income is determined independently of any discretionary fiscal policy that is predictable. Except for random disturbances, unemployment is always at the "natural" rate.

To fix ideas, consider the familiar identities from the national income accounts under the assumptions that the current account and the trade balance are the same and that foreign and domestic price levels are initially set equal to unity:

$$Y = C + I_d + G + X - R \cdot Z, \tag{9}$$

where Y is national income and $R \cdot Z$ is the domestic currency value of imports; and exports X include net interest, dividends, and other remittances. Suppose G is only government consumption, and public-sector investment is incorporated into the variable I_d.

Then, define social saving to be

$$S = Y - C - G \tag{10}$$

so that

$$S - I_d = X - R \cdot Z = I_f \tag{11}$$

where I_d is domestic investment and I_f is net foreign investment—the buildup of claims on foreigners. Any positive difference between social saving and domestic investment results, ex post, in a trade surplus and net investment abroad. Now divide social saving into private saving S_p, and government saving S_g. If T is total tax collections less transfers, then public-sector saving is

$$S_g = T - G. \tag{12}$$

Finally, we have

$$S_p + (T - G) - I_d = X - R \cdot Z. \tag{13}$$

The elasticities approach focused on the direct determinants of exports and imports on the right-hand side of equation (13). However, from the left-hand side, any improvement in the trade balance must involve a rise in private saving, a rise in government saving, or a fall in domestic investment. From our assumption of a perfectly integrated capital market, domestic firms and households see correct international rates of interest. Net savers take these rates into account in their intertemporal allocation of consumption and current acquisition of financial claims, and enterprises compare this cost of capital to their internal rates of return in making purely domestic investments and in issuing new financial liabilities. If a gap exists—say, saving exceeds domestic investment on private account (put the government to one side for a moment)—a net accumulation of claims on foreigners occurs through a trade surplus.[3]

But government (dis)saving—as measured by the fiscal deficit or surplus in equation (12)—may well enter as a wedge. If a fiscal deficit and foreign borrowing reflect a deliberate intertemporal choice by the government, then this official contribution to the external trade deficit does not represent a disequilibrium warranting official action. However, suppose the governmental deficit is unplanned insofar as the resulting debt issue is associated neither with public-sector capital formation nor with an "automatic" stabilizer designed to compensate for an unusual shortfall in private investment spending in the domestic economy—as in the trough of a business cycle. (Of course, in this last case I_d would fall along with $T - G$ to leave no net effect on the trade balance.) Then, any current-account deficit does represent an unwarranted disequilibrium—but hardly calls for a change in the exchange rate, as uncritical use of the old elasticities model would seem to suggest. W. M. Corden puts the matter thus:

> The current-account deficit of a country is the sum of the private financial deficit (excess of investment over savings) and the public deficit. If the current-account deficit increases this may be because the private deficit has risen—which is not a matter for public-policy concern—or because the public deficit has risen—which may indeed be a matter for concern. But the balance-of-payments figures in themselves will not tell one whether there is a problem. One must go directly

to the public-sector (including central-bank) figures, so making the balance-of-payments figures redundant. (Corden 1977, p. 51)

To illustrate the principles involved, consider the macroeconomic information available early in 1977 when American officials, most notably Treasury Secretary W. Michael Blumenthal, responded to a U.S. trade deficit (and Japanese trade surplus of the same order of magnitude) by trying to talk the dollar down and the yen upward. Although this jawboning by itself was by no means fully responsible for the subsequent loss of monetary control, as explained later on, the dollar did eventually depreciate from about 290 yen in January 1977, to 240 yen in December 1977, to about 190 yen in October 1978, as shown in table 13.4. In crisis circumstances, a major international rescue operation was launched on 1 November 1978, to prevent the dollar from falling further.

To reproduce the situation facing American authorities at the time, consider first U.S. saving and investment data only through 1977. Between 1975 and 1977, there is a rather definite decline in the U.S. current account: from +0.6 percent of GNP in 1975 to −1.5 percent of GNP in 1977 according to the data in table 13.2. But just as definite is the sharp rise in domestic investment spending, from 12.4 percent of GNP in 1975 to 16 percent in 1977—as the United States recovered rather sooner than other industrial countries from the worldwide depression of the mid 1970s. However, American "counter-cyclical" fiscal policy seems out of line with the investment recovery. True, government dissaving rose sharply in 1975 to almost 5 percent of GNP to offset the sharp fall in investment from 1973 to 1975. But as investment recovered from 1976 to 1977, the government deficit did not diminish commensurately: indeed the government continued to be a large dissaver in the inflationary boom from 1977 to 1979. Not surprisingly, this deficit showed up in the balance of trade as the American economy utilized the savings of foreigners, particularly friendly Japanese (table 13.3), to finance its "normal" level of investment expenditures. But instead of welcoming this financial support from abroad that helped keep the lid on American inflation in 1976 and 1977, American authorities responded in the mode of the old Keynes-Meade analyses by "talking down" the exchange rate in conjunction with an expansionary monetary policy as discussed below.

Table 13.2
Gross Investment and Government Financing Saving in the United States as a Proportion of GNP

	1971	1972	1973	1974	1975	1976	1977	1978	1979
Private gross domestic investment[a]	.150	.161	.168	.152	.124	.143	.160	.165	.163
Government-financed saving[b]	−.023	−.015	−.007	−.009	−.049	−.033	−.027	−.021	−.012
Current-account trade surplus[c]	−.005	−.009	−.001	−.006	+.006	−.003	−.015	−.015	−.013

Source: International Monetary Fund, *International Financial Statisics*, 1980 Yearbook, USA, Country Table.
[a]Lines 99ee and 93i.
[b]Line 80.
[c]Line 90c − line 98c.

The Ambiguous Effect of Devaluation on the Trade Balance

Departing even further from the elasticities approach with its implied official control over domestic internal aggregate demand, it appears that the 25 percent real (35 percent nominal) devaluation of the dollar against the yen in 1977–78 had no predictable effect on the net U.S. trade balance with Japan. Even afterward one cannot assess its impact on the balance between exports and imports. Of course, dollar devaluation may influence other variables such as the rate of price inflation, the demand for money, and even the level of investment.

To see the analytical dilemma, suppose the real exchange rate $\bar{R}$—as defined in equation (1)—is exogenously determined by official policy or by monetary variables yet to be considered. How then should the various saving, investment, and trade variables in equation (13) respond to a changed $\bar{R}$? How would $\bar{R}$ influence the net trade balance on the right side and, pari passu, the difference between social saving and investment on the left? Obviously, some economic structure must be imposed on the accounting identity.

The elasticities model focuses explicitly on the right side of equation (13). An increase in $\bar{R}$ makes domestic exports more competitive on world markets and makes domestic imports seem expensive to domestic nationals as outlined in equations (3) to (6). But for the trade balance to improve, this model requires internal demand restraint—say a reduction in government spending or "tight" money—to release the requisite resources from domestic absorption.

Let us now throw out these implicit assumptions and posit that throughout 1977–78 the American government applied neither fiscal nor monetary restraint. That fiscal policy was not restraining is obvious from table 13.2 because private investment recovered much more sharply than the fiscal deficit was reduced, and the assumption of passive or even expansive monetary policy is justified later on. Now look at the effect on the trade deficit of an increase in $\bar{R}$ from the viewpoint of the left side of equation (13): the balance between saving and investment.

Suppose private saving, S_p, is a statistically stable proportion of American GNP and, hence, is not much influenced by $\bar{R}$ in one direction or another. Once one integrates the saving behavior of households with that of firms, the historical evidence suggests

Table 13.3
Gross Investment and Government Financial Saving in Japan as a Proportion of GNP

	1971	1972	1973	1974	1975	1976	1977	1978	1979
Gross domestic investment[a]	.367	.366	.399	.381	.323	.315	.307	.308	.326
Government surplus[b]	−.002	−.016	−.016	−.016	−.048	−.020	−.062	−.065	−.053
Current-account trade surplus[c]	+.026	+.023	.000	−.010	−.001	+.007	+.016	+.018	−.008

Source: International Monetary Fund, *International Financial Statistics*, 1980 Yearbook, USA, Country Table.
Note: All entries in tables 13.2 and 13.3 have been standardized for the level of GNP appearing on line 99a.
[a]Lines 93e and 93i.
[b]Line 80.
[c]Line 90c − line 98c.

that aggregate gross private saving has been remarkably stable as a proportion of gross national product (David and Scadding 1974). However, this evidence seems to conflict with the common presumption in theoretical models of open economies: that devaluation increases private saving by reducing the real value of domestic cash balances. If the "law of one price" holds continuously across all commodities—as described below by equation (16)—and the devaluing economy is small, then the domestic price level will increase by the full amount of the devaluation. With fixed nominal cash balances, real balances will decline and private saving will increase (at least temporarily) if inflationary expectations are stationary (Michaely 1960; Tsiang 1961).

However, this real balance effect was offset in the 1977–78 devaluation of the dollar by at least two important influences. First, the unanticipated devaluation did not immediately affect domestic prices of nontradables or the dollar prices of tradable "fixprice" manufactures produced in the United States. Thus, the sticky American price level rose by much less than the nominal devaluation: 10 percent versus 35 percent, respectively. (The distinction between anticipated and unanticipated exchange-rate changes, and between fixprice and flexprice goods, is analyzed in more detail below.) Secondly, the initial shock of dollar devaluation itself heightened people's inflationary expectations about the future. They anticipated that the U.S. price level would eventually adjust upward. Indeed, some speculated that U.S. monetary policy might be out of control (as analyzed more fully below), so that further devaluation was possible. With these unstable expectations, a natural reaction of private owners of financial assets is to consume now rather than later; both the demand for money and private saving decrease.

A priori, therefore, one cannot project how private saving will respond to an unanticipated devaluation, and the evidence we have from tables 13.2 and 13.3 is that private saving—i.e., the sum of gross domestic investment plus the balance on current account, less government saving—in both the United States and Japan remained a fairly stable share of GNP throughout the 1970s.

Suppose, henceforth, that private saving is largely unaffected by $\bar{R}$; then the effect of devaluation on the trade balance (net foreign investment) depends on how $\bar{R}$ influences net public sector saving *or* private investment, as in equation (13). Taking the exchange rate as exogenously given by financial considerations that remain to be spelled out, I hypothesize that

$$T - G = S_g = S_g(\overline{R}) \qquad \text{where } S_g' > 0 \tag{14}$$

and

$$I_d = I_d(\overline{R}) \qquad \text{where } I_d' > 0. \tag{15}$$

That is, real devaluation yields some tendency for the public-sector deficit to diminish but also for gross domestic investment to increase. Hence, there is no presumption as to which way the net trade balance will move (McKinnon 1980b, and chapter 13).

Obviously, equations (14) and (15) hardly constitute a fully specified model of how the economy responds to a change in $\overline{R}$. But they can be rationalized in a way that is consistent with the experience of both Japan and the United States during the fall of the dollar in 1977–78. In an integrated world, an unanticipated real devaluation will (1) cause direct inflationary pressure from international commodity arbitrage; and (2) stimulate real output, including exports and domestic investment, because the country becomes a low-cost international supplier. Insofar as any resource slack exists, multinational and national enterprises will shift manufacturing production to that country with the undervalued currency and away from that country whose currency is overvalued. (In contrast, a fully anticipated nominal devaluation will be fully offset by internal price inflation.)

Both the higher price inflation (implying higher real marginal rates of income tax) and higher real output tend to increase government revenue more than expenditures. Hence, social saving tends to increase on government account in the devaluing country.

But the same forces stimulate a (relative) investment boom in the undervalued country. Business firms operating internationally are anxious to invest in plant, equipment, and inventories while the cost of doing so is artificially (and perhaps temporarily) reduced (chapter 13). Gross domestic investment in the United States did recover from the 1975 depression to achieve "normal" historical levels in 1977–78 (table 13.2), whereas gross investment in Japan (table 13.3) in 1977–78 remained sharply depressed, below historical levels, as if it were indeed a high-cost country with an overvalued currency. With this investment effect operating in both countries to offset changes in government saving, the U.S. trade deficit and Japanese trade surplus remained unresponsive to the exchange-rate change in 1978. (The second oil crisis in 1979 injected a third-party effect that makes the trade statistics impossible to interpret in a bilateral setting.) This is not to deny that the dollar devaluation was not extraordinarily unsettling for the world economy—as is discussed in more detail below. Rather, for open economies the exchange rate is simply not suitable for determining the balance between national saving and investment as the old elasticities model would seem to suggest.

Readers will be justifiably uneasy over coming to such a strong conclusion based on such slender empirical evidence: the 1977–78 fall of the dollar against the yen. However, a number of authors have identified devaluation episodes over many economies from the early 1950s to the early 1970s, and then done a before-and-after analysis of the response of the trade balance and of the balance of payments. Marc Miles (1979) studied 16 devaluations for 14 industrial and less developed countries in the 1960s and concluded there was no predictable effect on the net trade balance. In an examination of the 1973 breakdown of fixed exchange rates among industrial countries, Erich Spitaller (1980) found the trade balances of those that devalued actually worsened for the first year afterward. Finally, in the quite different context of quota restrictions on foreign trade, Anne Krueger (1978) studied the consequences of 22 discrete devaluations in 10 less developed countries from 1950 to 1970. She found no consistent response pattern for the net position of the current account, even for countries where the devaluation was ultimately considered to be "successful" in the sense of restoring international competitiveness. However, Miles and Krueger did generally find that the *overall* balance of payments of the devaluing countries improved. This is a result consistent with the monetary approach to the balance of payments but one that must be carefully qualified, as we shall see.

In summary, in open economies, the view now developing is that the most direct instrument of official policy for influencing the trade balance is the state of the public finances: the balance between revenues and expenditures. The consequences of adjusting the exchange rate are unpredictable. In contrast with the neo-Keynesian insular models, therefore, both theoretical considerations and empirical investigations run to the conclusion that the net balance on current account does not itself indicate any disequilibrium warranting official exchange-rate changes.

The Monetary Approach to Floating Exchange Rates

If exchange-rate changes have no predictable effect on the trade balance in the absence of supporting government macro policy, then the responsiveness of net exports by itself cannot be expected to determine the exchange rate. How then is a freely "floating" exchange rate made determinate? To solve this problem, exchange-rate theory has moved away from the elasticities approach and commodity flows to appeal to asset markets in general, and the market for monies in particular. Rather than go back to Hume and Ricardo to sketch all the historical antecedents of the monetary approach, I shall, with certain amendments, utilize John Bilson's (1979) summary of the state of theory evolving out of the seminal work of Jacob Frenkel and Harry Johnson (1976) and Robert Mundell (1968, chap. 8).

Initially, suppose that absolute purchasing power parity prevails but not necessarily balanced trade. International commodity arbitrage is sufficiently robust over the relevant time horizon so that

$$P = R \cdot P^* \quad \text{where } P \text{ is the domestic price level} \quad (16)$$
$$\text{and } P^* \text{ is the foreign.}$$

This "law of one price" is a commonly used analytical simplification. When R changes unexpectedly, however, it can only hold literally when all commodities are tradable and "flexprice" in the Hicksian sense: homogeneous primary commodities that are internationally traded on auction markets. (The case of "fixprice" manufactures and nontradables is treated in a later section when deviations from purchasing power parity are analyzed.) However, when exchange-rate changes are fully anticipated as with continuing internal price inflation accompanied by continual devaluations, equation (16) may apply to all goods and services (Frenkel 1976).

On the asset side, maintain the simplifying assumption of "perfect" capital mobility for the international exchange of *interest-bearing* debt (or equity) denominated in differing convertible national currencies. Bonds can be aggregated across all currencies because people behave as if interest differentials accurately reflect expected exchange-rate changes, thus making them perfect substitutes. Because trade surpluses or deficits are automatically financed by this nonmonetary interest-bearing debt, one can suppress direct consideration of current-account imbalances between countries *and* escape precisely specifying outstanding stocks of national bonds.

Unlike this perfect international fungibility in the bond market, working cash balances in national monies are less—possibly much less—than perfect substitutes in demand across countries. That is, define "money" rather narrowly to be the *national* medium of exchange: coin and currency or checking accounts for making payments to third parties. Because of legal tender provisions and the influence of tradition, nearly all commerce within each country is denominated in the national currency—the demand for which is closely related to GNP. These working balances are commonly assumed to be non-interest-bearing, an uncomfortable tradition followed here. The nominal rate of interest on domestic bonds, possibly influenced by exchange-rate expectations, remains the opportunity cost of holding each national money under the monetary approach. Direct displacement of one money by another does not occur—even when exchange rates are volatile.

On the supply side, suppose each central bank absorbs that part of the commercial banking system providing the means of payment. The effect is to have 100 percent reserve money. Let M and M^* denote the given domestic and foreign money supplies, respectively. Consider the remainder of each national system of commercial banks—those whose liabilities are time and savings deposits with flexible market-determined rates of interest—to be part of the perfect international bond market. Let i be the rate of interest on bonds denominated in the domestic currency and let i^* be that on foreign currency bonds such that

$$\frac{M}{P} = L(i, Y) \qquad \text{Demand for domestic money,} \qquad (17)$$

and

$$\frac{M^*}{P^*} = L^* (i^*, Y^*) \qquad \text{Demand for foreign money.} \qquad (18)$$

Using the common international price level from equation (16), and given supplies of each money to which their respective demands adjust, as in equations (17) and (18), we have

$$R = \frac{M \cdot L(i^*, Y^*)}{M^* \cdot L(i, Y)} \qquad \text{Equilibrium exchange rate.} \qquad (19)$$

The exchange rate is the relative price of two monies and is determined by the relative demand and supply of the two currencies (Mussa 1976). This theory of exchange-rate determination is simplicity itself. If the demand for foreign money suddenly increases, the equilibrium exchange rate R will increase and foreign prices decrease. If the supply of domestic money increases, R again increases but domestic prices rise. The exchange rate is determined jointly with the alignment of foreign and domestic price levels without any explicit reference to the net trade balance as in the old elasticities model. Hence, at first glance, this monetary approach would seem to rescue the old Friedman-Johnson advocacy of floating exchange rates for increasingly open economies.

Nothing has been said about how the national rates of interest i and i^* are determined in equation (19). But clearly the presence of "perfect" international interest arbitrage makes them closely related. Incorporating the forward rate of exchange, R_t^f at time t,[4] let us close the model by assuming that

$$i = i^* + \log (R_t^f/R_t) \qquad \text{Interest-rate parity,} \qquad (20)$$

and

$$E[R_t + 1] = R_t^f \qquad \text{Unbiased forward rate.} \qquad (21)$$

Because covered interest arbitrage in the unrestricted part of the international financial markets—principally the vast domain of Eurocurrency transacting—is virtually risk-free, the interest-rate parity theorem holds almost exactly in practice (Aliber 1973). More controversial is the proposition in equation (21) that the forward rate is an unbiased predictor of the future spot exchange rate. Although, in practice, the proportion of unexplained statistical variance in exchange rates is high, the null hypothesis that the forward rate, on average, neither under nor over predicts the future spot rate is difficult to reject (Frenkel and Mussa 1980). To advance the argument, therefore, let us assume that equation (21) is true, and combine it with equation (20) to get:

$$i - i^* = E \left[\frac{dR_t}{dt} \right] \quad \text{Fisher Open.} \tag{22}$$

At very short term, the interest differential measures the expected rate of change in the exchange rate: the Fisher Open theory (Aliber 1978). If the domestic currency is expected to depreciate, then the domestic interest rate increases and the foreign interest rate decreases. Fisher Open thus establishes an extremely important link between *anticipated* monetary policies and fluctuations in the *current* exchange rate.

To illustrate, start from a stationary equilibrium with nongrowing GNPs, given money supplies, and no anticipated change in the exchange rate, such that $i = i^*$. Now suppose the market comes to believe that domestic (but not foreign) monetary policy will become more expansionary and that the domestic currency will start depreciating. To fix ideas, suppose the market shifts to the view that both M and R_t will begin increasing continuously at 5 percent per year but with no discrete change in the domestic money stock. These revised exchange market expectations will immediately cause i to rise by 5 percentage points to offset expected domestic price inflation. Referring back to equation (19), the spot demand for the domestic currency falls discontinuously. Hence R_t increases *discretely* along with the domestic price level.

In a "free float," therefore, the prevailing spot exchange rate is very sensitive to anticipated monetary policies unless authorities dampen these expectations by demonstrating a willingness to adjust current money supplies to maintain the spot exchange rate within a small neighborhood or "norm" into the indefinite future—thereby keeping interest differentials close to zero—as with a virtually fixed exchange rate. Even if the law of one price does not hold, this sensitivity of the exchange rate to monetary policy remains important, as shown below.

Rigidity in National Price Levels and Stabilizing Speculation

The preceding analysis of the monetary approach suggested that exchange-rate expectations may easily become cumulative, particularly if observed changes are unidirectional, leading people to expect persistently higher inflation in one country. Without such sustained differences in inflation patterns, however, most observers have the impression that *expectations are normally regressive:* an anticipated depreciation sets up the expectation of an appreciation—possibly gradual—back to "equilibrium." What is the empirical basis for this presumption? First, national central banks usually protest that price (and exchange-rate) stability is an objective. Secondly, in industrial countries, regressive expectations are more consistent with observed price-level stickiness. Despite the unexpected large—but mainly cyclical—10 to 25 percent variations in exchange rates since 1973, ratios of national wholesale or consumer price indices have moved within a much narrower range. Hence, most of these exchange fluctuations violated the law of one price, perhaps only temporarily (Isard 1977). If the dollar/DM rate *unexpectedly* moves one percent in a day or five percent in a week, one hardly expects the ratio of German and American prices to move an offsetting amount.

This residual insularity between national price levels rests on the basic Hicksian distinction between fixprice goods—mainly brand-name and manufactured products—and flexprice homogeneous primary commodities such as wheat or copper, which are sold on open auction markets. Fixprice goods dominate the export bills of the industrial countries and, typically, are invoiced for given periods in the home currency of the exporter (Grassman 1973). Moreover, such a rigid pricing strategy is commercially desirable for both domestic and export sales (McKinnon 1979, chap. 4). Hence, firms have little or no immediate incentive to change the domestic invoice price of tradable manufactures or nontradable services in response to an unexpected and possibly temporary devaluation.

In contrast, homogenous primary commodities are typically invoiced in a single international currency: the U.S. dollar. For a "small" country, domestic currency prices potentially increase in proportion to any devaluation of its own currency. I say *potentially,* because international arbitrage in agricultural commodities is often truncated by quota restrictions.

Do these continual violations of purchasing power parity for the more numerous fixprice goods undermine the monetary approach to exchange-rate determination? Quite the contrary. Because national price levels are so easily detached from the law of one price, relatively modest changes in money-market conditions at home or abroad may move the exchange rate a great deal depending on the views of financial speculators, who must now be formally introduced into the analysis. No longer may one rely on commodity arbitrage by merchants to keep the exchange rate aligned with national price levels as in equation (16).

Indeed, if financial speculators were absent, the rigid pricing of manufactured exports would make the market for foreign exchange completely unstable! During the short run, when quantities already ordered cannot be altered, an unexpected depreciation necessarily worsens the flow of current payments: foreign-exchange earnings from exports decline, whereas foreign currency payments for imports remain unchanged. This is the famous J-curve effect (MaGee 1973). Without support from speculators, the depreciating currency falls through the floor. The old argument about whether exchange speculation is stabilizing or destabilizing is wrongly posed; speculation in the end must be stabilizing if the market exists at all (McKinnon 1979, chap. 7). The important question is whether the supply of stabilizing speculation is adequate to prevent very large cumulative movements in one direction. And the answer depends critically on how speculators view the operations of the monetary authorities.

Monetary Instability, the Overshooting Effect, and Keynesian Liquidity Preference

In this milieu of (temporarily) rigid and possibly detached national price levels and (mainly) regressive exchange-rate expectations, governments retain control, in the short run, of their real money stocks. Indeed, the familiar Keynesian theory of liquidity preference is now the most appropriate monetary model for describing how short-term rates of interest are determined in the national money market *jointly* with the current and expected exchange rate when the economy remains financially open. Although discarding the instantaneous purchasing power parity condition of equation (16), one may retain all the portfolio equilibrium equations of the monetary approach leading to the Fisher Open condition of equation (22).

Now, how does monetary policy influence the interest rate? Begin with full equilibrium in the domestic money market: foreign and domestic nominal interest rates are equal, and the stable domestic price level is aligned with foreign prices according to the principle of purchasing power parity. Then suppose a sudden increase, say 2 percent, in the national money supply, arising from an open-market purchase of Treasury securities by the domestic central bank. Because domestic prices do not change in the short run, the real money supply also increases by 2 percent. Hence, the short-term (say, 90-day) rate of interest on domestic bonds is driven down, say 1 percent, in order to persuade domestic transactors to hold the increased real balances. The economy is "small" so that the foreign nominal rate of interest remains unchanged.

How must the foreign-exchange market react? First, the exchange rate must accommodate both the 1 percent fall in the interest rate *and* the Fisher Open principle by depreciating discretely at time zero. This sets up the expectation that the domestic currency will appreciate smoothly by 1 percent, leaving bond holders with no further incentive to purchase foreign bonds (Dornbusch 1976). But this principle only establishes the *minimum amount*—1 percent in this case—by which the spot rate must initially depreciate. If speculators confidently expect the monetary authority to reverse itself in the near future, they will prevent further depreciation by acquiring domestic currency in sufficient quantities to offset the J-curve effect (McKinnon 1979, chap. 8). In the lowest graph of figure 13.2, the exchange rate jumps discretely from A to B by 1 percentage point, followed by a gradual fall of 1 percentage point over 90 days to point E, when the initial full equilibrium is restored. The money supply and interest rates return to their initial levels with unchanged domestic prices. Under these strongly regressive expectations, the market behaves *as if* the monetary authorities were committed to maintaining the exchange rate within a band of 1 percent on either side of the "parity" or normal rate.

If under more weakly regressive expectations, the 2 percent money-supply increase was thought to be permanent, the exchange rate would discretely jump 3 percentage points and then smoothly fall back 1: the solid line *ACF* in figure 13.2. The domestic price level would gradually move upward by 2 percent over 90 days to reduce the excess real cash balance and restore the domestic rate of interest to the international level. Finally, if a second money increase of 2 percent was anticipated in 90 days with no further money supply adjustments, the exchange rate would jump 6 percentage points at time zero and smoothly fall back 2 over the course of the next 180 days. Similarly, the price level would increase smoothly by 4 percent over 180 days until the initial interest rate was restored.

These modest "overshooting" effects in the presence of regressive expectations have been analyzed by Rudiger Dornbusch (1976). They occur under the assumption that speculators have full information regarding the future intentions of the authorities. Under uncertainty, however, a transitory 2 percent shock in the domestic money supply may lead at time zero to a depreciation much greater than the 1 percent fall in the interest rate. Speculators are much less likely to commit capital to support the devalued domestic currency under pressure from the J-curve effect. Hence, the new path for the exchange rate could be represented by the dashed lines: either from A to C to E or from A to D to G. Because uncertainty limits the supply of risk capital available for stabilizing the exchange rate (McKinnon 1979, chap. 7), the spot exchange rate now moves much more widely than predicted by changing international interest differentials.

In summary, to explain the marked cyclical exchange-rate instability since 1973, one need not appeal to extrapolative expectations or vicious circles—although these may be important, on occasion, as we demonstrate below with the 1977–78 fall of the dollar. Because national price levels can easily be detached from each other, monetary shocks—in the domestic supply of, or demand for, money—can cause sharp fluctuations in the exchange rate even when the views of speculators are (weakly) regressive and essentially stabilizing.

The Fall of the Dollar Against the Yen, 1977–78

Our theoretical development of the monetary approach has gone far enough to help us understand certain important events somewhat better than when the theory of exchange rates and interest-rate relationships proceeded from more insular assumptions. The dramatic fall of the dollar against the yen in 1977–78 can be used to illustrate both the interpretation to which we are now led and why monetary authorities, whose operating theories were still insular, went wrong.

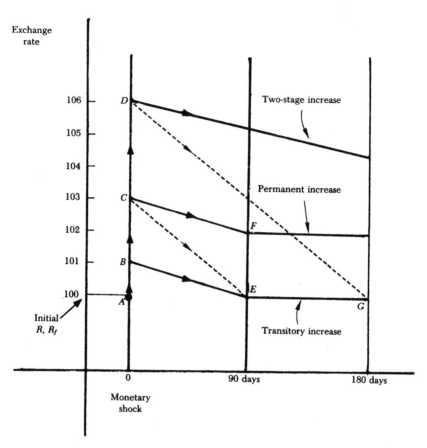

Figure 13.2
Alternative exchange-rate paths from a discrete 2 percent increase in the money
supply leading to a 1 percent decrease in the domestic interest rate.
Note: The exchange rate R = domestic currency/foreign currency. Hence an
increase in R represents a depreciation of the domestic currency.

To recapitulate briefly, early in 1977 there were strong signals
from officials in the Carter administration alleging that the dollar
was overvalued against the yen because of the emerging American trade deficit and Japanese trade surplus. (Above, we established that, for open economies, that is insufficient reason for
believing that the exchange rate was misaligned.) However, this
strong political signal to the exchange market, coupled with an
internal loss of monetary control in the United States, to be
described below, weakened the regressive exchange-rate expec-

tations that normally prevailed. Once dollar devaluation began, further depreciation was anticipated as was evidenced by a widening of the forward discount on the dollar—equation (21). This led to covered interest arbitrage, equation (20), in the international capital market with the remarkable adjustments in short-term money-market rates of interest in the United States and in Japan, depicted in table 13.4. In December 1976, the U.S. federal funds rate was 4.65 percent and the Japanese interbank call-money rate, which traditionally has been higher, was 7.11 percent. By the end of October 1978, the U.S. rate had moved persistently upward to 8.96 percent, whereas the Japanese rate had actually fallen to 4.18 percent: a change in the uncovered interest differential of more than 7 percentage points!

How did this interest-rate realignment—due mainly to changing foreign-exchange expectations—contribute to the loss of monetary control in the United States and make the cumulative dollar depreciation greater than intended? The short answer is that the higher American rate of interest reduced the demand for non-interest-bearing dollar balances (equation 17) while, at the same time, the Federal Reserve failed to reduce the supply of base money commensurately. In 1977–78, the American monetary authorities were still keying on the federal funds interest rate as their insular short-run instrument of monetary control. Hence, when pressure from the foreign-exchange market nudged American short-term interest rates upward because of the flight from the dollar, the immediate response of the Federal Reserve Bank was perverse: it purchased Treasury bills in a (vain) attempt to prevent interest rates from rising further and thereby increased the supply of money. With a lag of a week or two, foreign-exchange traders would see the new money supply statistics and become even more nervous. The stage was then set for further dollar depreciation, higher interest rates, and another maladroit monetary increase.

Why was the dollar's 35 percent devaluation against the yen prolonged over almost two years? Under a "pure" exchange-rate float, newly formed expectations of higher inflation in the United States would lead to an immediate discrete devaluation. First, expectations did not adjust all at once. More importantly, foreign central banks—notably the Bank of Japan—began intervening rather heavily to support the dollar and slow its rate

Table 13.4
Exchange Rates and Short-Term Interest Rates in Japan and the United States: 1977–78

		(1) Nominal Exchange Rate (Yen/$)	(2) U.S. Rate of Interest[a]	(3) Japanese Interest Rate[b]	(4) Interest Differential
1976	December	294.7	4.65	7.11	+2.45
1977	February	285.1	4.68	7.00	+2.32
	April	275.1	4.73	5.87	+1.14
	June	273.0	5.39	5.48	+.09
	August	266.6	5.90	5.57	−.33
	October	255.1	6.47	4.92	−1.55
	December	241.3	6.56	5.01	−1.55
1978	February	240.3	6.78	4.80	−1.98
	April	221.7	6.89	4.14	−2.75
	June	214.3	7.60	4.11	−3.49
	August	188.5	8.04	4.39	−3.65
	October	184.1	8.96	4.18	−4.78
→ Stabilization Plan of November 1st ←					
	December	196.3	10.03	4.57	−5.46

Source: International Monetary Fund, *International Financial Statistics* (various issues).
[a]Interest rate on federal funds (period average).
[b]Interbank call money rate of interest (period average).

of devaluation. This rather indefinite support in the spot but not the forward market may well have accentuated the forward discount on the dollar with the consequential interest-rate adjustments alluded to above. Moreover, these spot-dollar purchases caused many foreign central banks to lose control over their domestic money supplies in the 1977–78 period, thus contributing further to the great world inflation of 1979–80 (see chapters 7, 8, and 9).

In summary, during most of 1977–78 the Federal Reserve Bank was responding to signals in the American money market as if they were not dominated by expected dollar depreciation. Both Keynesians who relied on an interest-rate target, and monetarists who utilized a fixed money-growth rule, failed to spot the highly expansionary nature of American monetary policy in 1977–78 after the demand for dollars had fallen. Only after a major slide in the dollar's international value did the Fed enter with a convincing stabilization program on 1 November 1978, in which the domestic monetary base contracted by the amount of the official intervention. The interest-rate criterion was dropped temporarily (and then ostensibly discarded altogether in an official change of policy in another crisis on 6 October 1979) as was the proximate target of smooth domestic monetary growth. Although U.S. monetary authorities now respond to such major foreign-exchange crises, a procedure—or even a theory—is lacking for dealing with the foreign exchanges on a week-to-week basis. Federal Reserve operating procedures are still largely insular in nature.

The Real Appreciation of Sterling, 1979–80

Consider now another example of a government adopting a fixed money-growth rule as if the demand for money was not influenced by foreign exchange considerations. After the Conservative government was elected in Britain in May 1979, sterling was perceived (perhaps incorrectly) to be a "safe" petrocurrency because of the Iranian oil crisis and the lower inflation targets of the new government. There was a surge in demand for sterling assets—both money and bonds. But the new government had committed itself to an insular, monetarist growth rule and resisted increasing the British monetary base to accommodate this extraordinary new demand. With limited supply but increased demand for sterling, it appreciated by about 20 percent in nominal terms from December 1978 to the fall of 1980. This appreciation was considerably more in real terms after adjusting for the domestic wage explosion that occurred in 1979–80. The liquidity squeeze in the domestic British capital market sharply increased sterling rates of interest. The combined result of sterling appreciation and monetary stringency was a violent contraction in British manufacturing that still continues (November 1980).

The British misfortune is complicated by huge fiscal deficits associated with large wage increases for civil servants and the absence of any consistent policy toward the trade unions. Nevertheless, with the abolition in October 1979 of the exchange controls that had insulated the domestic money market in sterling from Eurocurrency transacting centered in London, the British economy is now highly vulnerable to currency substitution in either direction. With the resulting instability in the demand for sterling cash balances and a fixed rule for domestic money growth, the sterling exchange rate may become increasingly erratic (indeterminate?), and confidence in the sustainability of any money-growth rule itself may erode.

The moral of the newer perception of the relations between exchange rates and macro policy is that the Bank of England should redefine what it means by "tight" money. The sterling exchange rate could be fixed to some hard currency such as the deutsche mark—possibly in the guise of joining the European Monetary System (McKinnon 1981). Then, through purchases and sales of foreign exchange, the Bank of England could automatically adjust the supply of base money in sterling in the shifting demand for it. Moreover, a convincingly fixed exchange rate, coupled with free commodity arbitrage, would give the desired long-run signal to the market: that the British government is determined to phase inflation out of the system while recognizing the fact that Britain is an open rather than insular economy.

Some readers might object that Britain in the 1950s and 1960s was on a fixed exchange rate that was not successful: macroeconomic policy was on a stop-go basis, replete with periodic sterling crises. Through hindsight, however, we know that the Bank of England did not allow the British monetary base to adjust by the amount of its foreign-exchange interventions (Hodgman 1974). Because of the rules of its Exchange Rate Equalization Account, the Bank automatically sterilized the monetary impact of any reduction in dollar reserves by purchasing U.K. Treasury bills. At the present time, however, the Bank of England could use the exchange rate as the proximate indicator of whether the demand for sterling was "strong" or "weak." The process of stabilizing the exchange rate, without sterilizing official interventions, would then be the Bank's primary instrument for determining the U.K. money supply.

13.4 Conclusion

The first objective of this chapter has been to identify models of exchange-rate determination and macroeconomic management based, largely implicitly, on the concept of an insular economy. The two most influential have been, and still are, to some extent, the old Keynes-Meade model of internal versus external balance and the elasticities approach to "adjusting" the exchange rate to keep the balance of trade close to zero. These ideas were more or less fully worked out in the 1940s and 1950s. On their own terms, where both financial and commodity arbitrage with the outside world is limited, these early models remain logically consistent and appropriate guides to policymaking.

However, for macroeconomic control and exchange-rate determination in fully open economies, these older models became quite inappropriate and may lead policymakers astray as with the fall of the dollar in 1977–78. In particular, a persistent deficit or surplus in a country's balance of trade no longer indicates that its currency should be depreciated or appreciated. Instead, any "inappropriate" trade deficit or surplus likely reflects an inappropriate deficit or surplus in the country's public finances. Any official attempt to adjust the exchange rate in such circumstances is likely to generate serious financial instability while having no predictable effect on the trade balance.

What then determines the equilibrium exchange rate between open economies? The central insight of the monetary approach is to associate foreign-exchange turbulence in the 1970s with erratically differing national monetary policies. At first blush, this may suggest that it would be sufficient for governments to stabilize their domestic money supplies in order for deviations from purchasing power parity to be small and for the exchange rate to be determinate and potentially stable. The case for floating exchange rates and independent national monetary policies is apparently rescued from the insular nonmonetary foundations of the elasticities model.

But appearances are deceiving. The monetarists' advocacy of floating, combined with unchanging growth in some domestic monetary aggregate, implicitly presumes that the demand for each national money is stable and not much influenced by events in the foreign-exchange market. If, from time to time, national monetary systems are buffeted by individuals and firms, switching from one convertible currency to another—for reasons that may or may not be justified—then official action to stabilize the (nominal) exchange rate is warranted. In effect, the exchange rate (or other measures of pressure in the foreign-exchange market) is a valuable short-run indicator to the authorities of whether domestic money-market conditions are unduly easy or tight.

Putting the point more strongly, national monetary authorities can only ignore wide swings in their exchange rates at their peril—as recent experiences in the United States and Britain attest. However, only a smallish open economy like Britain could feasibly use a stable exchange rate as the principal pillar of its monetary policy. Such a country can ignore its own contribution to the growth of the world's money supply and to the increase of the international price level. The United States has the intrinsically more difficult problem of reconciling exchange stability with the need to maintain an independent anchor for its own price level and for the world dollar standard. In the long run, at least one convertible-currency country, or a small inner group of them, must evolve a purely internal system of monetary control to which others may adjust.[5]

Notes

I am indebted to Moses Abramovitz, John Bilson, John Cuddington, Tibor Scitovsky, and Beth Van Zummeren for helpful comments on earlier drafts.

1. A remarkable omission since J. M. Keynes had given the foreign exchanges center stage in his earlier books, such as *A Tract On Monetary Reform* (1923).

2. One of many authors who derived this precise expression was Joan Robinson (1937). But Arnold Harberger (1950) spelled out rather more carefully the required assumption that internal aggregate demand is being managed so as to keep the economy close to full employment.

3. For a contrary view that, in practice, national economies remain quite insular so that increments to national saving are primarily converted to increments in national investment, see Martin Feldstein and Charles Horioka (1980).

4. The single forward rate is defined with the same term to maturity as the relevant interest rate—say, over three months. Space does not permit consideration of how the whole term structure of forward exchange and interest rates is jointly determined.

5. This is a story for another time. Some of the problems involved are covered in McKinnon (1980b) and in chapter 22.

References

Aliber, Robert Z. "The Interest Rate Parity Theorem: A Reinterpretation," *J. Polit. Econ.*, Nov./Dec. 1973, *81*(6), pp. 1451–59.

———. *Exchange risk and corporate international finance*. London: Macmillan, 1978.

Bilson, John F. "Recent Developments in Monetary Models of Exchange Rate Determination," *International Monetary Fund staff papers*, June 1979, 26(2), pp. 201–23.

Caves, Richard E., and Jones, Ronald W. *World trade and payments: An introduction*, 2nd ed. Boston: Little, Brown, 1977.

Corden, W. M. *Inflation, exchange rates, and the world economy: Lectures on international monetary economics*. Chicago: University of Chicago Press, 1977.

David, Paul A., and Scadding, John. "Private Savings: Ultrarationality, Aggregation, and 'Denison's Law,'" *J. Polit. Econ.*, Part I, March/April 1974, 82(2), pp. 225–49.

Dornbusch, Rudiger. "Expectations and Exchange Rate Dynamics," *J. Polit. Econ.*, Dec. 1976, 84(6), pp. 1161–76.

Feldstein, Martin, and Horioka, Charles. "Domestic Saving and International Capital Flows," *Econ. J.*, June 1980, 90(358), pp. 314–29.

Frenkel, Jacob. "A Monetary Approach to the Exchange Rate: Doctrinal Aspects and Empirical Evidence," *Scan. J. Econ.*, 1976, 78(2), pp. 200–224.

Frenkel, Jacob, and Johnson, Harry G., eds. *The monetary approach to the balance of payments*. London: Allen & Unwin, 1976.

Frenkel, Jacob, and Mussa, Michael L. "The Efficiency of the Foreign Exchange Market and Measures of Turbulence," *Amer. Econ. Rev., Papers and Proceedings*, May 1980, 70(2), pp. 374–81.

Friedman, Milton. "The Case for Flexible Exchange Rates," in *Essays in positive economics*. Chicago: University of Chicago Press, 1953, pp. 157–203.

———. "The Role of Monetary Policy," *Amer. Econ. Rev.*, March 1968, 58(1), pp. 1–17.

Grassman, Sven. "A Fundamental Symmetry in International Payment Patterns," *J. Int. Econ.*, May 1973, 3(2), pp. 105–16.

Haberler, Gottfried. "The Market for Foreign Exchange and the Stability of the Balance of Payments: A Theoretical Analysis," *Kyklos*, 1949, 3, pp. 193–218.

Harberger, Arnold C. "Currency Depreciation, Income, and the Balance of Trade," *J. Polit. Econ.*, Feb. 1950, 58(1), pp. 47–60.

Hodgman, Donald R. *National monetary policies and international monetary cooperation*. Boston: Little, Brown, 1974.

International Financial Statistics, International Monetary Fund (various issues).

Isard, Peter. "How Far Can We Push the 'Law of One Price'?," *Amer. Econ. Rev.*, Dec. 1977, 67(5), pp. 942–48.

Johnson, Harry G. "Towards a General Theory of the Balance of Payments," in *International trade and economic growth: Studies in pure theory*. Cambridge: Harvard University Press, 1961, pp. 153–68.

———. "The Case for Flexible Exchange Rates, 1969," in *Further essays in monetary economics*. Cambridge: Harvard University Press, 1972, pp. 198–228.

Keynes, John Maynard. *A tract on monetary reform.* London: Macmillan, 1923.

————. *The general theory of employment, interest, and money.* London: Macmillan, 1936.

Kindleberger, Charles P., and Lindert, Peter H. *International economics,* 6th ed. Homewood, Ill.: Irwin, 1978.

Krueger, Anne O. *Liberalization attempts and consequences.* National Bureau of Economic Research. Cambridge, Mass.: Ballinger, 1978.

Lindbeck, Assar, ed. *Inflation and employment in open economies.* New York: North-Holland, 1979.

Machlup, Fritz. "The Theory of Foreign Exchanges," *Economica,* Nov. 1939, N.S. 6(24), pp. 375–97, and Feb. 1940, N.S. 7(25), pp. 23–49. Reprinted in American Economic Association, *Readings in the theory of international trade.* Edited by Howard S. Ellis and Lloyd A. Metzler. Philadelphia: Blakiston, 1949, pp. 104–58.

————. *International trade and the national income multiplier.* Philadelphia: Blakiston, 1943.

————. *The alignment of foreign exchange rates.* New York: Praeger, 1972.

MaGee, Stephen P. "Currency Contracts, Pass-Through, and Devaluation," *Brookings Pap. Econ. Act.,* 1973, (1), pp. 303–23.

Mathieson, Donald J., and McKinnon, Ronald I. "Instability in Underdeveloped Countries: The Impact of the International Economy," in *Nations and households in economic growth: Essays in honor of Moses Abramovitz.* Edited by Paul David and Melvin Reder. New York: Academic Press, 1974, pp. 315–31.

McKinnon, Ronald I. "Optimum Currency Areas," *Amer. Econ. Rev.,* Sept. 1963, 53(4), pp. 717–25.

————. *Money in international exchange: The convertible currency system.* New York: Oxford University Press, 1979.

————. "Exchange-Rate Instability, Trade Imbalances, and Monetary Policies in Japan, Europe and the United States," in *Issues in international economics.* Edited by Peter Oppenheimer. Oxford International Symposia, Vol. V. Boston: Routledge & Kegan Paul, 1980a, pp. 225–50.

————. "Dollar Stabilization and American Monetary Policy," *Amer. Econ. Rev., Papers and Proceedings,* May 1980b, 70(2), pp. 382–87.

————. "Offshore Markets in Foreign Currencies and National Monetary Control: Britain, Singapore and the United States," in *The international monetary system under stress.* Edited by Dreyer, Habesher, Willet. Washington, D.C.: The American Enterprise Institute, 1981.

————. "Currency Substitution and Instability in the World Dollar Standard," *Amer. Econ. Rev.* 72(3) June 1982, pp. 320–333.

Meade, J. E. *The balance of payments.* London: Oxford University Press, 1951.

————. "The Case for Variable Exchange Rates," *Three Banks Rev.,* Sept. 1955, (27), pp. 3–27.

Michaely, Michael. "Relative–Price and Income–Absorption Approaches to Devaluation: A Partial Reconciliation," *Amer. Econ. Rev.*, March 1960, *50*(1), pp. 144–47.

Miles, Marc. "The Effects of Devaluation on the Trade Balance and the Balance of Payments: Some New Results," *J. Polit. Econ.*, June 1979, *87*(3), pp. 600–620.

Mundell, Robert A. "The Monetary Dynamics of International Adjustment under Fixed and Flexible Exchange Rates," *Quart. J. Econ.*, May 1960, *74*(2), pp. 227–57.

———. "The International Disequilibrium System," *Kyklos*, 1961a, *14*(2), pp. 153–70.

———. "A Theory of Optimum Currency Areas," *Amer. Econ. Rev.*, Sept. 1961b, *51*(4), pp. 657–65.

———. *International economics*. New York: Macmillan, 1968.

Mussa, Michael. "The Exchange Rate, the Balance of Payments and Monetary and Fiscal Policy under a Regime of Controlled Floating," *Scan. J. Econ.*, 1976, *78*(2), pp. 229–48.

Robinson, Joan. "The Foreign Exchanges," in *Essays in the theory of employment*, Part III, Ch. 1. New York: Macmillan, 1937.

Sodersten, Bo. *International economics*, 2nd ed. New York: St. Martin's Press, 1981.

Spitaller, Erich. "Short-Run Effects of Exchange Rate Changes on Terms of Trade and Trade Balance," *International Monetary Fund staff papers*, June 1980, *27*(2), pp. 320–48.

Stern, Robert M. *The balance of payments*. Chicago: Aldine, 1973.

Swan, Trevor. "Longer-Run Problems of the Balance of Payments," in *The Australian economy: A volume of readings*. Edited by Arndt and Corden. Melbourne: F. W. Cheshire Press, 1963, pp. 384–95.

Tsiang, S. C. "The Role of Money in Trade-Balance Stability: Synthesis of the Elasticity and Absorption Approaches," *Amer. Econ. Rev.*, Dec. 1961, *51*(5), pp. 912–36.

14

Exchange-Rate Instability, Trade Imbalances, and Monetary Policies in Japan and the United States

14.1 Multinational Investment and the Real Exchange Rate

Many readers will grant our J-curve argument that the exchange rate cannot be determined by commodity flows within the short run of days or weeks. But in the intermediate or long run—say months or years—shouldn't the balance of trade respond positively to a depreciation if the exchange market can hang on that long? In particular, suppose the "real" exchange rate depreciates: the external value of a currency falls proportionately more than its relative internal rate of price inflation thus causing a prolonged departure from purchasing power parity. Shouldn't quantities of exports now flexibly adjust upwards, and quantities of imports adjust downwards, enough to overcome their higher invoice prices?

I shall argue that such longer-run "stabilizing" adjustments in the goods market are unlikely to occur. When capital is mobile internationally, investment and output can be sufficiently buoyed in response to a real depreciation that the balance of trade need not improve at all. The likely result is the mercantilist effect of having domestic output and consumption artificially stimulated at the expense of trading partners'. The underlying problem of exchange-rate instability remains unresolved.

To illustrate this general proposition, let us focus on bilateral trade between Japan and the United States over the past two years or so. The monthly real exchange rates in table 14.1 are

Originally published, in slightly longer form, in *Issues in International Economics*, ed. Peter Oppenheimer (Routledge and Kegan Paul Ltd., 1980): 225–250. Reprinted with permission.

Table 14.1
The Yen/Dollar Exchange Rate for 1977–78 (monthly averages)

	Nominal Exchange Rates		Price Indices (1953 = 100)		Real Exchange Rate	
	(1)	(2)	(3)	(4)	(5)	(6)
1977	Current (Yen/$)	1953 = 100	WPI Japan / WPI (U.S.)	CPI (Japan) / CPI (U.S.)	(2)/(3)	(2)/(4)
Jan	291.1	80.7	88.9	179.6	0.908	0.449
Feb	285.1	79.0	88.2	178.6	0.896	0.442
Mar	280.6	77.8	87.3	178.7	0.890	0.435
April	275.1	76.2	86.2	180.1	0.884	0.423
May	277.6	76.9	86.0	180.8	0.895	0.425
June	273.0	75.7	86.1	178.7	0.879	0.423
July	264.8	73.4	85.4	177.4	0.859	0.414
Aug	266.6	73.9	85.7	176.8	0.863	0.418
Sept	267.0	74.0	85.5	179.3	0.866	0.413
Oct	255.1	70.7	84.8	179.6	0.833	0.394
Nov	244.8	67.9	84.0	176.7	0.808	0.384
Dec	241.3	66.9	83.1	175.7	0.804	0.381
1978						
Jan	241.1	66.8	82.3	175.3	0.811	0.381
Feb	240.3	66.6	81.6	174.9	0.816	0.380
Mar	231.5	64.2	80.8	175.3	0.794	0.366
April	221.7	61.4	79.5	175.7	0.773	0.350
May	226.4	62.7	79.1	174.9	0.793	0.358
June	214.3	59.3	78.3	172.0	0.757	0.345
July	199.9	55.3	77.1	171.6	0.717	0.322
Aug	188.5	52.2	76.5	170.8	0.682	0.306

Source: *International Financial Statistics*, IMF (various issues), compiled by
Masahiro Kawai.

calculated on the principle of relative purchasing power parity
using 1953 as the (arbitrary) base year. Movements in the nominal
yen/dollar exchange rate are deflated either by relative wholesale price indices (WPIs) or by relative consumer price indices
(CPIs) in order to give alternative estimates of movements in
the real exchange rate. Because wholesale prices cover a more
or less representative basket of tradable goods, whereas the CPI
includes nontradable services, I shall use only the WPI in the
subsequent analysis.[1]

Despite the monetary turmoil of the early 1970s, the real yen/ dollar exchange rate was still about 91 percent of its 1953 parity as of January 1977. And this real exchange rate had not moved significantly further from unity during the previous 24 years. From January 1977 to August 1978, however, a substantial real depreciation of the dollar of 25 percent was accompanied by a nominal depreciation against the yen of 35 percent. I hypothesize that this real depreciation could not of itself have been expected to reduce the Japanese trade surplus or American trade deficit in 1979.

In contrast, the traditional analytical response is to distinguish between tradable and nontradable goods (Salter 1958; Dornbusch 1974), and to consider the appreciation of the yen to depress the production of tradable goods in Japan while raising the demand for them—and vice versa in the United States. Unfortunately, this traditional analysis depends heavily on the law of one price holding in the market for tradable goods. In reality, deviations from purchasing power parity are particularly pronounced under floating exchange rates, as table 14.1 makes abundantly clear. Because of sticky invoice prices, the appreciation of the yen forces the prices of Japanese goods—both tradable and nontradable—to rise above their American equivalents. Moreover, this traditional Salter analysis is static in the sense that the ongoing flow of investment and saving is not formally modeled, although Salter stresses the need to increase domestic absorption if the trade surplus is to be reduced.

Instead, consider modeling just the Japanese side of the adjustment process (on the understanding that the American response to the exchange rate is approximately the inverse) on a "fixed-price" basis. Note that the internal yen prices of Japanese goods are indeed sticky: Japanese wholesale prices in June 1978 were the same as in 1976 and were stable within a margin of one or two percentage points in the interim. Consumer prices were also remarkably stable, perhaps because the Japanese economy was depressed. Thus the yen value of output in Japan in 1976–78 provides a stable real numeraire on which to build a Keynesian-type income-expenditure model, where real and nominal values are virtually the same.

Then, in yen per dollar, movements in the nominal exchange rate e are equivalent to real changes because of the constancy of the Japanese price level. Dollar price inflation in the United

States would be equivalent to a rise in e, but otherwise foreign repercussions to income-expenditure changes in Japan are ignored in the algebraic model.[2] What is essential about this model, however, is that e is initially given from "outside" by financial considerations not yet formally considered. One can then test whether the flow of commodity trade eventually responds in a stabilizing fashion to, say, a fall in e: an appreciation of the yen like that portrayed in table 14.1.

The four basic behavioral equations are:

$$X = X(e) \text{ where } X'(e) > 0 \qquad \text{Exports} \qquad (1)$$

$$eM = mY \text{ where } 0 < m < 1 \qquad \text{Imports} \qquad (2)$$

$$I = I(e, i; \alpha) \text{ where } \frac{\delta I}{\delta e} > 0 \text{ and } \frac{\delta I}{\delta i} < 0 \quad \text{Investment} \qquad (3)$$

$$S = sY \text{ where } 0 < s < 1 \qquad \text{Saving} \qquad (4)$$

To these we add the accounting identities:

$$Y = C + I + X - eM \quad \text{Gross national product} \qquad (5)$$

$$S = Y - C \qquad \text{Saving-Consumption} \qquad (6)$$

$$T_d = X - eM \qquad \text{Trade balance in domestic currency} \quad (7)$$

$$T_f = \frac{X}{e} - M \qquad \text{Trade balance in foreign currency} \quad (8)$$

Within these eight equations, we have eight endogenous flow variables: Y, C, S, I, X, M, T_d and T_f. The exchange rate e and the interest rate i are given by financial considerations outside the model.

The yen export function—equation (I)—is straightforward for a Keynesian "fixprice" world. Japanese goods are invoiced in yen, and important costs of production like money wages are fixed in yen, so that the yen prices of manufactures are quite rigid even beyond the period of currency contract. Thus, when e declines in the "intermediate run," Japanese goods are seen to be more expensive so that world demand for them falls.

M is the dollar value of imports (fix price) so that their yen value, eM, declines with e unless M increases. For simplicity, I have assumed in equation (2) that the demand for imports is proportional to income with a unit (yen) price elasticity of demand.

The investment function—equation (3)—is the more novel part of the model, and is basically responsible for the unconventional results that are obtained. Investment *I* is strongly and positively influenced by the real exchange rate *e*. (The usual rate of interest also appears but it is not manipulated.) That is, a change in *e* lasting a few months or a year or two is perceived to be permanent by nonspeculative investors with stationary expectations. Thus Japanese costs of production—wages and locally produced intermediate materials—are raised above world levels by the general appreciation of the yen. Japan is perceived to be a high-cost country for producing internationally tradable goods in the *future*, so that multinational firms reduce *current* investment there or set up subsidiaries in low-wage countries like the United States. Within the world economy, I am hypothesizing that the real exchange rate has a first-order effect on where new private physical investment is located. *e* is an index of profitability of producing (cost of production) of internationally tradable goods.

Finally, in equation (4), the yen value of saving is proportional to national income. Because the government is not represented explicitly, *S* and *I* in the model have both private and public components.

Solving equations (1) through (6), the equilibrium level of national income Y^* is simply

$$Y^* = \frac{I(e) + X(e)}{m + s} \tag{9}$$

where

$$\frac{dY^*}{de} = \frac{1}{m + s} \left[\underset{+}{\frac{\delta I}{\delta e}} + \underset{+}{\frac{\delta X}{\delta e}} \right] > 0. \tag{10}$$

Because both the yen value of exports and investment fall as *e* declines, one expects the real appreciation of the yen exhibited in table 14.1 to depress national income in Japan (and contribute to a business boom in the United States). And, as of September 1978, this is indeed the case. *Private* investment in Japan is depressed, and industrial output has barely returned to what it was at the end of 1973. Unemployment has become a significant problem for the first time in the postwar period.

However, the main rationale for this intermediate-term model is to examine the impact on the trade balance of a real change in the exchange rate. In terms of the domestic currency (yen) we have

$$T_d = X - eM \tag{11}$$

and

$$\frac{dT_d}{de} = \frac{s}{m+s}\frac{\delta X}{\delta e} - \frac{m}{m+s}\frac{\delta I}{\delta e} \underset{<}{\overset{>}{}} 0. \tag{12}$$

$$\phantom{\frac{dT_d}{de} =}\ +\ \qquad\quad +$$

From equation (12), the indeterminant response of the yen trade balance to a change in e is a weighted sum of the export and investment responses. In the case of an appreciation where e falls, exports decrease but if investment falls sufficiently, imports (in yen) could decrease even more, whence the indeterminant sign in equation (12):

But we simplify further in assessing the relative importance of the export and investment responses. Suppose trade is approximately balanced, and hence domestic saving approximately equals domestic investment, such that

$$X \approx mY \text{ and } I \approx sY. \tag{13}$$

Further, define the *elasticities* of both the export and investment responses to be:

$$E_x = \frac{dX}{de}\cdot\frac{e}{X} \text{ and } E_I = \frac{dI}{de}\cdot\frac{e}{I} \tag{14}$$

Then substituting equations (13) and (14) into (12), we obtain a remarkably simple expression for the sensitivity of trade balance in domestic currency to the real exchange rate:

$$\frac{dT_d}{de} = \frac{sm}{m+s}\cdot\frac{Y}{e}(E_x - E_I). \tag{15}$$

Thus $dT_d/de > 0$ only if $E_x > E_I$. In the case of balanced trade, only if the elasticity of the export response exceeds that of investment do we get the "normal" effect of a devaluation (rise in e) improving the balance of trade.

The upshot is that an appreciation of the yen relative to the dollar *could* depress income and investment in Japan so that the trade surplus does not fall. Similarly, investment and income could be stimulated in the United States so that the American trade deficit widens. The goods market may remain incapable of determining an equilibrium rate,[3] even for a time horizon of months or years beyond that ordinarily associated with the J-curve effect.

14.2 The Absorption Approach to the Trade Balance and Financial Dissaving by the Government

How then is an equilibrium flow of imports and exports to be established among countries with floating convertible currencies and no detailed exchange controls or pervasive tariffs on commodity trade? Again we can appeal to the integration of the world capital market and simply consider the balance between saving and investment in individual countries—which necessarily spills out into the balance of trade as the difference between exports and imports. To fix ideas, consider the familiar identities from the national income accounts:

$$S - I = X - eM \tag{16}$$

$$S = S_p + S_g \text{ where } S_g = R - G \tag{17}$$

where

I is private investment
S_p is private saving
S_g is government financial saving
R is government tax revenue
G is government expenditures.

Leaving the export, import, and investment function as defined in equations (1), (2), and (3), let us modify equation (4), the saving function. Suppose only *private* saving is a constant fraction of national income:

$$S_p = s_p Y \text{ where } 0 < s_p < 1. \tag{4'}$$

Further, let us depart from the usual practice of treating the government surplus S_g as if it were endogenous. Rather suppose S_g is exogenously given a policy variable. (I realize that government revenue is dependent on the level of national income. Nevertheless, a government can adjust expenditures and tax rates in important ways so as to dominate S_g.) By this means we bring fiscal policy explicitly into the analysis. In looking at the recent Japanese experience, it proves very convenient to think of government financial saving S_g (or financial dissaving if $S_g < 0$) to be an important policy parameter, without worrying about the precise mix of expenditures and taxes.[4]

Now making use of the functional equations (1), (2), (3) and (4)'—and substituting these into the identities (16) and (17)—the equilibrium level of income is

$$Y^* = \cdot \frac{X(e) + I(e) - S_g}{m + s_p} \tag{18}$$

Not only does the real exchange rate e influence Y through the export and investment functions, but the level of government financial saving is negatively related to Y with a multiplier effect of $1/(m + s_p)$. Within our very simple Keynesian income-expenditure framework with fixed prices, only private saving and imports are endogenous leakages in the process of income generation. Some readers may find it more familiar to think of $-S_g$ as the vertical intercept of a consumption function that includes government consumption. So an increase in government "dissaving" (through reduced taxes or increased expenditures) shifts upward the whole flow of spending in the economy. Notice that the asset structure—including the money supply—has not been specified so that neither the interest rate nor the exchange rate can be determined within the model.

However, the state of the trade balance is determinate. In domestic currency we have

$$T_d = X - eM = \frac{s_p X(e) - m I(e) + m S_g.}{m + s_p} \tag{19}$$

Not only private saving, investment, and exports, but now the level of government saving S_g influences the trade surplus. Note, however, that T_d and S_g are not related on a one-to-one basis. The multiplier effect of S_g on T_d is simply $\frac{m}{(m+s_p)} < 1$. That is, an increase in public saving reduces income and private saving so that the trade surplus does not rise as much as the public finances improve. Nevertheless, they are positively related. Indeed, as the private propensity to save, s_p, becomes "small" as in the United States, deficits or surpluses in the government budget at the margin could dominate changes in the trade balance. And this idea is important in interpreting the current Japanese-American trade imbalance.

In recent experience, private saving propensities for each country have been fairly stable. Japanese household saving as a proportion of household disposable income has been about three times that prevailing in the United States. Discrepancies in gross savings rates—including retained earnings, capital consumption allowances, and government—are less pronounced but still striking. From 1960 to 1975, Japanese gross domestic saving averaged about 36 percent of GNP, whereas in the United States gross saving from all domestic sources averaged about 18 percent, or half as much.[5] And, with some cyclical variation, gross investment matched gross saving in both countries so there was no need to run trade surpluses or deficits on a sustained basis, i.e., no need for sustained *net* capital inflows or outflows.

However, beginning with the energy crisis in 1974 and the world recession in 1975, private investment in Japan slumped and has not recovered. The gross figures that are available in the IMF statistics, as displayed in table 13.3, fail to show the full extent of the fall in private investment because they include publicly financed fixed capital formation. Even so, by 1977 the fall is impressive: investment is 6 to 7 percent of GNP less than in 1970. If private saving were a constant proportion of GNP, one would have expected the trade balance to go into surplus by the amount investment falls if there were no other offsets in the Japanese economy.

The emergence of a trade surplus is quite definite by 1977 and the beginning of 1978—but it is still only of an order of magnitude of about 2 percent of GNP. Somewhat surprisingly, Japanese fiscal offsets are large and growing. The government financial deficit was over 6 percent of GNP in 1977. Otherwise the Japanese trade surplus would be even larger. (Insofar as the gross investment series includes new publicly financed capital accumulation that has been increasing strongly in Japan, one cannot exactly offset the fall of investment in the first row with the rise in the public-sector deficit in the second in netting out the effect on the trade balance.) So the trade surplus is not "large"; measured as a proportion of the yen value of GNP, it is back to where it was in the early 1970s. Nevertheless, the trade surplus might seem formidable to foreigners because the Japanese economy is bigger than in the early 1970s, and the yen has appreciated so much.

If one believes with the American government that the Japanese trade surplus is in need of "correction," one response is for the Japanese government to increase the volume of financial dissaving as represented by $S_g < 0$. And in 1978 the Japanese government's fiscal deficit is even larger than the 6.2 percent of GNP recorded in table 13.3 for 1977. On the other hand, we have established that further real appreciation of the yen would be worse than useless—private investment in Japan would slump even further. Indeed, the sharp appreciation in 1977–78 seems to have contributed significantly to the depressed condition (and trade surplus) of the Japanese economy.

On the other side of the coin, just the inverse of this analysis applies to the United States. America is experiencing a business cycle boom where, unlike Japan, private investment[6] as a proportion of GNP is now substantially greater than in 1975 as indicated in table 13.2. Government financial dissaving, however, has been reduced only slightly in response to the upsurge in investment in 1977 and 1978 (see table 13.2). Combined with the fact that private saving (not shown) in the United States is a percentage point less than its historical norm, this government deficit leaves a savings gap that is covered by drawing on foreign saving. And indeed the government deficit of $50 billion or so per year in 1977 and 1978 is large relative to the current-account deficit of about $30 billion per year. This deficiency of saving in the United States is being made good, in part, by the transfer of surplus saving from Japan.

One could even say that this transfer of savings from abroad has helped to sustain the current business boom in the United States. Without foreign central banks buying U.S. Treasury securities (they now hold about 20 percent of total U.S. government debt), a crunch in the American capital market could already have occurred. Therefore, the American trade deficit has probably been a benign influence during 1977–78 in preventing more inflationary pressure from developing in the United States.

Two further aspects of this income-expenditure approach to the Japanese-American trade balance are important to note. First, "unfair" Japanese trade practices are not responsible. For example, removing high barriers on agricultural imports into Japan would simply alter the composition of Japanese imports without much affecting the net surplus. A similar rationalization of American energy policy would probably reduce imports of fossil fuels into the United States, but would be offset elsewhere as long as America is deficient in saving. The microeconomic details of trade in this or that commodity are dominated by broad investment-saving considerations—unlike current heated political discussions of these issues would suggest.

14.3   Japan, a Natural International Creditor?

In order to understand the "unbalanced" economic relationship between the two countries one must look at *financial* considerations rather than commodity trade. The principal anomaly about the present situation is that the Tokyo capital market remains too inaccessible to foreigners. The natural counterpart of the surplus of saving in Japan, displayed in table 13.3, is that foreigners be able to issue bonds and stocks freely in Tokyo. Restraints on their doing so have been recently relaxed but are not yet removed. Even more importantly, exchange controls on Japanese firms and households that inhibit them from buying financial assets abroad are still considerable.[7] The commercial banks play a dominant role in domestic financial intermediation between investors and savers, and the rather tight restraints by the Bank of Japan on their acquisition of foreign (dollar) assets could well be eliminated.

With such controls on private capital outflows, how then is Japan's large trade surplus financed? If the current-account surplus exists, there must be a counterpart buildup of financial claims on foreigners if only from the principle of double-entry bookkeeping. Because private capital outflows are less than the trade surplus, there is chronic incipient upward pressure on the yen (in terms of dollars). To prevent the yen from rising as much as it would otherwise, the Japanese government enters the foreign-exchange market to buy dollars and sell yen. The dollars so purchased are then invested in U.S. Treasury bonds or bills, whose recent buildup in Japanese official exchange reserves has been quite rapid. The Japanese government is thus forced into being an unwilling financial intermediary for the trade surplus, and by international convention is trapped into acquiring U.S. government debt whose yield is not particularly attractive. But, with much unnecessary upward pressure on the yen, there is (must be) a capital outflow that exactly matches the Japanese trade surplus.

With the important caveat that this serious imperfection in the private Japanese capital market be removed, I see nothing wrong with Japan becoming a major international creditor like the U.S. was from the 1940s to the early 1960s, or like Britain prior to 1914. Personal saving in Japan is very high relative to that of other industrial countries. Because Japan is now at the frontier of new technology along with other OECD countries, it may be difficult to sustain the profitability of the high levels of domestic investment that occurred in the 1950s and 1960s. Hence, investment abroad could be socially useful given the needs of less developed countries and the fact that the net surpluses of the OPEC countries are coming to an end in the foreseeable future. Alternatively, a less satisfactory adjustment mechanism is to reduce the Japanese trade surplus by having the Japanese government increase its already large fiscal deficit so that government dissaving offsets private saving.

Notes

1. Economists have disputed the circumstances under which one or another price index is appropriate. (McKinnon 1979, chap. 6; Dornbusch and Jaffee 1978) Fortunately, in the Japanese-American case for 1977–78, it makes little difference which deflator is used.

2. Nontechnical readers can skip the algebra without losing the main thread of the argument.

3. The conditions for the "normal" effect of an appreciation reducing the trade balance in foreign currency are less stringent if there is a trade deficit

$$\frac{dT_f}{de} = \frac{T_d}{e^2} + \frac{dT_d}{de}$$

Clearly if the trade balance deficit is sufficiently large, we get the "normal" effect of a decrease in e reducing T_f and vice versa. This asymmetry in the algebra between trade deficit and surplus situations arises because the model is incomplete: the response of trading partners has not been explicitly taken into account. A full analysis of the conditions for stability in the foreign exchange market leads to look at the export and import responses from both sides. Even with a more complex two-country model, however, our qualitative results remain the same.

4. Notice that S_g is not a measure of total government saving. Real capital accumulation could be tax financed and not appear in S_g. Rather, $-S_g$ is simply the amount that expenditures for goods and services exceed tax collections.

5. These figures are computed from the *United Nations Statistical Yearbook* (1976).

6. Unlike Japan, a separate series on private investment does appear in the *International Financial Statistics* for the United States.

7. See the *28th Annual Report on Exchange Restrictions*, International Monetary Fund, Washington, D.C., 1977.

References

Dornbusch, Rudiger, "Real and Monetary Aspects of the Effects of Exchange-Rate Changes," pp. 64–81 in *National Monetary Policies and the International Financial System*, edited by Robert Z. Aliber, University of Chicago Press, 1974.

Dornbusch, R., and Jaffee, D., et al., "Purchasing Power Parity: A Symposium," *Journal of International Economics*, Vol. 8, May 1978.

Grassman, Sven, "A Fundamental Symmetry in International Payments Patterns," *Journal of International Economics*, May 1973.

Grassman, Sven, "Currency Distribution and Forward Cover in Foreign Trade: Sweden Revisited," *Journal of International Economics*, May 1976.

IMF, *International Financial Statistics* (various issues).

IMF, *28th Annual Report on Exchange Restrictions*, 1977.

McKinnon, Ronald I., *Money in International Exchange: The Convertible Currency System*, Oxford University Press, 1979.

Salter, W. E., "Internal and External Balance: The Role of Price and Expenditure Effects," *Economic Record* 36, March 1960.

United Nations Statistical Yearbook 1976, 1977.

15   Monetary Control and the Crawling Peg

Why have several less developed countries, but no industrial economies, adopted a crawling peg? As Williamson (1981) notes, academic discussion in the 1960s and 1970s was centred on applying the crawling peg to industrial economies as a modification of the dollar-based Bretton Woods method of setting official parities. Yet since 1973 many industrial economies have opted for floating, and none for crawling. Correspondingly, no less developed countries (LDCs), who typically limit the convertibility of their currencies, have opted for free floating, but since 1965 several have allowed their official parities to crawl smoothly downward through time.

The paradox can be explained if exchange-rate policy is treated simply as an adjunct of monetary policy, and not as an independent instrument for adjusting the trade balance. In executing monetary policy, different countries find it more or less convenient to rely on foreign-exchange transactions to determine jointly the domestic price of tradable goods and the monetary base.

The first part of this chapter explains why many industrial economies have opted to float but not to crawl, and why adventures in crawling according to commonly accepted indicator rules are likely seriously to destabilise an open monetary system that would otherwise be stable.

The second part of the chapter deals with two important facets of monetary policy in LDCs: (1) how best to live with ongoing inflation in an economy with repressed foreign trade and a repressed domestic financial system; and (2) how to maintain mon-

Originally published in *The Crawling Peg: Past Performance and Future Prospects*, ed. J. Williamson (Macmillan, 1981): 38–49. Reprinted with permission.

etary control during and after a major financial and trade liberalisation (possibly associated with a discrete devaluation) where
the public finances have improved to the point of allowing the
inflation tax to be phased out.

As we shall see, the crawling peg can greatly simplify monetary
management in both cases. Under (1), *passive* crawling to offset
movements in domestic prices can protect foreign trade against
domestic inflation. Under (2), a successful liberalisation requires
a change to *active* crawling that converges to a virtually fixed
exchange rate, and becomes the principal monetary instrument
for securing the domestic price level.

15.1   Regressive Expectations and Floating Exchange Rates among Industrial Economies

Unlike LDCs, most industrial economies have sufficiently convertible currencies that free floating is at least technically feasible. Foreign-exchange departments of authorised commercial
banks—henceforth simply dealers—are allowed to take the open
positions in foreign exchange necessary actually to make the
market. Although many industrial countries still restrict the
rights of individual citizens to hold interest-bearing securities
in foreign monies, large trading corporations and commercial
banks are quite free to hold forward positions or Eurocurrency
positions[1] as a means of covering their foreign currency exposures. This active flow of short-term capital between the currencies of any two industrial countries is essential to develop a
vigorous forward market on the one hand, and to minimise the
capital constraints on dealer-speculators taking balancing spot
positions in foreign exchange on the other.[2] In contrast, in order
to prevent capital outflows, LDCs typically go to considerable
lengths to prevent firms and banks—as well as individuals—
from buying foreign securities, thus making a free float virtually impossible.

The proposition complementary to this idea that only industrial economies have the option of floating, is that they both
desire monetary autonomy and have the internal financial *means*
for exercising monetary control on a day-to-day or week-to-week
basis. Except for the United States, this autonomy was quite
severely abridged during the fixed exchange-rate period from

about 1950 to 1970. Thereafter, monetary instability in the United States became greater than the authorities in other industrial economies believed they could accept, leading to their severing their fixed exchange rate with the U.S. dollar. To facilitate domestic monetary control after floating became more general, direct open-market operations and discounting with the central bank were necessary. They were easier to carry out in the 1970s than in the late 1940s or early 1950s when the free operation of domestic capital markets in Europe and Japan had not yet recovered from the war. This gave monetary authorities the capability of matching the supply of base money to the demand for it independently of the foreign-exchange market. Domestic financial maturity, therefore, is another precondition for independent floating.

Before the central bank in a financially mature economy can independently stabilise its own price level, however, one further condition is needed. Private expectations regarding the "normal" exchange rate should be mainly *regressive*. That is, if the spot value of the domestic currency unexpectedly depreciates in the foreign exchanges, traders anticipate an appreciation to near the normal level. Reflecting these regressive expectations, the forward value of the newly depreciated currency should be above the spot rate. These regressive expectations are consistent with domestic prices remaining largely invariant to exchange-rate fluctuations that have no definite trend. In this case, merchants do not bother to change price tags on domestic goods in response to short-run variations in the exchange rate. Similarly, a surprise domestic monetary expansion will reduce short-term nominal (and real) rates of interest according to the Keynesian model of liquidity preference, and increase aggregate demand for goods and services (McKinnon 1971). The spot exchange rate depreciates relative to the forward rate according to the interest parity theorem.

Of course, regressive expectations and the idea of a "normal" level of internal prices imply that traders are confident that the monetary authority will not embark on a wildly inflationary or deflationary policy over prolonged periods of time. By their past behaviour and perceived commitment to a modicum of price stability, authorities in industrial economies are confined to short-run and quite transitory fine-tuning of their money supplies. Otherwise, they run a substantial risk of upsetting the private expectations that are necessary to stabilise the market. Among industrial countries, such confidence is not absolute, and people in Germany may possess it in a higher degree than those in, say, Italy. With these caveats in mind, a no-par floating exchange rate is not only feasible for an industrial economy, but permits the limited exercise of monetary independence with some control over aggregate demand.

15.2 Variable Crawling, Extrapolative Expectations and the Loss of Monetary Control

Suppose instead our industrial economy had adopted a peg that crawled according to any of the various indicator rules reviewed in Williamson (1981). Then any surprise short-run monetary manipulations by the authorities would be frustrated. The problem is that the crawling peg is geared more to extrapolative expectations: exchange movements that persist in the same direction, rather than regressive expectations that presume a reversal.

Under a crawling peg with a narrow band around it, consider again a surprise monetary expansion engineered by, for example, a domestic open-market purchase of Treasury bonds. The increased liquidity and associated outflow of capital will then depreciate the domestic currency to the bottom of its band, causing a deficit in the trade balance from the J-curve effect, and reduce the foreign reserve holdings of commercial banks and/or the exchange-stabilisation fund. All the indicator rules proposed by various writers to initiate a smooth downward crawl in the domestic currency would then point in the same direction: reserves and the rate of reserve accumulation would diminish, the market value of the domestic currency would fall on the foreign exchanges, and the trade balance would show an increased deficit. Authorities who were committed to crawling would then announce an indefinite downward crawl of the parity. The same downward crawl would ensue if authorities were committed to passively indexing the exchange rate against any increase in domestic price inflation above the foreign rate.

But this official announcement would conflict with the market's natural tendency toward regressive expectations! That is, the projected or extrapolated downward crawl in domestic parity could easily undermine the idea that there is a normal parity—

and associated stable domestic price level—to which the exchange rate will return and to which the authorities are committed. Hence, under the downward-crawling parity, forward rates of exchange may well fall *below* the spot rate after a surprise monetary expansion. From covered interest arbitrage, domestic short-term rates of interest would then rise rather than fall. The normal Keynesian effect of a fall in the short-term rate of interest from an internal monetary expansion is then frustrated, and the monetary scope for fine-tuning the level of aggregate demand is thereby attenuated.

More than merely frustrating short-term attempts at Keynesian fine tuning (which may well deserve frustration) is involved. Suppose the crawling peg—using one of the indicator rules referred to above—is introduced into an economy that is basically stable with regressive expectations regarding the normal exchange rate, a stable demand for non-interest-bearing domestic cash balances, and a monetary base well under the control of the authorities. In response to short-run perturbations in the foreign exchanges or in some domestic price index, suppose a downward crawl is initiated; then the market naturally projects the crawl into the future so that the forward rate falls below the spot for all terms to maturity (say two years) for which an active forward market exists. Because of this upward pressure on domestic nominal rates of interest at all terms to maturity, the demand for *non-interest-bearing* domestic cash balances would fall and cause even further reserve losses.[3] A needless downward spiral in the exchange rate, coupled with more internal price inflation, could easily result.

Similarly, suppose an unexpected balance-of-payments surplus—perhaps resulting from monetary contraction—triggered an upward crawl. Interest rates would tend to fall at all terms to maturity; the demand for domestic non-interest-bearing cash balances then would increase and could well trigger capital inflows that augment official reserves and falsely signal that further upward crawling is warranted. These sharp shifts in the demand for base money—upward or downward depending on the direction of crawl—could wreak havoc with the authorities' efforts to tailor independently the supply of money to the demand for it, and would needlessly upset their foreign-reserve position.

Even if the market sees crawling taking place in only one direction, variations in the rate of crawl and the associated international capital flows would lead to the same kind of domestic monetary instability.

Why then was flexible crawling in either direction proposed[4] in the 1960s and early 1970s for the industrial economies? Most writers simply did not focus on the seriously destabilising effects that inappropriate movements in the foreign-exchange rate might have on the domestic demand for money in economies that are financially open. Rather, influenced by the older elasticities approach, the prevailing view was that the exchange rate—a policy instrument separate from (or in addition to) monetary policy—can be safely assigned to adjusting the balance of trade. Essentially, crawling was viewed as a smooth and nontraumatic means of adjusting the *real* exchange rate while retaining elements of a parity system that limited mercantilist rivalry among nations or conflict among central banks.

Now, however, there is greater appreciation that trade deficits or surpluses among industrial nations need not be due to real exchange-rate misalignment, nor do they signal the need for an official policy to vary the nominal exchange rate (McKinnon 1978). In the world of floating convertible currencies where capital can move relatively freely, a trade deficit simply indicates that domestic investment exceeds net domestic saving that, in turn, may well reflect the fact that government expenditures exceed tax revenues.[5]

15.3 Financial Immaturity and the Need for a Pegged Exchange Rate in LDCs

Most less developed countries limit the convertibility of their currencies so that domestic banks and trading companies cannot freely take positions in foreign exchange: the possibility of floating in a legally organised market is simply eliminated.

Financial immaturity, or more active domestic financial repression, is clearly linked with maintaining tight controls over foreign-exchange transactions. If, as in most LDCs, domestic financial assets are illiquid and bear a low real rate of return for that degree of liquidity, then domestic nationals will prefer to hold liquid assets abroad unless prevented by official restrictions.

These exchange controls are usually tightened in a situation of ongoing price inflation, an important aspect of which is to collect a tax from the domestic banking system. Because the tax is levied on domestic currency and deposits,[6] the purchase of foreign bonds or working balances of foreign exchange erodes the tax base. These resources not only elude the government's inflation tax but in doing so cause a further socially unwarranted capital outflow from the domestic economy. Given the initial distortion of a repressed domestic financial system, therefore, a detailed web of exchange controls is a perfectly rational—indeed necessary—policy response.

A high and variable rate of domestic inflation also destroys the idea of a "normal" exchange rate around which regressive private expectations might have some chance of stabilising the market. Not only is the supply of domestic base money in the future unknown, but the demand for currency and deposits is likely to be quite unstable in immature financial systems where money/GNP ratios are subject to frequent changes. Hence the equilibrium exchange rate and domestic price level, which just clear the domestic money market, are unknown to potential private speculators. Even in the absence of exchange controls, therefore, exchange rate instability experienced by a typical less developed economy under floating would be much greater than fluctuations already experienced by the industrial economies in more favourable circumstances.

These difficulties with pure floating lead authorities in almost all LDCs to adopt some version of a pegged exchange rate. The central bank itself becomes responsible for making the market on a day-to-day basis, and for providing forward cover to merchants—insofar as any such cover exists. With the central bank buying and selling foreign exchange directly, there is no point in having even a narrow band around the official parity.[7] While usually subject to ongoing inflationary pressure, the domestic price level is made somewhat more stable and the difficulties experienced by merchant traders are minimised. The only question is whether the pegged exchange rate is kept rigid for several months or years before some traumatic devaluation is undertaken as per the "adjustable peg," or whether devaluation proceeds smoothly according to the precepts of a downward crawling peg. Clearly, the distortions inherent in delayed and massive discrete devaluations are so well known[8] that I simply discard the adjustable peg as a desirable policy option.

But instead of hitting the reader with an elaborate taxonomy of all the circumstances in which a downward crawl is warranted, and all the possible indicator rules by which that crawl could be effected, let me consider but *two* empirically important leading cases:

1. *Passive* downward crawling in a repressed economy. Ongoing and uncertain secular inflation is associated with restrictions on foreign trade and on domestic financial processes.

2. *Active* downward crawling accompanied by trade and financial liberalisation. The government has a definite programme in mind for ending economic repression and bringing inflation under control.

Although difficult to identify precise flesh-and-blood prototypes in each category, the experience of the last twelve years or so in Colombia and Brazil approximates category (1), whereas the experience of Chile from 1977 to 1979 is an example of category (2).

Passive Downward Crawling in a Repressed Economy

By "passive" I mean that the government adjusts the pace of downward crawling, ex post facto, to whatever domestic inflation turns out to be. The rate of inflation is out of control and, ex ante, cannot be predicted with any accuracy. The main objective is to index the real exchange rate roughly at purchasing power parity with the outside world to avoid destabilising foreign trade. The political obstacle to adopting passive downward crawling is to get governments to admit that inflation will continue indefinitely and is unpredictable. Typically, only countries having long experience with high inflation—Chile in the 1960s, or Colombia or Brazil more recently—can bring themselves to adopt passive downward crawling as a way of insulating foreign trade against the worst effects of inflation. In effect, officially fixing the exchange rate is no longer a credible device for convincing the populace that the authorities intend to bring inflation under control, or indeed are capable of maintaining an unchanging foreign parity.

By a "repressed" economy, I mean one with widespread restrictions on foreign trade and domestic finance. Much of the current flow of imports and exports is repressed by quota restrictions (QRs) and redundantly high tariffs.[9] These QRs create a large body of "pseudo nontradables" whose domestic currency prices are detached from those prevailing in world markets. Although the exchange rate is pegged, increases in aggregate demand in the domestic economy raise the prices of genuinely nontradable services and also increase the domestic currency prices of a wide variety of primary products and manufactured goods that are pseudo nontradables. Because additional imports in the QR categories are prevented from entering the economy in response to inflationary pressure, their domestic prices are simply bid up.

The converse is also true: exchange-rate changes have little direct impact on the domestic prices of pseudo nontradables (McKinnon 1979b). The macoeconomic result is that the domestic price level is, in the short and intermediate runs, determined largely independently of exchange-rate policy when foreign trade is repressed by QRs. It is this price-level independence that makes passive crawling feasible *without* contributing to dynamic instability in the rate of price inflation. The causality moves clearly from the domestic price level to the exchange rate, and not vice versa.

Consider an example of passive crawling to illustrate this point. Each month, suppose that the authorities of an inflation-prone Latin American country calculate the increase in the domestic wholesale price index (in pesos) relative to the monthly increase in the U.S. wholesale price index (in dollars). Insofar as peso prices increase by, say, 3 percent, whereas U.S. prices increase by, say, 1 percent, the authorities would announce a 2 percent downward crawl in the peso in several small steps for the month following, and perhaps averaged forward for a somewhat longer period. In this sense, the exchange rate is adjusted ex post facto to domestic inflationary pressure. Alternatively, the authorities may simply project into the future a rate of crawling consistent with what they expect domestic inflation to be relative to foreign inflation. Although this downward crawl does nothing to mitigate inflation, neither does it exacerbate inflationary pressure beyond what domestic impulses would warrant. At the

same time, exporters (and producers of import substitutes outside of the QR categories) are given invaluable forward assurance
that the real exchange rate will not turn sharply against them.
Diaz Alejandro (1976) indicates that this kind of policy has been
an important ingredient in the substantial growth of "minor"
exports from Colombia in the late 1960s and early 1970s.

The second relevant aspect of a repressed economy is the state
of its financial system. Rigid ceilings on nominal rates of interest
on sight and time deposits are set below the rate of inflation,
and/or heavy official reserve requirements are imposed. Both
are part of the mechanism for actually collecting the inflation,
tax from the banking system. Except for fringe markets, little or
nothing exists in the way of open markets in nonmonetary debt
where interest rates are free to move on a day-to-day basis.
Therefore, the interest rate on "bonds" that defines the opportunity cost of holding money—in standard Keynesian or monetarist
macroeconomic models—simply does not exist. To be sure, people worry about the ebb and flow of domestic price inflation,
and arbitrage slowly between goods and money in determining
what level of real cash balances to hold. However, they have no
opportunity to arbitrage quickly between money and "bonds"
in response to what must be purely hypothetical variations in
some open-market rate of interest. With varying degrees of success, the government then tries to encompass the repressed domestic financial system with a cordon sanitaire of exchange
controls that prevents arbitrage with foreign capital markets.

Whatever the very substantial economic distortions of running
a repressed financial system might be (McKinnon 1973), it nicely
complements a downward crawl in the exchange rate that passively reflects a variable rate of domestic price inflation. Earlier,
we ruled out downward crawling by a convertible currency
precisely because extrapolative expectations associated with a
variable crawl would cause destabilising movements out of the
domestic money into foreign exchange; or variations in nominal
rates of interest on domestic bonds (also incorporating extrapolative exchange rate expectations) would destabilise the demand
for money on the part of purely domestic transactors. But money
holders in repressed financial systems do not have these options!
True, people can go into nonfinancial inflation hedges such as
real estate or hoards of grain as their expectations shift regarding
the future rate of inflation. Even so, authorities need have much

less fear of a variable downward crawl further destabilising the demand for money in a repressed financial system in comparison to an open one.

For example, suppose the domestic price inflation and downward crawl speed up unexpectedly so as to heighten inflationary expectations about the future. The resulting fall in demand for real money balances and augmented inflationary pressure (with some leakage into losses of foreign reserves) would be proportionately less in a repressed financial system than in a liberalised one, where bond rates of interest are free to vary and accurately reflect the rate of crawl. In practice, however, financial and foreign-trade repression are usually incomplete, and exchange controls on capital flows are somewhat porous. Thus, countries like Colombia must still worry about the destabilising monetary consequences of changing the rate of crawl (Hanson 1979), but not as much as the typical European country with a convertible currency would have to worry.

In summary, suppose we start with an unfortunate economic datum: a continuing and uncontrolled domestic inflation arising out of fiscal incapacity that requires the government to tax the banking system. From that follows a certain logical consistency to having quota restrictions on foreign trade, exchange controls on capital movements, a repressed domestic financial system, and a passive downward crawl in the exchange rate. Then the internal inflation rate can be used as an indicator of how fast the peg should crawl, in order to protect exporters, without further endangering the macroeconomic stability of the economy. Indeed, it might be quite dangerous to partially liberalise either foreign trade or domestic finance by itself because the economy may become more dynamically unstable. Bringing inflation under control through fiscal reforms, and eliminating economic repression in domestic capital markets and in foreign trade, should proceed hand in hand. And to the tricky problem of managing such a balanced liberalisation I now turn.

Active Downward Crawling during the Liberalisation of Trade and Finance

By "active" I have a very specific policy meaning in mind. Suppose now the government brings the public finances under sufficient control that the inflation tax can be phased out. With its newly gained credibility, the monetary authority pre-announces the rate of downward crawl for the next several months to a year into the future. This actively projected downward crawl may now diverge from recent inflationary experience; it is no longer tied to movements in last month's price index. Indeed, the objective is to transform the exchange rate into an instrument for reducing inflation and then ending it.

As already implied, this newly found fiscal and monetary control is compatible with ending the repression of foreign trade and domestic finance. In order to avoid an unending taxonomy of cases, therefore, let me simply assume that the government's new economic programme also includes: (1) the elimination of high tariffs and quota restrictions on foreign trade; (2) the lifting of usury restrictions on domestic rates of interest, the reduction of official reserve requirements on commercial and savings banks, and the development of an open capital market in domestic bonds (nonmonetary debt); and (3) the relaxation of exchange controls over capital inflows and outflows, possibly with a significant lag behind measures (1) and (2).

Such a sharp change towards economic liberalisation corresponds roughly to events in Korea in 1964–65 (apart from the downward crawl) and to Chile in 1976–77. How should the exchange rate and other domestic instruments of monetary policy be managed during, and for a year or two following, major financial and trade liberalisation so that those liberalisations are sustained?

At the time general liberalisation occurs, suppose that the *real* exchange rate has been successfully adjusted so it is not far from its "equilibrium" (purchasing power parity) level. In Chile, this was accomplished largely by passive downward crawling during massive inflation from 1975 to 1977; in Korea the exchange rate was discretely devalued and unified in 1964 to compensate for a sharp inflation over the previous two years. Hence in our model economy, the authorities need not plan for further significant realignments in the real exchange rate. Moreover, assume that trade liberalisation, particularly the elimination of QRs, has progressed to the point where the domestic price level is now much more closely linked through the exchange rate to prices prevailing in foreign markets.

In Chile in 1977 and Korea in 1965, however, the newly liberalised domestic financial system was by no means under control.

Severe difficulties arose out of the need to raise sharply the nominal rates of interest on domestic bank deposits and loans in order to compensate for lingering inflationary expectations. In both countries, the real size of the organised financial system had been badly squeezed by past inflation and usury restrictions. Because the ratio of money—broadly defined to include interest-bearing deposits as well as coin and currency—to GNP had fallen very low, the flow of private financial saving available for new industrial or agricultural investments was quite inadequate. Hence, the authorities in each country encouraged rapid growth in loanable funds from the banking system, at high equilibrium rates of interest, to finance capital accumulation during liberalisation. The principal means was to raise sharply the real yields on bank deposits available to domestic savers, a strategy that became feasible once inflation could be phased out and the government stopped tapping the banking system as a fiscal resource.

However necessary for rationalising the domestic financial system[10] and compensating for lingering inflationary expectations, the sudden sharp increase from low pegs to higher pegs in nominal rates of interest on some classes of bank deposits—and the complete freeing of interest rates on some other money-market instruments—created potentially overwhelming incentives for capital inflows that, under a fixed exchange rate, would cause authorities to lose control over the monetary base. If instead the exchange rate was floated, the resulting sharp appreciation would damage the newly liberalised export- and import-competing sectors. A financial imbalance existed: the difference between foreign and domestic interest rates was greater than expected exchange depreciation in both Chile and Korea. The nominal rate of interest, necessary to assure households and small savers that real yields on domestic time and savings deposits were now positive, was far above the margin of risk perceived by foreign-exchange traders and merchants regarding the likelihood of devaluation of the officially pegged exchange rate. As confidence in the sustained character of the liberalisation came first to the foreign exchanges, a massive inflow of foreign financial capital emerged in both countries.

One help would be to tighten controls on capital *inflows* during the transition, as both countries eventually did. However, going very far in this direction defeats the basic idea of economic liberalisation.

Far better to use an active downward crawling peg over a sharply proscribed period of time—say a year or two—in order to reduce the "real" yield seen by foreigners (whose monetary habitat is a foreign currency) of investing in domestic financial assets. The government could simply pre-announce a downward rate of crawl roughly equal to the difference between foreign and domestic rates of interest adjusted for risk. The rate of crawling would be progressively reduced along with parallel reductions in domestic interest rates, until a permanently fixed exchange rate could be established. At this termination of the downward crawl, interest rates at home and abroad would be correctly aligned with inflationary expectations completely wrung out of the domestic economy. This exchange-rate regime would then become the principal device for determining the domestic price level because of newly freed commodity arbitrage between foreign and domestic markets. The domestic money supply would be endogenous.

Chile appears to have successfully used such a strategy in 1978 and 1979. Trade and finance were substantially liberalised during 1976 and 1977, when passive downward crawling was employed to compensate for extremely high and variable inflation. Then with liberalisation virtually complete, but with domestic real rates of interest still much higher than those prevailing abroad, on 3 February 1978 the authorities announced a schedule of exchange rates which would apply from February 6 to December 31. As announced, the peso did depreciate from 28.91 pesos/dollar to 33.95 pesos/dollar, or 17.4 percent, bringing its total nominal depreciation for the whole year to 21.4 percent. In 1979, the peso was initially scheduled to depreciate by 14.76 percent in small steps before going to a completely fixed exchange rate in 1980. To be sure, the Chileans experienced heavier capital inflows in some months of 1978 and 1979 than they would like, but the active downward crawl was a deterrent.

Having no previous experience with a crawling peg, the Koreans did not manage their foreign-exchange policy so deftly. After very successful financial reforms in 1965, when nominal and real rates of interest were raised very sharply, the Koreans tried to maintain an absolutely fixed exchange rate. Huge inflows of foreign capital caused an unduly rapid increase in the domestic monetary base. In part because foreign trade liberalisation was incomplete, domestic inflationary pressure rekindled and forced unplanned devaluations over the next several years. A temporary, but active, downward crawl in 1966 and 1967 might well have helped the Korean authorities better to maintain internal monetary control (McKinnon 1973, chap. 11) in an otherwise successful series of liberalisation measures.

15.4 A Concluding Note

Proper concern for monetary control in an open economy greatly narrows the scope for using a formally crawling peg in any country maintaining a convertible currency and a stable domestic monetary system. Nevertheless, there remain two well-defined sets of circumstances where downward crawling is warranted.

First, in response to high and variable domestically generated inflation, the monetary authority can *passively* adjust the exchange rate in small steps without contributing further to dynamic instability only if (i) many importables (and possibly some exportables) are insulated from world prices by quota restrictions, and (ii) the domestic financial system is "repressed" and isolated from the world capital market. Although seemingly extreme, these circumstances have a certain mutual consistency and are applicable to several less developed countries at the present time. But once trade and financial liberalisation occur, the rationale for passive crawling disappears and retaining it could be dangerously unsettling.

Secondly, in the course of general liberalisation aimed at ending price inflation altogether, *active* downward crawling at ever decreasing rates can be a useful—even indispensable—temporary device for maintaining monetary control during rapid financial transformation. In paradoxical contrast to passive crawling, active crawling terminating with a fixed exchange rate is effective as a stabilising instrument only if trade is relatively free and quota restrictions are absent.

Notes

1. A more complete description of the role of Euromarkets in foreign exchange trading can be found in McKinnon (1979a, chap. 9).

2. The capital constraint on dealers and the key relationship between unrestricted capital flows and the forward market is developed in some detail in McKinnon (1979a, chaps. 5 and 7).

3. This kind of instability could well be mitigated if a (variable) rate of interest was paid both on demand deposits and commercial bank reserves held with the central bank.

4. See the survey of such proposals by Williamson (1981).

5. When the price level is not stable, and an ongoing inflation tax is used, the connection between government budgetary deficits and the trade deficit need not be so close.

6. The government may collect the tax by direct borrowing from the banking system at zero or low rates of interest through the "reserve" requirements it imposes. Alternatively, the government may implicitly assign revenue from the tax to a few favoured private borrowers who receive loans at less than market rates of interest.

7. The main point of a narrow band is to allow the central bank to devolve the clearing of foreign payments to commercial banks (McKinnon 1979a, chap. 2).

8. Anne Krueger (1978) analyses exchange-rate policy in ten LDCs over the period from 1950 to 1972. She identifies and analyses 22 discrete devaluations, and the associated attempts to liberalise trade restrictions built up prior to each devaluation.

9. Such regimes have been described in some detail in the massive ten-country studies by Bhagwati (1978) and Krueger (1978).

10. A more complete account of domestic financial liberalisation can be found in McKinnon (1973) and (1980).

References

Bhagwati, Jagdish, *Anatomy and Consequences of Exchange-Control Regimes* (National Bureau of Economic Research, Ballinger, Cambridge, 1978).

Diaz Alejandro, Carlos, *Foreign Trade Regimes and Economic Development: Colombia* (NBER, New York, 1976).

Hanson, James, "The Colombian Experience with Financial Repression and Incomplete Liberalisation: Stagnation, Growth and Instability 1950–1978" presented to First International Conference on the Financial Development of Latin America and the Caribbean, Coraballeada, Venezuela, February 1979.

Krueger, Anne, *Liberalisation Attempts and Consequences* (National Bureau of Economic Research, Ballinger, Cambridge, 1978).

McKinnon, Ronald I., *Monetary Theory and Controlled Flexibility in the Foreign Exchanges,* Princeton Essays in International Finance No. 84, 1971.

———. *Money and Capital in Economic Development* (The Brookings Institution, Washington, DC, 1978).

————. "Exchange-Rate Instability, Trade Imbalances, and Monetary Policies in Japan, Europe, and the United States," presented to a conference honouring Harry Johnson, Oxford University, September 1978.

————. *Money in International Exchange: The Convertible Currency System* (Oxford University Press, New York, 1979a).

————. "Foreign Trade Regimes and Economic Development: A Review Article," *Journal of International Economics*, August 1979b.

————. "Financial Repression and the Liberalisation Problem Within Less Developed Countries," in S. Grassman and E. Lundberg (eds.), *The Past and Prospects of the World Economic Order* (Macmillan, 1981, pp. 365–86).

Williamson, John, "The Crawling Peg in Historical Perspective," in J. Williamson (ed.), *Exchange Rate Rules* (Macmillan, 1981, pp. 3–30).

16

Two Concepts of International Currency Substitution

The concept of international currency substitution is useful for explaining why floating exchange rates have been so volatile. Moreover, where exchange rates are left to float freely, continually shifting portfolio preferences from one national money to another can cause sharp inflations or deflations in any open economy. But currency substitution is also treacherous semantically. People differ on its proper interpretation. In this chapter, the semantic problem is resolved by distinguishing "direct" from "indirect" currency substitution—each being treated separately in the two sections below.

Direct currency substitution means that two (or more) currencies compete as a means of payment within the same commodity domain. People hold transaction balances in both, say pesos and dollars, and switch freely between them. In its pure form this situation is unusual, if only because it is highly unstable: there is a strong tendency for one fiat money to displace the other. Previously only direct currency substitution has been analyzed in order to show that a floating exchange rate is inherently indeterminant. Empirically, however, this previous literature may have claimed too much: direct currency substitution is unlikely to affect financial relationships between mature industrial economies, although it is sometimes important within less developed countries (LDCs).

Indirect currency substitution refers to investors switching between nonmonetary financial assets, say "bonds," denominated in different currencies in a way that indirectly influences the

Originally published in *The Economics of the Caribbean Basin,* ed. Michael B. Connolly and John McDermott (Praeger, 1985), 101–118. Revised September 1994. Reprinted with permission.

domestic demand for transaction balances. Among industrial countries, the margin of international risk between bonds denominated in, say, sterling and dollars varies continually for unpredictable political and economic reasons. If such commonplace shifts in international risk assessments between nonmonetary assets effectively destabilize the demand for each domestic money, each central bank's monetary policy should be oriented toward stabilizing its exchange rate. This proposition remains true even for those industrial countries where direct currency substitution is not significant.

But first let us consider the more straightforward problem of how direct currency substitution tends to undermine domestic monetary control.

16.1   Direct Currency Substitution

Consider two fiat monies, A and B, neither of which has any intrinsic value, competing in the same commodity domain as a medium of exchange. They are *direct* substitutes in the sense that any storekeeper will potentially accept payment in either money. No geographic separation exists where purely domestic commerce in one region is denominated in currency A, and in another region is denominated solely in currency B. Nor do they have other distinguishing physical characteristics such as one currency being more useful for making small change or paying taxes than the other. Instead, both currencies circulate in common so that any good for sale in any locale could be invoiced and paid for in either A or B. Then, by this rather artificial construction, instantaneous purchasing power parity (PPP) exists between the two monies however the commonly quoted exchange rate might vary. That is,

$$P_a = SP_b \tag{1}$$

where S is the spot exchange rate of currency A/currency B, P_a is the common price level in currency A, and P_b is the common price level in currency B.

Whenever S increases, whether or not the change was expected, gimlet-eyed shopkeepers will immediately mark up invoice prices in currency A relative to those in currency B over the whole range of merchandise available to our geographically undifferentiated consumers. Goods need not even be arbitraged geographically (in response to exchange-rate changes) in order for absolute purchasing power parity to be maintained.

By our artificial construction, currencies A and B are direct and "perfect" monetary substitutes with the same real purchasing power over commodities at the prevailing exchange rate. Therefore, a *necessary* condition for their mutual coexistence is that prices of holding each of them be equal. If primary security markets are well organized, the relevant opportunity cost for holding non-interest-bearing transaction balances is *the* short-run nominal interest rate on bonds denominated in that currency.[1] Thus coexistence requires the nominal rates of interest on bonds denominated in currency A and currency B to be the same:

$$i_a = i_b \quad \text{where } i_a = \pi_a + r \text{ and } i_b = \pi_b + r \tag{2}$$

Within our unified commodity domain with a common real interest rate, r, nominal interest rates can only be equated if expected commodity price inflation in each currency is identical, that is, $\pi_a = \pi_b$. Only then will the "Fisher" components—reflecting anticipated inflation—in each nominal interest rate be equalized. But actual rates of price inflation will only be equal if the nominal exchange rate S is unchanging. Hence, a fixed exchange rate—likely imposed by some monetary authority—is a necessary condition for nonnegligible amounts of transaction balances in both currencies to be willingly held.

Suppose instead that S was free to fluctuate, and a market view developed (whether or not it was well founded) that currency A was going to depreciate against currency B, leading to anticipated relative inflation in all prices denominated in currency A. As interest rates on bonds denominated in currency A rose relative to those denominated in currency B, everyone would try to dump non-interest-bearing transaction balances in A and hold only B. The result would be a self-sustaining hyperinflation in currency A, driving real transaction balances toward zero as it fell into disuse. The demand for real balances in currency B, on the other hand, would increase sharply as people substituted directly out of currency A. Sharp deflation in commodity prices, measured in currency B, could only be avoided if the stock of nominal cash balances of currency B was expeditiously increased. In effect, with both circulating jointly, the demand for either currency would be highly unstable.

A fixed exchange rate, at which the monetary authority stands ready to withdraw one money from circulation as the other is injected (nonsterilized interventions), would prevent this kind of extreme currency instability from occurring. The relative supply of each currency would be adjusted automatically to changes in relative demands.

Even with a fixed exchange rate, however, having just one money in a unified commodity (and financial) domain is more convenient—the standard natural monopoly argument. Transaction costs are minimized if one currency is used as a standard of value for pricing commodities and as a means of payment. Price tags need only be stated in one currency, and people can consolidate and thereby minimize their non-interest-bearing transaction balances in achieving any given level of pecuniary convenience. In short, the great economies of scale from using only one money ensures that eventually one of our two currencies will replace the other—a "corner solution." But, if a fixed exchange rate is used during the transition, the severe financial trauma associated with competition among fiat monies in a floating-rate regime would be eliminated.

Gresham's Law II

Our hypothetical construction where two fiat currencies A and B were initially posited to circulate in common, but where only one could survive in the same commodity domain, reflects the operation of what shall be called Gresham's law II. This idea was well understood by authors writing about unstable currency relationships and bimetallism in the nineteenth century. Gresham's law was initially formulated for metallic currencies where coins minted with a particular metal might have a lower market value than (but the same face value as) those minted with a different metal. Then this "bad" money would drive out "good," as the superior coins were taken out of circulation (perhaps) to be melted down. With paper money, however, Alfred Marshall noted (1922, 61–62) that the opposite tendency would prevail.

Stronger fiat currencies would tend to drive out weaker ones: our Gresham's Law II. Calvo and Végh (1992) quote the League of Nations on the post–World War I currency experience:

Thus, in advanced inflation, "Gresham's Law" was reversed: good money tended to drive out bad, and not the other way round: the reason being the irreducible need for a serviceable medium of exchange in any modern economy based on division of labor and interchange of goods and services. (League of Nations 1946, 41)

Subsequently, several writers (Boyer 1978; Girton and Roper 1981; Kareken and Wallace 1981) have rediscovered Gresham's law II. Coming at the problem from how equilibrium exchange rates are determined in a free float, they find serious problems of instability (indeterminacy) when the two national fiat monies circulate in parallel, with agents holding some of each. But, under the seemingly innocent guise of a model that assumed a single homogeneous consumption good across two countries, Kareken and Wallace (implicitly) imposed instantaneous purchasing power parity (PPP). They then (are forced to) conclude that, with no portfolio restrictions on individuals taking open positions in other countries currencies, a floating exchange-rate regime is not economically feasible.

But Kareken and Wallace go too far. Their theoretical analysis does not apply to most pairs of countries, where PPP does not hold and goods are largely invoiced only in the currency of the country where they are produced—and these domestic prices remain "sticky" (invariant in the short run) when the exchange rate changes. Gresham's law II applies only in the few (but very interesting) cases where two fiat monies literally circulate in the same commodity domain and have the same purchasing power at every exchange rate.

Imperfect approximations to this highly unstable situation occur when dollars (largely U.S. $100 bills) circulate in parallel with pesos in Mexico and Argentina, soles in Peru, or shekels in Israel as in the late 1970s and early 1980s, or in Russia and Ukraine in the 1990s. The historical origins and quasi legality of this dual circulation vary from one country to another. It often arises because the domestic currency has been rendered unattractive as a store of value due to inflation, but the government still wishes to attract remittances from abroad by allowing remitters to hold dollar balances, or invest them in dollar-indexed deposits, domestically. These dollars then become acceptable as a general means of payment— sometimes in spite of restrictions designed to prevent it. Then, of course, Gresham's law II comes into force with a vengeance. Demand for the weaker domestic currency falls even further, price inflation (measured in the domestic currency) likely accelerates.

In late 1977 after years of exchange controls designed to prevent citizens from acquiring foreign-currency balances, Israel suddenly legalized foreign-exchange holding both inside and outside the country. The rapid substitution of dollar for shekel balances converted what had been modest ongoing price inflation (the decline in the shekel's purchasing power) of 15 to 20 percent per year into a very rapid inflation of over 100 percent. After several failed attempts, a comprehensive stabilization program was finally put in place in 1985 that included the reimposition of exchange controls with a deliberate phasing out of domestically held dollar deposits.

Exchange Controls versus Currency Displacement during Inflation

Exchange controls on foreign capital outflows *and* inflows are necessary to preserve the domain of the domestic currency when its holders are subject to the inflation tax (see chapter 15 above and McKinnon, 1993). They suggest that dollars (or some other hard money) should not be permitted to circulate in parallel with a weak domestic currency as a medium of exchange. Otherwise, individuals and firms will simply abandon the taxed domestic currency (pesos) in favor of the untaxed foreign currency (dollars). To prevent such currency displacement and the erosion of the government's tax base for financing an otherwise uncovered fiscal deficit, there is a strong second-best argument for imposing exchange controls when the government is unavoidably committed to inflationary policies as a means of raising revenue.

With such exchange controls in place, however, the government must then take responsibility for "making" the foreign-exchange market by standing ready to buy or sell foreign exchange on demand. Pure "floating" is not feasible because private financial institutions can no longer legally take the open positions in foreign exchange necessary to balance the flow of international commodity payments at a stable exchange rate. Kareken and Wallace (1981) make a serious logical error by suggesting that exchange controls, what they call portfolio autarky, would be sufficient to restore exchange-rate determinacy *without* official exchange intervention. But if short-term flows of private capital are blocked, merchants cannot hedge against foreign exchange risk nor can dealers clear international payments (McKinnon 1979, chaps. 5 and 7). With portfolio autarky, a floating exchange rate would still be highly unstable—albeit for somewhat different reasons.

In effect, a government that commits itself to a high inflation rate and the exchange controls that naturally go with it must itself make the foreign-exchange market. This explains why governments in many LDCs peg their exchange rates (although not always by using a formal exchange parity), whereas their brethren in industrial countries without exchange controls have the option of floating or not floating. In countries suffering from chronic inflation, however, an officially announced downward crawling peg—fully indexing the exchange rate to reflect domestic inflation—would seem to be the preferred technique for making the best of a difficult situation (as discussed in chapter 15 above).

This combination of capital-account controls plus indexing the exchange rate against a "hard" foreign money keeps the medium-of-exchange function for the domestic money but assigns the longer-term unit-of-account function to the foreign money. The heavy cost to a highly inflationary economy of not having its own stable standard of deferred payment for intermediate- and longer-term transactions is thereby mitigated; meanwhile the inflation tax base, that is, transactions balances on which the government depends fiscally, is preserved.

But neither indexing nor capital controls are ever perfect. Because price-level data usually take a month or so to collect, there remains short-term uncertainty in the unit-of-account function of domestic money during a high and variable inflation. Also, indexing the nominal exchange rate through continuous smooth "mini" devaluations, associated with a preannounced indexing procedure, makes the economy's real exchange rate unduly rigid. Thus, to adjust the real exchange rate, countries ostensibly following such indexing procedures often punctuate them with occasional unannounced "maxi" depreciations or appreciations—thus making long-term contracting more difficult. In addition, domestic nationals will always hold some foreign-currency balances illicitly to avoid the inflation tax. Nevertheless, exchange-rate indexing plus capital controls remains a second-best technique for limiting inflation on the one hand, and limiting some of the damage it does on the other.[2]

This argument for trying to limit direct currency substitution has been challenged by Jacek Rostkowski (1992). In his article with the revealing title "The Benefits of Currency Substitution during High Inflation and Stabilization," he correctly emphasizes the distortions and output-reducing effects from high and variable inflation. In order to provide households and firms with a more stable money, he then argues in favor of letting currency substitution occur freely through, presumably, a floating exchange rate. But this leaves the government's underlying fiscal problem unresolved. Incredibly, Rostkowski argues further that favorable effects of such currency substitution on output could mean that the government need not lose seigniorage net when substitution occurs.

However, Rostkowski's main example of the Russian hyperinflation of 1922–24 doesn't really support this latter hypothesis. In 1923, the introduction of the relatively stable new *chervonets* currency in parallel with the rapidly depreciating *sovznak* currency succeeded in increasing output, the total real monetary base, and seigniorage to the government. But the Soviet government controlled both currencies and received revenue from each—using the former for large denomination notes and the latter for small change. Indeed, the successful introduction of the chervonets was simply the first step in a successful currency stabilization where the old money was phased out.

If, instead, the new hard money had been a foreign currency—like dollars or sterling—the Soviet government of the early 1920s surely would have lost revenue net if free currency substitution was permitted. Indeed, seventy years later in 1992, Russia initiated general price decontrol in the absence of any effective foreign-exchange controls on capital flows or of an exchange-rate peg (even a crawling one). This led to a massive capital flight by enterprises into foreign exchange—largely dollars—resulting an incredible undervaluation of the ruble. Thus, direct currency substitution contributed to Russia's massive internal inflationary explosion in 1992, and Russia's subsequent loss of monetary control through 1995—although currency substitution was not the only factor involved (McKinnon 1993, chaps. 11 and 13).

One could argue in favor of unrestricted currency substitution in favor of a foreign money as a method of limiting the "revenue" raising capabilities of a fiscally weak domestic government—possibly with the objective of forcing fiscal reform or even overthrowing it! But short of this, our second-best policy of capital controls with a crawling exchange rate peg is preferred. Once the government became serious about reasserting fiscal control and ending its dependence on the inflation tax, it could consider fixing the exchange rate as the nominal anchor for the price level. But successfully converging to price stability remains a tricky problem.

Currency Boards and Gresham's Law II

In the extreme, replacing the central bank with a currency board could increase greatly the credibility of the government's commitment to a fixed exchange rate. But the economy must be small and naturally open—like Hong Kong, Panama, and more recently (1992) Estonia, all of which have operative currency boards—so that (1) direct currency substitution from foreign monies is always a "threat," and (2) pegging the exchange rate is itself sufficient to stabilize the domestic price level. Then the economy could actually benefit from the operation of Gresham's law II.

By allowing domestic nationals to hold foreign monies freely while standing ready to purchase the most important one at a fixed rate of exchange, a currency board essentially institutionalizes direct currency substitution. Because domestic bank notes (or base money in less primitive systems) are injected into the economy only in response to private demand for them at the fixed exchange rate, the outstanding domestic money supply is endogenously determined. The authorities give up any pretense of having an independent monetary policy in general, and close the door against ever (again) resorting to the inflation tax in particular. Credibility is high because the method of domestic money creation leaves 100 percent of the domestic note issue backed by foreign exchange reserves.[3]

With (at least) two monies potentially in circulation in the same domain and a fixed rate of exchange, we argued above that a corner solution is likely, that is, direct currency substitution will tend to drive out one or the other. But now that the government need no longer resort to the inflation tax, it is relatively easy for the currency board to make the home money just slightly more attractive. Domestic bills of various denominations, including small change, can made more readily available, with better protection against counterfeiting, and greater convenience in using domestic money in payment of taxes. These should then be sufficient to tilt the whole economy to a virtual corner solution where domestic money dominates as the means of payment. Ironically, noninflationary seigniorage accruing to the government can be quite substantial if the (now large) foreign-exchange reserves backing the (non-interest-bearing) domestic note issue are invested at interest in foreign currency bonds or Euro accounts. This is the potentially benign face of Gresham's law II.

In summary, faced with the threat of direct substitution between two currencies within a single commodity domain, Gresham's law II suggests that a government relying on the inflation tax—or other methods of taxing the domesic banking system—needs direct controls to prevent such substitution from occurring, that is, to prevent the encroachment of foreign currencies on the domain of the domestic one. But a fiscally strong government needs no such constraints for its own money to become dominant. Either way, however, the case for a laissez-faire policy of letting the exchange rate float is rejected.

Although not uncommon, the threat of direct currency substitution remains somewhat pathological. Of more analytical and wider empirical interest are the exchange relationships among "hard" convertible currencies—such as the yen, dollar, deutsche mark, guilder, etc.—where governments seriously strive for price-level stabililty, where foreign currencies do not circulate in domestic commerce, and where exchange controls are weak or absent. How does the case for free floating hold up in these more favorable circumstances?

16.2 Indirect Currency Substitution

To model accurately our experience with floating exchange rates since 1973, what salient features of finance and trade among market-oriented industrial economics with "hard" currencies should be incorporated?

First, in any one country the domestic demand for foreign money is largely *indirect*. Domestic firms or individuals wishing to pay for imports typically don't directly hold significant transaction balances in foreign currencies. Rather, they order necessary foreign exchange for any individual payment from their bank; or, more simply, they order their bank to make the foreign payment and to debit their account by the domestic-currency equivalent. In turn commercial banks enjoy scale economies and can offset purchases and sales of foreign exchange in the huge interbank market. So even the aggregate of commercial banks' M1-type transaction balances of foreign exchange—largely non-interest-bearing demand deposits in foreign banks—remains small in comparison with foreign and domestic money supplies.[4] However, domestic nationals may well hold significant interest-bearing securities—term deposits, bonds, or commercial bills—denominated in foreign currency.

Second, domestic commerce is denominated only in the national currency, which is the natural monetary habitat of domestic residents. In addition, each Western industrial economy (but not LDCs) typically invoices exports of manufactured goods and services—what are sometimes called Hicksian fixprice goods—in their home currency (Grassman 1973). (Exports of flexibly priced primary products, on the other hand, are generally invoiced in the accepted international vehicle currency, i.e., the U.S. dollar.) Because most goods produced in an industrial economy behave as if they were Hicksian fixprice goods, the domestic price level is not immediately influenced by unexpected exchange-rate changes.[5] Given the cyclical 20 to 25 percent changes in nominal exchange rates seen in the last decade, purchasing power parity (PPP) across hard-currency countries might not be restored for months, quarters, or even years (Isard 1977)—unlike the simple model of direct currency substitution with instantaneous PPP presented in section 16.1. Because of this observed stickiness in domestic prices, it makes no empirical sense to assume a unified commodity domain, a single good that is uniformly priced in either currency, as did Kareken and Wallace and other authors.

Third, by confining our analysis to hard-currency countries that need not resort to the inflation tax, we may plausibly assume that exchange controls on international capital flows are weak or absent.

Under these three conditions, how is the equilibrium exchange rate determined? Because both domestic output and prices are not immediately sensitive to exchange-rate fluctuations, any model of short-run exchange-rate determination must be explicitly financial in nature—whence the idea that the exchange rate behaves as if it were a "forward-looking" asset price (Frenkel and Mussa 1980). In contrast, the older literature advocating floating exchange rates presumed that commodity arbitrage would respond elastically to exchange-rate changes. If the domestic currency depreciated, they presumed that exports would quickly increase and imports decline to stabilize the foreign exchange market (Friedman 1953). But our actual experience with floating exchange rates has been quite different. Exports respond sluggishly, and because they are largely invoiced in the home currency, the immediate effect of a devaluation is a decline in the net trade balance measured in foreign exchange—the oft-noted J-curve effect (MaGee 1973). Hence, in the short run, exchange-rate determinacy depends heavily on stabilizing capital flows, which in turn depends on portfolio reactions in domestic and foreign financial markets to unexpected movements in exchange rates.

On the basis of these stylized facts, let us first consider how domestic monetary equilibrium can be upset by changes in international preferences between nonmonetary assets such as bonds. For reasons that will become clear, I call such bond-market demand shifts *indirect* currency substitution. Secondly, among the mature industrial economies, how does this indirect currency substitution affect the case for or against floating exchange rates? (By "floating," we mean that the monetary authorities neither intervene in the foreign-exchange market, nor adjust the domestic money supply to smooth exchange-rate fluctuations.)

The Exchange Rate as a Monetary Indicator

The primary job of any central bank is to balance the demand and supply of domestic money at a stable price level. For hard-currency industrial economies whose central banks control the rate of domestic money issue,[6] accurately predicting when the short-run demand for domestic money is changing—perhaps cyclically—is the key operational problem. Only by accommodating these changes in money demand can the central bank avoid unexpected inflation or deflation.

In financially open economies, changes in the exchange rate against stable-valued foreign currencies indicate shifts in domestic money demand generated *indirectly* through the international bond market. But why should the demand for domestic transactions balances— and the derived demand for base money—increase just because the international demand for domestic bonds suddenly increases?

Suppose countries A and B are in domestic and international portfolio balance, domestic prices are stable, and the exchange rate is maintaining purchasing power parity (PPP) between the two national price levels. Let S = currency A/currency B be the actual exchange rate, and let S^{PPP} be its equilibrium rate. Initially we have $S = S^{PPP}$. Although A's and B's bond markets are joined, each country's narrow money—coin and currency plus checking deposits—circulates only at home.

Now suppose international investors respond to some sudden political or economic news by shifting their desired portfolio from B_a (bonds denominated in currrency A) to B_b (bonds denominated in currency B). If some force—either the government itself or the belief of private foreign exchange dealers that the government is committed to defending exchange equilibrium—temporarily maintains $S = S^{PPP}$, i_a will tend to increase, and i_b to decline. But this upward pressure on i_a is then transmitted through the domestic liquidity preference function to the demand for non-interest-bearing narrow money, M_a. This incipient increase in i_a has thus caused an incipient fall in the demand for M_a. Disturbances in the international bond market are thereby transmitted to the national money market.

However, A's private sector cannot reduce its actual money holdings unless the government intervenes to withdraw some of M_a from circulation. With M_a unchanging, the attempt by domestic transactors to switch from M_a to B_a simply drives i_a back down to where it started as if it was in a liquidity trap. Because the initial decline in the demand for M_a cannot be realized, the temporary increase in i_a (reflecting the risk premia being required by international investors to hold bonds denominated in currency A) cannot be sustained. Nor can our equilibrium exchange rate. Currency A must depreciate with S rising sufficiently far above S^{ppp} until future exchange-rate expectations become regressive. That is, disturbed international investors come to believe that some significant future decline (appreciation of currency A) is likely so that their willingness to hold B_a is restored at the original unchanged constellation of (short-term) interest rates—as shown more formally in chapter 17 below.

For a closed economy, we know that a fall in the demand for money is inflationary if its supply remains unchanged. And in our open economy A, a shift in international portfolio preference from B_a to B_b is also inflationary—unless the national money supply is contracted. The primary mechanism of inflation is the depreciated value of A's currency in the foreign exchanges—the direct inflationary impact on the prices of internationally traded commodities and the unmistakable signal that price inflation will be greater in the future. On the other hand, an unexpected deflation in country B occurs—as if the demand for money had sharply risen there—unless its central bank increases M_b in an offsetting fashion.

In summary, the shift from B_a to B_b in the international bond market has the effect of indirect currency substitution; as if private agents collectively were reducing their demand for M_a and increasing their demand for M_b. Fortunately, the exchange rate acts a monetary indicator telling the authorities with a strong currency to expand and a weak currency to contract. The easiest way to do this is to intervene directly and let the domestic money supply vary accordingly. Alternatively, money creation through domestic open-market purchases or sales of Treasury bonds could be geared to how weak or strong the national currency was in the foreign exchanges.

However, simply maintaining a fixed exchange rate between them is not enough. This process of indirect currency substitution also suggests why fuller international coordination of A's and B's monetary policies may be important. To stabilize their common price level, the symmetry of the situation suggests that, institutional arrangements being equivalent, the supply of one country's money should fall by as much as that of the other increases. If only A's central bank were active in the foreign exchanges so that M_a would fall with no offsetting expansion in M_b, our two-country world would experience unexpected net deflation—even though S remained stable.

This unfortunate asymmetry existed under the world dollar standard of the 1970s through 1984, as analyzed by McKinnon (see chapters 2 and 7 above). In the face of massive changes in the collective demand for dollar bonds in favor of those denominated in marks, yen, sterling, and so on, central banks outside the United States ironed out the wilder fluctuations in their dollar exchange rates by adjusting their national money supplies upward to support these interventions. But the U.S. Federal Reserve System failed to adjust American money growth downward in a symmetrical, offsetting fashion. The upshot was synchronized, and thus unusually virulent, international business cycles from 1971 through 1984. (See chapters 7, 8, and 9 above.) But, with the Plaza and Louvre Accords of 1985 and 1987, intervention in the foreign-exchange markets has become much more symmetrical because the United States acts—at least through 1995—in concert with the other industrial countries. Consequently, national business cycles across North America, Europe, and Japan have become desynchronized and less pronounced since 1985 (OECD 1994). (See chapter 22 below.)

Within the European Monetary System (EMS), a similar problem exists because of the asymmetrical position of Germany. A major shift in portfolio preferences in the intra-European bond market for or against DM bonds can force inappropriate contraction in the monetary base for the EMS as a whole. Because of the unusual costs associated with German reunification in 1991 and afterward, deficit financing of massive new expenditures by the German government had the effect of shifting European portfolio preferences toward German bonds. To maintain their exchange rates in the face of a tight money policy by the Bundesbank, other European countries like France or Britain were forced into monetary contraction. The upshot was a Europe-wide cyclical downturn in 1992–93 and a forced break in the exchange-rate commitments of the partner countries—with Britain and Italy falling out in September 1992, and the remaining countries having to greatly widen their exchange-rate bands in another major foreign-exchange crisis in the late summer of 1993.

Real versus Monetary Disturbances

Let us simplify the analysis further by considering just one small country that has a negligible effect on the rest of the world but whose bond market is open to international investors. Many readers may object to the idea of keying on the nominal exchange rate against stable valued foreign monies[7] as a monetary indicator: adjusting the domestic monetary base to keep the nominal exchange rate stable. After all, shouldn't the nominal exchange rate be free to fluctuate to compensate for "real" disturbances in international trade?

Surprisingly, no. As long as domestic monetary policy is convincingly subordinated to maintaining a stable nominal exchange rate, international flows of financial capital will automatically offset deficits or surpluses in the balance of trade. However, if the exchange rate is floating, "real" shocks in international trade or capital movements are likely to upset the economy's monetary equilibrium! In effect, so-called real shocks tend to be telescoped into exaggerated shifts in portfolio preferences in the international bond market that generate indirect currency substitution.

To see this important point, let us take representative examples of both monetary and real shocks of the kind that have hit individual industrial economies over the past several decades. What exogenous disturbances, or "news," might upset the portfolio balance of international investors and cause indirect currency substitution? Consider the following three "shocks" that would make domestic bonds seem riskier and, with unchanging spot exchange and interest rates in the short run, induce a capital outflow:

1. *Political risk* is fear of exchange controls, wealth taxes, or other factors that bear on the convenience of holding assets in the domestic currency as distinct from foreign money.

2. *Inflation risk* in the longer term is an assessment of increased future domestic price inflation, with exchange depreciation, relative to that prevailing in alternative hard-currency countries.

3. *Real exchange-rate risk* is due to an unexpected decline in the international terms of trade and in future current-account surpluses. For example, a fall in the price of oil reduces the attractiveness of assets denominated in a "petrocurrency."

Often, individual investors might not distinguish sharply between political risk and inflation risk. Suppose the future election of a radical populist government suddenly appears more likely as the present government stumbles. Domestic investors don't really know what will hit them harder: new taxes on wealth or future exchange depreciation. Whether or not they make this distinction, their willingness to hold domestic financial assets falls sharply. Unless the central bank contracts the national money supply and allows domestic short-term interest rates to rise and compensate for the increased riskiness of holding domestic financial assets, exchange depreciation and a precipitate price inflation will ensue—as shown algebraically in chapter 17 below.

Consider now an unexpected real shock to an oil-exporting country that is the inverse of the third point above. In 1979, Britons suddenly found that the anticipated future stream of foreign-exchange earnings were substantially greater because of an unexpected increase in the international price of oil. Because sterling was floating, international investors projected that the future foreign-exchange value of sterling would be higher. They immediately telescoped this information back into 1979 and sharply bid up the nominal (and real) exchange rate for sterling. The result of sterling overvaluation in 1980–81 was a sharper fall in the inflation rate than the British authorities had expected, and a severe economic downturn.

Clearly, the correct response by the Bank of England to this real disturbance would have been to increase the British money supply beyond its preplanned rate of growth, in order to stabilize the nominal exchange rate. Interest rates on sterling bonds would have fallen, correctly reflecting the lessened exchange risk perceived by investors. The unexpectedly sharp decline in economic activity would then have been avoided. Most important, if international investors had known ex ante that the British government was committed to a stable nominal exchange rate for sterling, they wouldn't have anticipated a sterling appreciation in response to the oil shock. Thus the shift in their portfolio preferences toward sterling bonds would not have been so precipitate.

Conclusion

Monetary authorities in an open economy cannot easily distinguish direct from indirect currency substitution. They simply observe pressure for the nominal exchange rate to move up or down depending on portfolio shifts in currency preferences. International investors continually change their relative risk assessments of future price inflation, political stability, the terms of trade, and so forth—and all of this is (potentially) telescoped into fluctuations in the spot exchange rate if it is untethered. At any point in time, the central bank cannot know with any confidence what is dominating the demand for its (base) money. If a stable international monetary standard exists, the correct monetary strategy for any one country does not require any such omniscience. The spot exchange rate, measured against a stable-valued foreign currency (representing the international standard) is a rather sensitive forward-looking indicator of what the private sector anticipates might happen to the domestic economy in the future. By focusing on the nominal exchange rate, the central bank can better match the supply of its monetary base to the shifting direct and indirect demand for it. Provided that the economy is starting from a position of monetary and exchange-rate equilibrium,[8] the national money supply should expand above its norm when the currency became unexpectedly strong in the foreign exchanges and contract when it is weak. Whether or not the underlying disturbances are real or monetary does not matter. This rule is surprisingly robust in mitigating unexpected inflations or deflations, and has the incidental advantage of making foreign trade more efficient by smoothing exchange-rate fluctuations.

If followed by a "small" open economy whose own money supply is negligible in relationship to the relevant hard-currency outside world, such an exchange-rate rule by itself is sufficient to maintain monetary equilibrium. However, among larger countries, whose financial assets are quantitatively significant and substitutable in the portfolios of international investors, further international monetary coordination may be necessary to maintain stable growth in their aggregate money supply in order to properly anchor their common price level. This problem of sustaining worldwide monetary equilibrium is taken up in part III of this book.

Notes

This chapter is an extensively revised and updated version of McKinnon (1985). Thanks to Jürgen Schröder of the University of Mannheim and Paul Mizen of the University of Nottingham for their help with the revision.

1. The implications for long rates of interest are discussed separately in chapter 3 above.

2. The first best response is, of course, is to reassert control over the public finances so that inflation can be phased out altogether.

3. In practice, if there is an intramarginal "fiduciary" note issue, foreign-exchange reserves need not be a full 100 percent. Also, the problem of securing these exchange reserves against predator governments in the future requires some careful thinking—but it is not insurmountable.

4. If commercial banks want to speculate by a net open position in foreign exchange, adjusting their net forward positions—or holdings of interest-bearing foreign term deposits—is more convenient.

5. Remember that this is a phenomenon associated with hard convertible currencies. In highly inflationary situations, such as Brazil in the 1980s, or the German hyperinflation of the early 1920s, merchants often take exchange-rate movements as the best indicator of how they should alter prices in domestic commerce.

6. The central bank need not continually monetize public debt issues or mandatory private credits, but instead is free to determine—by open-market operations, discounting, or foreign-exchange purchases—the level of the domestic monetary base.

7. There is of course ambiguity if exchange rates among major industrial countries themselves fluctuate. Perhaps we should consider the case where there exists an international monetary standard that is known to be stable—as with the fixed-rate dollar standard of the 1950s and most of the 1960s—or that of a small European country keying the DM when there was no unusual fiscal upheaval in Germany.

8. If the economy is not starting from an equilibrium exchange rate or is on a higher inflation trajectory than the international standard, then there exists a severe problem of converging to a fixed exchange rate without provoking destabilizing international capital flows. Britain's (in)famous attempt to shadow the deutsche mark in 1986–87 touched off an unsustainable credit-led consumption and property boom fed by foreign capital inflows that led to a crash in 1990–91 (Walters 1986, 1990). However, this "overborrowing syndrome" in the face of apparently successful domestic economic reforms is much more than just a question of getting foreign-exchange policy right—and requires separate treatment (McKinnon and Pill 1996).

References

Boyer, R. 1978. "Currency Mobility and Balance of Payments Adjustment." In *The Monetary Approach to International Adjustment*, ed. B. H. Putnam and D. S. Wilford. New York: Praeger.

Calvo, G. and C. Végh. 1992. "Currency Substitution in Developing Countries: An Introduction." *Revista de Análisis Económico*, 7(1)(June): 3–27.

Frenkel, J., and M. Mussa. 1980. "The Efficiency of the Foreign Exchange Market and Measures of Turbulence." *American Economic Review* 70(2): 374–81.

Friedman, M. 1953. "The Case for Flexible Exchange Rates." In *Essays in Positive Economics*, 157–203. Chicago: University of Chicago Press.

Girton, L., and D. Roper. 1981. "Theory and Implications of International Currency Substitution." *Journal of Money, Credit, and Banking* 13: 12–30.

Grassman, S. 1973. "A Fundamental Symmetry in International Payments Patterns." *Journal of International Economics* (5): 105–16.

Isard, P. 1977. "How Far Can We Push the Law of One Price?" *American Economic Review* 67: 942–48.

Kareken, J., and N. Wallace. 1981."On the Indeterminacy of Equilibrium Exchange Rates." *Quarterly Journal of Economics* 96: 207–22.

League of Nations. 1946. *The Course and Control of Inflation: A Review of Monetary Experience in Europe after World War I.* Geneva: Economic, Financial and Transit Department.

MaGee, S. 1973. "Currency Contract, Pass Through, and Devaluation." *Brookings Papers on Economic Activity* 1: 303–23.

Marshall, A. 1922. *Money, Credit and Commerce.* Reprint. New York: Augustus M. Kelly, Publishers, 1965.

McKinnon, R. 1979. *Money in International Exchange: The Convertible Currency System.* New York: Oxford University Press.

———. 1985. "Two Concepts of International Currency Substitution." In eds, *The Economics of the Carribbean Basin,* ed. M. Connolly and J. McDermott, 101–18. New York: Praeger.

———. 1993. *The Order of Economic Liberalization: Financial Control in the Transition to a Market Economy* (2nd ed.). Baltimore: Johns Hopkins University Press.

McKinnon, R., and H. Pill. 1996. "Credible Liberalizations and International Capital Flows: The Overborrowing Syndrome." NBER Fifth Annual Asian Seminar on Economics, ed. A. Krueger and T. Ito. Chicago: University of Chicago Press.

OECD. 1994. "The Desynchronization of International Business Cycles." *Economic Outlook* (June): 37–43.

Rostkowski, Jacek. 1992. "The Benefits of Currency Substitution during High Inflation and Stabilization." *Revista de Análisis Económico* 7(1)(June): 91–107.

Walters, A. A. 1986. *Britain's Economic Renaissance.* Oxford: Oxford University Press.

———. 1990. *Sterling in Danger.* London: Fontana, for the Institute for Economic Affairs.

17

Why Floating
Exchange Rates Fail:
A Reconsideration
of the Liquidity Trap

How well do interest rates on bonds denominated in different currencies register international risk? I shall argue that, under floating exchange rates, short-term interest rates are pinned down in each separate national money market. Thus, in the short run when investor perceptions of international risk can change sharply, short-term interest rates fail to act as shock absorbers for offsetting that risk. The result is overshooting or "excess" volatility in spot exchange rates, changes that must bear the brunt of keeping asset portfolios in balance.

In addition, because short-term interest rates are caught in national liquidity traps, open interest parity fails when the system is disturbed by "news." Under floating, neither short-term interest differentials, nor premia or discounts in the forward exchange market, reflect observed short-run changes in exchange rates. Why, among the major industrial economies, the forward exchange rate contains no useful information on subsequent short-term movements in the spot exchange rate is a puzzling phenomenon explored in great empirical detail by Goodhart (1988).

In effect, the international capital market is inherently inefficient in adjusting for risk when, on the one hand, international flows of goods and interest-bearing financial capital are quite free, while, on the other hand, there is no common monetary standard under which this massive interchange of goods and financial assets takes place.

Originally published in *Open Economies Review*, 1, 3 (September 1990): 229–250. Reprinted with permission.

17.1   Separate Currency Domains: Some Stylized Facts

The relevant world economy is divided into several distinct currency domains separated by floating exchange rates. The monetary authority in each country (domain) fixes its national money supply (or domestic rate of money growth) independently of pressure for or against its currency in the foreign exchanges. However, international investors choose portfolios of bonds, equities, and real assets across countries (blocs) without restraint, and the economies in question are integrated in commodity trade.

As with the industrial economies today, such separate currency domains imply that:

A. Within each country, domestic currency prices are "sticky": they are not immediately sensitive to exchange-rate changes; and

B. Domestic transactors hold virtually all of the supply of (narrow) money—coin and currency, checking accounts, and so on—within each country. Foreigners might hold domestic bonds and equities, but not significant transactions balances in the domestic currency.[1]

(A) and (B) are complementary. In market economies, firms producing brand-name goods and services find it convenient to fix invoice prices in the domestic currency for weeks or months at a time.[2] And such Hicksian fixprice goods and services constitute the bulk of consumption and production in the industrial economics. Thus only domestic transactions generate demand for the national money narrowly defined. Should the need arise for foreign exchange, this is intermediated by banks—thus making direct holdings of foreign transactions balance by domestic nationals unnecessary (or negligibly small).

Although the domestic price level in each industrial country remains rigid—at least for finite periods of time—exchange rates are highly flexible as international investors switch their preferences between foreign and domestic securities. Unlike the situation when a common monetary standard prevails—as with the classical gold standard before 1914 or the calmer periods under the Bretton Woods system of fixed official exchange parities from 1950 to 1970—each investor must continually guess the course of each country's exchange rate and compare it with the differing interest yields on dollar, mark, yen, or sterling assets. The spot exchange rate behaves as a forward-looking asset price that is extremely sensitive to "news" regarding, say, how much the future money supply in country A might be expanded vis-à-vis country B, or how future taxes on assets in A might be levied, or how A's prospective terms of trade and future foreign exchange earnings might change and so on (Frenkel and Mussa 1980). Thus, the exchange rate appears to fluctuate randomly; it can't be predicted on the basis of past information on money growth, trade deficits, GNP growth and so on (Meese and Rogoff 1983).

One important casualty of this turbulence on the foreign exchange markets is the law of one price. Because similar (or even the same) brand-name goods are invoiced for discrete periods of time in the national currency for each country, they will be more or less always out of alignment with each other as the exchange rate fluctuates. Producers in country A find that they are continually subject to exchange risk in selling to country B—risk against which it is impossible to hedge fully (chapter 20). At a more macroeconomic level, continual price-level misalignments will develop. For example, the devaluation of the dollar from 1986–88 drove the American price level (for tradable goods) far below its European and Japanese counterparts.

In the much longer run, however, arbitrage in international goods markets tends to restore purchasing power parity—although many years might elapse before the price level in the country with the undervalued currency increases sufficiently (McKinnon and Ohno 1989). For example, the greater U.S. price inflation in 1990 compared to hard-currency Europe and Japan is a consequence of the earlier undervaluation of the dollar. But new "exogenous" exchange-rate fluctuations will prevent complete price-level alignment from finally occurring. Slow-to-adjust goods markets are always more or less out of equilibrium while exchange rates swing around to balance rapidly shifting asset preferences.

17.2 The Model

Our model of the liquidity trap, showing the failure of open-interest parity and excessive exchange-rate volatility, is confined to a single industrial country such that the rest of the world remains passive. Nevertheless, the principles involved easily generalise to mutual (non)adjustment of short-term interest rates across many countries.[3]

Although holdings of narrow money M1 by nonbanks are confined to nationals of the country in question, let us assume "perfect" capital mobility in the international bond market. No exchange controls impede international capital movements, and default risk on the chosen short-term instruments at home and abroad is assumed to be negligible. Domestic nationals *and* foreigners shuffle freely between domestic and foreign (short-term) bonds so that covered interest parity always holds

$$i - i^* = f = \frac{F - S}{S} \tag{1}$$

where

i is the domestic (short-term) interest rate.
i^* is the equivalent foreign interest rate.
S is the spot exchange rate:
     domestic currency/foreign currency.
F is the forward exchange rate.
f is the forward premium on foreign exchange with the
     same term to maturity as i and i^*.

Because this covered interest arbitrage is risk-free, the empirical robustness of (1) for Eurocurrency deposits is well established (Aliber 1973; Goodhart 1988).

Nevertheless, in our "forward-looking" asset portfolios, foreign and domestic bonds are *not* perfect substitutes. i need not be equal to i^* nor need $i - i^*$ equal the expected change in the spot exchange rate. Currency risk and political uncertainty combine to drive a wedge between domestic and foreign interest rates—a wedge that varies through time. To capture this effect, let us complete our basic model by using a set of equations provided by Schröder (1990) simplifying an earlier model of McKinnon (1983), which is a generalization of an approach pioneered by Dornbusch (1976). Except for i, lowercase letters denote logarithms.

$$\dot{p} = \delta(s - p - k) \qquad \text{with } \delta > 0 \qquad \text{Goods Market} \tag{2}$$

$$i = i^* + \theta(\bar{s} - s) + z \quad \text{with } \theta > 0 \qquad \text{Bond Market} \qquad (4)$$

For our small open economy, $s - p - k$ in equation (2) is the deviation of the real exchange rate, $s - p$, from purchasing power parity (PPP). If the foreign price level, P^*, is unchanging, then k can be considered a constant. Second, assume the domestic real output, y, is given at the full employment level. Financial shocks affect domestic absorption ex ante (the demand for goods and services) and thus the domestic price level, p, but not real output.

In response to exogenous shifts in s, the coefficient δ in equation (2) gives the speed of adjustment of the domestic price level, p, in restoring PPP at $s - p = k$. The greater the deviation of the real exchange rate from k, the greater the pressure on domestic prices to adjust. Being part of the same forward-looking process by which the exchange rate is determined, the prices of tradable and nontradable goods are presumed to adjust at the same rate. For example, an inflationary scare, which suddenly depreciates the domestic currency (increases s), will set in motion a broad price inflation across all sectors of the domestic economy.[4]

In equation (3), the money demand function is narrowly defined. Direct currency substitution between domestic non-interest-bearing money and foreign cash balances or foreign bonds is initially ruled out—although that possibility is considered later. Neither $\dot{s}^e$ (expected change in the exchange rate) nor i^* (the foreign interest rate) affect domestic liquidity preference—which is wholly determined by the domestic (short-term) rate of interest, i as long as y is given. Later on, this simplifying assumption of no direct currency substitution will be relaxed.

In equation (4), the parameter z introduces risk explicitly into the international bond market. When "news" arrives about, say, an increased threat of future inflation at home or higher future taxes on holders of domestic assets, the index z increases as international investors switch their asset preferences from domestic to foreign bonds. z is a measure of the risk premium, or the increased yield, international investors require to hold the now riskier domestic bonds into the indefinite future. Thus, if the exchange rate remains unchanged when news arrives, portfolio balance in the international bond market requires that

$$i = i^* + z. \tag{5}$$

Only if (5) holds continuously through time as z varies would relative interest rates do their job as shock absorbers for balancing international bond portfolios. Indeed, as we shall see, (5) is the "long-run" equilibrium condition for determining short-term interest rates in the international bond market for any given information set available to international investors.

17.3 The Liquidity Trap

Under floating exchange rates, however, (5) does not hold in the short run. Rather, i is "trapped" by the unchanging domestic liquidity preference function, and unchanging national money supply, shown in equation (3). Because p and y are also sticky (do not jump) when news arrives, i is the only endogenous variable in equation (3).

For example, suppose we start from a portfolio equilibrium where foreign and domestic bonds are equally risky, i.e. $z = 0$ and $i = i^*$ and the exchange rate is not expected to change. The international bond market is in balance. Now suppose that news arrives that raises z. i is still fully determined by equation (3): it remains pegged at i^*. Thus, in the short run

$$i < i^* + z \tag{5a}$$

even though domestic bonds are now perceived to be riskier.

Similarly, if the model were generalized to two or more countries, foreign short-term interest rates would be pinned down in foreign money markets by each national liquidity preference function. This Keynesian-type problem of nonadjusting short-term interest rates arises because the domains of circulation for narrow monies are separated by national boundaries. Under floating exchange rates, narrow money can't leave that country whose assets are perceived to be riskier—thus preventing its short-term interest rates from rising; nor is the supply of narrow money in safer countries naturally increased in order to permit its short-term interest rates to fall.[5]

In developing an argument for the nonadjustment of short-term interest rates to international "news," domestic monetary policy under floating exchange rates was defined simply as keeping the national money supply, M, fixed. Then, with an unchanging national money demand function, i.e., given parameters in equation (3), short-term rates of interest were caught in a national liquidity trap. In practice, short-term interest rates could still fluctuate with the demand or supply of the national money. However, these interest rate fluctuations are not responses to changes in perceived risk in the international bond market.

Alternatively, national monetary authorities could choose to exercise their independence under floating by keying domestic open-market or discount operations on some principal short-term interest rate in the national money market. Through much of its history, the U.S. Federal Reserve System has chosen to smooth short-run fluctuations in either the Treasury bill rate or—in more recent times—the interest rate on federal funds (the rate at which banks borrow or lend reserves to each other) irrespective of pressure on the dollar in the foreign-exchange market.[6] Then, even if the national money demand function does shift when news arrives and is digested by investors in the international bond market, domestic short-term interest rates would still fail to respond.

17.4 Exchange-Rate Expectations and "News"

So far, the idea of the liquidity trap has been developed without modelling how exchange rates respond to new information. And the basic idea of nonadjusting interest rates in the very short run remains valid for a variety of possible movements in the exchange rate—some of which we shall now consider.

When news arrives as indicated by an increase in z, s and possibly $\bar{s}$ jump discretely—even though the short-term interest-rate is immobile. $\bar{s}$ is the "long-run" equilibrium value for the exchange rate (in the minds of international investors) toward which s then subsequently gravitates smoothly—as described by the adjustment parameter θ in equation (4). But the nature of this long-run equilibrium is highly dependent on the qualitative nature of the new information. Is the change in z permanent or transitory? Does it reflect an expected change in domestic monetary policy, in future taxes, or in the country's terms of trade?

Rather than give a complete taxonomy of all possible forms that news might take, let us explore a few leading examples where the news itself is fairly transparent to international investors. Bubbles or bandwagon effects—where individual investors project that the exchange rate will continue moving in the same direction perhaps because they believe others are privy to information they don't have—are presumed to be absent. In practice, however, bandwagon effects seem to have been important in explaining both short- and intermediate-term movements in the dollar exchange rate in the 1970s and 1980s (Frankel and Froot 1986; Woo 1987).

However, in assessing whether floating exchange rates are inherently excessively volatile, I shall take the conservative course of omitting bandwagon effects from the formal analysis. If floating rates are shown to be excessively volatile in the absence of bandwagon effects, then the situation can only be worsened if such effects are present.

Once bandwagon effects are ruled out, purely transitory shocks to z would seem to have no great economic significance for exchange-rate movements. Let us, therefore, confine our analysis to "permanent" changes in the riskiness of domestic bonds: news increasing z which international investors believe will persist indefinitely and which eventually force an increase in domestic interest rates. In case I, we shall analyze a representative nonmonetary shock—a change in taxation—which leads to once-and-for-all changes in $\bar{s}$ and $\bar{p}$ as people move from domestic to foreign bonds. In case II, we consider more general "country" risk where concern for future inflation or political stability induces people to shift out of both domestic money and bonds.

Case I: Increased Taxation of Foreigner's Domestic Investments

Start again from a stationary equilibrium where $i = i^*$ and $\dot{p}_e = \dot{s}_e = 0$. Let z_1 denote an increase in risk that is not monetary in origin. For example, a threat to increase future taxes on domestic investments owned by foreigners—say, a domestic withholding tax on interest and dividends flowing abroad—would increase z_1. In the short run, international investors now shift their preferences away from domestic to foreign assets, thus depreciating the domestic currency until effective yields—interest rates plus expected change in the exchange rate—compensate for the higher taxes on domestic bonds. Rewriting equation (4), we have

$$i = i^* + \theta(\bar{s} - s) + z_1. \tag{4a}$$

First consider the economy's new long-run equilibrium associated with exchange-rate depreciation and inflation, and then work backward to look at the short and intermediate runs.[7] Because the nominal money supply remains, and is anticipated to remain, anchored, the exchange rate and the domestic price level are stationary in the long run:

$$s = \bar{s} \tag{6}$$

$$p = \bar{p} \tag{7}$$

$$\dot{p} = 0. \tag{8}$$

Substituting (6) through (8) into (2), (3), and (4a) gives the new long-run values of the interest rate, the price level, and the exchange rate when the system is again at rest. Substituting (6) into (4a) determines the long-run interest rate.

$$\bar{i} = i^* + z_1, \quad \text{and} \quad \frac{d\bar{i}}{dz_1} = 1. \tag{5b}$$

The domestic interest rate eventually increases by the full amount of the perceived increase in risk.

Then substituting (7) and (5b) into (3) yields the price level in long-run equilibrium

$$\bar{p} = m - \eta y + \varepsilon(i^* + z_1) \tag{9}$$

where

$$\frac{d\bar{p}}{dz_1} = \varepsilon. \tag{9'}$$

After z increases, price inflation ensues until real cash balances are reduced sufficiently to release i from its liquidity trap. Only after rising to $\bar{i}$, does i fully reflect the greater risk of holding domestic bonds. Through this inflation process, there has been *indirect currency substitution* (chapters 7 and 16). Real cash balances have been reduced, in favour of domestic bonds, by an increase in the price level.

Finally, substituting (6), (7), and (8) into (2) yields

$$\bar{s} = \bar{p} + k. \tag{10}$$

Because the real exchange rate remains unchanged when purchasing power parity is restored, the long-run equilibrium value for the nominal exchange rate depreciates proportionately to the increase in the price level:

$$\frac{d\bar{s}}{dz_1} = \frac{d\bar{p}}{dz_1} = \varepsilon. \tag{10a}$$

The path the economy takes towards this new equilibrium is portrayed in figure 17.1. Because the price level, real money stock, and nominal short term interest rate do not jump when news arrives, the exchange rate must depreciate sufficiently sharply to keep the international bond market in balance. Figure 17.1 shows the exchange rate jumping immediately from a to b and overshooting its long-run equilibrium at c. Regressive expectations are thereby established for subsequent (slow) appreciation from b down to c. Note that the zero interest differential $(i - i^*)$ at b does *not* reflect this expected movement in the exchange rate. Because i is immobilized in the domestic money market, open interest parity fails: the forward rate does not equal the expected future spot exchange rate.[8]

The exchange rate's initial jump from a to b (figure 17.1) can be calculated by substituting (10a) into (4a) to get

$$\frac{ds}{dz_1} = \varepsilon + \frac{1}{\theta}. \tag{11}$$

For a given increase in the risk premium z_1, the exchange rate jumps according to the elasticity of the demand for money and inversely to the perceived speed of adjustment θ: the rate at which s approaches $\bar{s}$. And, in turn, θ will depend on the rate of increase in domestic prices, and thus on the speed with which the domestic nominal interest rate is released from its liquidity trap—as shown in the upper panel of figure 17.1.

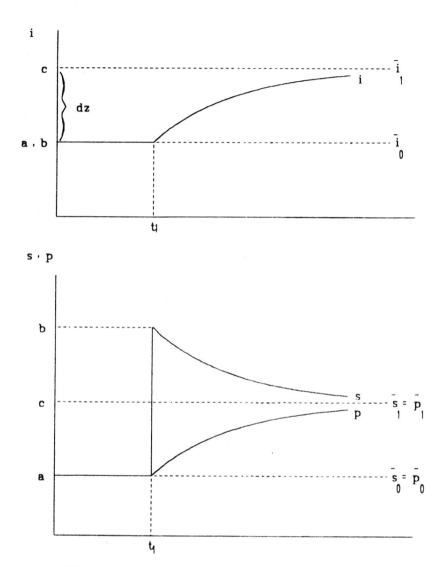

Figure 17.1
Exchange-rate overshooting with interest rate immobile in short run.

Although not necessary for the overshooting argument, suppose that the price level—in increasing from $\bar{p}_0$ to its new long-run equilibrium at $\bar{p}_1$—adjusts at the same rate as the exchange rate regresses (appreciates) from its short-run equilibrium at b to its new long-run equilibrium at $\bar{s}_1$: in equations (2) and (4), the adjustment parameters are such that $\delta \approx \theta$. Then, from the geometric symmetry in the lower panel of figure 17.1, we see that the degree of exchange-rate overshooting cb is about the same as the jump ac in the long-run equilibrium of the exchange rate (and price level).

Apart from the high degree of volatility in the exchange rate, however, the domestic price level has been destabilized by a *nonmonetary* shock that happened to change international asset preferences. Because the national central bank remained passive in the face of a depreciating currency, the (threatened) withholding tax on foreign investors forced an increase in the domestic price level as an alternative means whereby domestic short-term interest rates could increase. And other "nonmonetary" shifts in international asset preferences—say because of some perceived shift in a country's terms of trade—can similarly destabilize the domestic price level when exchange rates are left free to float.[9]

Case II: Generalized Country Risk

Changes in risk were confined to the international bond market in case I: a threatened increase in the withholding tax on foreign investors did not directly affect the demand for money by domestic transactors (equation 3).

However, more generalized political risk in any one country could induce domestic bond *and* money holders to alter their international asset positions (Schröder 1990). The emerging threat of a new, more populist government could make domestic wealth owners uneasy about future exchange controls, or higher wealth taxes, or higher price inflation, and so on. Although not knowing which of these possibilities is most likely, wealth owners could shift away from domestic money and bonds into foreign-exchange assets.

Start again from zero inflation where domestic prices and interest rates are aligned internationally. Suppose news arrives that country-specific political risk has increased. Investors now demand the risk premium z_2 on domestic financial assets. In any new long-run equilibrium, with an unchanging nominal exchange rate, the domestic interest rate must increase by z_2 to keep the international bond market in balance:

$$\bar{i} = i^* + z_2 \tag{5c}$$

similar to case I. Before this final equilibrium is reached, continuous bond-market equilibrium still requires

$$i = i^* = \theta(\bar{s} - s) + z_2. \tag{4b}$$

Equilibrium in the national money market, however, differs from case I. To incorporate this country-specific political risk, let us replace equation (3) with (3a) to get

$$m - p = \eta y - \varepsilon i - \gamma z_2 - \gamma[\theta(\bar{s} - s) + i^*]. \tag{3a}$$

In equation (3a), the behavior of money holders has been internationalized in two closely related respects. First, domestic transactors directly respond to political news by reducing their demand for (domestic) money by γz_2. Such direct currency substitution out of domestic money into foreign exchange breaks down the previously assumed insularity of the national money demand function. Second, logical consistency requires that domestic transactors also respond to the foreign interest rate and to expected changes in the exchange rate. Thus the far right-hand term in (3a) is also modified by the parameter γ.

Because money holders are mainly concerned with making payments for goods and services invoiced in the domestic currency, they are *less* prone to switch into foreign exchange than are yield-seeking foreign or domestic holders of the country's bonds. Thus we impose the condition that $\gamma < \varepsilon$. Money holders remain somewhat insular: the demand for money is more strongly influenced by changes in i (the return on bonds denominated in the same currecy) than by i^*, or by expected exchange-rate changes.[10] Algebraically, case I is case II taken to the limit where $\gamma \to 0$.

For case II where $p = \bar{p}$ and $s = \bar{s}$, the price level and exchange rate may be solved by substituting (5c) into (3a) to get

$$\bar{p} = m - \eta y + (\varepsilon + \gamma)(i^* + z_2). \tag{12}$$

Noting that $\dot{p} = 0$ in final equilibrium, equation (2) then yields

$$\bar{s} = \bar{p} + k. \tag{10}$$

For any change in generalized country risk, the corresponding changes in the long-run values of the interest rate, price level, and exchange rate are

$$\frac{d\bar{i}}{dz_2} = 1 \tag{13}$$

$$\frac{d\bar{p}}{dz_2} = \varepsilon + \gamma \tag{14}$$

$$\frac{d\bar{s}}{dz_2} = \varepsilon + \gamma. \tag{15}$$

The domestic price level increases—and the exchange rate depreciates—by more than ε. Country risk in case II induces an additional decline in demand for domestic money—as measured by γ. The increase in the price level and exchange rate is represented in the lower panel of figure 17.1—but now the distance ac—the increase in prices and the exchange rate in long-run equilibrium—is $\varepsilon + \gamma$, rather than just ε as in case I.

When the monetary authority leaves the national money supply m unchanged in face of increased country risk (case II), price inflation will be generated by the eventual risk-adjusted increase in the nominal interest rate *and* by direct currency substitution. The more elastic the demand for domestic money from either effect is, the greater this price inflation will be. In comparison to a financially closed economy, the presence of foreign portfolio alternatives magnifies these elasticities—thus accentuating the inflationary impact of heightened domestic political risk.

Although the long-run price level and exchange-rate increase more in case II than in case I, exchange-rate "overshooting" in the short run remains proportionally the same because the underlying equations for the goods, money, and bond markets are logarithmic. To see this, remember that m and y are fixed, and p is unchanging when news arrives. Then differentiate the bond market equation (4b) and the money market equation (3a) with respect to z_2, and solve simultaneously to get

$$\frac{di}{dz_2} = 0 \quad \text{and} \tag{16}$$

$$\frac{ds}{dz_2} = \varepsilon + \gamma + \frac{1}{\theta}. \tag{17}$$

Because the interest rate remains caught in its liquidity trap in the short run, the degree of exchange-rate overshooting is again determined by $1/\theta$—as in case I. Although the direct substitution away from domestic money now tends to reduce i, the expected exchange appreciation arising out of the overshooting tends to increase i. The two effects cancel to leave the domestic interest rate unchanged when news arrives—as in the upper panel of figure 17.1. Presuming again that the price level and the exchange rate subsequently adjust at the same speed, the symmetrically proportionate overshooting of the exchange rate in case II can also be represented by the distance cb in the lower panel of figure 17.1—with its absolute magnitude now greater because of the presence of direct currency substitution.

17.5 Perverse Changes in Short-Term Interest Rates and Aggravated Overshooting in the Foreign Exchanges

In response to some sudden change in international risk, whether similar to case I or case II, are there plausible circumstances where short-term interest rates could adjust the "wrong" way—and thus aggravate exchange-rate volatility?

Even if domestic money holders don't see foreign exchange assets as a convenient portfolio alternative, i.e., $\gamma \to 0$, they could well be sensitive to *expected* future domestic price inflation signalled by a discrete devaluation of the exchange rate. Being in direct contact with goods markets, cash-balance holders could move out of domestic money into (inventories of) commodities. As long as the price inflation was expected to continue, the demand for domestic money could be substantially reduced.

The actual rate of price inflation is determined by the deviation of the spot exchange rate from purchasing power parity—as per equation (2). Let us presume that expected inflation, π, is equal to actual inflation:

$$\pi(s) = \dot{p} \text{ where } \frac{d\pi}{ds} = \delta > 0 \text{ from equation (2).} \tag{18}$$

Combining the approach of Schröder (1990) with that of Sung (1988), the money demand function is further generalized to

$$m - p = \eta y - \varepsilon i - \alpha\pi - \gamma[z_2 + \theta(\bar{s} - s) + i^*]. \tag{3b}$$

α denotes the direct elasticity of money demand with respect to anticipated domestic inflation. Tanzi (1982) shows that expected inflation directly influences the demand for money in the United States—although his empirical analysis doesn't use the exchange rate as a forward signal.

Let arriving news of general country risk again be denoted by z_2. Because subsequent domestic price inflation is confined to the intermediate run, long-run increases in the domestic price level, exchange and interest rates remain as described in equations (13), (14) and (15) for case II.

However, the short-run response of the interest rate to an increase in z_2 is now very different. From the immediate depreciation of the domestic currency, inflationary expectations rise—possibly quite sharply. People reduce their demand for money according to the parameter α. But, in the short run, real cash balances can't change because the price level is sticky and the stock of nominal money is given. To keep the domestic money market in balance in the face of excess liquidity, therefore, i must fall immediately when z_2 increases—which accentuates capital flight into foreign bonds. This initially perverse movement in the short-term interest rate, when news arrives, is shown in the upper panel of figure 17.2.

This perverse movement in the short-term interest rate then *aggravates* the overshooting (depreciation) of the exchange rate above its long-run equilibrium value. To see this algebraically, differentiate the bond market equation (4b) and money market equation (3b) with respect to z_2, insert the new long-run equilibrium values for $\bar{i}$, $\bar{p}$ and $\bar{s}$, and then solve simultaneously for the short-run impacts on the exchange and interest rates:

$$\frac{di}{dz_2} = -\frac{\alpha\delta}{(\varepsilon + \alpha)} \cdot \frac{ds}{dz_2} < \quad \text{if} \quad \frac{ds}{dz_2} > 0 \tag{19}$$

$$\frac{ds}{dz_2} = \frac{\varepsilon + \gamma + 1/\theta}{\Delta} \quad \text{where} \quad \Delta = 1 - \frac{\alpha\delta}{\theta(\varepsilon + \gamma)}. \tag{20}$$

When news arrives, equation (19) shows how the domestic interest rate falls as the exchange rate depreciates. Moreover, with inflationary expectations now influencing money demand directly, a stable short-run equilibrium for the exchange rate might not exist. Additional capital flight from the falling interest rate may induce a vicious circle of exchange depreciation,

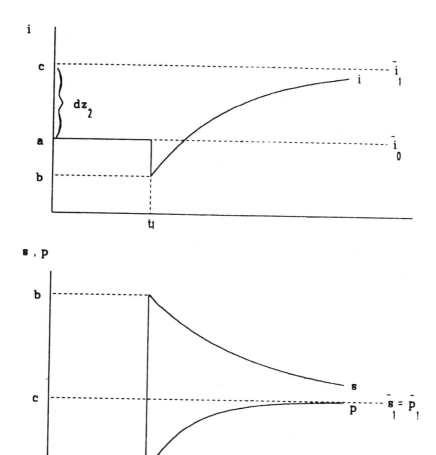

Figure 17.2
Aggravated exchange rate overshooting with perverse short-run adjustment in interest rate.

a rising price level, and increasing inflationary expectations (Sung 1988).

Although such vicious circles may be economically plausible in some circumstances, let us rule them out in our formal model. To ensure that the system will come to rest at its long-run equilibrium values defined by equations (13), (14), and (15), let us impose the stability condition that $0 < \Delta < 1$. This requires

$$\frac{\alpha \delta}{\theta (\varepsilon + \gamma)} < 1. \tag{21}$$

If condition (21) holds, the short-run exchange depreciation—the increase in s—is bounded. To further understand the meaning of (21), again suppose that $\delta \approx \theta$: the pressure on the exchange rate to converge to its long-run equilibrium is similar to that on the price level. Then, the jump in the short-run exchange rate varies directly with α; and, indeed, the stability condition reduces to $\alpha < (\varepsilon + \gamma)$. This condition could be violated if the domestic money demand function remains insular with $\gamma \to 0$ and its interest elasticity ε is small. However, α is almost certain to be less than ε because domestic bonds are usually a more convenient alternative to holding money than are commodity inventories. Thus, unless bandwagon effects or bubbles are present, a vicious circle can be ruled out.

Nevertheless, perverse adjustments in short-term interest rates greatly increase the volatility of "equilibrium" movements in the exchange rate—whether responding to changes in tax risk (case I), or to generalized country risk (case II). This "exaggerated" overshooting of the exchange rate is plotted in the lower panel of figure 17.2 where the vertical distance cb now exceeds that of ac. The erratic path for the short-term interest rate—first falling sharply, and then rising gradually as inflation reduces real cash balances—can be seen in the upper panel.

17.6 Optimal Monetary Policy in the Face of Direct and Indirect Currency Substitution

In a "free float," monetary policy is not used to smooth fluctuations in the exchange rate. Implicitly, the central bank has other, more purely domestic goals—traditionally the most important being to stabilize the domestic price level.

Let us accept this traditional objective in its own right. In a hypothetical social utility function, suppose that reducing exchange-rate volatility per se is given no weight. However, the authorities aim to stabilize the average level of domestic-currency prices.

Then, the central bank's technical mandate is to balance the (possibly) fluctuating demand for the domestic money by varying its supply so that the national price level remains fairly constant. But changes in the ex ante demand for domestic money are difficult to measure; and the consequences of getting the balance wrong are evident only with a lag—perhaps after price inflation develops and is hard to stop. Thus, to gauge whether or not the current demand for domestic money is shifting, central bankers often look to immediately available prices in auction markets—interest rates, foreign-exchange rates, primary commodity prices, and so on—for guidance.[11]

Suppose our economy is too small to influence primary commodity prices on a worldwide basis. The preferred monetary indicator then boils down to a choice between the domestic short-term rate of interest and the foreign-exchange rate(s) against some "hard" foreign currency(s). Can the model developed above then throw light on which more accurately indicates whether current monetary policy is too tight or too easy?

In both cases I and II, the news that shifted portfolio preferences was "expectational" or "forward-looking": the perceived increase in future risk required an eventual increase in the interest rate on domestic bonds in order to rebalance international asset portfolios. Once long-run equilibrium was reestablished with a higher price level, the reduction in the real stock of money finally permitted the necessary increase in interest rates.

Suppose now the central bank had chosen to key on the short-term domestic interest rate as its monetary indicator. In the traditional manner, the monetary authority expands the domestic money supply when facing (incipient) upward pressure on the interest rate—and vice versa. For either case I or case II, the central bank would be resisting the natural increase in the interest rate on domestic bonds needed to offset the higher domestic risk—as shown in the upper panel of figure 17.1. If the domestic money supply began to increase after news arrived, the exchange rate would depreciate even more sharply. Stronger and more immediate inflationary pressure would develop in the domestic economy. As long as the central bank tries to prevent the interest rate from increasing, no long-run equilibrium for the price level or for the exchange rate would be sustainable.

Suppose the interest rate initially moved "perversely", i.e., it fell when international risk increased as shown by the movement from a to b in the upper panel of figure 17.2. At first, the monetary authorities would be induced to contract the money supply. But this correct response would be overridden some weeks or months later when the interest rate rose above a en route to its new long-run equilibrium at point c. Targeting the domestic interest rate, when international risk premia change continually, is too treacherous.

In contrast, suppose that the central bank keyed on the exchange rate itself—provided that a rate close to purchasing power parity with a "hard" currency trading partner(s) was properly selected (McKinnon and Ohno 1988). Then, changes in the nominal money supply could allow the short-term interest rate to compensate directly for perceived changes in international risk—without disturbing the exchange rate or the price level.

To see this, consider again the country risk case where z_2 suddenly increases. From equation (4b), the exchange rate would stay constant if the interest rate immediately rose to

$$di = dz_2. \tag{18}$$

Following Schröder (1990), the necessary monetary contraction for satisfying (18) is found by totally differentiating equation (3a) to get

$$dm = -(\varepsilon + \gamma)dz_2 < 0. \tag{19}$$

The supply of nominal money is reduced to match the fall in the "effective" demand for real money. And this fall in effective demand can be partitioned into *direct* currency substitution as indicated by the parameter γ for case II, and by *indirect* currency substitution through the impact of the increased domestic interest rate as indicated by the semi-elasticity ε for both cases I and II. One way or another, such currency substitution will eventually take place. If the nominal stock of money is not immediately decreased, then we have seen how price inflation will ensue so as to reduce the real stock.

However, this necessity of reducing the real money stock as z^2 increases is more neatly accomplished by following a fixed exchange-rate rule. As the exchange rate tends to depreciate, the central bank would reduce the nominal (and real) stock of money directly by selling off foreign-exchange reserves or by open-market sales of bonds. Either approach satisfies equation (19)—thus leaving higher short-term interest rates without otherwise disturbing the economy's macroeconomic equilibrium.

The beauty of so targeting the exchange rate is that the authorities need not have good estimates of ε or γ—or know how much the interest rate must increase in final equilibrium. They may not be able to distinguish between case I and case II as the source of the financial disturbance. Nevertheless, by simply reducing the money supply and raising short-term interest rates by whatever is necessary to defend the exchange rate, they succeed in reducing the (real) stock of money in line with the reduced demand for it while leaving the domestic price level undisturbed.

17.7   A Concluding Note on the Prevalence of International Risk

By stabilizing the exchange rate, the monetary authorities free the domestic short-term interest rate to better reflect shifting assessments of international risk. The liquidity trap, or perverse short-run movements in interest rates, are avoided. Therefore, the international bond market works more efficiently when the exchange rate is fixed than when it is floating.

In contrast to the above analysis that took (shifting) risk premia to be exogenously determined, the *prevalence* of this expectational risk—the frequency and magnitude of shifts in the parameters z_1 and z_2—itself may depend on the nature of the exchange-rate regime in place.

The probability of experiencing "nonmonetary" shocks, such as the tax changes analyzed in case I, could well be independent of whether the exchange rate was fixed or floating. That is, such shocks are no more or less likely to occur under fixed as compared to floating exchange rates. Nevertheless, under a fixed exchange rate they are much less likely to destabilize the domestic price level when they do occur.

However, the probability of shocks in the form of "country risk"—as per case II—would seem to be much less likely once the exchange rate was known to be safely fixed in the context of a generally accepted common monetary standard—as laid out in part III of the book. Then, the domestic rate of price inflation would be constrained to that prevailing in the hard-currency outside world. Because people no longer need fear that the exchange rate 20 years from now will differ much from today's, their international portfolio preferences would be less volatile in the face of current changes in the domestic political scene.

Notes

I would like to thank Jürgen Schröder of the University of Mannheim for his invaluable help in simplifying the algebra, and greatly clarifying the economic arguments, in this chapter. Thanks also to David Robinson for catching a few more ambiguities.

1. In practice, "direct" currency substitution between the narrow monies of the industrial countries is minimal. For transactions purposes, Americans hold few yen, and Japanese few dollars. Within some LDCs, on the other hand, foreign currencies circulate in parallel with the national one—with highly destabilizing consequences for the domestic price level (chapter 16).

2. See McKinnon (1979, chap. 4) for a detailed analysis of why this invoicing is economically rational.

3. A more serious analytical simplification is the omission of long-term interest rates, which are not tied down by each national money market. Under floating exchange rates, long-term interest rates have been exceedingly volatile compared to the gold standard before 1914 and compared to the fixed exchange-rate dollar standard of the 1950s and 1960s. Excess volatility in long-term interest rates is analyzed in chapter 3.

4. Possibly consistent with John Taylor's (1980) model of staggered labor contracts—although the labor market is not explicitly modelled in this chapter. Note that these inflationary consequences don't depend on an increase in the trade surplus. Indeed, there is no predictable relationship between such a devaluation and the net trade balance (McKinnon 1990a). Hence, I have chosen to omit the details of net trade flows from the model.

5. Under a symmetrical fixed exchange-rate regime maintained by nonsterilized intervention in the foreign exchanges or by "equivalent" domestic open-market operations, the money supply would automatically contract in the riskier country (allowing its short-term interest rate to rise) and would rise in the country seen to be a safe haven—thus allowing its short-term interest rates to fall.

6. October 1979 through the summer of 1982 was the only time that the Federal Reserve Bank attempted to execute American monetary policy without targeting—or trying to smooth—some short-term interest rate (Heller 1988). Instead, they aimed, not very successfully, for a fixed rate of growth in M1. But this resulted in such extreme volatility in short-run interest rates that this policy was subsequently discontinued.

7. The algebraic development of case I follows that suggested by Schröder (1990).

8. In Dornbusch's (1976) model, where shocks are confined to the national money market rather than the international bond market, open interest parity holds after the exchange rate overshoots and regressive expectations set in.

9. For example, a permanent fall in the price of oil could induce exchange depreciation and a severe price inflation in an oil-exporting country—although the precise analytics might differ from the above analysis of a withholding tax on foreign interest and dividends. Indeed, equation (2) representing the goods market would have to be altered to distinguish between tradable and nontradable goods—in order to properly represent the impact of changes in the equilibrium "real" exchange rate.

10. Schröder (1990) has a very similar, although not identical, formulation for the demand for money in (3a). He allows γ to take on different values according to whether it modifies z_2 or $\theta(\bar{s} - s) + i^*$. However, the foreign-exchange risk margin seems similar for both terms. Being hard-pressed to come up with any intuitive argument on why they should differ, I adopt the simpler notation—the single parameter γ—which presumes they do not.

11. The position of a pure domestic monetarist is somewhat different. In this view, the demand for money is subject to small, unpredictable random fluctuations but is otherwise fairly stable through time. In particular, major expectational shifts in international asset preferences don't significantly impact the demand for the national money. Thus, in order to minimize volatility in inflationary expectations, the central bank does best to keep domestic money growth within a prespecified narrow range.

References

Aliber, Robert (1973) "The Interest-Rate Parity Theorem: A Reinterpretation," *Journal of Political Economy* 81(6), 1451–59.

Dornbusch, Rudiger (1976) "Expectations and Exchange Rate Dynamics," *Journal of Political Economy* 84, 1161–76.

Frankel, Jeffrey A., and Kenneth Froot (1986) "Understanding the U.S. Dollar in the Eighties: A Tale of Chartists and Fundamentalists," *Economic Record* (Special Issue), 24–38.

Frenkel, Jacob, and Michael L. Mussa (1980) "The Efficiency of Foreign Exchange Markets and Measures of Turbulence," *American Economic Review* 70, 374–81.

Goodhart, Charles (1988) "The Foreign Exchange Market: A Random Walk with a Dragging Anchor," *Economica* (55), No. 220, 437–60.

Heller, Robert (1988) "The Making of U.S. Monetary Policy," Seminar for Economic Policy, The University of Cologne, West Germany, April.

Keynes, John M. (1936) *The General Theory of Employment, Interest and Money*, London: Macmillan.

———. (1937) "The Ex-Ante Theory of the Rate of Interest," *Economic Journal* 47, 663–69.

McKinnon, Ronald I. (1979) *Money in International Exchange: The Convertible Currency System.* New York: Oxford University Press.

———. (1983) "Why Floating Exchange Rates Fail," *Working Paper* E-83-12 Hoover Institution, Stanford University.

———. (1985) "Two Concepts of International Currency Substitution." In Michael B. Connolly and John McDermott (eds.), *The Economics of the Caribbean Basin.* Praeger, pp. 101–18.

———. (1988a) "Monetary and Exchange Rate Policy for International Financial Stability: A Proposal," *Journal of Economic Perspectives* 2(1), 83–103.

———. (1988b) "An International Gold Standard Without Gold," *The Cato Journal* 8, No. 2, 351–74.

———. (1990a) "The Exchange Rate and the Trade Balance: Insular Versus Open Economies," *Open Economies Review* 1, No. 1, 17–38.

———. (1990b) "Interest Rate Volatility and Exchange Risk": New Rules for a Common Monetary Standard," *Contemporary Policy Issues*, (April).

McKinnon, Ronald I., and Kenichi Ohno (1989) "Purchasing Power Parity as a Monetary Standard." In O. Hamouda, R. Rowley, and B. Wolf (eds.), *The Future of the International Monetary System.* Aldershot: Edward Elgar, pp. 42–67.

Meese, Richard, and Kenneth Rogoff (1983) "Empirical Exchange Rate Models of the 1970s: Do They Fit Out of Sample," *Journal of International Economics* 14, 3–24.

Schröder, Jürgen (1990) "International Risk and Exchange Rate Overshooting," *Journal of International Money and Finance*, (June 1990).

Sung, Lap Man (1988) *Exchange-Rate Expectations and Interest Rates in Financially Integrated Economies.* Ph.D. dissertation, Stanford University.

Tanzi, Vito (1982) "Inflationary Expectations, Taxes and the Demand for Money in the U.S.," IMF *Staff Papers* 29, No. 2.

Taylor, John (1980) "Aggregate Dynamics and Staggered Contracts," *Journal of Political Economy* 88, 1–23.

Woo, W. T. (1987) "Some Evidence on Speculative Bubbles in the Foreign Exchange Market," *Journal of Money, Credit and Banking* 19(4), 499–514.

18

Floating Exchange Rates and the New Interbloc Protectionism: Tariffs versus Quotas

18.1 Introduction

I regard as a key advantage of free exchange rates the likelihood that they will lead to freer world trade, will promote a dismantling of exchange controls and import quotas and a reduction of tariffs.

—Milton Friedman, *The Balance of Payments*

The removal of the balance-of-payments (objective) is an important positive contribution that the adoption of flexible exchange rates could make to the achievement of the liberal objective of an integrated international economy.

—Harry Johnson, *The Case for Flexible Exchange Rates*

Earlier arguments in defense of floating exchange rates often contained high hopes that by allowing the exchange rate to adjust naturally in response to the ebb and flow of international payments, there would be no need for the government to intervene to correct balance-of-payments disequilibria. International payments adjustment would become virtually automatic. This was taken to imply, among other things, that there would be less likelihood that protectionist policies such as tariffs and quotas would be used. In other words, floating exchange rates should lead to free trade, or at a minimum, freer trade within the world economy.

Behind the earlier textbook arguments for the linking of free trade to floating exchange rates were two closely related as-

Originally published in *Protectionism and World Welfare*, ed. D. Salvatore (Cambridge University Press, 1993), 221–243, with K. C. Fung. Reprinted with permission.

sumptions. First, it was presumed that exchange rates would adjust toward market equilibrium in a smooth and orderly fashion. Milton Friedman argued that destabilizing speculators would on average incur losses while stabilizing speculators made profits—thus ensuring that stabilizing speculation would predominate.

The second presumption was that the "equilibrium" exchange rate for which stabilizing speculators would aim is governed by conditions in the *current* account of the balance of payments. Taking the spot markets for international goods and services as the reference point, the traditional advocates of floating had it that the exchange rate would adjust smoothly toward an equilibrium that balanced "international competitiveness" in importing and exporting. Economists were somewhat divided as to whether this equilibrium exchange rate would (1) roughly balance flows of imports and exports as per the elasticities approach to the balance of trade or (2) roughly align national price levels for tradable goods as per the principle of purchasing power parity. Both groups, however, looked to current commodity flows, rather than to the capital account of the balance of payments, to determine equilibrium. Floating exchange rates, it was imagined, would limit trade deficits with but modest departures from purchasing power parity. Real exchange rates would remain fairly constant.

Therefore, continuously smooth adjustment in nominal exchange rates to balance international competitiveness was seen—from a macroeconomic perspective—as a way of eliminating the balance-of-trade motive for protection. A government need no longer worry about untoward deficits or surpluses in its balance of trade. At the microeconomic level, floating exchange rates were seen to insulate domestic producers from abrupt changes in their ability to compete on international markets—and thus make them less likely to petition the government to relieve their distress. The demand for protection would diminish.

With our experience of the floating exchange-rate system, we now know that many, if not all, of the elements of the pre-1973 textbook arguments for floating exchange rates are empirically and/or logically incorrect. Floating rates do *not* move smoothly, steadily, or in an orderly way. They move more sharply and more frequently than most economists had expected—as likely away from purchasing power parity as towared it in the short run. But domestic goods prices invoiced in home currencies evolve more slowly, i.e., they remain "sticky." The correspondingly large changes in real exchange rates have led, in the 1970s and 1980s, to abrupt changes in industrial competitiveness and increased demands for protection. (But, as we shall see, protection more in the form of quantitative restrictions on trade flows rather than tariffs.)

Where did the traditional arguments for floating go off the rails? By concentrating on commodity flows and the trade balance, floaters misjudged what would determine a sustainable equilibrium in the foreign exchanges in the short and intermediate runs. Instead, it is now well established (Frenkel and Mussa, 1980) that, under floating, the spot exchange rate behaves like a forward-looking asset price that is dominated by financial institutions holding portfolios of interest-bearing securities and money denominated in foreign and domestic currencies. But such portfolio holders are more concerned with the future evolution of the exchange rate than they are with any level that balances current commodity flows. Such an asset price is highly sensitive to "news" such as how much the future money supply in the U.S. might be expanded relative to that in Germany or Japan, or how the U.S. future capital gains tax may change or what the prospects for changes in a country's terms of trade may be. Without a common monetary standard and a par-value system for exchange rates, how national monetary policies will evolve vis-à-vis each other is essentially random. Thus, exchange rates fluctuate as "virtual" random walks in the short run. They cannot be predicted satisfactorily using past information of money growth, GNP growth, trade deficits, and so on (Meese and Rogoff 1983).

The sharp volatility of the exchange rates is vividly illustrated by episodes of dollar gyrations in the 1980s. After being undervalued in early 1980, by early 1985 the dollar had overshot any equilibrium defined with reference to the current state of the commodity markets, say, by the principle of purchasing power parity. Similarly, by the end of 1987, it had fallen far below purchasing power parity (McKinnon and Ohno 1989). Since then, the dollar has continued to gyrate—rising or falling 15 to 25 percent over a year against other major currencies.

The arguments set forth below will show that quantitative restrictions in the form of quotas, voluntary export restraints, and market-sharing schemes are increasingly relied upon to reduce exchange-rate risk as relative currency values become more volatile. One possible caveat to our analysis is that it is static. From a dynamic standpoint, one may be tempted to argue that a country can engage in intertemporal optimization under the floating exchange-rate system by hedging efficiently in the forward exchange market. If exchange risks are fully hedged, there will then be no need for quota protection to stabilize domestic prices. However, the crucial assumption in this line of thinking is that exchange risks can indeed be effectively hedged. As we will argue in chapter 20, under many circumstances, economic agents *cannot* fully offset currency risks by utilizing existing markets for forward exchange. First, however, let us consider the problem in the absence of forward hedging against exchange risk.

18.2   The Nonequivalence of Tariffs and Quotas in the Face of Exchange Fluctuations

In the face of severe exchange-rate volatility, countries will attempt to utilize policies that can minimize domestic price exposure to such fluctuations. We argue that traditional fixed-rate tariffs are ineffective in reducing exchange risk. Instead, import quotas and other market sharing schemes will reduce the domestic price instability induced by exchange-rate changes. Furthermore, the severity of the quantitative restrictions required increases as the degree of exchange variability rises. As an alternative, sliding-scale tariffs and export subsidies, e.g., as utilized by the European Common Agricultural Policy program, can act as substitutes for import and export quotas for preserving domestic price stability.

To focus our analysis, figure 18.1 shows an auction market under exchange uncertainty, e.g., a market for a homogeneous agricultural good where exchange-rate changes are fully passed through into the domestic prices. DD is the net import demand curve (domestic consumption less domestic production) and μ is the mean domestic price with the corresponding mean of the exchange rate E (domestic currency/foreign currency) set initially at one. As the exchange rate depreciates, the domestic

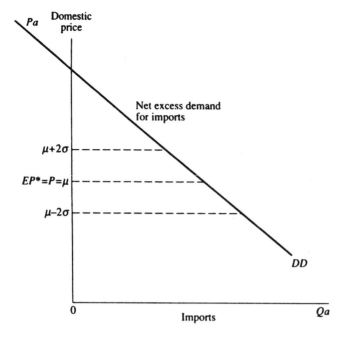

Figure 18.1
Exchange-rate and domestic price fluctuations under free trade.

price rises above μ while an exchange appreciation causes the domestic price to fall below μ. For illustrative purposes, we assume that under free trade, the domestic price varies from $\mu + 2\sigma$ to $\mu - 2\sigma$, with $P\varepsilon[\mu + 2\sigma, \mu - 2\sigma]$ and $E\varepsilon[1 + 2\sigma, 1 - 2\sigma]$. σ is the standard deviation of the exchange rate and of the domestic price.

If a fixed ad valorem tariff is imposed, the mean domestic price rises to $(1 + t)\mu$. But the variability is not reduced, with $P\varepsilon[1 + t)(\mu + 2\sigma), (1 + t)(\mu - 2\sigma)]$, as long as the tariff is not prohibitive. The spread of the domestic price is merely shifted up. The case of the fixed tariff is shown in figure 18.2.

Consider instead an import quota as illustrated in figure 18.3. First, suppose a quota of Q' is imposed coinciding with expected imports under free trade. Under this restriction, the domestic price is stabilized if the exchange rate appreciates above the initial $E = 1$. For example if the exchange rate is at E', the domestic price remains at μ rather than falling to P'. The discrepancy between the world price and the domestic price will create

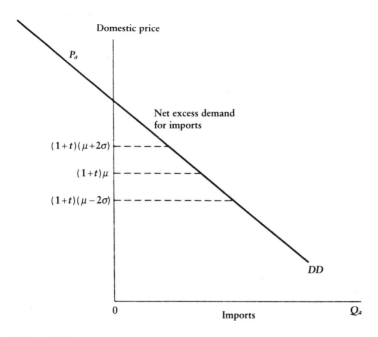

Figure 18.2
Exchange-rate and domestic price fluctuations under an ad valorem tariff.

a per unit quota rent of $\mu - P'$. Note however that if the exchange rate depreciates, the domestic price will still increase. An import quota of Q' will only preserve price stability for $E\varepsilon[1,1-2\sigma]$.

In order to stabilize prices over the range of $E\varepsilon[1+2\sigma, 1-2\sigma]$, the import quota must be more restrictive and set no higher than Q. Essentially the quota truncates the import demand curve, and the corresponding price acts like a price floor. From figure 18.3, it is easily seen that the restrictiveness of the quota necessary to stabilize domestic prices depends on the variability of the exchange rate. In other words, as the volatility of the exchange rate increases, the import quota must be reduced to keep the import price from fluctuating. Trade then becomes more and more restricted, and the average domestic price and the (variable) license rent get higher.

By focusing on the third quadrant of figure 18.3, we can further illustrate the case where the country is exporting instead of importing. This will be the situation if the average price is at

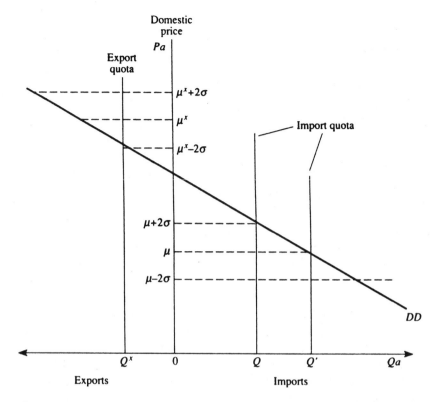

Figure 18.3
Exchange-rate and domestic price fluctuations under either import or export quotas.

μ^x with $P\ \varepsilon[\mu^x\ -\ 2\sigma,\ \mu^x\ +\ 2\sigma]$ under free trade. By similar argument as before, a restrictive export quota at Q^x will stabilize the domestic price at $\mu^x\ -\ 2\sigma$ or slightly below.

18.3 Empirical Overview

In parallel with the broad trend toward tariff reductions, there has been in the past fifteen years a serious move toward making interbloc quantitative restrictions more extensive. To underscore the growing importance of nontariff barriers, table 18.1 presents nontariff measures for OECD countries for the years 1981, 1983, and 1986.

Table 18.1 shows that, in 1981, hard-core nontariff barriers were used in 15.1 percent of OECD nonpetroleum imports. This

Table 18.1
The Share of OECD Country Nonpetroleum Imports Subject to Hard-Core Nontariff Barriers

Importers/Trade Partners	1981	1983	1986	1981–86 Change
OECD/world	15.1	16.7	17.7	+2.6
OECD/developed	14.3	16.3	17.5	+3.2
OECD/developing	18.8	19.6	20.6	+1.8
OECD/socialist	9.3	10.2	9.8	+0.5

Source: Laird and Yeats (1990).
Note: Hard-core nontariff barriers include variable import levies and product-specific charges; quotas; prohibitions; nonautomatic import authorizations including restrictive import licensing requirements; quantitative "voluntary" export restraints; and trade restraints under the Multifiber Agreement. OECD countries include: Belgium-Luxembourg, Denmark, France, West Germany, Great Britain, Greece, Ireland, Italy, Netherlands, Finland, Japan, New Zealand, Norway, and the U.S.

would mean that $80 billion in trade was affected by hard-core NTBs. Table 18.1 also shows that in 1981, 14.3 percent or $49 billion of OECD imports from other developed countries were affected by hard-core NTBs. More importantly, table 18.1 illustrates the rising importance of NTBs. Overall, from 1981 to 1986 the share of imports affected by hard-core NTBs rose by 2.6 percent, an increase equivalent to covering approximately an additional $14 billion in trade.

Table 18.2 further disaggregates the changes in the use of nontariff barriers in sixteen OECD countries. The individual country statistics show that the U.S. had the greatest expansion in new trade restrictions as the share of U.S. imports affected rose from 11.4 percent in 1981 to 17.3 percent in 1986. For the EEC, the index rises from 13.4 percent to 15.8 percent over the same five-year period.

True, the data in tables 18.1 and 18.2 cover only the relatively short time frame from 1981 to 1986. But we hypothesize that the increasing tendency to use NTBs in *interbloc* transacting has continued from the mid 1970s into the 1990s. Only within emerging trading blocs where countries have succeeded in stabilizing exchange rates among themselves—as within the EEC or North American Free Trade Area—have quantitative barriers to trade been reduced.

Table 18.2
Share of Nonpetroleum Imports Subject to Hard-Core Nontariff Barriers: Individual Countries

Importer	1981	1983	1986	1981–86 Change
Belgium-Luxembourg	12.6	15.4	14.3	1.7
Denmark	6.7	8.0	7.9	1.2
Germany, West	11.8	13.6	15.4	3.6
France	15.7	18.8	18.6	2.9
Greece	16.2	21.0	20.1	3.9
Great Britain	11.2	13.4	12.8	1.6
Ireland	8.2	9.7	9.7	1.5
Italy	17.2	18.7	18.2	1.0
Netherlands	19.9	21.4	21.4	1.5
EEC (10)	13.4	15.6	15.8	2.4
Switzerland	19.5	19.6	19.6	0.1
Finland	7.9	8.0	8.0	0.1
Japan	24.4	24.5	24.3	−0.1
Norway	15.2	14.7	14.2	−1.0
New Zealand	46.4	46.4	32.4	−14.0
United States	11.4	13.7	17.3	5.9
All above	15.1	16.7	17.7	2.6

Source: Laird and Yeats (1990).

In the last section, we demonstrated that fluctuating exchange rates are unpredictable and cannot be fully hedged. Sharp volatility of the exchange rates translates into big fluctuations in the domestic currency prices of tradable goods. This problem of exchange-rate induced price variability is magnified in some specific sectors such as agriculture, where the goods produced are homogeneous and the market structure is perfectly competitive. In the absence of quantitative restrictions on foreign trade, exchange-rate pass-through in agriculture is immediate and complete.[1]

18.4   Agricultural Protectionism within the EEC

The problem of exchange-rate changes and the domestic currency prices of agriculture is vividly illustrated by the experience in the EEC before exchange rates were effectively stabilized through the European Monetary System (EMS). As we will show, a dizzying array of policy instruments, including artificial exchange rates for agriculture ("green" rates) and border agricultural taxes and subsidies called Monetary Compensatory Amounts (MCAs), were employed to shield national farm prices from the effects of intra-EEC exchange-rate fluctuations and to deal with the consequences of such insulated prices.

Now, this complicated apparatus of sliding-scale import tariffs and export subsidies is mainly applied to external EEC agricultural trade with the rest of the world. Therefore, if international agricultural trade is liberalized between the U.S. and the EEC by, say, substituting modest fixed-rate ad valorem tariffs for the system of pseudo quotas (sliding-scale tariffs and export subsidies), national food prices will be directly affected by the volatile exchange rate between the U.S. dollar and the European currencies. The European objective of stabilizing agricultural prices will then become increasingly difficult, if not impossible.

Without a stable exchange-rate system, well-meaning talks of liberalizing the world trade of agriculture, as those sponsored by the GATT within the current Uruguay Round, will always run counter to the European (or Japanese) desire to maintain price stability in agriculture. This partly explains the great reluctance on the part of the EEC to negotiate for trade liberalization in agriculture.

To highlight the problems posed by exchange-rate variability for the agricultural sector, we will briefly describe the history, institutions, and policies of the European Common Market and the Common Agricultural Policy (CAP). As noted by Giavazzi and Giovannini (1990), "postwar European institutions—particularly the common agricultural market—depend for their survival on exchange rate stability."

The main objective of the CAP is to maintain uniform support prices in agriculture. The EEC in 1962 decided that the "European Unit of Account" (EUA) which was defined in terms of quantities of gold equal in value to 1 U.S. dollar, would be used for the determination of agricultural prices under the CAP. The official IMF exchange rates between the European currencies and the dollar would then be used to convert the CAP prices into each member's national currency.

In the early phases of the Bretton Woods fixed exchange-rate system, the EUA-based CAP prices worked well to preserve agricultural price stability. However, as exchange-rate realignments occurred more frequently in the late 1960s, domestic agricultural prices began to diverge among members of the EEC. Consequently, a system of compensating border taxes and subsidies was needed.

As described in detail by Gardiner and Josling (1991), the beginning of the exchange-rate problem for CAP occurred when France devalued its currency by 12.5 percent in August 1969. Before the devaluation, the minimum price floor for wheat in the EEC was 98.75 EUA/ton. Using the official exchange rates, the French and German governments can calculate their respective intervention prices. Intervention prices are domestic prices that the EEC guarantees to purchase from farmers.

After the French devaluation, agricultural prices in the EEC were kept fixed in terms of the EUA. Using the new franc exchange rate would mean an increase in agricultural prices in France of 12.5 percent.

At that time, the French government wished to avoid the political costs of food inflation in France. To stabilize agricultural support prices in domestic currency, France was allowed to use the predevaluation exchange rate to calculate the franc equivalent of the CAP prices. Thus a "green" exchange rate was "created" for the sole purpose of calculating agricultural support prices.

The use of the green rate led to lower agricultural prices in France compared to other EEC countries. The price divergence created arbitrage opportunities that would eventually defeat the purpose of containing food-price inflation in France. To prevent arbitrage, Monetary Compensatory Amounts (MCAs) were adopted. MCAs are border taxes and subsidies aimed at insulating the domestic-currency prices from exchange-rate realignments.

In this case for France, the MCAs took the form of export taxes and import subsidies and are called negative MCAs.[2] Basically MCAs are the difference in the French intervention prices before and after the franc devaluation. These taxes and subsidies were administered at the border posts.

The problem of exchange-rate realignment and agricultural prices was by no means unique to France. In October 1969, West Germany revalued the mark by 8.5 percent. In the case of wheat, this would imply a drop of the intervention price and a decline in the income of German farmers. Like the French, the West Germans decided to use the old rate to keep the food price stable in DM. As in the case of the French green rate, MCAs were needed to prevent arbitrage. Thus an import tax and an export subsidy were applied at the German border. West Germany, which maintains its support price above the uniform level, is said to have positive MCAs.[3]

Giavazzi and Giovannini (1990) provide a clear hypothetical example of how the MCAs work, which we modify for our illustration:

Suppose ... 1 EUA = 1 DM = 1 lira, and the intervention price for milk is 10 EUA liter. A realignment occurs, implying a 10% appreciation of the Deutsche mark and 10% depreciation of the lira, both relative to the EUA. The intervention price for milk is unaffected by the realignment. Therefore, the price for milk after the realignment should fall to 9 marks in Germany and rise to 11 lira in Italy. However, domestic currency prices are kept unchanged. After the realignment the price of milk in Germany stays at 10 DM, thus effectively rising from 10 to 11 EUAs; in Italy, it stays at 10 lira, thus falling from 10 to 9 EUAs. The EEC eliminates the possibility of arbitrage profits by taxing milk exports from Italy and subsidizing milk exports from Germany. For each liter of milk that a German farmer exports to Italy, he receives 1 EUA (a positive MCA) from the EEC that compensates him for the lower prices on the Italian market. Conversely, when an Italian farmer ships milk to Germany he is taxed; the tax rate is also equal to 1 EUA (a negative MCA).[4]

The MCAs, as discussed earlier, are designed as temporary devices to help stabilize farm prices and they are supposed to be removed over the long run. But the removal of the MCAs has proven to be uneven. In weak-currency countries such as France and Italy, negative MCAs are from time to time eliminated by domestic price increases. But for strong countries like West Germany and the Netherlands, the positive MCAs tend to persist.

Positive MCAs are difficult to remove because the required adjustment is one of domestic price decline. This would lead to a drop in farm income. Well-organized domestic farmers will lobby strongly against such measures. In contrast, the removal of negative MCAs leads to price rises, which will have the support of the farm community. Indeed, such asymmetric adjustment was codified in 1979 in the EEC's "Gentlemen's

Agreement," stating that any removal of MCAs should not lead to a drop of domestic farm prices.

Thus nominal exchange-rate changes interact with the political economy of the MCAs, leading to a real impact on agricultural production in Europe. Relatively speaking, farm production is stimulated in strong-currency countries while production is discouraged in weak-currency countries. The biased adjustments of MCAs create a ratchet effect on European farm prices. In fact, the average intervention prices have been rising over time. Overproduction of agricultural products worsens in Europe and this puts a further strain on the budget of the EEC. For example, in 1984, support for milk and dairy products was the single largest item on the EEC budget, accounting for 20 percent.

Green exchange rates, and positive and negative MCAs are the direct and indirect consequences of the Europeans' attempt to stabilize farm prices in the face of exchange-rate variability. The Europeans are well aware of the fact that exchange-rate fluctuations would endanger the CAP and the creation of a customs union. As early as 1969, the Barre Report stated "the commission estimates that a widening of the fluctuation margins for the exchange rates of member countries would pose important problems in the area of the common agricultural policy and in that of trade relations in the community, and especially that it would compromise the further integration of markets."

The EEC's concern for currency fluctuations and their impact on domestic prices is clearly reflected in the Uruguay Round talks on agriculture. Currently, a variable levy system is used in the Community to offset any changes in the world price of agricultural products. Given the dollar gyrations in the 1980s, it is safe to say that an important source, if not the dominant source of farm price instability, is currency variability. With their experience of recent exchange-rate changes, the Europeans are keen to protect agricultural producers and consumers from future fluctuations of exchange rates.

Given our discussions of the comparative insulation properties of tariffs and quantitative restrictions in section 18.2, one may ask why import levies are used by the EEC for external protection. However, as we will show next, a *variable* levy system is fundamentally different from a fixed-rate tariff. In terms of preserving internal price stability, sliding-scale import taxes are equivalent to quotas where the government appropriates the license fees or quota "rents." Thus as a substitute for a quota, we can examine the price effects of a sliding-scale tariff or a variable levy. If we can condition t to depend on σ and with $t < 0$ representing an import subsidy, then a sliding-scale tariff $t(\sigma)$ can fully preserve domestic price stability. For example, in figure 18.4, if the exchange rate appreciates and the corresponding domestic price incipiently falls to $\mu - 2\sigma$, a tariff of $t = 2\sigma$ will restore the price to μ. Similarly, if the domestic price incipiently rises to $\mu + 2\sigma$ from exchange depreciation, an import subsidy of $t = -2\sigma$ will lower the price back to μ.

If the industry in question is instead a natural exporter and operating at an initial price of μ^x with exchange and price variability measured by $P\varepsilon[\mu^x - 2\sigma, \mu_x + 2\sigma]$, then a sliding scale export subsidy $S(\sigma)$ can be used to stabilize export prices. For example, if the incipient price falls to $\mu^x - 2\sigma$ due to exchange appreciation, an export subsidy of 2σ can restore the mean export

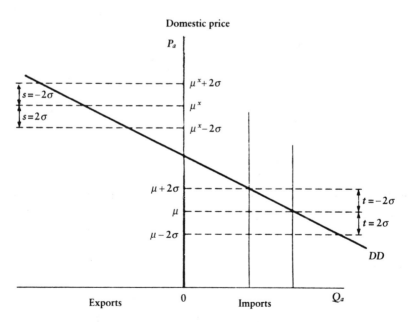

Figure 18.4
Exchange-rate fluctuations offset by sliding-scale tariffs and export subsidies.

price of μ^x. If instead the incipient price jumps up to $\mu^x + 2\sigma$, an export tax of 2σ can be used to preserve price stability.

18.5 Manufactures

In manufacturing industries, unlike the farm sector, the goods produced range from being homogeneous (for example, cement or low-cost garments) to highly differentiated (for example, consumer electronics or automobiles). The market structures in manufacturing are thus heterogeneous, with some industries having more monopolistic powers than others. Given such diversity, it is not surprising that exchange-rate volatility will have a much richer set of linkages with potential trade policy responses in manufactures.

The general impact of fluctuating exchange rates on the creation and the sustaining of trade barriers is, however, similar to that discussed in earlier sections. A nominal appreciation of the dollar, given the inertia in price levels, leads to a real U.S. exchange-rate appreciation. This has an adverse effect on the competitiveness of the U.S. import-competing and export sectors. For the perfectly competitive manufacturing industries, the effects of the dollar appreciation are well known. As stated before, a 10 percent exchange-rate appreciation is equivalent to a 10 percent export tax plus a 10 percent import subsidy. Even if the industry is oligopolistic, the effects are generally similar. The effects on competitiveness can be demonstrated in figure 18.5. For illustrative purposes, we focus on an international Cournot–Nash quantity-setting industry.

In figure 18.5, we describe a situation where the U.S. domestic firm, producing output X, is competing with a foreign firm, producing a differentiated product Y in the U.S. market. HH is the best response curve for the U.S. home firm, i.e., HH traces out the locus of the best output of the domestic firm, given the foreign output. FF is the best response curve for the foreign firm. A dollar appreciation will shift the best response curve of the foreign firm out, resulting in increased foreign market share and a reduction of the U.S. market share. At the initial equilibrium E, the foreign firm faces a given dollar marginal revenue curve but a lower dollar marginal cost curve due to the appreciation. This leads to increased foreign output. For the U.S. domestic

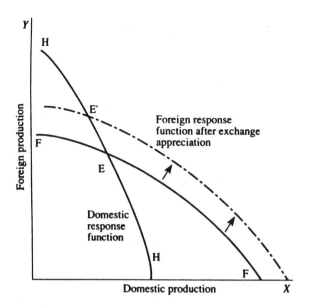

Figure 18.5
Exchange appreciation in a Cournot producer duopoly.

firm, market share, employment, and profits all decline. Figure
18.5 can also be used to describe a U.S. exporting firm competing
in the foreign market. The dollar appreciation will then have the
same effect on the U.S. firm in the export market as in the domestic market: a decline in U.S. sales, employment, and profits.

It is clear that industries are aware of the adverse competitive
effects of an appreciating currency. In 1983, the U.S. textile industry alleged that China's dual exchange rate constituted a Chinese
export subsidy. In 1984, the copper industries charged that one
of the ways in which Chile and other LDCs were subsidizing
their copper industries was by devaluing their currencies. As
the dollar rose in the first half of the 1980s, real textile exports
fell by 40 percent while imports almost doubled. In addition,
real apparel imports rose by 129 percent.

The squeeze in the export and the domestic markets caused
by the dollar appreciation led to intense lobbying by various
industries and labor groups. Unlike the scenario of multilateral
trade liberalization talks, which hurt import-competing industries but benefit the exporting industries, currency appreciation

hurts the entire tradable sector. This generates a strong coalition of industrialists and labor groups, which lobby for increased protection. For example, highly restrictive textile bills passed Congress in 1985 and in 1987. Though the bills were vetoed, the Administration responded to the lobbying pressure from the textile industry by imposing much tighter restrictions under existing arrangements and by tightening protection under the 1986 Multifiber Agreement. Protection in autos and steel was also continued. The Administration clearly understood the role of the exchange rate in increasing the protectionist sentiment. In September 1985, the Plaza Agreement was reached to coordinate actions of central banks to bring down the dollar.

An appreciating currency, as discussed earlier, creates great pressures on the government to sustain, increase, and erect trade barriers. But, in periods when the currency depreciates, it is much less likely that trade barriers will go down with the currency cycle. The reason rests again primarily on political economy grounds. With a lower home exchange rate, both producers in the home-exporting and import-competing industries tend to increase their competitiveness. From the domestic viewpoint, commercial policies to assist these firms are no longer needed. However, there are really no incentives for these producers unilaterally to give up import quotas or export subsidies. In fact, existing protectionist policies are rarely removed once they are installed since the producers and workers in the affected industries develop vested interests in these programs. The factors of production in the tradable sector will spend resources (time, money, and effort) to engage in the preservation of these policies. Furthermore, domestic producers will use the legitimate argument that new investment to reequip their industry will be too risky unless quantitative restrictions remain in place to offset the effect of any future exchange appreciation.

From the foreign country's viewpoint, the home currency's depreciation is the foreign country's exchange-rate appreciation. By the same logic described before, the foreign firms (whether they are perfectly competitive or oligopolistic) will lose market share. This leads to a drop in employment and profits. By the process of political lobbying, the foreign government will have to respond by increasing their own trade barriers.

Thus for each cycle of currency appreciation and depreciation, there will be a tendency for worldwide trade barriers to rise. Given the frequency and the magnitude of exchange-rate volatility under the floating-rate system, it is not hard to understand the increasing pressures that governments face in pursuing and sustaining various forms of trade policies.

In addition to the general tendencies of increasing pressures for adopting protectionist policies, volatility in exchange rates has also led to the adoption of specific forms of protectionism. We can describe American trade policies in the 1980s by three major tendencies: the proliferation of quantitative restrictions and other market-sharing schemes, the increased use of anti-dumping duties and countervailing duties, and unilateral trade actions (such as U.S. Super 301) in pursuit of "fair" trade.

We argue in earlier sections that the increased use of quotas, VERs, and other market-sharing schemes since the mid 1970s is a natural outcome of fluctuating exchange rates. As shown before, exchange-rate variability has the property that promotes a general rise of trade barriers. But domestic industries that seek to shield their industries from exchange-rate shocks will prefer quantitative restrictions rather than tariffs.

Unfortunately, from a welfare standpoint, the use of quantitative restrictions often leads to more pernicious effects than a fixed-rate tariff. The effects of tariffs are generally well understood. Tariffs are more transparent, and it is much easier for international negotiators to negotiate for lower tariffs.

In contrast, quantitative restrictions are much less understood, at least by the public. The lack of transparency makes it easier for the affected groups to sustain the barriers without much opposition. In the case of voluntary export restraints (VERs), the entire quota rents, i.e., the economic profits generated by the discrepancies between the domestic price and the world price, are given to the exporting country. This adds to the welfare loss of the home country. In the case of tariffs, the home country is able to capture the equivalence of the quota rents in the form of tariff revenue.

At least for some countries, there are additional reasons why countries will opt for quantitative restrictions (QRs) instead of tariffs to protect them from the fluctuating exchange rates. As discussed in McKinnon (1979), the answer may lie in politics:

"For countries with rather weak constitutional limits on the assertion of economic power by the government of the day, favorable QR allocations can reward one's political friends, and the denial of licenses—including the permission to export freely . . . can be economically devastating to groups who are politically unfriendly. And the pressures to distribute positive and negative patronage this way become more difficult to resist once a formal QR regime is put in place" (McKinnon 1991a, p. 101).

Who claims the quota rents depends on how the quantitative restrictions are administered and how the rights to import and export are licensed. In the case of VERs, the rights of the quota rents are automatically granted to the exporting country, even though who in the exporting country eventually captures the rents remains to be settled. In other instances of quotas, the importing country retains the claim to the rents.

The potential competing claims to these rents creates classic situations for rent-seeking activities, either at home or abroad. Important scarce resources including skilled professionals are diverted from production activities into lobbying and rent-seeking activities. Thus though QRs are rational responses by governments in a world of floating exchange rates, quotas and VERs generally distort the world economy to a larger degree than import taxes.

The prevalence of VERs, furthermore, can interact with old legislation such as the anti-dumping laws to generate further protectionist outcomes. As discussed earlier, VERs create economic rents that are captured by the exporting country. To allocate the rights to export, an often-practiced rule is to link the past export market share to the extent of quota licenses. Thus, if exporters perceive that a VER is probable, as perhaps due to new legislation by the U.S. Congress, then a multi-period profit-maximizing response would be to expand export sales immediately before any future VER is implemented. This is done in anticipation of future claims to the quota rents.

For perfectly competitive firms generally and for oligopolistic firms under some conditions, this will imply that foreign exporters sell in the U.S. market at below cost, thus constituting dumping.[5]

This type of dumping is not "predatory" in the usual sense, since it is not meant to drive out domestic competitors in order to establish an illegal monopoly. Rather anticipatory dumping here is a reaction to profit opportunities created by a legally sanctioned market-sharing arrangement (a VER).

Dumping, as induced by prospective VERs, will nonetheless injure domestic producers since home prices will drop. This will naturally trigger filing of anti-dumping complaints. Since there are actual dumpings, there can be one of two results. One is the imposition of an anti-dumping duty. But this may not be sufficient to deter dumping, depending on the foreign producers' perceived probable gains from the VERs. This can eventually lead to a curious mix of protection in the form of anti-dumping taxes and VERs.

Alternatively, the foreign firms can agree to the domestic producers' demand to raise export prices, thus settling the anti-dumping cases out of court. But this will have a potential effect of creating an implicit cartel between the domestic and the foreign firm. Indeed, out-of-court settlements of anti-dumping suits frequently take the form of the foreign exporter agreeing to limit his sale in the domestic market. Such a "legalized" cartel is thus sustained by an informal VER.

In either scenario, the interplay of potential VERs and anti-dumping legislation leads to further restrictive or protectionist acts. But, as mentioned before, the root of the phenomenon may lie in the floating exchange-rate system.

Another channel whereby floating exchange rates can lead to dumping is when an invoicing currency such as the U.S. dollar depreciates unexpectedly. It is fairly well known that, for a variety of differentiated manufactured goods, the export dollar prices of these goods in the U.S. are relatively fixed. But translated into dollars the price of the same good in the exporter's home country can fluctuate with the exchange rate. This can lead to price divergence. As a thought experiment, suppose a Japanese auto costs $10,000 in the U.S., 1,400,000 yen in Japan and the exchange rate is 1$ = 140 yen so that the law of one price holds initially. Now let the dollar depreciate to 1$ = 120 yen and assume that for a variety of reasons (e.g., pricing to market), the dollar price of the auto in the U.S. stays constant at $10,000. The yen price of the auto will likely be unchanged since Japanese producers have to pay wages and rents in yen. But the dollar price in Japan becomes $11,667. Thus the Japanese producers find themselves selling cheaper abroad than at home, i.e., they are dumping. This can cause complaints of dumping and can lead to anti-dumping duties.

Various countries' attempts to shield their markets from exchange-rate uncertainties feed the growing perception that these are "unfair" trade practices. The major piece of legislation used by the U.S. is the strengthened section 301 of the 1988 Omnibus Trade and Competitiveness Act: the so-called Super 301. It authorizes the Administration to retaliate against trading partners if successful negotiations are not concluded to open up their markets for U.S. exports.

As noted before, there are actual legitimate reasons why countries wish to protect their markets from exchange-rate fluctuations by means of quantitative restrictions and other market-sharing devices. On the other hand, it is also true that such attempts to shield their domestic markets can act as barriers against U.S. exports. Thus, legislation such as the Super 301 and its resulting trade tensions are companions of the current exchange-rate system.

18.6 A Concluding Note on Regional Trading Blocs

In the 1950s and 1960s, when par values for exchange rates were more or less fixed under a common monetary standard the industrial countries experienced an unprecedented increase in the growth rate of GNP and an expansion of world trade. Tariffs were reduced and quantitative restrictions were virtually eliminated. With the advent of the floating exchange-rate system after 1973, however, we witnessed an upsurge of "new" protectionist policies—including quotas, VERs, market-sharing schemes, anti-dumping, and countervailing duties.

In this chapter, we explored the hypothesis that the volatility of exchange rates contributes to the increase in these new forms of protectionism. We showed that, to maintain domestic price stability, quantitative restrictions will be preferred over fixed-rate tariffs, while sliding-scale tariffs or variable levies, as practiced in the agricultural sector in the EEC, have similar insulating properties as do quotas.

Thus does exchange-rate volatility erode the global free-trade ethic as envisioned in the GATT and its most favored nation

(MFN) principle. The tendency for the world to break down into regional trading blocs—within which more stable exchange rates based on a common monetary standard can more easily be established—has been greatly strengthened. For economies closely integrated in foreign trade, a zone of exchange-rate stability now seems necessary to preserve free trade in goods and services while reducing investment risk.

The EMS trading bloc in Europe is now paralleled by an emerging North American free trade area, where Canada and Mexico are curently orienting their domestic monetary policies toward keeping their exchange rates within a narrow range against the U.S. dollar. In the not-too-distant future, a yen-bloc among countries closely linked to the Japanese economy could well emerge.

While such regional trading blocs, each with its own common monetary standard, broaden the ambit of free trade (trade creation) internally, they are very much a second-best way of limiting the damage from global exchange-rate instability. Indeed, as long as untethered exchange rates among the major blocs of Europe, North America, and Japan continue to swing wildly of the order of 10 to 30 percent from one year to the next, interbloc protectionism in the form of quantitative restrictions, export subsidies, and generally heightened mercantilist rivalry may well be accentuated.

Notes

1. The added problem is that for some farm inputs (e.g., tractors), nominal contracts, menu costs, and pricing to markets can lead to delayed responses of input prices to exchange-rate changes. The differential responses of inputs and outputs in agriculture can greatly exacerbate the problem of income stability for farmers.

2. In trading with non-EEC countries, the MCA was subtracted from the external import levies and export subsidies.

3. Positive MCAs are added to the external import levies and export subsidies.

4. Note that, in the original example in Giavazzi and Giovannini (1990), ECUs instead of EUAs are used.

5. For references, see Yano (1989) and Anderson (1992).

References

Anderson, J. E. (1992), "Domino Dumping, I: Competitive Exporters," *American Economic Review*, March, pp. 65–88.

Dornbusch, R. (1976), "Expectations and Exchange Rate Dynamics," *Journal of Political Economy*, 84, 1161–76.

Frankel, J., and K. Froot (1988), "Chartists, Fundamentalists, and the Demand for Dollars," in Tony Courakis and Mark Taylor (eds.), *Policy Issues for Interdependent Economics*, London: Macmillan.

Frenkel, J., and M. Mussa (1980), "The Efficiency of the Foreign Exchange Market and Measures of Turbulence," *American Economic Association Papers and Proceedings*, 70, 374–81.

Friedman, M. (1967), *The Balance of Payments: Free versus Fixed Exchange Rates*, Washington, DC: American Enterprise Institute.

Gardiner, W. H., and T. E. Josling (1991), "Dismantling the EC's Agri Monetary System: Impacts on European Agriculture," mimeo, Stanford University.

Giavazzi, F., and A. Giovannini (1990), *Limiting Exchange Rate Flexibility: The European Monetary System*, Cambridge, Mass.: The MIT Press.

Johnson, H. G. (1973), "The Case for Flexible Exchange Rates," in *Further Essays in Monetary Economics*, Cambridge, Mass: Harvard University Press.

Laird, S., and A. Yeats (1990), *Quantitative Methods for Trade-Barrier Analysis*, London: Macmillan.

Meese, R., and K. Rogoff (1983), "Empirical Exchange Rate Models of the 1970s: Do They Fit Out of Sample," *Journal of International Economics*, 14, 3–24.

———. (1990), "Non-linear, Non-parametric, Non-essential Exchange Rate Estimation," *American Economic Review Papers and Proceedings*, 192–96.

McKinnon, R. I. (1979), *Money in International Exchange: The Convertible-Currency System*, New York: Oxford University Press.

———. (1991a), *The Order of Economic Liberalization: Financial Control in the Transition to a Market Economy*, Baltimore: Johns Hopkins Press.

———. (1991b), "Exchange Risk and Interest Rate Volatility in Historical Perspective," mimeo, Stanford University.

McKinnon, Ronald, and Kenichi Ohno (1989), "Purchasing Power Parity as Monetary Standard," in O. Hamouda, R. Rowley, and B. Wolf (eds.). *The Future of the International Monetary System: Change, Coordination or Instability?* Aldershot: Edward Elgar Publishing, pp. 42–67.

Morita, A. (1986), "Presentation to International Working Round on Exchange Rates and Coordination," Zurich, June 19.

Yano, M. (1989), "Voluntary Export Restraints and Expectations: An Analysis of Export Quotas in Oligopolistic Markets," *International Economic Review*, 30, 707–24.

III

International
Monetary Reform

19

A Common Monetary
Standard or a Common
Currency for Europe?
Fiscal Lessons from the
United States

19.1 Introduction

Consider an economically integrated group of countries that form an optimum currency area: the need for exchange stability is paramount.[1] As in the European Union (EU), political integration has progressed to the point where a federal system consisting of a central government and lower-level national or state governments has emerged. Under what fiscal circumstances should participating countries prefer a common currency to a common monetary standard? Once made, how does this choice constrain, or fail to constrain, each government's fiscal policies in the federal system?

Under a common monetary standard, national currencies remain in circulation. But member countries agree on a common monetary policy consistent with fixing exchange rates within narrow bands—say, 2 percent. Without disrupting trade or investment, these minor variations in exchange rates are sufficient to separate the domain of each national currency from the others, and the clearing of international payments typically devolves from central banks to commercial banks (McKinnon 1979). A common monetary standard can encompass a wide range of countries. The international gold standard from 1879 to 1914, and the fixed-rate dollar standard from 1950 to 1970, were virtually worldwide in scope.

Among the more closely integrated Western European economies, whether or not to dispense with exchange-rate bands

Originally published in *Scottish Journal of Political Economy*, 41, 4 (November 1994): 337–357. Reprinted with permission.

altogether and adopt a single currency is (was) the immediate concern. To the negotiators of the Single European Act of 1986 leading to the Maastricht Agreement in 1991, moving from a nascent common monetary standard to a common currency seemed a natural forward step to more complete financial and commodity market integration. Money-changing costs irritating tourists at airports—which are generally over 5 percent of the gross transaction value—would be eliminated.[2] In addition, fixed exchange rates would, seemingly, be better secured if national monies were completely withdrawn from circulation. The American monetary union with but one currency successfully circulating throughout the 50 states was the model.

But the right currency model for Europe is elusive. To prepare for full monetary integration in the late 1990s, the authorities in 1987 removed their remaining capital controls while pledging to keep exchange rates fixed henceforth—rather than leaving them adjustable. This proved to be "a bridge too far." Speculative attacks against the exchange rate pegs in 1992 and 1993 forced some members out of the European Exchange Rate Mechanism (ERM)—while others had to accept dramatically wider exchange-rate bands. The momentum for further integration in the EU was severely weakened. In 1994, once-burned European central bankers are loathe even to discuss the mutual stabilization of exchange rates—let alone discuss (re)establishing a common monetary standard with narrow bands (*Financial Times*, 11 April 1994, p. 3).

19.2 The Impossibility of Fixed Exchange Rates between National Currencies with Free Capital Mobility?

All too easily, one could draw the wrong lessons from these unfortunate episodes. Several writers, most particularly Barry Eichengreen (1993), now argue that fixed exchange rates can only be secured by complete monetary unification under a common currency. Richard Portes (1993, p. 2) puts this now prevailing view most strongly: "'Permanently' fixed exchange rates is an oxymoron." In the absence of capital controls, official par values for exchange rates between national currencies will invite speculative attack(s) that eventually undermine the currency pegs themselves. The only viable alternatives are floating without meaningful par values or complete monetary unification, i.e., a common currency without an exit option (Obstfeld 1992).

The failure of the EU countries to secure their exchange rates against speculative attack in 1992–93 seemed to vindicate this new wisdom. And, going one step further, Eichengreen (1993) argues that the gains from having a common currency aren't that great anyway. Among other things, the "lower" level national governments would be inhibited from taking countercyclical action against region-specific downturns; while the taxes and expenditures by the EU central government remain too small to provide automatic regional stabilization.[3] In contrast, the U.S. Federal Government's much larger flow of revenues and expenditures substantially cushions downturns in American regional incomes (Sala-i-Martin and Sachs 1992). Thus Eichengreen concludes:

There is no technical reason why a single currency is required to reap the benefits of a single market. In principle, factor- and product-market integration can proceed under floating exchange rates as well as under a common currency . . . (p. 1353).

In effect, the new wisdom goads the authorities either to push forward to the common-currency ideal or to live with virtually no-par floating—perhaps within very wide "soft" bands. And it suggests that a common monetary standard is not feasible.

. . . the one alternative that is not viable is fixed exchange rates between distinct national currencies (Eichengreen, p. 1354).

Here I take a different tack. By looking at the American economic model, I first show that a common currency in a federal system has potential advantages well beyond what the new wisdom suggests. Second, although fiscal conditions in Europe are not right for establishing a common currency, a common European monetary standard is feasible, and highly desirable.

19.3 Hard Budget Constraints in a Theory of Market-Preserving Federalism

If central, provincial, and local governments credibly commit themselves to suitably constrained competition with each other, this can generate what Barry Weingast calls "market-preserving federalism."

Market-preserving federalism limits the degree to which a political system can encroach on markets. . . . It simultaneously induces competition among the lower political jurisdictions while placing restrictions on the economic policy making of the national government. . . . It has played a central role in the economic rise of those nations which have been the richest in the world over the past several centuries: The Dutch Republic in the late 16th and early 17th centuries, England in the 18th century, and the United States in the mid-19th century (Weingast 1995, p. i).

Because government borrowing capacity depends heavily on the conditions of money and credit in the economy, market-preserving federalism depends as much on monetary arrangements at each level of government as it does on tax and expenditure assignments. Both monetary and fiscal conditions together then determine the hardness or softness of government budget constraints, and whether or not intergovernmental competition is appropriate.

In the formerly socialist economies of Asia and Eastern Europe, the problem of securing macroeconomic control is dominated by the need to harden, or reform, the "soft" budget constraints of enterprises (Kornai 1990; McKinnon 1993).

In the EU and U.S., as in most capitalist economies, the budget constraints of private enterprises are generally hard in Kornai's sense. However, the budget constraints on their governments could be "soft." Politicians usually have much shorter time horizons than needed for intertemporal optimization for the society as a whole—particularly if the welfare of future generations is considered (Buchanan 1987). Although endemic, this political short-termism can be kept under control if governments are subject to the following conditions:

1. No borrowing to finance current-account spending. Either current deficit spending is limited constitutionally, or by capital-market rationing (our main concern in this paper), or by some combination of the two. Without violating this condition, self-liquidating capital-account expenditures could still be deficit financed.

2. No residual finance from, or commingling of revenues with, other (levels of) government. Revenue sharing or equalization grants across governmental jurisdictions don't exist or are strictly delimited.

3. No restraints on the movement of industry, labour, or capital among government jurisdictions.

4. Open tax competition from other governments, similarly constrained financially, to attract industry, labour, or capital.

The familiar Tiebout model (1956) of efficient horizontal competition among local governments is reflected in conditions (3) and (4). No one government can levy taxes in its jurisdiction unless the revenue so generated finances efficient public goods production, or other commensurate benefits, for the region's taxpayers—who are otherwise free to move.

Tiebout implicitly presumed that conditions (1) and (2) were also satisfied—which need not be the case in practice. However, (1) and (2) are necessary conditions for assuring that (4) is welfare-improving. For tax competition to be benign rather than destructive, budget constraints on governments should be "virtually" hard, i.e., their borrowing capacity must be limited. Then, tax competition itself further restricts governmental borrowing capacity to finance current deficits.

If conditions (1) to (4) all hold, government budget constraints—in both the ability to tax and in access to credit—are then so hard that the short-termism of politicians is inconsequential.[4]

19.4 The Monetary System and Government Borrowing

In any federal system of government, a common currency under the secure jurisdiction of the central government (or other outside agent) can greatly harden the budgetary constraints on member governments. Once the lower governments can no longer issue their own money, or tap seigniorage from the central government's monetary system, or borrow or receive fiscal supplements (revenue sharing) from the central government, then their budget constraints become harder in the sense of satisfying conditions (1) and (2).

If, in addition, free trade is imposed within the union (condition (3) above) as within the EU and U.S., horizontal mercantile competition among member states then fully hardens governmental budget constraints while simultaneously improving resource allocation. Then, regulatory, tax, and expenditure competition among these subcentral governments becomes more benign than destructive. Within the American economic union, individual state governments are forced to withdraw economically unwise or inefficient tax and expenditure programmes (and other interventions) that distort labour and commodity markets—as illustrated below. I have called this horizontal fiscal competition among the states "market-preserving fiscal federalism" (McKinnon 1996).

But the U.S. Federal Government owns the central bank issuing the common currency. Because the Federal Reserve System now issues unbacked fiat money which is the definitive means of payment in the economy,[5] the federal government's budget constraint is inherently "soft" relative to that of the states. Why?

When the government owns its own central bank, everybody knows that, in a crisis, it can always "print money," i.e., use the inflation tax, to pay interest and principal and thus avoid outright default on the face value of its obligations.[6] Because owning the central bank greatly reduces any risk of outright default, the government can then preempt the national capital market to issue treasury securities at lower interest rates than can high-quality private borrowers whose debt is also denominated in the national curency.

Consequently, at every term to maturity, government bonds are considered to be the "safest" financial instruments denominated in the national currency. In the United States, the highest grade AAA corporate bonds usually pay an interest rate a percentage point or so higher than on long-term U.S. Treasury bonds—and B-grade corporate bonds pay about 2 percentage points higher while unrated "junk" bonds may pay 5 percentage points or more. After allowing for tax differences, interest rates on the debt of American state and local governments is also substantially higher than that on federal debt. The rationale for higher interest rates on private-sector or local government debt is that companies and lower governments are subject to commercial risk, i.e., the threat of bankruptcy, which the federal government is not, and holders of private securities (or those of local governments) face the same inflation risk as do holders of claims on the federal government.

Ownership of the central bank, when it is the source of definitive money in the system, confers a closely related financial advantage. When in fiscal distress, the central government doesn't face the threat of being rationed completely out of the national capital market.

In contrast, a state government or private borrower facing ongoing financial distress will have to pay a higher, and then a higher interest rate. If the crisis continues, at some point the putative borrower will be rationed out altogether no matter how high an interest rate he appears willing to pay. The higher interest rate is not credible because it makes default even more likely. The incentive for the bond issuer to repudiate his high-interest debt has become too high—so creditors refuse to lend on any terms.

But the money-issuing (central) government in distress need never be forced to repudiate domestic-currency debt. Even if highly inflationary and unpopular, it can always "print the money," or, like modern-day Brazil, issue highly liquid short-term financial assets that can be quickly converted into the definitive means of payment. Even when inflation becomes very high, a money-issuing government need not endure absolute credit rationing unless its currency is displaced by an alternative money controlled by some outside agency.

In the United States, therefore, the federal government can borrow "too easily" in the national capital markets—and much more easily than the state governments. Unless some other statutory or constitutional restraining device can be constructed to limit the federal government's direct and indirect borrowing, vertical competition between the American central and state governments tends to be unbalanced. The former encroaches too much on what once seemed to be the constitutionally protected residual powers of the states in ways that are *not*, by and large, market preserving. Whence the American constitutional dilemma: How to constrain the ambit of the federal leviathan when its budget constraint is much softer than those of the equally sovereign state governments.

In principle, shouldn't the nascent European federal system also benefit from more or less unrestricted horizontal competition among its national governments? Only if the European national governments had hard budget constraints similar to their American state counterparts. But as long as each issues its own fiat money under the control of its own central bank, European national governments also suffer (enjoy?) inherently soft budget constraints more like the American federal government's. Each can issue debt denominated in its national currency at the lowest interest rates—while avoiding the problem of being rationed out of the national capital market altogether.

(Fiscally weak European governments have gone one step further and used capital controls on foreign-exchange transactions in order to ensure that this preemption is complete. National savers are forced to buy the national government's bonds at lower interest rates than would otherwise prevail if they had the option to buy foreign bonds. In effect, capital controls are a back-door method of taxing national savers. In a wide variety of countries with capital controls, Giovannini and de Melo (1993) estimate that government revenue from this "financial repression" amounts to about 1 to 3 percent of GNP. The upshot is a further softening of the budget constraint on the government in question.)

Unrestricted competition among soft-budget governments then becomes suspect—and sometimes malign. In Europe for example, old inefficient state-owned industries are often heavily subsidized and new industry may receive unduly expensive tax exemptions. Whence the chronic political need within Europe to collectively restrain—by central government action or adjudication—the national governments' mercantilist instincts. For example, the EU Commission is always trying to force member governments to limit ongoing production subsidies, or to limit the number of times loss-making industries can be "recapitalized" by their respective national governments contributing more soft loans or equity capital.

In contrast, the American federal government pays little or no attention to mercantilist rivalry among the states—rivalry that is quite restrained by European standards. Important as the monetary mechanism itself might be in hardening the budget positions of the states, market-preserving federalism in the United States can only be fully appreciated if the division of fiscal and constitutional powers between the central government and the state governments is further spelled out.

19.5   Tax Assignments in the American Union and Competition among the States

Under the American Constitution, the federal government and the state governments are each sovereign in legislating taxes—with local governments being chartered or owned by their respective states. Are there significant constraints on the taxing powers of these various levels of government?

In 1913, the passage of the 16th Amendment to the U.S. Constitution permitted the central government to levy income taxes. (The state governments had not by law been similarly constrained.) Prior to 1913, the U.S. Federal Government was limited to customs duties or commodity excises. From the original Constitution, federal taxes must be uniform throughout the country, and export taxes are prohibited. The states are limited to taxing within their own jurisdictions, and they cannot interfere with interstate or foreign commerce. Beginning in the early 19th century, each state, except for one (Vermont) has amended its own constitution to limit, but not eliminate, its ability to issue general purpose debt.

Responsibility for the national defence, a national currency, and the financing of a federal judiciary was assigned to the central government. The Constitution was not explicit about state government spending obligations—other than to assign residual powers to the states. All governmental functions not explicitly specified in the original Constitution were to devolve to the states—provided there was no infringement on the freedom of interstate commerce.

Otherwise, the American federal system of taxation and public expenditures has been fairly free to evolve according to the ebb and flow of political pressures and market forces. Here I focus briefly on the current structure of taxes, and tax competition, arising out of this competitive interaction.

Courtesy of the Advisory Commission on Intergovernmental Relations (ACIR), figure 19.1 shows rather dramatically how taxes (not counting Social Security contributions) have come to be apportioned across all three levels of government.

At the Federal Government level, income taxes, both personal and corporate, account for almost 90 percent of revenue. Although states rely moderately on income taxation, the amount of

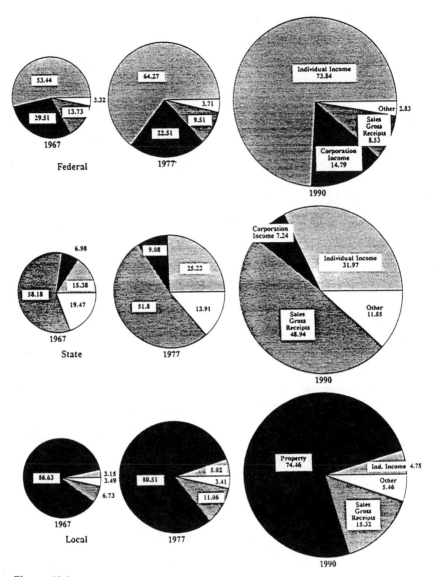

Figure 19.1
Specific taxes as a percentage of total tax revenue, selected years, 1967, 1977, 1990 (in percent).
Source: Taken from ACIR, *Significant Features of Fiscal Federalism,* vol. 2, 1992.

income redistribution that any one state can attempt is inherently limited by higher-income people migrating out of the state in question, and lower-income people moving in. That graduated personal income taxes (and redistributive transfers to the poor) should be assigned to the central government is one of the hoariest chestnuts in the theory of public finance—and is satisfied in the American case.[7]

(Although labour is not highly mobile internationally, capital is increasingly so. Thus international competition reduces the ability of even the U.S. Federal Government to tax capital. Figure 19.1 shows the share of corporate profits taxes falling from about 30 percent of total revenue before 1967 to 15 percent in 1990.)

At the "pure" state level, about half the revenue comes from the retail sales taxes (figure 19.1). Only in fairly mature market economies with relatively large "organized" retail outlets is it feasible to depend on just the retail stage for tax collection—and only then if the rates are kept modest within the 5–9 percent range. (The VAT rose to prominence in Europe in the 1950s because of the problems the French tax authorities had in collecting revenue from small shopkeepers!)

With the central government maintaining a hands-off policy, horizontal competition among states levying their own independent retail sales taxes promotes more efficient resource allocation. Individual states cannot levy a really high tax on any one consumer product because residents will buy it out of state. Interstate competition pushes states toward keeping rates moderate and the base broad. For example, a relatively modest 5 percent levy on all consumer goods and services gives little incentive for families to shop out of state—although evasion by interstate mail-order sales remains a problem that has only been partially corrected.

The same competitive arbitrage that prevents states from varying their sales tax rates limits local governments even more—to the point where local sales taxes are not used at all in most localities. Because the property tax base is much less mobile in the short and intermediate runs, the property tax has become the mainstay of local government public finance in the United States (figure 19.1).

What about sumptuary sales or excise taxes on "sin" goods, or consumption goods with very low price elasticities of demand? It is no accident that high taxes on tobacco, alcohol, and some jewelry are largely collected by the U.S. central government. (A high retail tax on gasoline would also fall more naturally into the central government's domain.) If any state levied an unusually high sumptuary tax on any one product, it would lose revenue as buyers shopped in those states whose rates were moderate.[8] So sumptuary taxes are best assigned to the central government.

In another dimension, tax competition for new industry can force individual states to rationalize their sales taxes by converting to a more pure "consumption" based format.

Once perfectly at home in Silicon Valley, Intel, the master of the microchip is now spreading outside of California, and is building a $1 billion semiconductor plant in New Mexico. The firm also saved itself $114m in hand outs from the New Mexico government, but that was not all. The firm also saved itself $65m by not having to pay sales tax for its new factory outside of Albuquerque. . . .

In California, where unemployment is running three percentage points higher than the national average, . . . assemblymen in Sacramento voted overwhelmingly in favor of a bill to eliminate the sales tax on production machinery. It will cost the cash strapped state $600m in lost revenue in the year ahead. But with luck, it might stop future Intels from moving out. (*The Economist*, 17 July 1993, p. 24)

Beyond taxation, interstate competition for industry encompasses the whole regulatory framework that states and local governments employ.

. . . between 1987 and 1992, California lost 107,000 jobs to surrounding states. Mexico was the biggest winner, gaining 21% of the California facilities, followed by Nevada with 11% and Texas with 10%. . . .

Most of the firms in the study blamed California's business climate. Health insurance premiums, which cost companies that pay them an annual $8,000 per year in California, are only half as much, on average in Nevada. Workers' compensation for injury or stress is typically 50% more important in California than in neighboring states.

What is (also) driving companies out of California is the frustration of having to comply with so many regulatory agencies at city, county, state, and federal levels. A company wanting to plant a tree in Los Angeles County has to get permission from 8 different agencies. To chop it down and make furniture from the timber requires 47 more permits. (op. cit., p. 24)

Subsequently, the State of California did make quite strenuous efforts to simplify its environmental regulations and limit claims for workers' compensation in ways that could be fairly described as "market preserving."

19.6 The Competitive Solution to the Problem of "Backward" Areas

What about backward or very poor areas? A hallmark of European fiscal policies is the idea that intergovernmental equalization grants or tax breaks for poor areas, which violate condition (2) above, are the normal mode of public finance. Won't unrestricted horizontal competition among the hard-budget governments simply lead to the rich getting richer and the poor getting poorer?

In the now unitary state of Great Britain, Whitehall provides almost all the finance for local-government spending—including intricate and detailed guidelines on how those funds should be spent.[9] Britain's postwar fiscal history is replete with "equalization" grants for almost every conceivable purpose—including grants for the preservation of crofting in Scotland that are virtually guaranteed to keep the rural highland areas poor. Uniformity in national tax rates was fractured. Enterprise zones with highly differentiated national tax rates under regional development boards proliferated to the point where even Margaret Thatcher had difficulty getting rid of them.

Similarly, within the now unitary state of Italy, local governments barely exist as fiscally autonomous entities. Even more than in Britain, variegated grants from postwar Italy's central government proliferated to all its municipalities—with special classes of subsidies for state-owned enterprises investing in poor regions. Since the early 1950s, this has aggregated to a huge net transfer—about 10 percent of GNP annually—from the wealthier north to the relatively poor Mezzogiorno. But, by the 1990s, the gap between the Italian north and south remains wide—and may be getting wider (Hilt 1994).

In the Federal Republic of Germany, condition (1) above seems fairly well satisfied: the lander governments are constitutionally restricted from borrowing. However, massive intergovernmental transfers—from wealthy lander to poorer ones, and increasingly from the federal government to the poorer eastern lander, are violating condition (2) and softening the budget constraints on the lower-level governments. Because these financial transfers are the fiscal props behind keeping wages high and unemployment benefits generous in the less developed east, they are also a major barrier to attracting industry into eastern Germany.

In Europe more generally, the principle of equalization grants across national governments from the wealthy members of the EU to Spain, Portugal, Greece, and Ireland seems well established. Below the national level, the EU development fund subsidizes poor regions throughout the Union.

In the American federal system by contrast, there are no block transfers from wealthy states to poor ones, and very little in the way of general purpose transfers (or revenue sharing) from the federal government to the state governments. The lower panel of figure 19.2 shows that only about 13 percent of revenues of states and localities combined comes from the federal government—and most of that is mandated aid to individuals which state or local governments are merely administering. Because intergovernmental transfers are not very important in the American federal system, condition (2) above is more or less satisfied.[10]

So how does horizontal competition among hard-budget American states deal with depressed or backward regions?

As late as 1950, the relative poverty of the southern American states was thought to be endemic. Everyone referred to the "poor South." But by making their labour markets more flexible by adopting right-to-work laws that outlawed the union shop and other restrictive labour practices so that initially wages were low, and by setting less generous welfare provisions resulting in lower payroll taxes than in the northern states, southern states attracted private corporate investment on a vast scale. Initially, the South's low-wage strategy encouraged net emigration. By the 1970s, much of the formerly backward region had become the prosperous "sunbelt" with net immigration—and incomes more on a par with the older industrial states in the North.

At the present time, wealthy large states like California and New York are in relative decline because rent-seeking groups—like trial lawyers—have seized control of regulatory agencies and government programmes such as worker compensation and health care. But as their industries are poached by states with less cumbersome labour practices and more efficiently administered public programmes, California and New York are forced to rationalize—and the poaching itself tends to level incomes across regions.

a.

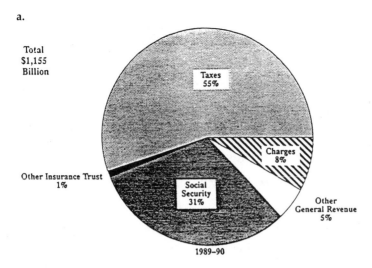

b.

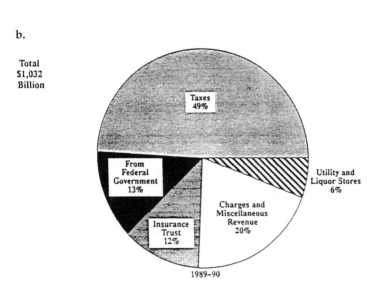

Figure 19.2
a. Federal government revenue by source, 1989–90. b. State and local government revenue by major financial sector and source, 1989–90.
Source: U.S. Department of Commerce, Bureau of the Census, *Government Finances in 1989–90.* Taken from ACIR, *Significant Features of Fiscal Federalism,* vol. 2, 1992.

19.7   Fiscal Constraints on Monetary Unification:
The Overhang of European National Debt

Europeans favouring a common currency cite the strong political symbolism, some reduction in long-run investment risk (without a common currency, you can never fully eliminate exchange risk), and elimination of money-changing costs of tourists moving from one European country to another. Perhaps the proposed European Central Bank (ECB) could ensure, on average, a more stable price level for the group than for most European countries acting alone.

Supplementing this familiar list, our analysis suggests an additional potential advantage: hardening the budget constraints on European national governments. Taking away their money-issuing authority while lodging it with the central government could be an important step toward limiting their borrowing capacities—condition (1) above. (The problem of European intergovernmental transfers violating condition (2) would still remain.) Doesn't the need to properly constrain mercantilist rivalry among Europe's national governments by hardening their budget constraints make an overwhelming case for pushing forward the Maastricht timetable on establishing a European currency?

Unfortunately no. Because of their huge debt overhangs, European national governments cannot presently afford to give up their money-issuing authority. This problem of the debt overhang is fundamental in the sense that it would continue to plague the putative monetary union even if initial "convergence" had been successfully achieved. Unlike the need for converging national rates of price inflation and interest rates, the basic fiscal problem is not simply one of convergence of public debts and deficits to some common level. The issue is more basic. National debt overhangs are simply too high in an absolute sense. Thus European governments cannot afford to cede control of their national central banks to some pan-European authority like the ECB.

The overhang of national debt in European economies now averages over 60 percent of GDP (table 19.1), which was the supposed target ceiling negotiated in the 1991 Maastricht Agreement before any member country could enter the common currency arrangement. But fiscal conditions among the member countries are very different—as table 19.1 also indicates. The ratio of debt/GDP is close to, or over, 100 percent for Belgium, Ireland, and Italy—while countries like Greece and Portugal only avoid explosions in their already large debt ratios by resorting to the inflation tax. Once accumulated, *public sector debts of this order of magnitude can only be safely managed if the government in question retains ownership of its central bank.*

But why might the rules of thumb suggested for Maastricht of, say, keeping debt ratios below 60 percent—or current public deficits below 3 percent—before joining a common currency, also be insufficient? For a substantially indebted national government, control over its own central bank confers two major advantages for debt management:

1. In the short run, major rollovers of existing debt are less risky if the central bank acts as the "government's banker," i.e., it provides liquidity to the market should something go awry.

2. In the long run, the perceived risk of outright default becomes negligible. Thus the "real" interest cost of government debt finance is reduced.

Together, (1) and (2) reduce the risk of a "run" on a highly indebted national government.

But this traditional low-cost financing of the national debt need not hold if the government loses control over its central bank. For example, in the late 1980s, the prospects of moving to a common currency in Europe with some finite probability seemed brighter than in 1994. The government of Italy faced some finite probability that it would lose control over the Bank of Italy, i.e., over its money-issuing authority, to the ECB. What then were the implications for the cost of servicing the government's debt?

Three Italian economists, Alesina, Prati, and Tabellini (1990), detected an inversion in this traditional relationship between interest rates on private and government debt in Italy. After exchange controls were removed in 1987, they found that the average yield on treasury bills was 1 to 3 percentage points higher (after adjusting for tax differences) than on "private" bank certificates of deposit of the same maturity. On medium-term maturities, two-year Italian government bonds yielded interest a percentage point or so higher than did 18- to 24-month bank certificates of deposit. Three heavily indebted European countries—Belgium, Italy, and the Netherlands—displayed this

Table 19.1
European Countries: Convergence Indicators for 1993 and 1994 (in %)

	1992 GDP Weights		Consumer Price Inflation		General Government Balance/GDP		Gross Government Debt/GDP[a]	Long-Term Interest Rates
	In EC	In World	1993	1994	1993	1994	1992	August 1993
EC countries								
France	19.2	3.6	2.2	2.2	−6.0	−5.9	52.6	6.4
Germany	23.2	4.3	4.6	2.9	−4.8	−3.5	42.5	6.4
Italy	18.4	3.4	4.5	4.6	−10.3	−9.2	115.1	10.3
United Kingdom[b]	17.7	3.3	3.2	3.8	−8.6	−7.4	35.1	7.0
Largest four countries[c]	78.5	14.6	3.7	3.3	−7.3	−6.3	60.3	7.4
Belgium	3.1	0.6	2.8	2.9	−6.7	−5.6	121.0	7.1
Denmark[d]	1.7	0.3	1.1	1.8	−3.5	−4.2	71.3	6.7
Greece[e]	1.7	0.3	14.3	9.5	−12.5	−13.3	108.6	20.3
Ireland	0.7	0.1	2.0	3.0	−3.4	−3.8	95.9	7.6
Luxembourg	0.1	0.0	4.0	3.3	0.1	0.0	5.8	6.8
Netherlands	4.7	0.9	2.0	2.8	−3.9	−3.9	79.0	6.2
Portugal	1.5	0.3	6.3	5.6	−6.4	−5.4	63.7	10.5
Spain	8.1	1.5	4.7	4.1	−6.3	−7.1	47.9	9.2
Smallest eight countries[c]	21.5	4.0	4.3	3.9	−6.0	−6.2	74.3	8.9
All EC[c]	100.0	18.6	3.8	3.5	−7.0	−6.3	63.4	7.8
Maastricht convergence criteria[f]	—		3.2	3.8	−3.0	−3.0	60.0	8.8

Non-EC countries								
Austria	—	0.4	3.7	2.5	-3.4	-3.0	49.4	6.5
Finland	—	0.3	2.8	4.1	-12.2	-9.5	39.5	7.7
Norway	—	0.3	2.5	2.3	-3.6	-3.4	43.0	6.2
Sweden	—	0.5	5.0	3.7	-13.5	-11.5	55.0	7.7
Switzerland	—	0.7	3.6	2.3	-2.4	-2.5	34.3	4.6
Five non-EC countries[c]	—	2.3	3.7	2.9	-6.6	-5.7	43.0	6.3

Source: International Monetary Fund. *World Economic Outlook.* October 1993.

[a]Debt data refer to end of year. They relate to general government but may not be consistent with the definition agreed at Maastricht.

[b]Retail price index excluding mortgage interest.

[c]Average weighted by 1992 GDP shares.

[d]The debt-GDP ratio would be below 60% if adjusted in line with the definition at Maastricht.

[e]General government balance includes capitalized interest: long-term interest rate is twelve-month Treasury bill rate.

[f]Unweighted averages. The Treaty does not indicate precisely how these indicators should be weighted across the reference countries.

interest-rate inversion in their domestic capital markets, while other potential members of the European common currency with lower debt ratios did not.

(In late 1992 into 1993 with Italy falling out of the ERM and its currency depreciating sharply—over 30 percent—against Germany and other "core" countries, one would expect this inversion to disappear as the possibility of Italy and other European countries joining together in a common currency arrangement became more remote.)

The Italian evidence discriminated between traditional inflation risk on lire-denominated debt and the risk of an outright public-sector restructuring or default. If investors believe(d) that a move to a common European currency will foreclose the possibility of the Italian government using the inflation tax to solve its debt problems, and if the government debt problem is severe enough, the risk premia incorporated in interest rates on Italian government debt could indeed exceed those on high-grade private debt. In the extreme, moving to a common currency in Europe could provoke a run on the Italian government, much of whose debt is already short-term and turns over every month.

But if a fiscal collapse in one country occurred, exit from the common currency agreement is virtually impossible. Thus the usual way of settling an untenable national debt overhang by devaluation and inflation is blocked.

19.8 Moral Hazard in Highly Indebted Governments in a Common-Currency Regime

Consequently, a country experiencing a fiscal breakdown would, under a common currency, have great leverage on the other member governments. To prevent possible Community-wide bank failures and financial dislocation arising out of that government's threatened default on its ecu debts, the solvent members of the Community might be forced to bail it out—whether by asking ECB to buy the troubled government's bonds, or by direct government-to-government lending. Knowing this ex ante, politicians in the errant country might become even less willing to take resolute fiscal action. Moral hazard would be uncomfortably high. Indeed, the EU has already agreed on large intergovernmental transfers to "distressed" areas and to equalization grants to poorer governments.

So what might we conclude about the fiscal impediments to a successful common currency in Europe? As long as the main taxing authority and main fiscal problems, i.e., the large debt overhangs, remain at the national level, giving up national control over national central banks is too costly. (In the extreme case, a fiscally weak government may not even be able to give up exchange controls on capital flows because of its need for revenue from financial repression—as discussed above). Government debts of this order of magnitude could only be accumulated in the first place because each national government in question owned its own central bank. Thus, to suddenly take away the central bank while leaving the debt residue would make debt management next to impossible.

In establishing a common currency, can this fiscal dilemma be avoided? Suppose the debts and much of the taxing authority of the national governments were transferred to the emerging European central government, which was also responsible for issuing the common currency. The fiscal regime would then be consistent with the monetary regime.

19.9 Government Debt in the American Monetary Union

Indeed, this is just the form of the American monetary union. Almost all general-obligation government debt is concentrated at the federal level, along with the money-issuing authority of the Federal Reserve System. Table 19.2 shows U.S. government debt to be 65 percent of GNP as of 1991, and by 1994 (not shown) it was close to 70 percent. Moreover, in the decade of the 1980s, the U.S. Federal Government's debt ratio was continually increasing—as if it had a very "soft" budget constraint.

In contrast, table 19.2 also shows that, in 1991, total state-government debt as a share of American GNP was just 5.8 percent, and combined state-local government debt was 15.6 percent Because state governments "own" and are responsible for local governments—counties, cities, and towns—the combined state-local debt is probably a better measure of the liabilities of the state governments. Unlike the U.S. government's debt, this combined debt shows no tendency to grow relative to GNP. In 1929, state-local debt was still between 15 and 16 percent of GNP. Not owning their own central banks, the state governments

Table 19.2
US Government: Federal, State, and Local Debt. Selected Years 1929–1991 (as % of GNP)

Year	Total[a]	Federal	State-Local	State	Local
1929	32.1	16.3	15.9	2.2	13.7
1939	66.3	44.2	22.0	3.8	18.2
1949	105.1	97.1	8.0	1.5	6.5
1954	83.1	72.7	10.4	2.6	7.9
1959	70.4	57.4	12.9	3.4	9.5
1964	62.9	48.8	14.2	3.8	10.3
1969[b]	51.9	38.1	13.9	4.1	9.8
1974	47.0	33.0	14.0	4.4	9.6
1979	45.4	33.2	12.1	4.5	7.7
1984	55.2	41.8	13.4	4.9	8.4
1985	59.7	45.5	14.2	5.3	9.0
1986	65.9	50.3	15.6	5.9	9.7
1987	67.9	52.5	15.9	5.9	10.0
1988	69.0	53.6	15.5	5.7	9.8
1989	70.1	54.9	15.2	5.6	9.6
1990	74.7	59.1	15.6	5.8	9.8
1991	81.1	65.0	16.2	6.1	10.1

Sources: Advisory Committee on the Intergovernmental Relations (ACIR). Federal debt figures include debt amounts held in government accounts. Table computed by ACIR in *Significant Features of Fiscal Federalism*, vol. 2, 1993.
[a]Total debt outstanding at the end of the fiscal year. These debt figures include all long-term credit obligations by the governments' full faith and credit, as well as nonguaranteed debts and all interest-bearing short-term credit obligations. Includes judgment, mortgage, and revenue bonds.
[b]During 1969, three government-sponsored enterprises became completely privately owned, and their debt was removed from the totals for the federal government. At the date of their conversion, federal debt was reduced by $10.7 billion.

did not have easy access to credit.[11] In order to maintain their creditworthiness, virtually all the American states have had to pass some form of constitutional or statutory restraint on government deficit financing. These restraints seem to have had some effect of further "hardening" the budget positions of American state governments. Comparing government indebtedness in table 19.2 to that in table 19.1, the outstanding general-obligation debts of the American states are very small by European standards.

Needless to say, transferring most of the huge debts of the European national governments to the European central government seems far beyond the realm of current political feasibility. Nevertheless, unless such a transfer was negotiated at the outset, the introduction of a common currency in Europe could precipitate debt crises at the national level.

19.10 A Common Monetary Standard without a Common Currency

Instead of the leap to a European common currency, national central banks and independently circulating national monies—separated by narrow exchange-rate margins—are best left in place. To shore up their revenue positions, fiscally weak countries outside the inner core might still retain some controls on capital account. Then a fiscal breakdown in any one country doesn't imperil the whole monetary mechanism. Although traumatic, the errant country can just exit from the exchange-rate agreement—perhaps to return some day. The electoral sanctions from losing fiscal control, inflating, and falling out of the monetary agreement fall mainly on the government of the country in question. Because that country's leverage for extracting concessions from the other members would be minimal, it would, ex ante, have more incentive to keep its fiscal house in order.[12]

Within the core group of noninflationary European countries, however, fixed par values and narrow bands for exchange rates can still operate indefinitely even if there are no capital controls in place. Indeed, as long as their monetary policies were credibly coordinated, stabilizing private flows of short-term capital make it easier to maintain par values for exchange rates without much direct intervention by central banks—as under the classical gold standard or the calm days of the postwar fixed-rate dollar standard (chapter 2). But how should such a monetary standard be organized?

First, a common price-level objective should be defined for internationally tradable goods within the core group as a whole—rather than just Germany in particular. Because it is consistent with the mutual commitment to fixed nominal exchange rates, zero inflation in a common producer price index[13] is the natural target for a common monetary policy in the core countries

(McKinnon and Ohno 1989; Ohno 1993). Here, German producer prices would be given no more weight than Germany's relative GNP would warrant. So the Bundesbank would be bound to a price-level rule which is at least partly external to Germany. But this would be an advantage to the German monetary authorities. The Bundesbank could more easily face down German trade unions if it had to maintain an externally sanctioned price-level objective that could not be easily modified by the Bundesbank itself. The problem of time inconsistency in German monetary policy would be mitigated by this external constraint on the Bundesbank's discretionary power.

Second, the core central banks should coordinate their monetary policies—mainly domestic credit expansion—in such a way as to achieve this price level objective for the EU as a whole. Although the monies of the core countries would continue to circulate separately within narrow exchange margins, each purely national rate of monetary expansion would be difficult to control or predict because of international currency substitution. Nevertheless, the collective money supply of the core group could be a helpful intermediate monetary indicator for targeting the common producer price level. But now the core central banks would act in concert to determine their domestic credit expansions with a more or less common strategy for adjusting short-term interest rates. Minor adjustments in relative interest rates would be assigned to stabilize exchange rates, whereas aggregate credit expansion would be assigned to stabilize the common producer price index (chapters 20 and 22).

Because national central banks would continue to collect monetary seigniorage at the national level, they would remain the natural "lenders-of-last-resort" to national banks in distress and the guarantors of the payments mechanism at the national level—while cooperating to supervise international clearing. Under guidelines similar to the international Basic Accord on capital requirements for reducing regulatory competition, they—or other designated national agencies—would retain supervisory responsibility for regulating banks against undue risk taking.

Needless to say, these proposed reforms of European monetary arrangements to secure better exchange-rate and price-level stability have many complications not covered here. Yet they are evolutionary and relatively modest compared to the "leap in the dark" of the Maastricht Agreement's push for a common currency. Because it respects the fiscal need to keep national central banks and national currencies in place in highly indebted European countries, such a common monetary standard is preferable to a common currency.

But remember, the budget constraints on European nation states will remain much softer than those on their American counterparts because European national currencies remain in place. Thus the EU Commission must chronically fight to constrain tax and subsidy competition among European national governments, while the U.S. Federal Government cheerfully ignores the ebb and flow of (benign) fiscal competition among the American states.

Notes

In its original form, this chapter was a paper presented as the twenty-ninth Annual Lecture of the Scottish Economic Society, at the Heriot-Watt University, on 7 April, 1994.

1. The old literature on optimum currency areas (Mundell 1961; McKinnon 1963) did not distinguish the case for fixed exchange rates from that for a common currency. The new literature (DeGrauwe 1992; Tavlas 1993) covers new theoretical arguments which, on net balance, increase the size of "optimum" currency areas. But it still does not resolve the issue of a common currency versus a common monetary standard.

2. In contrast, the money-changing costs of the vastly greater flow of commercial transactions by business firms are tiny by comparison—typically much less than one quarter of one per cent of the gross value of the transactions. However, firms face additional hedging costs and exchange risk (which hedging can't fully eliminate) when they contract forward.

3. Eichengreen also criticizes the Maastricht Agreement for not specifying how the putative European Central Bank's open-market and discounting operations would be conducted, i.e., which financial instruments would be chosen to avoid discriminating against one country or another. Responsibility for the prudential supervision for community-wide banking institutions also seems to have been left in limbo.

4. In transitional socialist economies such as China, interjurisdictional competition among local governments with hard budget constraints commits them to enforce harder budget constraints on the enterprises which they own (Montinola, Qian, and Weingast 1994; Qian and Roland 1994).

5. Which was not true when the U.S. was still on the gold standard. Before 1933, gold was the definitive means of settlement for the payment of debts (McKinnon 1996).

6. Apart from the inflation tax, there might remain some residual incentive for a surprise default—or capital levy—on the national debt if the government perceives that traditional methods of tax finance are becoming too expensive

and too distortionary (Alesina, de Broeck, and Tabellini, 1992). While true in principle, such a default has seldom occurred historically by any government that had access to the printing press. (In old Soviet Union, one could make a case that there had been instances of outright debt repudiation.) But I am treating this form of default risk to be negligible.

7. State personal income taxes are increasingly important, rising from about 15% of state tax revenue in 1967 to about 32% in 1990. But state income tax payments are deductible from the federal income tax base in a way that is advantageous to higher-income tax payers. This dampens the incentive to move to avoid the state income tax, and competition among the states in this dimension is thereby limited. Without federal deductibility, the states would rely much less heavily on the personal income tax.

8. Nor is restraint on interstate commerce an appropriate response—even if it was legal. In Canada, provincially owned liquor stores are given exclusive franchises to sell highly taxed liquor to final consumers—in part to limit the possibilities for interprovincial tax arbitrage. Once set up, however, these provincial government monopolies became very protectionist. They favoured stocking locally produced beer, wine, and spirits—until forced in 1987 to change by the Canadian-American Free Trade Agreement.

9. In great contrast to Weingast's (1995) characterization of 18th century Britain as a vibrant federal state within which horizontal competition among local governments encouraged industrial innovation to flourish—with parliament restraining the King from undue taxation or interference with domestic commerce.

10. But encroachment by the soft-budget federal government threatens the separation of economic powers of federal and state governments, and limits the market-preserving character of interstate competition. The U.S. federal government is now mandating more rules and regulations on local resource use—often accompanied by federal funding.

11. This is only a necessary but not sufficient condition to limit the ability of subnational governments to build up large debts. If revenue sharing and other transfers between the national and subnational governments are important, the capital markets will see that the subnational governments are not financially independent, and that they have an indirect pipeline to the central bank.

In Canada, provincial debts are large and about the same order of magnitude as that of the Canadian Federal Government. Revenue sharing and other intergovernmental transfers are much larger in Canada than in the United States. Because the Canadian government has not directly limited what the provinces can borrow, the capital markets see the Bank of Canada to be a potential lender of last resort for provincial debt.

12. To maximize the pressure on each member government to maintain fiscal restraint, I would argue that intergovernment transfers should be kept to a minimum within whatever form of fiscal federalism evolves in Europe. However, some influential authors (Eichengreen 1992) argue that such transfers are necessary to aid poor areas or to offset region-specific economic downturns.

13. In the presence of differential productivity growth, trying to align price indices that contain the prices of nontradables, such as national CPIs or GNP deflators, would not be consistent with fixed nominal exchange rates.

References

Advisory Committee on Intergovernmental Relations (1992). *Significant features on fiscal federalism,* vol. 2.

Alesina, A., Prati, A., and Tabellini, G. (1990). "Public confidence and debt management: a model and a case study of Italy." In R. Dornbusch and M. Draghi (eds.) *Public Debt Management: Theory and History.* Cambridge Univ. Press.

Alesina, A., de Broeck, M., and Tabellini, G. (1992). "Default risk." *Economic Policy: A European Forum,* 15, October, pp. 429–463.

Buchanan, J. (1987). "The constitution of economic policy." *American Economic Review,* 77, 3, June, pp. 243–50.

De Grauwe, P. (1992). *The Economics of Monetary Integration.* Oxford University Press, New York.

The Economist (1993). 17 July, pp. 23–24.

Eichengreen, B. (1992). "The political economy of fiscal policy after EMU." Center for International and Development Economics Research. University of California, Berkeley, December.

Eichengreen, B. (1993). "European monetary integration." *Journal of Economic Literature,* 31, 3, September, pp. 1321–57.

Giovannini, A., and de Melo, M. (1993). "Government revenue from financial repression." *American Economic Review,* 83, 4, September, pp. 953–63.

Hilt, A. (1994). "Southern models of eastern German development: lessons from the United States and Italy." Economics Department, Stanford University (unpublished).

Kornai, J. (1990). *The Road to a Free Economy.* New York, W. W. Norton.

McKinnon, R. I. (1963). "Optimum currency areas." *American Economic Review,* 53, pp. 717–724.

———. (1979). *Money in International Exchange: The Convertible Currency System.* Oxford Univ. Press.

———. (1991). *The Order of Economic Liberalization: Financial Control in the Transition to a Market Economy.* Johns Hopkins (2nd edition 1993).

———. (1993). "The rules of the game: International money in historical perspective." *Journal of Economic Literature,* XXXI, March, pp. 1–44.

———. (1996). "Market-preserving fiscal federalism in the American union." In Mario Blejer et al. (eds.) *Essays in Honor of Vito Tanzi,* International Monetary Fund, Washington, D.C.

McKinnon, R. I., and Ohno, K. (1989). "Purchasing power parity as a monetary standard." In O. Hamouda, R. Rowley, and B. Wolf (eds.) *The Future of the International Monetary System: Change, Coordination or Instability.* Edward Elgar, pp. 42–67.

Montinola, G., Qian, Y., and Weingast, B. (1994). "Federalism Chinese style: the political basis for economic success in China." Stanford University, February (unpublished).

Mundell, R. A. (1961). "A theory of optimum currency areas." *American Economic Review,* 51, pp. 657–64.

Obstfeld, M. (1992). "Destabilizing effects of exchange rate escape clauses." NBER Working Paper 3606.

Ohno, K. (1993). "The purchasing power parity criterion for stabilizing exchange rates." Ch. 19 in D. Das (ed.) *Foreign Exchange Markets and International Capital Flows,* pp. 394–415.

Portes, R. (1993). "The EMS and EMU after the fall." *The World Economy,* 16, pp. 1–16.

Qian, Y., and Roland, G. (1994). "Soft budget constraints in public enterprises and regional decentralization: the case of China." Stanford University, CEPR, February.

Sala-I-Martin, X., and Sachs, J. (1992). "Fiscal federalism and optimum currency areas: evidence for Europe from the United States." In M. Canzoneri,V. Grilli, and P. Masson (eds.), *Establishing a Central Bank: Issues in Europe and Lessons from the United States.* CEPR, Cambridge Univ. Press, pp. 195–220.

Tavlas, G. (1993). "The 'new' theory of optimum currency areas." *The World Economy,* November, pp. 663–85.

Weingast, B. (1995). "The economic role of political institutions." Hoover Institution, Stanford University, *Journal of Law, Economics and Organization,* 1995.

Monetary and
Exchange-Rate Policies
for International
Financial Stability:
A Proposal

Without a common monetary standard, the remarkable integration of Western European, North American, and the industrialized Asian economies in both commodity trade and financial flows is less efficient, and becoming untenable. Dissatisfaction with wildly fluctuating relative currency values, euphemistically called "floating" or "flexible" exchange rates, is a prime cause of the resurgence in protectionism.

In 1986–87, the overvalued yen forced Japanese industrialists to close factories, retire workers, and write off once valuable investments in plant and equipment. This parallels what their American counterparts were forced to do between 1981 and 1985, when the dollar suddenly became overvalued. Similarly, the paring down of the British manufacturing base was precipitated when the pound unexpectedly became a strong petrocurrency in 1979–81. In agriculture, Japan and European countries are determined to insulate their domestic prices of farm products from unsettling international influences, including volatile fluctuations in the yen/dollar or mark/dollar exchange rates. Thus, unless exchange stability is first achieved, the American government's attempt to broaden the General Agreement on Tariffs and Trade to encompass agriculture and services is likely to fail.

But what keeps the three major industrial blocs from developing a common monetary standard to prevent exchange-rate fluctuations? Although many people would point to political differences, doctrinal disputes among economists are more important. Well-intentioned politicians and government officials

Originally published, in slightly longer form, in *Journal of Economic Perspectives* 2, 1 (Winter 1988): 83–103. Reprinted with permission.

are stymied because of the differing theoretical perspectives of their economic advisers.

The first issue is whether or not a floating foreign-exchange market—where governments do not systematically target exchange rates—is "efficient." Because many economists believe that exchange risk can be effectively hedged in forward markets, they argue that international monetary reform is unnecessary.

Second, after a decade and a half of unremitting turbulence in the foreign-exchange markets, economists cannot agree on "equilibrium" or desirable official targets for exchange rates if they were to be stabilized. Two separate and contending principles—that of *purchasing power parity* and of *balanced trade*—yield very different estimates for the "correct" yen/dollar and mark/dollar exchange rates.

Third, if the three major blocs can agree to fix nominal exchange rates within narrow bands, by what working rule should the new monetary standard be anchored to prevent worldwide inflation or deflation?

After a brief consideration of some empirical evidence on the magnitude of exchange-rate fluctuations since floating began in the early 1970s, I analyze each of these conceptual issues in the course of demonstrating how the central banks of Japan, the United States, and Germany (representing the continental European bloc) can establish fixed exchange rates and international monetary stability.[1]

20.1 The Evidence

In figure 20.1, monthly data on the yen/dollar and mark/dollar exchange rates extend from the major breakdown in Bretton Woods parities in 1971 to March 1987. On the vertical scale, percentage changes may be read directly from one month to any other with the zero point representing the mean yen/dollar or mark/dollar exchange rates, 252 and 2.48 respectively, over this sixteen-year period. For example, at its trough of 1.72 marks in late 1979, the dollar was 37 percent below its period mean; at its recent peak of 3.31 marks in February 1985, the dollar was 28 percent above its mean. By late 1987, the dollar had fallen sharply below its 1979 lows.

Casual inspection of figure 20.1 indicates that movements in the yen/dollar and mark/dollar exchange rates were not only

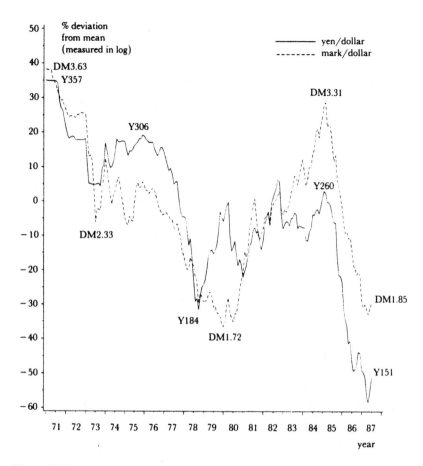

Figure 20.1
Mark/dollar and yen/dollar exchange rates: 1971–87 (monthly averages from daily data).
Note: Vertical scale shows percentage changes directly from one month to another. The zero point in the middle of the scale represents the period mean yen/dollar and mark/dollar exchange rates, 252 and 2.48, respectively, from 1971 to March 1987.

very large but were also positively correlated. Indeed, the simple coefficient of correlation is .67. In this respect, the unstable dollar is the main problem—suggesting that American monetary policy, in particular, has been insufficiently internationally oriented.

Yet divergent movements between the yen/dollar and mark/dollar exchange rates do occur, as a glance at figure 20.1 indicates. In March 1987, for example, the rate of 143 yen/dollar was 57 percent below its period mean, while the rate of 1.81

marks/dollar was "only" 32 percent below its mean. In this sense, in 1985–87 the yen had appreciated substantially against the mark as well as the dollar.

More generally, also including experiences of smaller "independent" floaters such as the United Kingdom or Australia, what are the stylized facts about currency fluctuations in world markets?

First, relative to profit margins on investment measured in any one national currency, exchange-rate changes have been very large: 1 percent in a day, 5 percent in a month, and 20 percent in a year are commonplace (IMF 1984).

Second, exchange fluctuations have been mainly unanticipated by the market, reflected neither in interest differentials across countries nor in forward premia or discounts in the exchange markets (Frenkel and Mussa 1980).

Third, these changes have been real in the sense that most domestic prices, including internationally tradable manufacturers, have remained relatively sticky. Because large cyclical fluctuations in exchange rates have not been offset by the much smaller, largely secular differences in domestic price inflation (Levich 1986), they induce abrupt changes in international competitiveness.

Fourth, despite the free flow of financial capital, large but variable real interest differentials of 3 to 4 percentage points between similar assets denominated in different currencies are commonplace (Frankel 1986).

20.2 Asset Pricing and Market Efficiency

What causes this great variance in floating exchange rates among industrial economies with open capital markets? The most convincing empirical description is that the exchange rate behaves like a forward-looking asset price: investors continually shift their preferences among yen, mark, dollar, and sterling assets according to how they imagine each exchange rate might move in the future (Frenkel and Mussa 1980). These expectations are then telescoped back into the spot market to produce the sharp changes shown in figure 20.1.

The floating foreign-exchange rate seems to be dominated by volatile asset preferences rather than adjusting passively to balance current flows of imports and exports. In the face of uncertainty about the future purchasing power of domestic money, liquid foreign-exchange assets are more easily substituted for domestic financial assets (money or bonds) than are physical assets such as real estate or stocks of commodities. Foreign bonds or bank accounts are also convenient hedges against possible future shifts in domestic, political, or commercial risk. These potential capital flows through the foreign exchanges on a daily basis are huge. Since they are so much greater than the value of commodity trade, they dominate observed movements in exchange rates.

When future exchange rates are uncertain, as under a free float, these portfolio preferences become highly sensitive to ongoing "news" about the exchange-rate consequences of how, say, future monetary or tax policy in one country might be conducted relative to another. Hence, virtually all the exchange rate variance shown in figure 20.1 comes from news that changes expectations—such as the American government's surprise leak to *The New York Times* in mid-January 1987 that it wanted the dollar to depreciate further despite attempts by the Bundesbank and Bank of Japan to support the American currency.

Correspondingly, little or none of the observed variance in the spot exchange rate is predictable from previous knowledge of forward rates (Levich 1986) or from generally available past information on national money supplies, interest rates, trade balances and so on (Meese and Rogoff 1983). In fact, the current spot rate seems to embody all relevant news up to that point, and subsequently moves like a random walk driven by new information coming in.[2] Because "excess" profits from speculating on the basis of common knowledge from the past are close to zero, the private foreign-exchange market seems to be highly efficient in processing the information available to it.

Nevertheless, I hypothesize that a floating foreign-exchange market is *socially inefficient* because private foreign-exchange traders face a huge gap in relevant information: the relative future purchasing powers of national fiat monies, none of which has any intrinsic value, are highly uncertain. Thus the assessments of international investors of whether dollar, or yen, or mark assets provide the best combination of yield and safety are unnecessarily volatile.

The appropriate solution to this portfolio instability would be for the U.S. Federal Reserve System, the Bank of Japan, and the Bundesbank to announce jointly that, henceforth, the three will adhere to a common monetary standard, thereby forgoing the option to inflate at different rates. In effect, they would seek to approximate the conditions prevailing within a single currency area where one monetary unit, say one dollar, would have roughly the same purchasing power over a broad basket of tradable goods in any participating region or country.

To help implement this new policy, fixed nominal targets for the yen/dollar and mark/dollar exchange rates (within narrow bands) would be officially announced, and set to approximate sustainable purchasing power parities. Once achieved, the three central banks would symmetrically adjust their domestic money supplies to maintain these nominal exchange parities and, concomitantly, maintain roughly the same rates of domestic price inflation in internationally tradable goods. Thus speculation on which nation's monetary policy will be the most inflationary becomes pointless, and a major source of instability in international currency preferences is eliminated once spculators know that future nominal exchange rates will be the same as today's.

Although there are many historical precedents, having countries give up some national autonomy over the supply of money in order to secure fixed exchange rates remains controversial. Hence, I shall first show how common arguments favoring exchange-rate flexibility become invalid once nations are highly integrated in finance and trade. Then more precise details on what having a "common" monetary policy means, and how it could be facilitated, are spelled out.

20.3 "Accidental" Monetary Disruptions from Real Disturbances

Are fixed nominal exchange rates appropriate if "real" shocks affect nations differentially? Most economists still believe that flexibility in nominal exchange rates is necessary to overcome domestic price-level rigidities to balance international payments properly—a belief analyzed in some detail later on. Here, however, consider the reverse problem: how do real shocks impinge on domestic monetary (price-level) stability when economies are highly open on both capital and trade accounts? Is a system of fixed or floating exchange rates the better shock absorber?

Under floating exchange rates, news about future exchange-rate movements also encompasses nonmonetary events. For example, a country might reduce its taxation of foreign corporations, or the price of its principal export could increase. If the economy of this country is highly open, these events wil not warrant a (nominal) appreciation of the country's exchange rate. Instead, if the country's exchange rate is left free to appreciate, such real disturbances would provoke an unexpected (and unwarranted) general price-level deflation in the country, as discussed in chapter 17. Consider a historical example.

With the worldwide increase in the price of oil in 1979, and Britain's emergence as a major oil exporter, investors projected that U.K. foreign-exchange earnings would be greater in the future. Moreover, they also knew that the Bank of England was committed to letting the exchange rate float while following a monetarist rule of limiting the rate of domestic money growth. Because of home currency preference by Britons to convert this future stream of earnings into pounds, sterling's future foreign-exchange value was seen to be higher by forward-looking international investors. This was immediately registered in the foreign-exchange market by a large increase in the demand for *spot* sterling in 1979. Thus, the nominal (and real) foreign-exchange value of sterling rose sharply, precipitately deflating the British economy and reducing international competitiveness so as to wipe out a large chunk of British manufacturing in 1980–81.

In contrast, under a rule of fixed exchange rates, the Bank of England would have stood ready to expand the sterling monetary base and reduce interest rates to satisfy any increased international demand for sterling assets at the agreed-on exchange rate. Moreover, because speculators would know that the Bank was committed to a fixed exchange rate, they would not have anticipated future sterling appreciation in response to the oil price increase. Thus, they would not have so sharply increased their demand for sterling assets in 1979!

The Dutch experience with the discovery and development of large natural gas fields in the early 1960s is an instructive comparison. Because everyone knew that under the old Bretton Woods system the guilder's foreign-exchange value was fixed in dollar (and mark) terms throughout the 1960s, no immediate international rush into guilder assets took place—and there was no precipitate exchange appreciation and deflation of the Dutch economy. To be sure, as the natural gas sector expanded and the tax revenues were spent for domestic goods and services thus bidding up wages, other Dutch tradable goods industries inevitably declined—the well-known phenomenon called the "Dutch Disease." But this decline was gradual. The fixed exchange rate avoided sharp appreciation and deflation—accompanied by heavy unemployment—of the kind that Britain was to suffer a decade later.

In summary, agreeing on a common monetary policy resulting in stable nominal exchange rates has two aspects. First, each central bank must give up *discretionary* power to persistently inflate its price level at a rate different from the common standard on which the group had agreed. Secondly, and less obviously, the cooperating central banks must stand ready to offset the portfolio consequences of internationally differentiated real disturbances to prevent them from *accidentally* disrupting any one country's nominal exchange rate and its price level—as in the British example above and in the American and Japanese cases to be described below.

Only when international investors have such forward assurance will the foreign-exchange market be informationally efficient in the social sense. Then private speculation will support the exchange-rate targets that the authorities announce.

20.4   Incomplete Forward Markets for Goods and Services: The Arrow-Debreu Dilemma

In response to the great turbulence over the past decade and a half, financial markets in Chicago, New York, London, Frankfurt, Tokyo, and so on have developed an amazing range of instruments for hedging both exchange and interest-rate risk. Now in the late 1980s, capital mobility among the three major blocs is virtually unrestricted, and industrial enterprises may freely borrow or lend foreign currencies directly at virtually any term to maturity. In the words of the Bank for International Settlements (1986, p. 1), "Innovation has improved the efficiency of international financial markets, mainly by offering a broader and more flexible range of instruments both for borrowing and for hedging interest-rate and exchange-rate exposures. These changes have clearly aided banks and their customers to cope with stresses associated with the greater volatility of exchange and interest rates in recent years."

After glancing at the dazzling array of financial instruments for taking forward exchange positions, most economists might rest assured that most international currency risk associated with trade and investment could be effectively hedged. Nevertheless, firms investing in physical plant or human capital find they have substantial exchange risk that *cannot* be hedged as long as exchange rates are free to fluctuate (Kindleberger 1972, 1985). Why the paradox?

The problem lies not so much with any inadequacies in the forward markets for foreign exchange, but rather is rooted in the incompleteness of forward contracting in markets for goods and services. We know that a manufacturer contemplating a new investment cannot make all his future production and sales decisions before the plant is built—then lay off the economic risks with a complete set of forward commodity contracts contingent on various uncertain states of nature. Arrow (1953) and Debreu (1959) have taught us the critical importance of forward commodity markets to hedge against price risk, coupled with insurance markets to offset production risk.

However, a dilemma arises because the transactions costs and moral hazard associated with contract enforcement of such contingent futures are generally prohibitive. Usually, producers cannot feasibly protect themselves with outside insurance policies against their inability to deliver, nor against unexpected changes in cost (Arrow 1973; Greenwald and Stiglitz 1986). A farmer would not necessarily want to sell his crop forward years—or even months—in advance if he cannot predict his own output or obtain crop insurance against a multiplicity of possible natural disasters (McKinnon 1967).

Thus producers typically sell forward only some of their output—and that but a few weeks or months in advance on a noncontingent basis. Many goods are simply held in inventory until customers come in to buy spot.[3] Because of these incomplete forward markets for commodities, therefore, fixed investments for producing internationally tradable goods and services cannot be hedged effectively against most foreign-exchange risk.

Let us illustrate this important point with the example of an industrialist contemplating where to build a new plant to produce laser disks. As in a common currency area, he must identify that geographic locale where (domestic currency) factor costs are relatively low compared to projected output prices—what I shall call the "economic fundamentals." But with floating exchange rates, he must also give positive weight to that country whose currency is relatively undervalued by the purchasing power parity criterion: the "real exchange rate" effect. Regardless of how our laser disk manufacturer balances the "economic fundamentals" with the "real exchange rate" to select a country for production, the choice can easily be made obsolete by currency fluctuation.

Only if the planned production of laser disks could be insured *and* sold forward over the lifetime of his plant could our industrialist absolve himself of exchange risk. Suppose these hypothetical forward prices for laser disks over a continuum of future dates were specified in all other relevant currencies. Then, the existing forward markets in foreign exchanges could be fully utilized. The industrialist could sell (go short) other currencies for the currency in the country of production at the various terms to maturity and amounts negotiated in any forward commodity contracts. Because of the Arrow-Debreu dilemma, however, such forward commodity contracts, fully insured against unexpected dislocations and delays in production, do not exist.

To be sure, a merchant exporter with inventories of already-produced goods can hedge aginst short-term exchange risk when he sells consignments abroad to be delivered in, say, 30 days or 6 months. After forward selling his goods for foreign money, he can effectively "double hedge" by selling foreign exchange forward to get safely back into the domestic currency (McKinnon 1979; Kawai and Zilcha 1986). And this type of forward currency transacting is very important in ameliorating short-term exchange risk.

But short-term hedging on a noncontingent basis covers only a small proportion of the potential longer-term exchange risk arising from investment decisions that are made today. In effect, incomplete forward commodity markets expose industrialists, with long-term fixed investments to foreign-exchange risk which they cannot avoid. Thus, random variance in exchange rates introduces new net risk into the world economy. In addition to the British overvaluation of 1979–81, consider more recent examples of this fundamental unhedgeability of long-term investment commitments against foreign exchange risk. When the dollar was generally weak in the 1970s, and became substantially undervalued from 1977 to 1980, American tradable good industries looked profitable, and "excessive" investments occurred in certain kinds of U.S. mining and manufacturing, with agriculture also becoming overcapitalized. As the dollar (unexpectedly) rose in 1981 and became overvalued until late 1985, these industries then suffered a big shakeout with bankruptcies and plant closures. Obviously, these companies did not (could not) hedge their foreign-exchange positions.[4]

The resulting avalanche of protectionist sentiment in the U.S. Congress is still with us. Although by 1986 and into 1987 the dollar is no longer overvalued against the yen and continental European bloc of currencies, industrialists see considerable future exchange-rate uncertainty in assessing whether or not to rebuild America's productive capacity in tradable goods industries. Investment is inhibited.

Similarly, as the yen rose incredibly from 260 yen/dollar in March 1985 to around 140 yen/dollar in the early part of 1987, Japanese industrial output turned down and much of her previously installed manufacturing capacity suddenly became unprofitable. In 1986, there occurred an unprecedented deflation of over 10 percent in the yen prices of Japanese industrial goods as measured by Japan's official wholesale price index (figure 20.2). The resulting industrial depression in Japan has prompted Japan's preeminent industrialist, Mr. Akio Morita (1986), President and Chairman of the Sony Corporation, to call for reforms such that national money becomes "a common scale of value internationally rather than just another speculative commodity." Otherwise, he cannot properly decide in which goods to invest, in which country to produce them, or how to arrange for future sales and supplies.

To be sure, neither American industrialists in 1977–80, nor Japanese industrialists prior to 1986–87, necessarily made wrong investment choices ex ante. Rather, they faced incomplete information regarding the future course of their own country's exchange rate—an information gap that turned out to be devastating.

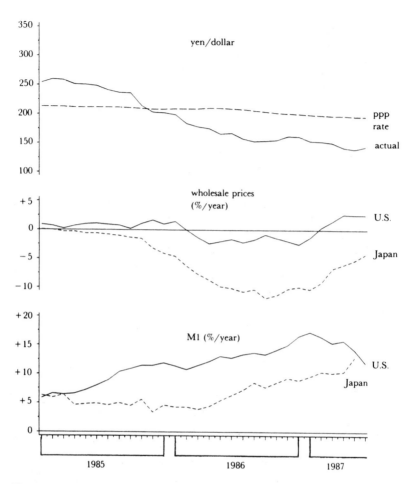

Figure 20.2
Exchange rates, prices, and money: Japan and the U.S.: 1985–87.
Note: Rates of change in money supplies and wholesale prices are year over year estimates taken from *The Economist*; estimates of purchasing power parity exchange rates (PPP) from Ohno (1987) (projected into 1987 from Japanese and American wholesale price indexes).

20.5   A Fleeting Vision of How Monetary Cooperation Could Work

When the dollar soared to 260 yen and 3.3 marks in late February 1985, the unsustainable loss in America's international competitiveness since 1981 had become so great as to be obvious to everybody. The Reagan Administration finally abandoned its long-standing refusal to treat the dollar exchange rate as a legitimate target for public policy.

For the rest of 1985, central banks cooperated to nudge the dollar down directly in the foreign-exchange markets—a policy that was announced and ratified by the Plaza Hotel Accord in September 1985. More important, their domestic money growth rates supported this objective. Figures 20.2 and 20.3 show that growth in M_1, the basic money supply, rose sharply in the U.S. to more than 10 percent per year, while Germany and Japan followed relatively tight money policies with M1 growth less than 5 percent.

At 200 yen and 2.3 marks by the end of 1985, the dollar was correctly aligned with the currencies of America's Japanese and European trading partners in two closely related respects. First, there was approximate purchasing power parity. One dollar could buy at the wholesale level a broad basket of manufactured goods in Japan and Europe similar to what it could buy at home (Ohno 1987).

Second, price inflation in tradable goods (as measured by changes in wholesale price indexes) were virtually the same in the three areas at the end of 1985, and close to zero. Being properly aligned, the yen/dollar and mark/dollar exchange rates were not themselves imposing any significant upward or downward pressure on the average price level of tradable goods in any of the three major blocs (figures 20.2 and 20.3).

Hence, late 1985 into early 1986 presented a wonderful opportunity for the finance ministers of the Group of Seven industrialized democracies to reinstitute a common monetary standard. At that time, a formally announced policy whereby the dollar would, henceforth, be kept within fixed narrow bands of, say, 190 to 210 yen and 2.2 to 2.4 marks, would have been easy to implement. If the dollar fell toward the lower intervention points, the U.S. Federal Reserve System would be obligated to tighten American monetary policy just as the Bank of Japan and Bundesbank (representing the European bloc) would be obligated to ease, and vice versa should the dollar become unduly strong.

To keep potentially volatile exchange rates within their prescribed bands, the three central banks must control *relative* short-term interest rates on a weekly basis, or even a daily one. Through open-market operations (or discounting), the weak currency

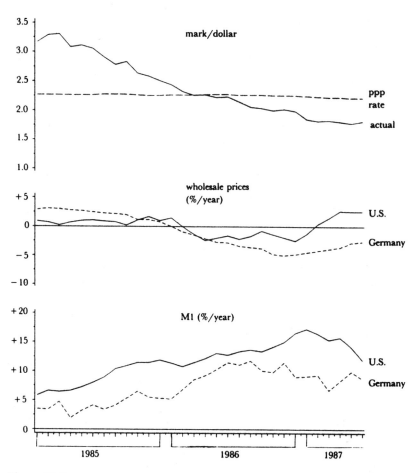

Figure 20.3
Exchange rates, prices, and money: Germany and the U.S.: 1985–1987.
Note: Rates of change in money supplies and wholesale prices are year over year estimates taken from *The Economist;* estimates of purchasing power parity exchange rates (PPP) from Ohno (1987) (projected into 1987 from German and American wholesale price indexes).

country would raise short-term interest rates to attract capital from abroad, and vice versa for the strong currency countries. With confidence in the official parities, very small changes in interest rates would attract (or repel) sufficient short-term capital to equilibrate the foreign exchanges.

Only as a last resort, or because of unusual financial turbulence, would substantial direct intervention in the foreign exchanges be necessary. Then, to be decisive, *symmetrically unsterilized intervention* is appropriate (see chapter 7). For example, if the Bank of Japan intervened at the lower bound for the dollar to purchase dollars and sell yen, the American monetary base would contract as the Japanese base expanded—leading to further equilibrating changes in relative interest rates in both countries.

Once speculators understood these new rules of the game, containing unambiguous information regarding the mutual intentions of the major central banks, then private short-term capital flows would help to stabilize exchange rates within their official bands. Very little actual monetary adjustment on a daily or even weekly basis would be necessary as long as everyone knew that decisive official action would be forthcoming if the need arose.

In the longer run, the three central banks would aim to keep constant their common (wholesale) price level in internationally tradable goods—whether measured in yen, dollars, or marks—as the nominal anchor for the system as a whole. For this purpose, aggregrate money growth, the sum of domestic credit expansions, could be targeted as an intermediate variable (McKinnon 1984). For example, if international deflation threatened, then joint money growth would be slowly accelerated.[5]

Unfortunately, this naive vision was not realized. Instead of being stabilized at its purchasing power parity level at the end of 1985, the dollar continued to fall throughout 1986 and then plunged below 140 yen and 1.8 marks in early 1987. Instead of feeding the foreign-exchange markets clear information regarding their mutual monetary intentions, governments criticized each other's alleged policy failure and then appeared to act at cross-purposes. Despite the weak dollar, growth in the American money supply throughout 1986 remained far in excess of that in Germany and Japan, as shown in figures 20.2 and 20.3.

20.6   The Exchange Rate and the Trade Balance

What provoked the American government to push and to keep pushing the dollar down so far—thus imposing undue deflationary pressure on Japan and continental Europe while risking the resurgence of inflation in the United States? The pursuit of what is now a false academic doctrine: that a once-and-for-all devaluation of a currency can systematically reduce that country's trade deficit as per the old Robinson (1937) and Meade (1951) elasticities approach to the balance of trade. When industrial economies were still fairly insulated from one another in the late 1930s into the 1950s, a devaluation could improve the trade balance. But among highly open economies of the 1970s and 1980s, exchange-rate changes have no predictable effect on the money value of net trade balances because of their more pervasive macroeconomic repercussions (Miles 1979; McKinnon and Ohno 1986). See also chapters 13 and 14.

After the sharp appreciations of the mark and yen over the past two years, most economists expected that the German and Japanese loss of "international competitiveness"—that is, relatively higher prices of their goods on world markets—would reduce their trade surpluses as measured in dollars. These direct price effects did not have a strong enough effect on the flow of imports and exports for several reasons.

First, their improved terms of trade meant that the Japanese and Europeans earned more dollars per unit of exports without paying any less per unit of imports.

Second, there were internal deflations in Japan and Germany (figures 20.2 and 20.3) that were a necessary consequence of their exchange appreciations. These deflations so depressed Japanese and German demand for imports and released more goods for export that the physical volume of exports relative to imports did not fall sufficiently (although substantial real adjustment did occur) to offset their more favorable terms of trade. Consequently, both the Japanese and German net trade surpluses measured in dollars actually increased in 1986 and 1987 in comparison to 1985.

Granted, the current huge excess of imports over exports in the American economy is unsustainable and must eventually be corrected one way or another. But this trade deficit of $150 billion to $200 billion a year merely reflects the saving-investment gap in the American economy created by the not coincidentally equally large U.S. fiscal deficit. Given the still-commanding reserve-currency status of the U.S. dollar in world finance, the American deficit acts as a huge vacuum cleaner that sucks up other countries' savings through the preemptive issue of the U.S. Treasury bonds in world financial markets. Consequential macroeconomic adjustments then force them to generate dollar surpluses in their commodity trade, whether or not they have appreciated their exchange rates. Getting rid of this chaos in the American public finances is the only satisfactory way to reduce the trade deficit. Because the great 1985–87 depreciation of the dollar has had, and will have, no substantial impact on this structural fiscal imbalance and consequent saving shortage in the American economy, it is incapable of correcting the U.S. trade deficit short of precipitating a major collapse of domestic investment within the United States.[6]

To be sure, the trade deficit is an important subject worthy of intense negotiation—but only in the context of assigning fiscal policies to resolve it. And in a world where real interest rates are still too high, there is little doubt that the United States should sharply cut its fiscal deficit to reduce its borrowing, rather than trying to persuade other governments to expand their expenditures and cut tax revenues.

For the international system to hold together, the U.S. government must give up its false, although widely held, view that dollar devaluation will itself substantially improve the dollar value of the net trade balance. For industrial countries, economists should jettison the whole elasticity approach relating the exchange rate to the balance of trade. Not only is this obsolete doctrine currently distorting relative currency values, but it suggests a "need" for continual exchange-rate flexibility—in order to balance ever-changing flows of imports and exports—thus making a common monetary standard impossible.

20.7 Purchasing Power Parity and the Nominal Anchor

But financial markets can be thrown into turmoil if participants believe that policymakers have half a mind to follow an incorrect theory and drive the dollar down. The foreign-exchange crisis from January through May 1987 is a case in point. Because the markets came to believe that American officials wanted the dollar to depreciate indefinitely, the normal inflow of private capital to cover the U.S. trade deficit dried up, thus necessitating massive official interventions by central banks to support the dollar. At the same time, long-term interest rates in American bond and mortgage markets rose sharply.

To get out of this unfortunate syndrome, we need an alternative theory of how exchange rates should be established. Purchasing power parity (PPP) can be an unambiguous theoretical guide for central banks and one with which the private financial markets can also feel comfortable.

The central idea behind PPP is to calculate nominal exchange rates that would align national price levels of internationally tradable goods as approximately measured by their respective producer or wholesale price indexes. Table 20.1 shows that concurrent purchasing power exchange rates in late 1987 are about 200 yen/dollar and 2.18 marks/dollar.[7] If the internal paths for price inflation were roughly the same (as they had been at the beginning of 1986) in Germany, Japan, and the United States, then these exchange rates (within narrow bands) should be the officially announced targets.

In 1986 and 1987, however, the prolonged undervaluation of the dollar—i.e., overvaluation of the yen and, to a lesser extent, the mark—has put the U.S. on a higher inflation path (figures 20.2 and 20.3). In Japan, deflationary pressure from the overvalued yen has caused a decline in a broad index of Japanese producer (and wholesale) prices and depressed the normal (high) rate of growth in Japanese money wages. Indeed, American money wages are now increasing one to two percentage points faster, despite Japan's higher trend in labor productivity.

Table 20.1
Exchange Rates, PPP Rates, and Target Rates

	Actual Exchange Rates (Quarterly Averages)		Purchasing Power Parity Rates	
	Yen/$	Mark/$	Yen/$	Mark/$
1986 IV	160	2.01	205	2.24
1987 I	153	1.84	202	2.22
I	143	1.81	199	2.18
III	147	1.84	201	2.18
IV	136[P]	1.68[P]	200[P]	2.17[P]
	Suggested target ranges			
1988	160 to 180	1.9 to 2.1	199[P]	2.16[P]

Source: OECD producer prices, IMF exchange rates. PPP calculations from McKinnon and Ohno (1987).
[P] indicates projected.

However, the momentum in these wage and price movements can only be altered with a lag. Thus, to facilitate smoother convergence to a common price level, exchange-rate targets should be set somewhat below current PPP levels, say in the neighborhood of 170 yen/dollar and 2.0 marks/dollar in late 1987. After the dollar had been nudged upward by relative monetary adjustments, unchanging official bands of, say, 160 to 180 yen/dollar and 1.9 to 2.1 marks/dollar could be established for early 1988 (see table 20.1). In 1988, if the exchange-rate misalignment with its differential inflation rates were to persist, then these target bands should be lowered somewhat.

Then, with exchange rates known to be fixed into the indefinite future, international commodity arbitrage and mutual monetary adjustment would ensure convergence to the same rate of commodity price inflation (preferably zero) in all three countries. Tradable goods prices (PPIs) would then be aligned close to purchasing power parity, and relative growth in national money wage claims would eventually reflect differentials in productivity growth, as had been the case in the 1960s under the old Bretton Woods system of pegged exchange rates when Japanese money wages grew much faster than those in the United States or Germany.

However, this proposal differs from the Bretton Woods Agreement, and also from subsequent American behavior, because the Fed would actively respond to the strength or weakness of the dollar against marks and yen, rather than simply waiting for the Bundesbank and the Bank of Japan to adjust. Although this will on occasion upset political sensibilities over short-term rates, it will pay political dividends in more stable long-term bond and mortgage yields once investors know that the dollar exchange rate will be roughly the same next year, or 10 years from now.

For example, for late 1987 into 1988, raising the yen/dollar and mark/dollar exchange rates toward their PPPs requires the U.S. Federal Reserve System to follow a relatively tight money policy while the Bank of Japan and the Bundesbank are more expansionary. As the mark and yen fall toward their PPP levels, inflationary pressure on prices and wages in the United States should slacken while it picks up in Japan and Europe. But the nominal anchor, the common price level measured at PPP exchange rates, would not be upset if this monetary adjustment were indeed symmetrical.

Announcement effects are important in order for private expectations to coalesce around the new exchange-rate targets. If the Fed simply tightens without revealing its foreign-exchange objectives, more severe monetary contraction and higher short-term interest rates might be necessary to boost the dollar toward PPP. Because expectations effects would be much less favorable, American long-term interest rates are less likely to come down as quickly.

Once exchange rates are properly aligned (according to PPP), representatives of the Fed, the Bank of Japan, and the EMS bloc should meet continually to monitor the behavior of their common price level in internationally tradable goods (as measured by PPIs or WPIs). Fortunately, information on commodity prices, even producer prices, becomes available much faster than the GNP statistics so widely watched today. Collective monetary expansion would be tailored downward or upward according to inflationary or deflationary trends in the common price level.

For example, the international integration of financial markets implies that stock market crashes, as occurred in October 1987, are felt in concert by all the industrial countries. In the face of such a deflationary threat, collective monetary expansion is warranted—without allowing any one country to get its currency undervalued and secure a mercantilistic advantage over its neighbors.

Even better as a nominal anchor for the system as a whole, a broadly based international price index, similar in scope to a PPI, could be priced out in each currency using a common set of representative weights for the industrial economies. A subcomponent consisting of homogeneous primary products, which are priced to market each day, could serve as an early warning indicator (Heller 1987) for movements in the broader index.

Participating central banks could use this nominal anchor as their own internal price-level target. For example, the Bundesbank could use the mark value of an international PPI as its target for "zero" domestic price inflation. If the Fed and Bank of Japan adopted similar internal targets based on the dollar and yen values of an international PPI, consistency between domestic price-level objectives and the obligation to maintain fixed exchange rates would be assured. (See chapter 22 for a more precise analysis.) When no such international index is available, existing national PPIs can approximate when the common price level is rising or falling (McKinnon and Ohno 1987).

Conversely, to prevent unnecessary conflict, countries should not adopt internal nominal anchors—such as the consumer price index or GNP deflator (both containing nontradable services) or growth in nominal GNP itself—that may be inconsistent with their obligation to maintain fixed nominal exchange rates.

Notes

1. A proposal first broached over a dozen years ago (McKinnon 1974) in response to the collapse of the Bretton Woods system of fixed exchange-rate parities.

2. This leaves open the question of whether new information, which shifts current expectations, is accurately borne out in the future. Because exchange-rate expectations are so difficult to measure, econometric testing of their accuracy is virtually impossible. Much new "information" about future monetary expansion—as, say, when the president of the central bank suddenly becomes ill—turns out to be ephemeral. Other news, such as changes in the tax laws affecting the relative profitability of holding foreign versus domestic securities, may prove well founded. Either accurate or inaccurate news, however, can move exchange rates, sometimes dramatically.

3. On the buyer's or consumer's side, a symmetrical inability to protect against future uncertain events—say the appearance of new and better products—limits their willingness to buy forward. Incomplete contingent forward markets push them toward buying spot.

4. Note that even companies that do not themselves engage in foreign trade can be highly vulnerable to such exchange-rate fluctuations (Hodder 1983).

5. Note that interest rates are much less useful as monetary indicators for the longer-run problem of securing price level stability for the group. Because of unstable inflationary expectations, sometimes called Fisher effects, absolute levels of nominal interest rates are ambiguous for measuring whether money is too "tight" or too "easy." Hence the need to pay attention to the aggregate money growth of the triumvirate to help anchor the common price level in the longer run, even while control over relative short-term interest rates is assigned to stabilizing exchange rates.

6. This ambiguous impact of an exchange-rate change on the trade balance is not just a short-run consequence of sticky invoice price for imports and exports—the familiar J-curve effect. In principle, adverse expenditure effects could offset direct price effects for several years (McKinnon 1981). In the very long run, of course, a devaluation simply washes out as internal price levels adjust and purchasing power parity is restored.

7. Without directly comparable national price indexes, calculating PPP exchange rates for internationally tradable goods can only be indirect and approximate. Nevertheless, new methods have been evolving (Ohno 1987; McKinnon and Ohno 1987) based on either WPIs or PPIs that, for the 1980s, seem to be significantly more efficient than the traditional technique based on the presumption that purchasing power parity held in some arbitrarily chosen base year.

References

Arrow, Kenneth, "The Role of Securities in the Optimal Allocation of Risk Bearing," *Review of Economic Studies,* 1964, *XXXI,* 91–96. (Translated from *Économétrie,* 1953).

———, *Essays in the Theory of Risk Bearing.* Chicago: Markham Press, 1973.

Bank for International Settlements, *Recent Innovations in International Banking,* Group of Ten Industrial Countries, April 1986.

Debreu, Gerard, *Theory of Value.* New York: John Wiley and Sons, 1959.

Frankel, Jeffrey, "International Capital Mobility and Crowding Out in the U.S. Economy." In Hafer, R., ed., *The Increasing Openness of the U.S. Economy.* Federal Reserve Bank of St. Louis, 1986, ch. 2, 33–69.

Frenkel, Jacob, and Michael L. Mussa, "The Efficiency of Foreign Exchange Markets and Measures of Turbulence," *American Economic Review,* May 1980, *70,* 374–81.

Greenwald, Bruce, and Joseph Stiglitz, "Externalities in Economies with Imperfect Information and Incomplete Markets," *Quarterly Journal of Economics,* May 1986, 229–264.

Heller, H. Robert, "Anchoring the International Monetary System," unpublished paper, Board of Governors of the Federal Reserve System. Washington, DC, March, 1987.

Hodder, J. E., "Exposure to Exchange-Rate Movements," *Journal of International Economics,* November 1982, *13,* 375–386.

International Monetary Fund, "Exchange Rate Volatility and World Trade," *Occasional Paper* 28, July 1984.

Kawai, Masahiro, and Itzhak Zilcha, "International Trade with Forward-Futures Markets Under Exchange-Rate and Price Uncertainty," *Journal of International Economics,* February 1986, *20,* 83–98.

Kindleberger, Charles P., "The Benefit of International Money," *Journal of International Economics,* September 1972, 425–42.

———, "The Dollar Yesterday, Today and Tomorrow," *Quarterly Review,* Banca Nazionale del Lavoro, December 1985, *2,* 295–308.

Levich, Richard, "Gauging the Evidence on Recent Movements in the Value of the Dollar." In *The U.S. Dollar: Recent Development, Outlook, and Policy Options,* Federal Reserve Bank of Kansas City, 1986, ch. 1, 1–28.

McKinnon, Ronald I., "The Exchange Rate and Macroeconomic Policy: Changing Postwar Perceptions," *Journal of Economic Literature*, June 1981, *XIX*, 531–57.

———, "Futures Markets, Buffer Stocks, and Income Stability for Primary Producers," *Journal of Political Economy*, December 1967, *75*, 844–61.

———, *An International Standard for Monetary Stabilization*. Washington, DC: Institute for International Economics, 1984.

———, *Money in International Exchange: The Convertible Currency System*. New York: Oxford University Press, 1979.

———, "A New Triparite Monetary Agreement or a Limping Dollar Standard?" *Essays in International Finance*, Princeton University, October 1974, *106*.

McKinnon, Ronald I., and Kenichi Ohno, "Getting the Exchange Rate Right: Insular Versus Open Economies," unpublished paper, Economics Department, Stanford University, December 1986.

———, "Purchasing Power Parity as a Monetary Standard" unpublished paper, Economics Department, Stanford University, September 1987.

Meade, James E., *The Balance of Payments*. London: Oxford University Press, 1951.

Meese, Richard, and Kenneth Rogoff, "Empirical Exchange Rate Models of the 1970s: Do They Fit Out of Sample," *Journal of International Economics*, February 1983, *14*, 3–24.

Miles, Marc A., "The Effects of Devaluation on the Trade Balance and the Balance of Payments: Some New Results," *Journal of Political Economy*, June 1979, *87*, 600–620.

Morita, Akio, presentation to *International Working Round on Exchange Rates and Coordination*, Zurich, Switzerland, June 19, 1986.

Ohno, Kenichi, "Estimating Purchasing Power Parities in the 1970s and '80s: The Price Pressure Approach," unpublished paper, Economics Department, Stanford University, September 1987.

Robinson, Joan, "The Foreign Exchanges." In *Essays in the Theory of Employment*. New York: Macmillan, 1937, ch. 1.

The Monetary Road to Postwar Prosperity: Marshall-Dodge or Bretton Woods?

Half a century after its signing in New Hampshire in 1944, the Bretton Woods Agreement on currency convertibility and exchange-rate stability holds its mystical allure. The great economist John Maynard Keynes was its inspiration, and played a major role—in conjunction with the American negotiators—in drafting the Articles of Agreement of the International Monetary Fund. The result is widely believed to have provided the monetary pillar—exchange rate and price stability—that supported the remarkable postwar prosperity of the 1950s and 1960s. (The other pillar was the 1947 General Agreement on Tariffs and Trade—now transformed into the World Trade Organization.)

In the industrial countries today—with resurgent protectionism, recurrent over- or undervalued exchange rates, volatile interest rates, higher average unemployment, and slower growth—people talk wistfully of recapturing the spirit of Bretton Woods. It seems a noble quest. But is the 1944 agreement the right starting point for international monetary reform today? The answer depends on whether the 1944 agreement, although formally ratified by member countries, was ever effectively implemented in practice. Were the intentions of the negotiators at Bretton Woods actually realized so that the IMF Agreement was indeed the basis for the postwar prosperity of the 1950s and 1960s?

After 1945, currencies in Western Europe and Japan remained inconvertible and in inflationary disarray. Trade remained bartered, narrowly bilateral, and so limited that output in Europe

Originally published as "Recapturing a Lost Spirit" in *Financial Times*, 21 June 1994, 12, in commemoration of the fiftieth anniversary of the Bretton Woods Agreement of 1944. Revised December 1994. Reprinted with permission.

and Japan stayed unnaturally depressed well into 1948. Furthermore, either because its mandate was incorrectly drawn or its financial resources were too slender, the International Monetary Fund did nothing to relieve this currency impasse and the postwar economic crisis. Faced with only anemic partial recovery by the late 1940s, Western Europe was ready to succumb to communism, and Japan faced high inflation and labor unrest.

The great rescue operation was engineered not by the IMF but by the Marshall Plan, from mid 1948 through early 1952, in Europe, and by the 1949 Dodge Plan in Japan. By 1951, the virtual elimination of inflation in Western Europe and Japan was followed by twenty years of stable (some would say unduly rigid) exchange rates based on the U.S. dollar—whose purchasing power over tradable goods also remained constant until about 1968. What can be called the "Marshall-Dodge fixed-rate dollar standard" led a healthy life until 1971, when President Nixon insisted that—to avoid disinflating the American economy—the dollar be devalued.

Both the Marshall and Dodge plans depended on direct dollar assistance from the United States. But surprisingly strong conditions—the elimination of fiscal deficits and inflation, and the step-by-step elimination of currency restrictions on current trade—were attached. In Europe, the capstone was the European Payments Union (EPU), established in September 1950 for securing full multilateral clearing among central banks of sixteen western European countries. To ensure credibility, the U.S. dollar was enthroned both as the unit of account and means of settlement within the EPU. European governments declared exact dollar parities (initially without even the flexibility of narrow bands around them) to facilitate the monthly clearing of international payments and to secure a "nominal anchor" for their warravaged financial systems. Similarly, Japan fixed the yen at 360 per dollar, secured by American credit lines under the Dodge Plan, as the anchor for its successful disinflation in 1949–50.

To maintain their dollar parities for the subsequent two decades, European countries and Japan subordinated their domestic monetary policies to their fixed exchange rates. More by accident than design, therefore, the United States alone had the monetary independence to provide a nominal anchor for the group. (Although by the late 1950s, American monetary policy was somewhat constrained by its residual link to gold.)

In what ways did the 1950–70 Marshall-Dodge standard differ from the spirit of Bretton Woods? Marshall-Dodge imposed a common monetary standard on the industrial countries at the outset of the policy of fixing exchange rates. Participating industrial countries experienced roughly the same low rate of price inflation in tradable goods—about 1 percent per year as measured by their wholesale price indexes (WPIs)—as did the United States.

Why deny that the negotiators at Bretton Woods in 1944 wanted a stable common monetary standard, or at least wished for something similar to Marshall-Dodge? Keynes, who dominated the thinking of the conferees, drew up the Bretton Woods articles to give each national government flexibility in choosing its own macroeconomic policy in order to secure full employment—while preventing spillover effects on its neighbors. Using precepts drawn from his *General Theory* (1936), Keynes wanted each government free to fine-tune its own monetary and fiscal policies to secure full employment—with differing inflation rates if need be. See rule box 2 in chapter 2.

Remembering the failure of the international gold standard in the interwar period, Keynes did not want to establish any common monetary standard. Nor, because of his concern with "hot" money flows in the 1920s and 1930s, did he want an unrestricted world capital market. He and his intellectual heirs subscribe to the principle of national macroeconomic autonomy. After the war, both Keynesians and monetarists rejected the idea that monetary autonomy of any industrial country be limited by international obligations. To be sure, each group had quite different ideas on how that autonomy should be exercised, but both wanted exchange-rate flexibility to make such autonomy feasible.

However, the Bretton Woods negotiators did want to restore normalcy in foreign trade on current account. Continual exchange-rate fluctuations and prolonged misalignments that upset a country's macroeconomic equilibrium were to be avoided. A new par-value system restricted short-run exchange-rate fluctuations within 1 percent on either side of "parity." These exchange parities would be easy to enforce as long as capital controls remained in place—as Keynes prescribed. "Beggar-thy-neighbor" policies from inappropriate exchange-rate fluctuations could thereby be prevented.

But Keynes also wanted the exchange par values to be adjustable. With economies insulated from each other on capital account, the main criterion for the IMF to agree on an exchange depreciation would be whether a country had an ongoing net trade deficit. For example, a country following a strategy of relatively high inflation for promoting increased employment could secure the IMF's permission for modest offsetting devaluations. While remaining pegged in the short run, exchange rates would be flexible—and national monetary policies quite differentiated—in the long run. Thus did the negotiators of 1944 imagine they had reconciled the principle of national macroeconomic autonomy with limitations upon exchange risk in international trade.

With hindsight (and Milton Friedman), we now know inflationary national monetary policies cannot sustain higher levels of employment. But that was not the prevailing view at Bretton Woods in 1944. Despite its great success in practice, the "accidental" advent of the fixed-rate Marshall-Dodge standard was a conceptual anathema to most professional economists in the 1950s and 1960s—with echoes to the present day.

How does this potted history matter for reforming today's international monetary system?

First, because international capital markets are now fully open, a trade deficit no longer warrants an exchange depreciation—which the old spirit of Bretton Woods encouraged. (See the analysis in chapters 13 and 14.) Recently, the ongoing U.S. current-account deficit has encouraged the American government to cajole the Japanese into two serious episodes of yen overvaluation—in 1986–87 and again in 1993–95. In both cases, a slump in private investment, because of the exchange overvaluation, caused a sharp downturn in the Japanese economy with no reduction in its current-account surplus—as shown in chapter 14 for the 1977–78 appreciation of the yen. In longer-term perspective, since 1971 the policy of forcing the yen to appreciate continually has imposed relative deflation in Japan without predictably influencing Japan's net trade surplus—as discussed in great detail in a related volume, *Dollar and Yen*, by McKinnon and Ohno (forthcoming).

Second, as with the Marshall-Dodge standard, securing more stable exchange and interest rates must proceed simultaneously with the international harmonization of national monetary policies. The keystone must be a low or zero rate of inflation in a broad basket of tradable goods.

As discussed in chapter 2, a second-best technique for providing a common nominal anchor is to turn the job over to a single dominant country whose own internal price level has been relatively stable. In some unusual historical circumstances, this may work well for a while. Yet any such asymmetrical standard remains vulnerable to upheavals in the center country. The (mild) American inflation of the late 1960s into the early 1970s, coupled with demands to devalue the dollar to restore international competitiveness, ended the Marshall-Dodge fixed-rate dollar standard. Within Europe after 1990, German fiscal deficits, coupled with tight money, undermined the commitments of partner countries to maintain their EMS narrow bands—with major speculative upheavals in exchange rates in 1992 and 1993.

Far better to negotiate a fully symmetrical agreement among hard-currency countries—like Japan, the United States, and the European bloc in the 1990s—for anchoring the price level of the group in a manner consistent with keeping nominal exchange rates stable into the indefinite future. And to this task we now turn in chapter 22.

Reference

McKinnon, Ronald, and Kenichi Ohno. Forthcoming. *Dollar and Yen: A Macroeconomic Approach to Resolving Conflict between the United States and Japan.* Cambridge, MA: MIT Press.

22

From Plaza-Louvre to a Common Monetary Standard for the Twenty-First Century

To reduce excessive financial volatility in today's international economy, the industrial economies must coordinate their monetary policies. But history matters, and any new reforms must be evolutionary rather than revolutionary. From chapter 2 and those following, the principal rules of the game for the classical gold standard before 1914, the Bretton Woods Agreement itself in 1944, the fixed- and floating-rate dollar standards from 1950 through 1984, the European Monetary System after 1979, and the Plaza-Louvre Accords holding since 1985 gave us important clues on how to proceed. In this concluding chapter, these ideas are brought together in a proposed new set of rules for reestablishing, and sustaining, a common monetary standard on a worldwide basis.

22.1 The Rules of the Game, 1985–95: The Plaza-Louvre Accords

Although the rules of the Plaza-Louvre regime are rather weak and informal, they still govern monetary relationships among Japan, North America, and Western Europe. Rule box 5, slightly revised from the McKinnon (1993) version, shows how the principal economies currently play the international money and exchange-rate game (page 68 or the appendix). Because these rules are the conditions from which evolutionary reform must start, let us briefly review their principal characteristics.

Originally appeared as a paper presented to the Reinventing Bretton Woods Committee, New York, 20 September 1994. Revised January 1995.

Unlike under the floating-rate dollar standard (1973–84), under Plaza-Louvre industrial countries now intervene in concert to limit unusually large fluctuations in the dollar's exchange rate against other major currencies; see rule III in box 5. After the spring of 1985, the United States dropped its previous hands-off policy toward the foreign exchanges. It began to hold foreign-exchange reserves of its own (rule IV), and to cooperate systematically with other central banks. Catte, Galli, and Rebecchini (1992) identified seventeen major "concerted" interventions, namely, those that included at least two of the G-3 central banks (Bank of Japan, Bundesbank, or U.S. Federal Reserve) between 1985 and 1991. Since the authors completed their path-breaking research, four further massive concerted interventions have occurred: from 20 July to 11 August 1992, in August 1993, in early May 1994, and in August 1995. An article in the *Financial Times*, 5 May 1994, reported the following:

Central banks yesterday intervened repeatedly, in concert, and on a large scale, to support the dollar. . . . In what dealers describe as the heaviest bout of intervention in several years, as many as 17 central banks were seen selling D-Marks and yen to buy dollars. The heavy support for the U.S. currency, coupled with the comments of senior officials, provided a clear indication that G-7 governments are unhappy with the recent weakness of the dollar. . . . One bank reported seeing 10 rounds of intervention by the Fed alone. Most European central banks, as well as the Bank of Japan, the Bank of England, and the Bank of Canada were also seen in the market. (P. 40)

Each of these four interventions succeeded in halting a precipitous decline of the dollar against the yen and mark—more by their signaling of future monetary policies (as Dominguez and Frankel [1993] had concluded for the earlier interventions) than their ability to seriously alter current private currency portfolios. Indeed, the immediate domestic monetary consequences of these (and previous) concerted interventions were largely sterilized—as per rule V in box 5.

Remarkably, central banks outside the G-3 were willing to buy dollars, not only with their own national currencies, but also with yen or marks—as per rule VII. At times of great pressure against the dollar, speculators typically opt mainly for marks or yen as "safe havens." Thus central banks other than the G-3 ones support stable exchange rates among Japan, Germany, and the United States to help prevent their own exchange rates from moving too much against one or more major currencies.

22.2 Plaza-Louvre and the World Business Cycle

Plaza-Louvre only weakly limits the more extreme annual or semiannual runs in the dollar's exchange rate; it does nothing to reduce short-run exchange volatility on a daily, weekly, or monthly basis. Nor does it eliminate the possibility of long-run drift in a country's exchange rate. Nevertheless, this fragile monetary order is surprisingly valuable in smoothing the world business cycle. From 1973 to 1984 under the floating-rate dollar standard, national business cycles were strongly and positively correlated. Since 1985, however, *Economic Outlook* (OECD 1994) confirms that national business cycles have become more desynchronized. Thus, over the past ten years, worldwide cyclical fluctuations have become less virulent because national business cycles tend to offset rather than reinforce each other. However, the OECD, the IMF in various publications, and the academic literature provide no systematic explanation for desychronization.

Why should this change in monetary regimes flatten the world business cycle? Under the floating-rate dollar standard—described in empirical detail in chapters 7, 8, and 9—the United States government neglected the foreign-exchange market and let other countries struggle *unilaterally* to smooth actual or incipient fluctuations in their dollar exchange rates. Because the dollar tended to be strong or weak more or less simultaneously against all other countries, they all built up dollar exchange reserves and expanded their national money supplies when the dollar was weak, as in 1971–73 or 1977–78; this expanded the world money supply and led to worldwide inflations in 1973–74 and 1979–80. Similarly, when the dollar became unnaturally strong, the other industrial countries were forced to draw down their dollar reserves and contract the rates of growth in their national money supplies—leading to synchronized international downturns, as in 1981–82.[1]

The switch to the Plaza-Louvre rules after 1985 ameliorated this problem in two related ways. First, because the U.S. Federal Reserve (at the storm center) would now enter obviously and in concert with other central banks to stop or dampen runs on the dollar (rule III), the signaling effect was stronger and less ambiguous. Rather than "benign" neglect, the private markets came to believe that American monetary policy, and the policies of other countries, would eventually be adjusted if necessary to stop a run on the currency—although policies were not generally adjusted in the near term (rule V). In particular, American monetary policy no longer perversely aggravated cycles in the dollar exchange rate and in world money.

Second, because the concerted interventions after 1985 were sufficiently successful in dampening extreme fluctuations in the dollar rate, foreign central banks no longer had to expand their money supplies when the dollar was weak (and vice versa) in order to make their interventions effective. Untoward fluctuations in world money were thereby dampened—along with cyclical fluctuations in the OECD countries as a group. Thus, in any reform program, the valuable positive aspect of the Plaza-Louvre regime—where the United States behaves symmetrically with respect to the other industrial countries in smoothing the dollar's exchange rate—should be preserved.

22.3 Plaza-Louvre and Excess Financial Volatility

Nevertheless, these current rules still tolerate excess volatility and long-term drift in exchange rates and, hence, in long-term interest rates. The weaknesses leading to this excess volatility and drift lie mainly in Plaza-Louvre rules II and VI (including VIa). They are closely related, but let us consider each in turn.

In box 5, rule II gives governments virtual carte blanche to decide unilaterally that the "fundamentals" for exchange-rate targets have changed. Consider a familiar example. From the early 1970s through the early 1990s, ever larger Japanese trade surpluses and American trade deficits provoked the U.S. government to "talk down" the yen/dollar rate—which fell erratically from 360 in early 1971 to less than 100 in mid 1995, when the U.S. trade deficit hit record levels.

The problem lies less with politicians and officials, and rather more with economic doctrine and economists—as discussed in chapter 20. The widely believed elasticities model of the balance of trade holds that a trade deficit can be corrected by exchange depreciation. But the elasticities model applies only in fairly special circumstances where economies are insular rather than open—see chapter 13, and McKinnon and Ohno (forthcoming). If exchange controls limit capital movements and if trade itself is a fringe activity, an economy is defined as "insular." At Bretton Woods in 1944 and for some years after, the elasticities doctine was empirically valid because controls on trade and capital flows were almost universal. In order to limit trade imbalances among what were then insular economies, the negotiators wanted pegged but adjustable exchange rates as reflected in rule II in box 2. If the spirit of the Bretton Woods Agreement had been effective, capital controls would have allowed national governments to change the pegs directly without being overwhelmed by anticipatory speculation. (But chapters 2 and 21 argue that the Bretton-Woods Agreement was quickly supplemented by the fixed-rate Marshall-Dodge Dollar Standard.)

Today, by contrast, capital and trade flows among the industrial economies are huge and virtually unrestricted. Rather than being directly controllable by Treasury authorities, any exchange rate is endogenously determined by the current and prospective monetary policies of the countries in question. No longer is the exchange rate an instrumental variable for controlling the net trade balance—or the current account—in a predictable fashion (chapters 13 and 14). Of course, countries with chronic inflation must continually depreciate to maintain balance in external payments. But, for a country starting with a stable price level, an exchange depreciation simply reflects a relatively easy money (high-spending) policy that stimulates economic activity overall. Exports and imports both increase, with no presumption about what happens to the net trade balance.

Consequently, in today's world of highly open economies, a flexible exchange rate is not an independent instrument for controlling trade flows. Instead, it is a potential source of monetary disharmony in the system.

For example, having the American authorities "talk the yen up" has forced outright deflation on Japan, that is, forced the Bank of Japan into an unduly tight national monetary policy (McKinnon and Ohno, forthcoming). The erratic fall in the Japanese wholesale price index (by more than 18 percent from 1985 through mid 1995) was accompanied by two major industrial recessions. The continual appreciation of the yen prevented the

Bank of Japan from anchoring its domestic price level—thus violating rule VI, even in the fairly weak form it appears in box 5. Yen appreciation with tight money so depressed the Japanese economy that the yen value of imports fell more than the yen value of exports. Rather than being corrected, Japan's current-account surplus increased.

Projected into the more distant future, uncertainty in exchange rates aggravates volatility in today's long-term interest rates—see chapter 3. Despite the world business cycle being less pronounced under Plaza-Louvre, the continued uncertain evolution of the yen/dollar and other important exchange rates ensures that long-term interest rates will remain excessively volatile in Japan, the United States, and the rest of the world.

22.4 Rules for the Twenty-First Century

Reducing excessive financial volatility, while properly anchoring national price levels, requires a strong mutual commitment by the industrial economies to stability in *nominal* exchange rates in the long run. However, the interaction goes both ways. If nominal exchange rates are to be fixed within narrow bands to reduce investor uncertainty, Plaza-Louvre's weak defense against price inflation must be strengthened.

Accordingly, suppose that, either by formal design or by evolutionary practice, the Plaza-Louvre rules are significantly enhanced. The central importance of Germany (representing a European bloc), Japan, and the United States is retained, but their symmetrical obligations to each other are spelled out more precisely—together with supporting obligations of other industrial countries. The resulting new rules for the game are laid out in box 8 under the title "A Common Monetary Standard for the Twenty-First Century"—or, more simply, CMS21. It would provide a monetary anchor for the world at large reminiscent of, but more secure than, the Marshall-Dodge dollar standard.

The logic of CMS21 can be best understood by contrasting its anchor rule with that under Plaza-Louvre. Among the G-3, an internationally consistent anchor for national price levels of tradable goods (rule VII in box 8) replaces diverse national monetary goals of simply keeping rates of price inflation "low," where no particular price index is specified (rule VI in box 5).

Rule Box 8
A Common Monetary Standard for the Twenty-First Century (CMS21)

Germany, Japan, and the United States (G-3)

   I. Announce target zones for yen/dollar and mark/dollar exchange rates of ± 5 percent to be sustained by mutual monetary adjustment. Base central rates on initial purchasing power parities that align wholesale price levels among G-3.

   II. Intervene in concert to reverse short-run trends in the dollar exchange rate that threaten to pierce zonal boundaries. Signal by not disguising these concerted interventions.

   III. Practice free currency convertibility on current and capital account, and hold official exchange reserves symmetrically in each other's currencies. U.S. government to complete its buildup of reserves in marks, yen, and possibly other convertible currencies.

   IV. Don't fully sterilize the immediate monetary impact of interventions in G-3 currencies. Let short-term interest rates and the domestic monetary base adjust modestly (Bagehot's Rule).

   V. Once inflation and longer-term interest rates are closely aligned across the G-3, harden and narrow zonal boundaries to ± 1 percent.

   VI. If rule I or rule V must be temporarily suspended, restore the country's "traditional" exchange rate as soon as practicable. If necessssary, deflate the domestic economy to the price level prevailing before suspension occurred.

   VIa. If the United States is forced to suspend rule I or rule V, change the numéraire currency for exchange rates to marks or yen— whichever one has the better record for maintaining its purchasing power under rule VII.

   VII. Assign domestic central bank credit to anchor the level of tradable goods prices in the long run. Use a national wholesale or producer price index as an approximate target until a WPI or PPI with internationally standardized weights becomes available.

   VIIa. Should undershooting or overshooting occur, do not rebase the price-level target.

   VIII. Remain passive, with no balance-of-payments or exchange-rate targets, with respect to countries outside the G-3. Sterilize (passively) the domestic monetary consequences of their foreign-exchange interventions.

Other Industrial Countries

   IX. Support, or not oppose, interventions by G-3 to keep the dollar within designated mark and yen zones. Buy dollars with the

Rule Box 8 (continued)

> national currency, or with yen and marks, when the dollar is weak, and vice versa.
>
> X.   Fix exchange rate against any G-3 currency by rules I, V, and VI above. If insufficient to anchor domestic price level, adopt rules VII and VIIa as well.

To reflect current practices by central banks, Plaza-Louvre's "rebasing" rule (VIa) allows differential drift in national price levels of tradable goods. If price inflation overshoots in any one decision period—whether it be over a quarter or a year, the national central bank simply rebases the relevant price index for targeting next period's inflation. By accepting the now changed dometic price level as the basis for future monetary targeting, the national monetary authority lets bygones be bygones. The result is price-level drift that differs from one country to the next so as to be inconsistent with long-term exchange stability.

In contrast, under the CMS21 price-level objective (rule VII in box 8), the Bundesbank, Bank of Japan, and Federal Reserve System each binds itself to deflate to some preassigned target for its national price level in the event that any one of them had mistakenly allowed some inflation to occur (rule VIIa). Procedures for correcting forecasting errors would have to be tightened so that if the targeted price level overshot in any one decision period, an offsetting downward correction would be required in subsequent period(s).[2] Once this basic anchoring mechanism is in place, the mark/dollar and yen/dollar exchange rates can be fixed at purchasing power parities (rule I), which align the targets for the national producer price indexes, and then sustained indefinitely.

Although a few scholars have advocated price-level targeting on purely domestic grounds, such a commitment would represent a significant change in the national monetary policies in the OECD countries in general and in our triumvirate in particular. But if the right price index is chosen, it would not represent a "major" change in current monetary practices. If a broad goods price index like the WPI or the PPI is targeted, then occasional deflation on a quarterly or annual basis is economically tenable and politically realistic. During the last decade of fairly low overall inflation in the industrial countries, all their WPIs (or PPIs) have recorded negative growth in occasional months or quarters—aside from the unduly prolonged deflation in Japan.

But national consumer price indexes (CPIs)—to which central banks now probably pay more, although not exclusive, attention—almost never exhibit downward movements, that is, show negative growth rates on a monthly or quarterly basis. The same is true for other broader price indexes—such as the GDP deflator—that include services as well as goods. The reasons are twofold. First, because measured productivity growth tends to be higher in goods-producing industries compared to services, CPIs naturally increase relative to WPIs in the longer run: a manifestation of the well-known Balassa-Samuelson effect. Except for occasional shorter-term booms in primary commodity prices, this gap tends to be of the order of 2 percentage points per year in mature industrial economies—but could be much greater in eras of rapid economic growth, such as Japan in the 1950s and 1960s (McKinnon and Ohno 1989). Second, because nominal wage rates are fairly rigid downward and services tend to be labor-intensive, any broad price index where services are heavily represented would also be rigid downward.

In summary, unless hit by unexpected exchange-rate changes, a national central bank in a mature industrial economy can relatively easily target the level of its domestic WPI or PPI in the steady state—while not necessarily reaching it every quarter or every year.[3] But, if successful, this would still leave modest upward drift in its CPI or GDP deflator that, under CMS21, it would ignore.

At the outset of the twenty-first-century reform program, existing national WPIs or PPIs would approximate a more general international price index for tradables. In large diversified industrial economies like Japan, Germany, or the United States, thousands of different goods enter each WPI or PPI. Because of large-number averaging, these national price indexes reflect general inflationary pressure very similarly—although their commodity or value weights vary somewhat from one country to another. For example, during the 1950s and 1960s, rates of price inflation in their WPIs were virtually the same: about 1 percent per year before 1968—as shown in chapter 2. In a new monetary pact, a more secure anchor would be a common WPI or PPI with internationally standardized weights, against which each national central bank aimed to stabilize the purchasing power of its own money.

Once price-level targets for national WPIs or PPIs are agreed on, then corresponding targets for nominal exchange rates can be calculated—rule I in box 8—according to the principle of purchasing power parity (PPP). These exchange rates would align national price levels (net of sales taxes or retail service margins) at the "factory gate."[4] In principle, these rates could be sustainable no matter what the now common rate of inflation in tradable goods happens to be. But the regime would only be satisfactory if the common price level was truly anchored in the long run so that each national monetary authority could report to its government that it was indeed stabilizing the domestic price level as well as the exchange rate.

22.5   G-3 Open-Market Operations and Domestic Credit in the Long Run

Under CMS21, how should German, Japanese, and American monetary policies be conducted in the long run? Rule VII specifies that the trend in each central bank's domestic credit expansion—the purchase of domestic securities or the discounting of commercial bank loans—be just sufficient to satisfy the domestic demand for base money when the producer price index is stable, real income is growing at its long-term trend, and broader price indexes like the CPI or GNP deflator drift upward at possibly different rates. Correspondingly, the net foreign-exchange reserves of any G-3 country, that is, the holdings of each other's currencies as per rule IV, would show no trend. The upshot is that no G-3 country would finance ongoing growth in its domestic base money by building up its net foreign-exchange reserves—although these reserves could show significant variance in the short run.

This is how Japan played the game under the Marshall-Dodge dollar standard when the yen/dollar rate was fixed at 360. In the 1950s and toward the end of the 1960s, Japan's net exchange reserves stayed fairly close to $2 billion—while the huge growth in demand for base money was financed entirely from domestic credit expansion by the Bank of Japan (chapter 2).

In contrast, by not expanding net domestic credit at all, the Bundesbank played the game differently—and inappropriately. In the 1950s and 1960s, a huge buildup of Germany's dollar reserves overaccounted for the very large increase in Germany's rapidly growing monetary base. Although the United States passively sterilized the impact of Germany's dollar buildup on the American monetary base (rule VII in box 3), eventually the restrictiveness of domestic credit expansion in Germany, coupled with overexpansiveness in the United States after 1968, undermined the credibility of the par value system. Beginning in 1969, foreign-exchange crises led to forced appreciations of the mark well before the more general depreciations of the dollar in August 1971.

Because the U.S. was so overwhelmingly large in the world economy in the 1950s and 1960s, the Federal Reserve was capable of pegging the common price level for the industrial world and many developing countries—as long as the Fed chose to direct its own rate of domestic credit expansion to that end, as per rule X in box 3.

In the 1990s, however, the U.S. economy is relatively smaller with a less favorable history from the 1970s and 1980s of anchoring its own price level. Thus, the anchoring job best devolves to the world's three major industrial and financial powers acting symmetrically and in concert. Under rules VII and VIIa of CMS21, the three central banks are to direct their domestic credit expansion to jointly anchor the common price level for tradable goods on the one hand, while maintaining the credibility of the exchange parities on the other. Rather than depending on the untrammeled hegemony of any one country, the new regime would depend on the three major financial powers to monitor each other.

What are the monetary mechanics? Each central bank must project the long-run growth in the demand for its monetary liabilities, that is, the domestic monetary base. For algebraic simplicity, assume that the long-run elasticity of demand for base money with respect to growth in nominal GNP is unity. Then domestic credit should grow by

$\Delta DC = \Delta Y + \Delta X$, where $\qquad\qquad\qquad\qquad\qquad\qquad$ (1)

ΔDC is the percentage change in domestic credit,
ΔY is the projected percentage growth in real GNP, and
ΔX is the projected percentage growth in the GNP
deflator assuming that the PPI is constant.

In the United States, where competition and productivity growth in services has been quite strong, ΔX would be quite modest, 1 to 2 percent per year. In Japan, where service prices were rising substantially compared to goods prices, ΔX would have been somewhat higher, 2 to 3 percent per year. Combined with projections of a naturally higher ΔY in Japan compared to the United States, domestic credit expansion by the Bank of Japan would be substantially higher than that of the Federal Reserve—as was the case when when the yen/dollar rate was fixed at 360. The natural rate of domestic credit expansion by the Bundesbank in the new regime would probably be closer to that of the United States—unlike Germany's behavior in the 1950s and 1960s.

Of course, these calculations assume that the elasticity of demand for base money with respect to increases in nominal GNP is unity in all three countries. My earlier proposals (McKinnon 1977, 1984) for coordinating domestic credit expansion to anchor price levels across our triumvirate showed misplaced confidence in the stability of the velocity of money. In the 1980s and 1990s, velocity proved surprisingly unpredictable—no matter which monetary aggregate one chose. Even so, the demand for the G-3's monetary base (including a stable European bloc around Germany) in the aggregate remains more stable than that for any one country. Because international currency substitution remains important (chapters 7 and 16), the triumvirate can do a better job of stabilizing the common price level in tradables jointly when exchange rates are tethered—under CMS21—than any one of the three can manage separately when continually hit by unpredictable exchange-rate fluctuations.

But the three central banks have to be flexible in using monetary instruments and selecting intermediate targets. Although each G-3 monetary authority cannot escape projecting domestic credit expansion similarly to equation (1), such projections must be continually revised to reach exchange-rate and price-level stability. For example, if one country builds up net foreign-exchange reserves relative to the other two, the former should nudge its rate of domestic credit expansion upward while the latter reduce theirs. Or, if the common producer price level begins to increase, all three central banks would reduce growth in domestic credit below previous projections.

What instrument of domestic monetary policy best maintains smooth secular growth in domestic credit as calculated in equation (1)? Because the United States, Germany, and Japan all have open and deep domestic bond markets, the natural instrument is open-market operations in government bonds. Because bond purchases occur at the discretion of each of our three central banks, they establish an independent monetary anchor for the group.

In contrast, in the 1950s and 1960s, Japan's monetary policy focused exclusively on maintaining the yen/dollar exchange rate while relying on the United States to anchor the common price level. In implementing this successful dependent monetary policy, the Bank of Japan relied mainly on its discount window for extending domestic credit. When commercial banks felt short of reserves, they showed up at the discount window and were generally accommodated. Thus, under the Marshall-Dodge dollar standard, Japanese money growth was endogenously determined and expansionary. But after the par-value system broke down in 1971–73, the syndrome of the ever higher yen has forced relative deflation on Japan (McKinnon and Ohno, forthcoming). Consequently, in the whole postwar period, the Bank of Japan has never been able to follow an independent monetary policy—whether under fixed or floating exchange rates.

Under CMS21, however, Japan—with Germany and the United States—will determine long-run growth in its own monetary base. This switch to discretionary open-market operations, with relatively minor reliance on discounting, will give the Bank of Japan a measure of independence greater than that under previous fixed or floating exchange-rate regimes.

22.6 G-3 Monetary Policies and Exchange-Rate Stability in the Short Run

Assuming that this long-run commitment to adjust domestic credit to anchor the common price level is in place, how would

the Bundesbank (representing monetary policy for a broader
European bloc), the Bank of Japan, and the U.S. Federal Reserve
System conduct their short-run monetary policies to assure
exchange-rate stability? Start by assuming steady-state equilibrium: each of the G-3's producer price levels is stable, and prevailing exchange rates are at their purchasing power parities (within
narrow bands), which align these national price levels—as was
the case under the Marshall-Dodge dollar standard. If the G-3
had been in this steady state for some time, longer-term interest
rates must also be closely aligned.

But short rates need not be. Because of the narrow bands
within which exchange rates can move, short-term rates could
differ temporarily across the three countries—as was clearly the
case under the pre-1914 gold standard. Indeed, under rule IV of
CMS21, short-term interest differentials are "assigned" to maintain the exchange-rate regime. Continual but modest variance in
short-term interest differentials, and in each country's monetary
base, would normally be effected by temporary deviations from
the projected trend in domestic credit in equation (1). For example, if the dollar weakened against the yen and mark and threatened to pierce its zonal boundaries, the U.S. Federal Reserve
System would (temporarily) nudge short dollar rates up while
the Bundesbank and Bank of Japan nudged the corresponding
mark and yen rates down.

In contrast, major concerted interventions in the foreign exchanges to defend the band limits (as per rule II in box 8) would
be infrequent—once or twice a year if Plaza-Louvre is any indication. If one became necessary, official reserve positions could
change substantially in the short run. But the short-term monetary effect would be partially sterilized by offsetting expansions
or contractions of domestic central bank credit. This is nothing
more than the application of Bagehot's Rule—as it operated under the gold and dollar standards (boxes 1 and 3). As under Plaza-
Louvre, these concerted interventions would still be effective
because they signal the authorities' long-run monetary intent.

The key idea is that the G-3 respond symmetrically and openly
to contain pressure in the foreign exchanges. If long-run monetary policy in each G-3 country is also correct, the exchange-
rate bands would be so credible that the necessary central bank
reactions to short-run pressure in the foreign exchanges would
remain modest.

The major stabilizing speculators in the foreign exchanges would—in the short run—be the commercial banks in their capacity as dealers clearing international payments on a day-to-day basis. If the ebb and flow of commercial payments by merchants and pension or mutual funds tended to push the dollar toward the bottom of its band(s) on any one trading day, commercial banks would simply draw down their modest dollar reserves to provide marks and yen to these nonspeculative "noise traders,"[5] and so stabilize the rate without official interventions. As long as the commercial banks knew that official support would be forthcoming if necessary, very little would be needed in practice. This was true under the Marshall-Dodge dollar standard after the European Payments Union, with its dependence on central bank clearing (weekly settlements), was terminated in 1958.[6]

Rather than being "hot" money, private short-term capital would regain the stabilizing role it played under the gold standard. Once the exchange-rate regime becomes credible, the fact that national capital markets are now so open to each other becomes an advantage in reducing financial volatility.

22.7   Other Industrial Countries in CMS21

To secure the monetary independence Germany, Japan, and the United States for anchoring the world price level, they must remain passive with respect to the balance-of-payments objectives, and foreign-exchange interventions, of other countries. By practicing free trade and open capital markets (rule III in box 8), the G-3 would benignly ignore the rest of the world. Correspondingly, rule VIII specifies that the monetary impact of changes in the official reserves of outside countries be fully sterilized. If other countries hold their foreign-exchange reserves in nonmonetary instruments—such as Treasury bills and bonds denominated in dollars, marks, or yen—this sterilization would be automatic, just as the United States passively sterilized the foreign-exchange interventions of all other countries under Marshall-Dodge (chapters 2 and 7).

In securing the overall success of CMS21, however, other industrial countries have important roles to play. By fixing their own exchange rates within narrow bands against the dollar, mark, or yen (rule X in box 8), they increase the ambit of exchange stability in the world economy. Not only is free trade is easier to sustain, but less-developed and transitional economies can better anchor their own price levels by adhering to CMS21. Once all financially important countries—that is, those with highly developed securities markets—belong to the same international monetary standard, portfolio churning and volatility in long-term interest rates worldwide would be dampened—see chapter 3.

Industrial countries outside the G-3 already implicitly recognize the importance of preventing major fluctuations in the mark/dollar and yen/dollar exchange rates. Under Plaza-Louvre, we saw how other industrial countries joined the concerted interventions of the G-3 to stabilize the dollar's exchange rate. When the dollar was weak, they bought dollars with their own currencies or by drawing down their reserves of marks and yen—as encapsulated in rule VII in box 5. And, under CMS21, these helpful support operations by countries outside the G-3 would continue—as per rule IX in box 8.

22.8   Exchange-Rate Parities

We have focused on mutual monetary adjustment among the inner core of G-3 countries to secure the common price level. Now it is time to discuss which regime of exchange parities is appropriate for all countries—large and small, rich and poor—wanting to join CMS21. Without first agreeing to harmonize national monetary policies, no system of exchange parities—central rates within a narrow band—can survive.

Yet some parity systems are better than others. Can the matrix of exchange rates among national currencies be established symmetrically? Which parity regimes are easily expansible to encompass new members? Which is most compatible with the anchoring mechanism? Fortunately, history provides useful guidelines. Consider four generic ways of setting par values among national currencies:

1. Use an external numéraire as under the gold standard.

2. Use a synthetic numéraire or currency basket.

3. Establish a bilateral parity grid with no single numéraire, as within the European Monetary System.

4. Use one national currency as numéraire as under the dollar standard.

The first three are either not feasible or not desirable, so our variant of (4), where the dollar is retained as numéraire (box 8), wins by default. Let us discuss each parity regime in turn.

Gold as Numéraire

By the late nineteenth century, when each major industrial country had proclaimed its gold parity, all national currencies had similar narrow ranges[7] of exchange variation defined by the gold points (chapter 2). Despite Britain's formidable position at the center of the world capital market, just one set of rules applied symmetrically to all participating countries (box 1). Undoubtedly, much of the political appeal of the gold standard rested on its formal symmetry, and new members could easily join by simply declaring their exchange parities against the politically neutral gold numéraire.

But choosing an outside numéraire also meant accepting its intrinsic purchasing power as the nominal anchor for the system overall. Gold's record was reasonably good, because nations could grow into a financially more sophisticated gold standard by the late nineteenth century from more primitive beginnings a century or so earlier, when precious metals were the primary instruments of monetary circulation. Gold's alternative uses in industry or as jewelry helped establish its purchasing power. But, by 1913, the superstructure of paper banknotes and deposit money had become huge relative to the narrow gold base of the system (chapter 4). In the 1920s, the world's gold base proved much too small to support Britain's attempt to reestablish traditional gold parities—leading to worldwide deflationary pressure and the Great Depression (chapter 2).

Today, when gold has been out of monetary circulation for many decades, estimating what the demand for it would be if its monetary role was restored is even more difficult. Any new set of "permanent" gold parities would have no defense against unpredictable systemwide inflation or deflation in the short or intermediate runs. In the late twentieth century, the velocity of virtually any monetary aggregate has become too volatile to rely on any one for anchoring the common price level. Nor is there any other international financial asset, with purchasing power more or less independent of what governments do, that can fill the bill as *the* external numéraire in a new system of exchange parities.

A Synthetic Numéraire?

Would a purely an accounting entity, which is not itself actively traded in private financial markets and has no independently determined purchasing power, be feasible for establishing the constellation of par values among "N" national currencies? In international treaties, this synthetic approach has been tried on at least two occasions.

First, in box 2 , for the Bretton Woods Agreement in 1945, rule I specifies gold to be the primary numéraire—even though at that time it was illegal to trade in private financial markets of the principal industrial countries and had been withdrawn from monetary circulation years before. In the event, this gold shadow of its former self never played—and could not have played—the numéraire role assigned to it in the treaty. As shown in chapter 2, the rules of the Bretton Woods treaty were quickly superseded by those of the fixed-rate dollar standard (box 3), where the dollar—which was actively traded against other currencies and had its own independently established purchasing power—became the numéraire and anchor.

Second, within the European Monetary System, a weighted basket of European currencies called the ecu (European Currency Unit) is the formal numéraire for defining par values—as per rule I in box 6 describing the "Spirit of the Treaty." The basket contains major and minor European currencies, some of which were subject to capital controls. Initially, it was thought that each member country would intervene to support its own currency when its market rate diverged too much from its central ecu rate according to an EMS divergence indicator. This proved awkward, because intervention did not take place with a basket of currencies. To enforce the band limits, governments preferred to hold and use major currencies like the mark (or even the dollar in the early stages of the EMS) with deep capital markets and no convertibility restrictions. Thus the divergence indicator quickly fell into disuse.[8]

Because of the greater credibility of the German monetary authorities, the EMS is usually depicted as a DM zone—where other countries willingly peg to the mark in order to better secure their own price levels.[9] Rather than the synthetic ecu, the anchor for the EMS thereby devolved asymmetrically to the Bundesbank—as per rule XV in box 7.

A Bilateral Parity Grid?

To achieve seeming political symmetry, however, Germany's important anchoring role in the EMS was (is) not properly reflected in its parity regime. Although EMS countries still formally define their central rates against the ecu, for defending band limits each focuses on its corresponding bilateral central rates with every other member—rule II in box 6 (or 7). At least before the upheavals of August 1993 forced a dramatic widening of the bands to a meaningless ±15 percent, European central banks had tried to defend the original ±2.25 percent bands around all bilateral parities: the so-called bilateral parity grid. Whenever any one bilateral band was at full stretch, the stronger currency country lent to the weaker one—as per rule III in box 6 (or 7)—to finance the official intervention. Rather than use the DM as the numéraire currency, official interventions were governed by attempts to preserve the bilateral parity grid.

More than just a curiosity, this disjointness between the symmetry of the EMS parity regime and Germany's asymmetrical role in providing the anchor currency was a major reason—although not the only one (chapter 19)—why the exchange parities proved so vulnerable to speculative attack. Pill (1995) has shown that adding new members to the pre-August 1993 bilateral parity grid increasingly constrained the effective range of exchange-rate variation to less than the formally permitted variation of ±2.25 percent between any two currencies. In Pill's words, the "effective" band became increasingly more restricted and narrower than the "notional" band.

In particular, any country that wanted to peg directly to the DM as the best and most convenient anchor for its own monetary policy continually found itself being bound by its bilateral obligations to member countries other than Germany. Pill cites the example of the peseta/sterling rate being a constraint on British monetary policy in the summer of 1992 because of the unusual strength (false, as it turns out) of the Spanish currency in this period. As membership increases, the core countries become more vulnerable to shocks on the periphery, and to peculiar gyrations in minor currencies.

Another way of appraising the bilateral parity grid is to note how the number of potential official interventions rises much faster than the increase in new members. Suppose there are N member countries in the EMS. Then if each pair has to maintain a bilateral parity (with a band around it), the total number of pairs is $\frac{1}{2} N(N-1)$. As the EMS membership increases, the number of potential official interventions increases by the order of N^2! This helps to explain why continual, and sometimes frenetic, official intervention was necessary to maintain the EMS parity grid before its seeming demise in August 1993. Even in times of relative calm, European central bankers phoned each other daily in order to identify which currencies were "strong" or "weak," and prepare to intervene in a multitude of different currencies—or to extend credit one way or another.

In addition, the formal symmetry in the EMS rules treating Germany's foreign exchange-rate obligations the same as any other's—in rules I and II (box 6)—posed a potential threat to Germany's monetary autonomy. Rule III in box 6 requires the strong-currency central bank to lend freely to a weak-currency central bank. If massive amounts of DM claims on the Bundesbank are sold to buy weak European currencies in some foreign-exchange crisis, Germany's ability to provide a stable anchor for the system is impaired if not unhinged altogether.

One National Currency as Numéraire?

Although not "politically correct," a more economically efficient method of setting exchange parities would be to recognize explicitly that the EMS was a DM zone. Other than Germany itself, each member country would only be responsible for one, and only one, exchange parity: that against the DM. There would be exactly $N-1$ official parities no matter what the membership. Without an official parity obligation, Germany would have the degree of monetary freedom necessary to anchor the price level. Each national currency could vary over the full range of its formal band with the DM, say ±2.25 percent or something narrower without being haphazardly restricted by the exchange interventions of other countries. New members could be added without complicating life for the old ones, that is, without cross effects from interventions in any one DM market to another. The EMS format would then look almost exactly like that of the Marshall-Dodge dollar standard of the 1950s and 1960s—where the Bretton Woods Article IV was interpreted so as to have all participants peg to the dollar, and the United States was left free to determine the common price level (rule box 3).

Surprisingly, the inner core of European countries may already have informally adopted this old Bretton Woods format. Pill (1995) interprets the events of August 1993 as informally establishing an exchange-rate regime consistent with the ideal of the EMS as a DM zone. By making the bands in the bilateral parity grid ridiculously wide, that is, ±15 percent, the EMS preserved political symmetry. But, within the stable inner core, these wider bands no longer were binding. In 1994, France, Belgium, Denmark, and the Netherlands pegged freely to the DM well within the old range of ±2.25 percent or less—and Germany could better manage its monetary policy—without being so disturbed by monetary events on the "periphery." In effect, turmoil in the foreign-exchange markets of other countries—Britain, Spain, Greece, Portugal, Italy, and newer members—no longer interferes with the inner core operating the regime as a DM zone.

Suppose lowercase "n" now represents the smaller number of EMS core currencies, where $n < N$. Then, under Pill's interpretation, just $n-1$ official targets for DM exchange rates now exist. The paradox of why the market exchange rates of the inner core moved so little after the wave of speculation demolished the old ±2.25 bands in the old bilateral parity grid is then explained. In effect, the EMS rules changed in August 1993 from an ostensibly symmetrical bilateral parity grid over the period 1979–92 to having the inner core of member countries peg directly to the mark.

But the rules of the EMS game for member countries on the periphery are harder to characterize. Because the unworkable bilateral parity grid is now in abeyance, some may eventually be drawn back into the core by directly pegging to the DM. Because the post-1993 EMS rules are still difficult to discern fully, the reader is spared yet another rule box to supersede box 7!

The problems with sustaining the bilateral parity grid in Europe have caused many economists (Eichengreen 1993; Obstfeld 1992; Portes 1993) to doubt the feasibility of any system of fixed exchange parities. As long as national currencies remain in circulation—thus giving an implicit exit option, they argue that the only way to avoid damaging speculative attacks is to move forward to a common currency or backward to no-par floating. In chapter 19, however, I showed that the huge debt overhangs lodged with the European national governments make it undesirable to transfer their money-issuing authority to the EU central government under a common currency. But, among the currencies of the inner core, a common monetary standard could be sustained indefinitely if their common price level in tradable goods was satisfactorily anchored.

In the light of Pill's results, we impose the additional condition that the parity regime be consistent with the anchoring mechanism. Although already in place informally for the inner core of member countries, the regime of formal exchange parities in the EMS should be changed to a simpler set of $N-1$ commitments to peg directly to the DM. Then, adding new members from northern or eastern Europe would pose no problems of monetary management for the core. From time to time, monetary instability in the peripheral countries might still force changes in their individual parities—but the whole EMS applecart need not be upset.

Similarly, a general bilateral parity grid would be inconsistent with the logic of CMS21 with N members, but which is anchored by just the G-3. Thus, rule I in box 8 specifies that the U.S. dollar be the numéraire currency for mark and yen parities. The dollar is still the international vehicle currency of choice in the spot and forward exchange markets, and the invoice currency for primary commodities in international markets. As such, it is the natural and most convenient numéraire against which the core members of CMS21 define their exchange parities. But unlike a pure dollar standard, the United States would now bend its own monetary policy, in conjunction with monetary authorities in Germany and Japan, to stabilize the yen/dollar and mark/dollar exchange rates—as per rules II, IV, and VII.

Under CMS21, countries outside the G-3 core would have a wider choice—under rule X, box 8—of pegging to any one of three currencies: the mark, yen, or dollar. The natural choice for European currencies would be the mark—as is already happening informally. In Asia, no such well-defined group exists for pegging to the yen, but any country that is highly integrated with the Japanese economy on current or capital account could choose the yen to satisfy its parity condition for membership. Other countries in the world would either return to a convenient dollar peg or be too unstable in a monetary sense to commit themselves to any fixed parities—or to CMS21.

Note that for those countries that choose a mark or yen parity, their band widths will be twice as wide with respect to the dollar. For example, suppose in steady-state equilibrium, all countries choose band widths of ±1 percent around their central parities—as per rule V in box 8. If France chose to peg to the DM, then the franc's range of variation would be ±2 percent with respect to the dollar, yen, and any other European currency pegged to the DM. Now suppose some Asian country, say Korea, chose to fix its parity against the yen. Then the range of variation of the franc against the won would be ±3 percent.

This band pyramiding is relatively insignificant if each country's primary band had indeed been narrowed to ±1 percent. However, if CMS21 starts with fairly broad bands, as per the ±5 percent indicated in rule 1, then pyramiding could lead to band widths as great as ±15 percent—a good reason for converging to narrower basic bands as soon as practicable.

But whatever band pyramiding occurs outside the G-3, the basic assignment of just one parity commitment to each member country still holds. Thus, CMS21 avoids the extraneous interference with each member fulfilling its primary parity obligation that was characteristic of the EMS bilateral parity grid.

Not only would CMS21 be consistent with the newly emerging structure of $n-1$ DM parities in the EMS, but it could anchor German monetary policy more securely. If the G-3 jointly establish a common price level in tradable goods (as measured by the PPI or WPI) through mutual adjustment and monitoring, this would put an effective limit on potentially erratic behavior by the Bundesbank. For example, in a world where the velocity of money has become difficult to predict, the Bundesbank could no longer pursue a growth target for M3 in a way that conflicts with the objective of stabilizing the German PPI. In addition,

CMS21 would force the Bundesbank to be more precise about its price-level target rather than arbitrarily picking and choosing among the German WPI, the CPI, money wages, or the GNP deflator.[10]

22.9 The Restoration Rule and Long-Term Interest Rates

After a successful transition (see below), suppose our new monetary standard was sustained for some time. Rules I through V and VII in box 8 were fully operational in fixing nominal exchange rates within narrow bands at a stable price level. However, because national currencies would remain in circulation under the control of national central banks, exit from the agreement is still possible. In the face of some financial or political crisis, a country could opt—or be forced—to leave.

The waves of speculation that swept the European Monetary System in September 1992 and again in August 1993 are indicative of what might happen to CMS21 in a broader context—although such disturbances would be less likely when the parity system was consistent with the anchoring mechanism. When international capital markets are wide open, such speculative attacks—warranted or unwarranted—on particular currencies can't be ruled out. Can the rules of the game be established so that such attacks, even when successful, are unlikely to fatally undermine the agreement itself?

The behavior of countries operating under the international gold standard before 1914 is instructive. In the face of a liquidity crises, a country would sometimes resort to the use of "gold devices," that is, it would raise the buying price for gold or interfere with its exportation (chapter 2). This amounted to a minor, temporary suspension of its traditional gold parity. In more major crises including wars, a few outright suspensions for some months or years occurred. In the long run, however, the gold standard was very successful in having countries adhere to their traditional exchange parities while anchoring the common price level. In early 1914, exchange rates and wholesale prices were virtually the same as they were in the late 1870s.

What gave the pre-1914 gold standard its long-run resilience? After any short-run crisis that forced the partial or complete suspension of gold parities, the unwritten "restoration" rule

(rule V in box 1) was that the country in question return to its traditional gold parity as soon as practicable. Even during a liquidity squeeze or other short-run trauma, longer-term exchange-rate expectations remained regressive with respect to these traditional parities. Correspondingly, long-term interest rates showed little volatility by modern standards and, without significant financial risk, their levels also remained low: about 3 percent in the United Kingdom and 4 percent in the United States.

Rule VI in box 8 is a modern version of the restoration rule. Within CMS21, suppose a crisis forces one country to abandon its dollar exchange parity, that is, rule I (or V) is suspended. But the country in question has precommitted itself to reestablishing its traditional exchange rate when the crisis is over. Because the remaining members maintain the value of their currencies in terms of tradable goods (rule VII), the errant country must eventually restore the real purchasing power of its own money.

(Of course, in the event of a complete fiscal breakdown and massive resort to the inflation tax, restoration of the traditional exchange parity would not be credible. Monetary harmonization within CMS21 would not be strong enough to foreclose the possibility of a fiscal breakdown in any one member country.)

If the crisis is more widespread and forces a general suspension of exchange parities in the short run, rule VII still anchors each country's price level so as to make a general restoration of traditional exchange parities feasible when calm returns. But calm will return that much sooner, or the crisis could even have been forestalled to begin with, if the markets knew that the authorities will follow the restoration rule as soon as they can. Then, long-term interest rates should sail through the crisis with minimal disruption.

But using the dollar as the numéraire currency makes CMS21 potentially more vulnerable to financial upheavals in the United States; hence the rationale for rule VIa. If the United States suspends its obligation to help maintain the dollar's exchange parities or the common price level, then the numéraire currency would shift to the mark or yen. The logical alternative would be that major country that best maintains the purchasing power of its money while keeping a fully open capital market where foreigners can transact freely.

22.10   Transition

What about problems of moving from the relatively loose rules associated with Plaza-Louvre to the much tighter ones, at least for the three center countries, associated with CMS21? Initially, if national rates of price inflation in tradable goods diverge significantly, and if long-term nominal interest rates are not aligned, then a serious convergence problem would exist.

For example, the syndrome of the ever higher yen (lower yen/dollar exchange rate) has forced Japanese prices and wages onto an unduly deflationary path vis-à-vis the United States, and has induced Japanese nominal interest rates to be lower than their American counterparts. Consequently, the PPP yen/dollar rate itself continually drifts downward. Even if the actual yen/dollar exchange rate was pegged as per rule 1, this downward drift would continue for awhile because of the inertia in domestic price-wage movements. So getting the correct yen/dollar rate to start with requires calculating the lags properly to ensure that American and Japanese price levels approximately converge at the starting exchange rate (Ohno 1990; McKinnon and Ohno forthcoming).

To illustrate, suppose CMS21 started when the yen was overvalued. As of January 1995, the spot yen/dollar is 100 per dollar whereas a best estimate of PPP would put it at 130. Because of the adjustment lags in rates of price inflation within Japan and the United States, a starting official target for the exchange-rate target should be somewhat less than its current PPP.

Similarly, in the transition, countries should not move to narrower target zones (rule V) until intermediate and long-term interest rates are fairly well aligned. The announcement of a serious new program for eventually harmonizing national monetary policies would itself tend to pull interest rates together. But if major interest gaps remain when the exchange rate is fixed, this could induce overborrowing and a loss of monetary control in the country with higher nominal interest rates (Walters 1986; McKinnon and Pill 1996). Instead, the authorities would do better to delay their final narrowing of the exchange-rate band until interest rates had adjusted sufficiently.

But the problem of when to implement the agreement could be posed more positively. Given the ebb and flow of financial events under floating exchange rates, situations occasionally arise where national rates of producer price inflation are virtually the same, and interest rates are fairly well aligned—see chapter 20. Any pair of national authorities could seize that window of opportunity to implement the agreement in its strong form.

At its outset, CMS21 need not encompass all the industrial countries. It could begin with, say, just Japan and the United States. Having being forced into two major deflations in the past nine years, the Bank of Japan certainly has a vested interest in better securing its price level in the future. Similarly, because Japan is the major marginal source of finance to the American economy, the Federal Reserve should worry about untoward interest-rate volatility on dollar assets that is heavily affected by uncertainty about the yen/dollar exchange rate. If their mutual interests were properly understood, a relatively tight CMS21 agreement between Japan and the United States could greatly benefit both countries.

But this need not preclude the continuation of the looser—but still very important—Plaza-Louvre regime. Continuing Plaza-Louvre more generally among the industrial countries would complement nicely closer cooperation between Japan and the United States under CMS21.

Although it might seem like overly radical pie in the sky, CMS21 could naturally evolve out of the Plaza-Louvre regime already in effect. True, the rules in box 8 require stronger commitments; but this structure is surprisingly similar to that in box 5. The key precept under Plaza-Louvre, of concerted action to stop untoward major runs for or against the dollar, carries over into CMS21. Like Plaza-Louvre, it would not require that the IMF's Articles be revised or any new IMF lending facilities such as Special Drawing Rights. Negotiations with the 150-plus diverse countries making up the IMF's current membership would be unnecessary.[11]

Instead, our common monetary standard need only be the direct concern of a small number of central banks in the industrial economies. Because of the importance of anchoring the common price level in tradable goods (rule VII), the initial focus of these core central banks should be on mutually adjusting their domestic monetary policies—rather than on promulgating tight bands for exchange rates. However, major exchange-rate misalignments, that is, departures from purchasing power parity, would have to be corrected at the outset.

22.11   What Not to Negotiate

In seeking to establish a common monetary standard, no less important is what should *not* be negotiated. The negotiators should leave many important economic issues entirely outside the agreement. Fiscal deficits or surpluses, and relative nationwide savings propensities more generally, determine net current-account balances. In financially open economies, monetary authorities cannot systematically affect net saving or trade imbalances—whatever the exchange-rate regime. However, as with the ever higher yen, monetary stability can be undermined if the authorities try to use the exchange rate as an instrumental variable for (falsely) pursuing a trade-balance objective. The upshot is that fiscal policies and trade imbalances are best left off the negotiating table for CMS21.[12]

Similarly, among countries where exchange controls have long since ceased to be used as protective devices, debate over commercial policies would serve no useful purpose in negotiating a monetary agreement for stabilizing prices and exchange rates. But the converse is not true. If an agreement like CMS21 is successfully concluded, the negotiating partners would have great incentive for removing the welter of quantitative trade restrictions in agriculture and industry that have been a response to volatile exchange rates—as shown in chapter 18.

22.12   Can CMS21 Be Sustained? A Concluding Note

Long-term interest-rate volatility—as well as exchange-rate fluctuations—would be reduced further if the common monetary standard applied to all industrial economies, and not just subgroups like the EU or Japan and the United States. Once banks, trust funds, insurance companies, pension funds, and so on, knew that each industrial country was on CMS21 indefinitely, no longer would they continually switch their holdings of long-term bonds denominated in different national currencies from one to the other. Their best guess for exchange rates in the long run would be what the rates are today.

In addition, "hot" money at the short end of the maturity spectrum would become less hot once the common monetary standard became general and narrow exchange bands became credible. As under the pre-1914 gold standard, short-term capital flows would again assume a more benign role as the balance wheel of international adjustment. The now well-known time (in)consistency problem in national macroeconomic decision making, where under floating exchange rates individuals worry that their government might hit them with a surprise inflation—would be ameliorated.

Although balance-of-payments adjustment among countries worked smoothly under the gold standard, the world economy itself was plagued with runs on the limited gold base—with consequently high volatility in short-term interest rates. But the monetary base of CMS21 would be the sum of the fiat monetary bases of Germany, Japan, and the United States. As under the Marshall-Dodge dollar standard when volatility in short-term interest rate was low, CMS21 would not be subject to the continual worldwide liquidity squeezes characteristic of the gold standard. New members could build up their dollar, mark, or yen reserves without forcing deflation on the system as a whole.

Can a very broad CMS21 pact be sustained? Once an inner core of major countries established a successful common monetary standard, others would willingly join. There was a worldwide rush to join Britain on the gold standard in the 1870s, and a similar rush among diverse countries to join the Marshall-Dodge standard in the late 1940s into the early 1950s. Once an international monetary standard appears to be working well, the sanctions against any government who fails to join it—or later abandons the accepted standard—become difficult for any politician to ignore.

Notes

1. This dollar-exchange-rate cum world-money explanation of synchronized world business cycles in the 1970s into the mid-1980s was further spelled out empirically in McKinnon (1984). It is the major feature that distinguishes the floating-rate dollar standard (box 4) from Plaza-Louvre (box 5), where "world" money growth has been much smoother.

2. This need not rule out rebasing intermediate monetary indicators if they go awry—as with the Bundesbank's recent extreme problems in having to

rebase M3, and the Fed's earlier dropping of all official targets for monetary aggregates. Unlike what I had advocated earlier (McKinnon 1984) the velocity of money in the 1990s has become too unstable to build definite targets for monetary aggregates into our cooperative procedures for establishing a common monetary standard.

3. Because of periodic booms and busts in primary commodity prices, countries like Canada and Australia would have more trouble stabilizing their PPIs. Then, more weight should be given to an external exchange-rate anchor.

4. An exchange rate that aligns producer prices net of commodity taxes and distribution costs is not the same as the purchasing power parity (PPP) commonly quoted in the financial press. The latter rate would equalize the cost of living across countries inclusive of indirect taxes and service costs. But it is the former PPP concept that is relevant for a common monetary standard, and is what actually, if implicitly, holds across the various regions of a common-currency area like the United States. In contrast, the cost of living in some American states can be lower than in others—South Dakota can be a cheaper place to live than New York—without upsetting the implicit one-to-one exchange rate between them.

5. Financial argot for those agents in the foreign exchanges who act for commercial reasons other than to speculate on the future course of the exchange rate.

6. Because exchange-rate bands separate the domains of national currencies, the clearing of international payments naturally devolves to commercial banks—which can profit from small exchange-rate variations within the bands. In contrast, across regions in a country with a single currency (no bands), the central bank clears interregional payments—as with the fedwire system in the United States.

7. Depending on distance and the costs of transporting gold, there were small differences in band widths across any pair of currencies.

8. Giavazzi and Giovannini (1989, 37) conclude, "While applauded by some as an important innovation, the indicator of divergence has played no role in the EMS."

9. Giavazzi and Giovannini (1989), De Grauwe (1991), Herz and Werner (1992).

10. In chapter 19, I suggested an alternative but complementary route for pinning down the Bundesbank. The core EMS members could collectively agree on a target for the common European price level in tradable goods—and then set up a European adjustment mechanism like that specified in CMS21 for achieving a common monetary standard.

11. This approach to CMS21 differs from the Bretton Woods Commission Report chaired by Paul Volcker, "Bretton Woods: Looking to the Future" (Volcker 1994). The report would assign international monetary reform to the IMF, while having it withdraw from much of its third-world and transitional-economy lending.

12. The huge and unsustainable buildup of public debt—inclusive of unfunded pension liabilities—by the industrial economies could lead to an inflationary explosion in the future. In chapter 19, I argued that any government issuing its own fiat money has a potentially "soft" budget constraint leading to excessive debt issue that victimizes future generations. CMS21 would not worsen

the problem, and might even harden budget constraints a bit. But, to limit significantly debt overhangs in the industrial economies, a harder money regime—or greater constitutional restraint—than dealt with here would be necessary.

References

Catte, Pietro, Giampaola Galli, and Salvatore Rebecchini. 1992. "Exchange Rates Can Be Managed!" *International Economic Insights* (September/October): 17–21.

De Grauwe, Paul. 1991. "Is the European Monetary System a DM-Zone?" In *Evolution of International and Interregional Monetary Systems,* ed. A. Steinherr and D. Wieserbs. London: Macmillan.

Dominguez, Kathryn, and Jeffrey Frankel. 1993. *Intervention Policy Reconsidered.* Washington, DC: Institute for International Economics.

Eichengreen, Barry. 1993. "The Economics of European Monetary Integration." *Journal of Economic Literature,* 31(3) (September): 1321–57.

Financial Times. 1994. "Banks Support Dollar". 5 May, 40.

Giavazzi, Francesco, and Alberto Giovannini. 1989. *Limiting Exchange Rate Flexibility: The European Monetary System,* Cambridge, MA: MIT Press.

Herz, Bernhard, and Roger Werner. 1992. "The EMS is a Greater Deutchemark Area." *European Economic Review* 36(7) (October): 1413–25.

McKinnon, Ronald I. 1977. "Beyond Fixed Parities: The Analytics of International Monetary Agreements." In *The Political Economy of Monetary Reform,* ed. R. Aliber, 42–56. London: MacMillan.

———. 1984. *An International Standard for Monetary Stabilization.* Washington, DC: Institute for International Economics.

———. 1993. "The Rules of the Game: International Money in Historical Perspective." *Journal of Economic Literature* (March): 1–44.

McKinnon, Ronald I., and Kenichi Ohno. 1989. "Purchasing Power Parity as a Monetary Standard." In *The Future of the International Monetary System,* ed. O. Hamouda et al., 42–67. Aldershot, UK: Edward Elgar.

———. Forthcoming. *Dollar and Yen: A Macroeconomic Approach to Resolving Conflict between the United States and Japan.* Cambridge, MA: MIT Press.

McKinnon, Ronald I., and Huw Pill. 1996. "Credible Liberalizations and International Capital Flows: The Overborrowing Syndrome." In *Financial Integration and Deregulation in East Asia,* ed. A. Krueger and T. Ito. NBER, University of Chicago Press.

Obstfeld, Maurice. 1992. "Destabilizing Effects of Exchange Rate Escape Clauses." NBER Working Paper 3606.

OECD. 1994. "The Desynchronization of International Business Cycles." *Economic Outlook* (June): 37–43.

Ohno, Kenichi. 1990. "Estimating Yen/Dollar and Mark/Dollar Purchasing Power Parities." *International Monetary Fund Staff Papers* 55 (September): 700–25.

Rule Box 1
The International Gold Standard, 1879–1913

All Countries

    I. Fix an official gold price or "mint parity," and convert freely between domestic money and gold at that price.

   II. Do not restrict the export of gold by private citizens, nor impose any other exchange restrictions on current or capital account transacting.

  III. Back national banknotes and coinage with earmarked gold reserves, and condition long-run growth in deposit money on availability of general gold reserves.

  IV. In short-run liquidity crises from an international gold drain, have the central bank lend freely to domestic banks at higher interest rates (Bagehot's Rule).

   V. If Rule I is temporarily suspended, restore convertibility at traditional mint parity as soon as practicable—if necessary by deflating the domestic economy.

  VI. Allow the common price level (nominal anchor) to be endogenously determined by the worldwide demand for, and supply of, gold.

Rule Box 2
The Bretton Woods Agreement in 1945: The Spirit of the Treaty

---

All Countries

    I. Fix a foreign par value for the domestic currency by using gold, or a currency tied to gold, as the numéraire; otherwise demonetize gold in all private transacting.

   II. In the short run, keep exchange rate within one percent of its par value; but leave its long-run par value unilaterally adjustable if the International Monetary Fund (IMF) concurs.

  III. Free currency convertibility for current-account payments; use capital controls to dampen currency speculation.

  IV. Use national monies symmetrically in foreign transacting, including dealings with the IMF.

   V. Buffer short-run payments imbalances by drawing on official exchange reserves and IMF credits; sterilize the domestic monetary impact of exchange-market interventions.

  VI. National macroeconomic autonomy: each member government to pursue its own price level and employment objectives unconstrained by a common nominal anchor or price rule.

Rule Box 3
The Fixed-Rate Dollar Standard, 1950–70

Industrial Countries Other than the United States

  I. Fix a par value for the national currency with the U.S. dollar as the numeraire, and keep exchange rate within 1 percent of this par value indefinitely.

 II. Free currency convertibility for current-account payments; use capital controls to insulate domestic financial markets, but begin liberalization.

III. Use the dollar as the intervention currency, and keep active official exchange reserves in the U.S. Treasury Bonds.

 IV. Subordinate long-run growth in the domestic money supply to the fixed exchange rate and to the prevailing rate of price inflation (in tradable goods) in the United States.

  V. Offset substantial short-run losses in exchange reserves by having the central bank purchase domestic assets to partially restore the liquidity of domestic banks and the money supply (Bagehot's Rule).

 VI. Limit current account imbalances by adjusting national fiscal policy (government net saving) to offset imbalances between private saving and investment.

The United States

 VII. Remain passive in the foreign exchanges: practice free trade with neither a balance-of-payments nor an exchange-rate target. Do not hold significant official reserves of foreign exchange, and (passively) sterilize the domestic monetary consequences of other countries' foreign exchange interventions.

VIII. Keep U.S. capital markets open to foreign governments and private residents as borrowers or depositors.

 IX. Maintain position as a net international creditor (in dollar denominated assets) and limit fiscal deficits.

  X. Anchor the dollar (world) price level for tradable goods by an independently chosen American monetary policy based on domestic credit expansion.

Rule Box 4
The Floating-Rate Dollar Standard, 1973–84

Industrial Countries Other than the United States

    I. Smooth near-term fluctuations in dollar exchange rate without committing to a par value or to long-term exchange stability.

    II. Free currency convertibility for current payments, while eventually eliminating remaining restrictions on capital account.

    III. Use the dollar as the intervention currency (except for some transactions to stabilize intra-European exchange rates), and keep official exchange reserves mainly in U.S. Treasury bonds.

    IV. Adjust short-run growth in the national money supply to support major exchange interventions: reduce when the national currency is weak against the dollar and expand when it is strong.

    V. Set long-run growth in the national price level and money supply independently of the United States, and allow corresponding secular adjustments in dollar exchange rate.

The United States

    VI. Remain passive in the foreign exchanges: free trade with neither a balance of payments nor exchange-rate target. Do not hold significant official reserves of foreign exchange, and (passively) sterilize the domestic monetary consequences of other countries' foreign-exchange interventions.

    VII. Keep U.S. capital markets open to foreign governments and private residents as borrowers or depositors.

    VIII. Pursue monetary policies independent of the foreign-exchange value of the dollar and of the rate of money growth in other industrial countries—without trying to anchor any common price level.

Rule Box 5
The Plaza-Louvre Intervention Accords for the Dollar Exchange
Rate, 1985–95

Germany, Japan, and the United States (G-3)

I. Set broad target zones for the mark/dollar and yen/dollar exchange rates of ± 12 percent. Do not announce the agreed-on central rates, and leave zonal boundaries flexible.

II. If disparities in economic "fundamentals" among the G-3 change substantially, adjust the (implicit) central rates.

III. Intervene in concert, but infrequently, to reverse short-run trends in the dollar exchange rate that threaten to pierce zonal boundaries. Signal the collective intent by not disguising these concerted interventions.

IV. Practice free currency convertibility on current and capital account, and hold official exchange reserves symmetrically in each other's currencies. U.S. government to begin building up its reserves in marks, yen, and possibly other convertible currencies.

V. Sterilize the immediate domestic monetary impact of foreign-exchange interventions by leaving short-term interest rates unchanged.

VI. Assign domestic monetary policy to achieve a zero or low rate of price inflation—as measured variously by the domestic CPI, or WPI, or GNP deflator. Do not commit to any one national price index, or attempt to coordinate inflation targets internationally.

VIa. If national inflation rates undershoot or overshoot their targets, rebase the price level for targeting next period's inflation. Allow cumulative drift in the national price level from past errors in forecasting inflation rates.

Other Industrial Countries

VII. Support, or not oppose, interventions by G-3 to keep the dollar within designated mark and yen zones. Buy dollars with the national curency, or with yen and marks, when the dollar is weak—and vice versa.

Rule Box 6
The European Monetary System (EMS) in 1979: The Spirit of the Treaty

---

All Member Countries

    I. Fix a par value for the exchange rate in terms of the European Currency Unit, a basket of EMS currencies weighted according to country size.

    II. Keep par value stable in the short run by symmetrically limiting range of variation in each bilateral exchange rate to 2.25 percent on either side of its central rate.

    III. When an exchange rate threatens to breech its bilateral limit, the strong-currency central bank must lend freely to the weak-currency central bank to support the rate.

    IV. Adjust par values in the intermediate term if necessary to realign national price levels—but only by collective agreement within the EMS.

    V. Work symmetrically toward convergence of national macroeconomic policies and unchanging long-run par values for exchange rates.

    VI. Keep free convertibility for current-account payments.

    VII. Hold reserves mainly as European Currency Units with the European Fund for Monetary Cooperation, and reduce dollar reserves. Avoid holding substantial reserves in other EMS currencies.

    VIII. Repay central bank debts quickly from exchange reserves, or by borrowing from the European Fund for Monetary Cooperation within strict longer-term credit limits.

    IX. No member country's money is to be a reserve currency, nor is its national monetary policy to be (asymmetrically) the nominal anchor for the group.

Rule Box 7
The European Monetary System as a Greater Deutsche Mark
Area: 1979–92

All Member Countries

    I. through V. Same as in EMS "Spirit of the Treaty" (Box 6).
   VI. Avoid using the credit facilities of the European Fund for Monetary Cooperation.

Member Countries Except Germany

  VII. Intervene intramarginally, within formal bilateral parity limits, to stabilize the national exchange rate vis-à-vis the DM. Increasingly intervene in DM rather than dollars.
 VIII. Keep active exchange reserves in interest-bearing DM open-market instruments such as Euromark deposits, as well as in dollar Treasury bonds.
   IX. Adjust short-term national money growth and/or short-term interest rates to support exchange market interventions—whether intramarginal or at the bilateral parity limits.
    X. Keep adjusting long-term money growth so that domestic price inflation (in tradable goods) converges to, or remains the same as, price inflation in Germany.
   XI. Progressively liberalize capital controls.

Germany

  XII. Remain passive in the foreign-exchange markets with other European (EMS) countries: free trade with neither a balance-of-payments nor an intramarginal exchange-rate target.
 XIII. Keep German capital markets open to foreign governments or private residents as borrowers or depositors.
 XIV. Sterilize (perhaps passively) the effects of German or other EMS countries' official interventions in the European foreign-exchange markets on the German monetary base.
  XV. Anchor the DM (EMS) price level for tradable goods by an independently chosen German monetary policy.

Rule Box 8
A Common Monetary Standard for the Twenty-First Century (CMS21)

Germany, Japan, and the United States (G-3)

    I. Announce target zones for yen/dollar and mark/dollar exchange rates of ± 5 percent to be sustained by mutual monetary adjustment. Base central rates on initial purchasing power parities that align wholesale price levels among G-3.

   II. Intervene in concert to reverse short-run trends in the dollar exchange rate that threaten to pierce zonal boundaries. Signal by not disguising these concerted interventions.

  III. Practice free currency convertibility on current and capital account, and hold official exchange reserves symmetrically in each other's currencies. U.S. government to complete its buildup of reserves in marks, yen, and possibly other convertible currencies.

  IV. Don't fully sterilize the immediate monetary impact of interventions in G-3 currencies. Let short-term interest rates and the domestic monetary base adjust modestly (Bagehot's Rule).

   V. Once inflation and longer-term interest rates are closely aligned across the G-3, harden and narrow zonal boundaries to ± 1 percent.

  VI. If rule I or rule V must be temporarily suspended, restore the country's "traditional" exchange rate as soon as practicable. If necesssary, deflate the domestic economy to the price level prevailing before suspension occurred.

 VIa. If the United States is forced to suspend rule I or rule V, change the numéraire currency for exchange rates to marks or yen— whichever one has the better record for maintaining its purchasing power under rule VII.

 VII. Assign domestic central bank credit to anchor the level of tradable goods prices in the long run. Use a national wholesale or producer price index as an approximate target until a WPI or PPI with internationally standardized weights becomes available.

VIIa. Should undershooting or overshooting occur, do not rebase the price-level target.

VIII. Remain passive, with no balance-of-payments or exchange-rate targets, with respect to countries outside the G-3. Sterilize (passively) the domestic monetary consequences of their foreign-exchange interventions.

Other Industrial Countries

  IX. Support, or not oppose, interventions by G-3 to keep the dollar within designated mark and yen zones. Buy dollars with the

Rule Box 8 (continued)

national currency, or with yen and marks, when the dollar is weak, and vice versa.

X. Fix exchange rate against any G-3 currency by rules I, V, and VI above. If insufficient to anchor domestic price level, adopt rules VII and VIIa as well.

Index